The Edge of Surrealism

THE EDGE OF SURREALISM

A Roger Caillois Reader

By ROGER CAILLOIS

Edited and with an Introduction by CLAUDINE FRANK

Translated by CLAUDINE FRANK *and* CAMILLE NAISH

DUKE UNIVERSITY PRESS   *Durham and London*   2003

© 2003 DUKE UNIVERSITY PRESS. *All rights reserved.*

Printed in the UNITED STATES OF AMERICA *on acid-free paper* ∞.

Designed by AMY RUTH BUCHANAN. *Typeset in* CARTER & CONE

GALLIARD *by* G&S TYPESETTERS. *Library of Congress Cataloging-*

in-Publication Data appear on the last printed page of this book.

TO BIG LITTLE HENRIK

CONTENTS

Acknowledgments

I am very grateful to the late René Chenon, Jacques Chavy, André Chastel, and Louis Dumont. I would also like to thank Olga Tabakmann, Esther Ambrosino, and Lia Andler. My thanks as well to Camille Naish and to Monique Kuntz and Pierre Bourgoin at the Bibliothèque Municipale de Vichy, Jean-Pierre Le Bouler, Denis Hollier, Michel Winock, Susan Suleiman, Laurent Jenny, Marina Galletti, and to all those who encouraged or helped my research, especially at Harvard University, the University of Chicago, and Barnard College. Catherine Rizea-Caillois and Jean-Marc Chavy and the Lawrence Krader heirs kindly granted me publication rights to family material. Let me also warmly thank my editors at Duke University Press, Judith Hoover, Leigh Anne Couch, Fiona Morgan, and Ken Wissoker, for all of their hard work and support. On a personal note, my gratitude goes to Michèle Cyna, Stéphane Berrebi, Brenda Fowler, John Farrell, Jon, and especially my parents—who frequented a philosophy reading group in postwar Paris that (although this was never mentioned) turns out to have included important former members of Acéphale.

Note to the Reader

A brief word about the translations. The primary goal of *The Edge of Surrealism: A Roger Caillois Reader* is to make Caillois's ideas accessible to an English-language audience. Thus, the translations strive for clarity without attempting to render the stylistic complexity, nuance, and shifts of his prose. Certain terms are difficult to translate, especially when Caillois uses them repeatedly or insistently. At times, I simply provide the English cognate of the French word, as in "connivance" and "resemblance"; at others, I provide the French term alongside the English, as in "accuracy" (*justesse*), which has the additional connotations of "soundness," "rightness," and "truth."

Camille Naish and I collaboratively translated Caillois's texts, with a few exceptions. "The Myth of Secret Treasures in Childhood" was translated by Lawrence Krader. And a few texts I translated alone: "The Birth of Lucifer," "Discussions of Sociological Topics: On Defense of the Republic," "The Nature and Structure of Totalitarian Regimes," "The Situation of Poetry," "Pythian Heritage (On the Nature of Poetic Inspiration)," "Loyola to the Rescue of Marx," and "The Image." Unless otherwise indicated, all translations within the body of the commentaries are mine.

Although I use endnotes for my own writing (introduction and commentaries), I have chosen to keep Caillois's footnotes in their original form; translator comments also appear as footnotes with brackets. And finally, the source note with each essay refers to the particular Caillois edition that was translated.

Introduction

This volume is a general introduction to Roger Caillois (1913–1978), an intriguing and obstinate French man of letters, whose oeuvre explored the mysteries of the individual, social, biological, and mineral "imagination" in a bewildering array of manifestations. In so doing, he nonetheless focused at all times on crucial issues of twentieth-century French intellectual life to engage in debates with some of its most prominent figures, among them, Bataille, Benda, Bachelard, Dumézil, Paulhan, and Lévi-Strauss. As a youth, Caillois was obsessed with resacralizing society, by which he meant restoring to atomized, individualistic modernity what the famous last chapter of Durkheim's *Elementary Forms of Religious Life* (1912) had lamented as lost, collective effervescence. In his last years, he sought to touch the distant, private minds of individual readers with meditative conjectures about the appearance of stones. Throughout, he was an independent and, intellectually speaking, rather lonely figure. "Caillois himself was not always acknowledged by the official specialists. He was interested in too many things," remarked Maurice Blanchot about Foucault's first editor, adding that he "was a conservative, an innovator, always somewhat apart; he did not figure in the number of those who held some form of recognized knowledge." [1]

Caillois is perhaps most familiar to contemporary American readers through his participation in the College of Sociology, which he codirected with Georges Bataille from 1937 to 1939, after a brief passage in the Surrealist movement during his student days at the Ecole Normale. [2] At this time, he favored revolutionary invocations of science and social science. During the war, he sought to foster culture as a bulwark of Western civilization and was known to some American readers through his French literary journal in support of Free France, *Les Lettres françaises*, published under the auspices of Victoria Ocampo's Argentine journal, *Sur*. Having spent the war years in Buenos Aires, Caillois returned to France where, in the 1940s, he demystified dominant ideologies of the left in the interests of authenticity, transparency, and cultural harmony, this last defined as "style." Ultimately, he pursued a nonacademic career in the international bureaucracy at UNESCO, which sought to promote peace through education and culture; here, he edited the influential journal *Diogène* (with an English-language edition, *Diogenes*), which allowed him to develop an interdisciplinary "diagonal science" in the 1950s and 1960s. He also belonged to the editorial *comité de lecture* at Gallimard and brought Borges to a French readership. In 1972 he was inducted into the chambers of the Académie Française; by this point, he had already turned to what *Pierres réfléchies* (1975) called the "materialist mysticism" of his lapidary reveries.[3]

Even in France, serious studies of this oeuvre have only begun to emerge in the past few years, and a definitive bibliography has not yet been established.[4] American readers have had available to them *The Necessity of Mind* (1932–1934), *Man and the Sacred* (1939), *Man, Play and Games* (1958), *The Dream and Human Societies* (1967), *The Writing of Stones* (1970), *The Mystery Novel* (Le Roman policier [1941]), *Pontius Pilate* (1960) and various articles.[5] However, if Caillois has received little significant French critical commentary, he is even less discussed at present in the Anglo-Saxon sphere. There are various reasons for this, first and foremost being the sheer difficulty and interdisciplinary scope of the corpus. When viewed as a whole, it stands as a beckoning enigma, a riddle. Is there an overarching unity? A key? Moreover, as readers of the present anthology may find, each text, when read in isolation, seems lucid but almost meaningless. What's the point? What is Caillois really saying here? Despite his premature death at 65, Caillois had time to complete a vast number of projects and collect his essays with prefatory frames, yet he never published any clear explanation or mapping of his writings overall.[6] In fact, by this point, he self-consciously cultivated the mysterious quality of his oeuvre. "Exploded portrait," states his preface to the collected essays in *Cases d'un échiquier* (Spaces on a chessboard; 1970).[7] As for his late lyrical autobiography, *Le Fleuve Alphée* (The River Alpha; 1978), this repudiates his participation in the discourse of French intellectual life and hence offers but a very partial view of his past.

Le Fleuve Alphée bears more than a superficial similarity to Sartre's *Les Mots* (1964), another autobiographical account of disaffection from the Parisian intelligentsia. It explicitly echoes as well Hoffmansthal's character Lord Chandos, who undergoes a decisive detachment from language, although, in contrast, the revealed purposelessness of language restored Caillois's own "reason for writing."[8] Indeed, Caillois utterly rejected any Romantic or contemporary cult of silence. Lecturing at the Collège de France in 1974, he declared, "A constant trait of poetry, throughout its history, is some elusive [*je ne sais quelle*] affinity with mystery but not at all with the inexpressible [*l'indicible*], as people too frequently claim. Poetry rather involves a sense of propriety, a voluntary reticence, a certain way of hushing what is essential, in order to merely lure the imagination, to let it develop the message as it might wish. Behind the letter of the message, something unexpressed seems to await the moment for delivering a secret—a secret known from the outset and which simply had to be roused."[9] But the purpose and meaning of such a secret is a complex affair. "I reconciled myself to writing only when I started to do so with the awareness that it was, in any case, a complete waste," writes this former member of the College of Sociology, who shared to some degree, as we shall see, Bataille's abiding anti-utilitarian orientation.[10]

Readers of *Le Fleuve Alphée* might well be enticed, then, by the lyrical mystery of its prose; however, they would still be hard-pressed to understand what Caillois's previous writings were all about. His autobiographical reverie seeks to recapture neither duration nor Rousseauvian pastoral, but the lost authenticity of the mineral realm. A melancholy gaze surveys the ravages of human progress and the death of man—not only as a construct but in a biological sense, as the death of the planet. The work is structured by an allegory of the mythical freshwater river Alpha, which coursed through the saltwater sea and emerged wholly untainted on the other shore. The sea represents the realm of science (technology), letters, and language. In contrast, the tenacious undercurrent—"some kind of rebellious or perverse instinct"—represents Caillois's latent lyricism or unmediated contact with the world, a "meager and personal existence, whose haunting memory I had preserved against currents and tides."[11] We learn that the late prose poems of his *Pierres* series thus enact a circular return to his childhood state of preliteracy, unduly prolonged by World War I, in solitary contact with objects, such as stones.[12] A second dominant metaphor of "bracketing," now drawn from phenomenology rather than mythology, stages this cycle: a gigantic parenthesis, also a bubble, brackets off his absorption in the saltwater sea to let him focus, in a literary *épochè*, on the essential origin and conclusion of his life. This is metaphorically and literally, then, a return to the source, which recalls a final passage of his anthropological study, *Man and the Sacred*: "The sacred is what gives life and takes it away, it is the source from which it flows, and the estuary in which it loses itself."[13] In this complex chain of analogies among inanimate nature, mythology, the "sacred," philosophical concepts, and his inner world, readers may well discern what Caillois called, in 1978, his "generalized poetics" (to which I will return). The true shape of his experiences, however, is something most readers will have to reconstruct for themselves.

The lack of attention to Caillois in France may also have to do with the rather intangible issue of intellectual distaste. His writing style, especially in the 1930s and 1940s, can seem at times very intransigent, pompous, or precious. More damaging is the fact that despite his interest in universal emotions and representations, Caillois is largely concerned with the responsibilities and thought patterns of an intellectual elite.[14] And then, during and after the war, while greatly admiring foreign cultures, in particular that of classical China, he was a vocal defender of the West, blithely insensitive to the problems of colonialism. In a heated exchange with Lévi-Strauss in 1954–1955, Caillois argued that the West, better in this respect than all the rest, could appreciate and reach out to other cultures—or to what he called the "fifteen to twenty centers of civilisation."[15] His biographer, Odile Felgine, insinuates a lack of interest on his part in African culture, which frustrated his UNESCO colleague, the Congolese poet Tchicaya U' Tamsi.[16]

More dubious, in my opinion, and of course more serious, are the accusations of fascist sympathies that have beset Caillois from the 1930s to the present.[17] I would even question Hollier's more moderate claim about his attitude toward fascism at the time of the College of Sociology, that "he sought to maintain a provocative political undecidability as long as possible, putting off the choice that he was being hard pressed to make by everything around him."[18] To the extent that Caillois's "political undecidability" characterizes a murky sense of just *what* he is opposing to fascism, I agree. For example, "Aggressiveness as a Value" is unacceptable to contemporary readers in any kind of political sense. Yet I reject the idea that Caillois cultivated some ambiguity about his hostility to fascism—as he defined it, in a way that first focused on its violence, irrationalism, and anti-intellectualism; subsequently, on its biological or racial hierarchies; and finally, on its nihilism (as we shall see). With regard to fascism stricto sensu, Caillois (with André Breton and Paul Vaillant-Couturier), drafted the Surrealists' pamphlet on the burning of the Reichstag in February 1933. He then spearheaded the antifascist intellectual group Contre-Attaque in 1935, signed a manifesto attacking Spanish fascism in 1936 while supporting the Popular Front that same year, and drafted the antipacifist, anti-Hitler declaration of the College of Sociology after Munich in 1938. Of course, the College of Sociology was itself specifically constituted in the context of antifascist intellectual vigilance. Caillois's vehement antinationalism may blur the picture. And his cult of masters, responding to Hitler's rise, may itself resound with fascistic overtones. He shared a traditional French fear that democracy could not live up to the radical egalitarianism of its own ideals (I later discuss this in relation to "La Hiérarchie des êtres" [The hierarchy of beings; 1939]). But that, as I have suggested, is another question.

A close look at the context of Caillois's writing can shed further light on the alleged "undecidability" of his political stance. I have in mind two instances of antifascist manifestos that he was unable to publish as such, one in 1935 and the other in 1939. The first was drafted to launch Contre-Attaque; however, Bataille wrote to Caillois that while he and Breton had both approved of the initial document, changes had been imposed by another member, Maurice

Heine, in light of the principle "Not to say but to do."[19] Caillois's correspondence reveals just how difficult it was to subsequently publish his "political pages" in the *Nouvelle revue française* and *Minotaure* (despite the backing of Jean Wahl).[20] Again, in 1939, when Caillois sought to publish an anti-Hitler manifesto, his correspondence reveals that Bataille and Paulhan found the text too plodding and unexciting: "We agree with the side you take," wrote Bataille, speaking for Paulhan as well, "we agree about the hatred of Hitlerism, but we also agree that you are not especially made for a task that requires, that *demands* more facility than rigor."[21] Bataille also wrote to Caillois what he was stating elsewhere at the time: "Since matters are inextricable, it is best to say nothing."[22] (And the pacifist Aldous Huxley chimed in: "With regard to signing a declaration about Hitler—I regret that I cannot do this, as I do not feel that politics [except such politics as are dictated by the need to 'make the world safe for mystical experience'] are my affair."[23])

Finally, on a purely theoretical front, Caillois has been frequently caricatured as a negative counterpoint to Bataille, whose rise to fame, Susan Suleiman reminds us, occurred right after his death in 1962. Acclaimed by *Tel Quel*, Derrida, Barthes, Foucault, and others, Bataille became a "central reference" when "the potential for a metaphoric equivalence between the violation of *sexual* taboos and the violation of *discursive* norms that we associate with the theory of textuality became fully elaborated."[24] More recently, David Coward, in a *Times Literary Supplement* review, evokes Bataille as one who "helped to explode culture and deconstruct its artefacts . . . a guiding spirit of post-modernism."[25] If his name is thus synonymous with "transgression" and "heterogeneity," Caillois, on the other hand, is often cited as the totalizing thinker, wielding the menace of scientific "homogeneity."[26] Some commentators cite his strong need for mastery over the irrational, unconscious drives and, more generally, mystery.[27] But even at the height of his voluntarist attitude in the late 1930s, as he later recalled, Caillois thrived on the challenge of obstacles: "Apollonianism is first and foremost a victory, but it presupposes monsters—it does not do away with them."[28] And he was always seeking out new monsters. More important, I view as an *intellectual* project—and not merely as an emotional, or emotionally driven one—Caillois's lifelong quest to integrate *savoir* and *non savoir*, lucidity and affect, the intelligible and the unintelligible. He did so in ways that generally entailed dynamic flexibility in the 1930s, and paradox or open-ended systems after the war; they were inspired from the start by Dumézil, Bachelard, and Paulhan.[29]

He first sought to grant objective status to the Surrealist inspiration (see "The Praying Mantis"). By 1937, at the College of Sociology, he was grappling with the "sacred"—in a tense and serious dialogue with Bataille's ideas.[30] During the war, Caillois moved, in conceptual terms, from sacred, or "contagious," ideation to the work of civilization, but he did not dismiss mystery or the Surrealist imagination altogether. In fact, his writing here is interesting to consider in relation to the projects of Paulhan and Borges, who had themselves evolved from Surrealism to cultural and aesthetic neoclassicism. After the war, deciding that the structuralist *sciences humaines* were really a form of false, Surrealist science, Caillois reinstated distinctions in his later writings that he had subverted in the 1930s, in particular, the dichotomy of poetry and science. By the 1960s and 1970s, if his "diagonal science" revived the Surrealist legacy in his own experience, it ultimately did so to articulate a nonscientific, poetic "science." In this regard, Caillois may be quite relevant, I suggest, to the current discussion launched by Alan Sokal and Jean Bricquemont's notorious *Impostures intellectuelles*, which addresses the status of scientific discourse in postwar French "theory."[31]

* * *

This introduction to Caillois presents him as an essayist who was deeply attentive to his time and who was very deliberate (albeit sometimes wrong) about the kinds of response, theoretical or other, that he sought to offer. This makes it quite interesting to try to understand the precise nature of his response. To this end, my commentary highlights two coordinated axes of interpretation, which I loosely call the dialogical and the self-reflexive. Caillois's writing is generally grappling with another body of thought; in their correspondence, Bataille refers to "the god Polemos."[32] While fending off others, though, Caillois also tends to build on, or rework, his own previous ideas. Yet such dialogical and self-reflexive aspects of his writings are rarely made clear to the reader. Why? Was he driven by an insidious love of secrecy? By a lifelong strategy of mystery and enigma? Are we perchance eavesdropping on the covert conversations of a philosophical elite?

Clearly, this question of intent is impossible to answer with any kind of certainty. That Caillois nurtured a predilection for a secret elite (see "The Myth of Secret Treasures in Childhood") is undeniable. That he was haunted by mystery, enigma, and secrecy is clear from the persistent recurrence of these terms throughout his oeuvre. This leads Hollier to pin him down with the image of the male mimetic insect masking or hiding its "difference" in "Mimicry and Legendary Psychasthenia," or with that of the reserved aristocratic elite in "The Winter Wind."[33] Yet this "sense of propriety" (*pudeur*), which Caillois ultimately attributes to poetry itself, never engenders the strategic coyness of his close friend, Paulhan, whose lengthy treatise, *Les Fleurs de Tarbes*, closes with "and finally, let's say I haven't said a thing."[34] Indeed, unlike Paulhan,

Caillois was compelled by scientific rigor before the war, by dictionaries and lexical accuracy thereafter. Despite his lifelong skepticism about what has traditionally been called "the masses" and their susceptibility to political demagoguery, his political writings from the war onward called for "*transparency* on the part of leaders" (see "The Nature and Structure of Totalitarian Regimes"). And if he dreamed about secret societies in the 1930s, he pointedly refused to participate in Bataille's secret group, Acéphale. His open advocacy of what he calls "Machiavellian" literary sociology in "Paris, a Modern Myth" is hardly a secretive move—although, as we shall see, he privately called "The Winter Wind" a "bluff." (Together with "The Birth of Lucifer," this text comes closest in Caillois's oeuvre to a form of "mythical" mystification.) But, generally speaking, I have never found an instance in which the hidden—that is to say, dialogical or self-reflexive—aspect of an essay contradicted its manifest expression, as in the Leo Straussian contradiction between a private Nietzschean and a public anti-Nietzschean meaning.[35] In a bittersweet eulogy, his lifelong friend, the wily René Etiemble, cast him for posterity as a "homo mendax" by recalling his comment in a late radio interview: "In life, I lie just as much as I breathe."[36] I would argue that this old philosophical chestnut marks Caillois more as a lover of paradox than as a liar; and then, he was publically broadcasting this esoteric conundrum to any listener willing to stop and think for a minute.

There may be several basic reasons why Caillois does not chart the full coordinates of his "conversation" and of his own conceptual evolution. One is the interdisciplinary scope of his early work. As a rule, most essays falling into James Clifford's large rubric of "ethnographic surrealism" lack any serious methodological and conceptual framing.[37] Like Caillois, these avant-garde writers were publishing for small clusters of informed, avant-garde readers of the Parisian "petites revues" (little journals). Moreover, by the latter part of the decade, many of Caillois's texts involved a conversation with Bataille about the latter's secret society, Acéphale. So strong was Caillois's sense of loyal discretion about this group—to which he was very close—that he did not publish anything about it in France until 1964 (see "Preamble to the Spirit of Sects"); prior to that, in 1960, he had published veiled allusions in his novel, *Ponce Pilate*, to which I will return. Secondly, Caillois's deep-seated intellectual orientation held to certain invariants that tended to obscure the polemical thrust of any particular argument, as well as the circumstances of its production. In particular, he shunned subjective and emotional outpourings, which I would distinguish from other presentations of the self, such as clinical introspection or poetic reverie. (Bataille continually reproached Caillois's lack of subjective, that is existential, involvement with the intellectual material at hand, most

prominently with the sacred.[38]) Aristocratic reserve or propriety notwithstanding, what Caillois also pursued was objectivity and accuracy; here he was
inspired by science rather than by Julien Benda's abstract ideals of humanity
or justice (see "Sociology of the Intellectual"). "It is harder to shake a correct
argument than a rock," he wrote in 1978.[39] This meant rejecting vanity and self-
interest, any quest for social reward or approval. "One should not live from
one's pen," Caillois declared, however naïvely, in 1938, while in 1948 he likened
intellectual *engagement* to the status of a "paid pampleteer."[40] A few years
earlier, in Argentina, he had declared, "An intellectual is an intellectual *on top
of* his professional occupation."[41] Finally, in its aspiration toward some substratum or grounding, both at the outset and at the close of his career, Caillois's ideal of objectivity moved far beyond accuracy and integrity. *Pierres
réfléchies* records that he sometimes wished for the "presumptuous" and exclusive reward of making a single contribution to "the sum total of proverbs,
which are anonymous and permanent; stones are immensely anonymous and
permanent."[42]

Over the years, I have developed more than a grudging appreciation for one
who idealized intellectual community and yet made the act of grasping (not
to mention sharing) his views such an arduous task. Perhaps from the start I
was intrigued by several comments from people who knew him well. For example, the philosopher Jean Wahl wrote to him in 1936, on reading his "political pages" (probably the first manifesto of Contre-Attaque): "There are few
people whom I trust as much as you." During the war, Breton wrote to Caillois that he was someone whose authenticity he had never stopped believing in
(despite their break in 1934). Finally, in 1974, Edmond Jabès wrote to him, "'I
learnt that whatever I might undertake, I will never do anything but persevere
. . .' That is the lesson you derive from your [own] books: the great (the only?)
teaching that a writer could transmit. . . . Your reflections remain important for
us: for nothing that is done—or undone—escapes your glance. To the 'perse-
vering' questioning that is yours, from one book to the other, one can only respond by a questioning that is sometimes different, but always parallel, fraternal."[43] This is a useful reminder of how intensely Caillois committed himself
to a life of essayistic inquiry sparked by the frenetic intellectual cauldron of
his youth—and in a way perhaps best compared to the lifelong projects of his
initial companions at the College of Sociology, Georges Bataille and Michel
Leiris.

*   *   *

The following seeks to recount both the inward and outward reach of Caillois's
systems, bridging academic research and the most extreme forms of avant-

garde thought. In 1929, this child of the provincial bourgeoisie set off from Reims to prepare for the Ecole Normale. By 1936, Caillois had obtained the competitive Agrégation de grammaire (classics); he also studied sociology of religion with Marcel Mauss and comparative mythology with Georges Dumézil and heard Marcel Granet applying Maussian sociology to the cultural imagination of ancient China.[44] His thesis for the Ecole des Hautes Etudes, written under the unofficial supervision of Dumézil, was titled *Noontime Demons* (1937; a brief sketch was published as the "The Noon Complex"). Much of his writing in these years—such as "The Function of Myth," social scientific reviews for the *Nouvelle revue française*, his essays in *Verve* and *Revue de l'histoire des religions*, and the lengthy study *Man and the Sacred*—were serious attempts to pursue the work of his Hautes Etudes mentors. "Dumézil spoke of him as the genius of our time," recounted André Chastel, his friend at the Ecole Normale."[45] As mentioned above, other important figures in his life were Bachelard and Paulhan, the prominent editor of the *Nouvelle revue française*.[46]

But Caillois was also shaped by members of the avant-garde, in the first instance by the poet Roger Gilbert-Lecomte. Originating from Caillois's hometown of Reims (also that of Bataille), Gilbert-Lecomte and other friends constituted Le Grand Jeu, a small literary group with a journal of the same name. Le Grand Jeu was a form of metaphysical dadaism or morbid *pataphysique*, led by Gilbert-Lecomte and René Daumal, who were both widely read in esotericism and mysticism.[47] Gérard de Cortanze has succinctly remarked about the group's mystical negative theology: "Le Grand Jeu aims to reach 'the empty point that sustains life and forms,' it opposes Surrealism which seeks, on the other hand, to 'fill up.'"[48] Caillois's experience with Le Grand Jeu may go far toward explaining his later ambivalent attraction to Acéphale. To this first group, in part, I trace his lifelong obsession with depersonalization, the dissolution of the self, and that *instinct d'abandon* (instinct of letting go) he explored from "Mimicry and Legendary Psychasthenia" to *Le Fleuve Alphée*.

Caillois sought to explore his imaginative experiences with Le Grand Jeu in his philosophical treatise, *The Necessity of Mind* (1932–1934), written after he had moved into the Surrealist camp.[49] Jean-François Sirinelli's monumental study of the Ecole Normale Supérieure explains that "Surrealism never really attracted students from the Ecole Normale. . . . Roger Caillois, the only such student who ever belonged to the Surrealist group, declared in 1972: 'People thought I was mad.'"[50] His 1973 reminiscence, "Testimony (Paul Eluard)," offers a lively self-portrait of the young Caillois joining forces with the Surrealist movement and hoping to do away with *la littérature* in the wake of Rimbaud and Freud. Caillois took part in the political turmoil of the early 1930s, when Breton was seeking a *redressement* (straightening up) to remedy Surrealism's internal conflicts and its difficult external relation to the Communist Party.[51] These political events apparently offered him early lessons about ineffectual political activism. In his writings at the time, though, Caillois was primarily intent to become the theorist or philosopher of Surrealist poetics—to grant its image a systematic, scientific ground. If he dismissed Surrealist automatism—from automatic writing to Dalí's "critical paranoia"—as arbitrary and subjective, Caillois did not reject automatism altogether but merely wished to make it more objective. *The Necessity of Mind* hence replaces *automatic writing* with *automatic thought*, and "lyricism" with automatized, lyrical *ideograms* (see "The Praying Mantis"). The project of *The Necessity of Mind* was not sociological, so it is somewhat difficult to understand Caillois's remark: "Now it must seem curious, but I didn't make any distinction between the study of religious sociology that I was pursuing with [Marcel] Mauss and my participation in the activities of the Surrealist group."[52] However, the art historian André Chastel told me that as he understood it, the theory of ideograms was a quest for fundamental structures of the individual and collective imagination. This was a "pre–Lévi-Straussian endeavor, which stemmed from Mauss, from the School of the Musée de l'Homme, and which sought to restrict the scope of trivial psychology derived from novels."[53] Indeed, Mauss was highly interested in the psychological and even biological aspects of the "total social fact": "Basically, here everything is mixed together, body, soul, society," he wrote in 1924, praising the studies of "instinct" as a collective factor, and also that mode of psychology "moving towards a kind of mental biology, a kind of true psychophysiology."[54] He heartily applauded "The Praying Mantis": "Your story of the mantis and the ghoul is perfectly interpreted. It's good mythology."[55] But Caillois would soon proceed to correlate biology and sociology to a much greater degree than his teacher would have wished (see "The Function of Myth").

Caillois broke with the Surrealists in 1934, right after the "incident of the Mexican jumping beans." This amusing and highly symbolic anecdote involved a crisis about the proper methodology for inspecting freshly arrived objets in the Surrealist orbit, a pair of jumping beans.[56] Caillois wanted to slice them open, to see what made them jump; yet out of principle, as he recounts, Breton refused to do so, for this would have destroyed "the mystery." Here was the triggering event for Caillois's monograph, *Art on Trial by Intellect*, framed by the "Letter to André Breton" and "Literature in Crisis"; however, these texts did not simply confirm the dichotomy of poetry and science, dismissing the first for the second. Inspired by German phenomenology and, closer to home, by Bachelard's *New Scientific Spirit*, Caillois was calling instead for a new, more imaginative science. Such an attitude would lead him to theorize creatively the perils attending modern scientific representation with his essay, "Mimicry and Legendary Psychasthenia."

Caillois's bold attempts to systematize the *imaginaire* of Le Grand Jeu, Surrealism, and theoretical physics launched his evolving theoretical models based on the quest for hidden identity—in 1978, he called this the "analogical wager."[57] In his famous article of 1946, "Le Sens moral de la sociologie" (The moral sense of sociology), Bataille said of Leiris, Caillois, and the *Collège*, "These young writers felt that society had lost the secret of its cohesion, and that here was precisely what the obscure, awkward and sterile efforts of poetic fever were seeking out." Hence they replaced Breton's literary quest with "scientific research."[58] For Bataille, the secret of social cohesion meant breaking individual and experiential barriers with effervescent, collective participation and categories of rational thought in favor of Lévy-Bruhl's "primitive mentality." But for Caillois, the secret of social cohesion partook of a much more wide-ranging form of alternative logic, largely derived from Baudelairean correspondences and scientific epistemology. He would develop these ideas in the 1930s, renounce them during the war, and thereafter reconsider them at great length.

In 1932, Caillois joined Breton's movement not just because it aspired to found a community but also because he viewed the Surrealist metaphor or image as a research method into what *The Necessity of Mind* calls the "empirical imagination."[59] Marc Eigeldinger writes, "Already for Victor Hugo, and then for Rimbaud and the Surrealists, the image was a tool of poetic knowledge at the same time that it was, according to Aragon, 'the greatest possible consciousness of the concrete.'"[60] For the Surrealists, in this regard, automatism was key. Breton's *First Manifesto* (1924) had voiced the hallowed principle of arbitrary associationism by echoing Pierre Reverdy's 1918 formulation: "The image is a pure creation of the mind. It cannot be born from a comparison but from a juxtaposition of two more or less distant realities. The more the relationships between the two juxtaposed realities are distant and true [*justes*], the stronger the image will be—the greater its emotional power and poetic reality."[61] However, as opposed to Reverdy's deliberate construction of poetic *justesse* [accuracy], Breton argued: "It is, as it were, from the fortuitous juxtaposition of the two terms that a particular light has sprung, *the light of the image*, to which we are infinitely sensitive. . . . Now, it is not within man's power, so far as I can tell, to effect the juxtaposition of two realities so far apart. The principle of the association of ideas, such as we conceive it, militates against it" (*Manifestoes*, 37). Five years later, his *Second Manifesto* would nevertheless suggest that the Surrealists' introspection should grant them a *"new consciousness"* of Freudian sublimation, hence a better grasp of inspiration, "and [that], from the moment they cease thinking of it as something sacred . . . they dream only of making it shed its final ties, or even—something no one had ever dared imagine—of making it submit to them" (*Manifestoes*, 161). In line with *The Second Manifesto*, Caillois's *The Necessity of Mind* did not pursue Reverdy's conscious poetic project but rather sought to explore the latent determinism of intellectual associationism. He imagined a universal, overdetermined network of *ideograms*: automatic crystallizations of representations, driven by the mechanisms of Freudian dreamwork and of obsessional, "psychasthenic" thought, as theorized by Pierre Janet and linked to the outlook of Le Grand Jeu (see "The Praying Mantis"). The *Necessity of Mind* also pursued the Surrealists' current drive in the early 1930s to objectively realize their dreams, since Caillois here imagined natural or *objective ideograms* (see "The Praying-Mantis"). In contrast, Reverdy had always described both the image and the emotion it provoked as a "pure creation of the mind" and a new "poetic reality."[62]

However, Caillois had not yet started to think about the secret hinge—correspondence, or identity—linking these representations. For the Surrealists, Baudelaire's legacy was anathema. Breton spoke of the *correspondances* as an "odious critical common-place," and Aragon's *Traité de style* (Treatise on style) inveighed against metaphor and analogy, "the crushing weight of Baudelairean *correspondances*."[63] Yet Caillois became interested in such questions, noting in *Art on Trial by Intellect* that "the realization of resemblance" was "the fundamental function of thought"; in fact, "there is no intellectual or affective process which is not based upon the phenomenon of resemblance."[64] He broke with Breton in part due to his new interest in scientific epistemology, which was encouraged by his new friend, Bachelard (see "Letter to André Breton"). I interpret the initial version of "Mimicry and Legendary Psychasthenia" (1935) as his reverie of a subversive, revolutionary New Science, predicated on a more imaginative "judgment of resemblance" than that of classical science or rationalism. He hoped to reform not only Surrealism but now science as well, under the aegis of German Romantic *Naturphilosophie*, that is, "Mme. de Staël's wish to take as a guide for experimental method 'a more extensive philosophy that would encompass the universe as a whole and would not scorn the nocturnal side of nature.'"[65]

In *Art on Trial by Intellect*, Caillois respectfully cites the philosopher of science, Emile Meyerson, whose major work, *Identité et realité* (Identity and Reality), challenged rationalism as the tautology of reason: its reduction to the same, to identity. Meyerson voiced the fear, as summarized by Louis de Broglie, that "the complete realization of that idea pursued by reason seems . . . chimerical, since it would involve resorbing all the qualitative diversity and progressive variations of the physical universe in one absolute identity and permanence."[66] Bataille hailed a related scene of reason's collapse on itself in "The Solar Anus" (1930): "Ever since sentences started to *circulate* in brains devoted to reflection, an effort at total identification has been made, because with the aid of a *copula* each sentence ties one thing to another; all things would be visibly connected if one could discover at a single glance and in its totality the tracings of an Ariadne's thread leading thought into its own labyrinth." His parodic, performative, realization of the copula then recast neo-Kantian logic as sexual participation: "When I scream I AM THE SUN an integral erection results, because the verb *to be* is the vehicle of amorous frenzy."[67] Here we find an early version of that "secret cohesion" or "sacred" collective "boiling point" to which Bataille aspired: "The sacred is only a privileged moment of communal unity, a moment of the convulsive communication of what is ordinarily stifled."[68]

However, as a student of the rationalist Mauss, Caillois was more inclined to question or even modify reason rather than to reject it outright. In 1938, he denied Lévy-Bruhl's notion of "primitive mentality," as did Mauss, but would further argue that "there is no logical mentality": it is merely an ideal model of reasoning, which the philosopher can never fully achieve given his human sensitivity and emotions. And he equates as two "philosophers" "the indigenous chieftain and the colonial administrator who is trying to make him see the light of reason."[69] Three years earlier, "Mimicry and Legendary Psychasthenia" challenged the idealist Bergsonian rationalism of Dominique Parodi's "Le Sentiment de ressemblance" [The feeling of resemblance], an article Caillois briefly refers to in *Art on Trial by Intellect*. Parodi had claimed that "the judgment of resemblance is the judgment of synthesis, by excellence. It is that properly intellectual act of unification or abstraction whereby we determine the world. . . . If . . . the origin and, in effect, the raw material of the judgment of *resemblance* is in the feeling of our spiritual life's unity and continuity, then all our knowledge and all our science are still nothing but the effort to ensure the very unity of thought's experience and continuity by discovering ever more secret and subtle relations or similarities in the world."[70] "Mimicry and Legendary Psychasthenia," on the contrary, reveals similarities that harbor disintegration. Still, the specter of total indistinction is kept at bay by the categories of nature and natural forces. Generally speaking, "Mimicry and Legendary Psychasthenia" recalls Schelling's Romantic *naturphilosophie* with its cosmic world-soul, informed by a universal *Urpolarität* (basic polarity) that constitutes, in the words of Walter D. Wetzels, "the principle of life throughout nature from crystals to man, render[ing] the formerly sharp distinctions between inorganic and organic nature, between man and the rest of creation, as mere gradual differentiations."[71] Caillois's tantalizingly obscure essay about mimicry explores "realizations of resemblance" in biology (the Lamarckian landscape imaging of insects), in anthropology (the mimetic magic of sorcerers), and in science (the spatial representations of modern physics). These mimetic insects, magicians, and scientists meet with nothing but depersonalization, disorientation, and general undoing along the way. Moreover, the essay itself is not exempt. Caillois's opening paragraph states the scientific imperative to resolve the dichotomies he will map out.[72] He then proceeds to reveal the secret cohesion or analogy among mimetic insects, magicians, and the epistemology of modern physics, which turns on the dissolution of the self and the *instinct d'abandon*. Does Caillois's delirious "judgment of resemblance" in this regard imply that he himself, as author, will be endangered as well? An allusion to aesthetic *correspondances* discreetly challenges Parodi's reassuring association of Baudelairean *correspondances* with the constitution and preservation of the self.[73]

Viewed in economic terms, Caillois's essay and its obsessional theory may well strike the reader as a somewhat "dangerous luxury," much like the mimicry he describes. Indeed, in its anti-Darwinian anti-utilitarianism, this essay shows strong traces of Caillois's new friend, Bataille, whom he had met by 1934, apparently through Jacques Lacan.[74] Caillois did not participate, like Bataille, in Boris Souvarine's Cercle Communiste Démocratique (Democratic communist circle). However, he read Souvarine's journal, *La Critique sociale*, where he had admired Bataille's essays, such as "The Notion of Expenditure."[75] This young student of Mauss and Dumézil was similarly drawn to the irrational and emotional motives of societies and political movements repressed by Enlightenment rationalism and utilitarianism (see "The Function of Myth") and with which classical Marxism did not contend. These issues had come to the fore by 1935, when politics was taking center stage after the fascist riots of February 1934. I have noted that Caillois initiated (and withdrew from) Contre-Attaque, which then met from September 1935 through May 1936 under the joint helm of Breton and Bataille. Hostile to party politics, fascism, communism, nationalism, and, later, the Popular Front's noninterventionism in the Spanish Civil War, Contre-Attaque derived its ideological outlook from Bataille's "La Structure psychologique du fascisme" (The psychological structure of fascism).[76] Its official manifesto proclaimed the urgent need, in the universal interests of mankind, to deploy the weapons wrought by fascism against fascism itself, "which was able to employ man's fundamental yearning for affective exaltation and fanaticism . . . [which is] infinitely more serious and explosive . . . than that of nationalists enslaved to social conservation and the selfish interests of fatherlands."[77] But Caillois was wary of Bataille's attempt to fight fire with fire. In an important letter to a friend, most likely written between 1935 and 1936, he declared:

> I don't think that my opinion on this topic is very valuable, since I am poorly informed, and I don't think anyone can be well-informed. It certainly seems that a kind of embryonic and shamefaced fascism is taking shape; but this is unlikely to become agressive unless the proletariat, if poorly led, gives it a pretext for doing so. In any case, the situation is totally different from what it was in Germany before Adolf Hitler's rise to power and, in my opinion, one should not expect such adventures here for the time being. I specify: for the time being, because people *over here as well as over there* are so hypnotized by them that we might very well end up by triggering similar events. But, to my knowledge, there is neither a serious fascist core among the workers nor a serious "red threat"; and so we have two very unfavorable circumstances for the instatement of a systematic and violent fascism.[78]

While Bataille's Contre-Attaque sought to fight fascism with its own weapons, such a "hypnotized" approach is precisely what Caillois wished to avoid, or so he claimed. In 1935–1936, his allegorical "L'Ordre et l'empire" unambiguously (if cryptically) depicted the violence, mythical irrationalism, and anti-intellectual tyranny of the fascist regime. This essay, and "The Function of Myth," suggest that he was groping for ways to revivify decadent social bonds—in this charged political context—without rejecting the Enlightenment. Although the thrust of his two conclusions is not entirely clear (Is he referring to Germany or to France? Is he describing or prescribing?), the point seems to be that Dionysianism and "the right to guilt," which have been repressed or displaced from the collective into the individual sphere by "rationalism," "skepticism," and "social utilitarianism," are now rightfully and ineluctably prepared to counterattack with the very weapons forged by "critical inquiry and systematic thinking." Indeed, *they* rather than reason—this "sorcerer's apprentice increasingly overwhelmed by the objects it has conjured up"—can currently avail themselves of "lucidity and science."[79] Such a response to Bataille's Dionysianism, as I see it, would characterize Caillois's approach throughout the period of the College of Sociology as well (see "Dionysian Virtues").

In early 1936, Caillois was specifically turning to Georges Sorel with these issues in mind, stating, "He shows such a concern to subordinate aesthetics to ethics in a world where frivolity rules and commands lack due respect that the *vox populi* no longer seems to be exaggerating when it unvaryingly recalls Sorel upon hearing the names of Lenin, Mussolini and Hitler."[80] My reading of this ambiguous remark is that he was here upholding the "serious" legacy of Sorel as a counterpoint to Contre-Attaque's aestheticized attempt to mirror and combat Nazi mass propaganda with Bataille's emotional "heterogeneity" and the Surrealist will-to-myth.[81] Indeed, Sorel's *Reflections on Violence* presented a modern counterpart to archaic myth with its program of the general socialist strike to rouse the proletariat, defined in Bergsonian and scientistic terms. Caillois, it should be said, shared neither Sorel's nationalism, Marxism, nor his agenda of applied, mythical irrationalism as a means of immediate revolutionary upheaval. In this last regard, I draw a sharp distinction between Caillois and his Sorelian friend of this period, the young Antillean sociologist, Jules Monnerot, who wished to scientifically trigger participatory, violent states, essentially conceived in terms of Lévy-Bruhl's category of "primitive mentality."[82] In contrast, Caillois imagined not only juxtaposing but integrating lucidity and emotion, science and myth with a "militant orthodoxy" poised somewhere between Marx and Durkheim, that is, between ideological superstructure and collective representation.

"For a Militant Orthodoxy" (1936) was written for the short-lived avant-garde group Inquisitions: Organe de Recherche de la Phénoménologie Humaine (Inquisitions: Organ of Research into Human Phenomenology; 1936), with a journal of the same name, which sought to uphold the Popular Front with ideological innovations reflecting the latest scientific breakthroughs. "A valiant journal," applauded Jean Wahl in 1936, "where the Marxist orthodoxy of one of the directors [Aragon] notwithstanding, the wish for rigor and orthodoxy on the part of the others, and of the collaborators, does not let itself be subordinated to any doctrine."[83] Caillois cofounded Inquisitions with the former Surrealists—now communists—Tristan Tzara and Louis Aragon, as well as Monnerot, Bachelard, and others (Paulhan also wanted to contribute). In group discussions published by *Inquisitions*, Caillois imagined a scientific aristocracy that would recuperate the revolutionary function of the nineteenth-century *maudits* (damned) poets, who had challenged the social order. In 1936, he argued, the obstacle had shifted from an oppressive social *order* to social *disorder*, for which the revolutionary remedy was the slow and hypothetical, indeed utopian construction of an ever-evolving "orthodoxy."[84] In this sense, "For a Militant Orthodoxy" can be seen as the initial manifesto of Caillois's "reactionary avant-gardism," to use the term applied to him by Meyer Schapiro in 1945.[85] Comparing *Inquisitions* to Bataille's new journal, *Acéphale*, Wahl added, "Caillois seeks rigor, Bataille appeals to the heart, to enthusiasm, to ecstasy, to the earth, to fire, to our guts."[86]

The rising tide of sociopolitical crisis led Caillois to make a more positive— or aggressive—use of modern science than he had with "Mimicry and Legendary Psychasthenia." Written and published more or less in tandem with Bachelard's "Le Surrationalisme," "For a Militant Orthodoxy" calls for an alternative logic, whose theoretical basis is outlined in Caillois's "L'Alternative (Naturphilosophie ou Wissenschaftlehre)" (Natural philosophy or the theory of science; 1937). Here, he draws on Meyerson and others to hail the breakthrough of modern physics:

> effectively instating . . . new conceptual frameworks and using the principle of continuous expansion to replace the closed logic of identity with a new logic—a logic of generalization. In this realm, there could be no question of any *a priori* respect for mystery; however, since nothing is ever lost, the reduction of mystery has transformed the explanatory principle just as the irrational residue transformed the rational modalities of the intellectual activity that accounted for it. Indeed, some kind of osmotic equilibrium always tends to establish itself between thought and its obstacle, since what does the explaining must necessarily be at more or less the same level as what is being explained.[87]

One definition of "generalization" is the following: "An operation whereby one discerns certain features shared by several singular objects and then unites the latter in terms of a single concept, whose [comprehension] is formed by these features."[88] Unlike the reduction to identity haunting Meyerson, generalization thus brings to light a secret or hidden similitude that resolves mystery while creating a new set of congruent elements.[89] In effect, "For a Militant Orthodoxy" transposes the "continuous expansion" of generalization into the social sphere as an ideological, collective order. This representation of heterodox orthodoxy, imbued with the contagious quality characterizing the sacred, courses through Caillois's subsequent models for intellectual activism during the next few years at the College of Sociology (1937–1939).[90]

Let me briefly note an acknowledged "cohesion" between Caillois and Paulhan, as the editor of *La Nouvelle revue française* was very interested in *Inquisitions*, and the first, 1936, version of his *Les Fleurs de Tarbes* ou *La Terreur dans les lettres* sought to bring a more rigorous and New Scientific focus to bear on Surrealism, literature, and orthodoxy. "For a Militant Orthodoxy" refers to the Russian mathematician Lobatchevsky as a model of generalization (as opposed to Hegelian dialectics); so too, Paulhan wrote to Jouhandeau that *Les Fleurs* sought to enact in the literary domain "the same revolution of the mind as that accomplished by Lobatchevsky in mathematics, and Riemann in geometry."[91] Indeed, Caillois's eulogy for Paulhan presents his thought as a mode of "open rationalism": "In his case, logic did not entail finding the flaw in any particular reasoning as much as it involved the capacity to modify, if not to reverse, the givens. He didn't try to show that the problem was poorly posed, but rather that one could pose it differently and that, to properly grasp its meaning, one had to admit and consider, at the same time, propositions that were symmetrical and contrary to it."[92] Paulhan's famous treatise on the prospect of literary orthodoxy, or of a shared rhetoric, focused on the dual nature of the cliché. At times a verbal obstacle to the transparent transmission of thought, it is also a potential site for the communion of souls, he argued. In the face of such unmanageable ambiguity, Paulhan then envisioned a vaster rationalism that might accommodate the shifts of the cliché and, more generally, of language itself. In this regard, the initial, 1936 version of *Les Fleurs* reveals the influence of Bachelard's *Le Nouvel Esprit scientifique*: "Here we must think," writes Paulhan, "of those scientists who refuse to dogmatically desire fundamental concepts; of physicists, who along with Einstein, take as their point of departure a *space-time* (as we do a *language-thought*); of microphysicists with their *movement-figure*; of geometers, with their non-Euclidian world. In their calculations, all of them thus replace clarity in itself with operational clarity." Moreover, Paulhan aligns Bachelard's New Science with theological models: "I don't know any definition of the *tâo*, of God or of the absolute, whose essence is not the identity of two terms that are just as contradictory as thought and language, space and time, movement and figure."[93]

Caillois himself would consider the bipolar ambiguities of the sacred in *Man and the Sacred*, as we shall see; however, in 1936, he was more interested in Fichte and the Vienna School. That is to say, "L'Alternative (Naturphilosophie ou Wissenschaftlehre)" retrospectively discerned in Fichte's debate with Schelling the twentieth-century conflict between "mysticism" and "science."[94] Caillois also revealed an interest in logical positivism that was unusual in the Parisian context. He thus rejected "the perceptible and intelligible forms of intuition," inveighing against "the school of Heidegger," "the literary," and "the poeticization of concepts."[95] In its place, he hailed scientific "systematization," defined along the lines of Carnap, Russell, and Reichenbach's *La Philosophie scientifique*, and defended "theoretical knowledge," that is, Reichenbach's epistemological *"concern to give a meaning, from the point of view of knowledge, to the methods used to know."*[96] "For a Militant Orthodoxy" illustrates this methodological focus when promoting generalization: "Nothing proves that we would not do better to conserve the current *syntax* of understanding on condition that we expand it whenever necessary" (emphasis added). For the logical positivists, such as Carnap, syntax involved logic as opposed to semantics: "A language consists of a vocabulary and a syntax, i.e. a set of words which have meanings and rules of sentence formation."[97] (The term syntax in this proto-structuralist sense would recur in Caillois's work, up to *Le Fleuve Alphée*: "Stones reconcile me for a moment with a syntax that extends beyond me everywhere."[98])

But Caillois's epistemological turn had an ascetic, ethical component as well; repudiating the model of the schizophrenic, depersonalized scientist of "Mimicry and Legendary Psychasthenia," Caillois would place deliberate self-bracketing at the heart of the scientific project. The visionary, he complained, merely enjoys the fruits of his private "sensibility," determined by factors of which he is unaware, such as health, temperament, education, and status; thus, "the immediate result of nature returns to nature without much having been gained in this circuit." On the contrary, the thoughts of the lucid scientist are self-consciously detached from such "self-indulgence" so they obey "impersonal" determinations.[99] And here is the glacial Zarathustrian lucidity outlined in "L'Aridité" (1938): "One is less interested in what one knows than in the way that one knows, and the effort of knowledge quickly takes this last as its exclusive object. One then reaches aridity; the investigation has no field above and beyond its own syntax."[100] In 1968, Caillois would describe "the emptying out of his inner self [putting to sleep his tastes and reactions] that the scientist must accept to perform his mission."[101] However, his ideal of lucidity, as rehearsed in the late 1930s, involved the passionate process of self-mastery rather than any real state of "scientific" being.

By early 1937, after "For a Militant Orthodoxy," Caillois's ethics of science had become a noxious brew of Nietzsche, Sorel, Loyola, de Maistre, and Corneille. The direct cause was the failure and, indeed, the collapse of Blum's government, which Caillois ascribed to Blum's personal ineptness for power. His writings in 1937, drawing on Frazer's *The Magical Origins of Kings*, suggest that what the contemporary world lacked, perhaps above and beyond Dionysian effervescence, was "pontifical power" and "despotism." Caillois's analysis of power entailed a simple binary system of tyrants and subjects, Nietzsche's master/slave dichotomy, later expressed in "La Hiérarchie des êtres" (The hierarchy of beings; 1939) as the distinction between those who sought "the arid pleasures of independence and power" and those who enjoyed all other "pleasures . . . those of the flesh and the mind."[102] Caillois also yoked this to Bergson and the tropism of the sacred. Power, he wrote, is "a mode of immediate datum of consciousness, towards which a being's elementary reaction is that of either attraction or repulsion." In Blum's case, for example, "every line of his writings indicates that he prefers being subjected to tyranny rather than exercising it himself." Caillois's cult of power was inflamed by the ideas of the right-wing romantic royalist, Joseph de Maistre concerning power's irreducible nature, with its divine source hidden in the mysteries of Christian sacrifice. "Clearly," writes Caillois, "for M. Blum, it's legality that establishes power. However, on the contrary, I am afraid that it is power that establishes legality." In this respect, Blum's conception of power as "administrative" or contractual rather than "pontifical" or "sacred" was a grievous and fatal flaw: "Saint-Just, who first asserted that one could not rule *innocently*, caused a king's head to fall because of this maxim."[103] (Yet, as we shall see, this did not signal Caillois's readiness to commit a human sacrifice.)

When Blum's fall was beyond repair in early 1937 Caillois had become deeply immersed in a "nonconformist" milieu lacking any faith in parliamentary democracy's capacity to withstand, using its own resources, Hitler's inevitable assault.[104] As extensively documented by Hollier, the College of Sociology was a complex meeting ground for left-wing intellectuals, many of whom had frequented the periphery of Surrealism, and whose deep sense of historical crisis in the face of imminent war led them to consider recasting "society" as "community" through sociological rather than political, nationalist, or racist mobilization. Caillois recounts that the term "college" referred not to an academic institution but to "the superior authority of a church," such as the "Sacré Collège" (Sacred College) of the Jesuits, adding that for the College of Sociology, "it was not economy that ruled the world but religious forces, which could be atheistic; it was the sacred that interested us, it was *not* theology."[105] This conception of the sacred as a form of psychological or emotional energy indissociable from the social order was loosely inspired by Durkheimian sociology, in particular by *The Elementary Forms of Religious Life* (1912): "If religion has given birth to all that is essential in society, it is because the idea of society is the soul of religion."[106] Jean Piel, Bataille's lifelong collaborator at *Critique*, after the war, cites Bataille's "Le Sens moral de la sociologie" to explain: "Bataille has shown that this project was essentially inspired by the 'solid' elements he had retained from Durkheim's doctrine; Durkheim had discovered, first of all, that 'society is a whole that is different from the sum of its parts,' and then that the sacred, in the sense given to it by primitive religions, was the bond, 'that is to say, the constitutive element of all that is society.'"[107] In its actual analyses, however, the College of Sociology drew less from Durkheim than from his nephew Mauss; from its recent discovery of *Gemeinschaft*, addressed by German sociology; and from Rudolf Otto's study of religious emotion, *The Sacred*.[108]

Caillois drafted, among other manifestoes, the group's declaration in November 1938 against the predominantly pro-Munich pacifist Parisian mood: "The College of Sociology regards the general absence of intense reaction in the face of war as a sign of man's *devirilization*. It does not hesitate to see the cause of this in the relaxation of society's current ties, which are practically nonexistent as a result of the development of bourgeois individualism."[109] This called for recreation rather than mere restructuring, for collective revolutionary action. Caillois did not analyze this social decay in precise Durkheimian terms, such as "organic" or "mechanical" "solidarity," which he would sometimes use during and after the war. In fact, he used images of various sorts to evoke the social havoc wrought by "individualism." Here is a "crumbling" world "that is menacing in the manner of a sponge" ("Aggressiveness as a Value"), while "The Winter Wind" talks of social "cohesion" as "a force that breaks any individual effort as if it were glass." Whether society is viewed as an oppressive block or as a sponge, what does remain consistent is Caillois's apocalyptic call for *supersocialization*. Rebellious individuals "must confront society on its own territory and attack it with its own arms. That is to say they must constitute themselves in a community."[110] Reflecting on such elite orders and their counterattack was his project for the next few years.

Comparing his response to that of Bataille and Acéphale, Hollier has coined the oft-cited contrast between Caillois's "will to power" and Bataille's "will to tragedy."[111] This distinction is undoubtedly apt. Yet neither power nor tragedy were so much ends in themselves as they were different means toward a similar end, namely, antinationalist social renewal or revolutionary resurrection. Although Caillois did write of despotism, his primary concern, and that of the College of Sociology, was the collective social order. "The Winter Wind" is prefaced by Nietzsche's sociological claim, which, notes Jean-Michel Heimonet, simultaneously appeared in the writings of Bataille and Monnerot: "The decay of society's morals is a condition under which the new ovule or new ovules appear—ovules (individuals) who contain the germ of new societies and units. The appearance of individuals is the sign that society has become capable of reproducing."[112] And both Bataille and Caillois were equally caught up in a fight against fascism that explicitly opposed bourgeois liberal democracy. They were haunted by the model of secret societies largely for their elective status, which, as Hollier evokes one of Bataille's talks, are thus "opposed on the one hand to de facto communities (the fact being geographical or racial) that made up the fascist regimes, but also on the other hand, to what can be called de facto absences of any community, that is to say, democracies."[113] Pierre Prévost, cited by Bataille, recalls that Bataille told the College of Sociology of his desire "to construct an (aristocratic) order that would take charge of the fate of human society!"[114] In *Acéphale*, he clearly stated, "The teaching of Nietzsche devises the faith of the sect or 'order' whose dominating will is to bring about free human destiny, severing it from both its rational enslavement to production and its irrational enslavement to the past."[115]

When considering this rejection of democracy, a historical caveat about the context and contemporaneous ideological spectrum is in order. Raymond Aron was himself calling for a reconsideration of democratic principles in 1939: "Today, it is no longer a matter of saving bourgeois, humanitarian or pacifist illusions. The excesses of irrationalism do not discredit—quite the contrary— that effort which is necessary in order to put into question progressivism, abstract moralism or the ideas of 1789. Like rationalism, democratic conservativism can only possibly save itself by renewing itself."[116] Yet, if Caillois sought to renew rationalism (however subversively), it could not be said that he wished to renew democracy. Certainly, he did not promote it as a valid means of challenging fascism. Having outlined Nazi violence and irrationalism at the time of Contre-Attaque, he further condemned Hitler's regime as a nationalist and racist community at the College of Sociology. In 1939, Caillois's essay "Naturaleza del hitlerismo" (The nature of Hitlerism) then attacked Nazism on conceptual grounds—in terms of its incoherence. Inspired by Hermann Rauschning's treatise, *The Revolution of Nihilism*, he dwells here on the Stalin-Hitler pact to highlight the opportunistic, ideological vacancy of Nazism. "In Germany, as elsewhere," states a concluding passage,

> each individual may have particular reasons for fighting Hitler's regime: one person is defending his ideal; another, his homeland; a third, his race, or his faith. Some people oppose him out of self-interest, others out of belief. These motives, which are different in every case, are all legitimate in their own spheres. But above and beyond any national, moral or doctrinarian sectarianism, we must face the fact that by its very nature a Hitlerian type of collective system threatens the independence and integrity of every individual and community. *Here is an apparatus of enslavement that does not justify itself in its own eyes*, which survives solely through conquest and excludes from the fruits of such conquest, furthermore, all who did not happen to be born into the privileged group.[117]

Given this appraisal of Nazism, it is interesting to note that several months earlier, Caillois had argued that democracy was weak in the face of fascism precisely due to its conceptual incoherence, to the contradictions inherent in the impracticable universal egalitarianism of 1789. "La Hiérarchie des êtres" declared, "Caught between the universality of its foundations and the egotistical concerns of its national interests, democracy is in a position of weakness vis-à-vis fascism which identifies for itself its own principles and ambitions. Fascism constantly makes democracy contradict itself without any possible way of doing the same thing in return. . . . So, when it comes to fascism, democracy has already lost ahead of time." Here defined as "anarcho-democratic," according to Etiemble, democracy must inevitably sacrifice its ideals and mimic the enemy it seeks to resist: "Democracy contains within itself an inevitability of fascism."[118] The problem, as Caillois outlined this ideological warfare, was to find an ideology that would "outclass" fascism as it had itself outclassed democracy, namely, one whose challenge to fascism would unmask the "deceptions" (*duperies*) or contradictions of this "pathological . . . perversion of democracy": an ideology of nationalist and racist egalitarianism that was in essence a will to power based on resentment. The conceptual clarity to which Caillois aspired he found, alas, in the "utopian" view of a universal community ruled by a Nietzschean master/slave meritocracy, or order: "Nothing limits their power except for the virtue they have available to ensure that it is respected." If this sounds idealistic, it was also pragmatic—from Caillois's perspective—to the extent that La Boétie had shown that the tyrant's power over his subject "was constituted by their obedience" (see "Aggressiveness as a Value").[119]

What emerges in Caillois's writing at this point is the need for an elective order of elite individuals who might themselves constitute and thereby purvey the sacred order or orthodoxy. The "secret of their cohesion" reflects what "The Winter Wind" describes as the "differential reflexes" of "likes and dislikes" between individuals, so that the very dynamics of their clustering is a kind of generalization, revealing their hitherto hidden identity—and their difference from others.[120] Such is the conceptual basis of the orders Caillois conceived between 1937 and 1939, in "Aggressiveness as a Value," "Dionysian Virtues," "The Winter Wind," "La Hiérarchie des êtres," and "Sociology of the Intellectual," whose self-selection remotivated racial, biological, or national distinctions on "elective" grounds and beckoned the reader (or listener) to join. "The Winter Wind" declared, for example, "Each of us, in relationships with other people, encounters some who show themselves to be of another moral species, almost of another race."[121] In effect, Caillois's terms curiously echo and rework a distinction coined by the great Dreyfusard Julien Benda, who described the rift between Dreyfusards and anti-Dreyfusards as the "combat of two moral races," as "a matter of biological self-interest, showing one's inaptitude or aptitude for life."[122] Benda thus contrasted, in the words of Michel Winock, La Boétie's "taste for voluntary servitude" to "the taste for freedom" as a "confrontation occuring in all historical crises." This taste for "voluntary servitude" characterized thinkers such as Barrès and Maurras who valued social homogeneity and the primacy of society over the individual, whereas, of course, the Dreyfusards instead valued the autonomy of the individual.[123] One might consider how Caillois seemingly tried to reconcile both categories.[124] Other intellectual ingredients included the Sorelian model of "active minorities" or revolutionary ideological elites.[125] Basing itself, in part, on the history of the Catholic Church, *Reflections on Violence* had declared that "the syndicates must search less for the greatest number of adherents than for the organization of the vigorous elements; revolutionary strikes are excellent for effecting a selection by weeding out the pacifists who would spoil the elite troups."[126] Caillois also loosely drew on Pareto's widely influential organicist theory of social revitalization from below, via the integration of dynamic elements from the lower classes.[127]

Despite his resistance to hypnotically counteracting Hitler's rise, he could or did not avoid some mimicry of the real enemy. Caillois wrote to Paulhan in 1939 that "the strength of Nazism came from the holy terror it dared to assume, in the wake of Jünger, Salomon, Nietzsche, etc. Were it not a form of decadence, the only way left to fight it would be to risk an even greater terror (because when it comes to mysticism, the strategy involves neither matching force, nor wearing down, but outbidding)." This letter may shed light on his earlier strategies—before he had come to see the Nazis' "decadence," or nihilist vacancy. Writing to Paulhan about "The Winter Wind" in November 1937, Caillois explained, "Since I didn't have the strength, I had to play with magical illusion [prestige], that is, gamble on mimicry. So even though I hate rhetorical flourish, I tried to use some, hoping that there might be some people who would be won over by the atmosphere and would join together, turning this atmosphere into an actual force."[128] ("Mimicry" here suggests Gabriel Tarde's definition of mimicry as the motor of social formations, and not that of "Mimicry and Legendary Psychasthenia.") In short, with its chivalric masters, "The Winter Wind" wittingly sought to hypnotize not the masses but the intellectual avant-garde—with the myth of lucidity and a paramilitary *saint effroi* (holy terror). Moreover, Caillois here explicitly echoes the Nazi propaganda machine in at least one respect. His 1940 lectures on "The Nature and Structure of Totalitarian Regimes" would cite (to condemn) the Nazi concept of *Wirbel* (whirlwind) "that expels its dead elements and makes popular leaders spring forth." Yet such social hygiene is clearly featured in "The Winter Wind," with its updated pagan rites of organic renewal, which Caillois likely drew from the studies of Dumézil but also found in the writings of the pre-Hitler writer, Moeller van den Brück.[129]

Hollier also shows that in 1938 Caillois drew the attention of the College of Sociology to a letter by Mauss about the Communist and Nazi Parties as "secret sects."[130] Yet we might note that even as the declarations of the Collège grew more antipacifist, voicing a greater "will to power," Caillois's own rhetoric was becoming increasingly temperate, that is, inclined toward spiritual and representational efficacy.[131] "La Hiérarchie des êtres" (which pointed to the Bolsheviks as a model of secret order) declared, "Any power that is not spiritual [mental] and pure finishes in blood. The only stable authority is that which constrains solely by means of example and is exclusively based on esteem and admiration."[132] "Sociology of the Intellectual" (1939) would then outline an utterly nonviolent, exemplary order, whose role was to produce "values" rather than master the world. In the absence of any clear causal explanation for Caillois's conceptual shift, it is helpful to note that in 1938 and 1939 he was writing *Man and the Sacred*, which proffers a specific model of "sacred" activism for the modern world, and of which "Sociology of the Intellectual" is an apparent illustration.

The binary tropism of likes and dislikes in "The Winter Wind" could perhaps be interpreted as an initial effort to systematize Bataille's anthropological views of the sacred as an ambiguous nucleus of attraction and repulsion, derived, in particular, from the ideas of Robert Hertz.[133] In any event, to "generalize" this theory was precisely the project, Caillois recounts, of his ensuing scholarly study, *Man and the Sacred*, which sought to outline the "syntax" of the sacred.[134] He first presents the sacred as a "category of feeling" investing sacred objects with an "aura"—such as that of *mana*, for example—and setting them apart from the profane as "taboo." The ambivalent attitudes of horror and love, or *tremendum* and *fascinans* (derived from Saint Augustine and Rudolf Otto), characterize man's apprehension of the sacred as a virtual force; Caillois uses the image of fire. However, "just as the fire produces both evil and good," when the sacred is put into effect in the world, it engenders "right and wrong action and is imbued with the opposing qualities of pure and impure, holy and sacrilegious."[135] The conceptual complexity of Caillois's model stems from the fact that although, when embodied or implemented, the sacred becomes polarized (into good or evil, pure to impure, holy or sacrilegious), each of these results gives rise to ambivalent feelings. "Every force animating [the sacred] tends to become dissociated," he writes; "its initial ambiguity tends to resolve itself into antagonistic and complementary elements to which can be tendered, respectively, feelings of awe and aversion—feelings of desire and fervor that are inspired by its completely ambiguous nature. But no sooner are these poles born of the extension of the sacred than they provoke, on their own part—and to the precise degree that they possess sacred character—the same ambivalent reactions that had originally isolated them from each other."[136] In short, Caillois is here providing a model of emotional paradox, in some sense grounded in the principle of identity and difference. Describing Saint Augustine's ambivalence toward the sacred, Caillois writes that Augustine "explains that his horror comes about by his realization of the absolute disparity between his being and that of the sacred, and he explains his ardor by his awareness of their fundamental identity."[137]

Although exploring such static conciliation of opposites would become an important feature of Caillois's theoretical imagination after the war, the real thrust of his "syntax" of the sacred in 1939 was the paradigm of its *oscillation* with respect to the social structure. "Bataille distinguished the Right and the Left sacred . . . the sacred of sanctity and the sacred of defilement," he recounted in 1971; "so I tried to systematize that and to show how in normal times, which is not festival, what counts is the sacred as respect. . . . On the contrary, in wartime, but *especially* during festival, there is transgression, because what was respected is now violated."[138] (Caillois recalls having lectured to the College of Sociology on the topic of war as the "black festival" of the modern world; however, this troubling equation of what he later described as two "total" collective phenomena did not appear in the prewar *Man and the Sacred*; see "Paroxysms of Society.") Thus *Man and the Sacred* generalizes the sacred's ambiguous bipolarity by theoretically unifying this within a single system of archaic social order, suggesting that both right and left sacred exist relative to the unique axis, or orthodoxy, of the *ordo rerum*. The right sacred, now "the sacred as respect," confirms the norm; the left sacred, now "the sacred as transgression," breaks with this norm, most dramatically during the period of festival and sacrifice.[139] The ordo rerum, then, is their common hidden identity bridging their polarized opposition. (Caillois's introduction notes that "if in this work a favored place is given to the concept of the *ordo rerum*, credit for this belongs to Mauss alone.")[140] The last three sections describe the modern experience of the sacred as one detached from the ordo rerum, as an interiorized and private attitude, sometimes "the specialty of a sect leading a semi-clandestine existence."[141] The modern mind must here choose between "the feared world of great conquests, the blessed world of great renunciations [abandons]" (see "Metamorphoses of Hell").[142] These two poles are distinct but conjoined as ambiguity in their difference from the profane. This last opposition itself reflects the world's essential ambiguity, one might say, for Caillois links the duality of sacred and profane to that of "inertia and movement, mass and force, matter and energy."[143]

Despite the obvious fact that Caillois is not discussing literature or language, let us briefly consider his generalization of the sacred in relation to Paulhan's view that language comprises complementary and antagonistic poles, such as "word" and "thought," conceptualized in terms of Einsteinian spacetime and theological antinomies, as mentioned earlier.[144] Especially interesting to consider here is Paulhan's argument that language is ambiguous in a virtual sense but polarized in practice—that only one aspect can be observed at any given time. As Laurent Jenny explains, "Language cannot be simultaneously apprehended as thought and as word. Although we constantly experience the indissociable nature of its two aspects, one of the two is always lacking."[145] As an alternation of "transgression" and "respect," the sacred's "applied" relation to the social structure likewise oscillates in its restricted expression of a single dimension. Let us note, though, that such pendulum swings are collective representations unrelated to private shifts of perspective by the participants, and they derive from the principle of norm and transgression, which Paulhan's oscillatory paradigm utterly lacks. As for the two sacred attitudes—sinner and saint—available to modernity, the individual does not alternate from one to the other. We shall see that Caillois's intellectual affinities with Paulhan would grow more pronounced during the war and thereafter. Yet his ever more literary approach to ambiguity derived from *Man and the Sacred* would generally continue to consider its collective dimension and its structures of transgression and paradox, rather than dwelling on the mysteriously mobile appearances and perceptions Paulhan ascribed to the apprehension of language itself. For Caillois, the *tremendum/fascinans* of the sacred affects its adherents as an emotional duality regardless of whether it is virtual or not.

In any event, his real interlocutor was Bataille. Unlike the profane world of egotistical self-preservation, the "supreme ends" of the contemporary sacred are those inducing a person to "*sacrifice* his life if necessary."[146] The lover, artist, scientist, miser, patriot, and revolutionary may illustrate such an "unconditional personal involvement, a similar asceticism and spirit of sacrifice." And what of reconstituting the social order through a sacred community? Although the rise of individualism has freed and protected the modern subject from all "psychic constraint," writes Caillois, "yet, the sacred persists to the degree that this liberation is incomplete, that is to say, whenever a value imposes itself as a *reason to live* upon a community and even an individual. For this value rapidly reveals itself to be a source of energy and a nucleus of contagion."[147] The prewar version cites two examples of such a "sacred milieu": the flame of the Unknown Soldier under the Arc de Triomphe and "certain aspects of the national-socialist movement in Germany."[148] "Sociology of the Intellectual" will suggest how the "unconditional commitment" of intellectuals can constitute such an order as well.

Let me underscore, then, that sacrifice and anti-utilitarian behavior are presented here as means, and virtual ones at that, rather than as ends in themselves. Caillois does not call for crime, transgression, or sacrifice; as the basis of sacred community, he highlights not death but a *reason to live*. Although Bataille's final letter in 1939 to Caillois about the College of Sociology generally concurred with Caillois's views of the sacred, his postwar review of *Man and the Sacred* sharply noted, "The sacred, in my opinion, first and foremost counters utility and those passions whose object conforms to reason. . . . At the basis of the *sacred*, we always find some prohibition forbidding behavior that is convulsive, foreign to selfish calculation, and that originates in the animal world." But this debate inevitably harkened back to the late 1930s, when Bataille was launching his secret society, Acéphale, driven by the project of human sacrifice. His important letter of 1939, marking in some sense the collapse of the College, noted of Caillois's desire to establish some form of "spiritual power" that, according to Caillois himself, society must "possess the forces, virtues, and seductions that demand and lead to sacrifice"; this last must therefore be true of "spiritual power" as well.[149]

One way to interpret Caillois's writings at the time is to highlight their difficult dialogue with a very local adversary.[150] His *Approches de l'imaginaire* (1974) cites Bataille's constant attempts to link Acéphale with the College of Sociology as an "explanation of, if not an excuse for" the "presumptuous and falsely pathetic tone" of "The Winter Wind" and other texts of the time.[151] Bataille and his secret society dreamed of an incandescent social communion that aimed to express perhaps more than to contend with the very real violence ahead. In 1935–1936, Caillois had refused to fight fascists in the streets while Bataille was urging just that. However, the roles were somewhat reversed in the next few years. After 1937, Bataille's group refused any instrumental appropriation or, as they said, "opportunistic use" of the group's "religious" energies, such as aggressiveness. In contrast, Caillois wrote in 1938 of "the immediate need for political struggle."[152] Bataille's aforementioned final letter to Caillois concerning the College recounts his public declaration of such discord to the group on July 4, 1939: "My emphasis on mysticism, drama, madness and death [strikes Caillois] as difficult to reconcile with the principles that we take as our point of departure."[153]

More or less coextensive with the College of Sociology, Acéphale (whose metaphorical name, "Headless," had in mind Nietzsche's "death of God" and "the headless crowd") anarchically attacked any kind of hierarchical system or structure topped by an individual summit: political, religious, sociological, philosophical, intellectual, and so on.[154] Acéphale maintained Contre-Attaque's anti-Hitler, anticommunist, and antinationalist stance, but had retreated from the world of politics, replacing Contre-Attaque's instrumental focus on mass psychology with a Kierkegaardian "religious" turn toward experiential angst. This small sect was composed of a core group of five young men in their early twenties, who had already been close friends for several years before falling under the spell of Bataille (roughly sixteen years older) at Souvarine's Cercle Communiste Démocratique. (One young member would refer to Bataille as "le boss."[155]) Inspired by two basic texts, Bataille's "Sacrifices" and "The Notion of Expenditure," the group spoke of reenchanting the world with secular myth and sacrifice, and they nurtured their apocalyptic sensibility with a Heidegger-inspired contemplation of death.[156] "Reproach of B.[ataille] to Heid[egger]. He reaches nothingness too *fast*," reads the marginal, handwritten annotation of an Acéphale member to an internal text of the group, Bataille's "Vingt propositions sur la mort de Dieu" (Twenty propositions on the death of God).[157]

To a certain extent, it is possible to discern a triangular structure with Bataille at the center, flanked by Caillois on one side and the small group of followers, the so-called friends of Bataille, on the other. Already in the founding days of Contre-Attaque, these opposed and competing influences began to emerge when Monnerot wrote to Caillois in November 1935, "In effect, Bataille has found a group—small though it might be—which agrees to make a program out of his ideas—I am not speaking of all the mutual concessions."[158] There is some evidence that Caillois was involved in Acéphale's early stages, in late 1936, a few months before it had fully taken shape as a secret society. One member, Georges Ambrosino, wrote to another in December 1936, "Acéphale? G. B. [Georges Bataille] under the influence of Caillois. Pffui—."[159] Then, in January 1937, Ambrosino and another member, Henri Dubief, wrote texts highly critical of Caillois: Ambrosino, "La Constitution de l'être est eminemment paradoxale" (The constitution of a being is highly paradoxical), and Dubief, "Critique d'une position de Roger Caillois" (Criticism of a position of Roger Caillois). Although it is not known just what they were responding to, and hence it is difficult to reconstruct the dialogue, they were clearly resisting Bataille's plans to join forces with Caillois and Monnerot. (According to the group's *Journal intérieur* [Private Journal], both texts focused on "the danger of opportunism and the possibilities of confusion."[160]) Ambrosino attacked Caillois's "wish for totality," which "can only mean the quest for a lucid totality." "The only quality that we wish to acknowledge, and constantly so, in a being is its scission, within and against itself," wrote this accolyte of Bataille.[161] Dubief's account suggests a talk in which Caillois claimed to share the group's goal of achieving "the highest degree of emotional tension"—but in a way that Dubief himself condemned: "Roger Caillois declares that he is awaiting a kind of 'state of grace.'" This reveals a lazy unawareness of his "fatal illness" (or human condition): "It is not by shutting his eyes upon himself and the world that he can hope to attain life." Dubief further claimed that Bataille and Caillois used the term "state of strife" in different ways: "For Bataille or for ourselves, this stems from feelings of 'weakness' or 'depressions,'" because only self-conscious despair will allow one to "overcome despair" and experience the "emotional tension" proper to the "taste for strife" and eventual triumph; on the contrary, "Caillois seems to experience this . . . in periods of intense activity, of success and euphoria" (see "Dionysian Virtues" and "Aggressiveness as a Value").[162]

The recent publication of Acéphale's internal documents illuminate the group's decision to go underground in February 1937 (without Caillois's awareness of this crucial event). They reveal its oddly bureaucratic structure and Bataille's increasing depression in 1938, after the death of his lover, Laure, which propelled the group toward the mystical quest outlined in his formula, "Joy in the Face of Death." Members were increasingly urged to focus, as in certain yoga techniques, on the moment of their own death: "I myself, destroying myself, consuming and butchering myself by means of my own avidity like fire."[163] What these documents avoid discussing in any explicit way is the question of human sacrifice, now generally accepted as one of the crucial aspects of the group. In 1944, Caillois's "Preamble to the Spirit of Sects" retrospectively discussed this project, meant to forge an indissoluble, leaderless bond, and which has been personally confirmed to me by a former member: "The fundamental thing," he explained, "was that there was to be a victim, killed, by one of the members of the group, who would have volunteered to do so. *But*, it didn't work for one simple reason, namely, it was not possible to find a volunteer to do the executing." He recalled that on becoming an adept of the group through a process of *adeption* (a term coined for this purpose), members signed a sacrificial contract (now lost): "Within the *group*, one committed oneself to being the *potential* victim and the *potential* assassin—but *with no* further specifications."[164]

"The goals and ambitions of Acéphale were very foreign to me," Caillois recounted in 1970, "and certainly, it is precisely because of the tension that revealed itself between Bataille and myself in the College of Sociology, in the face of my stubborn, obstinate refusal not to accept what was the basis of Bataille's life, what he valued most highly, that he may have been forced to found something apart, more secret, where this time there was no one who contradicted him and obliged him to greater prudence."[165] According to my informant, Caillois never actually participated in the rituals of Acéphale: "Caillois was informed about everything that happened in Acéphale but never wanted to take part in it." In 1974, Caillois further explained, "Bataille believed that accomplishing a human sacrifice would be an irreversible point, preventing any possible turning back. It came close to happening. The victim had been found, it was the sacrificer who was missing. Bataille offered me the role. Because I had written a panegyric about Saint-Just while still in high school, he probably supposed that I had the latter's inexorable character. Things didn't get beyond that."[166] Elsewhere in 1974, Caillois noted that Bataille "did not tell everything" and told him about Acéphale's plans for an "irreparable ritual gesture" only at the stage when the victim had already been found.[167] This is tempting to correlate with Marina Galletti's recent remark about a rumor that Michel Leiris, in a momentary state of suicidal depression (to which he was frequently prone), had offered himself as sacrificial victim.[168] Could Bataille have asked Caillois to execute Leiris?

As I suggested above, Caillois's *Man and the Sacred* and "Sociology of the Intellectual" describe the modern reconstitution of a "sacred milieu" in terms that implicitly challenge any strategic and foundational use of transgression, destruction, or sacrifice. Moreover, Caillois's parting shot in the immediate aftermath of Acéphale may be a review he discreetly published in Argentina in late 1939—in Spanish—assailing the use of Nietzsche as a "consolation." More specifically, he inveighed against the modern appropriation of primitivism, which merely projected the "mystery" and "depth" of something "probably rudimentary and poor": "No evidence confirms this backdrop painted with the vivid and coarse colors of sex and death, orgy and human sacrifice, against which 'savages' are posed in the eyes of 'civilized,' well-educated men."[169] But a more sustained dialogue with Acéphale at an earlier date can be partially reconstructed in "Dionysian Virtues," "Aggressiveness as a Value," "The Birth of Lucifer," "L'Aridité," and "The Sociology of the Executioner."

Written while Caillois was still somewhat involved with the initial stages of Acéphale, "Dionysian Virtues" suggests how to collectively harness *ivresse* (intoxication) instead of merely enjoying it in private; "Aggressiveness as Value" likewise argues for a conquering elite as opposed to unbound, wild aggression. Perhaps (but not necessarily) composed *after* Acéphale had gone underground, "The Birth of Lucifer," I suggest, includes a caricatural attack on Bataille, as well as his followers. A prototype of the rebellious nineteenth-century individualist who then unites with his fellows in "The Winter Wind," Lucifer is a Promethean Romantic writer, whose social revolt supersedes what Caillois calls Romantic Satanism (see "Paris, a Modern Myth"). In this last, it is not difficult to discern the figure of Bataille, whose founding speech to Acéphale evoked the legacy of "Romantic despair" when stating that each member should try to rediscover "primitive religious complexity" by confronting experientially "the violence that was nearby" and "his own aggressiveness." In my opinion, "Aggressiveness as a Value" already challenged Bataille's view that "despair here means that aggressiveness can be neither limited nor enslaved."[170] But "The Birth of Lucifer" then suggests overcoming this attitude, just as Lucifer overcomes Satan (in Caillois's idiosyncratic account), by combining scientific and Nietzschean self-mastery with Corneille's idea of "glory": "demonic pride, the feeling of supreme, private independence."[171]

Let me also speculate that two later essays, from 1938, might well bear directly on the projected human sacrifice. In 1970, Caillois recounted, "[Bataille] already had the victim and obtained from the latter (or was undertaking to obtain) a certificate intended for the law, and which exonerated the murderer ahead of time."[172] (Did Bataille ask Leiris to write a note excusing his assassin?) "Indeed, the executioner was supposed . . . to be protected from the law," recalled the former member of the group, "and there had indeed been discussions among ourselves to resolve . . . that it was something that was not right, trying to protect the person who would perform the murder."[173] I discern Caillois's response to this envisioned exercise in applied transgression in his essay "L'Aridité," where he distinguishes between "liberty" and "independence": "The Luciferian spirit considers this to be a crucial distinction, and a primary result of his critical reconsideration of the satanic state of mind. When an individual views the desire for liberty as nothing more than the demand to act exactly as he pleases and safe from any sanction—then this desire, in and of itself, is hardly capable of founding or even maintaining anything."[174] So much for Bataille's ploy. However, to the extent that, unlike Caillois, Bataille could still envision rekindling the sacred via an act of murder, Caillois's essay "Sociology of the Executioner" (presented to the College of Sociology) offered yet another response. Bataille and Acéphale sought to celebrate the execution of Louis XVI as an antecedent to their own sacrificial regeneration of the social order. However, drawing on his anthropological theory of the sacred and de Maistre, Caillois charted the "total social fact" of regicide, whose mythical structures still resonated in the Old Regime imagination—and even within modern France.[175] To refound society in this way, he implies, you cannot simply kill a willing friend in the suburban forest. Your actions must respect the deep-seated logic of execution, which involves the official executioner of the realm—and the king.

In 1960, Caillois's Borgesian novella, *Ponce Pilate*, told a story with some relation to these fantastic concerns of his youth. In this counterfactual tale, Pilate prevents the sacrifice of Christ despite the arguments of his Prefect—"It is not undesirable that one man die for the salvation of a people"—which Hollier describes as an expression of "sacrificial logic" proper to Caillois and others.[176] Yet it seems to me that such instrumental calculus—breaking eggs for omelettes—has little to do with the collective order of gods, men, and things outlined in *Man and the Sacred*. More interesting are the dialogues between Pilate and his utopian, visionary counselor, Mardouk, whose only belief is in belief itself, and who endorses sacrificing an innocent to bring about a new era and faith. In the 1930s, Caillois may have refused to align himself with Mardouk/Bataille's views largely for theoretical reasons: as being anachronistic, conceptually flawed, and unsound. Some sixty years later, and by the novella's conclusion, Pilate/Caillois rejects such injustice on stoic ethical grounds. Despite divine and human pressures, he remains free to follow his conscience.[177] In the intervening years had occurred, among other things, the war.

*   *   *

In Argentina, Caillois underwent a progressive intellectual, ideological, and cultural change, which left him a convert to "civilization"—or to what he had previously sought to overturn and destroy. "I had wished to unburden myself of this culture, as of a kind of load and enslavement," he wrote after the war. "I now recognized that it was fragile and difficult to conquer. Moreover, I understood that there was nothing outside of it that could justify the human adventure."[178] His journey through the sparsely populated region of Patagonia in March 1942 was emblematic of this humanist awakening (see "Patagonia"), which no longer sought to generalize biological, sociological, and individual drives, nor to draw on this theoretical unity to regenerate the modern world through apocalyptic revolution. If Caillois still defined lucidity and self-restraint as a means to individual freedom, this was not demonic "independence" but heroic autonomy from the "vertigo" of natural, unconscious, and collective forces; no longer did it involve the will to power over others.

During the war, Caillois's *La Communion des forts* (1943) republished certain of his writings on sects and élites linked to the College of Sociology. He tried to distinguish this "spiritual power" more explicitly from political power (see "Discussions of Sociological Topics: On 'Defense of the Republic'"). His new preface recast these essays as modes of intellectual resistance to demagoguery and fanaticized mass psychology, which inevitably engendered violence: "If only these masses were led by the slightest self-interest, but a collective entity lacks both the will and intelligence that sometimes help an individual control himself. [It is] completely rudimentary, blind, anonymous, and seem[s] capable only of fear, *ressentiment* or envy."[179] His new writings primarily focused, though, on the choices and efforts made in the Sisyphian project of producing civilization. The order Caillois envisioned was a new humanism whereby man and the human imagination stood alone in the world, participating less in society per se than in history. To this end, he cast aside science and generalization for the more restricted constructions of literature and culture. Significantly, his theory of the novel, *Puissances du roman* (1942), appears to transpose into secular terms Caillois's prior model of the sacred, for the novel swings between destroying and reconstructing the *city* or *polis*, as if he had generalized the novel's oscillation relative to this social axis. He also

rediscovered poetry, reserving a particular hostility for the poetic image—
to which he attributed the ills of Surrealism. Inspired by the careful selection
of "disparate wonders" making up the "total museum" of the poet Saint-John
Perse (Alexis Léger), he became a collector rather than a Romantic prophet of
totality.[180]

Caillois's prolonged stay in Argentina was the unplanned result of Victoria
Ocampo's invitation that he visit Buenos Aires for a three-month lecture series.
Significantly older and more experienced than he in the ways of romance,
Ocampo had admired his performance at the College of Sociology and then
quite literally carried him off to enlighten the cultural milieu she was working
hard to establish in Buenos Aires around her journal *Sur*. Caillois left Paris on
June 23, 1939; he returned in August 1945. After the Declaration of War on September 3, 1939, he was trapped in Argentina by the lack of sea traffic back to
France, but also, writes Felgine, because the French Embassy hoped to make
use of his intellectual qualifications: "he was the only *Normalien* who had
passed the Agregation exam of Letters on the subcontinent."[181] Moreover, he
had been officially declared physically unfit for military duty. Even so, Caillois
did at first plan to return to France. "Despite the fact that people tell me that I
will be more useful here than back there," he wrote to Paulhan on October 21,
1939, "I am not happy at the idea of staying."[182] Any hopes of going home became impossible, though, in the wake of the ten lectures he delivered in Mon-
tevideo against Hitler and Hitlerism in August 1940 at the behest of the British Embassy (Caillois had, by then, broken his ties with the Pétainist French
administration).[183] "I declare with great assurance that Hitler will fall with
a crash like Lucifer," he wrote to Ocampo.[184] The German Embassy in Buenos
Aires at once lodged a formal protest, as Argentina was a neutral country.
Therefore, "it was becoming very difficult for me to return to France," Caillois
explained in 1971. "I ran the risk of being arrested when I got off the boat." Besides lectures (including the "The Nature and Structure of Totalitarian Regimes") and essays (such as "The Nature of Hitlerism"), Caillois's strictly political response to the war was to play a founding role in the *Comité de De
Gaulle*, which he tried to hold back from a French nationalist outlook.[185]

As for his romance with Ocampo, this ended by early 1941 because Caillois's
prior girlfriend, Yvette Billod, had given birth to their daughter, Catherine,
out of wedlock, in France in 1940. Yvette and the baby moved to Argentina
in March 1941, where a marriage hastily ensued. But Caillois's extensive correspondence with Ocampo throughout his Argentine stay and thereafter
shows the deep and enduring nature of their bond. Above and beyond the
challenges of passion and Christian faith that Ocampo persistently leveled at

Caillois's "aridity," their dialogue flourished in the joint projects for Ocampo's journal *Sur* and for the French-language journal, *Les Lettres françaises* sponsored by *Sur*.[186]

Originally conceived by Waldo Frank, this cosmopolitan journal sought to define Argentine culture within its larger American and European context.[187] When Caillois reached Argentina, *Sur* was in its ninth year, and Ocampo was undoubtedly hoping to orient this intellectual milieu along the lines she had witnessed in Paris. By mid-1940, she had launched the Discussions of Sociological Topics, loosely inspired by the College of Sociology (see "Discussions of Sociological Topics: On 'Defense of the Republic'" and "The Nature and Structure of Totalitarian Regimes"). One current of the College was thus transplanted into a wholly new culture and world, of which two aspects are useful to keep in mind.[188] First, the other prevalent French influence at *Sur* was left-wing Catholicism, as purveyed by the "personalist" orientation of Denis de Rougemont, Emmanuel Mounier, and Jacques Maritain. John King's study explains: "Personalism appealed to *Sur*, because it rejected the twin poles of fascism and Marxism, individualism and collectivism, categories in which the 'person' became lost." He highlights the appeal of such a doctrine given *Sur*'s belief that thoughtful elites had an important role to play in fostering humanist values: "With a clear conscience the intellectual could be . . . the vigilant outsider, who could form a spiritual community with other like-minded 'persons.'"[189] However, Caillois did not join forces with the personalist strand at *Sur*. Preferring autonomy to divine authority, he founded his own journal, *Les Lettres françaises* (1941–1947), which remained in close contact with other journals of Free France, such as Raymond Aron's *La France libre* in London.

The second crucial point about *Sur* is that it had been unequivocally anti-Franco during the Spanish Civil War. With the advent of the Second World War, recounts King, "the magazine explicitly defended the Allied cause and frequently implied that the Argentine policy of neutrality was being formulated by fascist tendencies within the government."[190] The issue of October 1939, titled "La Guerra" (War) and voicing *Sur*'s belligerent response to Hitler's invasion of Poland, included Caillois's sociological analysis, "Naturaleza del hitlerismo" (The nature of Hitlerism): "This is intended to represent here the point of view of the College of Sociology where, for almost three years, Georges Bataille, Michel Leiris and I have been devoting ourselves to understanding European events and defining the most justified and ambitious stance to adopt towards them."[191] As noted earlier, Caillois also drafted an anti-Hitler manifesto, which he hoped to publish in the *Nouvelle revue française* as a declaration of the College of Sociology—but with many other signatures as well.

He wrote to Paulhan: "Here, it is signed by a sort of section of the C[ollège de] S[ociologie], formed by the same people as in Paris: professors of philosophy, writers and disciples of Maritain. I am, moreover, a bit alarmed by the sociology that they are pursuing: for it is gently taking the direction of forming an Argentinian imperialism that is very coherent and ambitious."[192]

More specifically, "The Nature and Structure of Totalitarian Regimes" condemned Nazism and communism as "totalitarianism" in the name of "the republic," "universal values," "the rights of individual conscience," and full, rational transparency: "The modern nation is not a religious community that must obey the revelations of a visionary. Politics is a matter neither of mystical ecstasies nor of blind faith. Both political leaders as well as their followers must have clear notions of what is being proposed." But what exactly was Caillois himself proposing? "Defensa de la republica" (Defense of the republic; first published in *Sur*, June 1940) defined the republic in terms of Rome, Venice, and France, "in those days when they were each losing their names to be called simply, all over the world, and without any possible misunderstanding, the Republic." This Republic and "classic democracy" was based on a system of elites, or open meritocracies, which, Caillois argued, was distinct from "the type of democracy that gives rise to totalitarian states."[193] Yet, it would have been helpful to clarify these terms; the categories of democracy and republic have entertained a long and complicated relationship in the history of French political philosophy.[194] Moreover, Caillois's essays in *La Communion des forts* and elsewhere echoed his fear of the masses and his prior belief that democracy's "only options seem to be either learning from its enemies or preparing for defeat." Still, in strong contrast to "La Hiérarchie des êtres" and closer to Aron's position, he concluded that unlike totalitarian regimes, "democracy, even if this is its only advantage, at least allows for hope. That is enough for us to defend and prize it as the means for pursuing the very enterprise that is working to transform it."[195] To the extent that he himself sought to bolster democracy, it was chiefly through *Les Lettres françaises*. In April 1942, Louis Tillier wrote about *Lettres françaises* for Aron's journal that it recalled Paulhan's *Nouvelle revue française* (prior to its collaborationist turn under Drieu la Rochelle):

> Even though Caillois is first and foremost interested in literature, it is not that he is seeking there some refuge from political anxiety: he simply believes that the man of thought and pen has enough to accomplish in his own sphere without encroaching upon those of the strategist or the economist. Literature for him is not a means of escape, a frivolous distraction but, above all, a way of waging war, which would not be "total" if it were not also a war of ideas. Caillois excellently defines the role that he intends

to perform in his 'Duties and Privileges of French Writers Abroad,' which serves as the editorial to the second number of *Lettres françaises*, and constitutes the manifesto of a journal that aims to be an organ of combat.[196]

"Duties and Privileges of French Writers Abroad" expressed a theory of commitment anticipating that of Sartre: the very act of writing or speaking or keeping silent is a political act. The journal's more general focus illustrated Caillois's belief, often voiced in these years, that the values of civilization must be forged outside the theater of war: "On battlefields, the reason of the one who is strongest is always the best."[197] This also took shape as the crucial dichotomy between civilization and barbarism, between Athens and Sparta, first sketched out in the preface to "Naturaleza del hitlerismo." The first is a society that subordinates "military virtues to civil [civic] virtues" (France); the second, one in which "military virtues" constitute an autonomous end in and of themselves (Germany).[198]

Most important for Caillois's turn to civilization, culture, and literature, Malraux embodied a parallel move away from rebellious Romantic satanism and the *maudits*, as Caillois evoked them. "This period will have led Malraux, like many others, to repudiate that deadly training leading one to believe that only evil and death are inexhaustible," he wrote; this writer and others aspire, instead, to "heavens against which the powers of hell cannot prevail."[199] Saint-Exupéry, as writer and aviator, best conveyed Caillois's new cult of individual heroism. "The Myth of Secret Treasures in Childhood," "The Situation of Poetry," and "Pythian Heritage" show that this shift was still largely a continued reaction against Surrealism—now in the name of a "mature" imagination. Caillois's *Le Roman policier* admired in this mass-cultural genre the duality of passive enjoyment and active research, sensitivity and intellect, social anarchy and regulation, freedom and constraint.[200] Such literary predilections squarely aligned him with Paulhan and with Borges, who personally reviewed *Le Roman policier* for *Sur* in 1942: "The literature of our time is exhausted by interjections and opinions, incoherences and confidences; the detective story represents order and the obligation to invent. Roger Caillois very well analyzes its role as rational game, lucid game."[201] Paulhan was similarly holding up the detective novel in *Les Fleurs de Tarbes* as a "glimmer of reconciliation" between *Terror* and *Rhetoric*: between the attack, since Romanticism, on literary language or form at the expense of thought or meaning and, conversely, a preoccupation with form and language at the expense of meaning or thought. "We are witnessing," Paulhan wrote, "the triumph and global spread of the only contemporary genre that obeys stricter rules than Voltairean tragedy or the ode of Malherbe."[202] Etiemble, who also reviewed *Le Roman policier* (after

Borges), drew an explicit connection to Paulhan in 1943, while underscoring Caillois's moral outlook: "He defines the outlines of a classicism; certainly not of a new classicism—that would be an academicism—but indeed of a classicism that is new. The details of the doctrine still remain to be specified; I would imagine that the theses of Paulhan in *Fleurs de Tarbes*, those of Focillon in *La Vie des formes*, would largely contribute to it. What Caillois is proposing, above all, is an ethics, more than an aesthetics."[203]

As noted above, Caillois's second "theory of the novel," *Puissances du roman*, transposes his anthropological model of the sacred and the ordo rerum into those literary terms of the novel's pendulum swing between destroying and reconstructing the polis. However, he still subordinates literary to social concerns, or literature to the social order. As escapist, individualist reverie, the novel can dissolve the society it is mirroring—a civilized problem that does not threaten "robust barbarians who do not delegate the care of living to imaginary beings." On the other hand (here referring to the writings of Hemingway, Montherlant, Saint-Exupéry, Faulkner, Malraux, Ch. Plisnier, and Ernst von Salomon—in that order), Caillois suggests that such contemporary novels "detach in the foreground of those societies whose decomposition they are hastening the heroes who invite it to rediscover its cohesion—this by dint of their public and private virtues." Such "exemplary" characters, or "'children of chaos' dream of engendering an order, these nomads dream of instating stability." Unlike the cohorts of "The Winter Wind," such individualists are not united by their shared Nietzschean status as masters. Rather, Caillois suggests that the "secret of their cohesion" is a form of "common faith": "This subterranean impatience expressed by the novel under so many different guises can only be termed religious. It marks the moment when these new and invisible forces still remain scattered, unknown to each other, albeit linked by some secret element *just like the readers of a book*."[204] So too, "Duties and Privileges of French Writers Abroad" had previously pointed to *Les Lettres françaises* as a means of creating the "organic solidarity" of intellectuals, specifically across the Atlantic divide.

This novelistic "recasting of collective life" outlined here creates an integrated unity wherein "the individual only thinks of *history*." It is nonetheless clear that the imaginative grip of the late 1930s, with its sociological ideal of community and an integral collective, was slow to fade. Caillois explained in an oft-cited remark in 1974 that *Puissances du roman* was still inspired by the College of Sociology's vision of a "'full' society . . . with no room for novels"—without yet realizing that this, in and of itself, was a novelistic dream.[205] As noted earlier, *La Communion des forts* recycled such essays as "The Winter Wind" and "La Hiérachie des êtres" framed in a new way. To this end, Caillois still drew on social considerations linked to the College of Sociology: "To in-state a spiritual power in society, one must gather and separate within it an entirely contrary society, that is also spiritual, from which it will emanate. To make itself heard, it will only have the magical prestige of the mind. Possessing no form of constraint, it will have to fascinate. Rejecting force, it will have to wield a certain magic or grace, in short some virtue that will be its principle and will appear to nature as supernatural."[206] Even in 1944, it appears that Caillois nurtured the idea of "spiritual power," or so we may gauge from correspon-dence with Jean Wahl (then teaching at Mount Holyoke College), to whom Caillois sent out a questionnaire on the topic. We may reconstruct the ques-tionnaire (now lost), from Wahl's answers to questions 2, 3, and 4: on "spiri-tual power," "strictly religious values," and an "elite" defined either as "nobil-ity or clergy" to sustain these values. Wahl wrote back on March 6, 1944:

> While reading your questionnaire, two memories inevitably come to my mind: that of a banquet of the journal, *Volontés*, from which the collabo-rationists Pelorson and Combelle emerged. . . . People there were very concerned with the quest for spiritual authority. And especially that of the College of Sociology, where, as you know better than I, two of the di-rectors, yourself and Michel Leiris, maintained an exemplary attitude, but the third [Bataille] was carried away, at least momentarily, by his cult for authority, his hatred of a kind of bourgeois anarchy, his idea of pre-cisely some sort of spiritual nobility, clergy, or monastic order, toward some questionable conceptions that were dangerous for the mind.
>
> There is something just as dangerous for the mind as the force being exerted against it: this is the force being exerted, or that claims it is being exerted, to protect it,—it is even more dangerous,—for the first oppresses the mind but leaves it intact,—the second risks corrupting the mind itself.[207]

Unfortunately, we may never know what Caillois wrote back to Wahl.

But several months later, he appeared to publish a formal repudiation of the ideal of sects, here linked to Acéphale and the College of Sociology, in "Actu-alité des sectes" (Topicality of sects) in *Lettres françaises* (October 1944), which became "Preamble to the Spirit of Sects." Its accompanying study, *Ensayo sobre el espíritu de las sectas* (Essay on the spirit of sects; 1945), asked in conclusion: "Is it possible to imagine a strictly spiritual fraternity? But isn't that like in-venting sainthood? And in the end, what could be more opposed to the pride-ful spirit of sects?" However, Caillois did not likewise reject "castes," a category he had long frequented in the works of Dumézil and which he seems to endorse in "The Nature and Structure of Totalitarian Regimes." By caste, he meant orders similar to the army or the church, namely, "traditional and respected forces. Hence they generally prove to be more passive than turbulent, concerned to defend recognized privileges rather than taking on daring projects or working to bring about radical upheavals. The pure spirit of adventure finds it hard to accept such inertia."[208]

Caillois's interest in "spiritual power" during the war may be historically comparable to the Ecole nationale des cadres de la jeunesse (National school for youth managers) inspired in part by personalism and set up in the Uriage Castle (Grenoble) in August 1940.[209] This neochivalric elite was engaged in "the quest for 'common values' above and beyond ideological divides," in the words of Bernard Comte. Uriage aimed to produce future leaders who would put "their intellectual capacities and technical expertise at the service of ethical and civic goals: the Fatherland and the national community, the 'revolution of the XXth century' inspired by Péguy, by linking Christian, Republican and Socialist ideals."[210] Yet, unlike Uriage, Caillois did not value nationalism, Catholicism, or socialism. He cited very different French models in Brazil in 1943, describing his Parisian years and those institutions where "every belief, every attitude was respected," such as the Ecole Normale, the *Nouvelle revue française*, and, in particular, the secular l'Abbaye de Pontigny (1910–1939), which served as a meeting ground for many of the most important, progressively minded intellectuals of its day.[211] Pontigny was run by Paul Desjardins (1859–1940), recently described as an "intolerant defender of intellectual tolerance and the freedom of peoples."[212] "It was in this Abbey," rather piously declaims the Brazilian summary of Caillois's guest lecture, "where the guests were subject to the discipline of a new monastic order, that Roger Caillois came to know the most important minds of the century who were peacefully dividing their time between fruitful meditations and discussions of proposed topics. Probity of mind, intellectual modesty, a thirst for knowledge, mutual tolerance, honest analysis—such is what one acquired at the Abbey of Pontigny."[213]

*   *   *

In the immediate aftermath of the war, on his return to Paris, Caillois was not at home. To Ocampo he listed some "new and pleasant" names: "Camus, Blin, Anglès, Picon, Devaulx, Druon, etc., but no one pays any attention to them (in general) and they are drowned in the crowd of those who are following the vogue of Aragon or of Sartre. I would have liked to found a journal with them. But how can I bring them together?"[214] He was involved with several journals (but neither *Les Temps modernes* nor *Critique*.)[215] By the end of the decade, he was on the editorial board of Gallimard and had started the Croix du Sud series, which introduced Latin American literature to the French public; his own translations of Borges began to appear in 1949.[216] His initial efforts to build an academic career in the social sciences were thwarted by problems gaining a foothold either in the Centre National de la Recherche Scientifique (CNRS) or at the Ecole Pratique des Hautes Etudes.[217] (According to Chastel, he unsuccessfully challenged Lévi-Strauss in 1946 for Marcel Mauss's Chair at Hautes Etudes—backed by Dumézil.)[218] Although Lucien Febvre did then offer Caillois a position in aesthetic sociology at Hautes Etudes in 1948, he had already accepted a bureaucratic post at UNESCO, first at the Bureau of Ideas and then in its Program of Representative Works.[219] Only in 1952 did he establish a real place for himself as chief editor of UNESCO's "transdisciplinary" journal *Diogenes*.[220]

Generally speaking, in the 1940s and early 1950s, Caillois was largely concerned with literature, civilization, and paradox. His *Babel: Orgueil, confusion et ruine de la littérature* (Babel: The pride, confusion and ruin of literature; 1948) continued to explore the thesis presented in *Puissances du roman* that literature could either destroy or build the polis. However, Caillois now described literature as merely one element among many: "In a civilization . . . everything must uphold everything else: the precept, poem and monument, garden, festival and virtue." Here, decadence was not conceived as social anomie or a loss of collective density but as a lapse of harmonious solidarity among these disciplines: "And first of all style disappears, which expressed the unity of the whole." Caillois's conclusion to this literary treatise proposed that the writer should entirely disregard his social surroundings and any chance of success to focus, instead, on "building some kind of order, instating some form of communion." Only then might he obtain, as a reward, "the ultimate grace of a style," which would be a miraculous coincidence with the collectivity.[221] In short, this complex creativity would capture the writer's ambivalence with respect to the social order or polis (thereby resolving literature's pendulum swing). It would also reflect the fusion of voluntary and involuntary processes. A contemporary reviewer described this little-read tract as a mode of literary *engagement* to "restore a classical order."[222] But in 1971, Caillois called it "Chinese classicism much more than Racinian classicism. . . . It is the Chinese sage who pursues his task . . . the architect, the painter . . . without worrying about what either the people, the prince, his friends . . . or even he himself . . . thinks."[223]

Caillois was now a solitary and provocative figure in the close entourage of Paulhan. Michel Beaujour has recently written, "It has never been said that anyone ever learnt how to write or practise criticism through Paulhan's essays."[224] Yet Caillois wrote to Paulhan in 1947, "I find that [Maurice] Blanchot imitates your style all too successfully."[225] Indeed, there may well have been a muted rivalry in this regard—with radically opposed orientations. The first version of *Les Fleurs de Tarbes* had hinted of some transcendent resolution to the pendulum swing between *Terror* and *Rhetoric* or "thought" and "word." Rather than seek any such resolution, Blanchot's "La Littérature et le droit à la mort" (Literature and the right to death) appeared to heighten this oscillation in an existential sense by adding Hegel to Paulhan and thereby replacing "word"/"thought" with "existence"/"nonexistence." That is, Blanchot describes how "the reality of words" can stand as "an obstacle," as the "ephemeral passage of non-existence"—but also as "a concrete lump, a block of existence." Here, such a pendulum swing has become the goal of literary, as opposed to common, language: "Literature is that language which has made itself ambiguity."[226] On the contrary, Caillois held high a model of linguistic and syntactical accuracy and transparency: "A strict language is a factor of truth, of liberty."[227] (In this respect, he sharply opposed the widespread use of Sartrean philosophical terms.) Unlike Paulhan, and Blanchot, in other words, Caillois never sought to cultivate the mysteries or paradoxes inherent in the virtualities or apprehension of language itself. He nonetheless pursued the model of literary oscillation between norm and transgression (see "The Image"). In so doing, he was seeking ways for the writer to capture this movement in a paradoxical form. For example, his remark that "a master-piece . . . is often an inimitable banality" hints at the combined effect of identity and difference, of habit and surprise: that is, the combined respect and violation of the commonplace or cliché.[228]

He also entered the polemical fray as a self-proclaimed "paradoxical intellectual," by which he meant nonconformist.[229] Intellectual and linguistic clarity were the norms by which he passed judgment on the Parisian postwar scene—not undertaking ideological demystification so much as tracking incoherence and obfuscation. "The majority of our intellectuals do not wish to give up anything," he wrote, because "yesterday, they wanted to be both Freudian and Marxist, Surrealists and Communists: today they would like to be Existentialists and Marxists or perfect disciples of Kafka as well as irreproachable workers of the proletarian revolution. They are not deterred by any acrobacy or dialectic in order to reconcile what is irreconcilable. Enough is enough."[230] In the heated debates of the *épuration* (purge), Caillois was solidly in step with Paulhan's *De la Paille et du grain* (1947–1948), which invoked the writer's "right to error" and decried the censorious strategies of the Comité National des Ecrivains in the épuration as a mimicry of fascist strategies.[231] (Caillois's "Responsabilité des écrivains" [The responsibility of writers; 1943] had already anticipated and condemned such an appropriation of Nazi "scaffolds" by Hitler's enemies.)[232] However, unlike Paulhan, Caillois clearly felt that the failings of the CNE had little to do with the ineffable nature of language. It was simply not being used authentically, he wrote; the actors were "partisan and engaged in a still ongoing struggle."[233] Such an approach informs his analysis of language and proverbs in *Description du Marxisme* (1950; see "Loyola to the Rescue of Marx"), a work poised between Jules Monnerot's *Sociologie du communisme* (1949) and Raymond Aron's *L'Opium des intellectuels* (1955).

Unlike Bataille, Caillois did not argue that communism—in its mystification both of its own people and of the outside world—was somehow more honest than anticommunism. For Bataille, this was so because he viewed anticommunism as a false sacred, whereas "for communism, *nothing is sacred*."[234] Thus to condemn a false sacred meant still holding to an ideal of the sacred. Indeed, Bataille still dreamed of *la vraie vie* (authentic life): "The world of the sacred is one of communication or contagion, where nothing is separated, where it takes an effort precisely to counter unlimited fusion." This definition of the sacred, which corresponds to Caillois's "sacred as transgression," was one that Bataille never criticized or repudiated in any way. Quite to the contrary, he never stopped faulting Caillois's objectivity, and that of French social science in general, for precluding any quest for the sacred or "the elusive."[235] Of course, by the time he founded *Critique* in 1946, Bataille had renounced much of his communitarian activism.[236] The inward turn occurred during the war, as he himself explained in *L'Expérience intérieure* (1942). And yet, as he wrote to his close friend Georges Ambrosino in November 1946, he hoped *Critique* would "serve as an introduction" to a college based on the principle "*whosoever does not essentially make a wasteful use of his time and [forces] is reducing himself to enslavement*." Unlike their prewar activities, he informed Ambrosino, "[the] organization should not have any perceptible stability: actually, the *college* should even be more an *absence of a college* than a *college*."[237] This negativity reflects Blanchot's influence on Bataille during and after the war, which taught the latter how to recast nostalgia for the sacred. In a well-known passage, he declared, "The man of the present is defined by his avid desire for myth, and if we add that he is also defined by the consciousness of not being able to achieve the possibility of creating a real myth, we will have defined a kind of myth that is *the absence of myth*."[238]

Caillois, on the other hand, did not share such nostalgia. He did not dream of communal fusion or apocalyptic festival proper to the regenerative "sacred as transgression"—that is, the preeminence of the collective over the individual (see "Paroxysms of Society"). But what had become of the sacred after the war? Some ten years after his return to France, Caillois gradually returned to social science as editor of *Diogenes*, bearing the mantle of Montesquieu and the more contemporary Mauss, whom he held up as a model of scientific inquiry, responsibly balancing imaginative risk and constraint to illuminate "some fundamental yearnings of human beings, which are obscure, tenacious, inextinguishable and, in a sense, recurrent in different guises at the various levels of civilization" (see "The Great Bridgemaker").[239] This echo of "generalization" was also present in Caillois's manifesto for his new interdisciplinary journal, which aspired to a kind of generalized comparative ethics: identifying the common worries, triumphs, and crimes proper to mankind as a whole. Yet, unlike Caillois's "militant orthodoxy" of 1936, this "authentic and militant expression of the scientists united in the International Council of Philosophy and Human Sciences" was scholarly, focused, and anything but revolutionary.[240]

In studies of what he called "contemporary sociology," to which he had returned by the 1950s, Caillois analyzed the modern "secular religions" associated with "death, chance, power [Hitler's charismatic power], and war."[241] Essentially inspired by the Maussian emphasis on recurrent human "yearnings," Caillois did not believe that the emotions linked to the sacred would disappear; unchanged from the pre- to postwar versions of *Man and the Sacred* is his discussion of the vestigial sacred in private experience. With "secular religions," Caillois was exploring belief systems that had, in fact, come to exist as collective phenomena and that were hence "sacred" or "authentically religious" in the Durkheimian sense; this did not mean that they were not inaccurate, misguided, or instrumentalized. The first essay, "La Représentation de la mort dans le cinéma américain" (The representation of death in American cinema), later became the historical panorama "Metamorphoses of Hell," in which Caillois declared, "I confess that I, for one, would have preferred to see Hell vanish simply through the workings of lucidity and justice," while admitting that this would never occur. The last essay, "Le Vertige de la guerre" (The vertigo of war), gave rise to *Bellone ou la pente de la guerre* (Bellone or the coming of war; 1963), a historical survey of the mythology of war, which won the Prix Médicis de la Paix and closed with "Paroxysms of Society." It is at the heart of the implicit debate between Bataille and Caillois in these years about war and modernity. First published as an appendix to the revised and enlarged edition of *Man and the Sacred* (1950), it would explore "modern war's hypertrophy and its mystique." Caillois tentatively attributed this compensatory, substitute sacred to the rise of profane utilitarianism, but also to industrialization and the mechanical—as opposed to organic—solidarity driving huge nation-states.[242] Most important, I would argue, he envisioned an alternative structure for contemporary needs, for "civilization."

The triadic model Caillois had devised for archaic societies in 1938 placed the profane as an equilibrium between the "sacred as respect" and its binary complement, the "sacred as transgression." Commenting on Huizinga's *Homo ludens* in an appendix to the postwar edition of *Man and the Sacred*, Caillois proposed a new triadic system, suggesting that only thus could modern societies resist the rise (or sacralization) of war. He was intent to make a distinction that Huizinga did not: between the ludic (games and play) and the sacred. *Homo ludens* had distinguished both from real—or profane—life as realms dominated by their own set of rules—or "as if." But it did not differentiate, notes Caillois, between the radically different attitudes of the people involved in the ludic and the sacred. The play/game sphere is one of "creative license," of playful transgression; it is an entirely human and formal creation marked by the freedom of deliberate self-constraint and self-defined norms. In contrast to this autotelic activity, the sacred overwhelms the individual with "pure content—an indivisible, ambiguous, fleeting and efficacious power." Civilization demands both. The ludic, according to Caillois, is the essence of civilization: "There is no civilization without play and rules of fair play, without conventions consciously established and freely respected. There is no culture in which knowing how to win or lose loyally, without reservations, with self-control in victory, and without rancor in defeat, is not desired. One wants to be a *beau joueur* [a good loser]." However, as a counterweight to this self-mastery, civilization also requires the sacred: "There is no morality, no mutual confidence, no respect for others—conditions for any thriving enterprise—if there do not subsist, above and beyond the individual's or group's profit, sacred commandments which no one dares debate, and which everybody thinks it is worth sacrificing their own lives to safeguard, or if necessary, risking the very existence of the collectivity they belong to."[243] In short, this contemporary social equilibrium would appear to replace the archaic duality of sacred "transgression" and "respect"; both ludic and sacred attitudes here frame the profane, utilitarian attitudes of work. However, ludic transgression is a fiction or simulacrum, and the contemporary power of the sacred rests in the individual conscience and its capacity for absolute commitment rather than the collective orthodoxy of the *ordo rerum*. A final, key difference is the lack of oscillation or transgression with respect to a single axis. Caillois envisions two different, and freely accepted, norms. (Although this initial discussion posits—as against Huizinga's theory—a radical distinction between the sacred and the ludic, Caillois does nonetheless state that the ludic could have emerged out of sacred forms of expression; see my introduction to "The Image.")

The divisions sketched out here may be loosely discerned in Caillois's own writings in the 1950s. His journal *Diogenes* comes closest to outlining some kind of sacred or "sacred commandments" with its "renewed Humanism" and the militant comparative ethics mentioned earlier. Although Bataille invited Caillois to participate in *Critique*, Caillois felt a journal should not comprise merely secondary, "critical texts"—and so he founded *Diogenes*, with "original texts" and a resistance to highly specialized studies and jargon.[244] On the other hand, Caillois explored civilized "creative license" or playful transgression in his numerous writings on play, art, and literature.[245] Under this rubric I would include the theory of the image (see "The Image") and, then, the fantastic (see "Fruitful Ambiguity"). Caillois's *Anthologie du fantastique* (1958) posited that in fairy tales no rules are violated, but in the literary fantastic, rules *must* be violated. "Fairy tales take place in a world where enchantment is taken for granted and magic is the rule," he wrote, whereas in the fantastic, the super-natural elements are transgressive, they "disrupt the stability of a world whose laws were hitherto considered strict and immutable. They constitute the Impossible, unexpectedly arising in a world that by definition excludes the Impossible."[246] Unlike Todorov's theory of the reader's "hesitation" with regard to competing explanations of a startling event, Caillois focuses on the slow process whereby for the reader, in conclusion, "what is unreasonable best seems to satisfy the demands of reason, and what is unintelligible those of the intellect."[247] While the historical literary fantastic thus transgresses the bound-ary of death, confirmed by science, Caillois later defined science fiction as a fan-tastic transgression of the boundary set by the human imagination—that is, the boundary of the unimaginable. Still closely related to Paulhan's own analy-ses, these postwar forms of paradoxical intellectual equilibrium were explicitly linked to the spirit of play/games: "An almost forgotten witticism of Madame du Deffand clearly sums up the state of mind typical of lovers of fantastic tales: 'Do you believe in ghosts?' 'No, but I'm afraid of them.' Here fear becomes a pleasure, a delicious game, a kind of wager with the invisible in which the in-visible—which nobody believes in—does not seem obliged to come and claim its due. Nonetheless a margin of uncertainty subsists, which the writer's talent tries to maintain."[248]

But the creative paradoxes of play and the fantastic challenged more than Bataille's nostalgia for "sacred transgression" with a civilized manner of inte-grating order and disorder, system and rupture. During the cold war, these lu-dic and aesthetic attitudes also defied what Caillois called "totalitarian" art and thought; by this he meant the loss of criteria, distinctions, and skepticism and an ensuing loss of freedom to determinisms of all kinds (mental, social, natu-ral, and ideological). His *Description du marxisme* thus explored the "intangible and adaptable" doctrine that its partisans deemed "invariable and infallible" (see "Loyola to the Rescue of Marx").[249] In the aesthetic realm, his "Actualité des Kenningars" (Topicality of the Kenningars; 1955) replayed his youthful at-tacks on Surrealist automatism in *The Necessity of Mind*; however, the alternative he now proposed was the paradoxical image rather than ideogrammatic associationism (see "The Image").[250] This essay challenged Breton's game *l'un dans l'autre* (one thing inside the other), a postwar version of the group's creative riddles, deriving any one thing from any other. Caillois used the term "totalitarian correspondences" to describe this infinite analogical extension lacking in clear definition: "Any reality whatsoever can be described on the basis of any other one and . . . hence, in theory, the powers of the image are boundless." Here, Caillois found "the culmination of the *parti pris* that [Paulhan] calls *Terror*." Shifting from Paulhan's term, *Terror*, to his own coinage, "totalitarian," he was implicitly updating the link between pathologies of expression or thought and political oppression. In 1957, psychoanalysis was another prime target: "There is nothing . . . that the doctrine does not explain or that it could not incorporate."[251] That same year, he discussed his long essay, *L'Incertitude qui vient des rêves* (The uncertainty that comes from dreams; 1957) at the Société Française de Philosophie, explaining that "the dreamer's consciousness" is "a fascinated consciousness," because "the dream always seems coherent. Moreover, for the dreamer its coherence is infinite, unquestionable. The reason is simple: dreams prevent consciousness from asking itself the slightest question."[252] His study concludes that he will never be able to know whether he is dreaming or not, and goes on to say "At the very instant that I am striving to establish this proposition, if I trust its truth, then I must wonder whether I am not dreaming."[253] Jenny cites this as "the collapse of distinctions," whereas I would say, on the contrary, that it is a paradoxical state of mind, which reestablishes precisely the intellectual self-consciousness and doubt, hence *freedom*, that dreaming denies.[254]

By the 1960s and 1970s, Caillois had withdrawn from the political forum, voicing Montesquieu's dictum about the gradual, multiply constrained workings of political change: "Politics is a most finely-grained file [*une lime sourde*], which wears things down and achieves its aim slowly."[255] Thus in June 1968, for example, he serenely explained that the students were merely engaged in age-appropriate behavior, while the "masses were behaving like 'great, calm forces,' using the events to improve their well-being in a society that they no longer rejected."[256] So perhaps the most immediate and important guise of "totalitarianism" for Caillois in these years was the structuralist sciences humaines. In 1975, Alain Peyrefitte privately praised his explicit stand, his "firm but nuanced reservation with respect to the incorrect use of certain sciences humaines, which intend to impose an exclusive and truly *totalitarian* hermeneutics upon those who are studying how societies or the psyche function."[257] Peyrefitte was referring to Caillois's vitriolic welcoming address for Lévi-

Strauss at the Académie Française the previous year, which was an unusually (for him) ad hominem attack on every aspect of the latter's work and career. Brandishing heavy artillery, Caillois cited Karl Popper's famous phrase, "A theory that presents itself as a science does so in vain when the very structure of the system makes it impossible to refute." And he recalled Popper's likening of Marxism and psychoanalysis to astrology rather than to astronomy: "In effect, such constructs assimilate everything: events and observations. It is only a matter of ingeniousness. Their ostensible capacity for absorption is infinite and irremediable. For this reason, they will never be more than para-scientific." [258]

Yet perhaps Caillois's hostility to totalitarian thought can also be seen as a reflection on the theoretical conceits of his youth, repudiating, for example, the infinitely expansive generalization of "For a Militant Orthodoxy." [259] Indeed, his dissection of Lévi-Strauss outlined at length their common intellectual origins in the Surrealist break with the West and Western logic. Already during their debates of 1954–1955, Caillois had written, "I admit that I myself shared the kind of hope that certain ethnographers placed in rituals such as Vodoo before actually becoming ethnographers." Highlighting the Surrealist tenor of the 1930s ethnographic imperative, he claimed, "They hated, but they didn't have enough detachment to compare." Members of this milieu, himself included, were driven by "the impassioned belief that their civilization [was] hypocritical, corrupt and repugnant, and that the purity and fullness for which the need [was] felt must be sought elsewhere, anywhere, and to be safe at the opposite ends of the geographical and cultural spectrum." [260] Both David Pace and Lévi-Strauss, in "Diogène couché," deemed this argument to be historically inaccurate and irrelevant. [261] Still, Lévi-Strauss elsewhere recounted that in 1928, without frequenting the Surrealists at all, he was nonetheless "completely enthused and seduced" by their movement: "I viewed myself as revolutionary in all fields at that time." [262] In any event, Caillois's tirade concluded with an allusion to his own past, worth citing in extenso:

> I was fourteen or fifteen when Roger Gilbert-Lecomte placed the first works of Lévy-Bruhl in my hands and explained that all of Western logic was doomed to sterility because it rested on the principle of contradiction: A is A, which could clearly not engender anything. On the contrary, the logic of participation proper to the primitive mentality allowed for all hopes. The reasoning struck me as peremptory. At that time, I didn't know that logic doesn't serve to invent but that, on the contrary, it is a kind of guarantee or assurance that the reasoner takes to prevent facile reasoning. I didn't realize that precisely because the logic of participation is immensely supple it is hence not at all a form of logic and that the prim-

itive mentality, for that very reason, is a kind of thinking totally lacking in rigor. But the *illusion of Gilbert-Lecomte* stems from the same lure as does the "*illusion of Saurat*" and the dialectic of Lévi-Strauss.[263]

If he was thus fending off the structuralist sciences humaines as a form of false, or astrological, science, Caillois was nonetheless more interesting than an embittered reactionary responding to the triumphs of Lévi-Strauss. In a kind of counterattack, one might say, against the Surrealist, or poetic, aspects of structuralism, he was himself drawing on Surrealism—or the Surrealist legacy in his own imagination—to theorize a speculative "diagonal science," followed by a "generalized aesthetics and poetics." By 1959, in the context of *Diogenes*, Caillois developed his first model of diagonal science to perpetuate the Maussian legacy by uniting scientists from different fields into one "fraternal" and "single perspective." Charting what he called the "shortcuts of nature" (*chemins de traverse*), diagonal science proposed an open series of new classifications based on creative, interdisciplinary taxonomies. In his first manifesto, he sharply opposed diagonal science to any aesthetic practice. Distinguishing the painter or poet from the scientist, he wrote, "For the scientist the real task involves . . . determining the hidden correspondences—invisible and unimaginable to the profane." He then strongly inveighed against "deceptive analogy" and "pure and simple metaphor," which only reflect the world of appearances—or what seems "evident, logical, and probable."[264] In this respect, he fully adhered to Bachelard's distinction between the hidden resemblances of science and the perceptible, or apparent, likenesses of metaphor and traditional reason (in particular, see Bachelard's *La Philosophie du non*, 1940).[265]

Yet, as Jenny notes in one of his insightful essays on Caillois's work, "It responds to science's rejection of appearances by vigorously reintegrating appearances into the scientific realm."[266] This may well have been true in the 1930s. Furthermore, when Caillois presented a second manifesto of diagonal science in 1970, it was to include analogies and correspondences available to poets and painters: in short, to the subjective, nonscientific imagination (see "A New Plea for Diagonal Science"). This theoretical agenda aimed for an endless plurality of cross-sections, with none claiming full, that is total, systematic value: partial generalizations, one might say. Focusing on dissymmetry, Caillois implicitly took to task structuralism's binding but supple binary oppositions, and reconsidering comparative categories disgarded by scientific progress, he dismissed utilitarian (Darwinian) models as he had in the 1930s, to favor universal motivations such as "abundance, play, *ivresse*, even aesthetics, or at least the need for ornament and decoration." What I would underscore, however, and as this essay's conclusion makes clear, nonutilitarian diagonal science was specifically defined as imaginative forays calling for rigorous verification, thereby leaving unscathed scientific practice itself—unlike the implications of "Mimicry and Legendary Psychasthenia" (1935).

In 1978, Caillois would call poetry the "science of feelings and sensations," as distinct from the real science of "measurable phenomena."[267] The conjectural scope of diagonal science would hence be largely poetic. Here, we must note that since the initial diagonal science, the following conceptual developments had marked his thinking about the literary and aesthetic imagination. In 1954, Caillois's *Poétique de Saint-John Perse* had described a form of poetic generalization: "The poet calls upon the world's totality to establish fragile and tenuous homologies in the infinite variety of available phenomena. The hidden *raison d'être* slowly appears, as the accumulating data increasingly betray and in the end bring to light the latent, middle term explaining the prodigious coalition."[268] Yet Caillois's theoretical view of poetry as a complementary science took shape only in 1968, with his important essay "Places et limites de la poésie jusqu'à, selon et depuis Baudelaire" (Places and limits of poetry until, according to, and since Baudelaire), where he defined it in the wake of this poet as a science of the "perceptible word," one that reflected a "common ground of the imagination." "The proper practice of poetic faculties," he wrote, "parallels the effort of scientific invention. It brings the same kinds of *ivresses* and illuminations, although these are always linked to a personal and transient experience. They could potentially be generalized but [for now] stand suspended and daring, lively and fluid, quivering and furtive, pure wagers of the imagination, which is training itself to achieve greater acuity and *justesse* [accuracy]. The poet is the scientist of appearances, of all those elusive and flighty things he must catch in the traps of language, since he is convinced that these, too, form a secret cloth with an ever-present weave." Redeeming the image from its Surrealist usage, as the proper tool of poetry, Caillois here indifferently called it an analogy, homology, metaphor, correspondence, or sign. It had become "the bridge drawn between two things that science, by vocation, must study independently, and certainly not in terms of their possible similarities—which it could only view as misleading appearances."[269] As if to further confirm the rift between poetry and science, he implicitly revised the earlier claim that the "homologies" of Saint-John Perse would slowly and inevitably reveal their "hidden raison d'être." By 1968, Caillois now voiced the more modest suggestion that the analogies of poetic science—virtually generalizable, as it were—harbored the mere potential for revelation.

Still subscribing to Surrealism's faith in the "world's unitary nature," Caillois qualified this apprehension of a finite cosmos with three key conceptual models.[270] In 1964, he presented a worldview derived from Borges, in essence positing man's epistemological limitations because he could never fully perceive the inevitable structure of circular time but only its "projections in the realms of space and causality: the labyrinth and recurrent creation."[271] Second, he turned to the Mendeleyevian combinatorial chart of the elements, which he described as the scientific counterpart to his own inquiry into the myriad permutations of the perceptible world. Finally, he developed the category of the "natural fantastic" to characterize his new "poetic generalizations" or correspondences (see "The Natural Fantastic"). "What I term the *'accurate imagination'* [*l'imagination juste*]," Caillois declared in 1974,

> means writing nothing that is not guaranteed by some kind of reality. . . .
> That is why my conception of the fantastic—what I call the fantastic in
> nature—is linked to poetry, which is the art of expressing and the science
> of perceiving the numerous relationships that elude quantitative analysis.
> The core of my thought is that since the world is finite, things necessarily
> recur, tally with each other, and overlap. And that is what allows for poetry, which is the science of the redundancies . . . in the universe; it is
> the science of these supercharged, and hence privileged, points and moments. . . . It is possible because the elements making up the world are
> finite in number and thus necessarily signal to one another [*se font des
> signes*], that is respond to one other. This view is close to Baudelaire's "*correspondences*," the difference being that I base myself less on Paracelsus
> than on Mendeleyev. . . . But it must be a surprising, scandalous *justesse*;
> one that is not merely a matter of course, that is useless. In this respect,
> I remain surrealist.[272]

The final phase of Caillois's generalization was increasingly Surrealist in this last sense. Generalization had been a tool of scientific mastery for him in the 1930s. But he would use the term almost parodically, or "pataphysically," with his "generalized aesthetics" of 1962 and then with his late "generalized poetics" in 1978. *Esthétique généralisée* (1962) emerged in tandem with his shift from the first, scientific diagonal sciences to the poetic and subjective version, as he was musing on the natural beauty of butterfly wings in *Méduse et Cie* (1960) and on stones in "Les Traces" (1961): "I call *art* that beauty which is deliberately produced by man, and *aesthetic* the appreciation of all beauty, that deriving from art as well as that which is accidentally encountered in the universe."[273] By 1978, Caillois thus illustrated his generalized poetics with *Le Champ des signes: récurrences dérobées* (The field of signs/The swan-song: Hidden recurrences), in which the writer features as merely one instance of a natural phenomenon: "Doesn't the drift of my reverie also belong to the general syntax that I am seeking to decipher?"[274] Such "syntax" predates images and language altogether: "In my opinion, it would diminish poetry to view it as a luxury or fantasy of the human species alone."[275] These final works proposed increasingly bold analogies, such as an anticipation of algebra in the designs of certain stones. Ever more bounded, though, by their epistemological constraints and brackets, Caillois's reveries sought not to subvert science but merely to incite the scientific imagination. This stance could recall the following words of Paul Ricoeur: "Poetry preserves, for science itself, an idea of truth according to which what is manifested is not at our disposal, is not manipulable, but remains a surprise, a gift."[276]

If diagonal science and generalized aesthetics and poetics fulfilled the Baudelairean aims Caillois had set out for poetry as a complement to real science, he was also providing a corrective to Surrealism itself, which he currently reproached for having betrayed its poetic aims, as a form of "astrological" poetry (see "Surrealism as a World of Signs"). Paul de Man has written about Mallarmé that "he inclined toward Hegel rather than toward Eliphas Lévi," in the sense of rejecting an "astrological" solution to the "specifically 'romantic' experience" of "poetic nothingness . . . Hegel's 'unhappy consciousness.'"[277] When Caillois now evokes his own "pursuit of surreality . . . (like an asymptote, I'm afraid, a curve drawing near without ever reaching)," he rejects Eliphas Lévi to opt not for nothingness, or Hegel, but for a full finitude that can never be reached. In a poetic appropriation of Popper, one might say, his late lyrical prose uses astrology scientifically, namely, as skeptical thought that makes clear its epistemological limitations and openness to revision—thus implicitly repudiating not only Surrealism but his own youthful efforts to make the Surrealist image scientific.[278]

But again, where had the sacred gone at this late date, when Caillois's writings thus turned on the dichotomy of poetry and science? Could this "recurrent yearning of mankind" have completely vanished from his own mind? On the one hand, it seems as if the progressive abstraction of his thought ultimately transmuted the sacred into secular, formal concepts unrelated to any kind of individual or collective experience of this phenomenon. Note how the prewar "sacred as transgression" inheres in the static paradox of the image, with its element of surprise; which is followed by the postwar "spirit of play" and the poetics of the fantastic; which cedes, in turn, to the formal designs of the natural fantastic. In 1972, Caillois's theory of universal dissymmetry would then formalize the fantastic in terms he finally applied to his analytical tool, analogy itself: "I am convinced today that the poetic image is, in its own way, a kind of dissymmetry."[279] On the other hand, his treatment of such forms is not "dehumanized" in the sense Ortega y Gasset gave to the term after Mallarmé.[280] To render Caillois's writing coherent in its own terms, I would recall, while reading these late prose writings, his early theory of the modern sacred as an absolute devotion that is private, interiorized, often secretive—and that can nonetheless give rise to community.

In this regard, Caillois's late pattern-seeking in the cosmos should perhaps be read against the backdrop of poststructuralism, as a counterpart to the "dehumanized" free play of the poststructuralist signifier. *Le Fleuve Alphée* and *Le Champ des signes* forge a mode of *différance*, a mimetic attentiveness to stones that does not seek to decode, unmask, or reveal but merely to translate the stones's appearance, "to obtain a form of verbal tracing." Yet this is a performative simulacrum because as Caillois says, it involves a brief gesture or "act of allegiance"—one complicated by the fact that with such interactions, the lyrical I achieves a level of self-deception rivaling the paradoxical ambiguity of Loyola's maxim (see "Loyola to the Rescue of Marx") or the spirit of play, as he is here both "duped and a willing player."[281] Perhaps we may then better grasp Starobinski's remark that "contrary to Romantic melancholy, which triggers irony and rupture,—it is at the moment of *return*, of restored presence . . . that a melancholy outpour occurs in Roger Caillois's writing."[282] Just as intricate as this gesture toward the mineral realm is the address Caillois twice proffered to his readers in 1978: "I only speak in my own name, but as if everyone were expressing themselves in my verse as much as I do myself. I am addressing an invisible interlocutor, but in such a way that everyone can have the illusion that my verses address him alone, or at least him first and foremost. They are confided secrets, but impersonal ones; they have neither a source nor an addressee. They are messages from one hidden ghost to anonymous ghosts."[283] In this final version of Caillois's elective elite, secret cohesion involves not the prereflective recognition of masters (as in "The Winter Wind"), nor some common literary faith (as in *Puissances du roman*), nor shared humanist orthodoxy (as in *Diogenes*). Rather, it calls on us to partake in a public game of lyrical intimacy—*hypocrite lecteur*. The reward might be that such intersections of objectivity and subjectivity could reveal something both obvious and yet surprising about our relation to literature, or about the emotion of analogy.

THEORY AND THE THIRTIES, 1934–1939

Surrealism and Its Environs

Introduction to "Testimony (Paul Eluard)"

In 1973, Caillois warned his audience that this evocation of his friendship with the poet Paul Eluard, and of his own experiences in the Surrealist movement, was inchoate at best. Yet such retrospection offers a lively roster of Caillois's aims and doubts with respect to Surrealism, which are interesting to compare with those voiced forty years earlier, in his "Letter to André Breton."

As recounted in "Testimony (Paul Eluard)," the young Caillois was deterred by the ambiguities of Surrealist politics. A full-fledged member from 1932 to 1934, he witnessed at close hand the difficult relations between the Surrealists and the French Communist Party (from which they were formally expelled in 1933); he also took part in the early stages of the antifascist intellectual mobilization of the Surrealists within the communist-led Association des Ecrivains et Artistes Révolutionnaires (AEAR) and, subsequently, the Comité de Vigilance des Intellectuels Anti-Fascistes, founded in March 1934 to align communists and noncommunists alike.[1]

In aesthetic terms, Caillois was bitterly disappointed that the experimental strategies of Surrealism, such as the practice of automatic writing, were more "literary" and less "scientific" than he had hoped. Although he was enthralled at first by Surrealist games purporting to explore the mechanisms of the imagination, he soon decided that these were deceptive social events in which the participants simply mimicked the common language of the group. He remarked in 1971 that this shortcoming had not escaped Breton's attention.[2] Moreover, "Testimony (Paul Eluard)" underscores the fact that Eluard's "*tentative* poetry," by deliberately feeling its way along, explicitly denied the principles of automatized composition.

This essay conveys the impassioned and ascetic intransigence of Caillois's youth, which was colored early on by the Romantic cult of Saint-Just. A few years later, the essays he published under the aegis of Surrealism (such as "The Praying Mantis") or right after his break with Breton (such as "Mimicry and Legendary Psychasthenia"), maintain a tone of almost exasperating scientific impersonality, even though these investigations, inspired by Freud and Pierre Janet, place emotion and obsession at their core. But "Testimony (Paul

"Témoignage," *Europe* 525 (1973): 79–84.

Eluard)" also reveals Caillois's sense of humor and irony, which would become all the more pronounced in his later years, especially when evoking his avant-garde allegiances of the 1930s.

TESTIMONY (PAUL ELUARD)

The author would like to stress that the following text was originally performed as an improvised speech, without any help from notes or chronological documents. We hope that the reader will take it as such and respond to the artless spontaneity of someone relying upon the good faith of this audience.

During yesterday's meeting I noticed that some of you, especially the scholars, were rather puzzled by the chronology of events between 1932 and 1935. I have tried to reconstruct this. My first intention was to speak of Eluard during the period when I knew him, that is, from 1931 until his death. However, after the war I frequented him less; we didn't meet almost daily as we had between 1932 and 1935. That was the period when political questions first began to present themselves, and in a very flexible and fluctuating way. In other words, people were taking positions that were being constantly reshuffled. And so I've tried to recreate this chronology—but without success. The recollections you'll be hearing are hence incomplete—not only piecemeal but also unconfirmed. I would be the first to urge you to check them before using them.

We must also remember to describe the witness. At that time I was a very young man . . . taking preparatory classes for the Ecole Normale Supérieure. I was naïve, doctrinaire, uncompromising, and rather aggressive.

I was born in Reims. I was a friend (at first, simply a neighbor on the same street) of several young men a few years older than myself: Vailland, Roger Gilbert-Lecomte, and Daumal. They were the ones who made me read Rimbaud and Lautréamont and drew my attention to Eluard. At the time, I'd read only one book by Eluard, *La Capitale de la douleur*, which I'd actually found rather disconcerting.

While a student at the lycée Louis-le-Grand, I was asked what kind of literature I liked for a survey by the newspaper, *L'Intransigeant*. I replied: "Romanticism, and the contemporary equivalent of Romanticism, namely Surrealism."

André Breton wrote me a note asking me to come see him; I did so, very excited, just at the time of the Aragon affair. Aragon had recently converted to communism and was returning from Russia. He had written a poem for which he had been greatly criticized. Certain lines had been interpreted as an incitement to commit murder. Breton had then put out a pamphlet demanding the dismissal of the "charges" against Aragon. Naturally, I signed this manifesto, which explained that poetry was not a serious matter. I remember that a few people (Bergery among them[1]) protested at this point, arguing that if poetry was to be taken only symbolically and figuratively, then perhaps it did not have the importance Surrealism claimed to ascribe to it.

What has been reported in books does not adequately convey the atmosphere surrounding those events. True, there is André Thirion's recent book [*Révolutionnaires sans révolution*; 1972], but I find that Thirion, whom I knew in those days, is very sketchy about the period. In addition, there are biased accounts that distort the facts, or at least make them too systematic.

So this was right after the break with Aragon. And yet, the group was not so much concerned with politics as with something entirely new: the arrival of Dali, and especially the emphasis on what he called paranoid-critical activity.

The important thing here was not the word *paranoia* (Breton and Eluard had already published their *Immaculate Conception*, with simulations of pathological deliria); it was the word *critical*. This was something quite new for the group, this idea that the simulation of delirious psychotic mechanisms could occur together with their critical examination and present itself as a *method*. For Paul Eluard—as we're speaking of him—the situation was doubly awkward. First, there was his personal relationship with Dali. His wife, Gala had left him and married Dali. Eluard was living with Nush. He loved her, and I may, perhaps, have a chance to describe how delicately he treated her. He was then suffering from tuberculosis and spent part of the year in sanatoria. And yet, if Nush dropped her glove or a piece of paper, he would rush to pick it up—even though he knew he wasn't supposed to make sudden moves. Still, despite his constant attentiveness to Nush, I always had the feeling that the memory of Gala (and not just her memory, for she was there in person) continued to fascinate him.

I found many things shocking in Surrealism, and when I withdrew from the movement after bearing with it for three years, it wasn't because I found it too strict, but because I thought it too indulgent. For example, I was surprised to discover that Eluard was not the poet's real name. I thought it unworthy of a poet (especially a Surrealist poet, theoretically opposed to all forms of convention and vanity) to choose a name that wasn't his own. His poem on the Gertrude Hoffmann girls shocked me too, not its contents but the title ["Les

1. [Gaston Bergery (1892–1974) was a nonconformist of the 30s. A deputy of the Radical Socialist Party (1928–1934) and then the "Frontiste" Party (1936–1942), which he founded with Jacques Izard, he also edited the party's journal, *La Flèche* (1935–1939).—Ed.]

Gertrude Hoffmann Girls"; 1926]; this did not impress me as a suitable topic for poetry but rather for reprehensible levity. I must say that I was then earnestly cultivating chastity and reserve. I did so not through inclination or morality but in order to imitate, I thought, my favorite hero, Saint-Just, about whom I'd written my first article when I was fifteen. This attitude irritated Eluard, who often reproached me in a friendly way for being more interested in ideas than in young women. But he could see that my case was hopeless. Perhaps he could also discern the affectation that entered into this naïve embodiment of the theorist, the "incorruptible" doctrinarian. When he wrote me postcards, he would often send me scantily clad girls. In my opinion, this was not entirely innocent.

Something else offended me. I had joined the Surrealist group believing in automatic writing, and then I realized that no one practiced it. Especially not Eluard, who openly disregarded it. Not only did he disregard it, but he was in the habit—and I found Supervielle did the same—of writing what I'll call *tentative* poetry. By that I mean, he would try out every single line on his friends. He would ask their opinion: "What do you think? Is it okay? Wouldn't it be better this way?" In point of fact, he would decide himself, and would do so alone. But what was characteristic (and it seemed to me the very opposite of automatic writing) was his constant care to grope his way along slowly and quite visibly.

I would often go to see him. I also used to meet him at the café Cyrano, on the Place Blanche, together with all the other members of the Surrealist group. They had their mandatory rituals. Whenever a woman arrived, Breton would get up and kiss her hand. Even the color of the drinks was ritualized: in winter it was tangerine-curaçao and in summer, pernod. To change color was almost a sign of opposition, as Monnerot pointed out to me.

It was at this point that I published my article on the praying mantis, first in *Minotaure*, which was practically a Surrealist review, and then in *Mesures*. I felt I'd rather inspired the habit of breeding praying mantises, which Breton and Eluard took to doing at Castellane.

There were also the postcards. This was when Eluard published part of his collection in *Minotaure*. Above all, there were the Surrealist games, which were the real cause of my break with Surrealism. There were questionnaires (irrational, of course) to which, in my naïveté, I ascribed some scientific intention. We were supposed to react as quickly as possible. Many of these questions and answers were published in numbers 5 and 6 of *Le Surréalisme au service de la révolution*. Thus the project's *literary* nature, in the worst sense of the word (indeed, its exclusively literary nature), is there for everyone to see.

This is what made me bristle, allowing me to see that my adherence to Surrealism was basically a misunderstanding. I had imagined that Surrealism was the end of literature but, in trying it out, I realized that it was an avatar of literature. The games revealed this to me, because the answers were almost always (not to say always) Surrealist clichés.

As for relations with revolutionary parties, I've already mentioned them with regard to Aragon's poem. Breton had defended it rather clumsily because his defense of Aragon essentially amounted to saying that because Aragon's text was poetic, it should not be taken seriously. Aragon rejected this defense (justifiably, in my view) and disowned Breton.

As a whole, the group joined the AEAR (Association des Ecrivains et Artistes Révolutionnaires). Breton carried things quite far at that point. There was a short-story competition for the worker-members. Breton was not only a member of the jury but also its formal spokesman. Upon reading these stories, which dismayed him, he took pains to discern their merits while expressing major reservations that could not deceive informed listeners. After that, the only Communist Party leader who approved of Breton was Gabriel Péri. Vaillant-Couturier was more of a writer and, at the same time, more political; it was thanks to him that the AEAR had been opened up. Breton here had a determined enemy, Fréville, the literary critic for *L'Humanité*, and Fréville won the battle. There was a memorable meeting of the AEAR. (I evoke this only for its atmosphere, because neither Eluard nor Aragon were there: Aragon never attended a single session of the Association while Breton was there.) Fréville delivered a real prosecution address against the Surrealist group. I am specifying this because the meeting took place behind closed doors and I don't think there was ever any record of it. First of all, Fréville attacked Breton on account of the *Vases communicants*. His argument went pretty much like this: "Comrade, do you admit that on page 24 of your book, you praise Lenin?" "Yes," replied Breton. "And that on page 18, you approve of the Marquis de Sade?"[2] "Yes," said Breton again. "Well, I rest my case: in my opinion, a book that puts Lenin on the same level as the Marquis de Sade is objectively counterrevolutionary." This was and still is a formidable turn of phrase.

Then Fréville spoke of Dali. Dali was attacked in far greater detail. He had painted Lenin with an inordinately long head resting on the kind of wooden fork used to prop up heavy branches. This was deemed sacrilegious. He had also painted six hallucinatory images of Lenin on a grand piano. He had sold a painting to a countess, who was said to be a niece of the Pope. And so on.

2. I'm guessing at the page numbers, of course; it's the principle that matters.

Above all, Dali had published an erotic dream in the sixth issue of *Le Sur-réalisme au service de la révolution*, in which he was masturbating with a roll of bread! This, apparently, was totally unacceptable. There was also (and this was one of the main items in Fréville's indictment) the hostile review of a Soviet film, *The Way of Life* (if I remember correctly) that demonstrated how hooligans were rehabilitated in the U.S.S.R. The article was signed by Ferdinand Alquié, and essentially concluded that the young delinquents were nonetheless preferable to the informers. This went too far. Fréville called on Breton to repudiate Dali and Alquié. Breton refused. The meeting ended in turmoil, but without resolutions to expel anyone.

At this very moment, the Reichstag was burned down and the Nazis came to power. I think that the gravity of the new situation was what changed Breton's attitude toward Dali. The AEAR published a newspaper page in black and red print, with a bloody swastika. To draft it, Vaillant-Couturier was selected from the majority group, and I myself from the Surrealist faction. This manifesto stated the AEAR's faith in the German proletariat. So then Dali became very angry and said he wouldn't sign a text like that, which he considered completely idiotic; that for his part, he would never have the slightest confidence in a proletariat that hadn't even been able to manage a "truly refined" and "truly subtle" general strike. This took place at Breton's home. I don't remember if it was before or after the publication of the page in question, but I remember Dali's adjectives. After this explosion, the people present seriously considered ousting Dali. To convey the mood of these quarrels, before coming here I unearthed the *pneu* [pneumatic letter] I received from Breton and Péret. Note the date, February 2, 1934; that is, four days before the demonstrations of February 6:

> Dear friend, we are absolutely counting on your presence at the meeting to be held on Monday, February 5, at 9 o'clock sharp, at Breton's residence, 42 rue Fontaine. Agenda: Dali having several times committed counterrevolutionary acts tending to glorify Hitlerian fascism, we the undersigned propose to expel him from Surrealism as a fascist element, this despite his declaration of January 25, 1934, and to oppose him in every possible way. Given that Yoyotte supports Dali in this confusional propaganda, which is disruptive to Surrealism's revolutionary ideology, we the undersigned propose to exclude him until he is able to keep his opinions to himself.
>
> Paris, February 2, 1934. Signed: Breton, Max Ernst, Tanguy . . .
>
> In the event that it is absolutely impossible for you to attend this meeting, please send us your vote, or convey it by proxy, with a written au-

thorization for a person present. In addition to those signing the above motion, and those in question (Dali and Yoyotte), we also summon Caillois, Char, and Maurice Henry.

Crevel, Eluard, Giacometti, and Tzara, being out of town, are requested to send in their decision by mail.

I went to the meeting. Dali was there. He literally went down on his knees in front of Breton, asking for a reprieve that was not granted, and he was expelled. I am certain that for Eluard, who did not attend this meeting for he was still in a sanatorium in Davos, this business was very distressing, because he always protected Dali. He did more than simply humor him, he defended him. Then came February 12[3]: we all went to the demonstration, and were carted off in police vans or pushed back into the Metro exits. Poor Tanguy had several teeth broken in the scuffle.

Shortly thereafter, I left the AEAR at the same time as Crevel, I believe; then Char, then Breton, and the rest of the group, who could all see the situation was impossible after Fréville's indictment. That December, for reasons unrelated to the preceding break, I quit the Surrealist group too. I didn't see Breton again until the war, when I got back in touch with him. I continued to see Eluard, Crevel, and Char. One fine day (this was, after all, a small world) I bumped into Aragon and Tzara. Together we founded the journal *Inquisitions*, with Monnerot as the fourth member. It had only one issue, because our positions were ultimately incompatible. I continued to see Eluard until my departure for Argentina, and then again after my return. In 1947–1948, I was busy with a journal founded by a Uruguayan woman, Susana Soca, called *La Licorne*. Eluard published there some poems about Nush. The journal had already gone to print when Nush died. He asked us to cross out his name and replace it with a pseudonym, Didier Desroches. In the issue containing these poems, the name Paul Eluard is illegible. It's covered over by a large stroke of mourning. Here is the last recollection of a somewhat personal nature that I can bring you of Paul Eluard.

---

3. [Fascist riots on February 6, 1934 triggered counterdemonstrations on February 12, which marked the historic rise of the *Front Populaire*. —*Ed*].

Introduction to "The Praying Mantis"

Caillois reworked and expanded his study of the praying mantis several times between 1934 and 1937, even lecturing on the topic to the College of Sociology.[1] The sexual power relations that he illustrates here, anchored in a biological substratum, will shape his discussions throughout the decade. In a way, this rather misogynist image became his trademark. It may echo, in automatized terms, what he calls Baudelaire's "sinister view" of "physical love": "an embrace inevitably involves a victim and an executioner, one who retains consciousness, stays alert and observes."[2] Moreover, we should recall that he was addressing (and seeking to systematize) a sexual emblem of the femme fatale, or of love and death that greatly compelled his immediate milieu: Breton, Eluard, and Dali.[3] To the extent that Surrealism involved some kind of scientific research, the praying mantis could well stand as one symbol of its prime mystery or object of study. Wrote Breton: "Despite the ways in which Sade and Freud, most memorably, have plumbed the depths of sexuality in the modern period, the latter still defies our wish to penetrate the world with its unshatterable core of *night*."[4]

Caillois tackles this problem through the praying mantis, which has an "objective capacity to act directly upon the emotions," given its "objective lyrical value."[5] He offers a long list of its varied effects on the human imagination: from classical Antiquity to the present (including the Surrealist milieu) and in a vast array of different societies. Why is this so? Caillois points to the insect's anthropomorphic aspect, which compels any human viewer. More important, the cannibalistic nuptial habits of the mantis express the interplay of love and death, or eros and thanatos, that Freud had most recently outlined in *Beyond the Pleasure Principle*. Our "ambivalent premonition of encountering one within the other," according to Caillois, cannot leave us unmoved by an insect that is endowed with additional bizarre attributes of death: movement after decapitation and a mimetic shift to a less vital natural state (which he later explores in "Mimicry and Legendary Psychasthenia"). In short, mythography and psychoanalysis should seek their origins in "comparative biology." The praying mantis does not affect us because mankind is subject to "castration

"La Mante religieuse," *Minotaure* 5 (1934): 23–26.

anxiety"; rather, men suffer this unconscious complex because they are afraid of being eaten. Yet, while seeking thus to make Surrealism more scientific, Caillois radically undermines science by describing a very dangerous object—one that transgresses its boundaries. We read that scientists lose "their professional dryness" and "scientific detachment" when inspecting the praying mantis. And although he himself does not indulge in emotional display, he outlines the limits of reason transgressed by the insect's fantastic behavior in a "decapitated state": "I am deliberately expressing myself in a roundabout way as it is so difficult, I think, both for language to express and for the mind to comprehend that the mantis, when dead, should be capable of simulating death." "The Praying Mantis" emerged from *L'Esprit des bêtes, zoologie passionnelle* (1853), written by a Fourierist, A. Toussenel. In 1971 Caillois recalled being struck by a "delirious" chapter on bats, which led him to think of the winged nocturnal creature as "a kind of *privileged basis* for the image, for the imagination, and hence, for poetry."[6]

With *The Necessity of Mind*, Caillois sought to reform Surrealism by creating a form of "poetry that renounces the use of its artistic privileges in order to present itself as a science."[7] Although the *First Manifesto* had outlined the *arbitrariness* of the Surrealist "image," six years later their *Second Manifesto* (1930) sought to synthesize Rimbaud and Marx. Their recent "will to objectify" led them from automatic writing to a more purposive grasp of reverie, dreams, and hallucinations.[8] Thus, Dali's "critical paranoia" took over the privileged place of hysteria, attempting to create "a coherent method of knowledge and creative interpretation of reality," according to Elisabeth Roudinesco; this controlled visual delirium, actively reshaping the world through desire, writes Maurice Nadeau, was a "perfect and coherent systematization, a means of achieving an all-powerful state."[9] *The Necessity of Mind* cites critical paranoia as the closest comparable theory in the Surrealist camp. However, Caillois felt that the images produced by critical paranoia lacked objective grounding, as they sought to replace the real world and were arbitrary and subjective. With the ideogrammatic image, on the contrary, he aimed for "absolute objectivity."[10]

The "lyrical overdetermination" he postulates in *The Necessity of Mind* was loosely derived from the psychological associationism proper to the psychiatric category of psychasthenia, coined by Pierre Janet, whose studies of unconscious automatism were well known in Surrealist circles. Caillois focused on *Les Névroses* (1909), which explained, "Psychasthenia is a form of mental depression characterized by a drop in psychological tension, by the lessening of those functions which enable one to act upon reality and perceive the real; these are replaced by inferior and exaggerated operations in the form of doubts, agitations, anxieties and obsessive ideas expressing the aforementioned problems, and which themselves present the same features." Janet's new pathological state, "psycholepsy" or "drop in mental energy," was heir to fin de siècle neurasthenia and forebear to Freud's obsessional neurosis.[11] Combining psychasthenia with the "overdetermination" of Freudian dreamwork, Caillois argued that certain representations crystallized through networks of overdetermined psychological associations into *ideograms*, or *objective ideograms*.[12] And he endowed them with a metaphysical scope. That is, objective ideograms, such as the praying mantis, revealed the "systematic overdetermination of the universe"—or rather, of a universal, psychasthenic imagination.[13] "Mimicry and Legendary Psychasthenia" shows at length that, unlike critical paranoia, psychasthenic obsessions fulfill neither desire nor a quest for power.

Caillois's fascination with the death instinct in "The Praying Mantis" stems from Le Grand Jeu and will draw him to Bataille in the following years. And it is what sets him apart from André Gide, whose *Corydon* (1924) also collapsed human and insect behavior in the wake of Bergson and Remy de Gourmont. Here, the narrator chats with Corydon, who seeks at one point to prove the natural status of homosexuality. Without fully breaking with Darwin, Corydon first highlights "the relatively constant overabundance of the male element in nature." He draws on de Gourmont, Bergson, and a certain Perrier, who proclaimed that "*the feminine gender is . . . in some sense that of physiological reserves; the masculine gender, that of luxurious but unproductive expenditure.*" For Corydon, such natural male "excess" compensates for "a certain indecisiveness in the sexual instinct," which is oriented toward *volupté* (sensual pleasure) rather than procreation. Hence, "the male [is] a creature of ostentatious display, song, art, sport, or intelligence—of *jeu* [play]." He thus enthuses:

> — . . . Oh Nature! For such an inconceivable victory over unorganized matter, over death, you are allowed to be lavishly prodigal indeed! No doubt this hardly entails any "ill-considered expenditure," no, for so much waste is not too high a price for your triumph. . . .
> —"Waste." You said it.
> —Yes, waste, from the viewpoint of utilitarian finality. But it is on such waste that art, thought and *le jeu* will be able to flower.

In short, Corydon finds cultural purposiveness in biological waste. But suddenly, the praying mantis stands out as a thorny counterexample, as one of the rare cases where "homosexual tastes" might be lacking in an animal species. Gide's narrator helpfully suggests that the female mantises' "extravagant consumption" of males shows that the sexual instinct is "overshooting its mark," that with the *mantis religiosa*, excessive expenditure is female (although the possible cultural value of such a phenomenon is left unclear).[14]

Caillois's "Praying Mantis" does not address the issue of finality, utilitarian or otherwise. It is only the following year, after his break with Breton, that he delves, as does *Corydon*, into the riddle of biological behavior. The insects of "Mimicry and Legendary Psychasthenia" here provide the biological ground for an anti-Darwinian, anti-utilitarian, universal *instinct d'abandon* (instinct of letting go). Important in this respect, most likely, was "The Notion of Expenditure" by Caillois's new acquaintance, Bataille. Any comparison with *Corydon* would have to consider the contract between Bataille's sacrificial (heterosexual) "expenditure" and Gide's ludic (homosexual) "waste."

THE PRAYING MANTIS:
FROM BIOLOGY TO PSYCHOANALYSIS

Certain objects and images are endowed with a comparatively high degree of lyrical force because their form or content is especially significant. This force affects many, if not all, people, and so it seems to be, in essence, an integral part of the given phenomenon. Consequently, this power appears to have as much claim to objective status as the phenomenon itself.[1]

It occurred to me that by virtue of its name, form, and habits, the praying mantis displayed this objective capacity to act directly on the emotions to an exceptional degree; this is very useful in helping us to understand how imaginative syntheses can be transmitted in a lyrical way. Therefore, I undertook some research to confirm my hypothesis regarding the insect. With this specific case, I was also trying to grasp how a representation could have a separate and,

1. These pages constitute the fifth chapter of a forthcoming work on *the mechanisms of overdetermination in automatic and lyrical thought and the development of affective themes in individual consciousness*. The book is titled *The Necessity of Mind* (*La Nécessité d'esprit*), and the following pages take on their full meaning only within this larger conceptual context. So I should clearly state that I am not claiming that men, after having carefully observed mantises, were deeply affected by their habits. I am merely stating that as both these insects and mankind are part of one and the same nature, I do not exclude the possibility of invoking the insects to explain, if need be, people's behavior in certain situations. For we must realize that man is a unique case only in his own eyes, and that this study is actually nothing but comparative biology. I have also chosen to summarize outside the body of the text (which remains unchanged) the few theoretical points that this study contains, I think, in and of itself.

as it were, secret effect upon each individual in the absence of any symbolic dimension, whose meaning was chiefly defined by its social usage, and whose emotional efficacy stemmed from its role in the collectivity.

Here are the results of my research. To avoid giving any grounds for skepticism by trying to demonstrate too much, they are presented without commentary; in any event, they speak for themselves.

The mantidae were probably the first insects on earth. This may be inferred from the fact that the *Mantis protogea*, whose fossil print was found in the Oeningen Myocena, belongs to the *Paleodictyoptera* group, which is defined by Scudder and can be traced back to the carboniferous age.

In his *Die Antike Tierwelt* (Leipzig, 1909–1913), Otto Keller includes the reproduction of a Proserpinian coin from Metaponte. Here, the image of a mantis appears next to an ear of the sacred corn that played such an important part in the Eleusinian mysteries. In his short commentary on this insect (2:460), the same author refers to the lexicographers and compilers Aristarchus and Suidus, who simply observe that the mantis lives in reeds. He also refers to Pseudodioskurides (*Mat. Medic.* 1:158), who adds that the Indian mantis is, according to Keller's translation, "ähnlich und als Heilsmittel wirksam" [similar, and with medicinal properties].

In a work I leafed through in the French edition (ed. J. Künckel d'Herculaïs, published by Baillère), A. E. Brehm points out that a sixteenth-century English naturalist named Thomas Mouffet proposed three different theories as to why this insect was named "mantis." All three are equally untenable and have no intrinsic interest, even as mistakes. This is most likely the same Thomas Mouffet who, in a passage quoted by J. H. Fabre (*Souvenirs entomologiques*, vol. 5, ch.20), notes that when a mantis is asked for directions by children who are lost, it shows them the way by pointing its finger (*sic*)—and rarely, if ever, does it mislead them (*Tam divina censetur bestiola ut puero interroganti de via, extento digito rectam monstret atque raro vel numquam fallat*). The passage is probably taken from his book *Insectorum vel minimorum animalium theatrum*, referred to by other authors[2]. One can find evidence of the same belief in the Languedoc region (see Sébillot, *Le Folklore de la France*, Guilmoto, 1906, 3:323, n. 1).

The insect is linked to the Marvelous in other ways as well. Referring to Nieremberg, A. de Chesnel thus declares that Saint Francis Xavier reportedly made a mantis sing a canticle. He also quotes the case of a man whom this

2. In fact, Eugène Rolland quotes it as such, referring to page 134 in the 1634 edition. His quotation has *altero pede* instead of *digito,* which seems more correct.

same animal supposedly warned, most opportunely, to return whence he came from.

J. H. Fabre (ibid.) says that he often noticed how in Provence the mantis's nest is considered a most effective remedy for chilblains and toothache—as long as it is gathered during a full moon. In *Le Folklore de la France* (3:330), Sébillot notes that around Menton it is thought to cure scurf. On the same topics, Eugène Rolland (*Faune populaire de la France*, 13:117) refers to Regius (*Mat. Medic.*, 32), but the list of popular terms he collected himself is particularly interesting. At times, the mantis is termed "Italian woman" or "specter" and at times, less explicably, "strawberry" or "madeleine." Generally speaking, we find here an ambivalent attitude. On the one hand, the insect is considered sacred, which explains its usual name of *prégo-Diéou* [pray-to-God], with variants and corresponding expressions in Parma, Portugal, the Tyrol, Germany, and Greece. On the other hand, it is at the same time considered diabolical, as manifest in the symmetrical name of *prégo-Diablé* [*pray-to-the-Devil*], which occurs, for example, in the saying *brassiéja coumo un prégo-Diablé* [to gesticulate like a pray-to-the-Devil] (see *Revue des langues romanes*, 1883, 295). The names *menteuse* [liar]; and *bigote* [bigot] noted in Villeneuve-sur-Fère (Aisne) also fall into this category.

If we now turn to the little expressions used by children when referring to the mantis, there seem to be two main themes. First, the insect is said to be a fortune-teller who knows everything—and, in particular, the Wolf's location.[3] Second, the mantis is believed to be praying because its mother died or was drowned. On this last point, testimony is unanimous.[4] It seems that we must generally abide by the views of De Bomare, who writes that the mantis is deemed sacred everywhere in Provence and that people are careful not to cause it the slightest harm.

3. Under the circumstances, can we not suppose that Italian peasants consider the grasshopper to be the supreme fortune-teller, as reported by A. de Gubernatis (*Zoological Mythology*, London, 1872, vol.1, ch. 7), due to a very understandable confusion between this insect and the mantis?

4. I shall quote the most explicit evidence, after Rolland: "*Prégo-Diéou, Bernardo, Bestieto segnado, veni près de iéou, que ta maryé es morto, sus un ped de porto, que toun payre est viéou, sus un ped d'ouliéou*" [Bernard the pray-God, sacred beast, come here, for your mother is dead, on a doorstep, for your father is old, on a step of olive-wood] (Arles); "*Prégo Diéou, marioto, ta may qu'es morto, débat un peu dé porto; te l'an réboundudo débat un ped de brugo*" [Pray to God, little Mary, your mother is dead; they buried her for you beneath a little bush] (Gascony); "*Prégo Diéou, Bernardo, que ta mayré s'es nagado*" [Pray God, Bernardo, for your mother has drowned herself] (Aude); "*Prego, Bernardo, qué Bernat es mort. Sus la porto del ort*" [Pray, Bernardo, for Bernard is dead. Under the garden gate] (Tarn).

This behavior is not unique. Phenomena recorded in northern Melanesia are even more pronounced. Indeed, the natives of Duke of York Island are divided into two clans. One of them takes as its totem *Ko gila le*, an insect so similar to the horse chestnut tree leaf that it could easily be mistaken for one. The other, the Pikalabas clan, takes as its totem *Kam*, "which is doubtless the *Mantis religiosus*" (J. G. Frazer, *Totemism and Exogamy*, 2:120 and following). As for the New World, Paul Eluard assured me that according to an ethnographic work whose title he could unfortunately not recall, certain native Mexican peoples view another mantid in exactly the same way.

The data from Africa, however, are the most significant. The happy mantis from the Cape of Good Hope is worshipped by the Hottentots (Khoi-Khoi) as a beneficent deity.[5]

In this connection, Georges Dumézil, professor of comparative mythography at the Ecole des Hautes Etudes, kindly showed me a passage from Andrew Lang's *Myth, Ritual and Religion* (London: Longman's, 1887) where the author analyzes the beliefs of the Hottentots and Bushmen.[6] According to them, the mantis (*Cagn*) is actually the supreme deity and creator of the world. Its amorous life is apparently "pleasurable," and the moon, which is fabricated out of an old shoe, is its own special possession. We should note, in particular, that its primary function seems to be that of obtaining food for those who beseech it. Furthermore, it was eaten and vomited alive by Kwaï-Hemm, the devouring god (Bleek, 68). So what clearly seems to be most emphasized is the digestive dimension; this should not surprise anyone familiar with the incredible voracity of this insect, prototype of the god. Among the latter's other avatars, let us note that he came back to life, with bones entirely reassembled, after having been killed by thorns (that were formerly men) and eaten by ants. This is an adventure in which digestion still plays a certain part, linking it to the rich mythical cycle of the dispersed and then resurrected god of the Osiris variety. As Lang remarks (*Myth, Ritual and Religion*), the mantis worshipped by the Bushmen should further be related to another mythical theme: the "detachable

---

5. At certain times of the year, these Hottentots engage in extremely lascivious dances, and the children fathered during this period are killed at birth (see E. S. Hartland, *Primitive Paternity*, London, 1910, 2: 213). In general, a more thorough study than the present sketch should take into account the sexual mores of the tribes that worship the mantis and what bonds may connect them to their mythological use of this insect as well as to its own habits.

6. For the Hottentots, Lang's main sources are Peter Kolb's essays of 1719, Thurnberg's writings of 1792, and the study by Halim: *Tsuni Goam, the Supreme Being of the Khoi-Khoi*. For the Bushmen, he refers to Bleek, *A Brief Account of Bushman Folklore* (London, 1975), and Orpen, "A Glimpse into the Mythology of the Maluti Bushmen," *Cape Monthly Magazine* (July 1874).

force" (for example, Minos's lock of hair, Samson's mane, etc.). Indeed, this mantis possesses a tooth, the seat of all its power, which it lends to whomever it wants. I find it significant that the mantis is particularly associated with teeth, both in Provence and in southern Africa. In my opinion, this relationship cannot simply be viewed in terms of the link between sexuality and nutrition that is proper to this insect, even though it may seem conclusive. Indeed, it is by now fully accepted that teeth play a major role in sexual imagery. Psychoanalysis holds that a dream involving tooth extraction refers either to masturbation, castration, or childbirth; according to the popular *Keys to Dreams*, it refers to death.[7] Moreover, among noncivilized peoples once again, a tooth extraction often replaces circumcision when this is not included in the initiation rites. Collectively, these phenomena present a remarkable degree of coherence, both in relation to each other and to the habits of the mantis, as we shall see further on.

So it would seem, generally speaking, that mankind has been highly struck by this insect.[8] No doubt this results from some obscure sense of identification, encouraged by the mantis's remarkably anthropomorphic appearance.[9] Let us now explore the possible reasons for both this identification and the insect's lyrical, emotionally affecting content.

According to the classification published in 1839 by Audinet-Serville, the

7. See S. Freud, *La Science des rêves,* trans. Meyerson (Alcan, 1926), 319, 346–350; *The Interpretation of Dreams,* trans. Strachey (New York: Avon 1965), 421–427. See especially the long remark by Otto Rank, quoted in a footnote, and the supporting linguistic examples. Similarly, mythographical data show that teeth are identified with the entirety or the essence of a person's being (see J. G. Frazer, *The Golden Bough,* vol.1). One thus finds the convergence that might be expected between the two kinds of research.

8. Even the Chinese have been emotionally affected by the mantis. Indeed, they keep mantises in bamboo cages and watch their fights with passionate interest (see Darwin, *La Descendance de l'homme et la sélection sexuelle,* trans. Barbier, Paris 1881, 318. Reference to Westwood's *Modern Classification of Insects,* 1:427). As for the Turks, they are convinced that mantises are always turned toward Mecca. See *Musée entomologique illustrée, Les Insectes* (Paris, 1878).

9. An item's anthropomorphic appearance seems to me an infallible source of its hold on human emotions. This is true, for example, of vampires, mandrakes, and the related legends. In my opinion, it's no coincidence that belief in bloodsucking specters finds a natural vehicle in a certain kind of bat. In fact, the anthropomorphism of the bat is especially far-reaching; it goes well beyond an overall structural similarity (the presence of real hands, with a thumb that can be pressed against the other fingers; pectoral breasts; periodic menstrual flow; and a free, dangling penis). As for the mandrake (*Atropa mandragora*), Theophrastus had already termed it an *anthropomorphon* and Columelle, a *semi-homo.* Its remarkable poisonous, soporific, etc. qualities and its power as an effective antidote to snake poison did all the rest. See interesting quotations in Gustave Le Rouge, *La Mandragore magique (Téraphin, golem, androïdes, homoncules),* ed. H. Daragon, 1912.

Mantidae family comes after the Blattariae, while preceding the Phasmidae, or Specters.[10] It comprises fourteen genuses; the eleventh is that of mantises, strictly speaking. These include the dessicated, superstitious, and herbaceous mantises; the brown-leaf mantis; the broad-appendix mantis (*Mantis latistylus*); the lobed, yellow-winged, and spotted mantises; the moon mantis; the simulacrum mantis; the patelliferous, pustular, neighboring, and varied mantises; the two-mamillae mantis (*Mantis bipapilla*); the long-necked mantis; the cuticular, spattered, sullied (*inquinata*), and black-veined mantises; the hairy-footed mantis; the ornate, pious, praying, prasine, preaching, and vitreous mantises; the belted mantis; the phryganoid, ringed-feet, multistriped, discolored mantises; the sister, the pleasant, and the steel-blue (*Mantis chalybea*) mantises; the red-hipped mantis (*Mantis rubro-coxata*); the nebulous mantis; and last of all, the bright mantis and Madagascan mantis.

This nomenclature is anything but superfluous. The least one can say is that it contains relatively few epithets with technical terms designating the variety's characteristics. Apart from the Madagascan mantis, not a single name indicates where the insect is most abundant or refers to the entomologist who discovered it (as often occurs in the natural sciences). There is no doubt about it: these terms, on the whole, are purely and simply lyrical.

The genus names are usually even more precise. For example, the twelfth is called *epaphrodites*, meaning literally "who are an invitation to love." As for the name of the first genus, *empusa*, it seems the most revealing, in my opinion. Nowadays the term refers both to this kind of mantis and to a kind of fungus parasitically attached to certain insects and that feeds off all their organs except for the digestive tract. In the language of sixteenth-century philosophers, according to the Littré, it also referred to fantastic imaginings. In antiquity, it was the name of a specter sent by Hecate that apparently was able to assume many forms but had only one foot (whence its name), according to Hesychios of Alexandria.[11] The *Etymological Magnum* points out that it is mentioned three times in Aristophanes (*The Frogs*, line 123; *Ecclesiazusae*, line 1056 [Assemblée des femmes]; and in fragment 426). It also quotes a lexicographer accord-

---

10. Audinet-Serville, *Histoire naturelle des insects: Orthoptères,* (De Roret, 1839), 133–214.

11. Hecate appears for the first time in the Homeric hymn to Demeter composed for the Eleusinian mysteries; this converges with the fact that on the coins from Metaponte reproduced in *Die antike Tierwelt,* the mantis is associated with the ear of corn. It is worth recalling that Hecate soon became the goddess of sorcerers and necromancers and would remain so during the entire Middle Ages, despite the efforts of the Church. See A. Maury, *La Magie et l'astrologie dans les antiquités et au moyen age* (Didier, 1884), 176. References in notes.

ing to whom the empusa was a hellish creature with one foot made of bronze and the other of donkey excrement.[12]

While I was thereupon reading *The Life of Apollonius of Tyana* by Flavius Philostratus (a book once thought likely to endanger the reputation of Jesus Christ as established by the Gospels), I was very surprised to run across a story about the adventures of an empusa and a young philosopher. This tale drew a particularly close comparison between the customs of these specters and the habits of the insects later known by the same name. It concerns a young man seduced by an amazingly beautiful woman. He is about to be married when Apollonius unmasks her by breaking her spell. Here are the two key passages: "This charming bride was one of those vampires [empuses] popularly called lamias or she-demons. They are very fond of love, and even fonder of human flesh. They use seduction to lure those whom they plan to devour." Then, a few lines later: "The ghost finally admitted that it was a vampire, and that he had been gorging Menippus with pleasures so as to devour him later; that it was his wont to feed upon handsome young men, because their blood is very fresh" (*The Life of Apollonius of Tyana*, 4:25).

One of Philostratus's translators, A. Chassang, points out that this story had some repercussions; in particular, it was adapted by Alexandre Dumas senior, in chapters 22 to 24 of his *Isaac Laquedam*.[13] It could be correlated, of course, with the medieval concepts of *incubi* and *succubi*. These are interesting in themselves. However, they derive from a completely different tradition and, most important, have but a formal, actually quite loose connection with the adventure of the empusa and the philosopher—as Chassang's quotations only help to confirm (447–450)—which itself seems much more linked to vampirism.[14] So we must instead compare this story to a double set of phenomena that is just as gripping: the habits of the mantises and human anguish about love (when viewed in light of the first, the second seems less senseless than one might like to think).

In my opinion, this feeling corresponds to a certain stage of emotional

---

12. For more detailed information, see the article entitled "Empusa" in Roscher's *Lexicon;* also Pauly-Wissowa's *Realencyclop* and J. C. Lawson's book *Modern Greek Folklore and Ancient Greek Folklore* (Cambridge, 1910), 174–175.

13. A. Chassang, introduction to Philostrate, *Apollonius de Tyane, savie, ses voyages, ses prodiges,* ed. and trans. Alexis Chassang (Paris: Didier et Cie, 1862), 14 n.2.

14. The story is also taken up by Flaubert in *La Tentation de Saint-Antoine,* ch.4. In the Renaissance it was taken up by Jean Bodin in his *De la Démonomanie des sorciers* (Paris, 1580), book 2, ch. 5, and by other demonographers of the period.

development. It is especially suited, I think, to becoming an all-exclusive passional theme. Thus Bychowski (*Ein Fall von oralem Verfolgnungswahn*) analyzes a case of persecution mania, in which a man is convinced that he will be devoured by a prostitute before he has even approached her. As for Baudelaire's well-known drawing of a woman, with the crucial caption, *Quaerens quem devoret* [Asking whom she is devouring] (see *Les Fleurs du Mal*, Payot, 1928 edition), its meaning is sufficiently clear to forgo further comment. More generally speaking, I would readily correlate these fantasies with the development of most castration complexes, which commonly originate in the fear of the toothed vagina, as everybody knows, given that in psychoanalysis it is classic, as it were, thus to identify the whole body with the male member and the mouth with the vagina.[15] So it would not be inconceivable that castration anxiety might be a specification of the male's fear of being devoured by the female during or after mating. This is perfectly represented in objective terms by the mantid nuptial habits—so great is the symmetry or, more accurately, the continuity between nature and the mind.[16] This example suffices in and of itself to account for both the possibility as well as the efficacy of objective ideograms. It also tends to corroborate a previously formulated hypothesis of mine concerning the systematic overdetermination of the universe.

As a matter of fact, people even today are unambiguously drawn to the praying mantis. I shall mention my own experiences further on, but there are many examples from my immediate circle illustrating this lyrical complicity. Thus, for example, André Breton bred praying mantises in Castellane for two straight years.[17] And when I asked Paul Eluard about the magnificent mantis collection in his home, he confessed that he viewed their habits as the ideal mode of sexual relationship. The act of love, he said, diminishes the male and aggrandizes the female; so it is natural that she should use her ephemeral superiority to devour, or at least to kill, the male. Dali's case is even better to use, given his paranoid-critical study of Millet's *Angelus*, which is a very complete

15. Mallarmé's sonnet "Une Négresse par le démon secouée" provides a striking example of this.

16. Moreover, these insects have another feature that could very well serve as a direct representation of castration: the ability to sever one of their limbs voluntarily (autonomy). See Edmond Bordage's reports in *Comptes rendus de l'Académie des Sciences* (1899), vol. 128 and *Bulletin Scientifique de France et de Belgique* (1905), vol. 39.

17. The same André Breton who wrote in *Ralentir travaux* (Editions surréalistes, 1930): "Celles qui dans l'amour entendent le vent passer dans les peupliers / Celles qui dans la haine sont plus élancées que les mantes religieuses" [Those women who, in love, hear the wind pass through the poplar trees / Those women who, in hate, are more outstretched than mantises—*Ed.*].

and impressive document on the relationship between love and cannibalism. He could hardly avoid citing the fearsome insect that actually unites these two savage desires.

Naturalists find in the praying mantis the most extreme form of the close bond that often seems to exist between the sensual pleasures of sexuality and those of nutrition. Dali outlined this connection in an utterly direct and intuitive way. On this topic, though, should at least be noted, following Léon Binet, the studies by Bristowe and Locket on the *Pisaura mirabilis cl.*: during coitus the female eats a fly offered by the male.[18] Hancock and Von Engelhardt have written on the *Oceanus Nivens*: the contents of a gland on its metathorax are absorbed by the female immediately before mating (this feature is shared by a kind of cockroach, the *Phyllodramia germanica*).[19] There are also Stitz's studies of the scorpion fly: during coitus, the female eats globules of saliva prepared for her by the male.[20] In similar circumstances, the female of the *cardiacephala myrmex* consumes food regurgitated by the male, who often transfers it from his mouth to hers. And the female of the white-headed dectique opens her companion's belly and extracts and devours the spermatic pouch.[21]

It has long been known that the mantis does not make do with such half measures. Indeed, in a *Journal de physique* of 1784, J. L. M. Poiret conveyed his observation of a female mantis that decapitated her male before mating and then completely devoured him after copulation. This story was recently corroborated in a fine account by Raphaël Dubois, with many details that aggravated the case. Paul Portier and others (see *Comptes rendus de la Société de Biolo-*

18. W. S. Bristowe and G. H. Lockett, "The Courtship of British Lycosid Spiders and Its Probable Significance," *Proceedings of the Zoological Society* (London, 1926). In my opinion, moreover, this example is only partially conclusive. We may no doubt observe that this insect feeds during the very act of coitus. But the more significant fact—that the female draws this nourishment from the body of the male, either by devouring him or by ingesting the contents of a special gland—cannot be detected here.

19. See B. B. Fulton, *The Tree-Crickets of New York: Life, History, and Bionomics* (1915).

20. See O. W. Richards, "Sexual selection and Other Problems of the Insects," *Biol. Review* 2 (1927).

21. If not manifest in human behavior, this relationship between sexuality and nutrition is nonetheless inherent, at the very least, in the human psyche; certain perversions attest to this. We might also cite the embryogenic development of the self-preservation and reproductive functions, and that of their organs—if the interpretation of such evidence were not still in doubt. It seems to me, furthermore, that attempting the psychoanalytical treatment of mental anorexia (when the subject refuses to eat, on various ethical or emotional grounds), and perhaps this has been done, might produce significant results in this regard. Finally, it is an oft-cited phenomenon that after coitus, women express and sometimes indulge a great desire to bite their lovers.

gie, vol. 32, 1919, with critical observations by Rabaud) had orginally thought that such cannibalism could be explained by the fact that the mantis needs albumin and protein to produce her eggs—and that she can find this in greatest quantity among her own species. This hypothesis was challenged by Rabaud, who noted, in particular, that the mantis does not eat the male just when she most needs this food. Thus, Raphaël Dubois's theory (which does not exclude the preceding ones, in my view), is more generally favored.[22] This naturalist observes that after having been decapitated, a cricket performs induced reflex and spasmodic movements both better and for a longer time than before.[23] Referring to the work to Goltz and H. Busquet (if one removes a frog's superior centers, it immediately assumes the coital position normally adopted only in the spring), he wonders whether the mantis's goal in beheading the male before mating might not be to obtain a better and longer performance of the spasmodic coital movements, through the removal of the brain's inhibitory centers. In the final analysis, it would hence be the pleasure principle that compels the female insect to murder her lover—whose body she begins to ingest, furthermore, in the course of lovemaking itself.[24]

These habits are so well-designed to disturb human beings that scientists for once, to their credit, have abandoned their professional dryness. For example, in his recent monograph, *La Vie de la mante religieuse*, Léon Binet, professor of physiology at the Faculté de Médecine in Paris, seems visibly affected by them.[25] In any event, it is quite surprising to see him briefly foreswear his scientific detachment to call the female a kind of "murderous mistress" (54), while venturing a most alarming literary quotation in this regard.[26] I myself shall take this revealing lapse as the basis for interpreting Binet's conclusion: "This insect really seems to be a machine with highly advanced parts, which can operate automatically." Indeed, it strikes me that likening the mantis to an automaton (to a female android, given the latter's anthropomorphism) reflects the same emotional theme, if (as I have every reason to believe) the notion of an artificial, mechanical, inanimate, and unconscious machine-

22. R. Dubois, "Sur les réflexes associés chez la mante religieuse," *C. R. de la Société de Biologie* (1929).

23. See the experiment of Daniel Auger and Alfred Fessard.

24. One can observe a photographic document representing this coital meal in J. H. Fabre's *Souvenirs entomologiques*.

25. Vigot Frères, 1931.

26. The quotation is as follows: "Elle épuise, elle tue, et n'en est que plus belle" [She exhausts, she kills, and this only makes her more beautiful—*Ed.*]. Alfred de Musset, *La Coupe et les lèvres*, 4:1.

woman—incommensurate with man and all other living creatures—does stem in some way from a specific view of the relations between love and death and, in particular, from an ambivalent premonition of encountering one within the other.[27]

For all that, I would not deny the existence of facts amply vindicating in and of themselves the conclusion called into question above. On the contrary, this kind of overlap would significantly heighten the praying mantis's objective lyrical value. Indeed, here again, reality exceeds our wildest expectations.

Above and beyond its jointed rigidity, which recalls a coat of armor or an automaton, it is a fact that there are very few reactions the mantis cannot perform in a decapitated state—that is, without any center of representation or of voluntary activity. In this condition, it can walk; regain its balance; sever a threatened limb; assume the spectral stance; engage in mating; lay eggs; build an ootheca; and (this is truly frightening) lapse into feigned *rigor mortis* in the face of danger or when the peripheral nervous system is stimulated.[28] I am deliberately expressing myself in a roundabout way as it is so difficult, I think, both for language to express and for the mind to grasp that the mantis, when dead, should be capable of simulating death.

Finally, let us not forget the mimicry of mantises, which illustrates, sometimes hauntingly, the human desire to recover its original insensate condition, a desire comparable to the pantheistic idea of becoming one with nature, which is itself the common literary and philosophical translation of returning to prenatal unconsciousness. There are numerous examples: the desert-colored *Luxor eremiaphileus*; the *Blepharis mendica*, speckled white on green like the leaves of the *Thymelia microphylla* upon which it lives; the *Theopompa heterochroa* of the Cameroons, which cannot be distinguished from the bark of a tree; the *Empusa egena* of Algeria, which, not content merely to look like a green anemone, gently stirs, imitating the wind's effect upon a flower; the *Idolum diabolicum* of Mozambique, whose petal-shaped, grasping tibia are aptly tinged with crimson, white, and bluish-green; the pale purple and rose-trimmed *Gongylus trachelophyllus* of India, which achieves "the picture of a dazzling flower that sways from time to time, turning its most beautiful colors to-

27. Those animal species in which the male dies immediately after fertilizing the female are too numerous to mention.

28. Moreover, every instance of such behavior tends to be viewed as purely automatic. E. L. Bouvier remarks, "This is a phenomenon of differential sensibility, limited to cataleptic tetanus, which is its main characteristic feature." *La Vie psychique des insectes* (Flammarion, 1918).

ward the brightest region of the sky"; and finally, the *Hymenopus bicornis*, which is hard to distinguish from a simple, marvellous orchid.[29]

Such floral transformations, whereby the insect loses its identity and returns to the plant kingdom, complement its astonishing capacity for automatism as well as its seemingly insouciant attitude toward death. These properties themselves complement other attributes that can jeopardize an individual's immediate sensitivity: such as the insect's name of mantis or empusa, that is, prophetess or vampire-specter; its shape, which, among all the rest, man can recognize as his own; its pose, either absorbed in prayer or engaged in the sexual act; and finally, its nuptial habits.[30]

We can now give an informed account of the lyrical objectivity of certain concrete representations and understand why they have the privilege of disturbing the affectivity of so many different types of people and, at the very least, of arousing in them a shared irrational curiosity.

Of course, it is hardly surprising that mankind's broadly uniform organic structure and biological development, and the common external conditions of his physical existence, should have a major impact on human psychology: one tending to produce in all people a minimum set of similar reactions and to engender, then, the same affective urges and primal emotional conflicts. In any event, this is akin to the way that, to a somewhat similar degree, uniform sensory mechanisms bring about uniform a priori forms of perception and representation. Besides, nothing in these remarks calls for the slightest explanatory hypothesis. On the contrary, the existence of elements that either partially or fully overlap with others does not seem preordained. That is, at first glance, it is quite possible to imagine the existence of a universe without objective ideograms. Yet, upon further reflection, one soon realizes that this raises the same insuperable obstacles as the idea of a world that is discontinuous and not overdetermined, albeit probably determined. Once again, it is utterly unthinkable that causal series could be totally distinct. This also contradicts experience, which constantly demonstrates their numerous intersections and sometimes supplies overwhelming, crushing expressions of their unfathomable solidarity. Although their meaning is hidden and ambiguous, such expressions never fail to reach their destination. In short, these are *objective ideograms, which concretely realize the lyrical and passional virtualities of the mind in the outside world.*

29. These examples are drawn from A. Lefèbvre, *Ann. de la Soc. entomologique de France,* vol.4; Léon Binet, *La Vie de la mante religieuse;* and Paul Vignon, *Introduction à la biologie expérimentale* (Paris, 1930).

30. Indeed, the mantis's usual posture is not one of prayer, as censors make us say (people do not pray in a prone position) but rather that of a man in the act of love. See Theocritus, *Idylls,* X, 18. The similarity could not be clearer.

Conclusion

Because this study was undertaken with the specific goal of demonstrating the existence of a certain lyrical objectivity, it did not have to be complete; it was enough to classify a few phenomena rather than exhausting the subject. And so, at times, I have made do with quotations from major reference works instead of directly quoting from actual sources (for example, with regard to the mythology of so-called primitive peoples). This has one important result: my argument is often supported by a choice of data that I did not make myself and that was, moreover, determined by concerns quite different from my own. So that in the last analysis, comparing the argument with the data may well add probative value rather than diminish richness and scope. Briefly put, it serves as a guarantee of accuracy that my demonstration could be carried out under conditions that were not designed for it.

Having said this, let us now analyze the theoretical conclusions it seems possible to draw with respect to the specific disciplines mentioned in this study.

First, as regards *mythography*, it appears that such research tends to establish that determinations caused by the social structure, however important, are not alone in influencing the content of myths. We must also take into account half-physiological, half-psychological factors such as man's inclination to be interested in, or even to identify with, anything whose external configuration suggests his own body—for example, the praying mantis or the bat. We should pay even more attention to certain basic emotional reactions and clusters that sometimes exist only as potentialities in human beings, but that correspond to phenomena explicitly and commonly observed throughout the rest of nature.

This brings us to the second discipline relevant to the present study: psychology, and more specifically *psychoanalysis*, which has brought to light the existence of such primal emotional constellations as the major complexes (the Oedipus complex, castration anxiety, etc.). It might perhaps be preferable to seek their origins in comparative biology rather than in the human mind alone. It seems that from this angle, we may achieve a closer approximation of the larger context within which these complexes should be viewed. Thus, the fear of being devoured by a woman (to use the phenomenon cited in this monograph) would no longer be deemed a transformation of castration anxiety. Quite the contrary. Castration anxiety would be a specification of the fear of being devoured. And because this fear may be considered the vestigial residue, in one species, of behavioral patterns observed in many others, it then has all the greater right to present itself as the original phenomenon. In other words, I think that these questions should ultimately be resolved by biology.

Introduction to "Letter to André Breton" and "Literature in Crisis"

These essays were, respectively, the introduction and conclusion of a mono-graph, *Procès intellectuel de l'art* (*Art on Trial by Intellect*), which Caillois pub-lished at his own expense in 1935, thereby stating his official break with Surre-alism. In 1946, the literary critic Gaëtan Picon remarked that Caillois's rejection of Surrealism was "inevitable": "One could expect that Surrealism would provide a new and decisive clarity that would infinitely push back the boundaries of darkness. Such is what Caillois was awaiting from it. But in Bre-ton, the love of the Marvellous obviously triumphed over this wish to unveil, and encouraged him to protect mystery much more than to unmask it."[1] In-deed, at first glance, the "Letter to André Breton" seems to articulate their di-vide in terms of poetry versus science, dramatized by the symbolic event of the Mexican jumping bean (see introduction). However, in the light of *Natur-philosophie*, dissecting the jumping bean need not necessarily have destroyed its mystery. "Here we have a form of the Marvellous that does not fear knowl-edge, but, on the contrary, thrives on it," writes Caillois. Given his interest in the fantastic attributes of the praying mantis, the act of revealing "an insect or a worm" in the bean could only, I suspect, have given rise to a new kind of wonder. After all, what makes these creatures jump around as they do, in per-manent darkness, quite literally in the "noctural side of nature"?[2]

Caillois also relates his implicit design to reform science to Gaston Bache-lard's "new science of the 'why not?'" set forth in *Le Nouvel Esprit scientifique* (1934). Aiming to revolutionize neo-Kantian philosophy of science, this in-fluential work stressed the imaginative aspect of contemporary inquiry, es-pecially of modern physics. *Le Nouvel Esprit scientifique* noted that contempo-rary science, severed from empirical perception and intuition, drove science to seek truth "despite what seems evident." Bachelard succinctly rephrased this changeover: "We will show that in scientific philosophy, the old philosophy of the *as if* has been superseded by the philosophy of the *why not*." Of course, this constructivist "why not" did not mean "anything goes"! Bachelard asserted that science "no longer . . . gives rise to a world by means of a magical impulse

"Lettre à André Breton" and "Crise de la littérature," in *Approches de l'imaginaire* (Paris: Galli-mard, 1974), 35–38, 52–54.

that is immanent to reality; it does so by means of a rational impulse that is immanent to the mind. After having formed a mode of reason in the world's image—during the initial efforts of the scientific spirit—the mental activity of modern science strives to construct a world in the image of reason."[3] We will next see that "Mimicry and Legendary Psychasthenia" radically questions the representational project of modern science, which is far more deranging to the scientist that Bachelard assumes.[4] ("For a Militant Orthodoxy" then praises modern physics as the most important fulfillment of such *dérèglement*.)

Art on Trial by Intellect was partially drafted during Caillois's Surrealist phase. It included "Décision préliminaire sur la métaphysique" (Preliminary decision about metaphysics), which "brackets" all metaphysical inquiry to define the observer "as the origin of the coordinate-system, and the only origin that counts for him, since it is the only one that registers and accounts for his *compromised status* in the world."[5] From this epistemological shift, Caillois then attacks "pure" science and art as modes of cognitive *resemblance* simply mirroring the abstract, formal structures of the self, its environment, and the universe.[6] In contrast to this, Caillois posits an "impure" mode of cognitive resemblance, where the self is center of its conceptual coordinate system. He finds this in "impure" art that expresses dreams, mental illness, myth, and "lyrical phenomena"; *lyrical* here means the actual or virtual contents of *consciousness*. "Notice sur l'impureté dans l'art" (Notice on impurity in art) argues that "one's personality is engaged by these *fantasies* in a much more deeply affecting way than it could be by the knowing smiles of harmony."[7]

A few years earlier, Ortega y Gasset had loudly endorsed, but for different reasons, what Caillois here describes as the crisis of literature.[8] Referring to the "dehumanization" of art, its loss of "human pathos," *The Dehumanization of Art* pointed to the thinning artistic ranks: "All peculiarities of modern art can be summed up in this one feature of its renouncing its importance—a feature which, in its turn, signifies nothing less than that art has changed its position in the hierarchy of human activities and interests. . . . Art which—like science and politics—used to be very near the axis of enthusiasm, that backbone of our person, has moved toward the outer rings. . . . It has become a minor issue. The trend toward pure art betrays not arrogance, as is often thought, but modesty. Art that has rid itself of human pathos is a thing without consequence—just art with no other pretenses."[9]

Ortega y Gasset urged dehumanized art to rest content with its authentic, if diminished, status, but Caillois dismissed it altogether. "Literature in Crisis" declares that the "simple formal structure" of "pure" art had been solved, or theoretically "absorbed," by "pure science." So Caillois calls instead for the scientific study of "impure" art, to establish a *general phenomenology of the imag-*

ination."[10] "Mimicry and Legendary Psychasthenia" suggests that what he really intends to create is an "impure" science.

LETTER TO ANDRÉ BRETON

27 December 1934

Dear Breton,

I had hoped that our two positions were not as deeply divided as they turned out to be during our conversation yesterday evening. In view of my particular stance, I had indeed felt that your activities contained both good and bad. Although I could not wholeheartedly endorse one of the two fields involved, I nonetheless found compensations in the other that allowed for such a sacrifice. Recently, the types of gratification I encountered while reading *Point du jour* made me definitively resign myself to seeing you with a foot in both camps: research and poetry (I am putting it crudely, of course, with no concern for nuance or overlap). After all, it was quite understandable—and considering your intellectual approach from the outset, I am tempted to write: it was all too understandable (meaning that Surrealism stems from a literary milieu)—that you should be inclined to strike an equal balance between the *satisfactions* offered by the first and the *jouissances* [pleasures] offered by the second, to use the two words arising almost simultaneously to our lips last night.

Given our conversation, however, it is clear to me that in your case there never was and probably never will be any equilibrium between the two spheres. For that matter, everything you have ever written or said proves this beyond the shadow of a doubt. You have presented several clear and consistent accounts of this attitude. It was hardly possible to misinterpret your position, as I had—without mistaking the expression of one's own desires for reality, which is a well-known human foible. So you are definitely on the side of intuition, poetry, and art—and of their privileges. Must I tell you that I prefer this kind of commitment to ambiguity? Yet as you know, I've taken the opposite stance—almost alone among those of my kind to do so. Indeed, strange though it may seem, people who do not indulge these weaknesses, and hence know them only from the outside, always view them with great superstitious respect; it is simply due to their naïveté. There is no need for me to expound my position, with which you are already familiar. It was fully set forth in the article *Spécification de la poésie*, which initiated my collaboration with Surrealism. Since then I've reasserted it on every occasion, up through the text of *Intervention surréaliste*, which, if I properly recall, you said revealed an antilyrical position ("antilyrical" has to be discussed) that was possibly of interest in some other context but certainly not here. Although I did not agree with you at the time, I must now admit that you were right.

I remain convinced that the point of contention is chiefly methodological, but for me this is a crucial question. After all, what do I care about illuminations that are scattered, unstable, and unconfirmed, that are meaningless without some prior act of faith—that are pleasurable, in fact, only because of the credence we attach to them? The irrational: granted. But first and foremost, it must be coherent (I am thinking of that coherence in favor of which logic had to yield all down the line in the exact sciences). I want the irrational to be continuously overdetermined, like the structure of coral; it must combine into one single system everything that until now has been systematically excluded by a mode of reason that is still incomplete.

It is also a question of age. How else can we explain the fact that your apperception of the day, of its demands, and of what is currently most compelling differs radically from my own? For instance, modern atomic theory is at present an adventure into the dark: somewhat like children raised in boxes, who are amazed to discover ferns (in the words of a physicist). This does not involve the *distress* or *jouissance* brought about by a *beautiful picture* but instead involves a sense of utter confusion; utter confusion in the face of what I choose to call the *debacle of the evident*. For there is nothing left of the old intuitions, and any philosophy that cannot fit together with this new science of the *why not* [*pourquoi pas*] is absurd. Of course, the results themselves are less in question than what they brought about: namely, their carnage of allegedly unsophisticated concepts. Here we have a form of the Marvellous that does not fear knowledge but, on the contrary, thrives on it. Just look how solidly it is upheld, and what an obstacle it confronts! When I compare this *great game* [*grand jeu*] with Gérard de Nerval's attitude, who refused to enter Palmyra so as not to spoil his preconceptions, or with your own, refusing to slice open a jumping bean that sometimes jolts about because you did not want to find an insect or a worm inside (that would have destroyed the mystery, you said), my mind is made up. Actually, it always was. As a child, I could never really have fun with toys; I was constantly ripping them open or dismantling them to find out "what they were like inside, how they worked."

If Surrealism can encompass this kind of attitude alongside others so radically opposed to it, then Surrealism is merely a word; and all the same, even at my own expense, I would like it to be more than that. And so I shall refrain from taking part in discussions where (unless I forced myself to be obliging) my outlook would be demoralizing at best and irritating at worst—in any case, undesirable. Likewise, for me, it is just as intolerable (to say the least) to be compromised by the activities of Victor Brauner or Georges Hugnet, for example; or by the biographical poetry that is becoming prominent in Surrealist writing (poems by Maurice Heine about Sade, by Hugnet about Onan, by you, by Eluard, and by various others about Violette Nozières; even Rosey's poem—epic poem—about you). Until now, my sense of solidarity has been strong enough grudgingly to defend all of this against outside attacks, however well-founded. That is why I had unhesitatingly accepted the clannish ethos of Surrealism. But I can no longer do so, as I disagree all too openly about the very basis of our accord.

Of course, you and I still share, for example, a great number of common exigencies. Even so, because we have totally different views as to the methods most likely to fulfill them, collaboration is out of the question; we can merely offer each other support. By which I mean that I, for my part, shall never rush to condemn your efforts. On the contrary, I shall be at your side if need be whenever my outlook is compatible with that of Surrealism: in matters of polemics, politics, or even the technical study of the imagination, if it is true that my ideas and ventures in this domain strike you as viable, as you asserted yesterday, perhaps even useful, after all.

You will say that I am basically consecrating what is a de facto state of affairs. I do not deny this, but you must admit that such consecration is probably a good idea. Don't you find that the Surrealist accord rests upon too many misunderstandings and mutual concessions, if not repressions? Nobody believes in intransigence or rigor any more. I for one have ceded as much ground as possible and would now like to redefine clearer lines. The position adopted by Maurice Heine, for example, strikes me as the possible model for a new alliance. Please let me remain nothing but some sort of corresponding member of Surrealism, as he does. That would be best for Surrealism and for me. Don't you agree?

Yours faithfully,
R. C.

LITERATURE IN CRISIS

Literature is undeniably undergoing a crisis among the youth of today. The best minds are leaving this type of activity for political or philosophical concerns. Granting that the best minds are also the most demanding, the reasons for such a choice are easy to understand.

First, in an era always on the brink of upheavals because of political, economic, and social problems, it is hardly suprising that some should view literature as an excessively innocent kind of distraction—untimely, in any event. They probably fail to recognize its lofty aims. Perhaps. Yet other people, who do acknowledge these ambitions, find that literature is far from having the means to realize them, and so they prefer to turn directly to stricter and more reliable disciplines.

Of course, there have always been young political theorists and philosophers. What is new and critical, however, is that the very people who seemed in every way most likely to become real artists or to pursue literary endeavors are the ones presently succumbing to such preoccupations. As a result, what gets produced is no longer worthy of consideration. Most books written by young people of the postwar period simply reveal their author's naïveté, as well as a clear lack of necessity.

This last word is important: for indeed, it would appear that art lapsed into its current sorry state due to some *inner necessity*. Little by little, it established itself as a privileged method for furthering knowledge and deemed that it could therefore embark upon increasingly risky, if not metaphysical, adventures without any precautions or safeguards. Among other things, this led art to question its own faith in itself and give a negative answer. Here, roughly outlined, is the conceptual evolution from Mallarmé to Dada, with Rimbaud containing it in a nutshell.

Poetry was hence afflicted in turn. To be saved, it had to be viewed either as an *exercise* only slightly superior to translating texts from the Greek or doing algebra (this was M. Paul Valéry's attitude, during his heroic period, although since then . . .) or as a *technique* for exploring the unconscious (this was Surrealism's attitude, when it was in the habit of confusing poems and automatic texts). The prestige still attached to the word "poetry" does not sufficiently protect it against those who have begun to condemn its heavy quota of nostalgic verboseness about passions that deserve better. Such people instead prefer to *isolate the poetic phenomenon*. Only in our moments of weakness are we still capable of applauding beauty. Times of tension demand a more nourishing substance, which would probably be science if we were not unshakeably drawn to the empirical imagination, with its fascinating questions lodged at the very threshold of consciousness, and which science studies poorly or not at all. However, we will not refrain from applying scientific method to the artistic domain, for scientific rigor here seems, in our opinion, more essential than elsewhere.

Until recently, the formal modeling of sounds, shapes, or colors (when analyzed in terms of its two subcategories, rhythm and harmony) was considered art's most unfathomable aspect. Art now turns out to involve a simple formal structure that has been more or less reduced to its constituent elements and is of little real interest. Above all, it requires no further explanation, as it has nothing more to offer than do natural phenomena themselves. Thus, one single mathematical ratio governs the morphology of most marine organisms and the perspectives of a monument or painting. One single law at the same time determines the modalities of chemical reactions, crystal formation, and the rhythm of a poem or a musical work. Dissymmetry is a phenomenon's precondition; symmetry, the precondition of its cessation. One could say that pure science has easily absorbed pure art.

But there is no science of impurity in art, no science of art's imaginative content, of the "subject" that people have worked so hard in varying instances to suppress. Even so, following Rimbaud, we must forsake any reverential attitude toward the disorder of the latter's mind. *The imagination does not make confessions on the grounds that it is wracked by guilt as readily as some guilty individual might do.* In any case, it does not confess to those who worship it but rather to those who oppress it. Therefore, it must be put to interrogation. The means are easily defined:

— Creation of experiments in which imaginative phenomena can be triggered under the best possible control conditions.
— Elaboration and criticism of techniques designed to reveal unconscious determinations.
— Objective and systematic study of every kind of conventionalism.
— Relative interpretation of phenomena occurring in the inner and outer spheres, so as to cast new light on the relationship between subjectivity and objectivity, by showing the basic homogeneity of the *Umwelt* [environment] and *Innenwelt* [inner world].
— Accounts (with or without commentaries) of states of depression, confusion, and anxiety, and of private emotional experiences.
— Update on the question of knowledge. Not so much in terms of modern theoretical revelations about matter's innermost structure. (Clearly, there is no common ground here; for example, it is nonsense to try to base psychological freedom on the intra-atomic indeterminacy relation). But rather in terms of those epistemological constructions required by the problems of contemporary scientific methodology.

Enough said. Let us consider that, as of now, this program is underway. Which means that the crisis of literature is entering its critical phase. Let's hope that it remains beyond repair.

Introduction to "Mimicry and Legendary Psychasthenia"

Art on Trial by Intellect had put "pure" art and science in the camp of "the in-stinct of self-preservation."[1] In short, here was Caillois's version of what Mey-erson and Bachelard, among others, attacked as the reduction to identity of traditional science.[2] He did not outline the instinct that, conversely, drove "im-pure" modes of cognitive resemblance, those that vitally "compromised" the self. "Mimicry and Legendary Psychasthenia" does so by positing an *instinct d'abandon* (instinct of letting go). And it does so largely in relation to what I would call "impure science." Caillois's praying mantis may have embodied the menacing object of scientific Surrealism; after his break with Breton, his mimetic insect seems to stand for the imperiled subject of a New (surreal) Sci-ence. Caillois correlates modern scientific epistemology with primitive anthro-pology (magical thinking) and insect mimicry. All three illustrate resemblance gone awry, as it were. At the core of his curious argument is a radically anti-Darwinian interpretation of mimicry as an anti-utilitarian "luxury" rather than as a mode of self-preservation or self-defense. Indeed, it entails a loss of energy and, at times, even death itself—Caillois evokes the wonderfully "miserable Phyllidae" mimetic insects, which engage in misguided collective cannibal-ism by mistaking each other for edible leaves.[3] As noted above, Bataille's sem-inal essay, "The Notion of Expenditure," had by now caught his attention. Un-like Bataille's theory of social and artistic "expenditure," however, Caillois focuses primarily on anti-utilitarian biology and science; and unlike Bataille's "limitless need for loss" and "desire to destroy" situated in the individual and collective unconscious, Caillois draws on Freud's *Beyond the Pleasure Principle* to invent *the inertia of the élan vital*, an instinct d'abandon as a kind of counter-force to Bergsonian vitalism.[4] Whereas expenditure for Bataille is a strictly hu-man phenomenon, Caillois extends it throughout all of nature, in a theoretical gesture that suggests, albeit without citing, the tradition of German Romantic *Naturphilosophie*.

In its assault on the Cartesian subject, I suggest that "Mimicry and Leg-endary Psychasthenia" also pursues the dialogue with Bachelard's New Science initiated in *Art on Trial by Intellect*. Focusing on this scientific dimension can

"Mimétisme et psychasthénie légendaire," *Minotaure* 7 (1935): 5–10.

illuminate Rosalind Krauss's discussion of the "optical unconscious," which she defines as an avant-garde "projection of the way that human vision can be thought to be less a master of all it surveys." Her study locates an important instance in "the group that formed around Bataille and his magazine *Documents* to conceive of doubling that would not be the generator of form. For example, Roger Caillois on animal mimicry." Caillois never participated in *Documents* (which was before his time), but Krauss is right to insist that Bataille's *informe* involved a "categorical, heterological [blur]," while for "Caillois it was perceptual, or rather a function of the axis between perception and representation."[5] This disjunction is precisely the question he implicitly puts to the euphoric new rationalism of Bachelard, who claimed that despite the conceptual difficulties of modern science, "one day, one realizes that one has understood. What is the new light leading us to acknowledge the value of these sudden syntheses? An inexpressible clarity that puts security and happiness in our reason."[6] In 1937, Bachelard's *L'Expérience de l'espace dans la physique contemporaine* attacked the "Realist," who clung to a world defined through his geometrical sense of "localization" in space, or of a "designated area in space," his "ontological center of gravity": "Challenge him a bit. Make the point that we know very little about this real which he claims to grasp as a given."[7] Whereas Bachelard sought to replace the empirical intuitions of Realism with the clarity of New Science, Caillois argues that the "represented spaces" of modern science inevitably "[undermine] . . . one's sense of personality," and he correlates them with Minkowski's psychiatric definition of schizophrenia, of "dark space," where the subject feels permeable to his surroundings.[8]

   The most notable response to "Mimicry and Legendary Psychasthenia" came from Lacan. First presented the following year, "Le Stade du miroir" ("The mirror-stage"), at least in its extant version of 1949, evokes Caillois's *mimicry* with regard to "psychological concepts" of mimicry, or "the problem of the signification of space for a living organism." Here, Lacan describes "how Roger Caillois . . . illuminated the subject by using the terms *legendary psychasthenia* to classify morphological mimicry as an obsession with space in its derealizing effect."[9] Perhaps less well known is Lacan's review of *Le Temps vécu* by Minkowski for the *Recherches philosophiques* of 1935–1936: "In our opinion, the most original form of intuition of this book, although it is barely broached, at the end, [is] that of another space besides geometrical space, namely, the *dark space* of groping, hallucination and music, which is the opposite of clear space, the framework of objectivity. We think that we can safely say that this takes us into the 'night of the senses,' that is, the 'obscure night' of the mystic."[10]

   So too, "Mimicry and Legendary Psychasthenia" suggests a form of spatial or materialist mysticism, situated somewhere between Le Grand Jeu and Caillois's final meditation on stones.

MIMICRY AND LEGENDARY PSYCHASTHENIA

Beware: Whoever pretends to be a ghost will eventually turn into one.

Ultimately, from whatever angle one may approach things, the fundamental question proves to be that of *distinction*: distinctions between what is real and imaginary, between wakefulness and sleep, between ignorance and knowledge, and so on. These are all distinctions, in short, that any acceptable project must seek to chart very precisely and, at the same time, insist on resolving. Certainly, no distinction is more pronounced than the one demarcating an organism from its environment; at least, none involves a more acutely perceptible sense of separation. We should pay particular attention to this phenomenon, and more specifically to what we must still call, given our limited information, its pathology (although here the term has a purely statistical meaning): namely, the set of phenomena referred to as mimicry.

For a long time, and for various reasons (often not very good ones), biologists have liked to focus on these facts with all sorts of ulterior motives. Some biologists sought to prove transformationism, which luckily has other foundations; others sought to prove the knowing providence of the celebrated God whose benevolence encompasses all of nature.[1]

Under these circumstances, a stringent method is absolutely necessary. First and foremost, these phenomena must be classified with great rigor, for past experience has shown that they have been confused with each other for all sorts of wrong reasons. As far as possible, one should even adopt a classification deriving from the phenomena themselves rather than from their interpretations, which may well be biased and which, anyway, are almost always controversial in every case. Therefore, I shall mention Giard's two categories—but without retaining them.[2] The first comprises *offensive mimicry*, meant to surprise one's prey, and *defensive mimicry*, either to hide oneself from an aggressor (concealing mimicry) or else to terrify the aggressor by means of one's deceptive appearance (frightening mimicry). The second category comprises *direct mim-*

1. A. R. Wallace, *Darwinism* (1889); L. Murat, *Les Merveilles du monde animal* (1914).
2. Giard, "Sur le mimétisme et la ressemblance protectrice," *Arch. de Zool. exp. et gén.* (1972) and *Bull. Scient*. 20 (1888).

icry, when the mimicking animal has an immediate interest in disguising itself, and *indirect mimicry*, when animals from different species display "professional resemblances," as it were, due to some comon adaptation, or *convergence*.[3]

* * *

(This was originally followed by a summary study of the elementary or secondary forms of mimicry, too lengthy to be included in the present article.)

* * *

It has been surmised that a harmless animal took on the guise of a formidable one in order to protect itself. Consider, for example, the *Trochilium* butterfly and the *Vespa crabro* wasp: both have the same smoky wings, the same legs and brown antennae, the same abdomen and thorax with yellow and black stripes, the same sturdy and noisy way of flying in broad daylight. Sometimes, the mimetic creature carries this further: for example, the *Choerocampa elpenor* caterpillar. This insect has two eye-shaped marks ringed with black on its first and fifth sections; when it is disturbed, the front rings retract and the fourth ring swells up sharply. It is claimed that the effect thus produced is a snake's head capable of tricking lizards and small birds, which are frightened by this brusque apparition.[4] According to Weissmann, when the *Smerinthus occellata* (which, like all sphinx moths, hides its lower wings in the state of repose) is in danger, it suddenly reveals these wings, whose two big blue "eyes" on a red background surprise and terrify the aggressor.[5]

With its wings outstretched, the butterfly thereby becomes the head of a great bird of prey. Certainly the clearest example of this kind is the *Caligo* butterfly of the Brazilian forests, which Vignon described as follows: "There is a bright spot surrounded by a palpebral ring, then overlapping circular rings of irregularly colored little radial feathers, all of which perfectly imitates the plumage of an owl, while the butterfly's body corresponds to its beak."[6] The

---

3. See also F. Le Dantec, *Lamarckiens et Darwiniens*, 3d ed. (Paris, 1908), 120 and following.

4. Cuénot, *La Genèse des espèces animales* (Paris, 1911), 470–473.

5. Weissmann, *Vorträge über Descendenztheorie*, 1: 78–79. This terrifying transformation is automatic. It may be compared to cutaneous reflexes, which do not always produce a color change meant to hide the animal but sometimes end up giving it a terrifying appearance. A cat's fur bristles at the sight of a dog so that, because it is terrified, it becomes terrifying. Le Dantec, who makes this observation (*Lamarckiens . . .*, 139), uses it to explain the human phenomenon termed *gooseflesh*, which especially occurs at times of great fright. It has persisted, even though the atrophy of the pilose system has made it obsolete.

6. P. Vignon, *Sur le matérialisme scientifique ou mécanisme anti-téléologique* (*Revue de philosophie*, 1904), 562. See Giard, *Traité d'entomologie*, 3: 201; A. Janet, *Les Papillons* (Paris, 1902), 331–336.

resemblance is so striking that the native inhabitants of Brazil nail the butterfly to their barn-doors as a substitute for the animal it mimics.

It is all too clear that anthropomorphism plays a decisive role in the foregoing cases: the resemblance exists solely in the eye of the beholder. The objective phenomenon is the fascination itself. This is illustrated, in particular, by the *Smerinthus ocellata*, which does not look like anything dangerous at all. Only the eye-shaped markings come into play: the behavior of the native Brazilian inhabitants simply serves to confirm this opinion. The "eyes" of the *Caligo* should probably be correlated with the apotropaic *Oculus indiviosus*, the *evil eye* that not only harms but can also protect once it has been turned against the evil powers to which it naturally belongs, as an organ of fascination par excellence.[7]

Here the anthropomorphic objection does not hold, for the eye is the vehicle of fascination throughout the entire animal kingdom. With regard to the tendentious claim of resemblance, on the contrary, the objection is decisive; moreover, even from a human perspective, no resemblance in this group is fully conclusive.

*   *   *

There are many examples of one form adapting to another (*homomorphy*). *Calappae* resemble rolled pebbles; *chlamydes*, seeds; *moenas*, gravel; and *palea*, sea wrack. The *Phyllopteryx* fish, from the Sargasso Sea, is merely a kind of "tattered seaweed shaped in floating strips," like the *Antennarius* and the *Pterophryné*.[8] The octopus retracts its tentacles, curves its back, adapts its color, and thus looks like a rock. The lower green-and-white wings of the *Dawn-Pierid* simulate umbelliferae, and the dents, nodules, and stria ribs of the *symbiotic lichnea* make it appear identical to the poplar tree bark on which it lives.

The *Lithinus nigrocristinus* of Madagascar and the Flatoides are indistinguishable from lichens.[9] Mantidae mimicry goes very far; with their feet simulating petals or else curling up into corolla, they look like flowers and imitate the effect of the wind on these plants with a gentle mechanical swaying.[10] The *Cilix compressa* resembles bird excrement, and the *Cerodeylus laceratus* of Borneo, with its foliaceous, light olive-green outgrowths, seems a moss-covered

7. On the evil eye and animals that use fascination, see Seligman's famous work, *Der böse Blick und Verwandtes* (Berlin, 1910) especially 2: 469. On the apotropaic use of the eye, see P. Perdrizet, *Negotium perambulans in tenebris* (Publ. de la Fac. de Lettres de Strasbourg, fasc. 6, Strasbourg, 1992).

8. Murat, *Les Merveilles*, 37–38; Cuénot, *La Genèse*, 453.

9. Cuénot, fig. 114.

10. See also references in Roger Caillois, "La Mante religieuse," *Minotaure*, no.5 (1934): 26.

stick. Everyone is familiar with the very leaf-like Phyllidae, which tend toward the perfect homomorphy found in certain butterflies. Above all, the *Oxydia* (see Rabaud's *Éléments*, 112, fig. 54), which attaches itself perpendicularly to the end of a branch and folds back its upper wings in a roof-like shape, thus looking like an outermost leaf—this is enhanced by a thin, dark line stretching across its four wings so as to simulate the leaf's major vein.

Other species are even more perfected: their lower wings are equipped with a loose appendage that they use as a leaf stalk, thereby gaining "a kind of access to the plant kingdom."[11] Together the two wings on each side form the lanceolate oval characteristic of the leaf; once again, a marking replaces the median vein, although here the spot is longitudinal and extends from one wing to the other. Thus, "the organo-motive force . . . must have skillfully cut out and arranged each of the wings, since it thus creates a shape not independently defined but rather in conjunction with the other wing."[12] The chief examples of this phenomena are the *Coenophlebia archidona* of Central America[13] and the different kinds of *Kallima* of India and Malaysia—which should be studied in greater detail. Following the arrangement noted above, the underside of their wings copies the leaf of their favorite landing site, the *Nephelium longanum*. Furthermore, according to a naturalist employed in Java by the house of Kirby and Company, London, to trade in these butterflies, each of the different *Kallima* varieties (*Kallima inachis, Kallima parallecta*) frequents a particular kind of shrub that it most closely resembles.[14] The imitation displayed by these butterflies is worked out in the most minute details: their wings actually have gray-green marks simulating the mildew on lichens. They also have shimmering areas that make them look like shredded, perforated leaves; they even have the "sphaeriaceous kind of mold stains scattered on the leaves of these plants: everything, even the transparent scars made by phytophagic insects, which lay bare the translucent epidermis as they devour patches of the leaves' parenchyma. The imitations are produced by pearly markings that correspond to similar markings on the upper surface of the wings."[15]

*   *   *

These extreme cases have inspired numerous attempts at explanation, though it should be said that none is fully adequate.

11. Vignon, *Sur le matérialisme scientifique*.
12. Ibid.
13. Delage and Goldsmith, *Les Théories de l'évolution* (Paris, 1909), 74, fig. 1.
14. Murat, *Les Merveilles*, 30.
15. R. Perrier, *Cours de zoologie*, 5th ed. (Paris, 1912); quoted in Murat, *Les Merveilles*, 27–28.

Even the phenomenon's mechanism has not been elucidated. Of course, we can note with E. L. Bouvier that ornamental additions are what make the mimetic species diverge from the normal types: "lateral expansions of the body and appendages in the Phyllidae; sculpted upper wings in the Flatoides; protuberant growths on many geometer moth caterpillars, etc."[16]But this is a singular misuse of the word "ornament"; above all, it describes rather more than it explains. As for the idea of *preadaptation* (the theory that insects seek out environments harmonizing with the early stages of their dominant coloring, or else that they adapt to the objects they most resemble), this is inadequate when confronted with such fine-grained phenomena. Arguments resorting to chance, even in Cuénot's discerning way, are even more inadequate. Cuénot first considers the case of certain Phyllidae of Java and Ceylon (*Ph. siccifolium* and *Ph. pulchrifolium*). Their favorite habitat is the guava tree, whose leaves they resemble owing to subterminal strangulation of their abdomens. And yet, the guava tree is not a native plant but was imported from America.

So, if this example involves similarity, it is by accident. Unconcerned by the exceptional—in fact, unique—nature of this occurrence, Cuénot suggests that the likeness of the Kallima butterfly is equally produced by chance; that it stems from the sheer accumulation of certain factors individually found in nonmimetic species, where they are insignificant (an appendage shaped like a leaf stalk, lanceolated upper wings, a median vein, transparent areas, and mirrors): "The similarity is thus achieved by compounding a certain number of small details. These are all quite unremarkable and occur singly in neighboring species; however, when combined, they produce an extraordinary imitation of a dry leaf. The success of this imitation depends upon the individual insects, which are all radically different. . . . This combination is just the same as any other; it is only astonishing because it looks like a particular object."[17] According to the same author, the *Urapteryx samqucaria* geometer moth caterpillar is likewise a *combination just the same as any other*, which unites a typical posture, a particular skin color, tegumentary roughness, and the instinct to live on certain plants. But this is precisely the point. It is difficult to believe that such combinations are *just the same as any other*, for these details could all be brought together without becoming assembled, without jointly working toward some specific resemblance. It is not the mere presence of such elements that is dis-

16. Bouvier, 146.

17. Cuénot, *La Genèse*, 464. In the most recent edition of his work (1932), Cuénot questions that this accumulation of small details could be directed by an "unknown factor" but still continues to view chance as the most likely hypothesis (252–253).

turbing and decisive; it is the fact of their *mutual arrangement*, their *reciprocal mapping*.

*   *   *

Under the circumstances, it is best to adopt a risky hypothesis that could be drawn from a remark by Le Dantec, which raises the possibility that certain workings of the cutaneous organs in the Kallima ancestors might have enabled them to simulate the blemishes on leaves.[18] The imitative mechanism would have disappeared after the acquisition of the morphological trait (in this case, as soon as the likeness had been achieved), in accordance, then, with the very law of Lamarck. Morphological mimicry could then be genuine photography, in the manner of chromatic mimicry, but photography of shape and relief, on the order of objects and not of images; a three-dimensional reproduction with volume and depth: sculpture-photography, or better yet *teleplasty*, if the word is shorn of all psychic content.

Certain more immediate reasons (and ones less vulnerable to the charge of sophistry) prevent us from viewing mimicry as a defensive reaction. First, this protection would solely serve against carnivores hunting by sight rather than by smell, as is often the case. Moreover, carnivores usually do not bother with motionless prey. Immobility would hence constitute a better defense in such cases, and, indeed, insects do not fail to make use of feigned *rigor mortis* (far from it).[19] There are other methods as well. To make itself invisible, a butterfly can simply use the tactics of the *Satyrid asiaticus* butterfly, whose lacquered wings at rest form a single line almost without thickness, that is imperceptible and perpendicular to the flower on which it lands; the line turns with its observer, who thus perceives only this minimal surface.[20] The experiments of Judd and Foucher have definitively settled the question.[21] Predators are not at all deceived either by homomorphy or homochromy: they eat acridians blended into the foliage of oak trees, or weevils resembling tiny pebbles, which are quite invisible to man's naked eye. The phasmid *Carausius morosus* (which uses its shape, color, and posture to simulate a plant twig) cannot be kept out in the open because sparrows immediately discover and devour it. Generally speaking, numerous remains of mimetic insects are found in the stomach of

18. Le Dantec, *Lamarckiens*, 143.
19. Cuénot, *La Genèse*, 461.
20. Murat, *Les Merveilles*, 46.
21. "Judd, The Efficiency of Some Protective Adaptations in Securing Insects from Birds," *The American Naturalist* 33 (1899); 461; Foucher, *Bull. soc. nat. acclim.* (Fr. 1916).

predators. So it should come as no surprise that these insects sometimes have other, more effective means of protection. Conversely, some inedible species (which therefore have nothing to fear) are mimetic. It seems we must therefore conclude with Cuénot that this is an "epiphenomenon," whose "usefulness as a form of defense appears to be nil."[22] Delage and Goldsmith had already noted an "excessively high number of protective features" in the Kallima.[23]

We are therefore dealing with a *luxury* and even with a dangerous luxury, as it does occur that mimicry makes the mimetic creature's condition deteriorate: geometer moth caterpillars so perfectly simulate shrub shoots that horticulturists prune them with shears.[24] The case of the Phyllidae is even more wretched. They graze on each other, literally mistaking other Phyllidae for real leaves.[25] Therefore, this could almost be viewed as some sort of collective masochism culminating in mutual homophagy—with the imitation of the leaf serving as an *incitement* to cannibalism in this particular kind of totemic feast.

Such an interpretation is less gratuitous than it might seem. Indeed, certain potentialities appear to subsist in man that strangely correspond to these phenomena. Even setting aside the issue of totemism, which it would be far too venturesome to address from this angle, there still remains the vast domain of mimetic magic according to which like produces like, and which is more or less the basis of all incantatory practice. It would be useless to rehearse every fact at this point; they have been sorted and classified in the classic works of Tylor, Hubert and Mauss, and Frazer. However, one important point should be mentioned: the correspondence successfully brought to light by these authors between the principles of magic and those governing the association of ideas. The law of magic, *Things that have once touched each other stay united*, corresponds to the principle of association by contiguity, just as the principle of association by similarity precisely corresponds to the *attractio similium* of magic: *Like produces like*.[26] Hence, identical principles govern, on the one hand, the subjective as-

<hr />

22. Cuénot, *La Genèse*, 463. On the efficacy of mimicry, see Davenport, "Elimination of Self-Colored Birds," *Nature* 78 (1898): 101; also Doflein, "*Uber Schutzanpassung durch Aehnlichkeit*," *Biol. Centr.* 28 (1908): 243; Pritchett, "Some Experiments in Feeding Lizards with Protectively Coloured Insects," *Biol. Bull.* 5 (1903): 271. See also the bibliography by Cuénot in *La Genèse*, 467.

23. Delage and Goldsmith, *Les Théories de l'évolution*, 74.

24. Murat, *Les Merveilles*, 36.

25. Murat; Bouvier, 142–143.

26. Naturally, the same correspondence exits between the association by opposites and the law of magic: *Opposites act on opposites*. In either domain, it is easy to reduce this case to one of similarity.

sociation of ideas and, on the other, the objective association of phenomena; that is, on the one hand, the chance or supposedly chance links between ideas and, on the other, the causal links between phenomena.[27]

The crucial point is that "primitive" man still has an urgent inclination to imitate, coupled with a belief in the effficacy of this imitation. Such an inclination remains quite strong in "civilized" man, for it persists as one of the two processes whereby his thought pursues its course when left to itself. To avoid overcomplicating the issue, I leave aside the general question of *resemblance*, which is far from being explained and plays a role that is sometimes crucial in emotional life and in aesthetics, where it is termed *correspondence*.

* * *

This tendency, whose universality thus becomes hard to deny, might have been the determining force behind the current morphology of mimetic insects, at a time when their body was more plastic than it is today (as we must anyhow assume, given the fact of transformationism). Mimicry could then accurately be defined as an *incantation frozen at its high point* and that has caught the sorcerer in his own trap. Let no one call it sheer madness to attribute magic to insects: this novel use of terms should not hide the utter simplicity of the matter itself. *Prestige-magic* and *fascination*: what else should we call the phenomena that were all grouped under the very category of mimicry? (As noted above, they were inaccurately classified because, in my opinion, the perceived similarities can here be too readily reduced to anthropomorphism; however, without these contestable cases and in their bare essentials such phenomena—or at least their early stages—are certainly analogous to real mimicry.) I have already offered a few examples of such phenomena (the *Smerinthus ocellata*, the *Caligo*, and the caterpillar *Choerocampa elpenor*), which are significantly illustrated, as well, by the mantis's sudden revelation of its ocelli when in the spectral stance, seeking to paralyze its prey.

In any event, resorting to the explanatory claim that magic always tends to seek out resemblance simply provides us with an initial approximation, as this too must be accounted for in turn. The search for similarity presents itself as a means, if not as an intermediary. It seems that the goal is indeed to *become assimilated into the environment*. And in this respect, instinct completes the work of morphology: the *Kallima* symmetrically aligns itself with a real leaf, its lower

27. See H. Hubert and M. Mauss, "Esquisse d'une théorie générale de la magie," *Année sociologique* (Paris, 1904), 7: 61–73.

wing appendage in the spot that a real leaf stalk would occupy. The *Oxydia* attaches itself perpendicularly to the tip of a branch, for the marks imitating the median vein require it to do so. The Brazilian *Cholia* butterflies settle in a row on little stalks so as to form bellflowers like those on lily of the valley sprigs, for example.[28]

*   *   *

It is thus a veritable *lure of space*.

Moreover, other phenomena work toward the same end, such as the so-called protective coatings. *Mayfly* larvae craft themselves a sheath case from twigs and gravel, and the *Chrysomelid* larvae use their own excrement in the same way. The *Oxyrhinchi* crabs or sea spiders randomly pick seaweed and polyps from their habitats and plant them on their shells. "The disguise seems to be a purely automatic gesture," for they garb themselves with whatever comes along, even with the most conspicuous items (see the experiments of Hermann Fol, 1886).[29] Moreover, this behavior requires vision, for it occurs neither at night nor after the ocular peduncles have been removed (experiments of Aurivillius, 1889)—which once again suggests that what we have here is a disorder of spatial perception.

In short, once we have established that mimicry cannot be a defense mechanism, then a disorder of spatial perception is the only thing it can be. Besides, perceiving space is certainly a complex phenomenon, as it is impossible to dissociate spatial perception and representation. In this respect, space is a double dihedron continuously changing its size and location:[30] it is a *dihedron of action*, with a horizontal plane determined by the ground and a vertical plane determined by the person who is walking and thus pulling the dihedron along at the same time; and it is also a *dihedron of representation*, shaped by the same horizontal plane as before (which is represented, though, rather than perceived) and cut by a vertical plane just where the object appears in the distance. Matters become critical with represented space because the living creature, the organism, is no longer located at the origin of the coordinate system but is simply one point among many. Dispossessed of its privilege, it quite literally *no longer knows what to do with itself*. This clearly recalls crucial aspects of the

28. Murat, *Les Merveilles*, 37.

29. Bouvier, 147–151. The same conclusion holds true with regard to insects: "Insects that disguise themselves need the contact of foreign bodies, and it scarcely matters what kind of body produces the contact" (151).

30. See also L. Lavelle, *La Perception visuelle de la profondeur* (Strasbourg, 1921), 13.

scientific outlook;[31] indeed, it is noteworthy that modern science has been producing increasing numbers of precisely such represented spaces: Finsler's spaces, Riemann-Christoffel's hyperspace, abstract spaces, generalized spaces, open, closed, dense, sparse, and so on. Under these conditions, one's sense of personality (as an awareness of the distinction between organism and environment and of the connection between the mind and a specific point in space) is quickly, seriously undermined. This, then, takes us into the realm of psychasthenic psychology or, more specifically, of *legendary psychasthenia*, if we thus term the disorder in the relationship between personality and space outlined above.

In the present essay, I can offer only a rough survey of the question; besides, Pierre Janet's clinical and theoretical works are readily available to all. For now, I shall primarily present a brief description of some personal experiences, which fully concur, moreover, with the findings published in medical literature: for example, the fact that when asked where they are, schizophrenics invariably reply, *I know where I am, but I don't feel that I am where I am*.[32] For dispossessed minds such as these, space seems to constitute a will to devour. Space chases, entraps, and digests them in a huge process of phagocytosis. Then, it ultimately takes their place. The body and mind thereupon become dissociated; the subject crosses the boundary of his own skin and stands outside of his senses. He tries to see *himself, from* some point in space. He feels that he is turning into space himself—*dark space into which things cannot be put*. He is similar; not similar to anything in particular, but simply *similar*. And he dreams up spaces that "spasmodically possess" him.

These expressions all bring to light one single process: *depersonalization through assimilation into space*.[33] In other words, what mimicry morphologically brings about in certain animal species. The magical (such as it can really be called without lexical misuse) ascendancy of night and of the dark, the *fear of darkness* also probably derive from the threat they pose to the organism/environment opposition. Minkowski's analyses are invaluable in this regard: darkness is not the mere absence of light; it has some positive quality. Whereas bright space disappears, giving way to the material concreteness of objects, darkness is "thick"; it directly touches a person, enfolds, penetrates, and even

31. One could almost claim that, for science, there is nothing but environment.

32. E. Minkowski, "Le Problème du temps en psychopathologie," *Recherches philosophiques* (1932–33): 239.

33. The expressions are drawn from introspective notes made during an attack of "legendary psychasthenia," deliberately exacerbated for ascetic and interpretative reasons.

passes through him. Thus the "self is *permeable* to the dark but not to light"; the feeling of mystery we experience at night probably stems from this. Minkowski, too, comes to speak of *dark space* and what is a near lack of distinction between environment and organism: "Since dark space enfolds me from all sides, and penetrates me much more deeply than does bright space, the role played by the inner/outer distinction and thus by the sensory organs as well (insofar as they enable external perception) is quite minimal."[34]

This assimilation into space is inevitably accompanied by a diminished sense of personality and vitality. In any event, it is noteworthy that among mimetic species, the phenomenon occurs only *in a single direction*: the animal mimics plant life (whether leaf, flower, or thorn) and hides or gives up those physiological functions linking it to its environment.[35] *Life withdraws to a lesser state.* Sometimes, the identification is more than superficial: Phasmidae eggs resemble seeds not only in shape and color but also in terms of their internal biological structure.[36] Moreover, cataleptic postures often help an insect's integration into the other kingdom. Weevils remain motionless; the bacillary Phasmidae let their long feet dangle—not to mention the vertical rigidity of the geometer moth caterpillars, which inevitably evokes hysterical contractions.[37] Conversely, doesn't the mechanical swaying of the mantises seem like a tic?

In the literary domain, Gustave Flaubert, among others, seems to have grasped the significance of this phenomenon, for *La Tentation de Saint-Antoine* closes with the scene of a generalized mimicry to which the hermit himself succumbs: "Now there is no longer any distinction between plants and animals. . . . Insects resembling rose petals adorn a shrub. . . . And plants have become confused with stones. Pebbles look like brains; stalactites like breasts; and outcrops of iron veins like tapestries with decorative designs." Thus witnessing the interpenetration of the three natural kingdoms, Anthony in turn falls prey to the lure of material space: he wants to disperse himself everywhere, to be within everything, "to penetrate each atom, to descend into the heart of matter—*to be* matter." Although Flaubert emphasizes the pantheistic, even

34. E. Minkowski, "Le temps vécu," in *Etudes phénoménologiques et psychopathologiques*, (Paris, 1933), 382–398: The question of hallucinations and spatial problems.

35. We have seen why it was appropriate to reject cases in which an animal imitated another animal: the similarities were not clearly, objectively established and the phenomena involved prestige-fascination rather than mimicry.

36. For the Phyllidae, see work done by Hennegay (1885).

37. Bouvier, 143.

magisterial aspect of this *descent into Hell*, here it nonetheless appears as a form of that process whereby *space is generalized* to the detriment of the individual, unless we should evoke, using psychoanalytic language, the return to an original insensate condition and prenatal unconsciousness—a mere question of terminology.

A look at the artistic domain reveals examples of similar phenomena. For instance, there are the extraordinary motifs in Slovakian folk decoration, which could equally well represent flowers with wings as birds with petals. And there are Salvador Dalí's paintings from around 1930. Whatever the artist may say, these men, sleeping women, horses, and lions (all of them invisible) result less from paranoid ambiguities and multiple meanings than from the mimetic assimilation of animate beings into the inanimate realm.[38]

Undeniably, some of the preceding accounts are far from offering absolute certainty. It might even seem reprehensible to compare such diverse types of realities as the external morphology of certain insects (in the case of homomorphism) with the actual behavior of people from a specific kind of civilization who may have a specific mode of thought (in the case of mimetic magic) and with the basic psychological needs of people whose civilization and mode of thought radically differ from theirs (in the case of psychasthenia). However, I consider that comparing such different occurrences is not only legitimate (after all, it is hardly possible to condemn comparative biology) but quite indispensable as soon as one addresses the obscure realm of unconscious determinations. Besides, the solution I have proposed covers nothing that could alarm a rigorous mind. It simply suggests that alongside the instinct of self-preservation that somehow attracts beings toward life, there proves to be a very widespread *instinct d'abandon* attracting them toward a kind of diminished existence; in its most extreme state, this would lack any degree of consciousness or feeling at all. I am referring, so to speak, to *the inertia of the élan vital*.

* * *

This is the perspective in which it may be acceptable to find a common origin for both mimetic phenomena—biological and magical[39]—as well as the psychasthenic experience, as the facts anyway seem to dictate one themselves. That origin is the *appeal of space*, which is just as elementary and mechanical as a tropism. Under its influence life seems to lose ground, to blur the line between

38. Salvador Dalí, *La Femme visible* (Paris, 1930), 15.
39. This parallel will seem justified if we consider that an instinct is produced by biological necessity. Or, failing that, the same necessity provides a type of imagination capable of filling the same role, that is, triggering similar behavior in the subject.

organism and environment as it withdraws, thereby *pushing back in equal mea-sure the bounds within which we may realize, as we should,* according to Pythago-ras, *that nature is everywhere the same.*[40]

40. In this rapid survey, I have had to omit certain related questions, such as obliterative coloring and flash coloring (see also Cuénot, *La genèse des espèces animales,* 3d ed., 1932). I have also omitted several discussions of secondary interest, for example, the connection between the instinct of giving up, such as I define it, and the death instinct defined by psychoanalysts. Above all, I have had to limit my examples. But here one need only refer to the striking and turbulent pages of P. Vignon's *Introduction à la biologie expérimentale* (Paris, 1930, *Encycl. Biol.,* 8: 310–459), and to the numerous accompanying illustrations. Readers will be especially in-terested in the section on the mimicry of caterpillars (362 and following); of mantises (374 and following); and of the grasshopper leaves (*Pterochrozes*) of Tropical America (422–459). The author shows that if mimicry is in each case a defense mechanism, it far exceeds its goal: it is "hypertelic." He therefore concludes that this is an infraconscious activity (one can follow him up to this point), pursuing a strictly aesthetic, decorative goal: "this is elegant, this is beauti-ful" (400). There is hardly any need to dispute such anthropomorphism. In any event, I my-self have nothing against the attempt to reduce the aesthetic instinct to the tendency to become transformed into an object or space. But is that really what M. Vignon intends?

Biology and Myth

Introduction to "Review of *L'Homme, cet inconnu,* by Dr. Alexis Carrel"

Alexis Carrel (1873–1944) was a French surgeon and cellular biologist who worked at the Rockefeller Institute for Medical Research in New York from 1906 until his retirement in 1939. His study, *L'Homme, cet inconnu* (Man, this unknown being; 1935), was a worldwide best-seller at the time, giving French expression to American eugenic theories—here as applied to the reproduction of elites. According to the current *Dictionnaire des intellectuels français*, Carrel was "obsessed by the degeneration of 'the civilized races' and influenced by neo-Lamarckian doctrine. . . . *L'Homme cet inconnu* aims to establish a 'Science of man' that would synthesize the different kinds of available knowledge and be entrusted to a 'hereditary biological aristocracy of scientists.'"[1] Carrel sought to implement this "science de l'homme" (science of man) at the Fondation Française pour l'Étude des Problèmes Humains (French Foundation for the Study of Human Questions, named Fondation Carrel), which Vichy created by decree in November 1941.

Caillois's brief review shows that his focus on biology as the basis for any study of man and the imagination did not lead him straight into the arms of biologizing sociology but actually left him quite vigilant with regard to the role of biological and racial discourse in the political sphere. His objections to Nazism at the time of the College of Sociology were specifically focused against a doctrine founded on biological and racial distinction. Even though his anti-Hitler strategies of the late 1930s always privileged some form of sociopolitical elite (as in "The Winter Wind"), Caillois defined this as a meritocracy whose elective structure defied the principle of a biological "hereditary aristocracy." A measure of his intellectual free-spiritedness can be seen in the concern voiced by Jean Paulhan, editor of the *Nouvelle revue française*, where the review appeared, about his vitriolic attack. "I am somewhat bothered about Carrel," Paulhan wrote his protégé on January 15, 1936. "I am sure that you are right, and yet, given all the talk (and favorable talk) about the book, I wish that

Review of *L'Homme, cet inconnu*, by Dr. Alexis Carrel, *Nouvelle revue française* (March 1936): 438–439.

you could be right with a little more proof. . . . Couldn't you develop and specify your objection to the work?"[2]

REVIEW OF *L'HOMME CET INCONNU,* BY DR. ALEXIS CARREL

This work addresses with shocking mediocrity a topic that deserved better. Few are as convinced as I that a thorough biological study of man could bring about decisive gains. Nothing, not even psychoanalysis, will prove to be more fundamentally researched. Nor is anything more likely to open up novel and yet well-founded paths for investigation. So it is a shame that the first exhaustive study of the question should turn out to be so intellectually crude that it seems designed to discourage rather than to stimulate any interest. Why spend so many pages recalling that Weber's law is not entirely accurate; that convalescents improve with a change in climate; that hope engenders action—and all sorts of propositions that make the wisdom of the ages suddenly seem like a series of mysterious hints and unfathomable paradoxes?

The work's final section seeks nothing less than to reform civilization and society. Here, we might well praise a certain open-mindedness, except for the fact that the author very quickly becomes irresponsible. On page 361, he writes: "Present-day proletarians owe their status to inherited intellectual and physical defects" (*sancta simplicitas*). And he suggests that this state of affairs should be accentuated through appropriate measures, so as to correlate social and biological inequalities more precisely. Society would then be directed by a hereditary aristocracy composed of descendants from the Crusaders, the heroes of the Revolution, the great criminals, the financial and industrial magnates (p. 360). On the contrary, a few pages later, and seemingly unaware of this sudden about-face, he considers doing away with the proletariat by requiring that all young people perform a stint of compulsory factory work (p. 385).

Enough. One almost regrets the printing press when we watch it adding such extravagant notions (that lack even the courtesy of mutual respect) to views that are already far too widespread. This work was very favorably received on the whole. But the reasons here are not those that would induce one to revise a severe judgment; nor are they themselves worth taking into account. The fact that certain people discovered biology in this book and others some means of political propaganda neither confirms nor detracts from its worth. For in these matters, the enthusiasm of both incompetence and self-interest are equally unacceptable. Besides, the work might focus attention, after all, on man's physical conditioning and encourage further study of the basic biological forces involved in the individualization of any living organism within an inanimate environment. These forces, similar to the laws governing fluid equilibrium, determine the tendencies causing the organism's creation, growth, and reproduction, as well as its return to an initial state of equilibrium. We still await that *general theory of instincts*, initiated in part by Moll and Weissmann, which already proves capable of explaining the most apparently baffling psychological *flaws* while resorting solely to such simple principles as, for example, contraction and dilation, tumescence and detumescence, paroxysm and release. The title of Dr. Carrel's work seemed to promise more from such types of studies than a vapid display of elementary knowledge. Too bad it was merely an advertisement.

Introduction to "The Function of Myth"

By 1935, Caillois was confronting the issue of sociopolitical militancy in Contre-Attaque by turning to Sorel (see introduction). His discussion of efficacious mythical crystallization as a "powerful investment of emotion" recalls the
myth of the general strike in *Reflections on Violence*: "a body of images capable
of evoking instinctively all the sentiments which correspond to the different
manifestations of the war undertaken by Socialism against modern Society.
Strikes have engendered in the proletariat the noblest, deepest, and most moving sentiments that they possess; the general strike groups them all in a coordinated picture, and, by bringing them together, gives to each one of them its
maximum of intensity. . . . We thus obtain that intuition of Socialism which
language cannot give us with perfect clearness—and we obtain it as a whole,
perceived instantaneously."[1] However, to the very real pressure by Bataille and
the Surrealists to wield myth as an immediate political tool, Caillois's essay
brings a note of scholarly calm and rigor.[2] This first draft of what would become the "sacred as transgression" in *Man and the Sacred* describes collective,
Dionysian festival and myth as a means of preserving the archaic social order.
Caillois's use of the term "function" reflects the social order of Mauss's "total
social fact" (see introduction), and his proto-structualist theory of mythical
logic or coherence should be read as a response to the theories of Lévy-Bruhl
and Dumézil in particular.

In 1969, Caillois's eulogy for Dumézil stressed that his teacher had always
related mythology to ritual and other forms of cultural expression, and that his
comparative mythology constituted a dynamic system. Here, "flexibility, tied
to erudition, culminates in a dizzying exercise of open classification, of conquering taxonomy, which is always in jeopardy but never at a loss. It is a fore-
gone conclusion that every aberration can be reduced to the system." This
confirmed Caillois's particular intellectual vein, "my taste for such a form of
uncertain stability. *He more than anyone else first gave me the idea that the realm
of the imagination had some kind of coherence.*"[3] In 1950, Etiemble had already
pinpointed for *Les Temps modernes* the seductive aspect of Dumézil's "coherent" sociocultural systems for those, such as he and Caillois, who were impa-

"Fonction du mythe," in *Le Mythe et l'homme* (Paris: Gallimard, 1938), 13–32.

tient with Surrealism. Evoking Dumézil's famous schema of triadic order linking divinities and social function in Indo-European thought, Etiemble flippantly wrote: "And so we understood: Ramnes, Tities, Luceres, you might as well say: brahmanes, kshatriya, vaiçya, the three blocks of the Vedic order, or to put it differently, if I've got it right: Mitra-Varuna=Odin=Jupiter-Fides=Romulus-Numa=Brahmanes=Flamines=Ramnes. . . . Which strikes me as infinitely more beautiful than the encounter on an operating table between an umbrella and one or two sewing machines."[4] Caillois's more earnest theoretical ambition in this regard was apparent from a review of Krappe's *Mythologie universelle* for the *Nouvelle revue française* of April 1936, a work that inspired him to dream of transcending thematic analogy in search of mythological "*structure*": a "sort of underlying identity between the elements that would be more architectonic than imaginative. . . . a universal mythology . . . which would merely outline the framework of a synthetic construction as Newton and Mendeleyev have done in other domains."[5]

Caillois's "mythical complex" has a more modest ambition: to transpose the *objective ideogram* into the sphere of mythology, as an overdetermined representation with a biological and social ground. Once again, this natural motor is anti-Darwinian and anti-utilitarian, but now Caillois has also read Nietzsche.[6] To self-destructive instincts in insects corresponds Nietzsche's *orgiastische Selbstvernichtung* (orgiastic self-destruction) in man, and the specific psychological drive of myth is humiliation or *ressentiment* at the social order, which induces the mythical hero to break the *taboo*, and the participant to identify with this "guilty" superman. (*Man and the Sacred* will list Napoleon, Faust, and Don Juan as modern mythical heroes.) Drawing on Dumézil's comparative mythology, Caillois argues that myth is always coordinated with collective ritual, such as festival, granting participants a real and not solely imagined satisfaction. He also devises a vast system for mythical plots composed by two intersecting axes: situations and heroic characters. This clearly challenges Freud's psychoanalytic anthropology of the universal Oedipal complex described in *Totem and Taboo*.

But what was the relation between the archaic past and the present? Mauss had concluded his *Essai sur le don* on the contemporary evanescence of such gift-giving patterns by cautiously noting that, perhaps, "by studying these obscure aspects of social life, we might be able somewhat to elucidate the path that our nations—their morality as well as their economy—should pursue."[7] Caillois's study of myth likewise notes the post-Enlightenment repression of Dionysian effervescence, which is vestigially present, he claims, among individuals utterly alienated from the social order. How such "instinctual and psychological potentials" should be effectively resocialized, and in a way proper to myth's coherence and logic, is a possibility Caillois merely raises; it is not one for which he provides any blueprint. His review at this time of Lord Raglan's *Le Tabou de l'inceste* was equally wary of applied anthropology. Caillois does confirm that such studies of human "fundamental yearnings," however "bloodthirsty and disorderly," had great political relevance: "For an act to be more than agitation, it must know how to strike only at the sensitive points." Nonetheless, he argued, careful scrutiny was required prior to any practical use: "Full light must be brought to bear on these issues: not to reduce but to discern, if need be to exalt." And it could be a slow process: "Therefore there is very much to be gained—*perhaps only in the long run, to be sure*—from works such as that of Lord Raglan."[8]

In my opinion, Caillois was thus resisting the call to anthropological arms of Bataille's Contre-Attaque. Moreover, Bataille's ecstatic writings on myth throughout the 1930s—from Mithra to Acéphale, as it were—differ dramatically from "The Function of Myth," which does not dwell on sacrifice, bloodshed, or death. Here is hardly what Bataille would call Nietzschean "tragedy" when laying the foundations for Acéphale.[9] Although Bataille's "The Sorcerer's Apprentice" at the College of Sociology echoed Caillois when discussing "myth ritually lived," his sense of how this "reveals no less than the true being" and "*total* existence" is quite far afield from the Maussian "total social fact."[10] Nor, for that matter, did the "dangerous" transgression he would describe after the war in *Literature and Evil*, in which he explicitly rejected any such social function: "Only literature could reveal the process of breaking the law—without which the law would have no purpose—*independently of the need to create order*. Literature cannot assume the task of regulating collective necessity."[11]

Et protégeant tout seul ma mère Amalécyte
Je ressème à ses pieds les dents du vieux dragon.
— Gérard de Nerval, "Antéros," *Les Chimères* [1]

It would seem that the capacity to invent or experience myths has not been replaced by that of accounting for them. At least, one must admit that exegetical attempts have almost always been disappointing. Just as time produced different cities of Troy, so too it indiscriminately compiled the strata of their ruins. This stratification is very instructive, nonetheless; a vertical slice could well reveal the broad outlines of some structure.

In this field, one major surprise is the great diversity of the phenomena that have to be analyzed. It seems that no single explanatory principle ever works twice in a row—from the same perspective and to the same extent. One almost wonders whether each myth might not require its own particular principle. As if each myth were an irreducibly unique structure, fully consubstantial with its explanatory principle, so that the latter could hence not be detached from it without suffering a major loss of density and scope. In any case, to view the world of myths as homogeneous and capable of being resolved by one single key, this is the idle fancy of a mind always intent to find the Same beneath the Other, the one beneath the many—but in this case, far too pressed for quick results. However, here as elsewhere, the result (when it can be foreseen through deduction, or when it is arbitrarily set in advance) matters less than the actual path taken to determine it.

In any event, it is certain that myth, positioned at the apex of society's superstructure and the mind's activity, by nature answers to the most varied demands, and simultaneously so. Therefore, they are imbricated within myth in a way that is inevitably very complex. An analysis of myth based on a single explanatory *system*, however well-founded, should and hence does leave us with a sense of insuperable inadequacy; in response, it is tempting to at once attribute a crucial importance to this irreducible residue.

Each system is thus true on account of what it suggests, and false on account of what it excludes; and the claim to total explanation can quickly propel the

---

1. ["And while I, all alone, protect my mother, Amalécyte / I sow afresh at her feet the old dragon's teeth." This poem is about Anteros, who, like Eros, was the son of Venus and Mars: Eros was the god of love; Anteros, that of passion. Nerval's poem begins: "You ask why there's so much rage in my heart / And why my flexible neck sports an untamed head" (Gérard de Nerval, *Oeuvres complètes,* ed. and intro. Albert Béguin and Jean Richer [Paris: Gallimard, 1960], 1:4).—*Ed.*]

system into a state of interpretative delirium, as occurred with the solar theories (Max Müller and his disciples), the astral theories (Stucken and the pan-Babylonic school), and, more recently, with the deplorable psychoanalytic endeavors (C. G. Jung, etc.). For that matter, such interpretative delirium may be quite legitimate in these fields; it may even occasionally seem like an effective method of research. Even so, it is still extremely dangerous, precisely because it seeks to be exclusive. This practice of research no longer involves checking a principle against every datum and keeping it sufficiently supple so that it can be enriched by the very resistance it encounters, in such a way that a certain exchange process during the course of analysis allows the principle gradually to master the object it is explaining. It is merely a matter of adapting the diversity of facts to a rigidly ossified principle that is held to be necessary and sufficient a priori. This is done by force and through a process of abstraction that divests phenomena of their specific features and, hence, of their basic reality. Furthermore, it is clear that mechanically extending an explanatory system ultimately makes it unable to determine anything with any kind of accuracy; it thus loses any explanatory function. In short, it is undermined. Nonetheless, if we take into account such lapses of intellectual judgment (that is, if we exclude those cases where an explanation is replaced by the forced adequation of fact to principle, and also where an explanatory principle is incorrectly deemed effective outside of its specific sphere of influence), it remains that no prior efforts in the realm of mythological exegesis deserve to be condemned without recall.

Each of these efforts applied to myths an increasingly fine-grained network of determinations, thus bringing to light the circumstances of their origin—involving such various factors as nature, history, society, and man himself. I shall not here chart the successive schools of thought, nor survey them critically once again. For that, one need only refer to the works that have already dealt with the topic with varying degrees of success.[2] It is enough for now to suggest the structural pattern of their evolution, which, broadly speaking, seems to proceed from the *outer to the inner*. Natural phenomena constitute the first level of determinations: the sun's daily course, the moon's phases, eclipses, and storms, all of these form a sort of outer casing, as it were, for myths. This material basis was universal; however, it did not have much direct influence. One should certainly not conclude that mythology is a kind of poetic transla-

2. See also J. Réville, *Les Phases successives de l'histoire des religions* (Paris, 1909); O. Gruppe, *Geschichte der Klassischen Mythologie und Religionensgeschichte* (Leipzig, 1921), H. Pinard de la Boullaye, *L'Etude comparée des religions* (Paris, 1922–1925).

tion of atmospheric phenomena[3]—following Schlegel, who defined it as a "hieroglyphic expression of environing nature transfigured by the imagination and love."[4] Natural phenomena function only as a frame, and should merely be viewed as an initial *terrestrial conditioning*[5] of the "myth-making faculty" [*fonction fabulatrice*] if not of the soul.[6] History, geography, and sociology each provide their own, convergent definitions of the circumstances in which myths originated and evolved. Aspects of physiology also illuminate the smallest details, from the mythology of nightmares to that of sneezing and yawns.[7] One can even determine the laws of mythical thinking and thereby delineate the psychological necessities of its structure.[8] It would be childish to deny that these different disciplines have made very important contributions. Mythical exegesis certainly has much to gain by drawing on historical and sociological data, in particular, and by using this to found its interpretations. Here, surely, lies the path to salvation. Historical and social facts constitute the essential casing of myths. And let us recall that research has been pursuing this direction ever more exclusively and with increasing success. Enough said. Its value is immediately obvious to anyone who is at all familiar with the works and methods of contemporary mythography. Nonetheless, despite all these efforts and

3. Likewise, one cannot seriously imagine that mythology represents a science that is referred to or expressed in allegorical fashion. Admittedly, it may be that Plato's supposed myths fulfill this role; but no one would consider confusing them with real mythology, mythology that is "finality without an end." Just as no one would designate as a myth the fiction of infinitely flat, curved beings, which currently serves to help us imagine a four-dimensional universe in expositions of relativistic physics.

4. Schlegel, *Rede über die Mythologie und Symbolische Anschauung*.

5. The term comes from C. G. Jung. See *Essais de psychologie analytique*.

6. [The term "fonction fabulatrice" was coined by Henri Bergson in *Deux sources de la morale et de la religion* (Paris: Ferdinard Alcan, 1932); I've used the translation found in Henri Bergson, *The Two Sources of Morality and Religion*, trans. R. Ashley Audra, Cloudesley Brereton, and W. Horsfall Carter (1935; Notre Dame, Indiana: University of Notre Dame Press, 1977)—*Ed.*]

7. See also W. H. Roscher, *Ephialtes, Eine pathologische-mythologische Abhandlung über die Alptrüume und Alpdämonen der klassischen Altertums (Abhandl. der ph. hist. kl. d. kgl/Säachs. Gesell. der Wiss.*, XX, ii, Leipzig, 1900); P. Saintyves. *L'Eternuement et le baillement dans la magie, l'ethnographie et le folklore médical* (Paris).

8. See also the works of Cassirer and L. Lévy-Bruhl. More boldly, Victor Henry writes: "Myth certainly predates man: for an organism endowed with some degree of consciousness, any apperception of an external fact is a potential myth. For the brain of a higher animal, the universe is expressed as a series of myths, that is, of instantaneous representations that vanish as soon as they occur. The more that memory and consciousness establish connections between these visual flashes of the non-self, the more the myth defines and asserts itself, and the animal climbs higher in the scale of beings." *La Magie dans l'Inde antique* (Paris, 1904) 242, n.1.

their remarkable results, there still remains an undeniable sense of some *gap*. Although we can see how the aforementioned determinations—natural, historical, or social—have all acted upon myths, the *sufficient cause* of this process is still a mystery. In other words, these determinations can operate only from the outside. They are the *outer components* of mythology, if you like. Yet to anyone who has some knowledge of myths, it appears that they *are also driven from within by a specific structure of autoreproduction and autocrystallization that is both its own motor and its own syntax*. Myth results from these two converging strands of determinations; it is the site of their mutual limitations and competing strengths. It is produced by the process whereby an inner necessity takes account of the outer demands and phenomena that offer, impose, or arrange matters—those demands and phenomena that, in the absence of any counterweight and despite our constant sense of frustration, have always generally seemed sufficient to furnish an adequate explanation of myths (barring any new information).

Nonetheless, they avoid the crux of the question: Why do myths have such an effect on sensitivity? What emotional needs are they meant to fulfill? What kinds of gratification are they supposed to provide? For after all, there was a time when entire societies believed in them and enacted them through ritual. And even now that they are dead, myths still continue to excite and cast their shadow on the imagination of mankind. Despite its erroneous ways, psychoanalysis must be given credit for having addressed the topic. As we know, its efforts were fruitless on the whole. It produced results that would be most blessed by eternal silence, given its need to transpose onto the analysis of myths, and by any means, an explanatory principle that could not even cover all aspects of psychology; its blind, mechanical use of an idiotic symbolic system; its complete unawareness of the problems specific to mythology; and its inadequate documentation, which allowed for amateurish carelessness. But one should not cite the failures of its faithful in order to refute the doctrine. The fact is that psychoanalysis posed the problem in all of its force, and that by defining the processes of displacement, condensation, and overdetermination it laid the foundations for a valid logic of the affective imagination. Above all, through the concept of a complex, it brought to light a profound psychological reality that might have a crucial role to play in the particular instance of explaining myths.

In any event, it certainly seems that this is the path to pursue to grasp the ultimate function of myths; that, venturing beyond psychoanalysis itself, we must look to biology and, if need be, interpret the meaning of such phenomena through their repercussions in the human psyche as presented by psychology. Comparing the most perfected examples of the two divergent evolutions in the animal kingdom (which respectively lead to man and to insects), it seems acceptable to seek correspondences between the two, and especially between *the behavior of the one and the mythology of the other*. Particularly so if, as M. Bergson would have it, mythical representation *(a quasi-hallucinatory image)* is meant to provoke, in the absence of instinct, the behavior that instinct itself would have triggered.[9] But this cannot involve *élan vital* or anything of the kind. Instinct is by no means in every case a force of salvation or preservation, nor does it always have a pragmatic effect of protection of defense. Mythology is beyond (or falls short of, if you prefer) the force impelling a being to sustain itself; it is beyond the instinct of self-preservation. Rationalism is responsible for this kind of a priori utilitarianism or, more exactly, the hypothesis that all living phenomena have a utilitarian end. Yet, as far as I know, rationalism has not yet resorbed mythology. And it *can only do so by giving ground*, either modifying itself or else extending itself by virtue of that osmotic equilibrium that, as noted above, always tends to become established between what is being explained and what is doing the explaining.[10] Myths are definitely not guardrails set up at each dangerous curve to prolong the life of the individual or of the human species.[11] To invoke the testimony of a man who certainly had some exact (philological) knowledge of mythology, let us recall that Nietzsche's *orgiastische Selbstvernichtung* assumed a whole gamut of exigencies oriented in the very opposite direction. In any case, this is a far cry from the all too renowned instinct of self-preservation.

Having thus clarified the general connections among mythology's basic de-

9. Henri Bergson, *Les Deux sources de la morale et de la religion* (Paris, 1932), 110 and following. It is hardly necessary to recall that for M. Bergson, it makes all the difference that man is governed by intelligence and the insect by instinct. Which amounts to saying, according to him, that "actions are pre-formed in the nature of insects, whereas only their function is preformed in man" (110).

10. Of course, this transformation, this adaptation, will not make rationalism stop being rationalism and from opposing as such a certain number of viewpoints. For it will never abandon any aspect of its fundamental axioms: determinism, internal systematization, the principle of economy, prohibition of recourse to any exteriority, etc. Utilitarianism derives far more from positivism than from rationalism, and rationalism could only benefit by excluding it from its axiomatics. For that matter, the work of science is directed toward the elimination of any final explanation.

11. On the contrary, there do exist instincts harmful to the individual and even to the species; for example, those found in certain species of ants, which feed the parasites that bring about their destruction. See also the articles by H. Piéron, "Les Instincts nuisibles à l'espèce devant les théories transformistes," *Scientia*, 9 (1911): 199 and following; "Les Problèmes actuelles de l'instinct,"*Revue philosophique* (1908): 329–369; *Bulletins et mémoires de la Société d'anthropologie* 4(1908): 503–539. A critical account of the problem and bibliography are also to be found in the classical work by W. Morton Wheeler, *Les Sociétés d'insectes* (Paris, 1926).

terminations, let us consider its structure. Here we find two systems of myth-making: *a form of vertical integration* and *a form of horizontal integration* (if it is not too bold to define this state of affairs using terms borrowed from economics). These entail two complementary frameworks, the interferences of which are relatively free (that is, anecdotal) because they seem to reflect only mythology's outer (historical) determinations rather than its inner (or psychological) necessities. This might explain why a certain mythical theme is never exclusively linked to one particular hero, and why, on the contrary, the connections between heroes and themes are readily rearranged.

It then becomes possible to distinguish *the mythology of situations* from *the mythology of heroes*. Mythical situations can be interpreted as the projection of psychological conflicts (that generally cover psychoanalytic complexes). The hero can be interpreted as the projection of the individual subject himself: *an ideal, compensatory image that imparts grandeur to his humiliated soul*. Indeed, a person is subject to psychological conflicts that naturally vary in accord with the civilization and kind of society to which he belongs (and do so to different degrees, depending on their type). He is usually unaware of these conflicts because they tend to be caused by the social structure itself and by the constraints thus imposed on his elementary desires. For this very reason, and all the more critically so, the individual cannot possibly escape these conflicts, for this would require an act that society, and hence he himself, have forbidden—indeed, his own conscience is strongly marked by and in some sense guarantees social prohibitions. *As a result, he is paralyzed before the taboo act and will entrust the task of carrying it out to the hero.*

Before addressing this aspect of the question, I would like to show through examples that not only folktale themes but also mythical themes, strictly speaking, can be reduced to *dramatic situations* that, in essence, *materialize certain crystallizations of psychological virtualities within a specific context*. There is, for example, the situation of Oedipus, who has murdered his father and married his own mother; or of Hercules, enslaved by Omphale. There is Polycrates, who throws his ring into the sea to ward off the dangers of excess happiness. One thinks of Abraham, Jephthah, and Agamemnon, kings who sacrifice their progeny; of Pandora, the artificial woman and the *Giftmädchen* [poison-maiden]. In any event, the very concepts of *hubris* and *nemesis*, which play such an important role in mythology, provide direct examples of this.[12]

We may now give its full sense to the concept of the hero, which is fundamentally implicated in the very existence of mythical situations. *By definition,*

12. Not only in Greek mythology: these two complementary concepts seem to outline the central constellation of all mythical psychology.

the hero is the one who can resolve these situations, with an outcome that is either successful or unsuccessful. For an individual most suffers from the fact that he can never escape the conflict in which he is enmeshed. Any solution seems desirable, however violent or dangerous, but because of social prohibitions it is also impossible, even more in a psychological than physical sense. Therefore, he delegates the hero in his place—and by nature, the hero is one who violates prohibitions. If he were human, he would be guilty, and as a mythical figure he still remains so. He is still tainted by his deed, and his purification—when called for—is never complete. *But in the special light of myth, that is, of grandeur, he stands unconditionally justified.*[13] The hero is thus the one who resolves the conflict with which the individual is struggling: whence his superior right not so much to crime as to *guilt*. The function of this ideal guilt is to pander to the person who desires it without being able, however, to assume it himself.[14]

Yet people cannot always be gratified with mere illusion; they must have the actual deed. That is, a person cannot forever restrict himself to virtually identifying with the hero, to an ideal satisfaction. Beyond that, he must have the experience of real identification and actual gratification. This is why myth is usually seconded by ritual, for although the violation of an interdiction may be required, it is only allowed in a mythical atmosphere, and ritual is what grants access to this. Here, we can discern the essence of festival: *it is a licensed form of excess whereby an individual is dramatized and thus turns into the hero.*[15] Ritual realizes the myth and allows people to experience it. This is why we find that myth and ritual are so frequently united; in fact, they are indissociable, and their divorce has always brought about their decline. Detached from ritual,

13. On the relationship between myth and the concept of grandeur, see R. Kassner, *Les Eléments de la grandeur humaine*, French trans. (Paris,1931), 92 and following. The essential idea is that grandeur must be defined as having a power of transmutation in ethical matters. When it affects guilt, this remains guilt but appears superior to the principle by virtue of which it is guilt. In this particular sense (which, I should add, is not Kassner's), grandeur is certainly the finality of myth.

14. It indulges more than it purifies: Aristotelian catharsis is definitely a notion that is too optimistic.

15. Excess as a feature of festivals and rituals has long been recognized. Freud simply echoes a classical definition when he writes: "A festival is an excess that is allowed, even decreed; the solemn violation of a prohibition. People do not commit excesses because they are joyfully predisposed to do so on account of some dictate: excess is inherent in the very nature of festival." *Totem and Taboo*, French trans. (Paris, 1924), 194. At present, all the movements that show mythological characteristics display a real hypertrophy of this festival or ritual function. Thus, the Hitlerian movement and the Ku Klux Klan, in which punitive rituals are clearly designed to give their members "that brief *ivresse* which an inferior man cannot conceal when for a few moments he feels powerful and frightening." See John Moffatt Mecklin, *The Ku Klux Klan*, French trans. (Paris, 1934). Moreover, it is certain that the representation of an "Invisible

myth loses most of its exalting force—its capacity to be lived—if not its raison d'être. It has become mere literature, like most Greek mythology of the Classical era, as transmitted by the poets—irremediably adulterated and normalized.

Yet, the relationship of literature and mythology cannot emerge in its true light until we have first defined mythology's function. For if mythology *compels* mankind only insofar as it expresses psychological conflicts structured in individual or social terms and then resolves these in an ideal way, it is hard to see why these conflicts would not directly have assumed the psychological language that is, in fact, their own; why instead they have assumed the setting—or should one say, the hypocrisy?—of myth-making. It would be useless to invoke a notion such as "prelogical," for here what needs to be justified is precisely the anteriority implied by the term "prelogical."[16] It is just as hard to rest with that alleged need for fantasy, reverie, or poetry one benevolently ascribes to mankind. Indeed, some people can do perfectly well without this need, while for others it simply reflects some weakness or is the price of a particular strength. And it is just as hard to believe that "censorship" has made myth-making necessary, *because an idea is rarely more deadly than its illustration*. Thus, we must apparently look elsewhere to grasp what renders it suitable. We must look to its actual properties, or more specifically, to the fact that a conflict's mythical projection is ambiguous in a way that allows for many different resonances; the mythical conflict is thus rendered disturbing on various accounts at once, and these resonances make it what it first seemed to be: *a powerful investment of emotion*.[17]

Here is the sense in which one may perhaps speak of internal mythology. Plutarch already seemed to have this concept in mind when he wrote:

> Just as mathematicians say that the rainbow is a picture of the sun variously colored by the latter's rays reflected in the clouds, so too the myth I have just recounted is the picture of a specific truth that reflects one single thought into different environments—as we may deduce from those rituals full of visible mourning and sorrow, from those architectural

---

empire that sees and hears everything," which served as a basis for the activity and spread of the Ku Klux Klan, is distinctly mythological.

16. [The term "prelogical" comes from Lucien Lévy-Bruhl, *The Primitive Mentality* (London: George Allen & Unwin, 1923)—*Ed.*]

17. G. Dumézil, one of those who have done the most to connect myths and rituals and to interpret them jointly in their mutual light, writes in a recent work: "The truth is that myths are born and flourish in conditions that are obscure but almost always accompanied by rituals. It's very likely that myths of 'bands of monsters' originated *with* rituals of disguise, and castration myths *with* ritual castrations." *Ouranos-Varuna* (Paris, 1934), 29.

arrangements of temples with different sections deployed either as wings, as open esplanades laid out in broad daylight, or else that are hidden underground, extending throughout the darkness with a series of rooms in which the gods are clothed, and which evoke both huts and tombs.[18]

A specific truth reflecting a single thought *into different environments*. Indeed, it does seem that mythology's syntax involves a structured play of perspectives spanning different levels of our affectivity. This is especially apparent in the analysis of the *noon complex*, with its clear stratification: under the midday sun, people renounce any action or will; sleep overcomes the senses and the mind; succubi perform erotic assaults; there is a generalized passivity and boredom with life *(acedia)*. All this while ghosts thirst for the blood of the living, who are now fully vulnerable because the shade is at its lowest point. This is the ghostly hour when the orb, at its zenith, encompasses nature with the high tide of death.[19]

Here we have the first structure of the mythical situation's repercussions: a *structure of emotional aggravation* (of a given phenomenon); second, there is a *structure of interference*. Most mythical situations partially cover at least one or several other such situations. Thus, to consider the preceding example, the noon complex culminates in the vampire phenomenon on the one hand, and in the vegetation demons on the other.[20] Similarly, the *Giftmädchen* theme is linked to that of the immortality potion, and the Polycrates complex to the

18. Plutarch, *Isis and Osiris*, § 20 trans. and ed. Mario Meunier (Paris: L'Artisan du Livre, 1924).

19. On this topic, see my articles published in the *Revue de l'histoire des religions* (Mar.–Dec. 1937) and the *Revue des études slaves* (1936–1937). Similarly, A.-W. Schlegel may be said to have analyzed the mythical overdetermination of the North when he viewed it as containing images of superiority and immobility, of the Polar star, the direction of the magnetic needle, immortality, identity, and self-knowledge. Another example of a thorough analysis of overdeterminations may be found in the study by J. Hubaux and M. Leroy on the wealth of emotive associations conjured up for the Ancients by the promise of Cinnamomus's abundant growth in Virgil's fourth *Eclogue*; also, the theme of resurrection and the phoenix; exotic legends in which an item is harvested with leaden arrows, or by means of chunks of meat that bring down the nests of the birds that collect it; birth in the furrows of the earth, surrounded by invincible serpents; connection with the cycles of Alexander and Bacchus, etc. See also *Mélanges Bidez*, 1: 505–530 (Brussels, 1934). "Vulgo nascetur amomum" [Assyrian spices shall grow all up and down (Virgil's *Eclogue* 4)—*Ed.*].

20. For the earth, source of all vegetation, is also the dwelling place of the dead. "All that lives emerged from her, and all that dies returns there; she is the nourishing earth, and also mankind's tomb. It is thus quite natural that the chthonian divinities, which preside over agriculture, should also reign over the dead." H. Weil, *Journal des savants* (1895), 305. Noon, the hour of the dead, must also be the hour of the vegetation demons.

Oedipus complex.[21] It hence befalls comparative mythology to distinguish between those cases where thematic links are anecdotal (caused by external factors), and those where they are caused by internal mythology. For a link that proves constant throughout several different civilizations could not possibly arise from the effect of their respective structures on the individual imagination.

In this way, the study of mythology can become a method of psychological prospecting. Indeed, the sufficient cause of myth is its overdetermination— namely, the fact that it is a knot of psychological processes, all coinciding in a way that can be neither fortuitous, occasional, nor personal. (For then, myth would not succeed as such; it would be merely a *Märchen* [fairy story].)[22] Nor can it be artificial (its determinations would be entirely different, as would its features and function).[23] So that uncovering the basic outline of the arrangement of these psychological processes will allow us to discern the unconscious determinations of human affectivity (more validly than psychoanalysis has done). Comparative biology should supply very valuable correlations as well, given that representation in certain cases replaces instinct, and that the actual behavior of an animal species can illuminate the psychological virtualities of man.

If we do not expect the study of myths to determine these instinctual or psychological virtualities, then it is not worth undertaking, for there surely exist disciplines that have a more immediate interest. And surely, nothing is more cumbersome, perhaps even more deadly, than a useless truth. It is merely *one* piece of knowledge—that is, all things considered, an especially critical obstacle for *knowledge* itself, which either is totalitarian or is not.

What is more, these instinctual virtualities have not died out. Persecuted and dispossessed, they continue to fill the imaginations of dreamers and, at times, the law courts and padded cells of insane asylums with repercussions that are "timid, incomplete, and rebellious." We should be aware that they are still capable of presenting their candidacy for the highest office. If times are

---

21. See G. Dumézil, *Le Festin d'immortalité* (Paris, 1924); P. Saintyves, *Essais de folklore biblique* (Paris, 1923), 377–381, ch. 8: "L'Anneau de Polycrate et le statère dans la bouche du poisson."

22. As is known, the *Märchen* during German Romanticism gave rise to many theories. It may be defined as a direct product (Novalis termed it necessary, ideal, and prophetic) of the imagination left up to its own devices. Goethe's *The Green Snake* and Hoffmansthal's *La Femme sans ombre* are the best-known examples.

23. We are then dealing with *literature*, which, from this point of view, would be an activity that replaces mythology after mythology has lost its necessity.

right, they can even obtain it. From humiliated to triumphant myths the path is perhaps shorter than we think. They would simply have to be socialized. And now that politics talks so readily of real-life experience and worldview, when it both punishes and honors basic violent emotions, and indeed resorts to symbols and rites, who would claim that this is impossible?

Introduction to "The Noon Complex"

This short piece encapsulates a lengthy thesis Caillois had been preparing for several years, briefly noted in "The Function of Myth," on the structure and historical decline of the noon hour's "mythical complex." The powerful "magic" exerted by the image or "the hour of noon upon human sensitivity" crystallized the emotions and states of Caillois's *instinct d'abandon*: running the gamut from depression to death, to which he now added sexual fantasy and ghosts.[1]

This research unearthed a crucial aspect of human experience that had been buried, or suppressed by modernity, so Caillois claimed, ever since the technique of chiming clocks had supplanted noon with midnight—or with what Gilbert and Sullivan call "the ghosts's high noon." Dumézil unofficially advised this thesis on Indo-European solar mythology, surveying Slavic demonology, Greco-Roman myth, and the malady of *acedia*—the sexual mysticism attributed to medieval priests, which is genealogically related to psychasthenia and, more commonly, to melancholy. For this project, Caillois undertook the only ethnographic work of his career.[2] Elsewhere in his thesis, he discusses vestigial traces of the noon complex in the modern mind, for example, in Schelling, Leconte de Lisle, Bourget, Nietzsche, and Jensen *(Gradiva)*, among others.[3] Closer to home, Caillois declares that "[even] the detective novel, a genre that is extremely revealing and valuable to study despite its exclusion from 'literature,' also makes use at times of 'Noon, King of Horrors.'"[4] Most importantly, and despite Philippe Borgeaud's recent discussion of this study's serious scholarly shortcomings, it offers a scholarly approach to a burning theme in Caillois's immediate milieu.[5] This sexual "plenitude which involves renouncing everything" requires no self-mutilation or identification with sacrificed gods. Solar mythology viewed as a form of Nirvana complex, anchored in biology, offers a tranquil counterpoint to Bataille's theories of violent solar sacrifice and "expenditure"—from "The Solar Anus" to Acéphale—that would culminate in the postwar cosmic potlatch of *La Part maudite*.[6]

Caillois's brief summation of his work was published in *Minotaure*, which had an interesting preface in October 1936, just after the Popular Front had

"Le Complexe de midi," *Minotaure* 9 (October 1936): 9–10.

come to power. Referring to "current events which are becoming more over-whelming day by day," it claimed that any "useful work" must express the "LA-TENT CONTENT" of its time.[7] Because Caillois was then a member of the re-search group Inquisitions, hewing to the Popular Front (see "For a Militant Orthodoxy"), could we—recalling Mauss's treatise on gift giving—relate this treatise on laziness to the leisure policies of Blum's minister Daladier? Could Caillois be charting, however ironically, those biological and archaic drives of liberal democracy that might legitimize the Popular Front and its paid vaca-tions? At various times, Caillois cited a question dear to the College of Sociol-ogy, namely, the issue of what replaced archaic festival—the regenerative mo-ment of the social order—in the modern world. Prior to defining war, together with Bataille at the College of Sociology, as modernity's "fête noire" (black fes-tival), he apparently thought of vacations (see "Paroxysms of Society"). How-ever, Caillois never explained just when or why he made that initial conjecture. Perhaps it had to do with the demons of noon. In any event, by 1939, having long lost hope for the Popular Front, he clearly saw a radical rift between lazi-ness and social revivification: "Is not the ephemeral pleasure of vacations one of those false senses of well-being that mask death throes from the dying?"[8]

THE NOON COMPLEX

Although there are many reasons for thinking that the hour of noon probably had major religious and mythological repercussions, especially in the fiery countries of the South, these have never been explored. And the reason is quite clear: the relevant texts are very few, widely dispersed, and make only glancing allusions to this phenomenon. But there is a decisive text by Servius, asserting that almost all the divinities appear at noon, which provides sufficient grounds for research.[1]

Besides, it is not difficult to uncover the causes of noon's prestige. This is the moment when the sun, at its zenith, divides the day into equal parts, each gov-erned by the opposing signs of rise and decline. This, then, is the moment when the forces of life and light yield to the powers of death and darkness. In ancient Greece, noon was in fact the *hour of transition* marking the boundary between the reign of the Uranian and of the infernal gods.[2] But noon is also

1. In Virgil's *Georgic*, IV, 401.
2. Eustathus, *In Iliad*, VIII, 66; *Schol. in Iliad*, VIII, 66; Etym. Magn., ed. Gaisford, 468; *Schol. in Apoll. Rh.*, 1, 587.

the time when shade is at a low point, and thus when the exposed soul is most vulnerable to dangers of all kinds. For similar reasons, noon is generally the hour when the dead make their appearance—*they who cast no shadow*. On the most elementary level, these are the reasons noon is preordained to witness the apparition of ghosts. Clearly, they require only those fantasies of the human imagination that are the most general and ancient: sympathetic magic and the principle of correspondence, the identification of the soul with the body's shadow.

Turning now from meteorology to physiology, we can observe that the hour of noon has here just as many reasons to command attention. The sun's burning heat is unforgiving at this suffocating time of day. Heatstroke, sunstroke, cerebral fever, and their attendant mental and physical ailments offered sufficient proof of demonic activity to persuade people that they existed. In Greece, these mishaps simply figured among the numerous other prerogatives of divinities or ghosts whose activities were not confined to this sphere: Pan, Hecate, the Eurpensus, the nymphs and Sirens. But elsewhere, in the Slavic domain, for example, where these demons bear the name of Noon, the sufficient cause of their creation is manifest in their function, whether they are ruthlessly brandishing a white-hot frying pan or tearing off somebody's head "like a flower."

Night has only the "silence and horror of darkness" with which to counter all of noon's constituent features. And, of course, this is hardly insignificant: our sense of mystery and anxiety in the dark is determined by the phenomonology of perception itself. But this does not mean that light does not possess those qualities enabling it to divulge specters. The creator sets atremble a blaze that fills light with countless troubling beings, who are always on the brink of visibility. Even so, the burning heat of day would not be the privileged time for the apparition of the infernal powers if midnight had an objectively perceptible status. Indeed, wherever clocks with chiming bells and their famous "twelve strokes of midnight" have allowed people to gauge the exact timing of the fateful hour, midday has given up its place to the deepest hour of darkness. Until then, midnight had no specific existence at night comparable to that of noon during the day. Because there was no sign such as the sun's positioning or the lack of shade to denote midnight, people therefore drew a contrast between the instant of noon and the undivided totality of the night. In any case, they could hardly define midnight as anything else besides the nocturnal counterpart to daytime's hour for ghosts. Thus, there never have been any specific midnight demons: none have been referred to in this way. The reason is obvious: midnight has no individualized status, and nothing in its physical conditioning makes it objectively dangerous or even noteworthy. Once striking clocks had endowed it with some specificity, midnight simply became a time of apparition when ghosts (basically all the same) revealed themselves as if by prior accord, but the hour lacked its own appointed phantoms. *In this way midnight welcomes specters, but does not dispatch them.*

A further, though entirely different determining factor has certainly contributed to the mythological decline of noon: the influence of Christianity. The Greeks did not attach moral qualities to light and darkness. Thus, they believed that demons indiscriminately appeared during both day and night.[3] But once light was held to express the principle of goodness, and darkness the very dominion of evil (a classification encouraged by Manichaeanism), people asserted that the demons had chosen shadow and, like bats, were spreading darkness about themselves and fleeing daylight.[4] It thus became apparent that the demons hated light. Harmless during the day when the salutary powers prevailed, they could reign supreme only under the cover of darkness.

In the circumstances, noon's preeminence insofar as ghosts were concerned quickly diminished. But such a source for determining factors of all sorts inevitably maintained its appeal for human emotion because the latter, in any case, could not stop finding a real satisfaction of its basic longings in that hour's image. At noon, it would seem that life takes a pause, organic matter returns to an inorganic state, and everything blazes pointlessly and without ardor in a futile desire for luxury and display. Activity of any kind seems to involve unpleasant and risible agitation. All heartbeats have come to a halt. The supreme triumph of the positive forces dissolves into renunciation, their surging forth into slumber and their plenitude into resignation. The will to live withdraws somewhere unknown, as if absorbed by thirsty sands. This silent exaltation of every abdication, like a flood invincibly overwhelming all morality, swiftly drowns any uncertain inclination or remorse it might find.

It is easy to perceive the seduction of such a scene for the asthenic personality—always prone to ask *What's the use?* Quite understandably, medieval doctors turned the noon demon into that of the *sinful sadness* or *acedia* afflicting monks in the middle of the day, with effects so serious that it was unhesitatingly classified among the deadly sins.[5]

3. See Lucien, *Philops.*, 17.
4. Eusebius, *Praep. evang.* VII, 16, 2; Grégoire de Naziance, *Part. Gr.* XXXII, 1376; Saint Basil, *Patr. Gr.*, XXX, 277.
5. Evagre de Pont, *Patr. Gr.*, XL, 1271; Nilus d'Ancyre, ibid., LXXIX 1159; Jean Climaque, ibid., LXXXVIII, 859, etc.

Cassian has given a very precise psychological description of this bane.[6] The ailing monk comes to feel an overwhelming revulsion for his life, for his monastery and companions. He is overcome with insuperable laziness. Daily work disheartens and repels him; even reading fills him with disgust. He is weary and yet ravenously hungry, with a kind of morbid need to sleep as the sixth hour is drawing near—the fearful hour of noon. At that time, he keeps on watching the sun, judging that its decline toward the horizon is too slow. For him, this is truly Plato's *motionless noon*. Here, then, is *acedia*: a state of clear-cut "psychological hypotension," with minor peculiarities connected with the dissipation of the intellect in every one of its forms.[7] Acedia is a sense of apathy toward life, the dull anxiety of a frustrated heart and an intellect confused by irrationality. It is not simply a matter of vague yearning but of real fits of abulia, keen states of psychological depression well-known to psychiatrists; such states differ from any other type of human experience.[8] And beneath it all, we find the lure of sexuality: the acedic subject would like to leave his monastery to visit a woman with no one to support her. Sometimes the sexual obsession is more explicit.[9] Alcuin views the acedic as a person overwhelmed by carnal desire, and Alain de Lille cites the impure acts of David, Samson, and Solomon as instances of sinful sadness: the sins of the just man, committed out of boredom.[10]

This is the final metamorphosis of the specters of noon, who were once vampires and succubi arising at the hour of the dead to feed on blood and sperm, who were purveyors of strength and life. We can thus observe how markedly they have been moralized. This evolution could be charted step by step. Here, though, I shall dwell only on its culmination: when the heavy, burning slumber of nature (with light's star at its zenith and in that state of fullness on the edge of decline) gives man at the same time the *justification, illustration*, and *exaltation* of life's letting go into its opposite.

Nothing can indulge an individual's basic longings more surely than the

6. Cassian, Instituta Coenobiorum, X, 2, 3.

7. See P. Alphandéry, *Journal de psychologie* (1929), 768–787: "De quelques documents médiévaux relatifs à des états psychasthéniques."

8. See ibid., 768. M. Alphandéry appropriately refers to certain descriptions by Pierre Janet.

9. There are numerous texts in which the demon of noon, disguised as a nun, assaults the monks during their siesta and "caresses them like a prostitute" (Césaire d'Heisterbach, *Dial. Mirac.* [The dialogue on miracles], V.33). But these are folktales whose analysis would exceed the scope of this summary article. I shall simply point out that the most developed among them is the story of Pope Sylvester II and the transparently named Meridiana (Gualterius Mayer, *Nugae Curialum*, IV, II).

10. Alcuin, *Patr. Lat.*, CI, 635; CCX, 127–128.

blazing lull of noon, that is, if it is true that mental life, and perhaps nervous life in general, tends toward abatement, invariance, and the suppression of "internal tension produced by excitations."[11] According to biologists, life and consciousness are burdensome conquests for unorganized matter which, for internal reasons, always tends toward the resumption of its primitive, inanimate state. This would explain the Nirvana complex—the essential desire to achieve a mode of being that is both a state of paroxysm and of resignation. No complex is more basic or irreducible. If the hour of noon supplies a tangible medium to this kind of need, then the hour may surely count on the loyal complicity of the human heart to guarantee its prestige. For "it should be said that sloth is a sort of beatitude of the soul, which consoles it for every loss and replaces every possession."[12]

11. Sigmund Freud, *Essays in Psychoanalysis*, French trans. (1927), 70. See also studies by A. Weissmann: *Uber die Dauer des Leben* (1882); *Uber Leben und Tod* (1892). Living substance contains a part that is always virtually dead, the *soma*, to which correspond the instincts leading from life to death. It also contains a part that is potentially immortal, the germinal cells, which tend to continuously surround themselves with a new *soma*, and which sustain the instincts directed toward the renewal of life.

12. La Rochefoucauld, *Réflexion* CCXC of the 1665 edition (eliminated in subsequent editions).

Introduction to "For a Militant Orthodoxy: The Immediate Tasks of Modern Thought"

"The Function of Myth" viewed mythical transgression as a functionalist response to the repressive constraints of collective order. "For a Militant Orthodoxy" defines the problem of contemporary France, on the contrary, as excessive disorder or anarchy (see introduction). Caillois's introduction to *Le Mythe et l'homme*, drafted in June 1937, in the early days of the College of Sociology, explained that the essays pursued a gradual progression from "indicative" to "imperative"—"as the object of study approached contemporary realities."[1] And although "For a Militant Orthodoxy" was not written after all the rest, its status as the conclusion cast it as the truly contemporary and *imperative* study. Here Caillois dreams of a scientific heterodox "orthodoxy"—or contemporary counterpart to myth—that might compel people's intellect as well as their emotions and thus remedy the decadent, that is to say, disintegrating, collectivity.

Favored by Bataille, who had recently drafted his own doctrinal guidelines for Acéphale (see "Aggressiveness as a Value"), this essay employs a brutally intemperate tone that likely echoes Baudelaire, who judged works not with "the nuances of a man of taste, but with the *pious rages [pieuses colères]* (that's his own expression) of a member of some Holy Office."[2] Thus wrote Caillois at the time, to underscore Baudelaire's ethical stance. As for the scientistic dimension of Caillois's project, this was quite typical of the group and journal for which it was conceived: *Inquisitions: Organe de recherche de la phénoménologie humaine* (see introduction). At the initial meeting on January 8, 1936, Tzara declared, "It is urgent that a new current of ideas should be able to take hold, chiefly characterized by its stirring, affective grip on people's emotions." The journal's task, he claimed, was to develop a theoretical superstructure based on the social sciences. Such a process of "generalization" (see introduction) would somehow operate as an intellectual branch of the Popular Front—as a correlative to the latter's transcendance, or overcoming, of sectarian politics. More-

"Pour une orthodoxie militante: les tâches immédiates de la pensée moderne," *Inquisitions* 1 (June 1936): 6–14.

over, because the "exact" sciences far surpassed the "human" sciences, Tzara declared, *Inquisitions* should apply the "cohesion" and "universalization" of the mathematical sciences to the study of human phenomenology. It would thus properly position man in the scheme of things and embrace the "totality" of interdisciplinary intellectual life "expressing the present revolutionary period." And although this project was aligned with the Popular Front, the members of Inquisitions were to abstain from politics as such, abiding in "the specific sphere of the superstructure."[3]

Much like Tzara's proposal, and like Bachelard's model of "surrationalism" in a prefatory article composed at Caillois's request, militant orthodoxy is an *open* and infinitely expandable structure. Rejecting Hegelian dialectics, "For a Militant Orthodoxy" articulates its basic form on the model of "generalization." However, unlike scientific or philosophical generalization, this systematization also had the emotional efficacy of Sorelian myth. Caillois explained in 1971:

> To my mind, the word "orthodoxy" is rather close to the word "inquisition," namely, I thought that if a doctrine developed in a rigorous way, then it could have, indeed it *should* have the ambition of becoming actual fact. Of course, this was sheer fantasy. . . . "For a Militant Orthodoxy" is the text that led to . . . the founding of the College of Sociology, which was fundamentally *activist*, as we said at the time. That is, we desired a mode of thought that would impress itself upon the real and would trigger a whole series of phenomena in the real—with the sacred being the chief one, the contagious spread of the sacred being the most important one.[4]

In 1936, logical positivist attacks on "the poeticization of concepts" notwithstanding (see introduction), Caillois envisioned "activist" doctrine. This term denoted the status of the theory itself relative to the world rather than any individual agency or ideological *engagement*. In this scientific sense, "activist" was the antonym of "determinist"; that is, it *produced* rather than *predicted* phenomena.[5] It also had an epidemiological connotation: "'Activist,' that is, meant to *secrete* and bring about a contagious activity," Caillois said in 1971; he offered another definition in 1963: "We were referring to chemistry and to the sudden, fusing, irresistible nature of certain reactions."[6]

As for the term "militant," "One could think of the act of a political militant," Caillois recalled in 1971, "but I was thinking of the three stages of the church: the church humbled, the church militant, and the church triumphant."[7] In the context of Durkheimian sociology, Caillois sought to construct a unifying faith, the secular religion or cement of a reordered society. As described here, this ideology takes shape in a sociopolitical vacuum: leaders, perhaps, but no subjects, and no enemies. Caillois was likely inspired by the utopian ideal of sovereignty described by the Durkheimian Marcel Granet in his studies of ancient China, which *Man and the Sacred* puts to frequent use. In the Golden Age of "perfect humanity" before the dynasties, explains *La Civilisation chinoise*, the sovereign "is, basically, the author of an accurate and salutary calendar. His ministers act, inspired by his Virtue. He himself reigns, without thinking to govern. He works to create, or better, to secrete order. This order is moral, above all, but it covers everything."[8] It is the Maussian *ordo rerum* at the heart of Caillois's *Man and the Sacred*.

FOR A MILITANT ORTHODOXY:
THE IMMEDIATE TASKS OF MODERN THOUGHT

> In the confusion of these times, a few men who are déclassé, world-weary and idle but rich in native ability can conceive the project of founding a new type of aristocracy, which will be all the more difficult to sunder insofar as it rests upon the rarest and most indestructible faculties, and upon the celestial gifts that neither work nor money can confer.
> —Baudelaire

Anyone who undertakes to survey the modern world will feel averse to almost everything he sees. We know only too well how things stand in the economic and social spheres and, more generally speaking, in that of human relations: there is nothing to keep, everything must be changed. However, in the narrower sphere of intellectual matters, the crisis is equally profound. After years of praiseworthy efforts, the advanced forms of literature and art, indeed the very ones that had sought to liberate the mind, such as Surrealism, are now engaging it in semi-aesthetic activities that have ultimately become obsessional and purely ritualistic. Philosophy had always been focused on one single goal. Yet its complete lack of method or authority has now scattered its perspectives and concerns. This anarchical and uncoordinated research, which is incapable of cooperating usefully to establish a conception of the world, discourages the best will and firmest hopes. As for science, it is caught up in unprecedented problems that are making it question its most well-established principles. Things have reached such a stage that the rationalist spirit, which gave birth to science, now views it with horror as if it were some monstrous and unnatural, albeit voracious, creation. The rationalist spirit is very frightened by discoveries and theories in domains ranging from physics to psychopathology that poetic fantasy (which is so free) could not even dream up—to its shame. Methodical investigation has been forced to invent them whether or not it wished to, precisely because it is not free.[1] Indeed, its strictest duty is to undertake a thorough and continuous process of transformation; it must constantly alter its innermost structure by incorporating the particular nature of the obstacles it is reducing.

However, describing the shadows of this scene already lets us foresee potential light. For some of these very shadows indicate the *orientation* and others the *constituent elements* of what, we hope, will be a salutary reform.

Indeed, in a world where confusion usually replaces depth, where laziness and chance replace daring and lucidity, where carelessness is a maxim for government, and the most unfounded arrogance passes for genius—a certain vigorous resolve and strict implementation should suffice to win all the votes that count. As for the rest, it is in their nature to submit and follow suit.

* * *

In intellectual matters, the reform must be absolute. To put this into effect will take intransigent firmness. A while back I wrote: "There have been no limits to the audacity of *laisser-aller*. It would even have set itself up as a system, if the organic weakness of *laisser-aller* were not precisely that it can never, under any circumstances, become a system. But this does not matter. We must be just as rigorous today as others were complacent yesterday." I will never tire of repeating this slogan. *Nonetheless, we must consider every aspect of the problem*. A certain abstract and crudely reductive mentality (the terms "rationalist" and "positivist" here denote this sufficiently well) has obtained nothing by expelling into outer darkness all the irreducible elements of real-life experience that did not fit into its narrow framework. Such an uncomprehending attitude, which bore the seeds of its own demise, inevitably brought about various kinds of deadly results.

Indeed, the mind has always grappled with extraordinarily disturbing ques-

---

1. In any case, it is significant that the boldest and best-led attempts to destroy the *forms of sensitivity* and the *projections of perception* came not from poetry but from science, especially from relativistic physics. It has thus provided the most important contribution toward the enactment of the *long, immense, et raisonné dérèglement de tous les sens* [long, immense, and reasoned derangement of all the senses] called for by Rimbaud.

tions that it seems driven to resolve. *There is, in man, a full mantle of shadow that spreads its nocturnal empire over most of his emotional reactions and imaginative processes, and his being cannot stop contending and struggling with this darkness for an instant.* Man's stubborn curiosity is immediately drawn to these mysteries, which so strangely border on his fully conscious state. He rightly feels that any form of knowledge that denies them credence and attention, that deliberately rejects or neglects them out of indifference, thus irremediably betrays its own purpose. When positivism excluded these emotive obstacles from methodical research, they became the exclusive monopoly of emotional and sentimental forces that were unable to control them and, instead, found satisfaction in making them divine.

And so came about the disastrous tendency to endow whatever seemed marvellous and bizarre with every possible virtue, and to make it one's task to keep it marvellous and bizarre. Following Rimbaud, people took pleasure in viewing their mind's disorder as quite sacred; unlike Rimbaud, though, they were not lucid enough to admit this bluntly, nor did they have the courage to withdraw from this futile game. It is high time we broke with this form of intellectual hedonism. Of course, mystery has much to account for, and many confessions to make. But this can be obtained neither by indulging it nor by adopting some sort of ecstatic stance, for here, once again, heaven belongs to the violent.

It is true that certain other people show themselves favorably inclined toward the pointless pleasures of conceding to the unknown a particular transcendant superiority over discursive modes of thought. They claim to supersede these modes, gaining direct access to the unintelligible through some *sudden shift*, in a radical break with the continuous deployment of the intellect.

However, it is hard to see what principle would allow us to conclude that something not understood is therefore incomprehensible. At the very least, this approach shows too little faith in the mind's perfectibility, and it is too attached to current intellectual frameworks that it unwisely thinks cannot be expanded. *Moreover, it is unlikely that a world that presents itself as a universe in every respect should contain an insuperable rift between what is perceived and the forms of apperception.* Last, transcendental apprehension, in practice, involves abruptly and fully discarding prior intellectual frameworks, while nothing proves that we would not do better to conserve the current syntax of understanding on condition that we expand it whenever necessary. It is unwise, to say the very least, to give up what we possess for what we merely imagine: the result could be very disappointing. Above and beyond the various kinds of suspicion that systematized thought has successfully brought to bear on the intellectual modes claiming to supersede it, it is in any case more expedient not to forsake an operational base that provides a very adequate starting point for an indefinite process of theoretical expansion.[2]

Besides, it is a fact that modern circumstances no longer allow us to rest content with the *illuminations* that I have elsewhere described, scarcely improving upon Fichte, as scattered, unstable, and unconfirmed; that are nothing without some prior act of faith—that are pleasurable, in fact, only because of the credence we attach to them.[3] It is futile to oppose them as such to logic or to a systematic mode of thought. The adversary must be defeated with its own weapons, by means of more rigorous coherence and more fine-grained systematization: by means of a construction that both implicates and explicates its object, rather than itself being reduced and decomposed by the latter. This process of *generalization*, whereby Riemann's geometry resorbed Euclidian geometry and relativist physics that of Newton, taking them as particular cases of a more comprehensive synthesis, shows the real path to pursue.[4] There is no longer any doubt in any field as to the outcome of the rivalry between the systematic and the rational—meaning, by this latter term, the formal nature of intellectual intuition vis-à-vis the content of experience.[5] The rational gave in to the exigencies of systematization on every count. It could not have been otherwise, for systematization is what determines the different stages of the rational. Knowledge never makes any such advance without becoming enriched through its conquests and assimilating the main part of their substance. Due to this continuous process of integration, the explanatory principle is always in every way superior to what it is explaining, and it thus always possesses the fundamental character of legitimate research. That which, in the *battle of*

2. I shall not retain these suspicions here, for when two modes of thought are opposed, it is pointless to draw an argument from one against the other, and vice versa. It is preferable to examine the drawbacks intrinsic to each one.

3. See Fichte, *Grundzüge des gegenwärtigen Zeitalters,* 8th lesson. I have summarized the philosopher's argument and commented on it in a special issue of *Cahiers du Sud* devoted to German Romanticism (1937). Roger Caillois, *Procès intellectuel de l'art,* 1st ed. (1935), 10.

4. Because too many people are still attached, if not to Aristotelian logic, then at least to the Hegelian dialectic, I would underscore that Bolyai and Lobatchevsky do not negate Euclid, nor does Einstein negate Newton, and that the conversion of contradictories does not permit us to move from the system of one thinker to that of another. I am referring, rather, to *generalization,* which is completely different. See also Gaston Bachelard, *Le Nouvel Esprit scientifique* (Paris, 1934).

5. Ph. Frank similarly defines common sense as the desire to make experimental facts fit the cosmology of classical philosophy. *Théorie de la connaissance et physique moderne* (Paris, 1934), 18.

strengths, guarantees its prestigious supremacy: *that it accounts for everything, while nothing accounts for it.*

Given such firm foundations, methodical research has nothing to fear either from the so-called more positive systems or from the various intuitionisms, and it may aspire to laying down the law for them both. It is in this sense that, without seeming too arrogant, one might speak of a *militant orthodoxy* that would exclusively derive its authority from the firmness of its principles, the rigor of their implementation, *and the appeal of its demands*. This would mean splendidly burning all bridges to distinguish oneself from mediocrity and counterfeit. In fact, there is no reason not to be brutal, for it is the very negation of order that rye grass should enjoy the same rights as good wheat, and a sound mind shudders at the prospect that weakness or inconsistency (if granted the same respect as strength and coherence) should ever submerge them with the volume and weight of their daily output. To be sure, not everyone applauds the wish to apply Nietzsche's injunction "Be harsh" to the intellectual sphere. But those who oppose it are all too justified in dreading its enactment. As for those who have nothing to fear, they would be at fault if they did not use it to decry and rightly vilify their adversaries.

* * *

We must therefore deal very strictly with people who prove incapable of weaning themselves. If we do not want our work to be pointless, we must view this intellectual reform as one that can be *generalized to all fields of human activity*, and we must work toward that end. It is not irrelevant to consider this goal, however premature it may seem, for grasping a project's full extent usually generates some energy that can immediately be put to use.

Besides, real intellectual intransigence cannot help but align itself with moral intrasigence. No intellectual movement is ever founded without forging a tight bond between these two forms of rigor. It is significant that in the past century, the writers whose intellectual stance developed the greatest attractive force—Baudelaire, Rimbaud, and Lautréamont—were also the ones whose moral position often strikes us as exemplary, given the characteristics of their time. However, there no longer exists any order or authority that would indict an intellectual who transgresses reason or mores, because licence passes for virtue in these matters, and *le dérèglement* [derangement] is deemed admirable fantasy. Therefore, *neither great creative genius nor great courage is required to turn revolt into some kind of civil status*. For this merely means assuming a comfortable position that still enjoys the prestige it acquired in heroic times on account of men who would currently repudiate (for their routine lives and complacency) those most eagerly claiming to succeed them. In fact, all three writers seem to have deliberately and dramatically disavowed such people ahead of time. The first with his entire critical corpus; the second with his *Saison en enfer*; and the third with his *Préface aux poésies*.

The moral values they defended (violent ones, to be sure, but also of loyalty and honor) were insurrectional only by force of circumstance, when they met with the unbearable oppression of unworthy constraints. At present, the field is clear and the most sustained efforts seem solely focused on perpetuating anarchy. Hence, the values with greatest plenitude and purest prestige are the ones that should go on the attack and ensure that *the worldview they reflect be seen not as a disordered chaos of conflicting demands, but rather as the only one capable of founding an order that could take account of man's irreducible needs.*

This moral rigor must be immediately put into effect in the realm of intellectual research, which from the outset requires probity that resists seduction and firmness that does not readily tolerate the desire to please. Indeed, there is an ethics of knowledge without which knowledge deserves neither tribute nor sacrifice—and could obtain neither. For a particular knowledge to merit being elevated to the status of *orthodoxy*, it is not sufficient that it be immune to all methodological criticism. Far from being irrelevant to human sensitivity, furthermore, it has to *exert a direct and imperative attraction on the latter and prove capable of mobilizing it instantly.*[6]

This is why moral guarantees are just as crucial as intellectual ones. Besides, how could one maintain and furnish intellectual guarantees if these were no longer being kept up by the strictest conscience in the whole conduct of one's life? Indeed, because man's constitution is so *unitary*, a concession on any one point would inevitably entail laxity toward the others.

As a matter of fact, to hope for an *orthodoxy* simply means *presuming that there exists an ideal unitary undertaking*, that which aims to put man's *full being* into play so that its different functions partake in a process of vital and continuous creation. This would especially gratify man's basic urges because instead of granting them partial, disparate, and scattered sustenance, it would be capable of organically binding together their honor just as it had united their efforts. Their demands would thereby gain more certitude and force, as their coherence and solidarity would now be clearly tried and true.

6. Indeed, the only difference between ordinary scientific knowledge and the particular kind of knowledge described here is that any result of the latter is also, by definition, a question of values and thus exerts some influence on the emotions. Whence the *aggressive* aspect of every orthodoxy.

This involves the most distant prospect, the most unlikely expectation. The immediate task at hand, which currently demands our energies, is just as modest and specific as these aims seem grandiose and, perhaps, vague. Nevertheless, the point of departure and the final goal share a common axiom of rigor. This should already suffice for their filiation to stand out quite clearly against the general complacency. From the very moment that war was declared, its ends had to be made clear: the slow and sound elaboration of a doctrine whose exactness lies not only in the sphere of philosophical truth but also in that of affective gratification and which, while granting to each individual *the certitude of his destiny*, also provides him with a moral injunction for all conflicts and the technical solution to all difficulties.

Lucifer at the College of Sociology

Introduction to "Interview with Gilles Lapouge, June 1970"

Conducted eight years before Caillois's death, this interview offers an intimate portrait of Bataille and of the College of Sociology. It highlights their crucial disagreement about reenchanting modernity in Paris between 1937 and 1939. To use Schiller's familiar distinction, if Caillois was "sentimental," Bataille was "naïve." Influential in this regard was the Russian-born philosopher Alexandre Kojève, whose renowned Hegel seminar in the 1930s launched a new current of Hegelianism in the French avant-garde. Caillois was not a follower of Kojève. There is little evidence that he attended the seminars on Hegel's *Phenomenology of Spirit*, and he portrayed the master/slave relationship in a manner clearly hostile to any Kojèvian/Hegelian approach (see "Agressiveness as a Value"). And yet, Caillois was struck—if not fully swayed—by Kojève's skepticism regarding the College of Sociology and, in particular, Acéphale. Here is a slightly expanded version (also from 1970) of the crucial dialogue he recounts between Bataille and Kojève: "Bataille barely hid his intent to recreate a virulent and devastating sacred, whose epidemic contagious spread would ultimately overcome and exalt the person who had first strewn its seeds. During one of our private meetings, he revealed this to Alexandre Kojevnikov . . . [who] answered that such a miracle worker could not possibly be transported, in his turn, by the sacred he had wittingly triggered any more than a magician could ever convince himself that magic existed by marvelling at his own tricks." As for the question of human sacrifice and the exonerating note from the consenting victim acquired by Bataille (see introduction), Caillois also recalled in 1970, "Such a ploy, although certainly quite useful, did not fit well with the savage explosion of the sacred that was supposed to reinvigorate a society without fervor. I thought back on Kojevnikov's objection and became even more reticent."[1]

Caillois and Kojève were hardly alone in resisting the call of the sacred proffered by Bataille. Perhaps most striking were the arguments voiced after the fact by a former member of Acéphale, Pierre Andler (alias Harry Dugan), who

---

"Entretien avec Gilles Lapouge," in *Roger Caillois: "Cahiers de Chronos,"* ed. Jean-Clarence Lambert (Paris: Editions de la Différence, 1991).

wrote to another former member in 1947: "There is necessarily a lie at the basis of any 'acephalic' attempt—no discipline (made up of consciousness) lets one destroy consciousness. To consciously deny consciousness borders on the grotesque. (In ecstasy, it is not the head that disappears, it's the body. We are constituted as consciousness of what we are, we are nothing but consciousness. The death of God does not create the Acéphale; on the contrary, it makes the head weigh heavily on the shoulders. The dagger and the flame and the skull and the labyrinth are nowhere if not inside this head, which does not only reason, or see—but which looks.)"[2]

INTERVIEW WITH GILLES LAPOUGE, JUNE 1970

The College of Sociology was one of the crucial stages in the itinerary of Georges Bataille. The year was 1937: Roger Caillois and Michel Leiris, who had both left Surrealism a few years earlier, joined Bataille in founding the College. It was devoted to the study of closed groups: societies of men in primitive populations, initiatory communities, heretical or orgiastic sects, and monastic or military orders. Regular meetings were held during 1937, 1938, and 1939; but then the war interrupted its activities. After the war, Caillois and Bataille met up again. Their paths would henceforth diverge, but their friendship endured. In agreeing to tell us about the brief but fascinating experience of the College of Sociology, Roger Caillois has also drawn a portrait of Georges Bataille.

How did we meet? I had already left the Surrealist group. It was around 1934–1935, and an article that Bataille wrote in *Critique sociale* on the idea of expenditure struck me as very revealing. It prefigured the main books Bataille would write later on, such as *La Part maudite* [The accursed share]. Bataille, for his part, had noticed an article I'd published in the review *Inquisitions*. The editors of this review were four former Surrealists: two were militant communists—Aragon and Tzara—and the other two, Monnerot and myself, were more reticent. Perhaps there were too many editors; in any case, only one issue was ever published. In that issue, the leading article was by Bachelard, whom I'd introduced to Surrealism by having him read Eluard, Aragon, and especially Lautréamont. As for my article, I'd entitled it "For a Militant Orthodoxy," which shows how committed it was. I was envisioning a form of revolutionary thought that would not be restricted to the intellectual sphere, but would open out onto real life. Two other texts I'd written previously, *The Praying Mantis* and *Paris, a Modern Myth*, had also caught Bataille's attention. We thus had many things in common. Both of us thought it was necessary to set about transforming society through revolutionary action. We were, you might say, more communist than Marxist, or even anti-Marxist. Marxism seemed to us inspired by an excessively narrow rationalism, for it takes very little account of relationships that are instinctive, emotional, religious, etc. Revolution based on economic factors interested us less than revolution in the emotional sphere. We both attributed a great deal of importance to emotional effervescence, and this drew us together.

I first met Bataille at Jacques Lacan's home. After that we met fairly often, and together with Michel Leiris we had the idea of founding a study group, which then became the College of Sociology. We tried to enlist the help of Kojève, who was, as you know, the leading interpreter of Hegel in France. Kojève exerted a quite extraordinary intellectual ascendancy over our generation. I must say that he did not favor our project. I remember: it was in Bataille's apartment on the rue de Rennes that we explained our project to Kojève. He asked us what, exactly, we wanted to do. We explained. We wanted to conduct philosophical research, but philosophy was in some sense merely a front, or a form. The real project was to reestablish the sacred in a society that tended to reject it. We were determined to unleash some dangerous currents and knew that we would probably be their first victims—or at least, be swept away in the possible flood.

Kojève listened to us, but dismissed our idea. In his view, we were putting ourselves in the position of a conjurer who expected his own tricks to make him believe in magic. But we did maintain close ties with Kojève. He even gave a lecture at the College, on Hegel. This lecture amazed us, both on account of Kojève's intellectual power and its conclusion. You remember that Hegel refers to the man on horseback, who marks the closing point of history and philosophy. For Hegel, this man was Napoleon. Well! That day Kojève revealed to us that Hegel had been right, but had got the century wrong: the man who marked the end of history was not Napoleon, but Stalin.

But let's return to the College. We held firmly to the term *college*. It conveyed our desire to develop a mode of thought that would strive to impose itself in the temporal world, as it was obvious that the spiritual dominated the temporal. Our meetings began. The first took place in the dusty café of the Palais Royal, which is what the Grand Véfour was in those days. Bataille discussed the sorcerer's apprentice. I gave a talk on "The Winter Wind." Later, meetings were held in a bookstore on the rue Gay-Lussac. To give you an idea of the titles of these talks: there was *Sacred Sociology*, by Bataille and myself; *The*

Sacred in Daily Life, by Michel Leiris; *Attraction and Repulsion*, by Bataille; *The Structures and Functions of the Army*, by Bataille. I myself lectured on animal societies, spiritual power, and the sociology of executioners.

It soon became clear to us that, although Bataille and I fully agreed on the subject of research, we did not have the same way of dealing with it and drawing conclusions from it. Between Bataille and myself there was a very unusual communion of minds, a kind of osmosis with respect to basic issues—so much so that our respective contributions were often difficult to tell apart. But we disagreed as to what we wished to make of this research. Bataille was always inclined to move toward the realm of mystical experience.

I'll give you an example. Levitsky gave two talks on shamanism. The topic fascinated me, because in my scheme of things (that of Mauss), there was a complete antinomy between magic and religion. Magic is a theurgical act that forces the supernatural powers to obey, whereas religion essentially entails submitting to God. At that time I felt very Luciferian; I viewed Lucifer as the truly effective rebel. Thus, shamanism mattered to me inasmuch as it represented a synthesis of religious powers and the domain of things infernal. For his part, Bataille felt much the same way. The difference was that Bataille genuinely wanted to become a shaman.

This explains why Bataille always sought to couple the College with a sect possessing very precise rituals. In his view, the Sacred could reappear only through the celebration of rites. Some of these rites were rather impractical, such as the idea of celebrating the death of Louis XVI on January 21 on the Place de la Concorde. Others were less complicated, for example, the obligation—to which we held—of refusing to shake hands with anti-Semites.

There was another idea, hatched by Bataille, that the action of a group could be fully efficacious only if the initial pact of alliance among its members was truly irremediable. And he was convinced that to bind their energies together, it was necessary to perform a human sacrifice. I here refer to an episode that had less to do with the College of Sociology than with another group, Acéphale. Bataille was its driving force, and its sectarian activities have remained absolutely secret. I am not at all sure what transpired with regard to this projected human sacrifice. What is clear, though, is that it was easier to find a volunteer victim than a sacrificer, and so things went no further. I refer to this episode in *Instincts and Society*, after an article on the subject appeared in New York—an article containing totally inaccurate information.

This episode helps us to clarify the picture of Bataille. For him, this was no mere intellectual game or provocative slogan, it was a carefully pondered action. There was nothing in common between the "simplest Surrealist act" as defined by Breton—an act of randomly shooting into a crowd—and the ritual sacrifice of a consenting victim that Bataille had in mind.

In this sense, the power wielded by Bataille was not at all a quasi-political power, such as Breton exercised over the Surrealist group. Bataille's power was more charismatic in nature: a form of influence. He was a strange, placid, almost clumsy man, but his very awkwardness had something fascinating about it. The oddest thing was this: though not irascible, this man was capable of flying into a rage at will, almost as a matter of technique and by himself. With no apparent provocation, he would fly into a temper that was simultaneously artificial and sincere—and extremely disturbing. There were numerous signs that, for Bataille, the College's theoretical research was simply a path toward an ecstasy that can only be termed religious or mystical—given, of course, that he was an atheistic mystic. Bataille's eroticism must be understood in a similar light. So too should his idea of laughter, an essential idea for him, of which he retained only the negative aspect: a kind of opening onto nothingness; in any event, a rupture, an "explosion."

Shortly thereafter, we were separated by the war. In 1944, when I returned to Paris, I read Bataille's book *L'Expérience intérieure*. The war had shown us just how inane the College of Sociology's endeavor had been. The dark forces we had dreamed of setting off had unleashed themselves entirely of their own accord, with results quite different from what we had expected. The war had probably made Bataille retreat into some inner world. For him, the pursuit of ecstasy took on mounting importance.

I saw him again. Our friendship had remained intact. At that time he was thinking of launching a new review and wanted to involve me in his project. But I wasn't satisfied with the formula he proposed. I didn't approve of his wish to publish only critical texts. I thought that we should publish original texts as well. This, by the way, explains the difference between *Diogène* and *Critique*.

Today, I view that entire period with detachment, but without the slightest sense of irony. Many of the ideas we upheld seem to me to have retained their force; for example, the recognition that Marxism, because of its basically "economic" emphasis, is ill-equipped to account for the different forces that deeply shape society. We wanted to arrive at an entirely new kind of society, in which the imperatives of instinct, emotion, and desire took precedence over economic ones.

Bataille was a good and kindly man. His unselfishness and generosity were boundless. He was as unlike a man of letters as could be. He always proceeded with great rigor. While his curiosity led him into extremely varied domains, ranging from eroticism to anthropology, from mysticism to political economy, he was certainly no dilettante. His culture and knowledge were vast and well-founded. I've tried to tell you the points we strongly agreed on, as well as those marking our differences. I must also say that, until the very end of his life, I always entertained the warmest friendship for him and an esteem that has never been belied.

10

Introduction to "First Lecture: Sacred Sociology and the Relationships among 'Society,' 'Organism,' and 'Being'"

These sketchy notes, which were taken by the young Jacques Chavy, a member of Acéphale, finally give us a clear sense of what Caillois presented on November 20, 1937, at the first public session of the College of Sociology. What Hollier tells us is that Bataille thanked "the previous speaker for the 'historical survey of sociological thought' that he presented," and that he was displeased, after the fact, by their lack of coordination.[1] Bataille complained to his young colleague that they had not achieved a united performance: "I suppose you were aware that the way we presented things yesterday was not equally well-prepared in every respect. It was altogether too improvised, it seems to me, too uncoordinated."[2] We now learn from Chavy's notes that Caillois was responsible for the "Bibliography" and Bataille for the "Metaphysics."

Caillois apparently framed his bibliography with opening remarks on "constraint" as constitutive of "the social"; with some unexplained references to E. Pittard's *Les Races et l'histoire* and François Simiand's *Statistique et expérience: Remarques de méthode*; and with a survey of "organicist" and "formalist" sociology. Here Armand Cuvillier's *Introduction à la sociologie* (1936) is very helpful, as its subsections on "Organicism" and "Formalist Sociology" offer roughly the same list of names as those mentioned by Caillois.[3] Moreover, Cuvillier cites Pittard and Simiand in the same breath when discussing the counterintuitive thrust of their sociological analyses: *Les Races et l'histoire* showed that terrible famines did not always trigger migrations; *Statistique et expérience* disproved Adam Smith's claim that the least pleasant professions commanded the highest salaries. Cuvillier then cites Simiand's remark about "patently collective" social phenomena: "If our results are not those expected by common sense, nor what armchair reasoning might predict, it is not that the reality they reflect is not 'reasonable'; it's that this reality involves *another*

Handwritten notes by Jacques Chavy, personal archives of Jacques Chavy. I have enhanced the notes by replacing abbreviations with full sentences or full titles whenever possible. When no title is indicated, I have provided summary bibliographical references drawn from Caillois's *Man and the Sacred,* his reviews of the cited authors, and Armand Cuvillier, *Introduction à la sociologie,* 6th edition (1936; Paris: Armand Colin, 1960).

order of reason."[4] Welcome to the College of Sociology! As for his closing allusion to the biological view of life as a "sequence of states of imbalance," this may look ahead to the "statics and dynamics of the sacred" with which Caillois will conclude the first version of *Man and the Sacred*.[5]

The following bibliography—broken down into "Animal Societies," "The Crowd," "The Relation between Societies and Individuals," "Power," "Secret Societies," and "Sacred Sociology of Modern Forms"—is quite important, for Bataille later described it as their "point of departure."[6] This extant record of Caillois's list makes it look quite earnest, excepting, perhaps, the crucial rubric "Sacred Sociology of Modern Forms." This includes little besides Sorel and Wilhelm Reich's *The Mass Psychology of Fascism*, which, curiously, is otherwise absent from the available documents of the College of Sociology.[7] As for the reference to Don Juan and Faust, this is clarified by *Man and the Sacred*, which features the pair (together with Napoleon in the prewar version) as "concrete symbols of the kind of grandeur and perdition reserved for those who violate taboos and are immoderate in feeling, intelligence, and desire" (see "The Birth of Lucifer").[8] The presence of Sorel's name in this category confirms his importance for Caillois. However, when I recently asked Chavy if Sorel had been of interest to him and his friends at Acéphale, he very clearly indicated that to their mind, Sorel and his ideas belonged to a bygone era: "No, he was a fellow from the nineteenth century!"[9]

FIRST LECTURE: SACRED SOCIOLOGY AND THE RELATIONSHIPS AMONG "SOCIETY," "ORGANISM," AND "BEING"

Caillois: Introduction

Need to study social questions
General ignorance of the results achieved by the sociological sciences. Urgency of these studies.
Until now they primarily addressed primitive [rudimentary][1] societies.

1. *Bibliography*. Objective presentation, which doesn't mean without any guiding ideas.

All notes in this chapter are the editor's.
1. Crossed out.

Above and overleaf: Undated pencil sketches of Roger Caillois made by Jacques Chavy during a meeting of the Contre-Attaque group (1935 or 1936).

2. *Metaphysics* [Bataille]

Social: What is marked by constraint (generally external) [in all domains (ext.)² nonfatal like a physical law].

Constraint—Sanction
Mystical sanctions: curse; excommunication, blacklist [index].³
Legal sanctions: execution; damages.
Moral sanctions: blame; disapproval.
Satirical sanctions: laughter; mockery.

E. Pittard. *Les Races et l'histoire* [Races and history].⁴
François Simiand. *Statistique et expérience: Remarques de méthode* [Statistics and experience: Methodological remarks].⁵

Organicism. Biologists:
(Henri Milne-Edwards).
Lilienfeld (Russian).
Herbert Spencer; Espinas.
A. Schaeffle.⁶

Formalist Sociology, which studies relationships and not customs.
Ferdinand Tönnies.
Max Weber.
Georg Simmel.

2. Crossed out.
3. The term "index" might also refer to the Church Index.
4. Eugène Pittard, *Les Races et l'histoire* (Paris: Renaissance du livre, 1924).
5. François Simiand, *Statistique et expérience: Remarques de méthode* (Paris: Rivière, 1922).
6. Henri Milne-Edwards, *Leçons sur la physiologie et l'anatomie comparée de l'homme et des animaux faites à la Faculté des sciences de Paris* (Paris: V. Masson, 1857); cited in Cuvillier, 32. Paul de Lilienfeld, *Pensées sur la science sociale de l'avenir* (1873–1881); cited in Cuvillier, 32. Herbert Spencer, *Principes de sociologie* [1876 Eng. ed.] (Paris: G. Ballières, 1879); cited in Cuvillier, 33. Alfred Espinas, *Des sociétés animales* [1877 1st ed.] (Paris: F. Alcan, 1924); cited in Cuvillier, 35. Albert Schaeffle, *Structure et vie du corps social* (1875–1878); *Esquisse d'une sociologie* (1906); cited in Cuvillier, 35.

A. Vierkandt.

L. von Wiese—relational sociology; concrete mass–abstract mass.[7]

Bibliography

1. Animal Societies
   W. Morton Wheeler? ants[8]

2. The Crowd

3. The Relation between Societies and Individuals
   Fr. Nietzsche. *The Will to Power*
   Emile Durkheim. *Suicide: A Study in Sociology*; and Maurice Halb-
   wachs. *Les Causes du suicide*.
   Edward A. Westermarck. *The Origin and Development of Moral Ideas*.
   E. Durkheim. *The Elementary Forms of Religious Life*.
   Lucien Lévy-Bruhl.
   Robert Hertz. "Prééminence de la main droite" (1907) [Preeminence
   of the right hand].
   Hubert and Mauss.
   J. G. Frazer. "The Scapegoat."
   Ph. de Felice. *Poisons sacrés et ivresses divines* [Sacred poisons and divine
   ivresses], religion and sexuality.
   Mythology: Tchernowsky; Marcel Granet.[9]

---

7. For Tönnies, see Charmet, rev. of *La Sociologie allemande contemporaine*, by Raymond
Aron. Weber was added in pencil. Georg Simmel, *Soziale Differenzierung* (1890), *Soziologie*
(1908); cited in Cuvillier, 57; see also Georg Simmel, *The Sociology of George Simmel*, trans. and
ed. Kurt H. Wolff (Glencoe, Il: Free Press, 1950). Alfred Vierkandt, *Kleine Gesellschaftslehre*
(Leipzig, 1923); cited in Cuvillier, 58; the bibliography to *Man and the Sacred* cites his "Das
heilige in den primitiven Religionen," *Die Dioskuren* (1922). Leopold von Wiese, *System der all-
gemeinen soziologie*, 2 vols. (1924; Munich, 1929) and *Soziologie: Geschichte und Hauptprobleme*
(Berlin, 1926); cited in Cuvillier, 59.

8. When Caillois argues, in "The Praying Mantis," that "myths are definitely not guardrails
set up at each dangerous curve in order to prolong the life of the individual or of the human
species," he cites "the classical work by W. Morton Wheeler, *Les Sociétés d'insectes* (Paris, 1926)."

9. See Friedrich Nietzsche, *Volonté de puissance*, ed. Würzbach, trans. Geneviève Bianquis
(Paris: Gallimard, 1936); see also Roger Caillois, rev. of *La Volonté de puissance*, by F. Nietzsche,
Inquisitions 1 (June 1936): 55. Emile Durkheim, *Le Suicide* (1897; Paris: Presses Universitaires
de France, 1999). Maurice Halbwachs, *Les Causes du suicide* (Paris: Félix Alcan, 1930). Edward
A. Westermarck, *The Origin and Development of Moral Ideas*, 2 vols. (London: Macmillan,
1906–1908). Emile Durkheim, *The Elementary Forms of Religious Life*, trans. Joseph Ward
Swain (1912; Glencoe, Il: Free Press, 1954). For Lévy-Bruhl, see Roger Caillois, rev. of *La
Mythologie primitive, le monde mythique des australiens et des papous*, by Lucien Lévy-Bruhl,

[4.] Power

J. G. Frazer. *The Magic Art and the Evolution of Kings.*
Joseph de Maistre. *Du Pape* [The pope].
Georges Dumézil. *Ouranos-Varuna.*
G. Davy. *La Foi jurée* [Pledging one's word].
Maurice Davie. *La Guerre dans les sociétés primitives* [War in primitive societies].
Marcel Mauss. *Seasonal Variations of the Eskimo.*[10]

[5.] Secret Societies

[6.] Sacred Sociology of Modern Forms

Don Juan?
Geneviève Bianquis. *Faust à travers quatre siècles* [Faust over four centuries].

Cahiers du Sud (Apr. 1935): 332–334, and rev. of *L'Expérience mystique et les symboles chez les primitifs: Pages choisies*, by Lucien Lévy-Bruhl, *Nouvelle revue française* (Aug. 1938): 321–324; the bibliography to *Man and the Sacred* cites only his *Le Surnaturel et le sacré dans la mentalité primitive* (Paris, 1931). Robert Hertz, *Mélanges de sociologie religieuse et de folklore* (Paris: Alcan, 1928); see Robert Hertz, *Death and the Right Hand* (Aberdeen: University Press, 1960). See the numerous references to Hubert and Mauss in the bibliography of *Man and the Sacred.* James Frazer, *The Scapegoat* (London: Macmillan, 1913); see also Roger Caillois, rev. of *Le Bouc émissaire*, by J. G. Frazer, *Cahiers du Sud* (Nov. 1936): 848–850. Philippe de Felice, *Poisons sacrés et ivresses divines* (Paris: Albin Michel, 1936); see also Roger Caillois, rev. of *Poisons sacrés, ivresses divines*, by Ph. de Felice, *Cahiers du Sud* (Apr. 1937): 304–306. Reference to Mythology: Tchernowsky or perhaps reference to Václav Černy—see below. The bibliography in *Man and the Sacred* (1939) refers to Marcel Granet, *La Civilisation chinoise* (Paris, 1925) and to Granet's *Fêtes et chansons anciennes de la Chine* (Paris, 1919).

10. James Frazer, *Les Origines magiques de la royauté* (Paris: P. Geuthner, 1920); trans. of James Frazer, *The Magic Art and the Evolution of Kings* (London: Macmillan, 1911). Joseph de Maistre, *Du Pape* (Lyon: Rusand, 1819); see also Joseph de Maistre, *The Pope* (London: C. Dolman, 1850); Caillois also cites his *Traité sur les sacrifices*, 12th ed. (Lyon, 1881) in *Man and the Sacred* and refers to de Maistre in "Sociologie du bourreau" (Sociology of the executioner) (1939); rpt. in *Instincts et sociétés* (Paris: Gonthier, 1964). Georges Dumézil, *Ouranos-Varuna* (Paris: Adrien-Maisonneuve, 1934); see also Roger Caillois, rev. of *Ouranos-Varuna*, by Georges Dumézil, *Cahiers du Sud* (June 1935): 499–501. Geoges Davy, *La Foi jurée* (Paris: F. Alcan, 1922); see also A. Moret and G. Davy, *From Tribe to Empire: Social Organization among Primitives and in the Ancient East* (1st French ed. 1926; New York: Cooper Square, 1971), cited in the bibliography to *Man and the Sacred*; see also Hollier, *Le Collège de sociologie*, 35. Maurice Davie, *La Guerre dans les sociétés primitives* (Paris: Payot, 1931); see also Roger Caillois, rev. of *La Guerre dans les sociétés primitives*, by Maurice Davie, *Nouvelle revue française* (Aug. 1936): 384–386. See Marcel Mauss: "Variations saisonnières dans les sociétés eskimos" (1904–1905), in *Sociologie et anthropologie*, ed. Georges Gurvitch (Paris: Presses Universitaires de France, 1989), 389–477; see also Marcel Mauss, *Seasonal Variations of the Eskimo* (Boston: Routledge and Kegan Paul, 1979).

Titanism.
Georges Sorel—
Wilhelm Reich. *The Mass Psychology of Fascism*.[11]

_____

Hubert and Mauss. *The Gift: Forms and Functions of Exchange in Archaic Societies*.[12]
Gifts with the constraint of giving back.
Not individuals, but collectivities.
Total phenomenon: religious; judicial; artistic.
Wealth, strength, prestige, mana.
Not only gift, but also solemn destruction.

_____

Life is a sequence of states of imbalance (biologist cited by Simiand).[13]

11. See Gendarme de Bévotte, *La Légende de don Juan* (1st ed. 1906; Geneva: Slatkine Reprints, 1993), cited in the bibliography to *Man and the Sacred*. Geneviève Bianquis, *Faust à travers quatre siècles* (Paris: Librairie E. Droz, 1935), cited in the bibliography to *Man and the Sacred*. For Titanism, see Václav Černy, *Essai sur le titanisme dans la poésie romantique occidentale entre 1815 et 1850* (Prague: Orbis, 1935); see also Roger Caillois, rev. of *Essai sur le titanisme dans la poésie romantique occidentale entre 1815 et 1850*, by Václav Černy, *Nouvelle revue française* (Nov. 1937): 847–849; rpt. in *Les Cahiers de Chronos: Roger Caillois*. See Sorel, *Reflections on Violence*; see also Roger Caillois, rev. of *Propos de Georges Sorel*, by Jean Variot, *Nouvelle revue française* (Apr. 1936): 600–602. Michel Winock writes that Sorel was invoked by many different political orientations: "Italian fascists, French fascists (both the real and the false ones) . . . partisans of Workers Socialism, who were opposed to State Socialism, Socialism of 'the intellectuals,' and Parliamentary Socialism." *Nationalisme, anti-sémitisme et fascisme en France* (Paris: Seuil, 1990), 334. Reich, *Mass Psychology*.

12. See Marcel Mauss, *The Gift: Forms and Functions of Exchange in Archaic Societies*, trans. Ian Cunnison (1907; New York: Norton, 1967).

13. Cuvillier cites Simiand's quotation of the biologist who claimed, "'In my generation, we had started out with a mechanical view of life; we were forced to acknowledge and seek to understand life as *a sequence of states of imbalance*.' And Simiand adds that this last formula . . . in his opinion expresses what is 'specific to and central in economic development' and in social life, generally speaking" (191).

11

Introduction to "Dionysian Virtues"

Why Dionysus? Manfred Frank tells us that well before Nietzsche's *Birth of Tragedy*, "already, in Euripides, Dionysus was called the 'new god' or the 'god to come': the god of future times to come, who safeguards the essence of religious hope for later generations after a mythical period has come to an end, and in the context of a rationalist view of life." But the return to archaic myth on the part of a disenchanted modernity seeks not "what is beyond perception" but merely *l'ivresse*, adds Frank. If this remark perhaps applies to Bataille's Dionysus, Caillois was closer, I think, to Ernst Bloch, who believed that the authentic Dionysus was hostile neither to the Enlightenment nor reason: "his conflict is only with the forces of permanence, being, established order and exclusion."[1] Of course, Caillois's intellectual framework was much more sociological and also exclusionary, as we have seen.

In "Dionysian Virtues," the term "virtue" (like "value" in "Aggressiveness as a Value") is void of ethical connotations: "virtue" is "*what binds together*" and "vice" is "*what dissolves* [loosens]." Roughly contemporaneous with "The Winter Wind" and "Aggressiveness as a Value" in the first half of 1937, this is the only essay that Caillois contributed to Bataille's journal, *Acéphale*. At a time when he himself was less interested in Dionysianism than in repressed "pontifical" power, Caillois seems to be primarily offering a response or corrective to Bataille. The preceding issue had specifically addressed Nietzsche and fascism: Bataille talked of Nietzschean festival as "the aggressive and gratuitous gift of oneself to the future, as opposed to chauvinist avarice, chained to the past," which Jacques Le Rider, citing Bataille's anthropological scope, calls a form of "Afro-Dionysianism."[2] Caillois's response, as in "The Function of Myth," is to proffer a historical caveat about the distinction between archaic and modern society. He had earlier argued that vestigial, modern Dionysianism was relegated to the alienated, individual mind; now "Dionysian Virtues" further insists that it undermines rather than reaffirms social cohesion when "enjoyed in a purely individual way." *Ivresse* does not intrinsically open up the individual to other subjectivities: it is a total state, which gives one the illusion

"Les Vertus dionysiaques," *Acéphale* 3–4 (July 1937): 24–26.

of power and existential intensity and fosters a violent attitude toward society. Unlike the "intellect," oriented toward conquest, *ivresse* opts out.

But what about religious ecstasy? In his concurrent review of Felice's *Poisons sacrés, ivresses divines*, Caillois emphasizes—against Felice—the distinction between *ivresse* and mysticism. If the first entails "an *isolating state*," showing up a certain lack in the individual's relation to society, "the mystic is an *isolated person* as well; and yet, viewed as a whole and in terms of its function, religion essentially seems to be a force of uniting, of communing; rather than a force of social scattering, on the contrary, it seems to be one of *supersocialization*, if I may risk coining a term, since the presence of the sacred is precisely what makes a community impossible to sunder." How can the mystic achieve a state of ecstasy that avoids the alienation of *ivresse*? Caillois draws a "fundamental contrast" between the *"function"* of the private, modern consumption of drugs or alcohol and "the shared consumption of the same toxic substances during ritual ceremonies in antiquity and in 'primitive' societies."[3]

We actually find Caillois praising the ritual usage of *peyotl* in a contemporaneous article. Reviewing Louis Lewin's *Les Paradis artificiels*, he first condemns the obsessional, unconstrained imagination that he implicitly ascribes to Surrealism: "Every delirium . . . is a world that is closed, unimaginable and inaccessible to other people, and which is itself unable either to affect or imagine them." (In contrast, consciousness is "supple enough to pursue the specific quirks of every folly, and aggressive enough to profit from this every time, thereby enlarging its domain.") And he also proceeds to enthusiastically endorse the *ivresse* of peyotl, claiming that this drug is harmless, nontoxic, and nonaddictive, and is nonetheless, "the most scorned of all. Of course, it does not provide any euphoria, or cheap sense of well-being." In peyotl's favor, Caillois argues that its hallucinations most deeply affect "the very structure of perception," without undermining "the faculties of introspection," and thus provide the only "truly usable" research into the imagination.[4] Moreover, an "unusually fascinating" study of the drug includes ethnographic discussions of the Huichol Mexican Indians, who, "made the plant into some kind of God and consume it ritually in the course of a prolonged collective quest and a series of magico-religious ceremonies."[5]

Approches de l'imaginaire (1974) recalls that he envisioned the modern world at the time through the works of Durkheim, Mauss, and Dumézil "that I would oddly mix with reveries culled from novelistic works, especially from D. H. Lawrence's *The Plumed Serpent*."[6] Could his initial fantasies of Acéphale, before it took shape as Bataille's secret society and perhaps more in line with Le Grand Jeu, have included some ritualistic consumption of the "lucid" hallucinogenic, peyotl? In fact, Bataille's group never used any drugs at all.[7]

However, Bataille and Acéphale may have been hard-pressed to avoid what "Dionysian Virtues" (and Baudelaire's *Paradis artificiels*) consider the real risk and temptation: the private pursuit of ecstasy. A former member of the group recounted to me that Acéphale "was something *nonviolent*, in the end, absolutely! . . . If it is possible to speak of excess it was insofar as each one of us could . . . move toward . . . seeking . . . let's say, ecstasy—*which* I did not reach, and which certainly *few* participants in Acéphale did reach. But that was the direction in which we were going."[8] Furthermore, Acephale's increasing secrecy and retreat from all sociopolitical action aligned it with what Caillois here calls the traditional "closed, local cults of the towns"—as opposed to revolutionary, historical Dionysianism, which was "open and universal."

DIONYSIAN VIRTUES

When the mind adopts a very severe form of self-discipline and laws that are *very strict at the very least*, it must apparently pay equal attention to *ivresses* and be disturbed by the mere fact of their existence. Indeed, it can never be fully sure that it will never experience any temptation or remorse on their account. In private, the mind can always keep itself in check and retain full control over any instinctual anticipations. In public, it can restrict the workings of its faculties to merely stating the obvious; proposing whatever can be expressed and defined; proceeding over fully conquered and assimilated ground; and suggesting only what is verifiable and already part of some systematic framework. Quite rightly, such austerity confers boundless power, and the austere mind acquires a cohesion that makes it impenetrable, like an army whose every tactical element benefits from the integral power of its total strength. Nonetheless, such a mind still feels the constant appeal of *ivresses*. As a matter of fact, it is likely to be even more vulnerable in this regard because a mind so tightly bound always gets swept away as a whole; it is too unified to divide itself up, thereby *cutting its losses* at the onset of vertigo. It could not conceivably remain any less integral in a spasmodic state than when engaged in cool calculation. Such a mind is just as ready for the first as it is practiced in the second, and it feels a sense of release that seems so explosive simply because it follows on an excessively high degree of tension.

Moreover, *l'ivresse* presents itself as a *total state*, whose domain encompasses the full range of human activities, at least in a virtual sense, as they all submit and fall silent even when it only arouses a single one. If we add that *semi-ivresse of superior lucidity*, described by Baudelaire, to those defined by Nietzsche, namely, the three intoxicating forces—strong liquor, love, and cruelty—we see at once that ecstasy can arise on the basis of anything whatsoever, and this without in any way altering its characteristically forceful sense of power. Whatever the deep effects of ecstasy might be, and whatever value one ascribes to them, they certainly entrance people, giving them the impression of having achieved the highest intensity of being (except, in a certain sense, for a few paralyzing toxins—which also nonetheless provide a feeling of intense and calm, albeit contemplative, superiority). And so people prefer these rare moments, which they immediately yearn to renew, over the rest of their lives.

Thus, beyond the fact that the various *ivresses* concern the individual in his most indefeasible self, they also seem to entail for him, in a natural way, a *violent* attitude toward society, and they may reflect certain problems in his adjustment to collective life. Here again we find an opposition (perhaps not the least important) between the *ivresses* and the intellect: the intellect is destined to conquer, and the *ivresses* are scornfully resigned to flaring up in isolation, exclusively for themselves.

Yet history suggests that this opposition is not at all absolute. To the extent that society cannot grant Dionysian virtues their fair share, that it mistrusts and persecutes instead of integrating them, people are reduced to acquiring— despite society—the gratifications that should properly come from society, and from society alone. Indeed, the essential value of Dionysianism was precisely that it brought people together by socializing something that, when enjoyed in a strictly individual way, divides them more than anything else does. Better yet, for Dionysianism, participating in ecstasy and a communal apprehension of the *sacred* was the *sole* cement of the collectivity it was founding; for the mysteries of Dionysus were open and universal, unlike the closed, local cults of the towns. Thus, Dionysianism placed the sovereign forms of turbulence at the very core of the social organism; when they started to decompose, society drove them out into the wastelands of its structure's outer periphery, where it expelled anything that could possibly threaten its cohesiveness.[1] The former development involved nothing less than the most radical revolution. And it is significant that Dionysianism coincided with the upsurge of the rural populace against the urban patriciate, and that the spread of infernal cults at the expense of the Uranian religion was due to the victory of the lower social strata over the traditional aristocracies. At the same time, the values switched signs: the two

---

1. In fact, in ancient Rome, Bacchanalia were prohibited, as being both contrary to the mores and harmful to the security of the State. As for Greece, Euripides' *Bacchae* (a document that, it should be said, is extremely tricky to use as evidence) shows clearly enough that the spread of the Dionysian cult did not take place without challenging the authorities.

poles of the sacred—the base and the holy—changed places. What had been marginal, with all the interesting opprobrium attached to this epithet, now became constitutive of order and *nodal*, as it were. What was asocial (or seemed so) united the collective energies, crystallizing and exciting them—it ostensibly served as a *supersocializing* force.

In light of this survey, we may now refer to *Dionysian virtues*—taking virtue to mean *what binds together* and vice *what dissolves* [loosens]. For it is enough that a single collectivity should use Dionysian virtues as its emotional foundation and make them the unique basis of its members' solidarity (precluding all forms of geographical, historical, racial, or linguistic predetermination).[2] This will ensure that the people they attract will deem Dionysian virtues unjustly thwarted in a society that seeks to ignore them, and which cannot suppress them; to make such people wish, and believe it possible, to unite by means of these virtues into an organic formation that can be neither reduced nor assimilated; and finally, to heighten their resolve to adopt this strategy, which is always available.

2. Here we should refer to an entire sociology of *brotherhoods*, which is unfortunately still quite undeveloped. We must point out two characteristics: brotherhoods exist as strong structures in a loose social milieu. They are formed by replacing factual determinations (birth, etc.), upon which the cohesiveness of this milieu normally depends, with a free act of choice that is consecrated by a kind of initiation and solemn admission into the group. They tend to consider this acquired kinship as equivalent to blood relationship (whence the constant use of the term *brother* among adepts). This makes the resulting bond stronger than any other and guarantees its primacy in the event of any conflict.

Introduction to "Aggressiveness as a Value"

With the demise of the Popular Front, Caillois would call for a group, or order, as a vehicle for "militant orthodoxy." Sorel was most likely paramount. "It is with elite troops," Sorel states in *Reflections on Violence*, "perfectly trained by monastic life, ready to brave all obstacles, and filled with an absolute confidence in victory, that Catholicism has been able, until now, to triumph over its enemies. Each time that a formidable peril has arisen for the Church, men, particularly adept, like the great captains, at discerning the weak points of an opposing army, created new religious orders, appropriate to the tactics demanded by the new struggle."[1] "Aggressiveness as a Value" thus offers a theoretical model for an elective community, which is a theoretical backbone of "The Winter Wind," presented to the College of Sociology shortly thereafter. The constitution of "an order" should suffice, in and of itself, Caillois argues, to create "order" (read: "militant orthodoxy") and rather magnetically "recompose social decay." The idea of aggressiveness is only aggressive—by which Caillois means conquering or contagious—when translated through the self-consciousness of a group into "value." But here again, as with Dionysian virtue, we confront a (Durkheimian) conceptual vacancy because such value merely expresses the social order itself. The initial set of eleven doctrinal guidelines for Acéphale (drafted by Bataille on April 4, 1936) had opened with an equally circular Durkheimian injunction: "To form a community that creates values, values that create cohesiveness." It closed with the Nietzchean command: "Assert the value of violence and the will to be aggressive inasmuch as they are at the basis of all power."[2] However, Caillois's theory of aggression was diametrically opposed to Bataille's.

On February 9, 1937, the document that gave Acéphale its explicit form, the

---

"L'Agressivité comme valeur," *L'Ordre nouveau* (June 1937): 56–58. Jean Grenier wrote about Aron and Dandieu's *L'Ordre nouveau*, that it, "has several things in common with *Esprit*. Both would like to block the formation of new totalitarian States—whether fascist or communist—where the individual is nothing more than one unit in the mass, a mere instrument at the hands of the State, 'the coldest of all the cold monsters,' Nietzsche used to say" ("*L'Ordre nouveau*," *Nouvelle revue française* 263 [August 1935]: 297).

Constitution du journal intérieur (Constitution of an internal diary), did not list Caillois as a member. Yet it revealed that an important meeting had occurred two days earlier, "in which Caillois took part [and where he stated] the principles that should, in his view, direct the formation of a group. After Caillois's talk, Bataille tried to show what a man in the throes of aggressiveness should experience in the wake of the reductions that Christianity and Socialism had sought to bring about."[3] Bataille read "Ce que j'ai à dire" (What I have to say), expounding at length on the need to live aggressiveness in a free and experiential rather than instrumental fashion (i.e., as harnessed to religion or to the fatherland): "It is likely that now more than at any other point in time, human existence needs to face the highly wrenching and overwhelming reality of aggressiveness."[4] Vincent Descombes has explained, in general terms, how Bataille's schema—conflating Durkheim and Nietzsche, or the profane with reason and the sacred with violence—is one in which "violence, just like the sacred, becomes a condition of human life. The philosopher who chooses reason over violence figures as a 'platonist,' an 'ascetic,' an 'enemy of life.'"[5]

At this session, Caillois undoubtedly read some version of "Aggressiveness as a Value" because Bataille wrote to Jean Rollin on July 17, 1937: "'If we are truly united, if we form a true community,' Caillois asserted in front of us, 'nothing will be able to resist us.' Caillois is unaware that we already form a true community but, in improvising, he expressed a belief that, in practice, turns out to be unfounded. Given the fact that the community among us already exists, we ourselves can witness the resistance which it encounters."[6] (This confirms Caillois's status as an outsider to Acéphale by mid-1937.) Moreover, "Aggressiveness as a Value" quite clearly contradicts Bataille by upholding self-mastery and self-discipline as opposed to unleashed turbulence. Here and elsewhere in his writings at the time, he recasts the Nietzschean categories of master and slave into those of "producer" and "consumer," which, as critics have noted, contain Saint-Simonian associations. "The Winter Wind" explains that these terms are more relevant than are master/slave to the contemporary world because they "simultaneously evoke the economic substratum and translate a vital attitude that, without being completely determined by this substratum, is often merely its direct result in the simplest cases."[7] For Caillois, the distinction first and foremost reflects the status of desire: "The quality of individuals can chiefly be measured in terms of how much they will give up for the mere possibility of greater self-mastery." This is quite antithetical to what he calls "the extravagantly optimistic belief that self-abandonment is sufficient to conquer the skies," in which we can discern a criticism of Bataille's Nietzschean elite.[8] Hollier correlates Kojève's Marxist and anthropological reading of Hegel with Bataille's notion of "unproductive expenditure," because in the initial fight to the death for recognition, the master—unlike the slave—is ready to give up his life.[9]

By 1938, citing La Boétie's theory of voluntary "servitude" (see introduction), Caillois was likewise concerned with the first stage of the master/slave dialectic, but specifically with the master's "existential impasse": the slave must be free for his recognition or submission to be valid.[10] Indeed, Caillois's "L'Aridité" thus states: "One works to free those beings whom one seeks to enslave and to render obedient only to oneself."[11] "Witty phrase no doubt directly inspired by Kojève's seminar!" writes Le Rider, while for Walter Benjamin, "[Caillois] has thus very simply described the fascistic Praxis.—It is sad to see a wide muddy stream spewing forth from a lofty source."[12] Neither commentator seems familiar with Caillois's attempts to explore this impasse in terms of gender relations in several texts, including a lyrical novella, *L'Aile froide* (1938)—through the prism of Corneille and Montesquieu's *Persian Letters*.[13] Let us first recall Kojève's influential sexual translation of Hegelian recognition: the master desires not the body but the free "desire" of the slave. It is perhaps not irrelevant, then, that Caillois speaks of imposed *jouissance*, which Hollier terms "rose-tinted sadism."[14] More charitably, though, Caillois applauds "that ethics of love depicted by Corneille's extraordinary *Place Royale*" where the hero "loves enough to wish, first and foremost, that his beloved should achieve independence and self-control—to wish to see her proud rather than humiliated." Caillois discerns this in André Rouveyre's novel *Silence*, where the female character by the end "understands the meaning of the stringent training imposed by her lover; and once she has become a predator like him, she thanks him for having forced her to endure this severe healing-process."[15] His own novella, *L'Aile froide*, on the other hand, depicts the tortured "existential impasse" of a despot with respect to his harem because he cannot bring about the paradox of a free slave. "Everything can be reduced to a matter of power and possession," declares "L'Aridité," "and here prevail relationships that are cruel, irreversible, and implacable."[16]

Indeed, "The Winter Wind" explicitly rejects the ensuing stages of the master/slave dialectic. For Kojève, the master is a consumer and his slave is a producer—which is precisely why the latter can dialectically "overcome" enslavement through work: "The complete, absolutely free man . . . will be the Slave who has 'overcome' his Slavery. If idle Mastery is an impasse, laborious Slavery, in contrast, is the source of all human, social, historical progress. History is the history of the working slave."[17] Such an evolution is what Caillois's static categories, grounded in the biology of the praying mantis, will categorically deny.

This essay expresses the author's personal opinion—rather similar to ours—about a crucial question. We suggested the topic to Roger Caillois, who was willing to voice his views. He is thus the first to do so from among those who, without being members of L'Ordre nouveau, nonetheless also believe that the current structure of society is unacceptable. (Editors' note)

A tradition of empty revolt and mechanical disobedience *should* currently make those destined for any kind of action view aggressiveness in a negative light, and rightly so. Given the attempt to make aggressiveness a virtue at all times, it has simply become an irritating habit, which seems both the mask as well as the revenge of impotence and weakness. It is hard to imagine anything quite so sterile as these fits of temper, which force themselves to disdain the intellect merely because they sense that they have all to fear from it. Some of these turbulent disorders, hailed as exemplary ways of life, lack any purpose or future; they do not really seek either. They attract attention (and only this) with their pleasant little scandals—equally made up of coquettishness and nervous tension. In the circumstances, anyone wishing to turn aggressiveness into a value has an initial duty to dissociate his own actions from these loud, episodic events. Turbulence can never serve as a strategic means of combat. Political parties thus renounce terrorism on an individual scale as soon as they see any real chance of coming to power. Certain kinds of sobriety are more fearsome than the lack of restraint.

The deep, irreducible root of aggressiveness lies in the will to boundless expansion that is inherent in any idea clearly grasped by the intellect and capable as well of exerting effective motor control over the emotions. There is no judgment that does not directly want to pass into action. Indeed, it should be said (against those who, with shameful indulgence, separate knowledge from action) that there is so little actual discontinuity between the two that any new realization as such means accepting one's responsibility and firmly deciding to act. Of course, it should be noted that ideas are born into a world that is dangerously receptive, with a truly excessive capacity for absorption. Thus, ideas do not have to contend with a sharp opposition that would force them to be more clear-cut and decisively to choose between surrender or resistance. Instead, they receive a welcome that is far too liberal and are hence assimilated (more securely than if by constraint) into what they were precisely supposed to fight. So the aggressiveness at their core is what serves to keep them independent, nonetheless, and to make them last. Yet aggressiveness cannot take on its full signification without a great effort of constant lucidity, even though it is determined by necessity. It must be just as transparent, coherent, sustained, and disciplined as people, on the contrary, enjoy imagining it as dark and murky, fleeting and capricious, indiscreet and agitated. In every one of his actions, an individual must know just what he is advancing and just what he is holding back. And what ensues from these principles must imperatively guide his stance on each specific point. The only valid and fertile aggressiveness is that of a cohesive, *unified* being, regardless of how brutal and unsteady this unification might be at the outset—and remain.

Both movements and ideologies can thereby acquire a measure of hardness that is abnormal but necessary in a crumbling world, a world that is menacing in the manner of a sponge rather than a wall. Thus, in a society with a tottering and loose structure, bodies can take shape that are almost foreign, utterly indigestible, stubborn, and opposed to the surrounding decay. In contrast (however small they themselves might be), their strong structure tends to disorganize and recompose this decay about itself according to its lines of force—just as large masses irresistibly attract less weighty and dense bodies into their own orbit.

Various considerations (economic ones being the least significant) lead one to divide people into moral categories as well, into those of *producers* and *consumers*. Therefore, it is important to stress above all that the consumers are infinitely malleable relative to the resistant nature of the producers. Indeed, at any given moment, the producers know precisely what they can concede and what they must preserve. They guarantee their life's worth through the value of the work to which it is devoted and find themselves in a situation where it would be wrong for them to maintain any fatal neutrality. For their opponents (whose chief strength is their number and inertia) would never trigger hostilities in which they would have everything to lose and which would reveal their deepest frailties. The lessons of history attest to this. Whenever a community of men has come together as the deliberate result of a mutual decision, a voiced common will, and a shared goal to pursue—rather than due to the enslaving or skillful effects of the past, or due to chance—this community (whether the Society of Jesus or the Ku Klux Klan) has always been ridiculously small at the outset. Yet it enjoyed a measure of success oddly disproportionate to such origins, and this success could hardly have been foreseen. Of course, these communities were aggressive by nature. But one should note that this reflects their structure's extreme density and unitary form, as if, to create order, it were first necessary to constitute *an order* in the concrete sense of the term, as when referring to a monastic or military organization. Hence, it is as if order and health tended to propagate themselves, *gaining ground* from one thing to another, like rot and decay, through a process of contagion.

For that matter, it is only right that the primacy of strength over weakness, of self-restraint over *laisser-aller*, of the organic over the inorganic should impose itself solely by virtue of the qualities inherent in their respective natures. And then, if there should remain—and there inevitably will remain—a residual set of people who are unmoved by example, it is no less right that once this form of persuasion has been exhausted, they should be subject to that of constraint—even if this might grant them the cohesiveness that they lacked, put them on the path that led their victors to triumph, and make them become conscious of themselves.

Aggressiveness is an obligation tied to circumstances and to the demands of an inner imperative. Yet leaving aside these two complementary aspects, aggressiveness has basically a single definition: namely, it is the attribute not of triumph but of legitimate conquest. It is hard to see, besides, what fatal sense of propriety would make an orthodoxy refrain from resorting to the secular arm.

Introduction to "The Birth of Lucifer"

Caillois's important preface to *Le Mythe et l'homme* (June 1937) echoes Mauss's *A General Theory of Magic* in defining the magician as a rebellious individual whose behavior, albeit infused with collective belief and superstition, is "disorderly, elective, criminal." Caillois, like Mauss, contrasts such private motivation with that of religion and its purveyor, which is "systematic, orderly, and required."[1] Caillois adduces to magic, though, Frazer's ideas about the pontifical will to power.[2] The opposition he draws here between magic and religion thus contrasts the "attitude of conquest" with "mysticism," or the "will to power" and "intelligence" with "sensitivity" and "passivity." Religion is "theopathic," whereas magic is "an attempt to extend the field of awareness to incorporate the suprasensible realm. This aspect, both aggressive and scientific, is why it is termed theurgical."[3] With the figure of Lucifer—prideful, fallen "light-bearer" of the Old Testament—he would seek to combine both.

"The Birth of Lucifer" paints a detailed picture of the transgressive Romantic individualist whose job in the late 1930s, according to "The Winter Wind," is to regroup with his fellow masters and fight society on its own terms. Was this lavishly illustrated text, painting Lucifer's turn from literature to action, both describing—and itself seeking to embody—the move from escapist to effective, and fascinating, literary exemplum or myth (see introduction)? In 1939, *Man and the Sacred* pointed to the devil as an incarnation of the sacred endowed with the dual powers of attraction and repulsion: "the tormentor also appears as the seducer and, if need be, as the comforter. Romantic literature, in exalting Satan and Lucifer, in endowing both with every charm, has merely developed their true nature, according to the very logic of the sacred."[4] Citing "The Birth of Lucifer" as one of his favorite essays, in 1971 Caillois specified: "For me, Lucifer, as his name suggests, is the demon or angel of lucidity. And I have always made a great distinction between Satanic and Luciferian."[5] Ambiguous though he may be, in other words, Lucifer is not Satan. He marks the move from "profaning" to "making sacred" described in "The Winter Wind," where Caillois calls for training an impulsive "sense of re-

"La Naissance de Lucifer," *Verve* (Paris) 1 (December 1937): 150–71.

volt" with "discipline, strategy and patience" so that the Satanic "spirit of riot-ing" will become the spirit of Luciferian conquest.[6]

"The Birth of Lucifer" provides a historical, theoretical, and mythical por-trait of such a persona, describing the rise of the *intellectual* in terms of Ro-mantic alienation. Whereas the Enlightenment philosophes, sponsored by the Court and grandees, lacked intellectual autonomy, postrevolutionary thinkers lost patronage but gained intellectual authority. The first generation of Ro-mantics took up the "compensatory" image of Satan: "the Angel of Evil, mo-tivated by the best sentiments." Their "ineffectual recriminations" were then replaced by the second, Luciferian generation of Romantics, in particular Balzac and Baudelaire (see "Paris, a Modern Myth"). This echoes Caillois's re-view of Václav Černy's magisterial *Essai sur le titanisme dans la poésie romantique occidentale entre 1815 et 1850*, on the Romantic rejection of Kantian collective morality for Promethean individualism. Caillois had harshly condemned Černy for disregarding the rise of social romanticism in 1850, when "literature, strictly speaking, brutally gives way to an entirely different activity, which is lit-erary only as a matter of tradition, convenience or blindness."[7] In a less his-torical sense, Lucifer also stems from Corneille and the Jesuits, who gave the playwright, notes Caillois elsewhere, "his theory of liberty, energy and of sub-ordinating one's will, instincts and feelings in order to carry out a chosen goal, despite every obstacle." He makes clear the current relevance of such a tradi-tion when he reviews Brasillach's biography, *Corneille*, and sharply faults the extreme right-wing writer's light treatment of the sociohistorical context, such as La Fronde—adding, "our time is witnessing the rise of other, more solid reasons, to be prepared."[8] Indeed, the whole tenor of "The Birth of Lucifer" is very grim; and when Caillois's Luciferian individuals bond together, they do so in the icy clime of "The Winter Wind," their only radiance being that "*sov-ereign irony at watching themselves live in the tragic moment*. This supreme de-tachment of strong men that Stirner mentions shows them their worth and as-sures them of the worthlessness of all those who would be incapable of equal elegance."[9] Such elegance is not sheer dandyism. In 1936, Caillois held up Montherlant as a key point of reference for the "honor-code of a moral aris-tocracy"[10]; however, by the late 1930s, he would assail the "fantasy," "mischie-vousness," "libertine behaviour," and "insouciant availability" of this writer's aristocratic stance.[11]

What kind of Satanism was Caillois seeking to supersede in 1937? I have suggested that it was largely Bataille and the "Romantic despair" of Acéphale (see introduction). The antithesis of Luciferian light and Satanic dark points almost too clearly to Bataille, given his first statement about Acéphale in June

1936: "What we are undertaking is a war. It is time to forsake the civilized world and its light. . . . Secretly or not, we must become entirely different or else cease to exist."[12] As for Caillois's highly critical comments about Satan's followers in "The Birth of Lucifer," emphasizing their ineffectual individualism, "lack of power, disorientation, and lack of practical sense," this tallies well with the available evidence regarding the conflict between Caillois and "the friends of Bataille" (see introduction). "The Birth of Lucifer" was published next to Bataille's "Van Gogh Prométhée." The two are interesting to compare. Over the next year, Caillois would imbue Lucifer with increasingly lunar connotations.[13] Even in this first sketch, however, the cerebral Luciferian self-mastery offers a radical antithesis to the solar, ecstatic self-sacrifice of Van Gogh's life and work: "what binds savage human fate to *radiance*, *explosion*, and *flame*, and only in this way to power."[14]

We might also consider the figure of Lucifer as a counterpart to the headless Acéphale, whose image, drawn by André Masson, adorned the cover of the publication, *Acéphale*. When thus viewed as a form of literary, avant-garde propaganda, like "The Winter Wind" (see introduction), Caillois's Lucifer could perhaps shed light on his aforementioned reveries inspired by D. H. Lawrence's *The Plumed Serpent* in the late 1930s. "It contained a whole theory of the sacred, and of the living sacred, the active sacred," he recalled about the novel in 1970, referring, in particular, to the "lyricism of its hymns."[15] It remains to be seen whether Lawrence's mysterious and provocative work about an artificial cult of Quetzalcoatl, launched by Mexican revolutionaries, and involving human sacrifice, played any role within Acéphale itself.[16] We have already noted Caillois's interest in the Mexican Huichol Indians' ritual use of *peyotl* (see "Dionysian Virtues"). However, this drug does not figure prominently, if at all, in *The Plumed Serpent*. A more immediate correlation is the rather demonic image of Quetzalcoatl, as embodied by the leader, Don Ramon, and as portrayed in the hymns Don Ramon creates for his countrymen: "Do you hear the rats of the darkness gnawing at your inside? / . . . / If the star shone within you / No rat of the dark dared gnaw you. / But I am Quetzalcoatl, of the Morning Star. / I am the living Quetzalcoatl. / And you are men who should be men of the Morning Star" (Lawrence 339). So too, Caillois's Lucifer, "more than ever represents the morning star in the sky of dawn."

Without addressing its deep causes for now, let us note that one of the psychological phenomena of the early nineteenth century with the greatest repercussions was the birth and spread of poetic Satanism, the fact that the writer readily sided with the Angel of Evil and felt that they shared specific affinities. From this perspective, romanticism appears in part as a *transmutation of values*. Gradually during the eighteenth century, then quite brutally after the French Revolution, the artist discovered that he was an outcast from the organized social structure. Because he had previously held his own place in society, he had remained there without exceeding its bounds: the pensions granted by the king and grandees freed him from all worries and let him dedicate himself to masterpieces, which were solely aimed at perfection. There could be no thought of contending with difficulties he did not even imagine. However, once the divorce between social structures and writer had occurred, the latter was abruptly left to his own devices; for the first time, he experienced anxiety and independence, the torment and pride of being isolated—or, as he expressed it, *misunderstood*. Confronted with problems, he acquired the ambition to solve them. Because he lacked any appointed position, he desired them all, but he did not wish to take upon himself any single one, strictly speaking, and become a sort of technician. He did not wish to renounce the right to pass judgment on all things, which he was beginning to view as his own role. Because he believed that he represented the intellect, he felt he had a word to say at all times and, if need be, a responsibility to assume. In so doing, he was already challenging those in power, running the risk of contradicting or hindering them, and already viewing them as a form of constraint.

Thus was born the *intellectual*, a type that would have been quite inconceivable at an earlier date. Although the task he sought to achieve was no doubt disinterested, he did not shun listening to the rumors of the forum. He was personally touched by the iniquities of the world and held some ideal authority accountable for them in the name of the intellect. To this turning point has been traced the end of art's status as a special finality. Thereafter, art would no longer constitute a self-sufficient activity. Thus was launched a crucial debate in the history of thought; it has not yet been fully resolved. Since that time, the relations between man and the world have been fundamentally unstable, in a way that currently overshadows all other aspects of the question.

The writer hence began to examine both himself and the world. He usurped the functions of priest, philosopher, and legislator; he tried to usurp those of the man of action and politician. The individual taken as the absolute point of reference and the highest authority was the point of departure and mainspring of Satanism, when—after European society had been recast by the ideas of the French Revolution and the Napoleonic Wars—it defined the program of a generation that had harbored extravagant ambitions and thought it possible to fulfill them, but then soon met with unforeseen, unacceptable, and disheartening obstacles. This dawning titanism was not the conceptual creation of a few isolated individuals. It was an authentic collective force searching for an image that could condense and *valorize* these acute and commonly shared aspirations, an image that would be a sign, incitement, and example. It was not long before the celestial projection of man's demands culminated in Satanic mythology. From Byron to Vigny the figure of the Angel of Evil took shape, driven by the best sentiments. He dispensed justice, was compassionate and humanitarian, and protected the weak; he was the born enemy of all power, scorned dogmas and morality, and was the divine representative of anarchical whims. He expected nothing from society and had no intention of sacrificing to it any independence, nor any of his most excessive and deadly impulses.

There was an underside to this coin. It seems that this ideal figure was merely a *compensatory image*—to which oppressed, maladjusted, and timid individuals would delegate a greatness that consoled them for their own mediocrity. This power and audacity were all the more grandiose as the individuals themselves were hesitant and weak.

And so, typically, this rebel's attitude was always purely defensive. Vanquished but not persuaded by God, he remained without any gain for himself, "a soul that dared make use of its immortality" and that, continually denouncing the wretchedness of the world and the injustice of the Creator, desperately opposed right to might.

Under the circumstances, Satanism first and foremost appeared as an instinctive and courageous, but heedless, revolt against the existence of evil and established powers. As an insurrection of sensitivity, Satanism regarded the intellect with suspicion and viewed the discipline it involved as unbearable chains. It held that any apprenticeship was a servitude, and that any constant effort meant the loss of some freedom. Proud and miserable, now seeking refuge in the nocturnal side of nature, Satan could there do little more than spread his tattered wings—those of a bat driven away by the light. Similarly, his followers seemed to assert the rights of the individual without being able to do more than despair of ever exercising them. Their disdain poorly masked their impotence, disorientation, and lack of practical sense.

Thereupon, a certain severity toward these ineffectual recriminations began to arise among more demanding individuals. They thought back to the unyielding energy of Corneille's heroes, the deliberate harshness of Montesquieu's *Sylla*. Balzac admired the Company of Jesus [the Jesuits] and wrote its history. Baudelaire, as a child, dreamed of becoming the Pope, but a "military Pope." The Luciferian spirit was born.

As his successor, Lucifer did not give up any of Satan's demands. However, he did stop performing the roles of the *maudits* and of the innocent victims of the latters' taste for justice. He accepted that force was the law of the world; he took stock of the rules of the game and, in adhering to them, became an adversary who was all the more formidable in that he thus remained less open to attack. Calculating and conquering, he did not believe that revolt was sufficient in and of itself, nor that bursts of instinct always led to victory. His lucidity, which he viewed as his primary and most powerful weapon, gave him a coolly detached and sometimes cynical indifference, which made him an accurate accountant of reality.

Lucifer is entirely focused on what is possible and undertakes it without delay. He is Satan in action; an intelligent Satan; and, in a certain sense, a courageous Satan. Like Satan, he is probably inclined to pessimism by nature; like Satan, he has probably been fed on various longings and indignations—which are not very dangerous to the extent that they already involve a kind of satisfaction. But with William the Taciturn, he knows that there is no need to hope in order to undertake—nor to succeed in order to persevere.[1] The single decision not to perish has made him decide to conquer and to make others perish. Although his passion drives him toward distant goals, he fixes the objectives of the day with a clear eye that nothing can blur. Discerning and enumerating the different means that will allow him to achieve these ends, he is as patient and precise as a geometer, as sparing of his moves as a chess player. He selects the one that is surest, most sober, as well as the most secret, or the most insolent. He is indulgent by design, disdainful by nature; he never forgives without visibly indicating his reserve, thus gaining the upper hand both by the understanding he displays and by the contempt he reveals. He is as troubling by virtue of the leniency he grants to others as by virtue of that which he rejects for himself. The principle of his authority is a severity applied only to himself. The ambition not to remain a slave makes him desire to be the master. A taste for not obeying gives him that for commanding; at the same time, it teaches him the necessity and nature of obedience. Having enough faith in his rebellion to

1. [William the Taciturn, or William the Silent (1533–1584), an extremely wealthy aristocrat, was renowned as the heroic liberator of Holland from Spanish rule. —*Ed.*]

view it as a future order, he does not tolerate any indiscipline, from any source, that might undermine it. Therefore, the full temper of domination inhabits this stubborn free spirit.

It is in this complex that the Luciferian spirit properly resides, as a force of darkness raging in the light. Perhaps one would not have thought that passion was more fearsome when methodical than when inflamed. Lucifer makes us perceive the extent of this error and, more than ever, represents the morning star in the sky of dawn.

14

Introduction to "Paris, a Modern Myth"

"Paris, a Modern Myth" develops Caillois's discussion of Romantic individualism in "The Birth of Lucifer" regarding the second-generation Romantics, such as Baudelaire and Balzac, who replaced aesthetics with ethics, in his opinion, and made literature into something "serious at last."[1] But here, he also develops another crucial aspect of "The Winter Wind," namely, its argument in favor of elective, aristocratic communities—as the only means conceived by figures such as Baudelaire and Balzac, "when the individualists of the last century imagined a sort of conquest of society (which they never at all attempted to realize)."[2]

Victoria Ocampo's introductory speech about Caillois to the members of *Sur* in August 1939 defined the College of Sociology as an attempt to explore the questions raised by Surrealism but, unlike the latter, with intellectual rigor and lucidity: through a "slow, patient, scientific" approach that, nonetheless, did not neglect the "passionate," "basic instinctual needs" at their core. Ocampo further explained that "the 'College of Sociology' deems it necessary to take into account the influence of political events, chiefly of the large movements of the postwar, that is, Leninism, fascism and Hitlerism. Those collective phenomena show and prove that social movements, today, extend beyond individuals and that they have their own laws. The founders of the 'College of Sociology' believe that given these postulates, and under these conditions, mythology can be defined as an interface between blind social demands and certain obscure needs of the human soul, such as those which psychoanalysis has revealed to us."[3]

To the decade's common question—What is the counterpart to archaic myth in modern society?—"Paris, a Modern Myth" offers, on the one hand, the standard reply that it could not be literature. Literature is precisely what happens to myth divested of its moral authority or collective coercive force, that has become mere aesthetic pleasure.[4] Yet, Caillois speaks, on the other hand, of the Luciferian literary sociologist, who strategically explores the collective, mythical dynamics of the nineteenth-century literary imagination. "The Noon Complex" and the research from which it stemmed had revealed

"Paris, mythe moderne," in *Le Mythe et l'homme* (Paris: Gallimard, 1938).

the mythical emotions associated with a specific hour throughout Indo-European history. "Paris, a Modern Myth" explores those tied to a specific place—presumably the reader's own home—and to a recent past.

Besides highlighting in general the emergence of a mass reading public, Caillois offers a historical, sociodemographic argument for the general shift in the representation of Paris around 1840, for what he calls the poeticization of urban life. This fantastic and epic cityscape inevitably gives rise, in turn, to the Hero who will undertake its conquest. The point is that "the elevation of urban life to mythical status immediately meant a keen commitment to *modernity*," that is, to reality, instead of the escapist strategies of the previous writers. As against the *mal du siècle*, and concomittant with the mass serial novels of the time, Baudelaire imagines a heroic, elective aristocracy, which resurrects the archaic *sacred guilt* of myth (see "The Function of Myth"). However, this transgression thrives on the return of repressed "pontifical" energy—which seems Apollonian rather than Dionysian. Left somewhat unclear is what effect, if any, these new literary myths actually had on their time. Generally speaking, with Baudelaire's "legendary translation of external life," Caillois is seeking to theorize an aggressive representation of society, which restores repressed instincts for power and aggression into reality, and which stands, in some sense, as the obverse of "legendary psychasthenia" with its dissolving effects. This duality foreshadows Caillois's theory of the novel as genre in *Puissances du roman* (1942) as a representation that alternatively undermines or reconstructs society.[5]

And then, despite Caillois's closing call for a "dramaturgical aesthetics" coupled with research into literary sociology and mass culture, it may be hard to grasp what he was proposing to his readers in 1937.[6] Perhaps the most apparent message concerns the well-known contemporaneous myths he leaves out and, thus, implicitly resists. Absent, one might note, is any Dionysian sacrifice. Absent, as well, are the great Parisian flâneurs of the Surrealist camp, such as Aragon and Breton—a Romantic "poetry of refuge and escape"? Elsewhere he clarifies the sense of "dramaturgy" by opposing it to "description," and of "exemplary" by opposing it to "objective."[7] Caillois wrote about Balzac: "The novelist thinks about the problems inherent in his society; and he suggests living solutions that are deadly or salutary in the form of his characters. To these, he restores the sense of the mythological hero: to provide in the realm of the sacred a precedent for dangerous and engaging action."[8] If Caillois sought to incite his intellectual milieu with such exemplary precedents as "The Birth of Lucifer" and "The Winter Wind," then "Paris, a Modern Myth" should perhaps be retitled "Baudelaire and Balzac, a Modern Myth"—as sacred precedents for the Luciferian sociologist. In any case, the essay certainly urges us to resume and fulfill, however lucidly, the dreams of past dreamers (and of D. H. Lawrence), rather than to awaken and free ourselves from them.

Readers familiar with Walter Benjamin's various studies of Baudelaire and "Paris, Capital of the XIXth Century," written in the latter part of the 1930s, will be struck by the numerous similarities with "Paris, a Modern Myth" in terms of the references and documentation (detective novel, political conspiracies, etc.). Benjamin attended talks at the College of Sociology and published some brief, dismissive comments about Caillois's work.[9] His treatment of Baudelaire underscores a tragic dimension that markedly contrasts with the aristocratic heroism of Caillois's poet. Likewise bridging the intersection of different epochs, Benjamin's Baudelaire is anything but a triumphalist figure. Rather than the lynchpin of a return to myth, Baudelaire here suffers that mid-nineteenth-century crisis when, on the contrary, collective experience disappears. Benjamin's Marxist modernity is the moment when art becomes merchandise, when objects lose their "aura"—a blend of ritual, festival, and collective imagination—or, more generally, their association with *Gemeinschaft*. As Gerard Raulet presents Benjamin's Baudelaire, he is, on the one hand, an allegorical genius whose poetry can partially restore "aura" and, on the other, a passive flâneur, painfully revealing "the price for which the sensation of the modern age may be had: the disintegration of the aura in the experience of shock." His poetry also expresses the deep psychoanalytic conflicts of his epoch. "It reveals modernity's unconscious by forcing the clashing simultaneity of old and new within modern fantasmagoria to its highpoint," writes Raulet of Benjamin's interpretation.[10] Any comparison with Benjamin must keep in mind that Caillois was never interested in the avant-garde dynamics of montage and its revelatory "dialectical images," preferring instead the analogical tradition of Baudelairean *correspondance*. Insufficiently alert to the problems inherent in his cult of power and "voluntary servitude," furthermore, his Luciferian lucidity was seeking neither to demystify nor to deconstruct but rather to revolutionize the reveries of idiosyncratic, surrealizing intellectuals between Blum's fall and that of France.

Behold the Holy City, founded in the West!
—Arthur Rimbaud, *Paris se repeuple*

Modern myths are even less well understood than ancient ones, even though
we're consumed by myths.
—Balzac, *La Vieille fille*

Surely a most perplexing aspect of the problem of myths is the following: it is
a fact that in many civilizations, myths have answered to human needs that are
so fundamental it would be absurd to assume that they have disappeared.
However, it is not clear just how these needs are being met in modern society,
nor what has taken over the function of myth.

Because one considers myth in terms of the imagination, it is immediately
tempting to suggest that literature might be the answer to this question. Yet
we should be extremely careful. If myth does have a certain kind of value as
such, then it is by no means aesthetic. To offer an appropriate description of
the sort of interest books arouse and the mental attitude presupposed by the
act of reading, we must stress above all that the first involves enjoying beauty
and the second, seeking out masterpieces. Literature may seem out of the question on this account alone, for it has a crucial corollary: that the communication between the work and the public is never more than a matter of personal
liking or of similar affinities—a matter of taste, of style. Thus, the final verdict
always depends on the *individual*; not that society has no influence, but it pro-
poses without coercion. Myth, on the contrary, was a *collective* property by
definition; it justified, sustained, and inspired the existence and activity of a
community, people, professional body, or secret society. As a concrete example
of proper conduct and a *precedent*, legally speaking, in the sphere of *sacred guilt*,
which was very extensive at the time, it was invested with authority and coercive power for the group owing to this very fact. One can further pursue this
contrast and assert that it was precisely when myth lost its constraining moral
power that it turned into literature and became an object of aesthetic pleasure.
This is when Ovid wrote the *Metamorphoses*.

There is nonetheless a possible connection between the two, for in principle
there are several ways to conceive of literature. Focusing on masterpieces is but
one of them, all things considered. Instead of attending to its most unique
achievements, one can envisage literature in a general way, irrespective of style,
power, or beauty. For example, one can attach a heavy significance to sheer
print-run statistics. Of course, this means deliberately privileging quantity

and giving popular literature a massive advantage over the literature of well-read persons [*des lettrés*]. Yet the analyst thus regains some measure of certitude and can better gauge his chances of discerning the laws of the genre, its main themes, and, especially, its practical implications for the imagination, for emotions and behavior. In short, the question is restored to a collective scale. And although literature cannot yet properly be compared to myth, it thereby becomes a force as well, like the press, for example—but situated on a strictly imaginative level. No doubt its action is infinitely more indirect and diffuse; however, it exerts the same kind of pressure, which is almost equally widespread.

Under these conditions, people wishing to study the ways and customs and the social processes of the imagination (either through the disinterested aims of knowledge, or intending to find something that could directly benefit the efficacy of their own action) inevitably come to adopt this very particular view of literature. Artists will readily find it rather detached, cynical, or contemptuous and yet quite lucid in part, perhaps even Machiavellian or, in a word, *Luciferian*—which, in effect, it is. Roughly speaking, this view of aesthetic criticism is akin to sociology's attitude toward a priori morality and that of so-called scientific psychology toward the rules of syllogism. Should we wish to name it, this will hence involve a type of *literary sociology*. And it will have some positive results for the literature of the literati. The latter is here not distinguished from popular literature, and one expects to find in both similar inclinations and appeals (when they are produced in the same periods and countries), even similar *myths* if need be (as this strategy stems from the study of myth, after all). Yet the specific merits of the literature of the literati are here objectively acknowledged and studied as significant factors, as well they should be. In other words, technical skill is analyzed as a form of superior weaponry; the halo of prestige, as a kind of influence peddling; and, last, the highest form of consciousness is equated with the well-known royal status of one-eyed men among the blind.

That said, it may then be acceptable to claim that from this vantage point there exists a representation of the cityscape that exerts *such a powerful hold on the imagination that no one has actually ever questioned its accuracy*. Albeit thoroughly derived from books, it is now sufficiently widespread to be part of the collective mental atmosphere and thus have a certain constraining force. Here we may already discern some features of mythical representation.

Literary historians have not failed to note that the urban setting was thus elevated to epic status or, more precisely, that the realist depiction of a clearly defined city (more integrated than any other in readers' actual lives) was suddenly exalted along fantastic lines. This can be observed in the first half of the nineteenth century, when the tone becomes loftier as soon as Paris takes center stage. At that point, grandeur and heroism apparently no longer had to dress up like Racine's Greeks or Hugo's Spaniards to claim our attention; to seem tragic, the tragic scene no longer required the distancing effects of time and space. The transformation was complete. The world of supreme grandeurs and unforgivable crimes, of constant violent deeds and mysteries; the world in which everything, everywhere, is possible at all times, because the imagination has sent there its most extraordinary enticements ahead of time and discovers them at once—this world was no longer remote, inaccessible, and autonomous. It was the world in which people lived.

This phenomenon (contemporaneous with the rise of heavy industry and the formation of the urban proletariat) is associated above all (to address the most obvious first) with the transformation of the adventure novel into the detective novel. It is a fact that the City's metamorphosis stemmed from the transposition of the *savannahs* and *forests* of (James) Fenimore Cooper into the urban setting.[1] In his novels, every broken branch signifies a particular anxiety or hope, and every tree trunk conceals an enemy's rifle or the bow of an unseen, silent avenger. Starting with Balzac, all writers have clearly signaled this loan and dutifully repaid their debt to Cooper. Works such as A. Dumas's *Mohicans de Paris*, with its highly significant title, are very frequent. This transposition is well-established, but the Gothic Novel undoubtedly played a role as well. Indeed, the *Mystères de Paris* sometimes recall the *Mysteries of Udolpho*.[2] The mythical structure quickly evolved: confronting the City, with its countless millions, stands the legendary Hero who is destined to conquer it. In fact, few works of the period do not include some inspired address to the capital, and Rastignac's famous cry [*"A nous deux maintenant!"*] is unusually restrained, even though the episode does contain all of the theme's typical features.[3] The heroes of Ponson du Terrail are more lyrical in their inevitable speeches to the "modern Babylon" (Paris is no longer called anything else).[4] Consider, for example, the speech of Armand de Kergaz in *Drames de Paris*, and especially

1. See also Régis Messac, *Le "Detective novel" et l'influence de la pensée scientifique* (Paris, 1929), 416–440.

2. Notably, in the dominant role played by cellars and subterranean passages.

3. ["Now let's fight it out—you and I!" from Honoré de Balzac, *Le Père Goriot* (Paris: Gallimard, 1971), 364.—*Ed.*]

4. This name probably has its origin in the sermons of preachers frightened by the countless dangers of perdition that the big city offered. One could undertake a sizable study of the Church's role in creating the myth of Paris, and of how the myth of Paris itself inherited a partly mythical representation of Babylon.

the one by that evil genius, the false Sir Williams (*sic*), in the *Club des Valets de Coeur*:

> Oh Paris, Paris! You are the true Babylon, the true battlefield of intellects, the true temple wherein evil has its pontiffs and its cult, and I believe the breath of the archangel of darkness wafts eternally over you like breezes on the infinite expanse of the seas. Oh unmoving tempest, ocean of stone, in the midst of your wrathful waves I would be the black eagle who affronts the thunderbolt and sleeps smilingly upon the storm, his vast wing outstretched; I would be the evil genius, the vulture of the seas, of this most treacherous and turbulent of seas, that sea in which human passions are stirred up and unleashed.

In these lines, where Greek scholars will be surprised to recognize one of Pindar's best-known images, we can almost discern the *insane words, though filled with infernal grandeur*, of the Comte de Lautréamont.[5] M. Régis Messac has already pointed this out. And indeed, it does involve one and the same Paris, the Paris whose taverns were described by Eugène Sue, and whose subterranean labyrinths he populated with characters that immediately became famous: le Chourineur, Prince Rodolphe, Fleur de Marie, the Schoolmaster. The urban setting becomes part of the mystery. Let us recall the exquisite lamp with the silver spout that shines "white, like electricity," slowly drifting down the river Seine on its way through Paris in *Les Chants de Maldoror*. Later on, at the other end of the cycle, in *Fantômas*, the Seine is host to mysterious glowing lights floating in its depths, near the Quai de Javel. In this way, the mysteries of Paris persist and remain the same: myths are less evanescent than we might think.

All the while, new works were constantly appearing, with the city figuring as the primary, though diffuse, character. The name of Paris almost always appeared in the title, indicating that this pleased the general public.[6] Under these

---

5. Here I merely wish to suggest the kinship of lyrical style and language. Moreover, the connections between *Les Chants de Maldoror* and the serial novel are already too well-known to have to emphasize them here. Even so, a serious study of the subject has yet to be undertaken.

6. Some titles should be mentioned here. I have selected them from M. Messac's bibliography: H. Lucas, *Les Prisons de Paris*, 1851; Eugène Sue, *Les Mystères de Paris*, 1842–1843; Vidocq, *Les Vrais mystères de Paris*, 1844; M. Alhoy, *Les Prisons de Paris*, 1848; X. de Montepin, *Les Viveurs de Paris*, 1852–1856; A. Dumas, *Les Mohicans de Paris*, 1854; P. Bocage, *Les Puritains de Paris*, 1862; J. Clarétie, *Les Victimes de Paris*, 1864; Gaboriau, *Les Esclaves de Paris*, 1867; X. de Montepin, *Les Tragédies de Paris*, 1874; F. de Boisgobey, *Les Mystères du nouveau Paris*, 1876;

conditions, how could each reader fail to develop the intimate belief (still manifest today) that the Paris he knows is not the only one? Is not even the real one? That it is only a brilliantly lit decor, albeit far too *normal*, whose mechanical operators will never reveal themselves? A setting that conceals another Paris, the true Paris, a ghostly, nocturnal, intangible Paris that is all the more powerful insofar as it is more secret; a Paris that anywhere and at any time dangerously intrudes upon the other one? This strangely present world is ruled by certain characteristics of childlike thought, in particular by its artificiality: nothing happens here that has not been premeditated for a long time; nothing is as it seems; everything has been prepared for timely use by its master, the all-powerful hero. And this is the Paris we find depicted in the issues of *Fantômas*. M. Pierre Véry has brilliantly captured its atmosphere. The typical hero, in his account, is the Man-in-dark-glasses: "The criminal genius, emperor of horror, master of preposterous transformations, a man who alters his face at will and whose costume, which is forever changing, defies any description; a man to whom no portrait ever quite applies . . . , a man whom bullets never hit, against whom blades are blunted, a man who swallows poison the way others do milk." And here is a page from the hero's life, as seen by the same author:

> He was the man whose residence, full of trap-doors and devices, has amazing elevators that link it to the center of the earth. He turns up in the middle of a field. A farm girl walks by—a goose-girl who is, who can only be, a sleuth in disguise. The other senses danger and retreats underground. Every hundred meters or so, all along the subterranean passages, there are triple steel gates which he opens with his little finger by pressing on a button. He proceeds through dens crammed with weapons and jewels, laboratories equipped with retorts, bombs, and infernal machines: and then he resurfaces, at Notre-Dame, by night. An altar pivots. It's the man in dark glasses: he has the keys to the vestry, and the beadle, who is his accomplice, lights the way with a candle. Now, on to the Louvre Museum. The Mona Lisa moves aside, and the man in dark glasses reappears. He has the keys to the main door and the iron gate; the watchman, who is in his employ, lights the way with a dark lantern. Next, the cellars of po-

J. Clarétie, *Le Pavé de Paris*, 1881; G. Aymard, *Les Peaux-Rouges de Paris*, 1888, etc. Naturally, we should also add titles such as Léo Lespès's *Les Mystères du Grand Opéra*, where the name Paris is merely implicit, and *Les Mystères de Londres* (Paul Féval, 1844), where it has simply been transposed.

lice headquarters: it's still the same man. The policemen, who are all under his command, pretend to be asleep as he goes by. Here again, he has the keys. He has all the keys.

Then we find him in a café, ordering a glass of beer: the waiter, who would sell his soul out of loyalty, slips a note under the saucer. The man in dark glasses calmly walks to the door. (It was high time: behind him a troop of police inspectors, brandishing revolvers, bursts upon the premises; this time they are not part of his gang.) He, meanwhile . . . etc.[7]

I apologize for this lengthy quotation, but its dithyrambic aspect, so well-suited to the subject, makes it hard to abridge. Moreover, as we shall see, it fulfills the idea at the back of the mind of the genre's creators. Finally, it marks a new step in the mythical description of the capital: the imagined rift between the Paris of everyday appearances and the Paris of mysteries has been bridged. The two Parises, which originally coexisted without being confused, have now been reduced to one. The myth had first contented itself with the facilities afforded by the night and the urban outskirts, by unknown alleys and unexplored catacombs. But then it moved rapidly into broad daylight, into the very heart of the city. It came to *occupy* the most frequented, official, and reassuring buildings. Notre-Dame, the Louvre, the Préfecture de Police turned into its favored terrain. Nothing escaped the epidemic: everywhere, reality was contaminated by myth.

By 1901, Chesterton had already pointed out that this transformation of modern life was first and foremost due to the detective novel: "This view of the great city itself as a thing of striking strangeness certainly found its Iliad in the detective novel. No one can help observing that in these stories, the hero or the investigator crosses London utterly heedless of other men and with an insouciant manner comparable to that of some legendary prince travelling through the land of elves. In the course of this adventurous journey, the banal daily omnibus assumes the antedeluvian aspect of an enchanted ship. The city lights shine like the eyes of countless magic sprites . . ." etc.[8]

What we have, then, is the poeticization of urban civilization and a truly deep emotional attachment to the modern city—which, moreover, was acquir-

7. Pierre Véry, *Les Métamorphoses* (Paris: Nouvelle Revue Française, 1931), 178–179. In addition to many detective novels, M. Véry has a remarkable article that appeared recently in the *Revue européenne* (May–June–July 1930), which displays an exceptional grasp of the modern imagination and is well worth pointing out.

8. G. K. Chesterton, "Defense of the Detective Story," in *The Defendant* (London, 1901), 158. See also R. Messac, p. 11.

ing its modern-day appearance at exactly the same time. We must now determine whether this phenomenon signals a mental revolution of a more general nature. For if this transfiguration of the city is really a myth, then, like all myths, it should be something that can be interpreted, and that can reveal destinies.

We already know what constituted the sociodemographic substratum of the period: a major increase in industrial agglomeration, rural flight, and urban overpopulation; the rise of large department stores (*La Fille mal gardée, Les Deux magots, Le Diable boiteux*, etc.), of high finance (Rothschild, Fould, the Pereire brothers, etc.) and of joint stock companies, etc. In 1816 just seven securities were listed on the Paris stock exchange; by 1847, more than two hundred. Railroad construction was actively under way. The trend of proletarianization was provoking its first crises, and secret political societies were quickly spreading.

Such a radical change understandably produced some degree of intoxication in minds already affected by Romanticism. But this time the shock proceeded in the opposite direction. It was an urgent, though no less lyrical summons from reality and present-day life. In fact, for the most lucid individuals, the elevation of urban life to mythical status immediately meant a keen commitment to *modernity*. We know what an important idea this was for Baudelaire: not surprisingly, he proved to be a resolute, impassioned proponent of the new outlook. He claimed that, for him, this was the "principal and essential" question: namely, to find out if his era possessed "a particular beauty that was inherent in new passions." We know his answer: it forms the conclusion to his most considerable theoretical work, considerable at least in terms of size: "The Marvellous surrounds and sustains us like the atmosphere; but we don't see it. . . . For the heroes of the *Iliad* can't hold a candle to you, Vautrin, Rastignac, and Birotteau—nor to you, Fontanarès, who did not dare to publicly recount your woes beneath the funerary and convulsed tailcoat we all wear;— nor to you, Honoré de Balzac, you, the most heroic, unique, romantic and poetic of all the characters you've drawn from your own breast."[9]

This was the first version of a kind of theory regarding the epic nature of modern life. Although its consequences were as yet unforeseen, Baudelaire would nonetheless spend his whole life pursuing it.[10] *Les Fleurs du mal* offers but an inadequate illustration. Perhaps this was simply a temporary expedient for an author who was then thinking of writing *novels* (he left us only titles) and

9. Baudelaire, *Salon de 1846*, ch. 18, "De l'héroisme de la vie moderne."
10. See also "Le Peintre de la vie moderne," "l'École païenne," etc.

who confided to his mother in 1847:[11] "On New Year's Day I'm beginning a new career—that is, I will create works of pure imagination—the Novel. I hardly need to demonstrate to you the gravity, Beauty and infinite aspect of that particular art." Later on, he would consider swearing that *Les Fleurs du mal* was a "work of pure art," but at the same time warned that this act would involve lying "through his teeth."[12] So we understand the spirit in which he invoked Balzac who, more than anyone else, developed the myth of Paris in the Baudelairean sense. Victor Hugo, in turn, yielded to the trend and wrote *Les Misérables*, largely a Parisian epic, and thereby showed how far he had come from the flashy exoticism of *Les Orientales* and *Han d'Islande*.[13] Like Baudelaire, Hugo did not view Balzac as a realist: "All his books," he observed in the speech delivered at the novelist's grave, "form one single book, a vibrant, luminous, profound book, in which our entire contemporary civilization can be seen coming and going, walking and moving about, with a touch of something alarming and dreadful mixed in with what is real." And Baudelaire never revised his opinion on this point: "I have often been surprised that Balzac's great renown came from his reputation as an observer. It has always seemed to me that his principal merit was in being a visionary, and a passionate one."[14] Moreover, when Baudelaire established his own theory of modern heroism, he was thinking of the Paris of Sue and Balzac—or rather, he was already turning to news items: "With the spectacle of elegant society and of those thousands of lives adrift, circulating throughout the lower depths of the big city—criminals and kept women—the *Gazette des tribunaux* and *Le Moniteur* prove to us that we need only open our eyes to discover our heroism."[15] This taste for mo-

11. That is, ten years before *Les Fleurs du mal*. Despite the legend, it is clear that this work hardly represents the tyrannical vocation of an entire lifetime.

12. Baudelaire, *Lettres* (Paris, 1905), 522.

13. Later, in *L'Homme qui rit*, Hugo describes the atmosphere of a city at night: "The little wanderer was experiencing the undefinable pressure of the sleeping city. Such silence, like that of teeming hives presently stilled, is dizzying. These states of lethargy all intermingle their nightmares; these slumbers make up a crowd, etc."

14. Baudelaire, "Théophile Gautier" (1859) (See *Baudelaire as a Literary Critic: Selected Essays*, trans. Lois Boe Hyslop and Francis E. Hyslop Jr. [University Park: Pennsylvania State University Press, 1964]: 152–79)

15. Baudelaire, *Salon de 1846*, ch. 18. We should remember that *Les Mystères de Paris* dates from 1843. And the "millions of lives adrift, circulating throughout the lower depths of the big city," are, for a mind as critical as Baudelaire's, an *object of faith*. In and of itself, this already proves the mythical nature of the representation of Paris. And so it will remain throughout the poet's entire life. Consider the "Tableaux parisiens" in *Les Fleurs du mal*, and especially the *Salon de 1859*, where Baudelaire laments at length the absence of paintings representing the

dernity goes so far that Baudelaire, like Balzac, applies it to the most trivial details of fashion and clothing. Both study these things in and of themselves, and turn them into moral and philosophical issues,[16] for they represent immediate reality in its most acute, aggressive, and perhaps most irritating form; but also in the way that it is most commonly lived.[17] In addition, as E. R. Curtius has strongly underscored, these sartorial details reveal that "the pathetic and violent struggle between the new forces of the time had been transposed into capricious and smiling terms."[18]

It is not hard to see that this systematic attention to contemporary life meant rejecting, above all, the outward features of Romanticism: the taste for local color, for picturesque exoticism, for the Gothic, for ruins and ghosts. But on a deeper level, it also implied a radical departure from the *mal du siècle*—in any event from the notion of the sickly, dreamy, and maladjusted hero. Indeed, it takes a hero driven by the will to power—not to say Caesarism—to confront the mythical city, the *crucible of passions*, which alternately exalts and crushes the sturdiest dispositions. "A strong man's destiny is despotism," wrote Balzac, and one of his better analysts remarks that he portrayed "beings who had emerged from the turmoil and confusion of sentimental life, had been freed from their paralyzing revulsion for existence, to rediscover the path of moral responsibility, effective action, and the faith that conquers all obstacles."[19] Some of his novels are thus clearly marked responses to *René* or *Obermann*. In fact, dreaming and its substitutes do not play a major part in the lives of Balzac's characters. They would probably come close to treating dreams as scornfully as does D. H. Lawrence, who compares them to garbage and deems it a strange aberration not so much that they should arouse interest, but that they should have been accorded any *value* at all.[20] Yet, the characters of *La Comédie*

---

natural solemnity of a vast city, the *dark majesty of the most disturbing capital city*, that has only been properly depicted by a naval officer (ch. 8).

16. Baudelaire crossed swords several times on behalf of black dress [the *habit noir* of the Third Estate—*Ed.*] (see above), and Balzac wrote a *Physiologie de la cravate et du cigare* [A Physiology of neckties and cigars], a *Théorie du gant* [A Theory of Gloves], and a *Traité de la vie elégante* [A Treatise of elegant life].

17. Furthermore, for Baudelaire, these preoccupations are related to his important theory of *Dandyism*, which he treats precisely as a question of morals and modernity.

18. E. R. Curtius, *Balzac*, French trans., 194–195.

19. Curtius, *Balzac*, 303.

20. "It is beneath our dignity to attach any real importance to [these heterogenous odds and ends of images swept together accidentally by the besom of the night current]. It is always beneath our dignity to go degrading the integrity of the individual soul by cringing and scraping among the rag-tag of accident and of the inferior, mechanic coincidence and automatic

humaine, however committed to action, remain Romantics nevertheless. This is either because there is necessarily a Romantic side inherent in the hero's nature resulting from his sociological function, or, as Baudelaire points out (Balzac's accomplice, here and always, in this adventure of modernity), because Romanticism remains a "grace, celestial or infernal," that bestows "eternal stigmata."[21]

In any event, by the time Balzac's characters come to grips with "*la réalité rugueuse à étreindre*" [reality, which is rough to embrace][22] they generally trail behind them a somewhat murky past (whether they are civilizing heroes such as Benassis or conquering ones like Rastignac). It is a troubled or difficult past, resembling the lives of their predecessors at the height of Romanticism, a past that shaped and forever marked them, but from which they depart without regret. Given all these features, this past could correspond to the period known in Classical mythology as that of *concealment*, which always precedes the hero's period of ordeals and triumphs: Dionysos at Nysa, Apollo as a shepherd at Admetus, Oedipus before the Sphinx, Achilles among the women of Scyros. In this regard, nothing could be more instructive than the type represented by Vautrin, who is both a rebel and creator,[23] the *forçat intraitable sur qui se referme toujours le bagne* [defiant convict who always gets locked away (Rimbaud)— *Ed.*] and, at the same time, an intelligent and exact man of action, secretly pulling the strings of an intricate, grandiose intrigue.[24]

In short, neither the Romantic nor the *modern* hero is content with the lives that society would have him lead. But the first withdraws from society, while the second opts for its conquest. Therefore, Romanticism results in a theory of ennui, while the *modern* sense of life leads to a theory of power or, at least, of energy. In the transfigured Paris of Hugo and Balzac rapidly appear the figures of Enjolras and Z. Marcas—as the first representatives of the type of the chaste revolutionary (specifically French, according to Curtius). For these men, power is by definition ruthless and quasi-*pontifical*, as D. H. Lawrence

---

event. Only those events are significant which derive from or apply to the soul in its full integrity," D. H. Lawrence, *Psychoanalysis and the Unconscious: Fantasy of the Subconscious* (1921; New York: Viking Press, 1972), 194.

21. Baudelaire, *Salon de 1859*, ch. 6.

22. Rimbaud.

23. See Curtius's analysis, 159.

24. This complex is properly what I call the *Luciferian* outlook. It corresponds to the moment when revolt turns into the will to power and, without becoming any less passionate or subversive, grants a major role to the intellect and to a lucid, cynical vision of reality in the carrying out of its aims. It is the changeover from *agitation to action*.

has described this with such striking formulations.[25] For his part, Baudelaire imagined that the mere act of wielding power conferred "if not virtue, then a certain noble stance," thus anticipating the English novelist's idea that "someone has to exercise power, and those with a natural gift for it and some respect for its sanctity are the ones who should possess it."[26] Here, this *natural gift* curiously covers the *celestial gifts that can be conferred neither by work nor money*, gifts Baudelaire has in mind when he speaks of founding a *new kind of aristocracy*.[27] Again, this thought is echoed by Lawrence: "We shall found a chivalric order in which we shall all be princes, like angels. We must realize this dream, or at least give it life; give birth to it on an earth watched over by our old spirit of cunning, guided by our ancestral habits of mercenary militarism."[28] As for Balzac, to come full circle, we need only recall that his first work, or nearly, turns out to be an *Histoire impartiale des Jésuites*, which he deemed an homage to "the finest society ever established." At the same time he was the creator of Vautrin and the author of the *Histoire des Treize*, which begins with these memorable words: "In Paris at the time of the Empire there were thirteen men, who were equally struck by the same sentiment, who were energetic enough to remain faithful to the same idea . . . who were all so deeply politic as to conceal their sacred bonds, so vigorous as to set themselves above any laws, and bold enough to undertake anything whatsoever." So too, their leader had assumed that "society should entirely belong to distinguished men who, besides their natural intelligence, acquired wisdom, and wealth would also possess a sufficiently ardent fanaticism to fuse these various forces into one single torrent." Moreover, like the Dandies who inspired Baudelaire's thoughts of founding a new kind of aristocracy, these men were "superior, cold, and mocking," and they were "drawn to Oriental pleasures in a way that was all the more excessive since such desires, long dormant, thus raged more intensely upon being aroused."[29] What is more, both writers cited exactly the same examples:

25. The term is from Hugo, who describes Enjolras as having a *Pontifical, warrior-like nature*. The character, *angelically beautiful* furthermore, seems to have been rather precisely modeled on Saint-Just.

26. Baudelaire, *Salon de 1859*, ch. 6. D. H. Lawrence, *Kangaroo*. It should be emphasized that this concept of power radically differs from the Maurrassian theory of monarchy and closely resembles Frazer's conclusions in *The Magical Origins of Royalty*. It is, moreover, a good sign that it is situated in the realm of science and not of a priori construction.

27. Baudelaire, *Le Peintre de la vie moderne*, ch. 9, "Le Dandy."

28. D. H. Lawrence, letter to Lady Ottoline Morrel, February 1, 1915. See also *Selected Letters*, French trans. (Paris, 1934) 1: 122.

29. Balzac, *Histoire des Treize*, preface.

the Society of Jesus and the Old Man of the Mountain [leader of the Islamic "Assassins"—*Ed.*]. Indeed, like Baudelaire's *ambitious and humble sectarians*,[30] Balzac's mythical associates, who enjoy the "constant pleasure of secretly hating mankind," hold in their mysterious sway a Paris that Balzac lengthily describes in lyrical and physiognomical terms in his narrative's opening pages. Portrayed as "freebooters in yellow gloves and carriages," they already belonged to the domain of popular literature.[31] This, then, gives us a sense of that idea at the back of lucid and privileged minds, of founding a military and monastic order reserved for the elite, exempt from the common moral code, and devoted to conquest both by principle as well as instinct. It is the carefully constructed counterpart of the myth being disseminated by the serial novel at the very same time. This myth had already loosely impressed on the popular imagination the vision of a vast slumbering city, over which a gigantic, masked Fantômas, freshly shaven, in tails and top hat, foot resting on some building, stretched out his all-mighty hand. This is the pose everybody would later see on magazine covers.

In short, around 1840, there was a major change in the external surroundings, chiefly in the urban setting, and, at the same time, there emerged a distinctly mythical idea of the city, which made the hero evolve and strictly revised Romantic values. This revision aimed to do away with Romanticism's weaker side and to systematize, on the contrary, its aggressive, enterprising aspects. Indeed, Romanticism marked mankind's new awareness of a whole set of instincts that society was eager to repress. To a great extent, though, Romanticism indicated that the struggle had been abandoned and that there was even a refusal to fight. Thus, the Romantic writer readily had a defeatist attitude with respect to society. He turned to dream in its various forms, *toward a poetry of refuge and escape*. The project of Baudelaire and Balzac was exactly the reverse. It sought to *incorporate into real life* the exigencies that the Romantics had resigned themselves to satisfying on a strictly artistic level, and that sustained their verse. The endeavor of Baudelaire and Balzac was thus clearly related to myth, which *always involves granting the imagination a greater role in real life*, in that, by its nature, myth is capable of inciting people to action. On the other hand, a literature of refuge and escape remains thoroughly literary, for it serves to supply *the most ideal and harmless compensatory pleasures* and thus makes the imagination accordingly retreat when it comes to practical demands. Hence,

30. Baudelaire, *Le Peintre de la vie moderne*.
31. Balzac, *Histoire des Treize*.

the former style of Romanticism found itself, in essence, totally unable to produce myths. Of course, it obligingly created fairy tales and ghost stories and beguiled itself with the fantastic; however, in so doing, it actually drew further away from myth. For myth, which is *imperative and exemplary*, shares little with a taste for the supernatural that operates as a kind of *outlet*, which merely reveals social maladjustment rather than a collective, exalted, and rousing representation of society.

For the work of Balzac to appear genuinely mythical, on the contrary, let us simply recall that already during the writer's lifetime, clubs sprang up in both Venice and Russia with male and female members who assumed the roles of characters from *La Comédie humaine* and tried to pattern their lives on these models. Such events were childish, of course. Yet we should realize that we do not know enough about the nature of the ill-defined needs they presuppose; and it seems clear that one can rely on these needs as a sure means of influencing mankind.

I may then, finally, present a critical conclusion: the myth of Paris showed that literature has strange powers. It seems that art, or rather *the imagination as a whole*, relinquished its autonomous sphere to attempt what Baudelaire (to quote him one last time) luminously termed the "*legendary* translation of external life."[32] Upon analysis, what was written at the time, as the expression of a single society, reveals an unsuspected coherence on every level—and, hence, a capacity to persuade, if not to pressure and subjugate, that made literature into something serious at last. The pursuit of the Beautiful (which anyone who is not an aesthete considers such a suspect occupation) seems trivial when compared to the value of this general phenomenon; in contrast, Beauty could only be of interest, then, as an idle whim. This might perhaps represent a dead loss for art, in the strict sense of the term—although that is debatable. But anyway, this in itself is unimportant. Indeed, what truly matters is to imagine the possibility of orienting aesthetics toward *dramaturgy*, that is, toward exerting an effect on people through representations engendered by the very morphology of the society in which they live—representations inherent in their lives and specific problems. Even more important, though, is to realize that phenomena of this kind have actually occurred *ever since everybody has been able to read*.[33] For under these conditions, the question of myth must be ad-

---

32. Baudelaire, *Le Peintre de la vie moderne*, ch. 5. Baudelaire himself is the one who underlines the word *legendary*.

33. That is, ever since compulsory primary education was instated, which became veritably widespread at exactly the time that the myth of Paris was taking shape.

dressed and reckoned with once again. And, as might be expected, this invites us to consider many things in a new light.[34]

34. This study only seeks to show, through examples, the substantial benefits of studying literature free from any aesthetic viewpoint. Of considering, rather, its influential role, its social conditioning, and its function as myth in relation to newly emerging stages in the history of ideas and the evolution of environments. The study's documentation is fragmentary, and its analysis incomplete; the conclusions may need to be revised. But given the current state of research, things could not be otherwise. For it seems that interest in such questions, as yet, has only indirectly attracted general attention. It would have been very important to be well informed on the following points, each of which could be the subject of a monograph: (1) Descriptions of Paris before the nineteenth century, mainly by Marivaux and Restif de la Bretonne. (2) Role played by Paris in the Revolution; polemics between the Girondins and the Montagnards tending to oppose the capital and the provinces; how the great *Parisian* revolutionary "days" generally affected people's minds. (3) Development of the secret police during the Empire and Restoration: how this instilled a greater sense of urban mystery in people's imaginations. (4) Psychological depictions of Paris, and their evolution, by the principal writers of the time: Hugo, Balzac, Baudelaire. (5) Study of the objective descriptions of Paris: Dulaure, Maxime du Camp. (6) Poetic vision of Paris: Vigny, Hugo (especially the long historical-metaphysical panegyric of *L'Année terrible*: "Paris Destroyed by Fire [Paris incendié]"), Rimbaud, etc. Only after the completion of this inquiry can the question be addressed as it should. However, it is probably not too soon to outline the research and indicate its implications.

15

Introduction to "Sociology of the Intellectual"

In the introduction, I proposed that by 1938–1939, Caillois had taken a stand against Acéphale's project of human sacrifice (which he may not have known about in 1937). In this light, his *Man and the Sacred* and "Sociology of the Intellectual" can be interpreted as responses to Bataille's fantasies. In particular, the final sections of *Man and the Sacred* suggest that reconstituting a "sacred environment" in the modern world need not involve Bataille's favored motto of "la joie devant la mort" (joy in the face of death). Caillois here argues that an individual or collective in search of community should find a *raison de vivre*, to which they might then, if necessary, sacrifice their lives. In listing those capable of such "unconditional commitment," Caillois does not include the intellectual. And yet, *Man and the Sacred* does refer to contemporary intellectual objects of veneration. "These new conditions of the sacred have led to its assuming new forms," he writes. "Thus, it invades ethics and transforms such concepts as honesty, fidelity, justice, and respect for truth and promises into absolute values."[1] Focusing, then, on such "absolute values" (whose primary spokesman at the time was Julien Benda), "Sociology of the Intellectual" will articulate a new collective order.

Caillois reworks Benda's *La Trahison des clercs* (The treason of the intellectuals; 1927) in terms of the modern sociology of the sacred.[2] He was responding to a talk in March 1938 by the philosopher whose famous treatise assailed the descent of the twentieth-century French intellectual from the spheres of pure, abstract reason into those of factionalism, party politics, and worldly corruption.[3] Michel Winock reminds us, however, that "the treason of the intellectuals does not involve taking part in a public action—Benda glorifies Voltaire in the Calas Affair, and Zola in the Dreyfus Affair—but in subordinating the intellect to earthly *partis pris*." For Benda, intellectuals should be disinterested, or driven by abstract principles—such as "humanity" or "justice"—rather than giving intellectual expression to political passions such as those of race, class, or nationalism.[4] Sartre is generally deemed the philosopher who first challenged Benda by arguing, after the war, notes Allan Stoekl, that "the writer is always immersed in a milieu," that "Benda's cleric is himself already

"Sociologie du clerc," in *Approches de l'imaginaire* (Paris: Gallimard, 1974), 61–69.

committed, already partisan, even though he might think he represents only abstract truth—and he represents nothing other than the privileges of the élite class to which he belongs."[5] Well before Sartre, though, Caillois's "Sociology of the Intellectual" proffered a sociological rebuttal to Benda—reducing the intellectual to his church rather than to his class.

Caillois sent his essay to Jean Paulhan with the following comment: "Publish it as a report, or if it's too long, as the second part of 'The Winter Wind,' because the argument's structure is exactly the same: I try to explode a certain position from within and then set it against another one that completes and justifies it."[6] Caillois first dismantles Benda's opposition between "order," which is pragmatic, and "justice," which is abstract, to assert that intellectuals should not "measure the flaws [of the polis] on a scale of absolutes." Then he argues that their function is to produce historical "values to renew the century, values that are as un-abstract and un-eternal as possible, but no less ideal or uplifting." In French, the word *clerc* refers both to a religious cleric and to a learned scholar or intellectual. So Caillois restores intellectual identity to its "clerical" ground in a sociological and secularized sense, while upholding Benda's ideal of intellectual transcendance and authority, of detachment from contemporary passions.

In 1946, Caillois wrote that his high school teacher, Georges Bidault, had been outraged by "Sociology of the Intellectual": "When he returned it to me: '*Tu quoque, fili!*' [And thou too, my son!] he exclaimed. 'Your article is pure Maurras. Dear friend, you are pursuing a dangerous tack.'" Caillois went on to remark: "I was making claims that were frankly reckless, and which I have since rectified, on the relations between spiritual and secular power."[7] Twenty-five years later, he further clarified the intent of his essay: "It was inspired . . . by India especially, the brahman facing the *ksatriça*." Caillois was apparently drawing on Georges Dumézil's *Flamen-Brahman* (1935), a work that explored the analogies between the Indian brahman caste and the Roman corporation of the *flamen*. Both brahman and flamen served as sacred doubles or simulacra of the sovereign power. The brahman derived sanctity from its vestigial, prehistoric status as sacrificial victim, whereas the flamen was a "victim who was never sacrificed."[8] Thus, added Caillois (with an audible chuckle in this videotaped interview), "the cleric was the one who committed himself, who never took up arms, who was not allowed to perform the slightest act of violence, but who possessed spiritual authority in the face of secular power. Therefore, his only means was to pay with his own person. . . . It is the vassal, according to Japanese customs, who slits open his stomach to show the Lord that he is wrong. *That* is what I had in mind . . . and I do not believe it is either Comtiste, or Maurrassian."[9]

In a society based on the distinction between the temporal and the spiritual, the opposition of cleric and layman is a given fact; it is beyond dispute and, in a way, foundational. On the contrary, in a homogeneous social state, it cannot be unquestioningly accepted that certain people should seek to assume the clerical function on the grounds that they are serving values they deem abstract, eternal, and universal (in short, free from temporal interests). These people actually do uphold the exigencies of these values with, without, or against temporal interests. But does that make their stance acceptable and effective?

The values they defend—justice, reason, truth—challenge embodied ideals such as nation, state, or class, which by nature involve the unconditional pursuit of private gain. These last values are precisely the ones politicians promote to supervise the administration, preservation, and growth of the public wealth. Hence, it is clear how there could arise a conflict between entities rooted in history, forced to fight for their existence, and the abstract principles of the "clerics"—who either strive to instate them in society (with the risk of tainting gold with lowly lead) or else worship them peacefully, far from any strife, safeguarding their integrity and immutable form.

He who governs has no choice; like Goethe, he must prefer injustice to disorder. Here is the supreme maxim of politics. But there is a wide range of options for the citizens who are not responsible for the smooth workings of the countless mechanisms of social life, those required by a highly developed division of labor, and which actually allow those people criticizing their operation to remain so very detached. These critics can counter the painstaking efforts of politicians with a resounding *fiat justitia, ruat coelum* [let justice be done, though heaven shall fall]; and, should justice fail to be carried out in some specific case, they can invoke terrible catastrophes, or even universal destruction.

One should not deny the gravity, internal rigor, and, in a certain sense, the grandeur of such an attitude. Any relentless effort or steadfast stand against all odds harbors some wild attraction that compels our admiration. But then, neither obstinacy nor heroism can guarantee accuracy, and the death of martyrs does not prove the truth of any faith. Therefore, because error does not inevitably lack the strength of its convictions, we must be careful not to make conviction promise more than it can deliver. Let us merely note, for now, that if the distinction between cleric and layman has any meaning at all in a society lacking the distinction of the spiritual and the temporal, then it is insofar as such a distinction covers the rift between the two attitudes described above: for the first, everything is subordinate to order; and for the second, to justice.

The modern "cleric" rather flatters himself in claiming to uphold every supreme, eternal, and disinterested value, for he excludes many of them from his own domain, either through oversight or arbitrarily. He condemns specific values (such as some abstract notion of force in itself, for example) even though they possess all the features of values he actually favors. And he neglects other values, such as beauty, despite the fact that they fulfill his regular criteria. Besides, intellectually speaking, it is very hard to refer to an artist as a cleric. And this for an obvious reason. What the artist claims as his own value and the type of activity involved—aesthetic creation—have no practical application in the temporal world, nor are they likely to bring it any degree of moral resolve. Art can adapt to and beautify anything at all. Now, whereas the values of the "cleric" are held to be disinterested, they are nonetheless required to prove that they have enough real implications to motivate some degree of personal commitment. Matters have reached such a point that the "cleric" will not be fully granted the role of championing truth except (it goes without saying) insofar as truth and justice are linked by circumstance, and truth thus means taking a stand in the real debates of the day. It follows that a scientist is then not necessarily viewed as a "cleric", and he is not "clerical" to the extent that he is a scientist. So contesting a specific scientific theory is not generally deemed "clerical." On the contrary, the act of denouncing a false document that helped to condemn an innocent man, and thus of demanding a retrial—this is considered very "clerical" indeed. I need not underscore the great difference between this last stance and that of a handwriting expert who may offer his professional opinion about the evidence. The scientist never raises the question of value, never worries about what ought to be; that is why he is not truly "clerical."

Therefore, it is tempting to conclude that the "cleric" appears intent to safeguard one single value: justice. Among the so-called abstract and disinterested values, here is the only one that, in extremis, exists exclusively in terms of the temporal; that, when put into practice, engenders a course and politics of action; that, above all, makes us choose between itself and the polis. Because justice is not on easy terms with the world, it demands an explicit attitude of either total accord or frank hostility from the world, and the same from its own servants toward the world.

Here, our analysis reveals a second, more serious discrepancy between the claims of the "cleric" and his actual nature. Contrary to his assertion, it cannot be persistently maintained that justice is abstract, absolute, immutable, and a priori. There is nothing more variable, more conditioned by particular civilizations, or more contingent on time and place. In matters of justice, there are disagreements between Orientals and Europeans; men of classical antiquity and Christians; children and adults; nomads and sedentary peoples; between farmers and huntsmen. In the polar regions, winter and summer themselves can even give rise to seasonal legal systems that periodically replace each other in one and the same population. I would not deny that this last example involves two sides of a single coin. But it does show that there are inevitable adjustments between legal principles and systems—that can even stem from breaks in the circadian rhythm.

Of course, one can view morality as something unchanging. Loyalty and rectitude do not depend on climate. And everywhere, similar features distinguish generosity from greed and frankness from hypocrisy; the same holds true for many other qualities, both good and bad, that are assessed in relatively constant ways, regardless of time or place. But these virtues have only private implications. They concern only the soul. They have never been required by law, nor has public esteem always held them high. Everyone disagrees as to their value whenever some personal or public interest is at stake. Nothing legitimizes them. They are deeply personal. Their differences become more pronounced as soon as they are linked to the circumstances of collective life: legal systems and social customs stand opposed. As soon as a person's actions influence and reflect the group in which he lives, morality maps out for him varied and changeable duties and rights—however true to its principle morality might remain in the hearts of men. Whenever it finds its concrete application, the instinct of what is just and unjust quickly scatters into countless legislations that are all equally pressing, however vague or precise they may be.

Furthermore, the concept of justice is ambiguous in and of itself. Its different meanings have been enumerated many times. Whether people should receive according to their merit, their capacity, or their needs, and how such matters should be judged—this has been a topic of frequent debate. Enough said: this confusion is significant. The content of the idea of justice basically oscillates between the two poles more or less defined by the Greek concepts of *thémis* and *dikê*, or the Latin concepts of *fas* and *jus*: cosmic order and fair distribution. The first notion was inspired by observing nature and by experiencing a universal regularity that seems to set each phenomenon in its time and place. The second was apparently conceived by a mathematical mind [*esprit géometrique*] that favored exact divisions and scorned contingent facts. The "cleric" should be endlessly grateful for the imprecision of a language where the same word contains two different concepts: the world's basic equilibrium, which cannot be disturbed without automatically unleashing a compensatory force, and the distribution of rewards and punishments commensurate with actual deeds. This is a crucial problem. Indeed, on a cosmic level, justice and order are clearly the same, and public business (including the rights and duties of each individual) does not occur outside of the world's arrangement. Thus Goethe's maxim giving preference to order over justice (a maxim that the "cleric" directly opposes) suddenly turns out to be a legitimate, universal, and disinterested form of justice: in fact, the one that reflects the permanence of the universe's eternal order and that, far from thwarting the aims of distributive justice, grounds them in reason. No conservative would argue otherwise.

In its extreme consequences, this suggests that the idea of justice most eagerly acknowledged by the "cleric" is not the only legitimate one, for he can well adopt whichever he prefers, after all, without worrying about the existence of others. Yet, let us move on to a new argument from the fact that the concept is so deeply ambiguous, nearly impossible to grasp. It could almost be said that the word "justice" means whatever one wants it to. People agree about its content only after it has been reduced or rendered totally abstract, so that it can no longer be directly applied to any specific case. The bridges have been burned. There is no longer any direct path down from principle to event that is ineluctable, one-to-one, and necessary. Instead, we find contingent and multiple interpretations of the case in question, whereby each participant (who cannot rigorously return to the idea's definition) interposes between the idea and the concrete issue to be settled the forms of mediation that seem most opportune. This procedure was successively called sophistic, casuistic, and dialectical at the time when it was most in force. That is why "clerics" do not agree as to the demands of justice in every instance, and propose different solutions that nonetheless all claim to derive in equal measure from justice itself.

Let us consider the implications of this remark: the "cleric" is not the impartial critic of society he claims to be. He does not remain aloof from its evolution, directly subservient to the eternal principles he wishes to see triumph in society. Between those principles and his actual judgments there is a gap he cannot properly bridge, and through this gap slide the hypocritical pressures of his faction's interests and every prejudice he unwittingly shares. Even supposing that he might be exempt in this respect, his resolve would still be deterred, nonetheless, by the promptings of his amour-propre, and even by the secret pride, albeit the last one left: precisely, of being exempt. Under these conditions, in trying to be an angel, the "cleric" plays the fool. He is actually the pawn of the very determinations he claims to master from on high, and whose abjection he likes to proclaim in comparison to the supreme values. Rather than the pure perspective of the Eternal, what he provides are personal or sectarian opinions, which often arise from the least acceptable motives. To voice his view on all topics, as he does, as if this stood for reason, truth, and justice (when anybody else can legitimately do the same and frequently does, all too driven by vanity)—this is an intolerable and anarchical state of affairs, and a fresh catalyst of disorder and turmoil.

* * *

Does this mean we must reject the cleric's function altogether? The foregoing analyses show that its character is misleading only when we specifically consider a homogeneous society. In this context, moreover, the cleric's office has few repercussions; it is made to act as the fifth wheel of the wagon. For even if this society does not comprise the distinction between the spiritual and the temporal, its politicians are led to cloak their activity with the banner of the law. They are all lawyers, either by profession or occasionally, and they all invoke justice, the eternal and indefeasible values, to sanction decisions that are simply in their best interests. Each one of their actions needs some kind of justification, some allusion to ideal principles. So how can we choose between the justice of "clerics" and that of politicians? Among the rights they cite, how can we discern which is legitimate and which is usurped? Should we take into account the stance of "disinterestedness" to which the "cleric" attaches such importance? Aside from the fact that this quality is not always apparent, and that it is hard to imagine absolute disinterestedness, the assumption that disinterestedness guarantees truth is also a strange kind of reasoning because, in fact, it merely gives truth a chance. This would suggest that accurate judgment simply entailed lacking any direct stake in the debate, or else deciding against oneself.

Furthermore, this still involves the assumption that "clerics" and politicians take different sides. And yet politicians consistently define their positions by upholding views contrary to those of their opponents. So they turn out to be right or wrong strictly by chance, and without ceasing to defend the interests they represent, for that matter. As for the "clerics," we have seen that they cannot descend from principles to events without having recourse to some element of contingency. They, too, uphold opinions that are not exclusively dictated by justice alone. Almost unavoidably, "clerics" and politicians thus find themselves gathered in each other's camp.

Nothing could more clearly show the failure of "clerics" than the fact that they contradict each other and that it is impossible legitimately to prefer their opinions to the arguments of politicians. However, I should repeat that this assessment is valid only in those cases where the "cleric" has lost his attributes. His function is here strictly residual and devoid of real energy; given the form shaping social existence, it is then transferred to the rulers themselves.

On the contrary, when the cleric fulfills some function in society, he is invested with authority due to that very fact, not so much as an individual, but because he belongs to a very well-defined organization that is everywhere called a Church. This latter monopolizes clericalism, as it were, so that no competitor can acquire equal status or hinder its actions. Moreover, as Joseph de Maistre has superbly shown, the Church is autocratic and infallible in its essence; such a nature immediately calls for the most severe kind of discipline, even in the realm of thought. If things were otherwise (if everyone were free to have his own opinion, to express and uphold it whenever and however he pleased), then any form of prestige or efficacious authority would be inconceivable. The Church, which was a dense group by necessity, arose as a constituted and impenetrable body, which grew through a process of free affiliation or co-optation within society, while exceeding temporal bounds. From his membership in this undivided group, the cleric received the investiture of his office and the distinctive feature, either garment or tonsure, excluding him from the secular domain: the visible sign that he was a vessel of the sacred. His strength was not that of a man, but rather of the organism into which his own self had disappeared, and which his own person, however unworthy, wholly represented nonetheless. For in eliminating his own person, the cleric made room within himself for the Church, which henceforth expressed itself in his every word and embodied the full sum of its being in the wretched bodies of all its servants.

Once completely removed from the world of greed and passions, clerics could then address it from on high. While they were still emmeshed in it, their admonishments had no platform on which to rest.

This explains the role of the cleric in those societies where it has been most clearly apparent. In China, the scholar stood alongside the feudal lord, to approve or disapprove of his mode of rule; the Indian Brahman, guarantor of the divine order, assisted and advised the rajah; and in the Christian West, the monk faced the feudal lord while the pope confronted the emperor, armed with the thunderbolts of anathema, interdict, and excommunication. The prestige of the first category of men was never powerless when confronting the warriors of the second.

Only under these conditions does there exist a state of equilibrium between the spiritual and the temporal, and does the status of the cleric have meaning and power. But his authority does not derive solely from the Church. Another, more private and personal source must be added to this external one. The cleric offers a guarantee of the superiority of his function through the severity of his vows and voluntary constraints: in short, by consenting to lose his status as an individual, an alienation visibly expressed by his sacerdotal dress. The enjoyments he is giving up, the gratifications he rejects, whatever flesh, money, and worldly grandeur can provide (the object of human desire and of his own contempt)—all of these bestow on him some sort of essential right over those people content with what he disdains. The cleric renounces temporal benefit in order to acquire merit, and more as a kind of precaution than by distaste; still more because he may thus demand more from others by demanding so much from himself. In so doing, he gives irrefutable proof of his lofty soul and acquires infinitely more in the realm of being than what he loses in the realm of having.

We can now readily understand why certain laymen in modern society, stirred by memory or the imagination, pride themselves on assuming a function whose social necessity is now obsolete and which, furthermore, no one will contest. The benefits are obvious. Claiming to be clerics while remaining laymen, they believe they can sit on both sides of the fence and keep or obtain every benefit of a secular, if not worldly life (for their lack of awareness is unbounded), while they also hope to enjoy the halo of holiness and be heeded as spokesmen of the Eternal (or of some historical fatality) because of their borrowed name. They hope to appropriate for themselves the authority attached to the idea of the Church; to enjoy its privileges without taking on any of the corresponding duties; to claim the right to judge the government of public matters while refusing the function's attendant responsibilities; and last, to set themselves up as boundary stones when, in fact, they are shaken by the slightest breeze.

Here, we have a usurpation of title that would call for sharp reproof if it provoked any kind of serious disorder. But the imposture fails; its futility quickly returns to its own void. It is easier to hear voices crying in the wilderness than those raised at public fairgrounds. The proclamations of these churchless "clerics" are lost in the tumult of the public forum where, following their lead, everyone is holding forth, all equally sure that they are speaking for justice and the law—albeit without guaranteeing their credibility with anything to distinguish their own life from that of the common herd. Sometimes these "clerics" can be heard lamenting the fact that their words have no effect, even while they also applaud living in an era of blessed tolerance, when people no longer risk being burned at the stake for what they say. As if the one did not imply the other; as if it were natural for the crowd to listen passively and with rapt attention to words costing little to those who pronounce them—words committing these speakers to nothing at all.

The very reasons for which the ill-considered use of the cleric's title is a clear fraud by the same token define the conditions of an authentic clerical function.

They show that it is utterly at odds with a loose social formation in which people either ignore or fight each other. They confirm the need for a strictly constituted and hierarchical organization, which strips each member of his peace and freedom, leaving him unable to enjoy anything, and even to be present to himself. Alienated both from secular society and from themselves, these men will then form a strong community that stands apart. They will not intervene in the affairs of the polis to measure its flaws on a scale of absolutes. Instead, they will devote themselves to working out the values that will renew the century, values that are as un-abstract and un-eternal as possible, but no less uplifting or ideal for all that: in a word, historical values, subject to change and death, fulfilling the needs of the time and milieu, and perishing on account of their own victory. They represent the active projections of desires that, however ephemeral, always reflect the same demand for morality. They are truly the *ideas that lead the world*. Once they have died, once they have been superseded and fossilized, perhaps they too, in turn, will be used in a lean year by other men calling themselves "clerics," and who somewhat hopelessly uphold them when new values should be conceived instead.

Indeed, genuine clerics do not defend values; they create and supply them. Their history is always that of some Society of Jesus. They do not approve or condemn from the outside; rather, through influence and example, they propagate, extend, and make triumphant the faith that produced the initial miracle when it indissociably united them at the outset. They spread like a contagion. The seed is not differentiated in this early stage; thought and action are one; the same thing both states the rule and drives the secular arm. The only clerics are those of the Church, and they are formed by the Church Militant. Hence their destiny is not to hold on to words that are increasingly detached from things; rather, it is to grapple with reality and prepare its transformation by arranging the world in terms of their desire and by extending beyond themselves the order that has triumphed within.

II

WRITING FROM PATAGONIA,
1940 – 1945

After the College

16

Introduction to "Preamble to the Spirit of Sects"

"Preamble to the Spirit of Sects" discusses Acéphale as if Caillois had been a member himself. But a more legitimate recantation of Acéphale had already been publicly aired by former member Patrick Waldberg, who published letters to his wife, Isabelle (also close to the group) in the New York avant-garde journal *V.V.V.* (Feb. 1944). "How could we have fallen into Bataille's mystical trap for such a long time?" complained Waldberg at this point. "We started out with too many people. We also started out with too many words and too many objects. . . . We did not sufficiently determine the role of literary representation in everything that we did." Moreover, "we were wrong to commit ourselves without greater reservations to Bataille's Nietzscheism." And he states somewhat elliptically, "We must disqualify all that part of our activity whose theme was 'joy in the face of death.' There, more than elsewhere, we seriously failed in humor and dignity."[1]

Caillois is really dissecting, here, both Acéphale and his own aims at the College of Sociology, from which he underwent a gradual detachment during the war, pursuing no further contact with Bataille. This study of sects was a definitive and final break. A vainglorious sect dreaming of spiritual or intellectual power could not possibly be a "pure" or "saintly" elite (see introduction). The temporal was not the eternal. Partly because Caillois did not wish to publish revelations about Acéphale in France, *Essai sur l'esprit des sectes* did not appear there in toto until 1964.[2] At that late date, Caillois's preface was much friendlier toward sects and other social "fervors," which, like "hydra heads," he claimed, are always reborn: "Indeed, civilization is perhaps nothing other than the difficult enterprise of forcing wild saps and grasses, the origin and source of everything, to become fruitful and excellent. The dialectic that I establish between *sect* and *society* tries to define the chief mechanism governing the renewal of the social fabric. The essay was written in 1943; you can readily guess what kinds of fears inspired it."[3] "Preamble to the Spirit of Sects" did not equate the College of Sociology or Acéphale with any kind of political view. However, it did draw explicit parallels between the pre-Hitler culture of secret

"Préambule pour l'esprit des sectes," in *Approches de l'imaginaire* (Paris: Gallimard, 1974), 89–94.

societies and violence depicted by such writers as Ernst von Salomon—whom Caillois, in 1971, recalled having read with great interest—and the conspiratorial ethos of his Parisian circle in the late 1930s.[4]

In *Le Rocher de Sisyphe* (1946), Caillois said that his study of sects voiced "doctrinal arguments" against prior predilections, which were "novelistic," "personal," "imaginary," and "futile." But such a recantation had already started taking shape in one major, evolving text. The first stage, in 1940, itself conveyed an attitude that he would likewise condemn six years later as "a sort of examination of conscience" marked by "excessive romanticism," which he was republishing out of a sense of "integrity," to reveal "the temptations to which [he] had been susceptible" and to "suggest that the barbarian remains close at hand in those people most eager to define and vaunt civilization."[5] I am referring to "Etres du crepuscule" (Twilight creatures), which Caillois probably began to write in late 1939 but published after the armistice.[6] Its main tenor was a violent, apocalyptic sense of defeat, as well as an equally violent repudiation of his own prewar arrogance and inauthenticity— in which he also clearly targeted the College of Sociology, and probably Acéphale. Key passages have been translated in Hollier's *The College of Sociology 1937–39*, but I would like to highlight Caillois's basic argument, namely that this (unspecified) group of "highly cerebral natures" was incapable of *real* self-sacrifice: "We did not achieve that extreme state of despair in which misery and death seem a form of deliverance. We would have had to accept not only those sacrifices that flattered our pride, but those taking us by surprise, confounding our intelligence (which could not have imagined them) and confounding even our wish to withdraw (which intended to spot slights and failures only where it chose to). Our hearts drew more somber happiness from those strategically calculated defeats than from an all too brilliant success."[7] Perhaps the most pessimistic and damning lines that Caillois ever wrote were those trying to safeguard an intellectual place for himself and his friends in the new world that would exclude them: "We would like to work to define the barbarism that is now organizing itself and will turn into civilization; to chart its style; to propose its contents; and not to abandon it altogether to its inertia, inclination, and temptations. Without anyone to keep watch, it would risk getting caught on too much wreckage, [too many deadly vestiges].[8] It would be entirely built upon foundations that it should destroy. We must at least supervise this recasting of the world, as we lacked the strength for that ultimate renunciation that would, perhaps, have allowed us to lead it."[9] Quite fascinating to observe, in my opinion, is how Caillois refocuses the project of intellectual elitism at this crucial—unhinged—time, when he is moving from the cult of revolution to that of civilization, while remaining suspended somewhere between the two. Here, he comes closer than anywhere else to Vichy's creed of the National Revolution. And just *whom* is he addressing in the final passage: "Let others say the *yes* we never pronounced. If their will desires to achieve the goal it pursues and grows through the obstacles it meets; if it grows through its defeats; if it grows through its victories. Then, equally fed by triumph and defeat, these unified and pure beings will be graced and will suddenly gird the sword of the elect. We do not ask that they honor us; but we ask that, before condemning us as they should, if we were unable to precede or to follow them, they acknowledge that we recognized and dreamed them, that we defined their virtues, and that none of us mistook himself for one of them."[10] In developing this conclusion for *La Roca de Sísifo* (1942), Caillois conflated the "barbarians" with "the young, rough workers," while claiming for himself and his friends the rank of intellectual "proletariat."[11] This gives credence to George Auclair's remark that the barbarians and the heroes refer, "perhaps more than to the Nazis, to the communists who were beginning to emerge triumphant."[12] But did the original text of 1940 similarly reach out instead to the Nazis? A closer look shows that unlike the second version, the first does not refer in the same breath to the new barbarism and the new heroes, nor does it equate them in any explicit way. Indeed, my strong sense is that they were originally distinct, as befitting civilization's separation between warfare and culture (see introduction). I thus read Caillois's invocation of these "unified and pure beings"—yet to come—as a despairing expression of his elitist chivalric ideal, and of his persistent hope for victory over the Nazis in a war that he would prefer to be "courtly" rather than *total* (see "Paroxysms of Society").

PREAMBLE TO THE SPIRIT OF SECTS

Various writers, responding to the issues of the day, I would imagine, have drawn attention in the past to the role of sects. Some developed a theory; others portrayed sects at work in their narratives. Still others cited their own experiences, to derive from this some sort of lesson. I shall leave aside whatever is purely imaginative. There are enough novels (especially those for the youngest curious minds) depicting the exploits of some mysterious and all-powerful association that, in the depths of a forest or the heart of a capital city, performs the rituals of a bloodthirsty cult, exacts dire vengeance, supports law and virtue, or else seeks to gain mastery over the world. Brotherhoods of stranglers or pirates, fellowships of fanatics or ambitious men, of criminals or righters of wrongs—the variants all seem equally capable of indulging some natural tendency of childhood reverie to unite adventure with secrecy. But these are merely fantasies that adults, generally speaking, are ashamed to enjoy. Yet, there exist other fantasies that are destined for adults—and closely related to the fictions they so disdain. This time, their authors do not treat such fantasies lightly at all. They do not present them as gratuitous tales, composed at random and simply to entertain the reader. The authors claim to detect a need, to offer some means of salvation, to present a well-conceived doctrine or an applicable program. They consider that what they are setting forth is either real, possible, or desirable. For example, Jules Romains, a famous novelist, undertook to write the faithful and complete chronicle of his time, and he deemed it necessary to devote an entire volume of his work (significantly titled *The Quest for a Church*) to these surprising concerns. Here we find a character who interprets the complete history of the world in light of the power he attributes to sects. They alone, he explains, have been running everything. Sects have provoked or controlled decisive events as they pleased, albeit discreetly, by intelligently applying effective pressure to the right place on every occasion. He refers to the monastic and military orders, to the Templars and Teutonic Knights, Janissaries and Assassins, and then to the Jesuits and Freemasons—whose alliance should be underscored, in his opinion. This bold historian limits himself to conjecture. But others take action by providing long descriptions of mysterious doings by conspirators intent to stop wars, and who destroy those people jeopardizing the peace with their maneuvers, strategies, or recklessness.

In *The Magic Mountain* Thomas Mann likewise maps out a vast panorama of the political tendencies dividing the modern world; it is both a study and a general overview. One theorist stands out sharply. He upholds trenchant ideas with a lucidity and vigor that command acquiescence. He is a Jew, a disciple of the Jesuits who would have entered the Society himself if illness had not interrupted his novitiate. He counters the egalitarian aspirations of a liberal democrat with the idea of a communist, theocratic society that is governed by a hierarchy of implacable ascetics who rule by means of a holy Terror. Without further dwelling on this, I refer the reader to this dual and striking account. In any case, many less wide-ranging or famous works reveal similar anxieties.

Thus, everything suggests that many fine minds, especially today, feel the seduction of secret societies—at the very moment when both customs and institutions alike seem to be turning us away from them. These people seem to nurture the project of founding some type of Order, an organization that would start by uniting a few men who are dissatisfied with the world in which they live and seek to reform it; who conclude a pact of solidarity demanding infinitely more from each other than what they gave to their original milieu—

and infinitely more than this milieu ever thought to request. But it is this very discipline that attracts them. They see it as a guarantee of their efficacy. People imagine this community as one whose unimportance or absurdity initially protects it, and which then gradually increases its scope and power. Although it would always remain a minority of the elect, it would ultimately come to control the destinies of the whole country or of the world. At least, it would decisively influence how these bodies are ruled. Yet this would remain utterly hidden from the vain, pretentious, and narrow-minded multitude, which would submit to this extremely subtle yoke for its own slavish happiness.

These are reveries, of course, and ones that I am exaggerating furthermore, making them even more chimerical. But it would be wrong to disregard them altogether. They reveal a general malaise and may inspire good projects. Although we smile when meeting them in our readings, we may be frightened to find them elsewhere—even in real life. For it is in the nature of myth to seek realization and try to mold reality to its own image. We must resist automatic skepticism that is blinder than naïveté itself, and that would prevent us from witnessing the miraculous course of strange careers.

Even before the war of 1914, Germany was favorable terrain for adventures of this sort. Certainly, they were then little more than childish pranks. Still, various movements looked on them kindly or showed signs of such tendencies themselves. Young people, in gangs, more or less withdrew from society and set off along the roads, seeking a more favorable climate for some sort of desire for ardor and purity. First the war, then the ensuing defeat heightened these vague desires, which were still harmless and vague. The national humiliation showed how the old world (by now discredited) had failed. Many people had already decried its mediocrity, and it was trying to survive its own demise through futile institutional change. However, the scope of the disaster proclaimed the need for radical upheaval. At the same time, it offered a common, urgent, and grandiose goal for all this untrammeled, unfocused energy, which soon openly challenged the collapsing old order and was persecuted in return. It is well-known that secret associations of terrorism and revenge were flourishing at the time. Independent commando units kept war going at the borders. The Holy Vehmers were punishing traitors inside the country; Hitler's movement drew its best forces from their midst. Everything suggests that he later got rid of these men, who were far too unruly; but their somber mysticism presided over his early stages. There are eloquent accounts of this initial frenzy: Ernst von Salomon's *Les Réprouvés* is probably still the most direct and informative. The new master was subsequently able to get rid of those fanatics whose nearly religious temperament was misplaced in the political domain.

Certain turbulent virtues that are highly useful when engaged in the process of conquering power may become dangerous, though, after this has been achieved and there is a risk that they can be used against one in turn.

For now, however, let us simply consider the outset: when the original dreams could hardly let one foresee the terrible historical irruption that such effervescence would ultimately bring about, when their full force was shrewdly harnessed in the right circumstances and we suddenly saw an amazing avalanche terrorize and crush many nations.

In January 1941, a journal started reappearing in Paris—a city occupied, as a matter of fact, by the recent effects of such a cataclysm. In an early issue, Henry de Montherlant described an endeavor in which he had taken part with four other young men in 1919.[1] Their intent, he says, was to form "a rather codified and harsh club." The club itself was rather anodine, as were its aspirations—even though they could have been limitless. The author adorns his confidences with so many comments and references to more illustrious examples, such as medieval chivalry and the Nipponese Bushido, that one can sense him starting to get emotionally caught up once again. What could be prompting him to recall such trivial episodes from his long-forgotten youth twenty years later, if not the confused sense that they are somehow linked to the scenes and the historic events before his eyes?

One should also reread *La Gerbe des forces* by Alphonse de Chateaubriant. It has been noted that this work fostered a great deal of valuable sympathy for the new Germany among French officers. Strategically invited to visit the Third Reich, the author was clearly won over, most of all by certain attempts—being actively promoted at the time—to resurrect the old Orders of Knighthood. Indeed, there was a serious effort underway in several fortresses buried deep in the Black Forest or in Kurland to prepare an elite body of implacable and pure young leaders for the supreme role of managing the nation as well as the world it was destined to conquer. Apparently, the experiment had no tangible results. Most likely, the Party had its own ready candidates. But the project kindled more than one imagination.

This was especially true among those of us who had founded the College of Sociology, which was exclusively devoted to the study of closed groups: so-

---

1. [Caillois is referring to the first chapter, "Les Chevalries," of Montherlant's *Le Solstice de Juin*. Written in July 1940, this series of essays was first published in the *Nouvelle revue française* edited under German occupation by Drieu la Rochelle (see Henry de Montherlant, *L'Equinoxe de Septembre suivi de Le Solstice de juin et de Mémoire* [texte inédit] [Paris: Gallimard, 1975]).—*Ed.*]

cieties of men in primitive populations, initiatory communities, sacerdotal brotherhoods, heretical or orgiastic sects, monastic or military orders, terrorist organizations, and secret political associations of the Far East or from murky periods in European history.[2] We were enthralled by the resolve of those men who, from time to time throughout history, apparently wished to give firm laws to the undisciplined society that could not satisfy their desire for rigor. With sympathy we observed the progress of those people who withdrew from such a society in disgust and went to live elsewhere, under harsher institutions. However, some among us, who were full of fervor, could not readily resign themselves to merely interpreting; they were impatient to act for themselves. Our research had convinced them that will and faith could overcome any obstacle so long as the initial pact of the alliance proved to be truly indissoluble. In the heat of the moment, nothing less than a human sacrifice seemed capable of binding together our energies as profoundly as it was necessary to carry out some huge task—which, furthermore, did not have any clear goal. Just as the physicist of antiquity needed but one single fulcrum to lift up the world, for the new conspirators the act of solemnly putting to death one of their own members seemed a sufficient means of consecrating their cause and ensuring their eternal loyalty. By making their efforts invincible, this was supposed to deliver the world to them.

Would you believe it? It was easier to find a volunteer victim than a volunteer sacrificer. In the end, everything was left unresolved. At least, that's what I imagine, for I was one of the most reticent members, and things may have gone further than I knew.[3] We spurred each other on, though, with several examples, both ancient and modern, exotic or very local. And if nothing irremediable did occur to seal our conspiracy, this was due to simple cowardice and because of some doubt that remained unspoken as to the fruitfulness of such a bloodbath. We lacked heroism, and also, I think, conviction. Personally, I, at least, feared that this murder, which in some way was supposed to christen our faint hearts, would not grant us any of the virtues and ardor that let people move mountains. I was afraid it might leave us hesitant and timid, even more distraught as criminals than we had been as innocent men. In my opinion, it

2. The aims of this institution were expounded in three manifestoes that appeared simultaneously in *La Nouvelle revue française* of July 1, 1938, signed respectively by Georges Bataille, Michel Leiris, and myself.

3. I am referring to the group known as Acéphale. Bataille often spoke to me about it, and I always refused to belong, even while collaborating with the journal of the same name, which was its mouthpiece. There are some interesting revelations about this group, which insisted upon secrecy, in *V.V.V.* no. 4 (Feb. 1944): 41–49.

seems so futile to think that the horror of a shared crime could enact miraculous transformations in the soul, or that this in itself could bestow on a few men, who would suddenly agree to oppose all the rest, indomitable courage and an everlasting oath. This requires strength that no monstrous ritual can provide. It must be fully drawn from within oneself. For the person who has achieved it, crime and consecration merely confer superfluous unctions—even though he himself might believe that they provide (like Samson and his mane) the supernatural vigor taking him from one victory to another.

My only intent has been to add this account to the preceding ones and nothing more. Besides, I have no great illusions and fully recognize the wretched nature of these vain ambitions. But I would like to show that they are widespread under one guise or another, and that from the outset they tend toward astonishing extremes. The fact that they almost always give off hot air means neither that they do not exist nor that they do not probably signal a thought-provoking malaise. Besides, these reveries are not a recent phenomenon. Balzac and Baudelaire already took pleasure in imagining a company of mysterious, powerful freebooters who were nevertheless refined and ruthless, with a secret network of servants, spies, and righters of wrong spread throughout capital cities and all the apparatus of the major countries. Nothing could resist these invisible masters, whose strength lay in their unity and secrecy. Strange ramblings of this sort may be found in the *Histoire des Treize* and in Baudelaire's critical writings. And one could cite other names in succession over the course of the past century that meet up with Jules Romains and Henry de Montherlant.[4] Is it thus constant, this taste for shadow and power, this desire to arrange the world according to stronger laws? In any event, what is the source of such long-lived and permanent anxieties? In my opinion, here are some questions that require an urgent response.

4. I have collected the essential texts of Balzac, Baudelaire, and D. H. Lawrence touching on this question, in a chapter of my book *Le Mythe et l'homme* (Paris: Gallimard, 1938), 193–204.

17

Introduction to "Discussions of Sociological Topics: On 'Defense of the Republic'"

In June 1941, *Sur* presented a formal outline of the topics it would pursue in the "Debates sobre temas sociológicos": "Topics of national interest: The issue of government in our country; Need for a reform of secondary and higher education; Mission of SUR. Topics of general interest: The issue of religion in the contemporary world; Relations between current art and social ideas; State of right and totalitarian state; Primitive forms of mentality in modern society."[1] The "discussions" had actually been launched the previous year with a meeting devoted to Caillois's article, "Défense de la république" (see introduction). His persistent and demanding interlocutor in the excerpt presented here is Angelica Mendoza, one of many Argentinian intellectuals assembled for these gatherings by Ocampo.[2]

The other comments are voiced by Pedro Henríquez Ureña (1884–1946), an influential Latin American critic, scholar, and essayist; Enrique Anderson-Imbert (1910–2001), an Argentine author and scholar who would become the Victor Thomas Professor of Latin American Literature at Harvard University from 1965 until 1980; and José Bianco (1908–1986), a novelist and important editor at *Sur* for twenty-three years.

"Défense de la république" endorses the following meritocratic model:

Generally speaking, it is important, I think, to aim for an organization that gives power in every domain to intellectual competence and moral qualification; that is not ready to accept that these should bow down in the face of a majority opinion and even less that they should rest upon the quasi-unanimity of an intoxicated or terrorized mass. [Every leader] must be exclusively responsible to his peers gathered in a College, in whose midst [he must take] his place simply as one person among his equals. The point is to found a hierarchy and keep it open and mobile at all times, in order to constantly replace the external inequalities due to birth or fortune by those that are revealed in individuals, and of which

"Debates sobre temas sociológicos: En torno a 'Defensa de la república,'" *Sur* (July 1940): 86–104 (excerpts).

they can never be dispossessed. Such a regime aims to replace privileges with superiorities. It asserts that men are born equal in rights, but denies that they remain so: they rise or fall according to their capacities and their works. It wants to give everyone the same possibilities for trying his luck, but does not deem it at all desirable that the diverse results of gifts and efforts should be leveled off in order to compensate artificially for the differences caused by the very differences that exist between men. Everyone has the right to his own proper virtues, and the State should not have the power to confiscate them, nor should mediocrity be free to corrupt them.[3]

DISCUSSIONS OF SOCIOLOGICAL TOPICS: ON "DEFENSE OF THE REPUBLIC"

Angelica Mendoza: Don't you think that this ideal will turn into an aristocracy?

Caillois: That is precisely what I wanted to clarify. I do not much like the word "aristocracy." It too readily evokes a social class, and one that is, moreover, defined by birth and fortune. I would rather speak of a hierarchy of merits and rights.

Angelica Mendoza: How can one view an intellectual oligarchy as a means of saving democracy? For the ideal you are suggesting is that of an intellectual oligarchy.

Caillois: It involves a kind of *Order*, in the religious sense of the word, formed by men whose prestige reflects above all their moral and, needless to say, their intellectual qualifications.

Angelica Mendoza: Well, with this ideal we will end up with another dangerous totalitarianism.

Pedro Henríquez Ureña: Have you thought about what is to prevent this caste from degenerating into an oppressive one?

Caillois: This caste cannot possibly oppress, and for a very simple reason: it doesn't have any coercive power at all. Such power is in the hands of the State. However, the point is that this caste should exert a strong enough influence on public opinion for the State to have to take its position into account. Mme Mendoza will grant me that this dichotomy certainly constitutes more of an obstacle than an incitement with respect to the formation of totalitarianism.

Angelica Mendoza: No, no! I cannot accept that! And who would hold political power?

Caillois: Political power would be held by the men who practice politics, but who would not possess authority.

Enrique Anderson-Imbert: That is to say, like the Elders in Ancient Greece?

Pedro Henriquez Ureña: And do you think there is a way of convincing a modern society that such a regime is possible?

Caillois: Yes. I think so, yes. Why not? Besides, societies can be convinced only through revolution. I don't see any other way. And this one is not that bad. I don't reject it at all.

Pedro Heniquez Ureña: In the final account, that's the mechanism. But what about the ideals? I don't think it's so easy to convince a society that a certain regime is appropriate merely as a functional mechanism—there is also the question of what its purpose will be.

Caillois: There is no lack of an ideal: to establish an international order viewed as absolutely superior, in reality as much as on the level of values—*de facto* and *de jure*—to national prides and their shameless ambitions.

Pedro Henriquez Ureña: In short: what the Catholic Church should have been.

José Bianco: Or, to take a less illustrious example, the United Nations.

Caillois: No, not the United Nations, which was composed of diplomats and governmental delegates. The order I am thinking of must be—and I underscore this again—utterly independent from state organisms. It is autonomous, only responsible to itself. And that is why it has the right and the power to be international.

Angelica Mendoza: I say that it's a utopia.

Caillois: Of course, it is a utopia. Any project for the future is utopian. Especially revolutionary ambitions and, above all, those that put the greater trust in the will of men. . . .

Pedro Henriquez Ureña: So, moral authority, nothing else. These cases Caillois is talking about occur in history from time to time. There have been some in Argentina, for example. I am referring to Mitre, who exercised, as it was said, "el bartolato": a moral authority. And Sarmiento. . . .

Victoria Ocampo: I would like to say something: it seems to me that Gandhi is our clearest example of authority without power. Roger Caillois, what do you think?

Caillois: Yes, it's true; in our time, Gandhi is a splendid example of authority exercised without power. This example is all the more clear-cut insofar as it is extreme. If such results can be obtained by an isolated individual on account of his moral authority alone, just think how much more could be obtained by a fraternity specifically constituted for this purpose, and that society recognizes as holding a genuine social function.

18

Introduction to "The Nature and Structure of Totalitarian Regimes"

The fact that identical accounts of Caillois's lectures on "The Nature and Structure of Totalitarian Regimes" were simultaneously published in French and Spanish-language Buenos Aires newspapers suggests that these synopses were probably distributed by the speaker himself. Thus they usefully document Caillois's political outlook at the time. An initial announcement in *La Nación* listed the proposed series as follows: "The Nature and Structure of Totalitarian Regimes": "To What Do They Correspond?"; "How Did They Arise?"; "How Do They Function?"; "What Do They Threaten?" A more detailed description of Caillois's projected topics then ensued to entice participants who could openly enroll in these "private" conferences sponsored by *Sur*:

> The French Revolution and the idea of nation. The decadence of traditional values and the crisis of liberalism. The revolutions of the postwar. Precursors and theorists. The new myths: race, soil, blood. The nihilism of the "outlaws." National socialism as a form of decadence. Apostles and dictators: personalities and deeds. History of the parties. A new technique for conquering power. The totalitarian state: the ideal of a closed world without play. The fight against the universalisms: science, religion, intelligence, etc. Functioning of the system. Traditional army and praetorian guards. Triumph of the police. The cult and mystique of war. The problem of the "elites" and the need for an aristocratic and international structure.[1]

Even though the lectures tend to avoid bibliographical references, Hermann Rauschning's *Revolution of Nihilism* and Elie Halévy's *L'Ere des tyrannies* were certainly influential.[2] In July 1943, *Lettres françaises* declared that Halévy's

---

Lecture 1: *La Nación* (28 Aug. 1940); *La Vanguardia* (28 Aug. 1940). Lecture 2: *Courrier de la Plata* (30 Aug. 1940); *La Nación* (30 Aug. 1940). Lecture 3: *Courrier de la Plata* (4 Sept. 1940); *La Nación* (4 Sept. 1940). Lecture 4: *La Nación* (7 Sept. 1940). Lecture 5: *Courrier de la Plata* (11 Sept. 1940); *La Prensa* (11 Sept. 1940). Lecture 6: *Courrier de la Plata* (14 Sept. 1940); *El Mundo* (14 Sept. 1940). Lecture 7: *Courrier de la Plata* (18 Sept. 1940); *La Prensa* (18 Sept. 1940). Lecture 8: *Courrier de la Plata* (21 Sept. 1940). Lecture 9: *Courrier de la Plata* (25 Sept. 1940); *La Nación* (25 Sept. 1940). Lecture 10: *Courrier de la Plata* (28 Sept. 1940); *La Nación* (28 Sept. 1940).[1]

major historical study of democracy and socialism in the aftermath of WWI, correlating Bolshevism with the regimes of Mussolini and Hitler, was one "that best helps us to understand the world's current transformation."[3] Caillois's mapping of the relation between democracy and totalitarianism is also interesting to compare with Raymond Aron's lecture in June 1939, "Etats démocratiques et états totalitaires" (Democratic states and totalitarian states).[4] Aron believed that the real danger for democracy, in the words of François Furet, was its conservative adherence to "French revolutionary universalism," that is, "progressivism, abstract moralism or the ideas of 1789. Like rationalism, democratic conservatism can only possibly save itself by renewing itself" (see introduction).[5] Caillois's "La Hiérarchie des êtres" had sought to move beyond the dichotomy of democracy and fascism, as he then defined it, through a hierarchy of merit and choice. By 1940, however, he was arguing that *both* democracy as well as totalitarian states could be challenged in the name of the democratic "republic," the "example of the French Revolution," and "universal values."

Until now, the sole evidence of these lectures has been Francisco Ayala's "El Curso de Roger Caillois" (Roger Caillois's course) in *Sur* (November 1941). Exiled from Franco's Spain, the communist Spanish writer first noted that "the dramatic circumstances in which such political systems are being studied by a French writer have brought to these lectures an atmosphere of special sympathy," and he praised Caillois's "high level of thought and objectivity." However, Ayala did question the first lecture's analysis of the French Revolution as the original source of nationalism, and hence of totalitarianism, whose emergence he himself would have attributed to the nation-states or the Renaissance monarchies. He also strongly criticized Caillois's "equation of totalitarian regimes—that is to say, of the Nazi regime, the one constantly before the speaker's gaze, with the Russian Communist regime. [Caillois] is thus falling into a stance of political polemicizing that has lately arisen due to obvious circumstances, and whose explanation is usually (even if not in Caillois's case) nothing other than the *conservative* goal of fighting at the same time, and in the same struggle, both the class revolution threatening the Capitalist order and the National German revolution, which threatens the nations where that order prevails." On the whole, though, Ayala was quite favorable, and especially liked "the analysis of the new myths: earth and blood, and all the mysticism that constitutes the backdrop of Nazi ideology." He closed with these comments about the last lecture: "Departing from the expository and analytical mode, Caillois sketched out a few ideas about the form in which society should be organized, in his opinion, given that the future order should not be totalitarian, and given democracy's inability to resist the assault of such regimes. This involved very summary suggestions concerning the formation of independent *élites*, which produce a kind of social differentiation. His analysis would need to develop at further length the general outlook behind these ideas."[6]

Much less friendly was the right-wing paper *Crisol*, which attacked Caillois's "antitotalitarian" stance on September 22, 1940:

> The truth is entirely the opposite of what Professor Caillois claims. Totalitarian regimes do not curtail human liberty but rather regulate it and prevent libertine behavior. They do not repress religion but rather collaborate with it as we see in Italy, where Religion enjoys the highest prerogatives. The mind is not subjected to mechanical forces but rather the reverse; and what one attributes to totalitarian countries is the defect of democratic countries. Man, at the service of the authoritarian State, does not convert himself into an automaton; rather, that heresy only occurs in those crude democratic regimes which turn human society into a herd without hierarchy or personality. And in Italy, Spain and Germany, on the contrary, hierarchy, talent and virtue occupy the rank that befits them. Mr. Roger Caillois speaks out against totalitarian regimes, because he is no longer in accord with the New France, and because he is being paid here to speak precisely in this way.[7]

THE NATURE AND STRUCTURE OF TOTALITARIAN REGIMES

Lecture 1, August 28, 1940

He first presented the rules he would seek to follow to achieve valid results, explaining that he would refrain from any political stance and confine himself to the analysis of facts and concepts. Moreover, he would use only firsthand documents, and preferably those written by the partisans of the totalitarian regimes. He declared that he was not interested in biased attacks but rather in the definitions of their own work provided by the dictators themselves. He showed the crude confusions that easily arise when trying to define a totalitarian regime in relation to liberalism, democracy, socialism, or reactionary attitudes. It involves a remarkably more complicated and original phenomenon. A totalitarian regime is a political system in which a disinterested individual stance has become impossible; which tolerates no opposition or indifference toward the state; and in which a party organized as a state comes to power and replaces all the organisms of traditional administration. Thus, a regime is totalitarian when it holds the nation as the supreme value to which it seeks to subordinate everything else—equally so, both within and without. In this form, it is conquering and intransigent.

The idea of nation thus understood is quite recent. It was known to the eighteenth century. Rousseau is the one who defined it in the Social Contract, where he stated that the general will to all rights over individuals and over their actual lives was a "conditional gift" from the national community. He remarked that the first concern of the state should thus be to educate its citizens. The purpose he ascribed to this process was to "denature them," that is, to construct something conscious and homogeneous (the nation) out of parts of the whole.

The French Revolution sought to enact this plan. The club system, which served as doubles of government organs and as their overseer, gave the country a typically totalitarian structure. Above all, the education of children in schools and that of adults in civic festivals displayed concerns strikingly similar to the country's foreign policy. The proposed ideal was the same: to create a population of workers-warriors-citizens, whose only virtues, freedoms, and joy would come from their participation in collective virtue, freedom, and joy.

Does this means that the French Revolution was in all respects identical to the current totalitarian regimes? No. Its structure was the same, but the values of the French Revolution were reversed. In the French Revolution, the nation merely viewed itself as the point of application for universal values. It had no value in and of itself—except in relation to the latter. In the current regimes, on the contrary, each nation presents itself as an absolute value; instead of liberating the others, it must thus inevitably subjugate them. Here lies the difference: the French Revolution was an example for the world. The national totalitarian revolutions, which are necessarily oriented toward conquest, are a danger for the world.[1]

Lecture 2, August 30, 1940: The Concept of Leader

The speaker explained the "leader principle" *(Führerprinzip)*, which totalitarian regimes oppose to the liberal democratic system.

This principle consists in seizing responsibility and authority in one hand and placing them beyond the reach of any discussion or control.

Each person has a hierarchical superior. At the top is the leader, who is responsible to the people as a whole, even though it is unclear how this respon-

1. [Some of the Spanish-language versions of the lectures vary in length, but never in their content or significant wording.—*Ed.*]

sibility can take a concrete form. In any event, the precursors of national socialism all agree that the "leader" must lead the nation with a somnambulistic sense of security. He possesses an "inner sense" that he gets from "Our Lady of the Soil," and to which he must blindly entrust himself, as if he were in a hypnotic trance. From this stems the commonly held German image of the chancellor, accurate or not: he is idle, a dreamer, chaste, vegetarian, loves nature and birds. He lives in a state of isolation, lost in contemplation. He rarely shows himself and only on solemn occasions, to convey his fearsome decisions. So there is no point in wondering whether the Führer is a guide or a medium, an authoritarian dictator or a passive executor of the masses' desire. He defines himself as "a drum and a magnet." He is a tamer of wild animals who alternately seduces and wounds, but who also appears in the guise of some sort of savior, a redeemer who takes upon himself the entire anguish of a population and to whom all prayers are addressed. Everybody then feels light and free, unburdened of his fate.

After several comments on other features of the leader, the speaker concluded by saying that the Führer—the leader—is not a statesman, properly speaking. In fact, he is the contrary of an administrator, of one who governs in the usual sense of the word. He is a mystic, whose very function consists in brandishing lightning and running blindly toward a catastrophic fate.[2]

The modern nation is not a religious community that must obey the revelations of a visionary. Politics is not a matter of mystical ecstasies nor of blind faith. Both political leaders as well as their followers must have clear notions of what is being proposed. And indeed, in totalitarian states, the leader escapes everybody's control, and the masses follow his mandates without any criteria or judgment.[3]

Lecture 3, September 4, 1940: Race and Nation

In essence, racism has a religious basis: the fact that a population is convinced that it has been made to dominate the world and to fulfill a civilizing, historical mission in accordance with this dominion. This irrational conviction is coupled with a pseudoscientific construction, in particular with a fanciful anthropology and a rather delirious history, which over time become increasingly

2. [The following paragraph was included in the more expansive version of Lectures 1 and 2 published in "Al margen de las Conferencias de Roger Caillois: 'Los Regímenes Totalitarios Marcan un Retroceso,'" *La Vanguardia* (September 3, 1940)—*Ed.*]

3. [See also "Al margen de las Conferencias de Roger Caillois: 'Los Regimenes Totalitarios Marcan un Retroceso,'" *La Vanguardia* (September 3, 1940)—*Ed.*]

simplistic, all-encompassing, and unreasonable, somewhat in the manner, for example, of psychoanalytic interpretations.

In this way, one comes to assert, and of course to show, that any artistic achievement, scientific invention, great culture or civilization illustrates the superior qualities of the Nordic or Germanic race. One or several other races are similarly chosen to represent the principle of evil, ugliness, and destruction. The goal is to form a master race that will have at its disposal "all the resources of the planet."

Race is defined by blood and soil. It is the "obscure existential foundation from which we are separated by a clear mind and impersonal reason." The chief contemporary racist theoretician, Hans F. Gunther, defines it for his part as "the set of hereditary and collective abilities that are physical or psychological in nature." Race is not subject to the category of causality but to that of fate *(Schicksal)*. It thus stands opposed to the values of exchange, relation, and reason. The soul of the race *(Rassensch)* is chiefly hostile to money and science, which are universalist and rootless. It lives in the countryside, far from the corruption of the towns; it asserts the vital energy of a people in the face of capitalism and the intellect, and will ensure the victory of the Sword over money.

The race must be "given a form" in order to become a nation. This occurs when the people are seized by a "whirlwind" *(Wirbel)* that expels its dead elements and makes popular leaders spring forth. The people are then set up as an organic community that realizes a kind of national and military socialism by placing all persons and goods at the service of the expansionary force of the nation. The nation rejects the external influences that hindered its formation or birth, and especially Christianity (a factor of cowardice and a religion of slaves) as well as abstract right (which tends to place different races of unequal value at the same level). Thus rid of age-old errors, the totalitarian nation is ready to conquer the world and fulfill its mission.[4]

Lecture 4, September 7, 1940: The Mechanization of Nihilism

[Caillois] stated that for different reasons and in varying degrees, the current totalitarian regimes were preceded by a state of uncertainty and effervescence marked by radical nihilism. In Russia, this state is quite well-known, having been described by novelists of exceptional talent, such as Dostoyevsky, among others. Until 1920, the same mentality prevailed in Germany. Nihilism is characterized by its rejection of society and of the principles that society respects or

4. [See also "Al margen de las conferencias de Roger Caillois: 'Del Nihilismo al Hitlerismo,'" *La Vanguardia*, (September 10, 1940)—*Ed.*]

pretends to respect; it involves youth imbued with a spirit of negation toward everything that people generally revere. They are aware of their fall and enjoy their shame. As fatalists, they accept their cursed destiny and simply scorn all human life—including their own. They are thus led to terrorism and political crime, and turn these into a theory, as the only pure and constructive activities.

It was this state of affairs that gave rise to the "youth movement" in post-war Germany. Desperate men, officers who refused to lay down their arms when peace was restored, rushed to the Eastern borders, where they could still carry on the fight. These were brutal "lansquenets," who felt confident that they stood for the "path" of truth and life in the face of empty institutions and mediocre, timid managers. They grouped themselves in commando units, then later in secret societies of political assassins. They were both nationalists and communists. They fought against the Bolsheviks, while at the same time admiring and envying them. They soon had their great men and martyrs. Through that epical paroxysm, they learned the pleasures of destruction and cruelty, the joy of always exhausting their forces, without scruples or reservations—that they would never forget or abandon later. They felt nonconformist in the face of a hostile world, in the face of their own country, which they had failed to conquer.

It was among the mystical assassins, continued Mr. Caillois, that national socialism found its most dynamic elements, those who would ensure its triumph over parties that were larger but less resolute. They titled themselves representatives of the "Secret Germany." Later, they would return to a "manifest" but domesticated Germany, which had been mechanized by the needs of political action and by the discipline of a party drawing its active strength from the savage energy of a few men.

At first, they were the stated enemies of any principle, value, morality, or society. Perhaps if the powerful and wealthy had really given proof of courage and virtue instead of being hypocritical bon-vivants and fearful egoists, this radical, desperate negation would never have taken shape; nor would it have been capable of arousing "this destructive whirlwind full of resentment, skepticism and will to power which is today conquering Europe and destroying civilization."

Lecture 5, September 11, 1940: Strategy and Taking Power

The terrorist attacks of the nihilist period obviously did not yield any practical results. The military coups d'état turned out to be equally inoperative. Then one came to realize that it was necessary to kindle passions and to base oneself on the masses, and not merely engage in secret society activities. This was the originality of the National Socialist Party: the decision to remain legal or to feign an attachment to legality in order to bring about revolution after coming to power. Yet within the expandable framework of legality, all procedures seemed licit. One had to play on the passions and the emotions, and preferably on the base passions and strong emotions. Propaganda particularly addressed the "heart," that is to say, women, the very young, and frenetical individuals. It used speeches, music, violence, uniforms, and huge processions. All of this seems based on the crowd psychology of Gustave Le Bon.[5] The assembled and excited masses have a sense of invincible power and a feeling of anonymity that removes any fear of punishment or responsibility. They lose all sense of caution or instinct of self-preservation; every gesture spreads by some sort of immediate contagion. Every feeling is forceful at once. The slightest hint becomes certainty; the slightest antagonism, fierce hatred. The moment an idea is voiced, the suitably excited crowd wants to act without any regard for obstacles. It wants orders, and orders for immediate violence.

The strategy of the totalitarian party is to systematically exploit these phenomena, with propaganda playing a prominent role. It must attack one adversary at a time, tenaciously, and with many slanderous statements on marginal issues that are capable of arousing suspicion and hate. It doesn't matter if the accusations are lies; everything is justified by success. First discredit—that is the principle.

Violence is the second factor of success. The masses like violence; they dislike both objectivity and prudence, which they see as weakness. Hence, there is a systematic use of brutality, not by taste but out of tactical necessity, to frighten some people and seduce the rest. The other parties are blind and timid. They actually play the rules of the parliamentary and electoral game without wishing to consider that the totalitarian party doesn't respect these rules, and that it is only waiting to come to power to crush any kind of opposition, in line with the chief maxim of totalitarian action: "The strongest one must be the only one."

Lecture 6, September 14, 1940: The Functioning of the Totalitarian Party

Simply considering rules or laws, the totalitarian party or state is democratic: elections have their role to play at every level. Nonetheless, there is here something abnormal, and too perfect: unanimity. If everybody were truly free to

---

5. [Gustave Le Bon (1841–1931) was a French social-psychologist whose influential work, *La Psychologie des foules* (1895) outlined in critical fashion the collective minds of crowds and how these overwhelmed any single individual.—*Ed.*]

have his own opinion, then unanimity would be inconceivable. Unanimity is a sign of constraint. How is it exercised? How is unanimity achieved? These are the questions raised by the functioning of the totalitarian party.[6]

At its base, the party is formed by cells that are utterly isolated from each other. They receive directives from above. These are never discussed, only implemented. If anyone ever dared to criticize them, people would pay no attention to the value of the arguments but immediately question this person's sincerity, and he would be expelled as a saboteur. It can happen that one cell as a whole does disagree with party policy, but then, the rest don't know anything about it. Only the section, that is to say, the higher organ, is informed, and measures are immediately taken to resorb the evil or to strike it at its roots. Hence when there occurs one of the abrupt changes of orientation that characterize totalitarian parties (not enough attention is paid to this tendency), the new policy is unanimously ratified. A contrary policy would have been ratified with the same universal acquiescence. The point is that the lower levels are sufficiently well screened so that only hard-liners are sent to the Party Congress.

Likewise, the doctrine is limited to a well-defined role: it does not serve

---

6. [We find an amplified version of this talk in "Como funcionan los partidos totalitarios," *Democracia* (September 20, 1940), Caillois Archives, which recounts that in Caillois's previous lecture

he had shown that the totalitarian Nazi Party had employed the legal resources of democracy to harness public opinion and use the masses in its antidemocratic project. In this lecture, he illustrated the fact that totalitarian parties, because of their rigid structure, annul all democratic principles and defeat any attempt on the part of their constituent elements to act independently.

To illustrate his thesis, Mr. Roger Caillois took the French Communist Party as an example. He analyzed it in detail and established the premise that there was no basic difference between the internal workings of the communist, fascist, and Nazi parties. He noted that he was choosing the French Communist Party to illustrate his idea because he had had the opportunity to study it at close hand and possessed some official documents on this topic.

People belong to a party more by temperament than by ideas. Nowhere can this be seen better than in the extremist parties. In France, the Communist Party was an aggregate of people who came from all spheres of society, including the petty bourgeoisie and members of the dissolved reactionary *ligues*. The extremes meet up. And the temperamental similarity between a communist and a follower of the "Croix de feu" fascist cohorts is much greater than it is between a communist and a socialist.

This fact explains the extraordinary number of supporters that the French Communist Party was able to garner at a certain time: it was due to the obstacles barring the operations of the extreme right-wing *ligues*, fascist in essence, whose members [then] joined up.

—*Ed.*]

to determine policy, still less to verify it, but only to justify it—by means of phrases and quotations borrowed from the official theorists. These phrases and quotations naturally change according to shifts in party policy. Periodically, there are then secessions from the group by those who want to remain faithful to their ideas. However, this is never more than the departure of a few individuals who will soon disappear, while the party carries on—unfaithful, perhaps, but just as strong, combative, and vehement. For its real unity lies in its rigid structure and in a certain way of understanding politics. It is impossible to form a minority within a totalitarian party. To do so would show "divisive activity," which is the capital offense.

The elections are likewise an illusion. In reality, there are only nominations made by a higher organ of the hierarchy, controlled by a special committee, and ratified by a subsequent vote.

This is the apparatus ensuring the cohesiveness and discipline of the totalitarian party. It is an instrument well suited to the conquest of power. Alas, that is all it has left. Its members are no longer anything but the wheels of a machine; its doctrine, nothing but a supply of interchangeable slogans. Because it is freedom's enemy when it comes to its own members, by implication it will be all the more so for its enemies. Having achieved its goal by coming to power, its only options are bureaucratic stagnation or military adventure. For it never knew how to ask men to be anything more than civil servants or corporals.[7]

Lecture 7, September 18, 1940: Solidification of the Totalitarian Regime

To come to power, the totalitarian party relied on turbulence, audacity, and devotion—if not a certain spirit of nihilism and despair. But once it has become the government of the state, it assumes a completely different mentality: a distrustful and meticulous fierceness. It does not let any organism remain independent within the mass; on the contrary, the latter is rendered shapeless and inorganic in order to best direct its reactions. The party watches over the adults, creating a dual organization for every task and for every need, whose rivaling members mutually monitor and control one other. In addition, the state takes over full control of education. It intervenes in the economy, destroys the trade unions, deprives the employers of initiative or gain—all this in order to turn national production into a huge machine that complies with its orders. In

7. [See also "Como funcionan los partidos totalitarios," *Democracia*, (September 20, 1940), Caillois Archives.—*Ed.*]

agriculture, it insists on attaching the peasants to the soil and making them dependent and submissive by granting seeds, tools, and credits while establishing production quotas at the same time.

They have the same policy for the army and churches. In every instance, the point is to deny any autonomy and to bend everything to the will and needs of the state. Even the family is affected, for it constitutes a kind of intimacy that tends to detach man from the collectivity. So efforts are made to splinter the family by recruiting each of its members for a different political organism. The family then merely survives as some sort of reproductive cell meant to perpetuate and multiply the body of the anonymous servants of the state.

Propaganda, or else administrative or police coercion, has to accomplish whatever education does not. When persuasion is impossible, the regime makes promises or threats. It is upheld just as much by ambition and fear as it is by spontaneous or artificially sustained enthusiasm.

It takes particular care to crush the least sign of indiscipline or independence. The violent elements that did most to establish the regime are sacrificed in the interests of its stability: they are liquidated without pity, and for any pretext whatsoever, as in the summary executions of June 30, 1934 in Germany and the murky Moscow trials in Russia.[8] A totalitarian government does not tolerate centrifugal forces.

Everything is thus subordinated to the interests of the national collectivity, which then dedicates itself to exploiting its wealth (if some is still unused) or to conquering new riches (if it has used up its own). The totalitarian regime is industrial and military by necessity—but in varying degrees depending on its material resources. In any event, it tolerates only one type of man: the servant of the state who renounces any universal kind of concern or ambition. Mobilizing the energies of the nation to an extraordinary degree, it constantly increases its wealth and might and bans any disinterested enterprise. It dooms to disappearance those types of humanity represented by the scientist, the artist, the saint, and also the lover, the gambler, and the adventurer. It achieves a world that is regulated but mediocre, powerful but empty; one whose voracity is vast but never its contributions.

8. [The executions of June 30, 1934, otherwise known as the "Night of the Long Knives," involved Hitler's purge of Eric Roehm and other leaders of the stormtroopers (SA), who had assisted in his rise to power. Hitler feared they would try to seize power as head of a military government. The Moscow Trials, or the Great Purge, involved three highly public show-trials and several secret ones (August 1936 to March 1938) in which the Stalinist regime fabricated evidence to condemn leading Bolsheviks of treason.—*Ed.*]

Lecture 8, September 21, 1940:
The Totalitarian Nation: A Compact and Closed World

The totalitarian state is based on the identification of the part with the whole, of a party with the nation. In its usual form, though, a nation is a field of forces displaying a great waste of wealth and energy. The government keeps it coherent, but tolerates neutral zones and even trends hostile to its unity. There are some tacit divisions of power—for example, between the state and the churches. Moreover, the rights of individual conscience and of universal values are always left untouched. The pursuit of perfection, beauty, or truth are not seen as interests of the state; hence they should escape its control. The state can support but not enslave them.

By contrast, the totalitarian nation intends to capture all available energies, and domesticate neutral ones. Because it can dispose of all usable forces, it channels, distributes, multiplies, and accumulates them according to its needs. In the material realm, it assumes total control over production and allocation. In the spiritual realm, it fights any values that assert their autonomy, especially those expressing ambitions that transcend national limits. It attacks the churches above all, as these institute bonds differing from those of the racial community and represent an order to which one belongs by vocation and conversion—not by birth. Generally speaking, the totalitarian regime denies the independent reality of any fact or postulate that is not tied to the nation and that has not been subjugated to its needs. Therefore, art tends to be reduced to advertisement and scientific research to industrial applications.

Similarly, the universal value of law is no longer recognized: national utility determines what is just and unjust. There is even an attempt to destroy the code and traditions of the military caste in order to end its isolation within the nation and absorb it into the total and constant mobilization of the entire community.

In a liberal regime, liberty basically only derives from the structures' pluralism and mutual antagonism and from the variety of outlooks they reflect. The totalitarian regime, on the contrary, unifies and organizes the structures, turning them into a ruthless and rigid machine. All outlooks share the same goal: national power. The nation must suffice for everything: it is at one and the same time fact, fate and ideal, reality and a faith. Its purity must be protected against any foreign intrusion: spiritual autarky is coupled with material autarky. Boundaries become impenetrable barriers; they are the limit and point of departure for an expansionary force.

The totalitarian environment is thus an organized world that is tight and closed; inside it, there are no dead zones and no openings toward the outside.

It is a huge energy condenser, whose accumulated force can be released only by conquest. And because the conquered territory is immediately incorporated into a closed system, each annexation increases the tension and demands a new release of energy, that is to say, a new military venture. That is why the totalitarian regime is a regime of the preparation for war; and in war it finds its highest form of expression.

It is condemned to this by its very nature. War is its raison d'être, and the regime makes no secret of this fact.

Lecture 9, September 25, 1940: The Cult and Mystique of War

The totalitarian regime is materially and spiritually an enterprise of preparation for war. It represents a total mobilization of national energies, whose only possible aim is to expand and engage in armed conflict. That is why it is important to study its conception of war. Man has always found a gratification for some of his instincts in war: it allows him to cause damage. He can destroy to his heart's content. As war evolved, the more it moved away from chivalric games, tournaments, or duels, the closer it drew to its "absolute or abstract" form, as presented by Clausewitz and described theoretically in Ludendorff's work, "Total War."[9] War is then no longer politics by other means, exchanging the pen for the sword. It is the nation's supreme expression; peace is only an armistice, a time of lull, a waiting period. Banse defines the tasks of the state exclusively in view of war: selecting warriors by racist eugenics, military education, and accumulating military material and potential.[10] According to these theorists, war must be the citizen's "only passion, joy, vice, and sport."

This political philosophy is coupled with a vitalist metaphysics: war is the great and painful process of giving birth to civilizations. All fruitfulness, all progress come from war. Without war, man would turn into a fat, stupid ox, spending all his time chewing his cud, and his only ideal would be "security in property."

9. [Karl von Clausewitz (1780–1831) was a Prussian general, whose influential work on military strategy, *On War* (1832), presented the thesis that war is a form of political action rather than an end in itself. He also advocated "total war," by which he meant waging war on the enemy's entire territory, property, and population. Erich von Ludendorff (1865–1937), author of *Der totale Krieg* (Total war; 1936), was Germany's chief military strategist in the latter part of World War I.—*Ed.*]

10. [Ewald Banse, author of *Raum und Volk im Weltkriege* (Germany, Prepare for War!; 1932), was an important Pan-Germanist, expansionist theoretician. His ideas concerning geopolitics, or the theory that history is driven by geographical determinism, helped inspire Hitler's annexation of Austria and the Sudetenland.—*Ed.*]

In certain writings, such as those of Ernst Jünger, war is primarily described as an authentic divine revelation.[11] It realizes man. The baptism of fire is a real form of sacrament. It elevates the individual to a stage that neither science nor art could have let him attain. Modern war treats man as if he were matériel; it keeps him mired in mud and decay, intoxicates him with the smell of blood, smears him with liquefied corpses as if this were holy oil, keeps him on intimate terms with his excrement and vomit. War deindividualizes him, divests him of any pleasure, strength, or personal ambition; it turns him into the obscure and anonymous antihero represented by the Unknown Soldier—a perfect symbol of the interchangeably hideous fate of modern combatants, in which each individual can nevertheless recognize his own efforts, specific ordeals, and irreplaceable sacrifice.

For Jünger, war is beneficial in proportion to its horror and inhumanity. The *ivresse* of killing is equivalent to the spasm of love. It restores man to the world's fundamental principle, to its primordial prodigality. That is why the cause does not sanctify the fight; it is really the fight that sanctifies the cause. It doesn't matter if one fights for a mistake. The heroism is the same, and it lets the perishable being—who is continually perishing—overcome his fear in the same way. For a brief instant, it thus lets him attain immortality and identify with the force that moves the world—that gives birth to him and then makes him explode like a meteor. War preceded man's appearance on earth and will survive him, for it is the supreme and terrible expression of cosmic existence.

Having thus emerged from nihilism, the totalitarian regime returns to it with its conception of war—either as "hygiene of the peoples," in the Mussolinian formulation, or as revelation and ecstasy in the manner of the German lyric poets. Such a cult of orgiastic destruction is what crowns the edifice and forms the most intense, grandiose, and significant high point of this gospel of force.

Lecture 10, September 28, 1940: The Future Order

Totalitarian regimes subordinate every activity to the national power. It is not simply that the individual exists only in relation to the nation. Nothing specifically belongs to him—neither his arms, beliefs, nor pleasures. He exists

11. [Ernst Jünger (1895–1998), was a complex and prominent German novelist and essayist, whose early writings, such as *Stahlgewittern* (The storm of steel; 1920), or *Feuer und Blut* (Fire and blood; 1925), glorified his experience of trench warfare as a military officer during World

solely by dint of participating in the higher organism of the totalitarian nation, which opposes liberal nations in the way that wolves oppose lambs, and which opposes other totalitarian nations as wolves oppose other wolves. That is why war is not accidentally but essentially the mode of being for these regimes.

Whoever desires an order for the world must thus oppose to theirs a different kind of conception. It is inevitably futile to think of democracy, which finds itself disarmed in the face of systems emerging from its own vices, and whose strength comes from exaggerating and organizing the latter. Basically, democracy can fight totalitarian regimes only by imitating them. Its only options seem to be either learning from its enemies or preparing for defeat. Wisdom proceeds down the first path; events and democracy's inertia propel it down the second. Indeed, if the nation is viewed as the supreme or unique value, and if its role is indefinitely to increase its power, then, clearly, nothing in the world surpasses the totalitarian regime: it is a marvel of organization. That is why it can be properly countered only by its absolute opposite, negating the double base on which it rests: the divinization of the nation and of the popular community.

We must thus fight nationalism and demagoguery and form organic elites, grouped in bodies, without any attachments at all to the world, exclusively inspired by a solid and firm sense of caste and of dedication to their own ideal. We must conceive of these elites as multiple—in any case, as religious, military, and intellectual—and with their mission mapped out for them in the face of totalitarian regimes. It is to oppose their nationalist and racist delirium by restoring the idea and cult of universal values; to oppose their demagogic vertigo that sustains the popular frenzy and makes it a docile instrument in the handle of a leader who is nothing but the reflection, the projection of its blind furies.

Totalitarian doctrines are based on instinct and the release of obscure forces that are rebelling against the intellect; we must praise lucidity and self-mastery. Totalitarian doctrines lead to the creation of compact and closed worlds, filled with fears and petty desires—like everything that the human mind does not dominate. We must train ourselves in courage and generosity. Totalitarian regimes mean to unify everything inside each nation: each person gives everything to the state and receives everything from the state, including his ideas and emotions. We need men firmly resolved not to give the best part of them-

War I. His relation to Nazism remains murky. Indeed, he refused to join the Nazi Party in 1933, published a likely allegorical attack on Nazism, *Auf den Marmorklippen* (On the marble cliffs; 1939), and allegedly plotted against Hitler. However, during World War II he fought in the ranks of the Third Reich.—*Ed.*]

selves to the state; who are firmly resolved never to place gifts made for another use in the service of any material power; who are convinced, furthermore, that they can better serve the state by resisting it and not allowing themselves to be assimilated than by giving up everything to the blind demands of its insatiable and vain avidity.[12]

12. [See also "Al Margen de las Conferencias de R. Caillois: Culto y misticismo de la guerra"; "El Orden Futuro," *La Vanguardia*, (October 1, 1940), Caillois Archives. —*Ed.*]

Treasure and Culture

Introduction to "Duties and Privileges of French Writers Abroad"

"Were we as mute and silent as stones, our very passivity would be an act. . . . All speech has repercussions. And all silence."[1] Thus spoke Sartre in 1948, at a time when he was "concerned to rehabilitate literature, before the bar of the advancing revolution, which suspects that literature is useless," writes Anna Boschetti.[2] In 1941, Caillois was already uttering much the same thought, while rediscovering the value of literature, which the war rendered impossible.[3] And it was tied to his lingering aspiration for what he here calls an ideal, "organic solidarity that intellectuals have always lacked—a lack that has prevented them from having any effective spiritual power."

Despite its vast roster of contributors and authors, *Lettres françaises* was actually produced by a very small group of people whom *France libre* listed as Caillois, Etiemble, Emilie Noulet, and J. F. Ballière. Louis Tillier noted what he called its "in-house spirit that never degenerates into that of a clique; nor does the group of friends ever become a mutual-admiration society." Why not? Because the journal did not strive for "the 'happy' medium in the slightest; nobody fears categorical opinions, even if they run the risk of being unjust since they are human; and lies, even pious ones, are treated without mercy."[4] For one thing, *Lettres françaises* was fundamentally hostile to any celebration of French nationalism. It said the following about Henri Focillon's *Fonction universelle de la France*, published in *France libre* (April 6, 1941): "Text of a lecture given in New York in 1940. The author celebrates the civilizing mission of France with great strength of conviction. One wonders whether it would not be more appropriate to let such praise be voiced by others."[5] Furthermore, the journal's political condemnations—especially where Caillois's voice is present or discernable—aim for dispassionate clinical precision. For example, it praised "Au service de l'ennemi" (In the enemy's service) in *France libre* as "a calm, completely intellectual analysis of the cases of two 'collaborationist' writers: J. Chardonne, a grand bourgeois, skeptical, detached, and who then readily resigned himself to the simple rule of force; Drieu la Rochelle, a Romantic partisan of violence and of a unified and Nietzschean Europe. The author shows

"Devoirs et privilèges des écrivains français à l'étranger," *Lettres françaises* 2 (October 1941): 1–4.

very well how in both cases, each has had to contradict himself in order to defend his choice."[6]

As Caillois's journal has never been studied or discussed, let me cite extensively from the following review in the *Times Literary Supplement* (1942):

It is only outside France that the true voice of France can be heard. It is in reviews like *La France Libre* in London and *Lettres Françaises* of Buenos Aires, that the gagged French spirit can find expression, the silenced French conscience find a voice. *Lettres Françaises* is more purely literary than *La France Libre*. Indeed, its political flavor is only apparent in its literary criticism . . . in the "Revue des Revues" and the "Revues des Livres," and in the feature called "L'Actualité Littéraire." This chronicle of literary life in enslaved France gives its author admirable opportunities to make his points, often by mere juxtaposition. . . . Sometimes the arrow that is sent into the hides of the venal and the feeble is an arrow made and shot in France. . . . But more often [these arrows] come from the editors of the review and the barbs gain from the impartiality with which they are shot. It is not enough to be on the right side; there are duties of decorum, of proportion, of taste imposed more than ever on the representatives of the French mind in the free world. If the interesting review *La Nouvelle Relève*, published in Quebec, caters a little too much to local clericalism, that is noted. If an exile loses his sense of proportion it is noted. . . . But valuable as these negative protests are, the positive protests are more valuable still. Of such is the academic discourse of Paul Valéry on Bergson. . . . *Politique d'abord!* In a wider, deeper sense than that given to his slogan by Maurras, the editors of *Lettres Françaises* have not retreated to an ivory tower. But they have not forgotten the claims of pure letters either. The ordeal of exile, interpreted in two very different works by St.-J. Perse and Victor Serge, memories of Joyce, a plea for Chesterton, these are marginal cases. But pure poetry and pure letters, the poets of *Fontaine* and the historians of surrealism are admirably studied. And a series of "Textes à relire" [Texts to reread] from Montesquieu's "Conduite des Romains pour soumettre tous les peuples" [How the Romans went about subjugating all other populations] to Ernst Jünger serves a most useful purpose. The letter written by Renan to David Strauss in 1871 has, if anything, more force than it had then. What was then prophecy is now fact and a brutality and grossness far beyond the worst dreams of 1870–1871 has evoked a hatred, deeper and more universal than that whose rise Renan saw as the dread fruit of Germanic triumph and Germanic lack of moderation and self-criticism."[7]

In the review *Esprit* of March 1941, Emmanuel Mounier published an admirable speech on the misunderstandings that threaten to divide Frenchmen in the occupied and unoccupied zones: "During the months of war, we had raised the issue of the vanguard and the rear. After all, we do constitute a kind of rearguard—at least psychologically—with respect to the occupied zone. Today or tomorrow (after the fact) our every thoughtless deed, insouciant selfish gesture or blunder will be felt by people on the other side in exactly the same way that the combatant was affected by civilian carelessness or incomprehension. This could produce an unfortunate misunderstanding, for which we ourselves would hold the most responsibility since we are in the most privileged situation." Such cautionary measures are even more essential for French writers currently living abroad, in a free land, in America—whether by choice or by chance. The case of French writers residing in London, that is, in a country at risk, is certainly different. Those who are enjoying only the benefits of exile must remember how immensely privileged they are when compared to their fellow writers still in occupied or unoccupied France, a country that is everywhere enslaved. Therefore, their duty is to constantly recall the difficult living conditions with which the others are struggling. They already have much to atone for in being far away from them in times of ordeal; it would be criminal to behave as if they were émigrés, exclusively attentive to the new milieus that have generously welcomed them. Staying in touch with their friends is the least they can do. And this does not simply mean keeping up a correspondence or personal relationships. It means loyalty at all times. Writers who enjoy their full freedom of expression (and are being continually tempted by those around them and by their own feelings to abuse this freedom) must control themselves, out of solidarity with writers in France who are being coerced into a state of near silence. When some people are gagged, the rest should voluntarily refrain from excessive licence. They should not set about chattering and declaiming every which way, filled with indignation, boasts, or empty advice. Their advantages should only help those who are deprived of them; it would be shocking to put them to any other use. We all now live in a world where every gesture, every spoken or written word has ineluctable consequences. There are no longer any actions that leave one unscathed or that have no repercussions. Anyone who did not grasp this state of affairs would thus be excluding himself from the world of tomorrow; even today, he would simply be a puppet, more pitiful than worthy of blame.

We must also realize that this continued deference toward writers remaining in France does not demand any convenient prudence. Above all, it does not suggest that we remain neutral or silent. Can anyone really claim that the writers in France are neutral! Is someone else thereupon going to invoke the dictum that "silence is consent"? For this to be so, writers would at least have to be allowed to voice their objections if they wished to do so. Besides, they do speak, and will always speak, in a way that is more or less obscure or veiled—as concealed as necessary. It is inconceivable that a civil servant could be more intelligent than people whose intelligence is their profession; that he could outwit the very strategies that he himself has forced them to adopt.

This, then, is the duty of French writers abroad: to try to be careful interpreters of their fellow writers reduced to whispers. It is not true that they should refrain from all judgment, indignation, or action, on the grounds that they are distant and safe or that they do not share in the trials of those who are suffering. Indeed, such abstention is not what people forced to abstain expect from them. (For that matter, abstention rarely seems dictated by tact alone but also by clear-cut opportunism.) On the contrary: our loyalty toward them obliges each of us to be committed and to take sides. It forces every writer who does not want to be separated from his companions to adopt the position he thinks they would want him to adopt, on every issue. In this way there can arise a type of organic solidarity that intellectuals [clercs] have always lacked—a lack that has prevented them from having any effective spiritual influence.

Today, writers in France and abroad need each other. Writers back there, who can neither speak nor act, delegate the others to do it in their place and in line with their intent. We who are free must feel bound by this invisible chain and prevent it from becoming slack. Writers do not owe their loyalty and compliance outright to some other group. These they exclusively owe to their fellow writers, namely, to those with whom each writer feels that he shares in common the best part of himself. He need not have met them personally. It is enough that he should respect them and have sought to earn their respect in turn. It is enough that he should know they have jointly served the same cause; such is the secret and entirely ideal tribunal he must feel judging him at all times; such is the tribunal to which he must hold himself accountable.

In any event, this journal has adopted this kind of self-discipline. It is an attempt to keep French writers in touch with each other. It seeks to serve those who have remained in France, and to do so irrespective of any preference or personal liking for specific writers or movements. It will do whatever it can to prevent the emergence of any divide. It aims to express not only respect and understanding but also a spirit of obedience toward those who are proving their vigilance and courage in France. This journal wants to listen to them, observe them, repeat out loud the words they can only whisper, and make sure that the freedom it enjoys is truly put to the service of those from whom it was stolen. Here, at *Lettres françaises*, no one will feel free until these people are also free once more—except to the extent that it may help them achieve their freedom.

It is in this perspective, then, that the journal wishes to contribute to the influence of French culture. Its book and journal reviews, in particular, are written with this purpose in mind. They do not differ from those being currently published in France. They are just as eager to welcome anything that indicates a refusal to surrender and betray; just as merciless toward those who, with shameful satisfaction, take pleasure in repudiations that garner them glory and gain. These reviews are merely clearer, as their role demands. And it is in this spirit that the present issue reproduces a selection of poems and an article by Emmanuel Mounier from journals appearing in France. Let it never be said that these works, these worries, these voices were not passed along. Novelty can wait.

Introduction to "Patagonia"

Bataille presented the so-called Left Sacred to the College of Sociology as the motor, or magnetic source, as it were, of human society: "The social nucleus is, in fact, taboo, that is to say, untouchable and unspeakable; from the outset it partakes of the nature of corpses, menstrual blood, or pariahs." In this well-known talk, he suggested that, unlike other animals, "everything leads us to believe that early human beings were brought together by disgust and by common terror, by an insurmountable horror focused precisely on what originally was the central attraction of their union."[1] In the 1930s, Caillois, as we have seen, did not make such distinctions between the fundamental drives of men and animals. However, this changed during the war. "Patagonia," for example, draws a sharp contrast between the natural and the human response to death. In exploring the theme of the cemetery, though, Caillois's lyrical essay could not differ more radically from Bataille's discussion cited above. The natural windswept cemetery of the beach, with its carcasses of birds and sheep, takes shape against the carefully tended groves that instate the moment and place of human habitation. But for Caillois, the cemetery is not a magnetic, polarizing center of attraction and repulsion; it is a place of continuity, the locus of tradition, of remembrance and preparation for the future. Gaëtan Picon, in 1946, characterized the underlying idea of Caillois's wartime writings as a refutation of the "absurd" and "history" to reassert the role of human consciousness in recognizing its continuous identity over time: "man's intelligibility for himself throughout his entire evolution; something that is equally shattered by Hegelian, Marxist or Spenglerian models of history."[2] Here, perhaps, is the "secret cohesion" or humanist generalization to which Caillois now turned.

During the war, Caillois came to define literature and civilization as exemplary precedents, but without the "activist" aspects of myth. "Patagonia" exemplifies Caillois's view of civilization, which itself frames *Le Rocher de Sisyphe* (1946): "Always start everything over again? Yes, most likely. One simply has to know and accept this. Yet one should nonetheless try to firmly establish those light links whose fragility makes them very difficult to estab-

"Patagonie," *Renaissance* 1.3 (July–Sept. 1943): 419–428.

lish. . . . *There are no useless efforts. Sisyphus was strengthening his muscles.* For it is never the result that counts: any rough wind blows it away. What counts are the sacrifices and trouble one must suffer to obtain it, while knowing that it is transient; these will last, as exemplary precedents."[3] Such an ethics of effort places self-mastery, not power, at the source of civilization. Moreover, in marked contrast to the hygienic disposal of a decaying society in "The Winter Wind," civilization's worth is not lessened by the fact that the wind should blow it away. In fact, when "Patagonia" suggests that civilization has to do with such details as "whether to add cinnamon, ginger, or sugar [to bottled spirits] and, if sugar, then whether this should go into the bottom of the glass (and what shape this should be) or whether 'tis best to melt the sugar in a per-forated spoon while sprinkling it with some pure water," we hear echoes of Flaubert's *Bouvard et Pécuchet*. The value of fleeting and fragile civilization may lie precisely in its absurd futility.

"Patagonia" highlights the theme of treasure, which runs through much of Caillois's wartime writings, and stands for unproductive work—as opposed to unproductive "expenditure." He does not use the term "sacred." Nonetheless, what I call unproductive work, effort, or consecration is precisely how *Man and the Sacred* had characterized the crucial attitude of the modern sacred a few years earlier. The difference is that Caillois no longer seeks to constitute a "sa-cred milieu" but to foster, in this fashion, the impersonal and ephemeral mon-ument of civilization: each participant "shares in building a secret edifice, whose blueprint and dimensions he does not know." Discussing a "sacred lan-guage" with the College of Sociology in 1939, Paulhan had described a secret proverb society that Hollier links to his later comments, in *Le Clair et l'obscur*, about a "doubly secret" society, in which "the word forming the members into a group is still obscure for the most assiduous of them. A given man can be-long without even knowing it."[4] The secrecy Caillois evokes, however, does not relate to the fact of participating in a collective: people are aware of both their contribution and their individuation. In such a social order, what remains secret is not access or initiation but collective achievement. "The Myth of Se-cret Treasures in Childhood" describes the imaginative force of secrecy in a young child's unproductive play; "Patagonia" evokes an open or accepted form of secrecy whereby civilization transcends the adult individual—both literally and perhaps metaphorically as well. The concluding passage, in which Caillois aspires to "bring to the common treasure a minute speck of gold," seems to echo the conclusion to one of Germaine de Staël's most moving chapters in *De l'Allemagne*, "De l'influence de l'enthousiasme sur les lumières" (On the influ-ence of enthusiasm on the Enlightenment). Promoting tolerance, generosity, and conviction as a means of rebuilding postrevolutionary France in 1813, she had closed with this image: "The inhabitants of Mexico, as they pass along the great road, each carry a small stone to the grand pyramid which they are raising in the midst of their country. No individual will confer his name upon it, but all will have contributed to this monument, which must survive them all."[5]

After the war, Caillois explained the impact of his journey down the Argentine coastline and back up along the Chilean shore: "Faced with desert vastness, I felt just how uncertain founding and maintaining a human establishment actually was. I perceived some kind of crazy gamble in culture—that of the soil as well as that of the soul. I suddenly felt a tremendous respect for man's achievements, one that never left me."[6] In other words, the absence of man drew Caillois away from nature. Yet, quite striking in "Patagonia" is the complete lack of any reference to precolonial inhabitants, namely Indians, or to pre-Columbian civilization. Not surprisingly, his interlocutors at this "Discussion of Sociological Topics" gave Caillois a very hard time by recalling salient social and historical facts, specifically that Indians in Peru still made up 80 percent of the population. Of course, Argentina notoriously decimated its indigenous population in the nineteenth century. Caillois's correspondence to Ocampo shows that he was not oblivious to this issue, citing some rare encounters with Indians on his trip.[7] Then, his expanded version in 1949 evoked the "brutal and often exterminating conquest" of the continent.[8] A letter in 1947 from Malraux, then Minister of Culture, confirms Caillois's interest in promoting pre-Columbian civilization.[9] But it is clear that he was naïvely eager, at first, to view the American continent as the utopian realm of *truly elective* communities, based on antinationalist and republican ideals. His lecture in October 1941, "Tienen las Americas una historia común?" (Do the Americas share a common history?) described America as an immigrant community on a vast scale, where "the idea of nation has lost any traditional or hereditary character. It is a land of choice and adoption." In America, as opposed to Europe, the process of "becoming a nation and acquiring independence occurred simultaneously," he explained, so that "the idea of liberty is the essence of America, on an individual as well as national level."[10]

Saint-John Perse was "Patagonia"'s immediate recipient, and he wrote back about the work's "singular beauty."[11] Beyond their shared aesthetics of literary language and style, Caillois's description of Perse's *Exile* suggests a possible intertextual dialogue.[12] He writes that *Exile*'s

> sea, endlessly rolling "its sound of skulls upon the shores," insistently proclaims the world's vanity. The man who feels himself destined like the most solid monuments to the same wretched fate resolves to build pre-

cisely with those things which, being fragile and without a morrow, seem very close to having no existence. . . . If all things ceaselessly vanish here below, there is sureness only in the continuous dilapidation which forms the law of the world. The spirit, which is free, can accede to it instead of attempting to resist it: the spirit then no longer is subjected to it, but finds itself, as it were, in tune with eternity. Such is "Exile," that feeling of absence which pursues him who no longer recognizes his fatherland anywhere and who in his soul alone has chosen to discover his pleasures and his pains.[13]

The natural "vanitas" of the shoreline, the relentless demise opposed by man's most "fragile" constructions—these recall "Patagonia." However, in Caillois's lyrical prose, civilization takes shape and the poet does not retreat into spiritual exile from the world.

The work can also be read in the context of Caillois's attitude toward Valéry. As a possible allegory of the current destruction being wrought in Europe, "Patagonia" seems to stand as a realized metaphor of Valéry's most famous poem, "Cimetière marin." A note in *Lettres françaises* tends to confirm the likelihood of such a transposition when it describes Louis Lévy's "Toulon" in *France libre* as a "commemoration full of sympathy of the town, its amiable and fine inhabitants, and of the port, whose submerged fleet constitutes a new and unexpected 'Cimetière marin.'"[14] Caillois's lifelong friend, André Chastel, recalled about the pivotal years in Argentina that the "ideas of Valéry here intervened to repress, in some sense, the memory of Benda and Bataille."[15] Yet, after the war, Caillois wrote several major essays about Valéry, showing that despite certain newfound affinities, there was also deep discord. Most important, he rejected the poet's privileging of the intellect over "sensitivity," which was relegated to the role of "nature's diabolical mainspring." And in sharp contrast to Valéry's "disdain for the created universe" (in the words of Caillois), "Patagonia" dwells at length on the world.[16]

As depicted here, this is a world where even stones come to dust, "cannot keep their shape or hardness." But some thirty years later, *Pierres réfléchies* would imagine a natural burial for fossils: "Once life had been wrung out of them, the carcasses were restored to stone. . . . Many eons went by. A marble ossuary replaced the evaporated seas. The unflagging patience of a very slow chronology, the physics of tender, insistent pressures, the alchemy of metalliferous salts kept the subtle and adventurous discourse of forms from returning to original indistinction."[17] *Cimetière généralisée* (generalized cemetery).

PATAGONIA

For Victoria Ocampo

Here are the shores of a bleak and inhospitable expanse, swept by the fastest wind on earth. It blows in from the pole, with thousands upon thousands of icy arrows piercing through any kind of protection, cruelly melting into one's bones and veins, right where life's warmth seems to smoulder. Clad in the hides of the livestock he raises, man staggers under the gusts' driving force. His hands avidly seek any kind of support against the relentless violence of the storm. On the worst days, he must crawl. What vegetation can resist such blasts? Here and there, deep and fibrous roots full of viscous milk venture forth, above ground, their low, compact domes made of moss harder than stone. Far from chipping into it, pebbles splinter against this iron grass. And the sheep that must either gnaw it or die ruin their teeth in a year.

Some ships load the bales of wool piled up at intervals along the beaches of the estuaries and bays. In exchange, they deposit machines, furniture, books—whatever the first residents of a savage land may request from the distant ports of civilization.

*   *   *

Four days after setting out from the last trading post where these gifts from another world are put on board, the ship comes to a huge gate. High, glowing cliffs bar its path, leaving open only a narrow gorge, which seems very dark against their dazzling whiteness. The cliff's rising walls appear to enclose a mysterious paradise. But they quickly draw apart, fading into the distance, blending with the horizon, and reuniting then behind the boat, as if to trap it in a vast, exitless lake. Soon, their dark side is all that is visible, and the sun rising on the open sea reaches the bay's still somber waters through the slight, almost fragile cleft that is the only way in.

On the approaching shore can be discerned the most rudimentary dwellings ever built by civilized man. A mobile camp would have seemed more settled in its ways, more certain of its laws and permanence. These houses of corrugated iron, neatly aligned in rows of right-angled streets, seem to lack any kind of memories or intentions. They conform to a monotonous layout very different from the village design in more ancient lands, which is always idiosyncratic: villages clustered around churches like stars or else standing alongside a road, indicating that the geography is man-made and configured to the site. However, the people sheltered here did not think to grace these walls with any hint of their own tastes. No one stamped the sign of an individual soul upon these niches and sheds. It would have taken but a minimal effort. Just one single flower behind a curtain, or one curtain behind a windowpane. The issue here is not poverty but absence. These structures lack something found in a nomad's tent, or even an animal's den: they have not been shaped to reflect the particular being that lives inside; they do not express a few of its troubles and joys.

The same neglect prevails on the beach. One runs across the cadavers of sheep, which can be recognized by the few flocks of wool quivering on their skeletons. Further on, it is possible to make out a seal's remains; its dark fur has better withstood this bad weather. Its surface is marred only by the strong blades of its flippers, whose tips display the animal's parallel digits—still held tight as if warding off water. Or else there is a bird's carcass, more than half-buried in the wet sand; the wind is tearing off its last few feathers. It looks as if all the animals in creation have sent representatives to die here. A sea urchin shell lies on top of a passerine's skull. Bullock horns rest against a whale's vertebra. Countless animals of every size and species—some from the plain, some from the seas, still others from the skies—have gathered here to expire in a first and fatal intimacy. Fate, which had them live in contrary elements and gave them such various strengths, likes to unite them at their hour of death: a belated rendezvous fraternally restores the most dissimilar beings to the void. For one last moment, shells, wings, and cartilage still display their vain differences. The life for which these marvelous structures were created has now left them. The flesh they upheld and enclosed swiftly disappears into the ground, where everything dissolves. Even the toughest remnants, gently crushed by the ocean's useless energy, in turn become indistinct dust. They follow the feathers and scales that once covered them (each a superhuman masterpiece of material and color). They rejoin the soft substance that had rotted first—that had been considered warmer and more alive when, in fact, it was simply more perishable.

Here, even the stones get worn down and cannot keep their shape or hardness. That they do not breathe is not always of much help. This beach is implacable toward matter itself. It eloquently proclaims a law of universal and terrible destruction. Suddenly, the rumblings of war, carnage, and fires are no longer scandalous; rather, they appear to be some sort of unnecessary haste. As people with the taste for and religion of war have always maintained, such horrible massacres seem quite consistent with the order of things. They seem a sort of puerile impatience, a strange frenzy to turn time on its head and outpace the moment. The tranquil mass grave extending here gives them the appearance of some fever of nature—one that does not undo nature's secret order but simply quickens its beating heart, making it all violent and tumultuous.

The horror of battlefields was confirmed in this way by a peaceful expanse, in which each element would cooperate in restoring the many delicate structures, inhabited by a divine energy, to the very simplest types. Without hatred, the sun and salt dissolve their debris. Although we readily perceive the source and sign of life in this star and these crystals, we catch them busily erasing it, down to the very last trace.

*   *   *

In this ossuary, one corpse is missing: that of man, who gathers his companions' remains and tries to keep the shape of their bodies intact. He safeguards his own likeness against carnivores, surf, and wind. In vain, he protects an integrity that everything attacks and shatters. What prodigious care! If man believes that nothing remains of his being after death, then what scruple makes him bury or embalm a useless hull? If he imagines that something immaterial extends his life into some Beyond, this provides only one more reason to shed the importunate cover that imprisons life's spark. What is the source of this mysterious awe that both piety and skepticism almost equally bestow on a mass of flesh that is destined to scatter or rot, and that, like other corpses, probably contains some vestige that could be skillfully put to use if it were obtained in time? But neither the expectation of some Beyond nor the certitude of the void consent to deliver an inert substance to craftsmen who could draw some useful materials from it. Man, who likes nothing to go to waste, makes an exception when it comes to the bodies of other men. He considers it even more sacrilegious to use than to abandon them. And so, to protect them from any foreign attack, he sets them in an enclosed space where their solemn self-destruction is to proceed undisturbed. He attentively arranges a tidy haven for their disgusting flow, as if he sought to prevent this matter from mixing with the other, less kindred one into which it must inevitably fuse.

*   *   *

That is why human traces are the only ones absent from this macabre museum of bones, hides, and feathers. The rough inhabitants of this coast have obeyed the law of their species. Before building for themselves more stable dwellings than the houses built out of the tin cans that ships provided for their hunger, they set apart an enclosed plot for their dead. Behind a wall, they planted trees that uselessly impart to stones the shade of which the living remain deprived. They did not put the same work into their own homes. For them, man's time on earth probably seems too brief to be commensurate with a tree's patient growth. These transient creatures lack the time to await its future coolness, and so they reserve it for their remains, which will enjoy it in some less fleeting season. Slow foliage adorns the site of their final, lengthy leisure, as if to make it better and more seductive than the restful pause they sometimes grant themselves in the twilight, after a day spent working in shadeless fields. Those not yet born, though, will inherit the grove devoted to the dead, which founds in the solitude of nature the start of a human landscape.

*   *   *

The emigrant who settles there cannot bring along anything of what he leaves behind. He arrives naked and alone. He understands that here he must begin once again the history of mankind. No plants from any previous garden could adapt to this ground, because their soil has to have been tilled for a long time; and where no plough has ever passed, it is still too soon for rakes and spades. One must rediscover every clause of the compact governing the difficult management of human relationships, rediscover every rule of a secret, delicate syntax that was never formulated, but which centuries of use have made precise and hard. In this way, children acquire a sort of second language that gives both their meaning and quality to the words of others. The principles of hygiene and politeness, of gastronomy and *honnêteté* [civility]—all these fit together and uphold each other. The precepts for harnessing animals and pruning fruit trees, for lace patterns and embroidery stitches; the recipes for distilling and bottling spirits; advice on how and when to serve them, and on the proper way to drink them (all at once, or in small sips); advice on making compliments about them, on whether to add cinnamon, ginger, or sugar, and, if sugar, then whether this should go into the bottom of the glass (and what shape this should be) or whether it is best to melt the sugar in a perforated spoon while sprinkling it with some pure water; the rules of self-distrust for scientists and historians; the maxims of morality, which are always the most fragile and the easiest to respect merely in appearance; the commandments of tact that are not unusual to find surviving in hearts that have rebelled against all the rest, and in which they form there a kind of indelible deposit; how to do somebody a favor, and without ever making them aware or reminding them of it (how one offers a present and the mode of giving, as we know, is worth more than what is being given). These small codes of work, civility, and etiquette shape one's mind and teach it to resist the temptations of crudeness. Against the natural advantages of violence, ruse, and money, they establish another prestige that cannot be fully defeated by brutality, fraud, or wealth. They are what make possible every kind of glory. They make possible the existence of goods that cannot be obtained by means of money or lies, nor by fate or power.

They live in the soul, and are precisely the goods that make it strong and incorruptible, conferring a sort of grace that prevents it, at the very least, from yielding to fear or envy. But it may be imprecise to say that they live in the soul. They constitute it. For I know not what this word means, unless it is specifically a power that a man can gradually bring to fruition within; a refusal he is increasingly able to hold up to the fury of his own monsters, and to the threats and lures offered by the world to scare or seduce him. Everyone can clearly distinguish who (among the people he knows) cultivates this soul and who neglects it. I know not what we mean by civilization if it is not the habit of paying homage to these invisible treasures, and the delicacy of perception that allows people to appreciate their quality.

Is this the attribute of having a well-trained palate, a subtle sense of hearing, a hand knowing how to weigh, or of some more general capacity to discern the transparency and iridescence of things, virtues, pearls, or wines? This is not the time to propose an established hierarchy of the skills of the senses, intellect, or heart. For now, it does not matter to what end they are applied, as long as it is to the precious products of great patience. Even if all masterpieces do not equally deserve so much solicitude, it's already enough that none lets its excellence be grasped at once. Each makes the layman study in order to reproduce or appreciate it, and no education is useless. Even if the discipline pursued by the boor refines him only on a trivial point, it will foster a fruitful strictness both within and around him that can extend to higher ambitions. It is fortunate that the dazzling perfections observed in nature—which presents itself as immediate and definitive—are not man's prerogative. Just as he must take great care in forming his own treasures, he must be trained to perceive them as well. And he demands ever more perfect ones. Those that had just delighted him, and that he was proud to have achieved, disappoint him at once. They serve only to make him imagine others that, in turn, will give rise to more requirements than they themselves have satisfied. There is no marvel, temple, jewel, science, or sainthood that does not reward (whether through the sudden skill of genius or through some even more mysterious grace) at long last, an age-old gestation.

*   *   *

Of all the strands that elsewhere make up the frail network of constraints and applied efforts from which miracles ultimately arise, there is not one, on this deprived shore, that must not be woven anew. One must rediscover the necessity of every obligation at its source and also, after many trials and errors, how to define it correctly and formulate it precisely. The human heart is more difficult to seed than the soil. No magic spell can harvest it in one fell swoop. This delicate agriculture calls for a dynasty of master farmers. One cannot foresee what songs or dances so much love and persistence will bring, what words of greeting and farewell, what techniques of surveying and construction—or finally, what hierarchy of merits and virtues. Perhaps we shall witness the rise of strange customs, surprising buildings, or a legislation that is peculiar when compared to the arts and laws of another place or of today. Civilizations are diverse and do not allow for mutual understanding. Their evolution as a whole keeps them apart. Each strikes the other as monstrous and barbaric. When one of them admires enigmatic masterpieces, it is because it doubts the value of its own works or because it knows that this frivolous enthusiasm does not affect its deep preferences. Nonetheless, all styles are related, for they each require the same degree of steadfastness and discipline. They demonstrate that one effort continuously applied to the same end consecrates a human life to a task from which it draws its greatness. The generations following upon one another at the same work site are carrying out a long-term project that no single person could perform in the short time and with the feeble means he has available. He would waste his effort without prolonging or founding a single thing. One isolated individual cannot constitute the hinge between a tradition and an adventure. He does not continue or initiate anything at all. He cannot even revolt. What could his energy possibly rise up against? Someone who has received no inheritance, has been born into a desert, and has encountered no obstacles— he would have no yoke to shake off. Constrained to live for the moment, he would not leave behind any example to imitate or project to pursue—even for those dark workmen evoked by the *maudits* and who unmask hypocritical respect and false piety with righteous rage. They clear the terrain so that others may build; their rebellion demonstrates their great loyalty. But he (were he to exist) who stands alone, without historians or prophets, who has no memories and nurtures no projects—I doubt that he would deserve the name of man. His work and cries would be no more lasting than the twittering and nests of birds. His inarticulate voice would resemble the stupid and monotonous laughter of the seagulls flocking on these shores. And there would have been no reason for him to notice, among so many bones, fleeces, and feathers, the absence of his own corpse.

Throughout his life, he would share the unconsciousness of animals; his mind would be unable to embrace any stretch of time greater than what fate has allotted his existence. He would be restored to nature without ceremony or delay, delivered at once to the sun and the waves. Abandoned with indifference, his carcass would be just as untended as those of sheep and seals; it would wither away with them, disappearing as rapidly as the vain works of all fraternal living beings who endlessly renew the same life over again because they do not honor their dead.

By digging a grave for his remains, man founds his claim on the future. He does not consent to having his existence repeat that of his fathers—in the way the lives of other beings with nothing to receive or pass along eternally repeat themselves. He also shows that he can remember and prepare. He establishes a continuity. By linking his efforts to those of his contemporaries, he unwittingly unites them with those of a host of vanished or future beings. He thus shares in building a secret edifice, whose blueprint and dimensions he does not know. He does not know that his travails, quarrels, and daring—more fruitful than his docility—are what make the changing House that shelters him evolve from first draft to architectural completion. Imperceptibly, the workman's hand acquires unerring skill; the potter and the poet define the rules of their art; the sculptor can produce the purest curve and select the hardest material; and the heart learns the worth of daily virtues: steadfastness, discretion, delicacy, generosity, and certain others from which it may now suddenly choose. And then, finally, it can conceive the value of unique and perilous qualities that serve in difficult times and demand more greatness, courage, and hope.

*   *   *

This is how a civilization appears. Here is its pledge, in the garden dedicated to unfeeling remains, upon this severe shore. The stubborn trees and shade that men think they have raised here for other shades already offer, to a desolate land, the promise of the supernatural forests that will consecrate its valor and devotions.

Here, on a ground so harsh that one doubts man could ever take hold, an homage of leaves publicly testifies to his first victory. Who would not here perceive the fate of this untiring being? He will populate the infertile vastness and make it give rise to towns and harvests of all kinds.

There will always remain enough vast deserts for those whom no wealth can satisfy. And what would be the meaning of their contempt if they left nothing behind? These scornful individuals will have no lack of empty spaces with which to feed their soul on substantial absence. But such detachment, the final conquest by a few rare elect, is beyond what man must first be proud to have produced. I want him to advance toward destitution, working his way through the excess of cumbersome wealth brought about by his ardor and genius. I want him to reach a state of poverty, giving up the very talents and virtues most costly to obtain. As I enter into his solitary expanse, I wish fertility upon a miserable realm where only fishermen of souls and gold prospectors first set ashore. I would like to see their dual avidity rewarded and to contemplate this continent of promises covered with miraculous ears of corn.

*   *   *

Descending the coastline to one of its outermost points, I rediscover on the open seas the immortal gifts that no one has earned, and in the face of which actual civilizations themselves seem to last only one day: the sea, the cold polar wind, and that fixed constellation sprawling, chainlike, across the vastest sky. I will not rush to measure my life against their longevity. First, I must learn how to be worthy of the obscure workmen who are initiating here a perishable creation. Over there, the ancient effort of their predecessors made me affluent. Why would I be disloyal to them, for loyalty merely orders me to do well whatever I have set out to do? Showered with riches and born into the very warehouse in which history amassed them, I am too indebted to men to scorn their labor and refrain from taking part. As each of them has done, I must by dint of decency and rigor, on a good day and with some luck, bring to the common treasure a minute speck of gold. Only then will I no longer feel like a parasite or impostor but will stand tall in my place and rank. I will be able to address all the works of mankind on equal terms. I will even have won the right to distance myself and watch, then, how they grow smaller before disappearing altogether.

Introduction to "The Myth of Secret Treasures in Childhood"

In early 1941, Caillois wrote to Ocampo about his

> childhood pleasure in greeting people and especially in taking them back to the elevator. In the past, at home, I similarly liked to bring people who would come to our house all the way up to my room. You too: I drew you there when I first could, and moreover to show you my "treasures." Those were books. Prior to that, they were special stones hidden in the corner of the garden in the countryside or in a beam of the barn. There was a greater or lesser initiation to the treasures, according to the degree of favor I bestowed; the hiding places that I opened up were more or less numerous. . . . Here, once again, I have treasures and secrets (the two things merge). . . . An object that is, by nature, meant to be exhibited (a box of butterflies) cannot become a "treasure," even if I like it very much. If you wished, I could go on talking to you about this for a long time. It's my particular kind of childhood memories. I suppose they reveal a personality that is both exhibitionist and secret, and—already—the taste for an elite of "initiates." [1]

Clearly, Caillois attached some significance to this confession, as he wrote to Ocampo several days later: "I would not wish my 'letter about treasures' to get lost: I wrote it thinking that it would amuse you and that you would make comments." [2] Rather cruelly—and childishly?—he apparently neglects the fact that Ocampo had been greatly upset by his marriage the previous month. "Don't write to me any more," she unconvincingly insists, while responding that she, too, had possessed childhood treasures but that "basically, people are what made up my treasures. Perhaps you are right to love *things*. That gives less sadness." [3]

"The Myth of Secret Treasures in Childhood" considers certain aspects of the private, modern experience of the sacred, as defined in *Man and the Sacred*, where Caillois had described how cult and ritual were now distilled into the

"The Myth of Secret Treasures in Childhood," trans. Lawrence Krader, *V.V.V.* 1 (June 1942): 4–8.

mere acknowledgment of "a sacred element, surrounded by fervor and devotion, which one avoids talking about and tries to hide, for fear of exposing it to some sacrilege (insult, ridicule, or merely a critical attitude) on the part of the indifferent, or one's enemies who would not respect it."[4] In 1942, Caillois does not explore this with any explicit reference to the sacred but instead to the private "secret treasures" of childhood—which an adult must transcend and overcome to achieve the true, collective "treasure" of civilization (see "Patagonia").

Before the war, the figure of the miser had its place in Caillois's roster of the private, modern sacred, with a "fortitude" evoking the master's self-mastery in "L'Aridité": "the joy of pure possession, the sterile possession of riches held back from circulation, kept unproductive and that one prefers to destroy rather than turn into usefulness or happiness."[5] Benjamin had specifically criticized this passage in 1938, perhaps indirectly—or unintentionally—targeting Bataille as well. Among other things, he claimed that Caillois endorsed the praxis of "Monopolkapitals" (monopoly capitalism), which "prefers to destroy its resources 'rather than transform them into utility or happiness'" (this last phrase quoted from "L'Aridité").[6] In "The Myth of Secret Treasures in Childhood," though, such unproductive hoarding has shed its Bataillean associations with destruction and "expenditure." As a phenomenon of childhood, it helps constitute the burgeoning individual and thus set the stage for the "fortitude" and "unproductive work" of adulthood.

Of course, Caillois's view of childhood could not be more different from the Romanticism of Bataille, for whom "a return to childhood" would constitute the aim of literary transgression in *Literature and Evil*.[7] Beyond that, Caillois's treatise on childhood—or, implicitly, on maturity—challenges the idealization of childhood by the avant-garde, and specifically, by Breton and Leiris. (The recently renewed dialogue with Surrealism included Breton's letter to Caillois regretting their break and the latter's indictment of politically and morally insouciant French intellectuals exiled in New York; see "Duties and Privileges of French Writers Abroad").[8] Ambivalently, one might say, "The Myth of Secret Treasures in Childhood" gestures back to Surrealism by providing a roster of the movement's attitudes toward the "privileged object." Both the actions here described by Caillois and the article as a whole redeem the Surrealist aesthetics of mystery. Indeed, the scene of the child painstakingly hiding a small object in the wall could well seem to reverse—and thus negate?—Caillois's desire to dissect the famous Mexican jumping bean in 1934. But let us not forget that the adult narrator here has a normative perspective on such construction of secrecy, as something proper to childhood alone. Presumably, unlike Kojéve's magician, the child can be enchanted by his or her own tricks.

Caillois seems to address a similar commentary to Michel Leiris's founding text for the College of Sociology, "The Sacred in Everyday Life," which implicitly conflates the imagination of children and archaic cultures together with his own: "What, for me, is the *sacred*? To be more exact: what does *my* sacred consist of? What objects, places or occasions awake in me that mixture of fear and attachment, that ambiguous attitude caused by the approach of something simultaneously attractive and dangerous, prestigious and outcast—that combination of respect, desire, and terror that we take as the psychological sign of the sacred?"[9] For Leiris, the imaginative landscape mapped out during childhood will later constitute, more or less unchanged, the cherished basis of adult vertigo, or the "psychological" sense of the sacred. *Man and the Sacred* had noted, when describing the ambivalent or ambiguous attitudes triggered by the sacred, "The sacred stimulates in the believer exactly the same feelings as fire does in the child—the same fear of being burnt, and the same desire to light it."[10] However, "The Myth of Secret Treasures in Childhood" does not consider such ambivalence in its implicit correlation of childhood and the sacred, perhaps because Caillois is searching for the sources of moral and intellectual strength—as a bulwark against vertigo, whose lure he now frequently decries. "Yet that [the mind] should always be tempted by [vertigo]," he also writes at the time, "is what constitutes its greatness."[11]

Perhaps the closest analogy to Caillois's secret treasures may be found in Saint-Exupéry's *The Little Prince* (1943), written while the aviator was temporarily exiled in New York.[12] Recuperating a golden-haired myth of Rimbaud for Christian humanism and for the war, this fable evokes innocent and virtuous visionaries: "When I was a little boy I lived in an old house, and there was a legend that a treasure was buried in it somewhere. Of course, no one was ever able to find the treasure, perhaps no one even searched. But it cast a spell over that whole house. My house hid a secret in the depths of its heart."[13]

THE MYTH OF SECRET TREASURES IN CHILDHOOD

Muted and dim for the adult, the word "treasure" speaks eloquently to the child, and sparkles before his eyes with the most glowing power. These syllables, which age, experience, and reflection soon render unusable, shine in childhood with a splendor equaling the riches they represent. They scintillate like doubloons buried by pirates of old in the depths of caves, like rubies, emeralds, and so many brilliant stones at the moment when they are brought to light by earthly hands, which they fill with fire. Yet, can children be carried away by stories in which they recognize nothing of their own desires and sorrows, to which they are total strangers, which surprise instead of captivating them? Like the novels of adults, these tales would not please the children nearly so much if they did not speak to them of themselves, and if they did not describe to them their everyday concerns, distantly and dramatically veiled.

In fact, it is not so much that children believe in treasures. These they have. It is not just that they imagine that with courage, perseverance, and cleverness they will discover treasures in the depths of grottoes, where adventurers have left them. They themselves conquer and amass similar caches, which they jealously sentinel. Little do they know that the cares and tastes of freebooters are, for the most part, overzealous echoes of their own experience. Really, how are we to tell whether the child conducts himself as he does in imitation of the fictions he devours, or whether, on the contrary, these legends do not illustrate, in a romantic way, convictions natural to an awakening consciousness, habits and modes of behavior normal to a being who does not yet feel himself on the same scale as his environing world? It often happens that imagination and conduct serve each other as doubles, lend each other mutual support. Issued from the same source, they act jointly, and one does not know, as in the myth and the rite, which precedes and which follows, the posture or the belief. We must investigate the nature of this fictitious wealth, in which children perceive real benefits.

It is not a matter of riches, whose sum can be calculated in specie. Treasures are constituted by privileged objects. It is not the sale value of these objects that makes them precious: that is often nil. The fact that they are rare does not make them the more attractive: they may be commonplace; they are not required to be beautiful; they are not souvenirs. They have not belonged to any dear one. They recall no anniversary, joy, or pledge. They have neither been given nor taken as security. They are often found in the gutters. It is not that they are rare, but that they are coin of another realm. They are not beautiful, but brilliant. The child therefore keeps the tinfoil that wrapped his chocolate bar. He rates "steelies" above all other marbles. Mercury attracts him more than any other substance. Bodies of this sort possess a magnetism that sensibly enhances the somewhat mysterious character of their nature: here is a metal that folds, that crumples, with which one may cover and silver all things; there is another metal that eludes the grasp, that flows, that skids away in droplets, that is cold to the touch. What attributes may not be expected of such surprising substance? They are powerful and active, as the "steelie" that cracks the clay "immie" or sends it flying; as the polished glass stopper that isolates the wet and separates it from the dry better than a cork could. It alone can serve as a *hermetic seal*: the obscurity of the term proves the importance of the thing. It is fitting to keep under cover and apart any substance whose effects are terrible or deadly. These attributes bring it within the circle of privileged objects. For privileged objects are by their nature tokens of violent death. Whatever appears capable of killing surely must be treasured. An insignificant letter opener cuts the figure of a dagger. A bottle containing some harmless lotion becomes a vial filled with the most thundering poison. It is enough that it came from, and still possesses, the atmosphere of the pharmacy, in whose back rooms white-coated men mix potions that cure, and whose display windows are mysteriously decorated with immense globes of glass filled with colored liquids. How many children are not equally intrigued by the machinations of the young heroine of current fiction, who is described as "concocting fake poisons, hiding vials, pasting macabre labels, inventing dark names"? And what destiny is not promised by a bottle, a striking appearance, suggestive of important uses?

The administration of these treasures is no less singular than their nature. Often, some risk must be run to win them: the star pupil has to steal the mercury, drop by drop, during physics class, risking dread punishment. Or he will go the length of breaking thermometers at home. He thus uncovers the forbidden metal that becomes all the more precious to him because to replenish his stock of it he has sacrificed the principles of obedience and honesty. Moreover, the danger he runs of being caught redhanded in each new larceny adds to the charm of the magical substance, a charm further enhanced by the necessity to wait for occasions favorable to theft, by the care he must take to disguise on the spot so fleeting a thing without losing a drop, and by the difficulties that stand in the way of his carrying it off without too much loss. For one cannot stuff it into one's pocket or keep it in a poorly stopped bottle. It penetrates cork, is swallowed by all porous bodies, and little drops of it emerge when you press the stopper of any makeshift repository into which it has been poured. Above all, it must be kept from contact with other metals, for mercury unites with everything and corrupts everything, even honest gold. Nothing is more desirable than this liquid destroyer of substance reputed to be unalterable; besides, it is so difficult to capture and keep.

But even if it had not been dangerous to take hold of the alluring object, it would have required luck and time to find it. One may come across it in a needle of rock crystal, a spear point of gypsum, a block of solid perfume, a scented paste that suddenly becomes the prodigious poison with which the

Old Man of the Mountain intoxicated the Assassins.[1] But most envied is he who possesses a chip of the fabulous Iceland spar with the double refraction.

Chance, difficulty, and danger; these are the qualities that give prestige to the chosen objects. The child who makes them his treasure feels all the pride of possessing them: they serve him not just as fetishes and good luck pieces. They spirit him away to the world of adventure and distances, lead him over the least navigable, the least explored seas, the Sargasso Sea, floating graveyard of ships, and introduce him at last to fabled fastnesses hidden from sight by the bulk of mountains. They appear as booty lifted from a universe compared to which the real is weak and pale, a universe whose power and glory they keep intact. It is a question of glowing embers from an unquenchable fire within, of a magic snow brought down from inaccessible heights, a snow that no matter where you keep it, will never melt. It is as though the objects that the child treasures were able to retain within a small mass, ordinary enough in appearance, a beauty, a force, and a mystery that reside only in the essence of elements and at the limits of the habitable globe. So too in mythologies the other world is spoken of as containing the most powerful and least conceivable objects: golden apples, blue birds, singing streams. These exhibit exactly the qualities that the child's treasures recombine, in particular that quality of extreme intrinsic rarity that is not the direct contrary of multiplicity, that strangeness that seems to contravene miraculously all natural law, producing mixed species, like the hippocampus, steed of the seas, and precious stones that are diaphanous and hard, thus uniting the contradictory virtues of fire and water. Their appearance may be magnificent or wretched (you have to seize the giant ruby, the silver sword, but so, too, is an old lamp the prize, a bonnet with holes is the cap of invisibility, and of three caskets you must choose the shabbiest). Finally, the power invested in these objects enables you to go beyond what is normally possible: it permits you to disappear at will, to paralyze from a distance, to subdue without a struggle, to read thoughts, and to be carried in an instant wherever you want to go.

Magical objects, like the objects treasured by children, are not at the disposal of the first comer. To win them, you scale heights at swordpoint, fight dragons, swim fiery streams. Many extraordinary ordeals must be endured to prove oneself predestined, both by natural audacity and by the favor of the djinns. Luck and courage are firmly linked. A happy ending repays bravery;

1. [With their phrase, "The Old Man of the Mountain," the crusaders thus referred to the twelfth-century Syrian grand master of the "Assassins"—the legendary Rashid ad-Din as-Sinan. Derived from the term "haschisch," the Islamic "Assassin" sect (ca. 1100–1300) would allegedly ready itself for martyrdom by enjoying drug-induced visions of paradise.—*Ed.*]

but, on the other hand, one can be courageous only if one has faith in one's star. Here, more than anywhere else, fortune smiles on the audacious. Whoever is not sure of his destiny is not sure of himself; he lacks the self-control necessary to surmount the deadly perils awaiting him.

These costly marvels will not permit themselves to be seen or touched save by him who can carry them away. It is as if they would be profaned by vulgar contact and lose their virtues if not separated from common things and uses and from casual touch. Hence children seek for their chosen objects hiding places worthy of such privileged natures, places secret as the things themselves. For treasure is a secret. The notion of treasure and the notion of secret are almost completely complementary. It is not enough that the uninitiated cannot find the hiding place; he must be completely unaware of its existence. No doubt it can be revealed, but only with the proper solemnity. Then one conducts precisely the ceremony suited to the consecration of friendship. Surely you are not going to share a secret with him who is not worthy! The revelation of secret objects thus becomes for the child the supreme token of confidence and the cement of brotherhood. The Graal, appearing before its assembled servitors, does not unite them less and does not guarantee a firmer fidelity. The disclosure of the treasure to a friend will not only arouse his admiration and respect, but also bind him to silence about what he has seen, pledging him to maintain an unbreakable loyalty to the possessor. It amounts to a true initiation rite. The child who inducts into his secrets the one he has chosen from among all others, and who reveals in order the hierarchy of hiding places where the precious objects are ranged behind three, and even four, false fronts, conducts himself in a manner not essentially different from that of the priest presiding over the underworld of Eleusis or, in some African glade, revealing to the novice the secrets of his cult. He leads him through the various degrees of initiation, guiding him to ever more sacred and secret treasures, kept in the depths of an impenetrable sanctuary or buried in places set apart under stones of no value, which seem never to have been displaced by the hand of man.

As with mystical objects, the treasure owes its value to the fact that it is unknown. The child takes infinite precautions to lift the wallpaper, scrape out the plaster behind, place within the hollow his prodigious deposit, and to paste back, as best he can, the paper torn in what appears to be the most accidental way, or, conversely, in accordance with the pattern of the designs. It might be said that by this procedure he assures his own life and stows it safely away. He bases his personality on the possession of this imaginary secret. Comparison with the myth is once more revealing: here, too, the life, the power, and the courage of the hero is fastened to an external and material soul: a weapon or a mirror, a feather or an egg; to some magnificent or humble but always fragile object, guarded in the crook of a tree or locked in a sunken vessel, in a place not easy to recognize or reach. The mere disclosure of this external soul, or its destruction, always eventuates in the death or impotence of the hero. Like Samson, he loses thereby the magic faculties that raise him above common men.

This is the true meaning of treasures to the child. By means of them he escapes from the dependence in which the grown folk keep him. The treasures that he guards, without the knowledge of his parents, do not merely introduce him to the imaginary world of adventure and miracle. On the contrary, they found the child's autonomy and help him to gain a footing in the real world, whose adult pleasures he envies and access to which is prevented by so many humiliating prohibitions (don't play with fire, don't pick up knives). His gravest concerns are not taken seriously. Possession of the treasure gives him revenge and, also, an importance refused him until then. The objects that he alone recognizes, whose price and power he alone knows, that have been conquered in open war or that good fortune has placed in his path, of which he is the sole and mysterious master in a world where he is permitted to own only the playthings we pretend amuse him, confirm his new-born feelings of self-estimation and assure his young courage. These objects set conditions and yield rewards.

Far removed from economic concepts is the concept of treasure. It is their precise negation. It belongs to the realm of the magical. It evokes an inalienable opulence, not symbols of conventional exchange. Never has treasure been composed of notes and titles. A mother calls her son her treasure. The money of a banker is only wealth. The riches residing in treasures cannot be bargained for. They heighten the spirit of the discoverer. They have to glow with every kind of fire. They may have been acquired by crime, but not by avarice. Coins may be mixed with pearls and rubies, but they must have long since lost currency and have value only as gold. Where pirates have interred their splendid plunder an adventurer finds by chance a brilliance increased by shadowy depths. This is nothing that labor can amass. The conjunction of chance and daring is necessary, an exceptional victory, in which all forces, from destiny to merit, have coincided. A fabulous success has repaid faith in the impossible. The qualities employed to obtain it are clearly opposed to the patient, regular toil by means of which the workman in the fable helped his children acquire a treasure they had not dreamed of, precisely the kind of treasure that the defiant heart discounts.

Real treasures are not accumulated. No amount of obstinacy discovers them, no foresight expects them; they infinitely exceed the capital a life of privation and effort is able to amass. They are sudden bursts of splendor, and bestow less money than glory on the young hero who has conquered them. He takes from them only the pure certainty of his destiny, a sign that he is able to conquer nature and men.

There is no lack of stories flattering this strange faith. There is Edmond Dantès, suddenly transformed by a treasure into the powerful Count of Monte Cristo. Dungeon and riches make of him another man; his physical appearance is changed: he becomes handsome, suave, strong, and implacable. He knows all customs and speaks all tongues. In the vengeance he pursues he believes himself to be the instrument of fate. On another level, but in a genre that addresses itself equally to the imagination, in almost every one of the works of Villiers de l'Isle Adam, treasures play a role of the utmost importance and with their far reflections illuminate the whole story. They are always about and always active, working on the heroes like a charm. Their value as talisman, the magic power attributed to them, has never been so well or faithfully described. Finally, what is to be said of fairy tales? We know that they are filled with treasures that serve as the rewards destined for their favorites by gnomes, elves, and kobolds. Here dwarves hold mountains ajar and conduct the chosen into a subterranean world, where inconceivable gems have slept for centuries. The brilliance of these gems encloses God knows what curse and spell, which shows to what extent he who seeks treasure departs from the standard gauges of prosperity.

This is because treasures do not belong to the social world and have nothing to do with law or custom. They are the fruit of an inexplicable larceny or of a sacrilegious pact. They come from the dark and invest with virtues and rights that hardly facilitate the spirit of docility and resignation. They incite to adventure and sanction the ambition to be more than a man. Yet the child wants most of all to be a man, the equal of adults. And so, by means of the objects he has acquired and which he cares for with piety, he opposes to the world that neglects him the first offerings of a personal activity that seems all the more important insofar as the care taken to keep it secret renders it the less illicit. It takes the child from the circle of those who scorn him, and opens to him the gates of a world full of wonders, where his value is recognized and where he finds the employment refused him elsewhere. Imagination anticipates reality; it has not yet become the refuge of frustrated hopes and lost illusions; it is the lance of real conquests. These bits of glass, these drops of mercury, these rolling dice, simple images of chance, these tiny and ridiculous windfalls, these valueless vials of waste and odd-ends of adult occupations, but brilliant, rare, difficult to acquire, educate the child's spirit and teach it to be faithful first of all to itself. They help the child to affirm himself, to prize more than anything else certain personal goods that take their value only from the worth that he bestows on them. The world may scorn such miserable objects. They are sanctified by the sacrifices made for them. But by these laughable intermediaries the child tempers his spirit and is enabled to safeguard, with a little secret, the source and warrant of his future strength. It is his own ego that the child tends with such care. In its hiding place the material treasure already protects man's faith in his own task and in the favor of fate. Whoever would act must neither presume too much on his powers nor underrate them; he, above all, who does not believe that he needs to hope in order to begin or to succeed in order to persevere needs more than anyone else to feel within his own being an ultimate power, which no disaster can ruin, no triumph distort. It is enough not to expect at the hands of fate those goods that you first prize. It is enough to fear most of all the weaknesses of your own heart.

Introduction to "The Situation of Poetry"

"Among the urgent tasks that these times demand of the mind," Caillois had written in mid-1938, responding to an "Enquête sur la poésie indispensable" (Survey about indispensable poetry), "one of the most important is to restore poetry to its proper and mediocre function, to confine to its small domain this activity which is so presumptuously invading the great ones."[1] In a somewhat similar vein, "The Situation of poetry" declared, "These times will have witnessed poetry's attempt to become everything that it is not: magic, mysticism or music."[2] Yet there is a crucial difference between these two responses. The latter essay went on to introduce a special double issue of *Lettres françaises*—devoted to poetry.

Rehearsing the grounds of his hostility to poetry in the 1930s, Caillois outlines the two alternative choices at the time—confessional lyricism and pure poetry—which recall the distinction between "impure" and "pure" (or "dehumanized") art of *Art on Trial by Intellect*. But now, Caillois does not close with a gesture toward science. Instead, he opts to reconsider the difference between poetry and prose, to insist that poetry must share the transparency of prose—and to this should be added formal constraints and mystery, from which "it draws its most personal effects." Not a word here about the poetic image or metaphor, which Caillois shunned for a long time after his rift with Surrealism, before his slow reinstatement of its privileged place after the war.[3] In the preface to an anthology of French poetry published in Buenos Aires in 1944, Caillois spoke of the need to "humanize mystery, I mean to show everyone that mystery is relevant to him and enriches him." And while attacking overwrought poetic enigma, he praised "this surprising fusion of poems and songs—already noticeable before the war in the writings of very young poets—which with the war seems to have greatly accrued. Indeed, songs are the traditional genre that makes one easily accept the element of mystery and uncertainty which is still an essential, almost indispensable, attribute of poetry. It may bore or disorient people when it seems freely cultivated at will; but it is enchanting if one surmises that the only obscurity retained is that which always subsists in matters of life and destiny."[4] "The Situation of Poetry," though, laid

"Situation de la poésie," in *Approches de la poésie* (Paris: Gallimard, 1978), 23–27.

the grounds for its new poetic aspirations in the poems of Victor Hugo and Saint-John Perse. In 1952, Caillois evoked what had seemed so praiseworthy about Hugo during the war. What appealed to him were not the hallucinatory images, the "visionary" Hugo, but rather a more "daring" and, "as one says, more modern" aspect of the latter's poetics, by which Caillois meant the lack of signification: "These texts without meaning present themselves as fables without a moral, but they nonetheless retain—without losing any of it—what constitutes the intimate coherence, accuracy and authority of fables, legends, proverbs, of any image or sentence that can persuade us by means of prestige [marvel] and immediately so."[5] This brings to mind Jean Paulhan, whose life-long fascination with the impersonal and powerful rhetoric of proverbs, fables, and legends deeply influenced Caillois.[6]

If Hugo offered Caillois accessible, that is authentic, poetic mystery, Saint-John Perse gave him the basis for a new poetic apprehension of the world and, in particular, of objects.[7] In 1943, in his essay "The Art of Saint-John Perse," he wrote that the vocabulary and contents of the "songs" *Eloge, Anabase,* and *Exil* were so "disconcerting" that they seemed entirely invented but were actually based in fact: "One would swear that the things evoked by the poet were invented by an imagination given to fantasy and recognizing no other law than its own caprice. But one is soon led to recognize that everything is true to life and has been borrowed from various parts of the world and assembled here in a disparate collection of wonders. . . . The entire universe contributes to this total museum in which man's rarest and most moving conceptions are arrayed in long processions."[8] Caillois's fascination with the "processional" quality of Perse's poetry would develop into his extensive analysis of this lyrical *musée imaginaire* in *Poétique de Saint-John Perse* (1954), focusing on its "encyclopedic" structures (Borges, Jules Verne, and Toynbee are other "encyclopedists").[9] This analysis would later provide, in turn, the groundwork for Caillois's distinctions between the literary and the scientific imagination, between Saint-John Perse and Mendeleyev.[10]

THE SITUATION OF POETRY

Reports confirm that owing to France's misfortunes and defeat, many people are seeking in poetry the solace that has probably been hard to request from reality itself. According to André Gide, we must not be surprised that, "just like those who 'enter the religious life,' so many young people have entered the life of poetry, while preceded or joined in this 'clergyhood' by so many of their elders." Another witness recounts: "Since the armistice, there has been a continuous explosion of poetry. Many booklets are being produced every day (this common phenomenon is not limited to the past few months); in addition, poets are being welcomed by literary journals in a way suggesting that the current ones, without exaggeration, are all chiefly poetry journals. This welcome also reflects the public's desire. Poets are now being read in the way that one recently used to read fictionalized biographies: avidly. And reading is not enough. People talk about them; hold forth about them; bitterly argue about them. And this is happening everywhere: in the journals, of course, but also in the daily newspapers, which have now joined in." The fact is that during these somber times, many people, over there, find refuge and hope in poetry.

I do not know what such a preference augurs for literature. As far as I'm concerned, if this is the right place for a confession, I do not understand much about poetry and always felt more disposed to fight it rather than giving myself over to it. The poems that were being published were almost exclusively lyrical, and I do not much like lyricism. Moreover, it seems natural to consider oneself a poet. Or at least, this is what many people believe. They cannot experience any emotion without feeling it should be confided to verse. Hence the large number of naïve confessions, forced images, and pretentious expressions generally contained in poetry colllections. The bombastic vies with the mannered. Here more than elsewhere people seem convinced that sincerity replaces all effort and merit. Yet nothing comes of this but wind and foam. An art that seems inclined to favor only the most facile and futile qualities over strict, severe measures leading to excellence can hardly provoke much respect.

Furthermore, because the poets were giving up metrics and prosody as well as rhyme and caesura, their writings could usually be distinguished from prose solely on account of a typographical layout whose raison d'être was no longer apparent; a monotonous and loose syntax tending toward simple lists and, finally, a basic incoherence of dubious worth. In short, these poems struck me as bad prose, that is, as a lazy mode of self-expression. I vaguely suspected that often the writer was a poet merely to escape the requisite discipline of thought and style.

Insofar as he demanded less from work itself and entrusted more to inspiration, the poet would inflate his ambitions: calling himself a magus or prophet, a *voyant* or metaphysician. He believed that if his verse were unintelligible, this would suffice for it to contain some mysterious revelation, capable of astounding reason and ravishing the soul. Some people, on the other hand, driven by laudable aims, had thought of isolating poetry in the same way that a chemist extracts a pure species from the raw material being analyzed. This meant deriving a concentrated and precious essence from the crude compound within which it lay invisible and dissolved. A knowledgeable chemistry, or so people claimed, could thus disengage poetry from the various residuals that were altering it so extensively that its specific properties were destroyed. Once set free, made whole and unalloyed, poetry would be fully resplendant at last. People would come to know its true features. In every verse, its nature would be made manifest at its paroxystic height, instead of emerging here and there throughout the poem. The ambition was excellent, the result unsuccessful. Poetry, now disincarnate, had lost its power to move the reader, while gaining nothing in return. When all verses laid claim to equal status, the spell of a successful verse glistening against a neutral background became imperceptible. Even more important, once poetry had been carefully cleansed of the merits of prose and painstakingly reduced to its particular virtues, it appeared meager and quasi-skeletal. Its powers were equally diminished. It seemed as if this absolute divorce had left it without substance. In the end, this purity that uprooted poetry, driving it to mere acoustical effect (just as painting, at the same time, was content to produce abstract combinations of proportions and colors), was transforming it into an artificial discipline, whose sole interest was the one people were generously willing to grant it.

My own idea of poetry, on the contrary, is quite humble and trivial. I would not release any prey for its shadow, nor give up what is sure for the sake of some uncertain benefit. And so I envision poetry, above all, as a mode of writing that obeys not only the constraints of prose but also its own special constraints, such as number, rhythm, and the periodic repetition of sounds; its powers must consequently exceed those of prose. As you can see, nothing could be more prosaic than this idea. So I ask that poetry should have all the qualities required of prose, which first and foremost include those of bareness, precision, and clarity, and which all aim to eliminate the gap between language and thought. The poet must seek to express everything that he pleases, and only that. Taken to its extreme, this means that poetry should include nothing ineffable or suggestive, no evocative images, mystery, or ambiguous and prestigious verses whose meaning depends not on the author (who scandalously puts up with this uncertainty) but on the reader—and which thus vary according to his character, or perhaps his whim. I have always been surprised that Valéry's austere genius could have developed the theory of this strange abdication.

As opposed to such varied, and often legalized, abuses, I thus imagine a discourse that fully resembles prose but also possesses the perfections of poetry. These must involve a gain that is not offset elsewhere—a supplement of efficacy that is not paid for by less rigor or refinement. It may seem surprising that I am so relentlessly drawing poetry closer to prose. Some will assure me that if my wish were to be fulfilled, this would more surely kill poetry than would the hollowest delirium of its most fanatical supporters. But it would probably be discovered as well that many of the most beautiful lines, and the very ones appearing to contain the infinite (whether by Racine, Nerval, or Baudelaire), do not greatly contravene these exigencies. But what about music? What about the harmony produced by a simple syllabic assemblage that seems so spellbinding, and whose sounds appear self-sufficient, quite apart from the meaning of the words they form? When we listen to or pronounce such sounds, do we not have a sense of satisfaction that is suddenly fulfilling?

I hope that this is not so. For if the exclusive role of verse were to flatter the ear, then I would be able to distinguish it from song and music only in terms of its lacks and flaws. And I imagine that musicians would turn away from it, not finding there all they sought, just as readily as those who prefer the gratifications of the intellect to the transports of the senses.

We must therefore challenge these parasitical forms of prestige and deceptive charms. Yet it is nonetheless clear that poetry is better suited than prose when it comes to mystery, and it draws its most personal effects from this source. Some poems contain an enigmatic apologue that we believe to be true even though we do not know what inner situation could clarify or explain it. With only a premonition of what these parables might mean, we wait for events to elucidate or confirm this. Yet such a key might not open any door, or else we might never happen to be standing in front of the door that it does open. We will never uncover the lesson hidden in the omen: the right moment will never have come, and the omen will remain useless. This untitled poem by Victor Hugo, which begins, "Autrefois j'ai connu Ferdousi dans Mysore" (In bygone days, I knew Firdousi in Mysore), strikes me as the perfect model of those fables that are exemplary and edifying, or so we surmise, and yet we cannot discover with any certainty why this is so.[1] Kant, who let his rigorous doctrine rest on pure reason, defined beauty (it is well-known) as a finality without an end; he might perhaps have appreciated these signs that silence their signification.

At other times, the poet seems to describe distant climes, recounting the history of dynasties probably lost for centuries. He delights in painting foreign customs, curious gestures, and feelings that are hard to imagine. With these, he composes vast frescoes, which seem imaginary and gratuitous, full of a picturesqueness and exoticism created and reinforced at leisure. And it turns out we can grow accustomed to these invented civilizations that have the merit of becoming familiar and indispensable. Here we have worlds built by the mind

---

1. [See Victor Hugo, *La Légende des siècles*, 2 vols. (Paris: Flammarion, 1979). —*Ed.*]

alone, with their religious, military, and legal institutions, their marriages and funerals, their longings and secret pleasures; here they are, presenting themselves as the promised land, the recourse and desire of a desolate heart; here they are, offering both a maxim and course of action to aimless ardor. What are you telling me? That this was all an inner landscape? That these overseas expeditions were merely an illusion? That these sumptuous and arbitrary settings, this skillful disorientation merely served to erase what is ephemeral and local in man, so that the poet—Saint-John Perse in this instance—could attain the simplest nature of this malleable being. . . .

Such are a few of poetry's goals and achievements that can inspire respect on the part of the most recalcitrant individual. There are others—some quite rare and some more common.

I will not try to hide the fact that chance rather than deliberation presided over the assembly of the following texts. They just happened to be there: I did not choose them. They seemed to form a set that, despite its gaps and randomness, held some kind of lesson. This collection is probably ill-assorted and far from complete. The misfortune of these times is partly to blame; so too is the lack of preparation and of any guiding thought. I did not even allow my tastes, which do not deserve such an honor, to express themselves. In any event, I am only proposing this collection for what it's worth, and that is probably not greater than the value of each text it includes. But some are not bad at all.

Moreover, this journal, as you know, seeks to show on every possible occasion the solidarity that binds it to the writers who have remained in France. Let us recall its mission faithfully to reflect their worries and consolations: this motive that is indeed not aesthetic but moral, not to say emotional, overcame any final doubts.

Introduction to "Pythian Heritage (On the Nature of Poetic Inspiration)"

Together with "The Situation of Poetry," "Pythian Heritage" was a key essay in Caillois's *Les Impostures de la poésie* (Impostures of poetry, 1st ed; 1944). By "impostures," he had several rather Romantic tendencies in mind. The first, records his conclusion, "involves viewing poetry as superior to all earthly things and hence seeking to separate it from these to give it more brilliance and purity than it could possibly have." Second, and more directly relevant to "Pythian Heritage," was the cult of mystery and inspiration on the part of those claiming "that a supernatural breath inspires them and that they have learned everything directly from nature or from their heart. But they have actually been taught by their predecessors. This is easy to see. They are men of craft, whatever they may claim. Rimbaud alone—whom they unwisely take to be the most miraculous member of their troop and who tried out every style before forming his own—is proof enough."[1] Much of *Impostures de la poésie* expressed Caillois's continued feuding with Surrealism, the sharpest assault being an unsigned review of *V.V.V.* in the same issue of *Lettres françaises* as "Pythian Heritage," to which it seems to give an ad hominem, polemical edge. The reviewer cites Breton's *Situation du surréalisme entre les 2 guerres* (or "Speech to Yale Students")— *"I repeat that Surrealism stemmed from a declaration of limitless faith in youth's genius"*—to claim that the movement is far too well adapted to its audience: "In the past, people rather used to refer to the genius of childhood, if not of intrauterine life. When will somebody praise maturity? Besides, the text includes the most serious concessions. And one must note a strange misuse of the concept of liberty. Certainly, there are few ideas we must value as highly with regard to the affairs of the *polis*. But in *Lettres*, where everything is free from the start, where no constraint is required, and indeed where doing what pleases people is merely an act of laziness, nature, lack of daring, rigor, or ambition—doesn't liberty reside in creating enslavements to which the author chooses to submit in order to dominate a material that escapes and deludes him whenever he abandons himself to it?"[2]

"L'Héritage de la Pythie," in *Approches de la poésie* (Paris: Gallimard, 1978), 34–42.

Just as "The Situation of Poetry" dwelt on poetic mystery, "Pythian Heritage" focuses on poetic inspiration—all this going to show that Caillois's aesthetics of effort, poised though it might be against Surrealist laissez faire, sought to incorporate the imagination, that is, some unwilled dimension of aesthetic creation. His essay considers the hallowed distinction between inspiration (often referred to as enthusiasm) and effort or work. Traditionally, most theories of inspiration place it prior to the subsequent stage of work, but Caillois conversely argues that the poet's labor precedes his inspiration; in fact, the latter is an act of "restitution" for previous effort. This is hardly the same thing as the process of working to spark revelations from the unconsious, as Breton had urged in his *Second Manifesto*. Caillois's agenda may be closer to Valéry's ideas about increased sensibility: "Work would not lead to the solution. . . . However, it would increase the number of chances favorable to the artist's general project; he would momentarily become a very sensitive echo chamber for all the events of consciousness that could be useful to his project."[3] Unlike Valéry, though, Caillois offers a specifically causal economic model of the relation between work and compensatory product. Yet this defies any utilitarian interpretation because the poet is himself unaware of the connection. His work, then, is fundamentally disinterested.

But this has little to do with Kantian aesthetic contemplation, because beauty and form, as such, are not an issue here. Etiemble suggested that Caillois's aesthetics during the war were an ethics (see introduction). In this regard, I would underscore how the radical rift between man and nature in this outlook are at odds with his biological analogies of the 1930s and the "generalized aesthetics" of the 1960s. Indeed, they seem to echo a prior unsigned commentary in *Lettres françaises* on Jean Mahan's "Combat de l'homme" (Man's combat):

> First-rate contribution. The author shows very well that the doctrines being honored in Germany today represent a choice made in favor of the state of nature and its simple and brutal laws. He thereby explains, but without overdoing it, Hitlerian anti-Semitism: for the Jew is the legislator, the enemy of nature, which he is striving to subjugate and control. The main argument is a very accurate appreciation of morality. . . . "This word is synonymous with poetry; with a wild wish for humanity; with a stubborn persistence to want the impossible; with a desperate gamble. . . . Moral law, this invention of ours, is our desperate heroism. We do not wish to be what we are, and we wish to be what we are not. And all that for nothing. For nothing is obliging us to do so."[4]

It has always been difficult to gauge the relative parts of inspiration and labor in the work of art. Each artist actually does whatever he likes, and the results are neither better nor worse for all that. But things are different in the realm of theory, where many artists, not to mention philosophers, show their preference in these matters and make an example of it. Schools then challenge one another, and fanatics soon start to scorn the masterpieces shaped by principles that are not their own. One school finds beauty only in order, another in careless outpourings. These doctrines quickly become immutable laws. People now demand that all artistic creation should either be deliberately planned or else, on the contrary, lack any conscious intent.

This quarrel may seem surprising. These contending principles (which could not be more totally opposed) do not seem powerful enough to function effectively on their own. Clearly, attentive forethought can structure the architecture of a painting, sonnet, or fugue. It can produce an effective combination of colors, rhythms, and sounds; it can arouse and then gratify a specific need, interweave surprise with suspense, identify the proper means for any aesthetic end, and make an artwork a continuous joy for the mind and senses through skillful hints, repetitions, and careful progressions. However perfected, though, such skill is only regulatory; it manages wealth it could not possibly create by itself. Nor can it foresee the future results of its own artifice. I do not think that the intellect ever produces the material it tries to arrange, nor that the will ever creates the goal toward which it is tending. The intellect and will are simply tools when compared to the subject of the artwork. This we cannot do without—even if we were to focus exclusively on intellect and the will, even if we felt indifference or disdain toward this subject, or actually wished to destroy it. An artist will never find his work's substance in his alchemical rules, nor the idea for that triumph he has chosen to achieve.

On the other hand, though, what can we expect from inspiration? Where does it come from? If a reckless artist abandons himself to this mysterious impulse, can we be sure it will not lead him astray? We generally agree that the ancients were all too credulous in believing that a god governed poetic enthusiasm. But is it any less credulous to assume that a blind force lying deep within man, buried in a shadowy underworld, composes oracles that reveal to his stupefied intellect the secrets of both fate and the world? No hope could be more utterly vain. Of course, in the sea's abyss, it does occur that a mass of hideous, trembling flesh takes shape as a pearl under its roughened shell. And it does happen that wonders seem produced by chance or by fortuitous encounters in the depths of oblivion—which consciousness can barely reach, and which are bestrewn with fermenting shameful lusts and vague thoughts. But in fact, what people receive from inspiration is merely the fruit of their disquiet. Their sudden talent actually stems from sleepless nights. A musician composes a sonata in his dreams; a poet finds his verse in a spiritualistic seance. One scientist is taking a bath, another sees an apple fall: thus are revealed two basic laws of the universe. But these are totally personal and individual gifts; in other words, they seldom reach the wrong address. The whims of fate do not favor an unhinged mind. And no inventor or artist has ever received a sudden gift that he has not already imagined, desired, and tried to attain for a long time. The heavens, everywhere, help only him who has truly helped himself and who awaits nothing from divine intervention, relying solely on his own strength.

*   *   *

Upon examining the nature of inspiration, we thus realize that it is simply an act of restitution. Is the poet ever startled by an image or strophe seemingly whispered by some unknown voice, without cause, and that he never would have obtained through his own efforts (or so he thinks)? Then it is merely because he does not stop to think that today's miracle has been earned by yesterday's diligence. He sees no connection between such effort and such ease, even though the latter results from imperceptible work that remains unbroken, even in sleep.

This very special labor requires deep rest, and it is more like sleep than effort. All the faculties must be relaxed. If a single one stays awake, it would break the spell. The conscious mind must be distracted and the will at rest for the process to be successful. Then, the worker who has despaired about his skill will receive unexpected resources from his many wasted efforts, perseverance, and former ambitions—from his useless, confused impressions collected at random. Almost unwittingly, he has been acquiring these resources for his entire life. Indeed, his great devotion to his art has kept him attentive and subservient even when he flattered himself by thinking that he had escaped its constraints.

In calm waters, each suspended particle sinks and deposits itself according to its own weight. Thus, when our mind has long and pointlessly agitated its thoughts, it is best to release and forget these deft fugitives—rather than stubbornly trying to force them into docile submission. More will be achieved. The same holds true when one is struggling to remember something. It seems so close you can truthfully say it is on the tip of your tongue, but the very act of doing so seems to drive it away instead of calling it near. Each effort to apprehend this recollection pushes it further away, as becomes increasingly clear. You must wait until you are no longer thinking about it; and when your mind is idle or busy with something else, it will then perceive what its feverish focus could not grasp.

There is a common lesson to be drawn from this familiar experience, from these gifts of exaltation or reverie, from the discoveries attributed by legend to chance or to random events. This lesson is infinitely more modest than the fraud (perhaps a naïve one at that) perpetrated by people who highlight the sudden advent of sovereign favors in order to humiliate the careful achievements of the intellect and will. In fact, such gifts simply warn the worker that, from time to time, he should relax his desire for total control. At times, he should interrupt his calculations. A state of repose will bring the solution that method could not find. But such forms of self-abandonment are fruitful only after a great deal of thought; inspiration has never favored a poet above and beyond the merits of his own talent. Moreover, we should not imagine that he may not select from or else correct what he does receive. For inspiration supplies a large bounty, which becomes even larger on request. Before long, the project will have turned into a work of nature that is inevitably blind, vague, and confused. Any useful element is generally drowned in a mass of suggestive ones that are monstrous or absurd, or else sparkle deceptively. They could not be made admirable through skill. They can only arouse a kind of horror—which the indulgent, welcoming mind quickly views as the sign of their divinity.

A higher ambition knows that it can't make do with such an impure and unfinished harvest. Already on guard against dangerous fruitfulness, it still more carefully avoids waiting for the onslaught of wild grass, which grows without planting or cultivation. A lofty art expects the soil and sap to provide only the raw material for its task and the urgent thrust compelling it to work.

*   *   *

In art as in ethics, the crucial point is to flee nature, to replace its laws with principles reflecting a different kind of rigor. Nature is equally hostile to justice and to style. It destroys any order that does not involve external constraints, whether these are endured or imposed. It can express itself only through cries and sighs. Nature is surprised by skillful reserve, disconcerted by self-willed constraint. Therefore, whoever cultivates these will surely lighten his great burden and acquire an equal measure of freedom. There is no danger that such a taste for renunciation could make man forget his primitive avidity altogether; nor is it likely that a writer's stratagems would make him forget his transports of inspiration. Neither could fully untangle themselves from what constitutes their being. And yet, both would lack dignity if they did not aspire to enter into the realm of another rule.

By itself, the work of art seems to have some sort of strange desire to blossom and expand. It can neither be led nor stopped at will but instead demands its own completion; it aims to use up the force endowing it with the need to grow and explode. It seems driven by the desire to exist as much as it possibly can—either as an abrupt, uncontrollable gust, a kind of explosion carrying it to its peak and destroying it in one fell swoop; or like shells and trees, which unfold their spirals or trunks at a regular pace, quite patiently and until death. In these processes there prevails something that is simple and indefinite (whether imperceptible or brutal), that radically differs from the strict and closed order of lucidity. Indeed, in the state of nature, laws are nothing but some sort of impetus. Both their flexibility and violence seem fully adequate to their respective functions, and their ineluctable nature is like instinct in the sense that it appears to fulfill rather than oppress. The various discourses man uses to express himself, and that constitute the arts, always have a certain ease, or necessary flow; in this respect, they are no more exempt than the rest of the world. These discourses are just as deeply rooted in nature. Yet if man invokes nature by necessity, he need not entirely abandon himself to its lures nor view its sure and elementary ground as the highest virtue he might ever wish to acquire.

Of course, to avoid producing an ill-shaped or hybrid work of art, he must not contravene the laws of nature either gratuitously or out of ignorance. He must skillfully indulge her ways, while mastering them at the same time; he must submit in order to tame them, to make them serve his private ends. So let him then enjoy these earthly gifts, but without envying their perfection compared to his own creations. And they should not serve as his models. His vocation is to move away from them. Bird songs are not music and can never become music. Painting has a deeper motive than the mere desire to imitate the elegant forms and brilliant colors we see around us. In any event, this would be an impossible task because recovering their brightness would mean recreating life itself, and this privilege belongs to life alone, to perpetuate itself in every being without strain or special effort.

An artist has other ambitions. He may be seduced by the beauties flattering his gaze, yet he knows that he himself must produce something of a different kind, requiring him to take an opposite path. He is probably still tempted to appeal to those powers within, which are related, he feels, to the grace playfully creating wonders all around. Will he believe that these underground sources are divine? Will he surrender in the face of their mystery? Not content to merely draw on their thousand gifts, will he view inspiration as supernatural when it is more natural, in fact, than he is himself? This would mean giving up the single glory he can truly call his own: the right to hesitate and to choose. I hope that his heart will reject such an exchange and refuse to sell for the pleasures of intoxication, for the right to pronounce futile and obscure oracles, what is his fragile birthright, namely, this taste for immortality—which it is quite noble for him to maintain while knowing, as he does, that he must die.

III

POSTWAR STANCES, 1946–1978

The Moralist

Introduction to "Loyola to the Rescue of Marx"

This essay is a first sketch of Caillois's lengthier work, *Description du marxisme* (1950), which he ironically retitled in 1974 *Essai d'une description marxiste d'une idéologie promue vérité scientifique par une grande puissance* (Attempt to give a Marxist description of an ideology that has been promoted into a scientific truth by a major power).[1] Or, as the work's epigraph declared: "An orthodoxy is not an immutable truth, it's a political truth, that is, a truth resting on a political power and subject to political obligations." In the 1930s, Caillois had found communist ideology too rational, instrumental, and utilitarian—in effect, too "profane" in a sociological sense. As I interpret it, his "L'Ordre et l'empire" (1936) presents an allegory of the Marxist state (the Tcheou empire), which seeks to enact Kojève's "end of history"; it is a realm regimented by conservation, stability, and uniformity and by "immutable rites" reflecting the doctrinal slogans of "the Five Cardinal Principles and the Three Indispensable Virtues."[2] In 1950, he analyzed communism as a form of "secular sacred" (see introduction), in this case, one that strategically and falsely used the "sacred" prestige of science.

As noted in the introduction, this demystification of language in terms of its social or sociopolitical context set him apart from Paulhan, whose approach to the mysterious paradoxes of language essentially dealt with the individual or private experience of apprehending them. Caillois's analysis of Loyola's maxim, as I call it, is a good example of his contrasting method. After the war, this maxim inspired his definition of "the spirit of play and games" as a form of "detachment with respect to one's own action" with an ethical, almost utopian, cast: "To consider reality a game," he wrote, "to conquer more ground by means of these grand manners, which reduce stinginess, covetousness, and hatred—that is to enact civilization." And here he held up the exemplum of Loyola, "who taught that one should act while relying only on oneself, as if God did not exist, but while constantly reminding oneself that everything was dependent upon his will. *Le jeu* [play/game] is no less arduous a school; it commands the player to neglect nothing in order to triumph, while remaining detached at the same time."[3] But "Loyola to the Rescue of Marx" then claims

"Loyola au secours de Marx," *Liberté de l'esprit* 6 (summer 1949): 123–124.

that this is the very maxim used by the Communist Party to manipulate and control its own members. In short, when instrumentally imposed on others, the Loyolan belief system becomes a form of enslavement; when voluntarily adopted in a secular setting, it is the means to achieve a free and civilized society.

In his recent study *Le Siècle des intellectuels*, Michel Winock evokes the journal that published "Loyola to the Rescue of Marx" in the early days of the cold war: "The antitotalitarian camp already possessed at least one intellectual organ, the journal *Liberté de l'esprit*, Gaullist in orientation, which had been founded in 1949 and was run by Claude Mauriac." He explains that the "anticommunist analyses" of this "rather private journal" had enough "volunteers" but an insufficient "audience outside those circles already won over to the defense of capitalist interests and those ordinary conservatives who didn't need any expert demonstration to inveigh against communism." Winock adds that "*Preuves* . . . therefore became the French, liberal and democratic expression of intellectual anticommunism between 1951 and 1969."[4] Caillois's contributions to *Preuves* (funded by the Congress for Cultural Freedom) were on the topics of art, literature, and play/games.

LOYOLA TO THE RESCUE OF MARX

Were it not for the various communist parties and the Soviet state's power, Marxist doctrine would certainly long ago have become a mere object of curiosity that interested only a few scholars. Studying the early stages of political economy, these archaeologists would speak of Marx in the same way that historians of chemistry speak of Lavoisier, or as textbooks cite all theories of precursors: their naïve errors make us smile, but their accurate intuitions still compel our admiration. This would have been the inevitable fate of Marxism if it were indeed the scientific theory that its believers claim.

But it is neither a science nor even a method. At best, in its final and most degraded version, it is a form of sophistry, like those employed by the various conjectural sciences (such as, for example, astrology). It is possible, but not very responsible, to oblige it with the term dialectics. At the same time, Marxism is far more than a science. It is the ideology of a fearsome party, which uses it as a banner and pretends that the ideology makes it invincible, whereas, on the contrary, it is the number and valor of its troops that save the ideology from oblivion, that allow it to survive and be respected; without this formidable support, people would laugh at it instead.

Having established this relation, the raison d'être of every strange feature suddenly becomes perfectly clear:

1. *First, the dogmatism*: The prestige of science has nothing to fear from criticism or free inquiry. For its results are precisely the fruit of a research process in which everyone has been able to take part, and where debate not only is not shunned but is systematically provoked. By contrast, a doctrine guaranteed by the force of a faction that it seems to be protecting in turn, and whose strategy it serves to mask, must present a minimum degree of stability. In any case, it is out of the question that it could ever be refuted from the outside and be at the mercy of some discovery, experiment, or additional study or information. Whence the constant reference to the original texts, the exegetical disputes, and recourse to the argument of authority.

2. *Then the fact that not everyone who wishes can be Marxist*: One must be approved by the Party hierarchy, which alone has the power to decide (and this monopoly is indispensable) who the "real" Marxists are, namely, the people whose commentaries may be trusted. That is why, unlike science in the proper sense of the term, Marxism is the privilege of a faction that exclusively reserves the right to orthodox exegesis of the Scriptures and utterly rejects any outside interpretation. To be a renowned Marxist, a person must be a communist; or else, he is dealt with just as Bossuet dealt with Richard Simon and those who authored the first critical studies of the Bible: as sacrilege.

   I need not underscore how radically this attitude (a fatal one, furthermore) differs from the scientific spirit—which is necessarily open and universal.

3. *For similar reasons, it is a kind of article of faith that Marxism cannot be surpassed*: This is an extraordinary claim that, as before, categorically contradicts the nature of science, where progress is precisely a process of continual supersession. But here again, it should be understood that the Communist Party is really what people cannot politically seek to surpass without thereby becoming its enemy. Once more, it is important to make this transposition.

4. *Last, the doctrine is elevated to the supreme criterion of truth*: One does not invoke science to verify that Marxism is well-founded; on the contrary, Marxism is what decides whether some biological discovery or other is well-founded or not, whether some research in physics or psychology is opportune. One particular notion is denounced as guilty and bourgeois; another, on the contrary, is declared consistent with the interests of the

revolution and, hence, with truth. As for political economy after Marx, this is so roundly condemned that it is purely and simply eliminated, and in a way that somewhat recalls mathematicians who discard papers on squaring the circle without even reading them. Here again, this surprising inversion reflects the same urgent and simple need: to shelter ideology from science, that is to say, from a continuous possibility of renewal, led by outsiders who are inspired by the pursuit of a universally valid truth rather than by the concern for the triumph of any one particular faction.

* * *

It remains to be asked why this faction, which seems to give everything to the doctrine without receiving anything in return, cheerfully burdens itself with this rigid and vulnerable system, which can only hinder, mislead, and perhaps discredit its own action. For it is hard to see why a valid movement that has mobilized the best and greatest share of several nations' energy and devotion would persist in tying its fate to an idea made absurd and superstitious by the evolution of time and research. Does this simply reflect routine and the weight of a legacy people are afraid to cast off?

It is indeed plausible to point to the negative influence of a cumbersome heritage. But there is also much to be gained by elevating into dogma a doctrine of the Marxist type, with its favorable bias about the necessary unfolding of history.

Indeed, reduced to its essence, the system can be summarized by a simple proverb that is a also *simplistic* one: "Help yourself, and the heavens will help you." Of course, it takes the apparatus, vocabulary, and authority of science to endow this advice with the desired efficacy. In each militant's mind, the prestige of science—which has here become an object of credulity rather than a method of research—guarantees the value of a practical maxim that he takes pride in observing punctiliously, and which is the only lesson he retains from a complicated theory that is almost inaccessible to untutored minds. In fact, the troops only know it by hearsay. But they derive from it the certainty that they will triumph and the conviction that their action is consistent with the very order of the world due to some kind of divine right. Their energy is hence all the greater. However, this ardor must not be lulled in the lazy hope that a happy ending will propitiously occur without any work to speed its advent. Victory is marked by destiny only if the communists do not spare their own efforts. That is why, from the very start, the Party leaders reacted firmly against a quietist deviation asserting that the working class merely had to await the verdict of history, which could not fail to arrive and which could not fail to be in its favor.

From here, matters quickly swung to the opposite extreme. A maxim of Ignatius of Loyola was revived under a different guise—the one ordering people to act at all times as if God did not exist and to rely solely on their own strength (while knowing full well, however, that everything rests in divine hands). An admirable maxim: it gives man self-confidence, forbids him to depend on anyone but himself, demands his relentless efforts, and, at the same time, *it prevents him from despairing if he should fail or from blaming his own weaknesses or the incompetence of his leaders*. If he is defeated, then it was willed by the heavens or history. He must bow down and take heart once more for the heavens or history will recognize their own in the end.

We can see what a useful maxim this formulation is. It seems to foresee any objection, to console in advance for any defeat. It is quite natural that the communists should have adopted it, in turn. It is the only one that could help conspirators: confirming their legitimacy and fated success, while requiring them to keep their energies constantly and fully mobilized. In strictly political terms, who could ask for anything more?

Introduction to "Paroxysms of Society"

Much ink has been shed, and much confusion created, about Caillois's stand on the relation between war and festival. At stake is what he deemed the modern counterpart to festival, taken in its anthropological sense of revolutionary social renewal, to which the College of Sociology deeply aspired. The postwar preface to *Man and the Sacred* says that although Caillois had initially thought of vacations, he later rejected this analogy because they were a means of social dissolution rather than cohesion. But only the postwar edition goes on to suggest that war might be the modern correlative to festival. Hollier thus suggests: "Before the war, Caillois viewed the modern world, with disgust, as one sinking down into vacations, atrophying in a moldy slow dance that no festival would ever shake up again. On the contrary, after the war (and after the fact), he viewed the modern world as one doomed . . . to war." With terms Caillois uses to describe archaic or anthropological attitudes toward the sacred, Hollier then concludes that he shifts from a prewar "horror of putrefaction" to a postwar "fascination of flame."[1] This may be somewhat misleading.

Heightening the ambiguity, here, is that Caillois often forgoes quotation marks. This can be a problem when citing or paraphrasing Nazi sources; I am specifically thinking of the appendix to *Man and the Sacred* on "War and the Sacred." He also presupposes a reader who knows that he did not view WWII as a "blast." But most to blame is that although Caillois's prewar edition of *Man and the Sacred* did not equate war and festival, he apparently *did equate the two at this time*, as he himself recounted in 1971:

> For me, and for Bataille as well, festival was the time of great expenditure and frenzy, the time when all taboos were violated, and people spent all the accumulated wealth. What could correspond to festival in modern society? It could not be vacations—for in "primitive" societies, this festival lasted for fifteen days and everything vanished into a great frenetic fusion. There was only one thing that could correspond in terms of both its vastness and violence, its overturning of rules—that was war. Whence the

"Paroxysmes de la société," in *Bellone ou la pente de la guerre* (Bruxelles: Renaissance du livre, 1963; Paris: Nizet, 1973).

theory of war that emerged from the College of Sociology. It's also one of the lectures I gave, I believe, "The Theory of War Viewed as a Black Festival" ["La Théorie de la guerre conçue comme la fête noire"]. I think that that's the expression I used, "the black festival of the modern world" [la fête noire du monde moderne].[2]

Because Caillois's talk on the topic of festival has been lost (and Hollier instead reprints a chapter from *Man and the Sacred*), this comment is an important clarification. In short, Caillois, along with the College, held that modern war, in the wake of WWI, was the contemporary counterpart to the social apocalypse of archaic festival. Philippe Borgeaud writes that this notion of "war festival"—"which comes right out of Frazer," in his words—was "most likely widespread in the world of French Sociology, beyond the small circle of the College of Sociology uniting Caillois with Bataille and Leiris."[3]

Prior to the war, Caillois was thus riveted by the apocalyptic image of the imminent war, although solely "The Winter Wind" truly attests to this—and to a lesser degree, I would argue, than were Bataille and Acéphale.[4] But during and after the war, Caillois wrote repeatedly and urgently about the dangers inherent in this fascination with war, with modern *Totalkrieg*, as a form of "secular sacred" all too available to the modern imagination precisely because of those structural traits it shared with archaic festival. The postwar *Man and the Sacred* clearly states that the "meaning and content" of modern war and archaic festival utterly contradict each other but that war, like festival, is a "total phenomenon which makes modern society rise up as a whole and entirely transforms it."[5] Caillois's analytical comparison with festival pursues the analyses of "The Nature and Structure of Totalitarian Regimes" to offer a pessimistic, cold war appraisal of the dangerous "sacred" attraction of this collective phenomenon, which is therefore, in a strictly sociological sense, authentic.[6] Introducing *Quatre essais de sociologie contemporaine* (1951), he explains that "the symmetry of war and festival provides the key that best allows one to account for the cult and mystique of war, whose development we have witnessed during the course of the nineteenth century, and which seem to have attained their most heightened forms in the past few years. As the reality of war today dominates the full spectrum of the problems of civilized life, it is not surprising that it is in relation to war that we may observe, in their most extreme state, the feelings of amazement, paralysis and vertigo, the reactions of ecstasy and horror—which, to my mind, unmistakably reveal the presence and sway of the sacred."[7] This does not mean that Caillois cannot denounce "this absolute paroxysm of collective existence," endowed with its "character of a black festival, of an apotheosis in reverse." The tenets of its faithful are fundamentally wrong. "Here is what caters to palpitating hearts," he writes of modern war and its violence, "and persuades them that it opens the doors of an inferno for them that is truer and greater than a happy and peaceful life."[8] He would continue to dissect and combat the seductions of Hell in "Metamorphoses of Hell."

"Paroxysms of Society" is at the heart of the discord between Bataille and Caillois in the postwar era, emerging out of the College of Sociology. Bataille's review of *Man and the Sacred* and its new appendixes in 1951 made it clear that, unlike Caillois, he did not question the sacralization of war. The problem with atomic *total war* was not that it was sacred, in the terms outlined by Caillois, but that it could destroy mankind. Bataille concludes: "Studying the sacred gives one the sense of an insoluble problem and curse for mankind. Without the sacred, man cannot possess the totality of being's plenitude, he would thus only be a partial man; but the sacred, if it takes the form of war, threatens him with total annihilation."[9] Bataille was still nostalgic, in short, for what he called festival and "ancient wars" ("black festival"?). He wrote to Caillois in 1945, responding to what was likely an early draft of "War and the Sacred," that "war has lost the *sovereign* character it once shared with festival. Like industrial companies, it is nothing but a *subordinate* operation."[10] Caillois, he said, reduced "economics . . . to production": "It seems to me that you have not sufficiently stressed the difference between ancient wars and modern weapon industries: today companies are the ones fighting each other and discharging their potential." Indeed, *La Part maudite* (1949) had not relinquished the basic tenets of "The Notion of Expenditure." Bataille attributed the onset of modern warfare to the historical evanescence of "the great and free social forms of unproductive expenditure." He argued that modern societies should find adequate safety valves for the "free expenditure" of energy, "unproductive works, to dissipate energy that could not be accumulated in any way," that would otherwise fuel modern war's strategic and instrumental destructiveness, "a catastrophic expenditure of excess energy."[11]

In effect, Bataille and Caillois both believed that modern wars were genealogically related to potlatch, which, like Mauss, they both viewed with nostalgia; however, they had very different interpretations of this special festival. Bataille was referring to potlatch as defined through a rather idiosyncratic interpretation of Mauss's *The Gift*. "'The ideal,' indicates Mauss, would be to give a potlatch and not have it returned," Bataille states in "The Notion of Expenditure." "'This ideal is realized in certain forms of destruction to which custom allows no possible response.'"[12] However, Caillois's writings constantly sought to challenge and reorient Bataille toward a more orthodox reading of Mauss, based on the normal—rather than exceptional—procedures of potlatch. For Mauss, potlatch as a "total prestation" did not simply express some deep-seated, ineradicable drive to destroy, but rather was an archaic form of social order and arbitrage. Indeed, if we turn to the body of the text in which Mauss's footnote occurs, we read the following: "Outside pure destruction the obligation to repay is the essence of potlatch. Destruction is very often sacrificial, directed towards the spirits, and apparently does not require a return unconditionally, especially when it is the work of a superior clan chief or a clan already recognized as superior. [Here is the footnote: "The ideal is to give away property that is not to be returned. . . ."] *But normally the potlatch must be returned with interest like all other gifts.*"[13] Already, Caillois's "First Lecture" to the College of Sociology closed with a summary of *The Gift* in terms of "gifts with the constraint of giving back." And although *Man and the Sacred* cites potlatch in its discussion of festival, Caillois here quotes Mauss: "'Not by motives of generosity or chance, [but through reciprocity],' Mauss emphasizes, 'gift exchange results in producing an abundance of wealth.'"[14]

Caillois was hence nostalgic for potlatch conceived as a form of social order informing both festival and war, and which held neither incandescence nor sacred appeal. To this end, "Paroxysms of Society" actually distinguishes between ancient festival and potlatch by delineating three broad stages. First, in the most undeveloped societies, festival is the moment of collective, sacred regeneration, when subgroups come together; there is no analogous form of war. Second, in more "complex and diversified" societies akin to those of the Christian Middle Ages, festival is akin to war: it has evolved into the escalating rivalries of potlatch or courtly war. (Here is Caillois's ideal.) These elite activities do not precipitate any form of social paroxysm at all: "In this transitional era, the high point is no longer festival but is not yet war." Largely motored by the rise of nationalism and the nation-state, in the third stage, modern war then returns to archaic festival in some of its "functions," "attitudes," and "mythologies" while operating a "radical conversion" of "bond" into "conflict."

Caillois's additional comments on this topic in *Bellone ou la pente de la guerre* (1962) reveal his persistent skepticism about democracy, or Tocquevillian doubts about radical egalitarianism: "Either social inequalities between men are codified and upheld by rituals, customs and laws, and then wars are generally limited, courteous and relatively bloodless sorts of games and ceremonies; or else men have equal rights, they participate equally in public affairs and, in this case, wars tend to turn into unlimited, murderous and relentless clashes." More specifically, still nostalgic for the military "caste," he blames "the state's assimilation with the army" for the rise of "egalitarian, totalitarian nations"— a pitfall that classical China alone, he suggests, was able to avoid.[15]

In primitive societies, the time of the sacred was that of festivals. Although these festivals certainly involved well-ordered ceremonies, they first took place as vast explosions in which an entire populace gathered to expend its energy, squander its resources, assert its vitality, commemorate its ancestors, and welcome in the new generations; it celebrated and communed in a collective frenzy, from which it emerged both depleted and exalted. War has many features suggesting that in modern societies it fulfills the function performed by festival in undeveloped societies, despite the fact that its contents are different, if not radically opposed. It represents a phenomenon of equal scope and force; it overturns the economic, institutional, and psychological order to a similar degree. Thus, it is perhaps by comparing war with festival that we may best grasp exactly how and why war so markedly gives rise to the reactions that characterize the sacred.

Parallel Convulsions

The reality of war corresponds to that of festival. Moreover, the mind constructs quite similar mythologies on the basis of the two. War and festivals are both periods of movement and uproar, massive gatherings during which an economy of waste replaces one of accumulation. People consume and destroy whatever was previously put aside and acquired through the laborious efforts of commerce and skill. In addition, modern war and primitive festival are periods of intense emotion: intermittent, feverish crises disrupting the dull and peaceful monotony of everyday life. Personal and familial concerns give way to collective obsessions. The individual's independence is temporarily suspended. He merges into an organized and unanimous throng, where his physical, emotional, and even intellectual autonomy all disappear. He is no longer his own master, and all former distinctions are erased in light of a new hierarchy. The usual gestures of work, the minor obligations of private life, the regularity of everyday existence—these are all replaced by a rigorous and frenetic world, which strangely combines exuberance and discipline, anxiety and merriment, order and disorder. In festival, alongside tumultuous uproar and charivaris, there occur fasting, ritual silence, and all sorts of prohibitions. In war, matters are more meticulously organized to conclude in more widespread, thorough devastation; order and calculation are combined with the risk of death and the *ivresse* of destruction.

The cycle of war and peace reproduces the cycle of festive and profane time, with its alternating periods of concentration and dispersion, turbulence and work, waste and economy. This involves such a radical overturning of norms that it almost recalls the cycle of pilgrim crickets in the animal kingdom. A generation of nomadic and gregarious insects with powerful wings, which carry them away in dense cloud formations, usually follows on a sedentary generation, where each insect lives in its own hole with atrophied wings.

Furthermore, a radical reversal of moral commandments accompanies war and festival. In times of war, people can and must kill, even though murder in peacetime is the greatest crime of all. In times of war, truth and property are not respected, even though they were deemed equally sacred just a short while before. Similarly, during a festival, people can and must commit acts normally thought to be sacrilegious, such as eating the totemic animal or having sexual relations with a woman from the same clan. In times of war and festival, it becomes mandatory to perform criminal, extravagant acts, to break the usual laws. Both periods stand as monumental, prolonged debaucheries that naturally induce a climate of excess and escalating rivalry, in which the rules of civilization are temporarily abolished.

Bouts of drinking and carousing, rape and orgy, boasting, grimacing, obscenities and swearing, bets, challenges, brawls, and atrocities all feature in the daily agenda. They herald in the new regime, proclaiming its nature and advent. Any form of excess normally contained by the codes of decorum (whether gesture or speech, movement or noise, consumption or destruction) now has free rein, and gloriously so.

The worlds of war and festival inevitably invite such expressions by the mere fact of having violently broken with profane or secular existence. These basic similarities rest, first of all, on the economic significance of the two phenomena, and on the unusually privileged positions (sociologically speaking) that they equally hold in those societies where they occur in their most heightened form. But the analogy (and if only that, it is nonetheless instructive and illuminating) does not concern merely the substratum of collective life. It also has to do with the private attitude of the participant, who feels aggrandized in festival and war through his intimacy with the divine or with death. In both cases and in a similar way, the two symmetrical paroxysms unleash the instincts normally held in check.

The Epiphany of the Sacred

Under the circumstances, it is hardly surprising that related mythologies should have arisen from similar grounds. Indeed, the merits traditionally ascribed to war ever since it came to dominate the existence of societies perfectly correspond to the vivifying virtues that festivals of the past were supposed to elicit with heightened strength and renewed vigor.

War and festival (those periods when norms are in abeyance and real forces erupt) stand alike as the sole remedies for inevitable decay. Profane time and peacetime necessarily strengthen established positions, vested interests, conventional opinion, routine and laziness, selfishness and prejudice. Things become weighted down and ossified, tending toward immobility and death. On the contrary, war and festival discard dregs and waste, eliminate false values, and recover the source of primordial energies, reactivating their full and dangerous, but salutory, violence.

In both instances, people awaken to a time without order, conventions, or fixity. They feel transported back to the time of chaos and monstrous fertility, when everything engendered everything else. From this fountain of youth, nature and mankind both emerge renewed.

It is in the course of festival that a child becomes a full-fledged being: circumcision perfects the phallus; initiation and wearing masks consecrate the adolescent. He thus leaves the category of the people who become terrified to join the group that does the terrifying. Military service likewise turns a young man into an accomplished citizen, and the baptism of fire confers priceless prestige upon an adult. At the same time, given the scope of the sacrifices involved and the great, exhausting shake-up they provoke, war and festival institute a new order and reinvigorate society, removing all cumbersome, obsolete institutions. They instate the young leaders and usher in a new era.

The individual experiences his participation either in festival or in war as an epiphany as well as a sacrament. He believes that he is glimpsing into the heart of things, and he is thereby transformed. This carries him into an intense, authentic world, compared to which ordinary life afterward seems like a copy without color or depth. War's horror does not lessen the brilliance of the revelation but intensifies it. The more atrocious the war, the more dazzling the revelation.

After both festival and war alike, society settles down once more. The paints are wiped off and the masks are buried; uniforms are put away in closets and weapons stashed in the arsenals. Gods and ancestors fade away; people recover their place and their duties; social inertia bears down as it did before; prohibitions are restored; hierarchies are reasserted; work resumes after l'ivresse; and skill, now transformed, returns to peacetime applications. The period of excess ceremoniously comes to a close and ordinary life begins anew, with its numerous activities—including the preparations for the next explosion.

Society achieves its highest and most imperious glory in its moments of incandescence. The religious fascination once proper to festival is reproduced on behalf of war by the mingling of social classes, the loyalty shown to the dead, the general exaltation, the common faith in the group's destiny, and the strain of constant tension. From this particular perspective, it hardly matters that this experience involves a mystique of carnage and an apotheosis of destruction. The vertigo is the same. The absence of any effective initiative to avoid the fatal rendezvous vividly demonstrates war's paralyzing power. Ever since war became hyperbolic, it immediately subordinated an increasing share of the country's resources and energies to its future needs (once peace is restored). Ever since then, social determinisms have worked in its favor: in a way, they have demanded war. Because of its unceasing growth, war overrides any objections; in the end, its very immoderation is what makes it impossible to contest.

War stands as the severest fate: blind, absurd, as deadly as possible and also totally inhuman. And let us note that the sacred is exactly the same. Its values may vary but never its nature, which is incomprehensible, crushing, and beyond dispute. Man experiences as sacred whatever both eludes him and allows him to escape his own condition; the rapture that both exalts him and plunges him into despair, that seems to free him from the mediocrity in which he is mired—as it sends him, shuddering, into an intense and perilous world. This is what war has provided for mankind, ever since a decisive break of equilibrium assured it—against the general will—a kind of absolute preeminence in human affairs and it came to serve as the basis for almost all major governmental decisions.

From that point on, even dithyrambic praise has been insufficient to express the virtues of war—virtues that are measured by its horrors and that we need war to possess to offset its monstrosity.

From Festival to War

Nevertheless, war and festival radically differ from each other in certain basic respects. These oppositions are so obvious that they are hardly worth listing. In fact, the differences are so many and glaring that they have generally overshadowed the similarities, which stem from the identical function of these two major upheavals, in which society suddenly reveals its total power over the individual, de facto and de jure. Besides, we should be careful: here, what is most apparent is not the most important. On further analysis, the features one would tend to mention first—the recourse to violence and the death of the participants—do not seem to be the greatest point of contrast between war and festival. Some wars are not very bloody, and in many festivals blood flows freely. In Dahomey, the death of the king was accompanied by a kind of destructive fury: "The entire populace was gripped by wild unrest." The monarch's wives would destroy the furniture, jewelry, and utensils in the royal palace, and would then start killing each other so fiercely that several hundred victims would be counted when it was over: 595 in 1789.[1] This rage to destroy would cease only with the coronation of a new king. Can it be said that this was a ritual of mourning? Clearly, frenzy prevailed over ceremony. In Antiquity, the Attic cult gave rise to similar excesses. March 24 was the date set for the "day of blood": the high priest opened veins in his arm to sprinkle blood on the god's image. The other priests made cuts in their bodies. Overexcitement then reached its height: novices and spectators would seize hold of swords, tear off their clothes, and mutilate or emasculate themselves. Next day, the feast, of the Hilaria was a time of wild celebration; debauchery and delirious joy were required behavior. On March 27 a procession took place that served as an excuse for boisterous demonstrations and obscene songs.[2]

In ritual unrest, participants sometimes get crushed. With all the bustling and milling about, the collective excitement invariably causes a number of fatal accidents. Nobody tries to prevent them. On the contrary, it would seem that they add to the commotion and festive atmosphere. At times, the violence is deliberately provoked. On the anniversary of the murder of Ali and his two sons, Hassan and Hossain, Shiite Muslims are seized by a madness that makes them inflict dangerous wounds and mutilations upon themselves and their offspring; sometimes they do so after swallowing pellets of opium meant to inure them to pain. On the "day of blood" in Teheran, swords are handed out to the ecstatic faithful advancing in procession. They come and go, whirl round, step back or slip to one side, emitting dreadful shrieks. They brandish their knives and cut themselves on the head. Blood flows. The long shirts of the fanatics turn red. Gripped by madness, they lash out blindly and are soon slicing their own arteries and veins; they die on the spot, with pink foam streaming from their mouths. Meanwhile, the crowd draws the bloodied troop toward yet another crossroad, and the ranks are constantly swelled with new recruits—auxiliaries, or soldiers charged with maintaining the peace, who are overcome by the contagion and suddenly strip off their tunics, demanding weapons to participate in the slaughter.[3]

Such bloodbaths make it sufficiently clear that a festival is most of all a collective paroxysm, a herd movement in which participants may die or be horri-

1. Two hundred eighty-five on another occasion. See also Philippe de Félice, *Foules en délire, extases collectives* (Paris, 1937), 65–66, from Archibald Dalzel, *The History of Dahomey* (London, 1793), 150–151, 204–205.

2. De Felice, *Foules en délire*, 114–116.

3. De Felice, *Foules en délire*, 114–116.

bly mutilated. Hence, it is not on this account that we may best differentiate festival from war. Rather, it is the fact that festival, in essence, represents the will to commune, whereas war first and foremost represents the will to do harm. In festival, there is exaltation; in war, people seek to defeat and subjugate others. Hatred replaces cooperation, and the clash between two nations replaces the alliance forged between two fratrias. What once served to consecrate unbreakable bonds now maintains ruthless conflicts. Such a radical conversion is not due to some whim of fate: it can result only from broader historical transformations. Let us seek to uncover the broad outlines of this surprising evolution.

A primitive community is basically ill-defined. Even when settled in a fixed area—for cultivation, pasture, and hunting—it does not actually know its own boundaries. As people move further away from the village, their proprietary sense of the land decreases, unless some specific site has acquired particular importance: places of worship, watering holes, or game preserves. The shift from one tribe's territory to that of its neighbor occurs gradually. Besides, the real bonds are not caused by the fact that people live in the same territory but rather that they participate in the same mystical principle, which is embodied in the clan and generally passed on by the women. Each clan has its own totem, the emblem and source of this supernatural virtue. And the group is never isolated. It is linked to a symmetrical clan through ties of intermarriage; these ties confirm and renew the alliance with each following generation. Here lies the importance of the incest prohibition, that is, the law of exogamy: each individual must marry into the complementary clan. In fact, this rule merely reflects one specific instance of a system totally predicated on collaboration and exchange: the exchange of women, of course, but also that of food, services, and ceremonies. Each group views the antithetical group as the source of its survival, strength, fertility, and glory. Their relationship is governed by painstaking reciprocity. Each serves to ensure the other's life and prosperity.

And so, the paroxysm of such a society is necessarily that moment when the constitutive subgroups come together in a period of official promiscuity. Conjoined and intermingled by festival, their members enter into the vertiginous world of the sacred, myths, and dreams. They can relive the origin of things. They leave the realm of time and rules. All prohibitions are violated. Masked figures engage in fertility and initiation rites. Food is guaranteed for a new duration. A new generation is integrated into the collectivity. Disorder reaches its height as the society communes and asserts itself in a state of vivifying effervescence through a general expenditure of wealth, motion, and energy.

In a society of this type, without nation or state, war never exceeds the stage of ambushes, raids, and plunder or revenge expeditions. It can never become a crucial concern, and basically remains a scattered and random event; that is to say, it does not exist. Such a society achieves its incandescence during, and by means of, festival.

With the rise of a hierarchy and the individualization of power, as society becomes more complex and diversifies into specialized occupations—warriors, priests, blacksmiths, dancers, carpenters, healers, or other people with distinctive techniques founding their authority and determining their social role—a change takes place in the reciprocal prestations and the perfect equilibrium, that govern the relations of complementary groups. Under these conditions, the chief mainspring of the collective pact is no longer respect but prestige, whether this involves initiatory brotherhoods or hereditary castes. Societies of this type vary greatly. Nonetheless, they seem to pertain to some sort of generally feudal Middle Ages or, in any event, to present certain features that are similar to those of the Christian Middle Ages. And they may be permanently arrested at this developmental stage. I would define these societies by suggesting that class barriers are here more important than territorial boundaries. Indeed, class distinctions create the real barriers and divide the opposing communities. Thus, war becomes the privilege—almost the monopoly—of an aristocracy, which reserves for itself the right to bear arms and whose members fight among themselves, just as they marry into their own ranks.

This is the era of courtly war, which exists only in a hierarchical world and which opposes only people of equal rank, warriors by birth and destiny; the common people are merely their valets, auxiliaries, or victims. At this stage, war is a game with strict rules. Honor is the sovereign power, and it is acquired by issuing, accepting, and meeting challenges; by giving proof of valor, loyalty, and generosity; and by performing heroic deeds. Titles, banners, coats of arms, crests, and heraldic emblems of every kind proclaim a lord's nobility. His bravery and splendor diminish or increase its renown. War is a joust. It is close to a game, given the formalism of its conventions, and close to a sport, because it involves rivalry and competition. It is a physical exercise, in which champions must face each other with equal weapons, and where the best wins the prize. This concept of war did not emerge from the ambushes and raids of less differentiated populations. It stemmed directly from festival.

Festival changed along with society. It ceased to be a paroxysm of communing and became instead one of escalating rivalry, in which leaders sought recognition of their own preeminence. With much pomp and ceremony they would distribute or destroy as many riches as possible to assert their superiority over less opulent or generous rivals. The goal was no longer to preserve but rather to upset the equilibrium of favors received and rendered. In effect, each gift challenged the other leader to surpass it. It was the way to gain political authority, influence, supernatural secrets or tokens, coats of arms, talismans, prerogatives, names, myths, and songs or dances with magical properties. The Kwakiutl would say: "We do not fight with weapons, we fight by offering up our possessions."[4] The men would bring garlands, meant to represent the heads of their enemies, and throw them into the fire while shouting out their names. In fact, though, the garlands corresponded to the copper plates they had handed out, and the proclaimed names were those of rivals who had been defeated in the tournaments of generosity. Bombast and pointless expenditure were deemed signs of grandeur. A chief would burn up his oil reserves, rip up his canoes, shred his otter skins, and hurl his copper plates into the sea, all to humiliate his adversary. The obsession to be superior was constant and covered the entire socioeconomic system. Anything people could acquire by sacrificing their own wealth could also be gained by murdering its proprietor. They could just as readily obtain desired goods or privileges by killing the owner as by disqualifying him with a gift far too sumptuous for him to possibly reciprocate with the requisite interest.

Of course, the institution of "potlatch" is exceptional. But the psychology it derives from is present in most aristocratic societies (that is, precisely where war occurs in its courtly form), where splendor and feats (the "record") prove the valor of the well-born man. Here, war itself is luxurious: it is the festival in which people risk their lives. However, it divides instead of uniting them. It sets boundaries. It justifies the pride of the privileged minority devoted to this activity. Thus it does not stand as society's pinnacle at all. In this transitional era, the high point is no longer festival, but is not yet war.

War took on this status after the national whole had triumphed over all the other collective structures. The fraternity of noble warriors had been unconstrained by any borders. They had fought each other without hatred, with mutual esteem, in limited bouts that did not significantly weaken their instinctive solidarity or their arrogance toward the bourgeoisie and the peasants—in other words, toward civilians. But once the nation recognized only citizens with equal rights, to whom it granted political power while imposing mandatory military service, it became an indivisible and armed totality, necessarily distinct from and opposed to all other nations. It was exclusive, absolute, and increasingly vast as the state took over more services and exercised greater forms of control. In short, the more socialized the nation was, the more rigid and closed in upon itself it became.

4. Ruth Benedict, *Echantillon de civilisations*, French trans. (Paris, 1950), 206–234. See also Marcel Mauss, "Essai sur le don, forme archaïque de l'échange," *Année sociologique*, NS 1 (1923–1924).

Politics is then conducted with at least the fear, if not the expectation, of war. The government supervises, regulates, and takes charge of everything relating to the nation's moral and material strength. It constantly focuses on the prospect of armed conflict, so that war, for the state, is both an object of fascination and an absolute. However peaceable it may be, the state will ultimately sacrifice almost anything to war, whether preparing for it or fearing it. The nation cannot avoid this fate as long as it is composed as a whole and acknowledges no higher authority. Indeed, it finds itself in a natural state of constant competition with neighboring totalities. When the state mobilizes its resources in manpower, equipment, and energy to launch them against some rival nation, this is its period of incandescence, exaltation and expenditure, and extreme tension. When two such societies meet, it is no longer a communal coming together, as in the case of complementary groups from indeterminate societies without boundaries or states. It is a ruthless carnage, caused by the exercise of sovereignty that accepts no bounds—and is hence inevitably driven by selfishness, the wish to expand, and, if not the the will to power, then at least the concern for territorial integrity.

A state asserts and legitimizes itself, exalts and reinforces itself by confronting another totality. And this is why war resembles festival and constitutes a similar paroxysm. Following the example of festivals, war appears as an absolute, and, in the end, it provokes the same mythology with the same vertigo. This transforms even the violence of war, which, as we have seen, is not always absent from festival. In festivals, however, violence remained accidental; merely adding to the fertilizing effervescence from which it sprang through excessive vitality and which it then raised to a feverish pitch. In war, however, violence is the object of a systematic effort; it is mechanized and the deliberate goal of relentless hostility. If the state is born of war, it returns the favor by producing war in turn. The two evolve together. Whenever war is exacerbated, the state accordingly strengthens and extends its powers. Conversely, each new charge assumed by the state tends to increase the size and severity of war. The more the state controls, the more war consumes, and the state controls more and more so that war might consume more and more. The state's chief concern thus becomes the fight in which it may have to pit its strengths and resources against the neighboring state. By contrast, in a world with less rigid and nearly nonexistent structures, these encounters are occasions for gift exchange and carousing, festivals, fairs, and competitions. However, once the state has established and asserted itself, the spirit of competition prevails over that of fraternity. After an interlude of noble competition and courtly rivalry among privileged individuals, there swiftly appears the era of hate-filled and absolute disputes—ruthless conflicts that put into question the very existence of the opposed collectivities.

Orgy and carnage, festival and war: two symmetrical phenomena that are both violent. They perform the same supreme function in two different contexts and hence share a similar capacity to fascinate—the first attracts and the second terrifies—depending on whether the crisis is meant to fertilize or destroy, welcome or repulse. The path leading from festival to war merges with the evolution of technical progress and political organization. Everything has a price: the current forms of war were implicated in the very development of civilization. And we have reached a point where the latter must quickly find a way of parrying this domestic danger, which feeds on the achievements of civilization and threatens to destroy it.

Introduction to "Metamorphoses of Hell"

In 1937, Caillois had been promised a contract with Gallimard for an edition of the *Pléiade* that was to be titled *Mythologie*. In this comparative survey of world mythology, he planned to include Christianity; Gide thus vetoed the project.[1] Some forty years later, Caillois's genealogy of the Beyond set forth in "Metamorphoses of Hell" obliquely resumed this original plan, while giving greater historical breadth and scope to his lifelong meditation on the seductions of Satan. *Quatre essais de sociologie contemporaine*'s discussion of the "secular sacred" addressed not only the sacralization of war by pre-Hitler and Nazi writers but also the collective representations of a country like the United States, which, Caillois said, sought to be absolutely profane: "Can a civilization subsist without having recourse to the sentiment of the sacred? What masks does the sacred adopt in a civilization whose originality precisely consists in doing away with it to the utmost extent?" "La Mort dans le cinéma américain" contrasted the Mexican cult of death with the "negation of death's sanctity" in the United States, "country of reason and progress, where optimism is a cardinal virtue" and where a profane "mythology" of death seeks "to conjure [it] away." That is, the boundary between life and death has become indistinct. Last rites are like social visits with the deceased, and "the other world thus presents itself in a bureaucratic mode, which likens it to reality and extends the latter."[2] When Caillois returned to this essay in the 1970s, currently writing about modernity *à l'amèricaine* rather than about the United States stricto sensu, "Metamorphoses of Hell" explained that the prior mythological "model had been unsatisfactory. It seemed implausible since it was located in the Beyond; at the same time, it merely transposed there the dullest measures of everyday life." The modern mind still needed the emotional ambiguities of the "sacred"; indeed, "its yearning for marvelous pleasures, its fear of unbearable torments . . . but . . . found it unnecessary or unreasonable to situate these after death or even at the far corners of the universe."

Caillois's genealogy of modern Hell draws on numerous sources—such as film, science fiction, and an anthology by Borges and Bioy Casares—to explore

Excerpted from "Métamorphoses de l'enfer," in *Obliques: précédé de Images, Images* . . . (Paris: Gallimard, 1987), 213–47.

"how Heaven and Hell have declined as concrete entities, what this void has meant for the spontaneous exigencies of the human mind, and how makeshift fantasy has sought to fill in this dangerous gap." He concludes with a mythology of Hell (and Heaven) in the real world—not after death—that maintains the dichotomies of bliss and pain and of reward and punishment, while switching them around through mutual contamination. Through this permutation of sacred ambiguity, Heaven is residence to the pseudo-elect, who deserve no reward for virtue; they nonetheless bask in transgressive *jouissance*. In Hell, the damned are the truly virtuous ones, who do not merit punishment; yet they are condemned to suffer degrading torture.

As noted in the introduction, Caillois was unperturbed by May 1968, but in this essay he certainly seems irritated (if enticed) by mass culture, to which he attributes, in part, the feverish cult of transgression. But what of Bataille in all this? Generally speaking, of course, Bataille had displaced his prewar longing for "sacred" communion with his well-known theories of the individual literary imagination and its "hypermoral" grasp of Evil. "What suddenly comes to light in Emily Brontë's attitude," he wrote in *Literature and Evil*, "by means of an intangible moral solidity, is the dream of a sacred violence which no settlement with organised society can attenuate."[3] Does Caillois really blame Bataille's transvaluation of good and evil, with its cult of transgression, erotic or otherwise, for what "Metamorphoses of Hell" deems the current Heaven of transgression?[4] In any event, he certainly appears to recant his *own* allusions to imposed jouissance in the 1930s.[5]

One of the key features of Caillois's analysis is that death as a boundary or threshold separating life from Heaven or Hell does, effectively, disappear. In thus pointing to the evanescence of death, his argument has links to the larger, contemporary theme of death itself as taboo or forbidden. The idea that our experience of death is fundamentally transgressive runs through Bataille's postwar writings. But in his view, this interdict does not necessarily foster displacements. For example, his review of *Man and the Sacred* (1951) locates the vestigial *sacred* of modern life precisely in the private encounter with death: "When we see our fellow men alive, a certain face is sacred for me, in a sense, if death can't freeze its traits without making my heart bleed."[6] Blanchot's complex writings on death's inacessibility, though, included the idea that insofar as the experience of death "at the level of Hell" was concerned, "the true face of death" was papered over or hidden by the consoling, metaphysical illusions of Hell.[7] Closer to Caillois's analysis of metaphysical Hell's demise was Philippe Ariés's discussion "La Mort inversée. Le changement des attitudes devant la mort dans les sociétés occidentales" (Death reversed. The transformation of attitudes toward death in Western societies; 1967). Building on Caillois's "La

Mort dans le cinéma américain," Ariès cites Geoffrey Gorer's *Death, Grief and Mourning* (1965), which "shows in a striking way how death has replaced sex as the chief interdict in the twentieth century." In the "diffuse and anonymous anguish [that] has been spreading out to replace those words and signs multiplied by our ancestors," Ariès concludes by discerning a possible crisis of individualism.[8]

With the demise of death, Caillois seems less worried about the demise of rites (or individualism for that matter) than about the realization or enactment of myth in the world. (He had clearly moved far from "Paris, a Modern Myth.") At the core of this essay, albeit left relatively unexplored, is "the world of the concentration camps"—clearly denoting both Nazi and communist camps—as the basis for the modern conception of Hell. Here, he locates a *real* source for modern mythology, and this source is itself mythology come down to earth (for example, Solzhenitsyn's *First Circle*). Caillois's few, sparse comments provide little sociohistorical etiology for the camps, which he seems to link to the dominion of social atomization or the profane—"the general tendency of an impersonal society." In this phrase, and in the image of the "punctilious officials" with human "rancor" but deep impassivity, we might also hear an echo of Hannah Arendt's famous *Eichmann in Jerusalem* on the bureaucratic state and the "banality of evil." Most important, the absence of moral framework—the guards are "as devoid of guilt or innocence as their imaginary predecessors"—makes obvious the need for precisely that. When the mythology of Hell came down to earth, it lost any ethical significance it might ever have had.

It is interesting to consider this chilling absence of passion as against the views of Bataille, who viewed "the evil" *(le mal)* symbolized by Buchenwald as passion, here "bestiality," instrumentally deployed by reason, or by "the reason of State"—just as modern warfare arose from inadequate or instrumentalized "expenditure."[9] He wrote about the Nazi camps, reviewing David Rousset's novel *Jours de notre mort* (1947): "We cannot be *human* without having perceived in ourselves the possibility of suffering, and also that of abjection. But we are not only the possible victims of the executioners: the executioners are like us. We must go on to ask ourselves: Isn't there anything in our nature to make so much horror impossible? and we have no choice but to answer: Nothing indeed."[10] Without seeking to justify or exonerate these agents in any way, Bataille's "hypermoral" perspective outlines a common thread of emotion, inhuman though it might be, potentially uniting "us" with the executioners.[11] If Bataille finds an emotional basis for a stance beyond Good and Evil, Caillois rather dispassionately cites the guards' own lack of emotion to outline the perils of an immanent, rather than metaphysical, Heaven and Hell.

It goes without saying that learned and voluminous works have compiled and compared mankind's representations of the Beyond—of the types of lives, in other words, awaiting people after death. Sometimes the authors of these collections have tried to classify such imaginary worlds or latter-day dwellings of the dead and to uncover the secret laws by which they have been conceived, as well as the places—both near to and distinct from one another—in which they were located. Reaching these sites, however inevitable it might be, is not always easy. As for returning from them, this has been impossible except in a few legendary cases: Ishtar, a goddess; Orpheus, a legendary hero; and Lazarus, a man raised from the dead but about whom nothing else is known.

Furthermore, as far back as the oldest evidence goes, people have always imagined that the afterworld contained both a place of punishment for wrongs committed in this one and also, but less precisely, a region where praiseworthy actions were rewarded, especially if they had passed unacknowledged. Yet the belief, as old as history itself, has lately been fading away and even vanishing. From a certain perspective, confining ourselves to the West in the broad sense of the term (in the sense of any region in the world where there are universities, libraries, and laboratories), things have reached the point where our century may be remembered as the one marking the disappearance—at least the eclipse or metamorphosis—of Hell.

It does not seem premature to recall briefly the principal ways in which our species, more or less everywhere, has come to imagine this posthumous empire where the condemned suffer horrifying and specific tortures. I will then examine how this representation has evolved, and finally suggest some of the reasons that have prompted and still prompt mankind (almost everywhere and simultaneously, and after so many centuries) to forsake the deeply and widely entrenched idea of a concrete, punitive Beyond. . . .

*   *   *

[Caillois then surveys the myths of Heaven and Hell in the West and compares these with the belief systems of certain non-Western cultures]. Hell is nearly always varied, spectacular, paroxysmic, and individualized. Heaven is nearly always one single color, or at best, iridescent; harmonious or, in any case, without discord; monotonous, and thus potentially boring; and it is anonymous. That is, there is no bliss specifically tailored to an individual's well-earned merits in the same way that the punishments of Hell correspond to particular sins. Another equally important difference: readymade beatitude rewards an entire life of blameless virtue, whereas specific tortures usually punish one single, if glaring, misdeed. To grasp the full scope of this disparity, let us simply recall that the *Inferno* is the only section of Dante's poem ever to have reached a popular audience – and this because of the pictures of torture it purveyed.

* * *

However varied the traditional imagery may have been, it was always predicated on mankind's universal and tenacious need for a supernatural justice that would avenge people for the wrongs they had witnessed or suffered on earth. This demand proved so fierce that it made people demand that the joys and sorrows of the next world should last forever and be unbearably intense. This soon offended the spirit of charity, and then the credibility of the retribution lost ground as well. It made God seem so inordinately cruel that several doctors undertook to exonerate him from an accusation that was unacceptable, if not contradictory. They proposed that the sufferings of the damned were purely fictitious or merely imagined. The damned were mistaken about the reality of the fire that consumed them, which was actually sparked by their own remorse and certainty of deserving punishment. God had nothing to do with it. An immanent law was pursuing its ineluctable course. After Origen, Masilio Ficino supported this heresy.[1] Theology was a deductive science. The paradoxes generated by its rigor rival those of mathematical severity. Giordano Bruno therefore had to extend Ficino's thesis to its logical limit.[2] If Hell was nothing but a representation, then those who did not know about it or else refused to imagine it (pagans, atheists, skeptics, or cynics) would obviously remain unharmed for all eternity. For it was only from their earthly life that souls could have acquired the representations that were torturing them. Therefore, the sole effective means of safeguarding oneself against Hell was impiety, either naïve or strategic. But this also served to fuel an inextinguishable and questionable fire: the Inquisition arrested, judged, and condemned Giordano Bruno, who was burned alive in Rome one fine morning in the year 1600 by flames that were both ephemeral and real.

To approach this evolution from another perspective, it seems that there

1. [Masilio Ficino (1433–1499) was an Italian philosopher and theologian of the Renaissance, whose interpretation and revival of Platonism, integrating it with Christian theology, influenced European thought for centuries — giving rise, among other concepts, to "Platonic" love. —*Ed.*]

2. [Giordano Bruno (1548–1600), burned at the stake by the Inquisition for his unorthodox views regarding the infinite nature of the universe and the multiplicity of worlds, was an Italian philosopher, astrologer, mathematician, and Dominican priest. —*Ed.*]

exists in the world of emotions (as in the syntax of justice and *justesse* [accuracy]) a form of entropy akin to what is noted in physics: a similar tendency toward the equalization of all levels, tensions, and temperatures. In this instance as well, everything seems to have become reduced, to have reached a form of tepid equilibrium, of permanent indifference. Sufferings and delights lost all their intensity and even acuteness. Presently it was the soul, furthermore, rather than the flesh that had to be rewarded or tormented. Heaven became the term for a transforming union that dissolved personal identity within restored unity; Hell referred to the intimate curse barring the damned from the ecstasy that they were nevertheless burning to share. We find no imagery here: the first term indicates a state of fulfillment and the second of frustration. The two are no longer divided by anything more than a kind of sign change in an algebraic system that is just as theoretical and remote as that expressing the weak interactions of elementary particles. Heaven is not so very delectable nor Hell so agonizing. The void of *Nirvana* is not far off. Upon leaving the body, the soul currently seeks only tranquility, or eternal rest—that is, an absence or, at most, a pale euphoria. If Dante were alive today, he might have to reconcile Judas and Beatrice in the same final indistinction.

*   *   *

I think that this kind of assimilation as well as the concern to dissociate God's infinite goodness from any cruelty were primary factors in the slow decline of posthumous tortures. However, fantasy was still ruled by the same principles. The modern world's first representation of the Beyond was in its own image—as might be expected. It was bureaucratic and administrative, essentially derived from American films. People reached Hell by crossing some sort of meadow bathed in rising mist. Uniformed officials took charge of the new arrivals. Having done with the formalities, the newcomers then entered this new world, full of corridors, elevators, files, records, inventories, and catalogues. The atmosphere was that of some immense government agency, where, not surprisingly, no one was ever to be seen except for subaltern civil servants or, perhaps, a department head. The very picture of a complex, inextricable, and irresponsible organization. The god of the Dead, who remained invisible, had become a kind of Immigration Manager. Upon arrival, there was no sense of disorientation; people were treated exactly as they had been at their point of departure. There were no torments or ecstasies: monotony for all. The modern Beyond was not a world of extremes but one of dusk. Asphodels had simply been replaced by filing cabinets.

Apparently, this model turned out to be unsatisfactory. It seemed implausible because it was located in the Beyond; at the same time, it simply transposed there the dullest measures of everyday life. It extended into the next world a well-balanced monotony that was neither alluring nor frightening.

Modern consciousness did not, however, relinquish antitheses, despite its rejection of all posthumous worlds. It retained its yearning for Marvelous pleasures, its fear of unbearable torments. But the modern mind found it unnecessary or unreasonable to situate these after death or even at the far corners of the universe. It merely had to look around itself or extrapolate from the evidence of history or current events. Unbelief has no doubt depleted the Elysian fields and the shades of Tartarus, but the planet's recent past has had no trouble supplying equally eloquent pictures. The screen and the tabloid press give descriptions of *la dolce vita* that made it an enviable copy of the heavenly joys that had been called into question. Luxurious debauchery seems within reach; it hinges on some happy random event where a stroke of luck can compensate for lack of fortune, just as winning the lottery's first prize suddenly bestows that wealth rarely assured by a lifetime's work. Symmetrically, the world of the concentration camps furnished a terrible and immediate picture that did not simply refer back to some problematic Gehenna and that instilled more terror than any pangs of remorse could have done. The horrifying memory still expresses, if not the fate, at least the general tendency of an impersonal society where punctilious officials—as devoid of guilt or innocence as their imaginary predecessors—perform their role of depriving the mass of miserable people entrusted to their surveillance of all they have, including hope itself—it is their job to do so. Logically enough, and to indulge their own rancor, they consign the intractable ones to the nethermost circle of a domestic damnation where death, this time, is not a means of access but of escape.

Under these conditions, it seems that there was little the imagination could add to the scenario. In fact, what it did was to refine and complicate. Above all, it was quick to install the tortures of the ancient Hell within the modern world, with science and technology assigned the task of granting the tormentors a more efficient array of tools. At their disposal they now had electricity, acids, ultrasonics, lasers: a thousand machines and poisons that, rightly or wrongly, were thought to make suffering more acute and long-lasting. Neurologists and cardiologists were at their sides, regulating the pain to keep it just below the danger point. Orderlies and doctors revived the victim between two series of "interrogations." The rhetoric of hyperbole simply became more pronounced and ornate. The creativity of aesthetes produced a roster of new torments. Mass-produced films, the literature of mass consumption, and comic strips vied with each other to feed mankind's stubborn pleasure in cruelty, one long illustrated by Tibetan silks and the frescoes of Pisa. Bizarre alliances were forged. A precursor in this respect was *Le Jardin des supplices* [The garden of tortures]. Published in the last year of the nineteenth century, this novel depicted cruel tortures targeting sexuality, which used sexual pleasure itself, imposing and forcing it upon people, transforming it into a horrible and ultimately fatal form of suffering. The treacherous groves, the charming retreats of the sinister park have nowadays been replaced and reproduced by perfectly equipped soundproof cellars. Here, under the spotlights, practiced torturers who are artists at their trade handle throbbing flesh and raw nerves. And, as Baudelaire claimed about Goya, we do not fail to find

> quite naked young girls adjusting their stockings, to tempt the demons
> ["Les Phares," in *Spleen et idéal*].

They add spice to the torment with a mirage of lust. But they don't seek to distract the torturers themselves. Their role is secondary; they merely display themselves or, at most, hand over the instruments. They are present only to evoke sexual pleasure at the instant of suffering. By their seductiveness and docility, they usher into this sterilized underground, which significantly perpetuates the ancient site of Hell, the legendary heavenly courtesans, Moslem houris, and Indian apsaras. They are neither patients nor technicians, just servant girls in a state of undress. Their reserve and the generally self-effacing manner of the torturers prevent us from confusing these dreadful, glacial rituals with the real crimes of a Gilles de Rais or an Erzebet Bathory.[3] Even less can they be mistaken for Sade's scenes of obsession, featuring the torturers as the main protagonists. Here, the situation is reversed. Sexual gratification is secondary. In fact, it emerges only between the lines. The mission of the attractive assistants charged with awakening desire is merely to remind the victims that they are very near some Eden to which they would be immediately admitted if they made the very slightest concession—even a slight, but unforgivable, wink.

This is a very ancient combination. Indian ascetics and figures such as Saint Anthony in the early years of Christianity also had to be able to resist the torments of demons and the voluptuous delights proposed by immodest young exhibitionists. But at least, those scenes of torture and temptation occurred in

---

3. [Gilles de Rais (1404–1440) was a Breton aristocrat, who fought with Joan of Arc before retiring to his domain, where he developed an interest in Satanism and was ultimately hanged for allegedly kidnapping, torturing, and killing over 140 children. As Gilles de Rais is linked to the tale of Bluebeard, Erzebet Bathory inspired the tales of Dracula. This female Hungarian aristocrat (ca. 1560–1614) tortured and murdered countless young women, anywhere from sixty to six hundred.—*Ed.*]

the forest or desert, in some vague place, far from everything else. Moreover, they were distinctly hallucinatory in nature. And above all, they chiefly consisted in trials that opened the way to eternal salvation.

The same connivance still exists. Even if the setting is now familiar, almost trivial, the mainsprings remain identical. Philosophers unsuccessfully tried to dispel the phantasmagoria that naïve superstition as well as cautious theology had relegated beyond the grave at least, or to the distant ends of the inhabited world. "If you chase Hell away, it will gallop right back to you!" And it comes back even closer: on the street corner, at arm's length. Only rarely did Hell ever stand for a dark and shady ideal, which was hence all the more appealing. It was a dreaded and naïve kind of menace—hardly some repressed, unavowed, haunting, saturnine desire that one might easily fulfill by succumbing with little effort. Apparently, the current aim is to convince the rebel that he need only acquiesce, and he will leave an abyss of suffering for a pinnacle of delights. He merely has to take the first step. Once launched down this slope, it will take more than Heaven to bring him back: "Hell helps those who help themselves."

At a time when the tide of cruelty and eroticism is running high, it is hardly surprising that we should encounter such a hypertrophy of imposed suffering or of strictly sexual promised joys. Given the exceptional technical and industrial development of our time, it was inevitable that science would play a primary role in a Hell occurring before death—which now opens onto a void. Hence, the three main stars—violence, sex, and machines—are spontaneously arrayed in a way that combines their nearly unrivaled forms of fascination.

What has happened is that the hitherto supernatural spaces of rewards and punishments have now reciprocally contaminated each other, and so much so that they sometimes give the impression of switching places. Yet the accursed (or protected) sites still retain enough specific features to be identifiable; thus, some replace the vanished Empyreans and others the depreciated Gehennas.

They continue to appear as marginal abodes. Although they are close by, this proximity is somewhat offset by their near secrecy. Access is difficult, requiring passwords, strategic maneuvers, and accomplices on the inside. On the one hand, we have a world of luxury and lust, a mood of licentiousness and festival, heightened by jewels, furs, nudity, succulent dishes, wines, and lighting effects as well as aphrodisiac, euphoric, or hallucinogenic drugs. On the other, we have the setting of a surgical operating room, where glass cases display rows of dental, surgical, and welding instruments. Attentive and seemingly detached assistants are present in both places. In the first, musicians and footmen replace angels, or Hebe and Ganymede; in the second, human executioners quite skillfully take over from the torturing demons of yore. The end result is the same: a momentary loss of consciousness. This is marked by two opposing signs (ecstasy versus blackout, swoons due to pleasure versus pain), which both correspond, however, to excessive sensations that erase everything else, that transcend any state of consciousness one could express. It was once thought that this kind of experience could be achieved only by approaching the absolute.

Although many elements indicate a certain continuity, crucial differences in the character of the protagonists betray a significant palinode.

As Heaven and Hell have been acculturated into a mysterious universe of cellars and palaces, lost in the countryside or hidden in the heart of cities, the process has been accompanied by more than merely juxtaposing the sites of great sexual delights and overwhelming tortures. At present, innocent people or heroes are the ones being victimized by cruel, neuropathic jailers in horrifying dungeons; while in the neighboring boudoirs, the showoffs, the scoundrels and perverts indulge in prolonged, poisonous pleasures. The first sign of a crucial turning point may well be the fact that the pseudo-elect are no longer enjoying the contemplative beatitudes of Paradise: the new ecstasies are more spasmodic than serene. They often bring on madness and death, just like the brutalities of the torturers.

It is even doubtful that these accursed pleasures revive the joys of the blessed in another guise. Although they do not represent the underside of Hell, they nevertheless derive from the Devil's initial function: he first appears as a tempter before proving to be an executioner. Far from being serene, the pleasures of the privileged company are thus almost necessarily spasmodic, a constant alternation of orgasm and collapse. These *jouissances* have a seismic quality. They are not any kind of reward. They provide neither well-being nor appeasement. They clearly belong to the domain of transgression. Their pleasure arises from something close to blasphemy, or at least from a deliberate challenge to natural and permitted behavior, to mores and laws.

Elysian-style bliss became boring because it was bland. Hence it developed into orgiastic effervescence that is both stupefying and convulsive; it is ultimately contrary to the angelic happiness that was for so long the prerogative of the elect. Just as clearly, the tortures experienced by the victims do not represent any form of expiation. The tormentors want their victims to recant. They want to wrest from them a plea, a confession, a secret. Their goal is to make the victims give in or, as they say, *crack*. The pain they inflict does not redeem; it breaks people down and degrades them. The recent mythology purveyed by films and the popular press consequently reveals a double swing of the pendulum. The forbidden pleasures reserved for a wealthy or corrupt elite (whose luxury insults the humble as much as their debauchery does) stand opposite horrifying jails in which the just are tortured almost as a punishment for— and proportionally to—their integrity. In its descent to earth, the hallucinatory and symmetrical hinterworld once formed by Paradise and Hell has doubly reversed its vocation. In adjoining and communicating settings, an extravagant and insistent imagery depicts foul and triumphant depravity as well as the humbled, crushed courage of martyrs without haloes—partly Luciferian—who seem more prideful or obstinate than pious.

* * *

At this point in the argument, a scruple makes me hesitate. Can we really compare a purely fictional world, produced by countless scribblers and doodlers inventing whatever they personally please, with vast coordinated representations that are the object of quasi-unanimous faith, and that are upheld by religions, Churches, and theologies? On reflection, despite these obvious differences (which in any case, if I am right, are caused chiefly by the evolution of mores and ideas), Hell's earthly avatar in the end belongs less to the worldly and novelistic sphere (in short, to literature) than to mythology in its strict, rigorous sense. To ascertain this, let us examine the boundary separating myth from the arbitrary fictions that are produced by the imagination or creative minds.

First of all, myth is not individual. It has a widespread authority that it derives from itself. It transposes onto an awe-inspiring stage the reality from which it draws. Its heroes are barely superhuman and move in a world that merely magnifies everyday settings. Its exploits and trials do not seem purely fictional. They reflect a certain truth that, albeit approximate, blurred, changeable, and accepted in various versions, nonetheless gives rise to some kind of belief that is itself quite vague and obscure but, unlike a dogma, is neither specific nor compulsory. Second, the mythical environment, its characters, and their adventures all have the power to bewitch the person who enjoys such tales: he becomes an unwitting means of contagion. Each listener ensures and spreads the influence of myth; he tends to draw inspiration from myth and recreate it in his immediate surroundings, at least through daydreams. Above all, these fantasies are imperative, protean, superposable, secretly shared, and all the more exalting to the extent that they readily illustrate, and celebrate, forbidden behavior: lust, cruelty, murder, everything that society rejects and punishes. Myths radiate a kind of supernatural incandescence that seems to attach a fabulous and revered precedent to the model it holds out to the bold. I know very well that people only rarely follow this example and that things remain at the stage of reverie and vague desire. But this confused temptation, which is proper to myth, still continues to ferment, giving rise to concupiscence and shivers.

Like myths, the works of fiction purveying the new fable are more or less anonymous and collective—one rarely recalls their author's name. On the contrary, the heroes are highly individualized, like those of myths. Their style and manner are identifiable and unchanging. As in myths (or tales), they move between episodes that hardly vary. More to the point, rather than shattering our focus, the variety of the episodes confirms—by the similarity of their vicissitudes—the coherence and the stability of this ghostlike world that borders on ours and that is home to eternal suffering and delight.

The modes of being of Heaven and Hell, the fates of the elect and of the damned, were essentially no different from this. One can discern most of the features I have just tried to describe. Of course, the means of diffusion were quite different, each proper to its time. On the one hand, there were tales, fables, apologues, and sermons, capitals of columns and church portals, cathedral frescoes, wooden stages for mystery plays; or else, in antiquity, theogonies and epics, vase paintings, rituals and mimicry of festivals and processions, tragedies. Today, on the other hand (and equally powerful), we have the printing press and photography, film screens, radio, posters, serials, and television. The most widely read novels, those that put us into our most docile emotional state, are the ones we read with bated breath and beating heart, without thinking at all about their technique. When animated, luminous, and transient pictures are projected in the dark and we cannot pause to linger over them, it is hard to gauge their truth thoughtfully and appreciate their beauty with our sensibility; they are endowed with the best possible weapons for imposing their magic. And while we are viewing them, they are ideally safeguarded against the two attitudes that could potentially enable an audience to escape their grasp: critical detachment and aesthetic judgment. These faculties do take their revenge after the fact, but only among a very few professionals and film buffs. Indeed, the vast majority of viewers are left with their first impression; the channels purveying this effect are simply more persuasive than before.

It is through these channels that people now receive the current, profane representations of Heaven and Hell— no less abundantly and, at times, quasi-hypnotically. The new myths have inherited certain aspects of the fables of the past and taken their place. However, their orientation is almost diametrically opposed. They have been producing ever more scenes of harmful pleasures instead of radiant beatitudes and of unfair rather than expiatory sufferings. It remains that both joys and pains are henceforth simply located behind a thin curtain, and that to reach or confront them one no longer has to cross the threshold of death.

The transformation of an obsolete Beyond and the creation of a substitute in the realm of the living is probably due to a larger transformation. The religious and providential worldview was unseated by the triumph of analysis, control, and verification, and by the exclusion of the irrational and invisible—

so that the Kingdom of Heaven and the infernal abyss were refuted as well. The imagination was then forced to combine things, to coordinate hallucinatory events with those from the realm of the admissible; the fantastic quality of ghost stories, which had once disturbed people, thus became similar to the Marvelous quality of fairy tales, which delighted them. No longer could one create worlds teeming with prodigies and bristling with monsters, for these were denied by principles of physics and biology learned at school, confirmed by constant osmosis, and never challenged. Fantasy took an entirely different tack, one dictated by the only outlook shared by all—and that was unshakeable insofar as it was generally unstated.

At present, the realm of myth, located somewhere between faith and doubt, requires a scientific backdrop. To seduce credulity, it currently speaks of robots, electronics, self-replicating machines that free themselves from man and enslave him. Any other kind of fantastic has become mere empty distraction; it can no longer really arouse the least shred of doubt, the "but what if it were true" that briefly shuts down our ever vigilant skepticism.

Emptied of the supernatural, there is nothing left of outer space except for asteroids and galaxies; in the depths of the earth there is nothing but igneous rock and ore. Therefore, Heaven and Hell both have had to adapt themselves to the new rules of the game. Most people are quite convinced that it is only here on earth, and while we are still breathing, that our nerves can make us scream with pain or swoon with rapture.

I do not consider it far-fetched to suggest that this fundamental evolution is the slow-working and remote (I would say profound did I not distrust this adjective) cause of the emergence of an updated phantasmagoria. Of course, the two mythologies are so radically opposed (not only in their settings but also in ethical significance) that one first hesitates to compare them. Or else one wonders whether the human adventure, having reached the peak of some gigantic ridge, has not just started to descend the other side. After all, it is always in the nature of myths to feed upon the dreams of their day and provide a decodable spectrum for their observers.

Moreover, this about face would not be unprecedented. I shall cite only one. The earlier utopias—those of Plato, Thomas More, and Campanella—described ideal communities that had resolved all antinomies, admirably and durably instating general happiness. But readers have often remarked that, on the contrary, the recent utopias (those of Aldous Huxley and George Orwell) conjure up nightmarish societies that are monstrous and cold, founded on utter tyranny, horror, and automatism. Fear has replaced hope. That the two sorts of half-visionary representations underwent a sign change, a radical and similar reversal of orientation, seems hardly coincidental.

However, I am not convinced that we should be upset by such symptoms, even if their convergence is alarming. Perhaps they are only the vain simulacra of passing clouds, a short-lived interlude without a future. They are useful warnings nonetheless. And so they warranted the first elements of a "file" on the fables that have succeeded in gaining wide acceptance. I confess that I, for one, would have preferred to see Hell vanish simply through the workings of lucidity and justice, and especially without this sudden reversal (as a horrible and menacing counterpart), this semiabdication of the imaginary, which has invented a hybrid, nearby, and plausible substitute for the ancient, inaccessible dwelling place of the dead (out of bravado, spite, or despair). It is a substitute that serves to trigger and no longer to compensate—even in the manner of a flywheel designed to channel the ardor of wild, fruitful energy that is, perhaps, fruitful when harnessed but devastating when left to its own violence (not to say, provoked).

Signs and Images

Introduction to "The Image"

Written two years before *Babel*, *Vocabulaire esthétique* (1946) listed "fourteen articles of an aesthetic vocabulary" next to that of "Image": "Liberty, Rule, Sincerity, Order, Originality, Ineffability, Surprise, Form and Contents, Progress, Authority, Literary Criticism, Art for Art's Sake, Edifying Literature." Caillois's preface explained that he was publishing this prescriptive poetics because it countered the views of the day[1] During the war, Caillois shunned the image or metaphor, viewed as the Surrealist trope par excellence. However, after the war, and with "The Image," he steadily reinstated this category, which would eventually bridge his initial Surrealist "objective ideogram" (see "The Praying Mantis") and his formal lecture on poetry to the Collège de France in 1974. As the final chapter of *Approches de la poésie* (1978), this lecture was a much reworked version of "The Image"; it defined the crucial question about metaphorical similitude as knowing "which conditions the proposed relation must fulfill to satisfy not only the imagination, which is always easy to deceive for an instant, but a more lasting and rigorous exigency."[2]

In his essay of 1946, Caillois framed the topic by explaining that poetry has always required the "union of sound and meaning, of rhythm and an idea." However, according to him, modern poets have divested their writings of such constraints; and to compensate for this lack, to preserve the uniqueness or magic of poetry, they have thus focused on the image. What was previously ornamental has now become the "very essence" of poetry, and one whose sole function is "to surprise."[3] Deliberately or not, Caillois's postwar attempt to theorize the norms of adequation proper to an *accurate* imagination *(imagination juste)* was revisiting Reverdy's 1918 theory of conscious poetic creation, founded on the claim that, "an image is not strong because it is *brutal* or *fantastic*—but because the association of ideas spans a great distance and is *accurate [juste]*" (Reverdy 75). In the 1940s, Caillois likewise explored the careful equation of surprise and *justesse* within a successful image, but in so doing he emphasized the criterion of *justesse* to a much greater degree than Reverdy had.

Excerpted from "Image," in *Babel, précédé de Vocabulaire esthétique* (Paris: Gallimard, 1978), 66–69.

As for poetry's ontological status—objective image or Reverdy's "pure crea-tion of the mind"—Caillois did not address such questions at this time. In the 1960s and 1970s, though, he resumed his inquiry launched in the 1930s re-garding natural representations (see "Surrealism as a World of Signs" and "The Natural Fantastic").

A dialogue with Paulhan was perhaps Caillois's more pressing concern in "L'Image," which appeared shortly after Paulhan's *Clef de la poésie* (The key to poetry; 1944). This treatise explored how the conflicting laws of Terror and Rhetoric made readers of poetry alternatively perceive "thought" or "lan-guage," or "content" and "form," as Paulhan here used the terms almost inter-changeably. Such structural oscillation or "contradiction" was, he claimed, "unavoidable in any case (and any direct observation [of the poem] utterly out of the question)." Hence, the poet's task was to create the "most complex structure" of "words and ideas" without hoping to master "the strange drama of poetry" and "the mystery in some sense required by its regular workings and the constant breathing of our language." The solution, or "key," as it were, lay in the reader's ability to achieve an "accommodation" or "pact" with the image. "We may not be able to think overtly of form and content as one and the same thing," wrote Paulhan, "and that a word is an idea. Yet we may at least think of 'the hem of the airs' or 'the dew with a cat's head' *as if* the words were ideas, and the form were the content. We may think of them askew [*de biais*]. In fact, it is only askew that we may think of them at all."[4] The reader thus has the responsibility to address poetry's mystery and produce a strategic stasis by thinking askew.

For Caillois in the postwar era, as noted in the introduction, the literary text was the site of creative license or controlled transgression—the realm of "as if"—proper to the civilized spirit of "play and games." However, he paid little heed to those mysterious shifts in the appearance and perception of language that so fascinated Paulhan. In contradistinction to *Clef de la poésie*, "The Image" suggests that although the reader may experience poetry as a paradoxical equi-librium, the fabrication of such an event rests squarely and exclusively on the shoulders of the poet. Unlike Paulhan, Caillois would continue to insist on the writer's fundamental responsibility in this regard. For example, his subsequent "Actualité des Kenningar" would contrast the *kenningar* explored by Borges (traditional, fixed metaphors of Icelandic sagas) and Breton's Surrealist game, *l'un dans l'autre* (based on free association) by relating the first to Paulhan's *Rhetoric* and the second to Paulhan's *Terror*. These ritual riddles and surprising metaphors were radically distinct, Caillois argued. Rhetoric was aligned with traditional knowledge; Terror, with novel creation. He nonetheless called on the writer to coordinate these two extremes: "It is good to surprise, but mere arbitrariness or mismatching are nothing in and of themselves: one must surprise *accurately* [*justement*]."[5]

In 1958, refining the rift between sacred riddle and ludic poetic image as presented in "Actualité des Kenningar," Caillois suggested that the first might have given rise to the second. To stage the anthropological origin of the image, evolving out of and away from fixed ritual or Rhetoric, he evoked a Paulhanian scene: a "battle of riddles" around a brushfire. "Usually, everybody knows the answers," he wrote. "It's not a matter of finding the solution, but of innovating, of discovering other answers that can fit the proposed definition equally well. Each person tries to come up with new analogies that nonetheless can be accepted by all."[6] The poet's task in bridging the old and the new is clear, and it avoids the complex perspectival ambiguities outlined in Paulhan's famous talk to the College of Sociology on the anthropological apprehension of proverbs or "sacred language."[7] Still, over the next few decades, Caillois would grant the poet—and image—a significantly higher degree of involuntary fantasy and mystery (see "Fruitful Ambiguity" and "Surrealism as a World of Signs").

THE IMAGE

. . . Certainly, it is excellent for an image to be surprising: this is the precondition of its force. But it has to be *juste* [accurate] and impose itself. An image soon stops persuading or even making any impression at all if it disconcerts us at no cost, without any element of truth. It must fulfill two nearly incompatible duties: to present what is evident and to surprise. If surprise is sacrificed, then the image is weak; if obviousness is sacrificed, then the image is absurd, that is, meaningless and even weaker in the end. The terms it connects must summon each other on one level, and repel each other on another. Hence, I detect a serious mistake in modern poetry's maxim that an image is powerful to the extent that it springs from terms that are all the further apart. Distance is not enough: there must also be *justesse*. True, I do not find it very satisfying to compare an apple to an orange, but it is no better to compare a cat to a flute. In the second case, the distance is too great; in the first, the similarity. When pursuing only similarity or disparity, we give ourselves too vast a field. . . . Because infinity—for the eye—begins just a few meters away from the retina, it is possible to reject as arbitrary any relation that is not immediately apparent.

Conversely, a little effort and cleverness can ultimately establish or justify any similarity. But the game is not worth the candle [there's no point]; if poetic pleasure does exist, then I doubt it can be obtained by straining so hard and exerting so much ingenuity.

Actually, the only thing that endows an image with efficacy is a striking similarity that everything around it denies. The distance must be great and the obviousness beyond dispute: the shock stems from this. If the shock is powerful, then it is one that almost always has to have been prepared ahead of time. The context is what lets the image produce its most vivid discharge. I earlier said that comparing a cat to a flute did not satisfy me. I could have said the same thing about for example, a flower and a chair, or death and a brook. Nonetheless, when Rimbaud writes "Trouve des fleurs qui soient des chaises [Find flowers that are chairs]" and Mallarmé "Un peu profond ruisseau calomnié, la mort [Death, a shallow, slandered, brook]," I feel fulfilled above and beyond my expectations. But the point is that each time, the poet had subtly aroused in me an expectation, and more specifically, the expectation of the image he was about to propose. So it is not enough to say that I accept this image; rather, I demand it. And by referring to the premises that slowly made the comparison possible and almost necessary, I should be able to explain very clearly, should the occasion arise, why this is so.[1]

On the contrary, I could imagine the same images strewn at random, crudely presented in those lists that are wrongly being offered to us as poems devoid of artifice. And I could imagine those images reduced there to their simplest form (the brook of death, the chairs of flowers), in accordance with the mechanical, rough formula that poets seem to be favoring. The images would not have affected me as much had they been lost among other phrases of the same monotonous make in this rudimentary display; indeed, in and of themselves, they do not have much intellectual, lyrical, or formal significance. They owe what I acknowledged above to the artist who first carefully imbued them with a foreign virtue before then deftly presenting them. Such virtue de-

---

1. [In his revised version of this passage (1978), Caillois expands on this last point: "It is futile for a poet to compare a tangerine to an orange; a tiger to a jaguar; a caiman to an alligator. This is the task of the logician or scientist: to determine the neighboring genus and the specific difference. But it is just as futile for the poet to compare a flower to a chair, unless this encounter has been prepared and is therefore duly called for by the context, by a mediation that, in this case, would be the idea of welcome and rest. Indeed, this is precisely what Rimbaud's poem—where the reader seems called upon to accept the similarity—suggests ahead of time" (*Approches de la poésie*, 239).—*Ed.*]

rives neither from the terms the images unite nor from the union itself, but merely from the artistry thereby revealed.

* * *

In these images, it was the artist who so successfully reconciled obviousness with surprise that they seem to be almost mutually sustaining. And this is the goal to achieve: To reinforce one by means of the other, in an unforeseeable way, and by developing to their highest degree qualities that are unrelated and all but mutually exclusive. For this reason, verse has always required both rhythm and an idea; for this reason, every work requires a finished form and a robust content.

How can we not discern a permanent and rigorous aesthetic law in this obligation to pair diametrical opposites? Is there any artist who has not had to painstakingly comply with it at times? But to believe that the solution is always provided right from the start; . . . that obviousness itself provokes surprise; that form is . . . implied by content—this reflects such a crude naïveté that its effects cannot prosper for long. And yet, it is the naïveté of poets who are convinced that comparing two objects as dissimilar as possible is all it takes to produce a valuable image.

Introduction to "Fruitful Ambiguity"

An amusing exchange with the Surrealists took place when André Breton and Jean Schuster parodied Caillois's poetic treatise, *Art poétique, ou confession néga-tive* (Ars poetica, or negative confession; 1958). Rehearsing the technique Breton and Eluard had applied to Valéry in 1929, Breton and Schuster's "Art poétique" voiced vicious replies to each strophe of Caillois's "negative" injunctions, or models of lyrical self-restraint.[1] For instance, *Art poétique* declared: "Men's dreams, their deliria, have found a place in my poems, but to receive there a name, a form, a meaning. I have made order out of their confusion. I have stopped their flight. They are affixed in my words."[2] Breton and Schuster shot back: "Men's dreams, their deliria, have culminated in my poems. It was not for me to make them state their name; ever-changing, they possessed several meanings. I respected their confusion. I let their flight take its course. My words testify to their constant metamorphosis."[3] Yet Caillois's *Au coeur du fantastique* (At the heart of the fantastic; 1965) described the true Fantastic as something mysterious and involuntary, "a form of questioning that is just as anxious as it is anxiety-provoking, and that suddenly arose from some undetermined shadows; its own author had to take it just as it came, wishing, sometimes desperately, that he could respond."[4] In opposition to the Surrealists' willed unintelligibility, as he describes it, "Fruitful Ambiguity" thus tries to envision a more legitimate form of unwilled intelligibility.

Au Coeur du fantastique as a whole explored pictorial images, specifically "engraving and painting that characterize a certain Fantastic in the West between the Renaissance and Romanticism."[5] The brief excerpt translated here highlights literary examples, such as Raymond Roussel, whose creativity involved a very precise manipulation of chance—discussed by Breton, Leiris, and Foucault, among others. Caillois explores two types of images, the first of which he calls "infinite" or "null images"; the second is "blocked images." The first, typified by Surrealist images, "do not *want* to mean anything, or rather they want to say nothing, at the same time as they imply everything. They are

Excerpted from "Fertilité de l'ambigu," in *Cohérences aventureuses: Esthétique généralisée; au coeur du fantastique; la dissymétrie* (Paris: Gallimard, 1976), 184–190.

reverie traps, confusion machines, as perfectly suited to their task as possible. Nonetheless, they present one weakness, which is that they were deliberately conceived with this intent, and that we know it."[6] The second, "blocked images," include any form of tightly coded formal structure, such as *kenningar*, or allegory, that has lost its key. Caillois then posits some element intervening despite the artist's or writer's intent to instill mysterious order into "infinite images" or, conversely, some mysterious free play within "impeded images." Besides Roussel, the poet Gérard de Nerval is here a model: "I suspect . . . that he was not entirely clear about what he sought to convey." For the reader or viewer, the end product in either case involves an equilibrium of order and disorder.

Roussel was a key inspirational figure for Queneau's avant-garde group OULIPO, Ouvroir de littérature potentielle (Potential literature workshop), founded in 1960, which sought to apply mathematical concepts to literary form. In the 1930s, whereas Caillois had sought to better understand the determinism of Surrealist associationism through his scientistic "objective ideograms," Queneau at the time felt that modern literature and especially Surrealism were already far too intent on mimicking scientific research. Yet Queneau also criticized Surrealism in a way that could recall both Caillois's early criticism of Surrealist method and those later attacks voiced during his turn to "a classicism that is new" (to cite Etiemble). Indeed, in 1938, Queneau questioned Surrealism's conflation of "chance, automatism, and freedom," since, "*that* kind of inspiration which means blindly obeying every impulse is in fact an enslavement. The classical writer who writes his tragedy, while respecting a certain number of rules that he knows, is freer than the poet who writes whatever occurs to him and who is enslaved to other rules of which he is unaware."[7] By the 1960s, the positions of Queneau and Caillois concerning the literary use of science had switched to the extent that Queneau's OULIPO, however playfully, adopted an experimental scientific approach to literature while Caillois's playful "generalizations" were much more circumspect in this regard (see introduction). Yet both writers still entertained a dialogue with Surrealism. One OULIPO member, Jacques Roubaud explains that, "The intentional, voluntary nature of constraint upon which [Queneau] often insisted, and quite emphatically so, was for him indissociably tied to his strong rejection of chance and especially of the frequent correlation of chance and freedom."[8] That is, both Caillois and Queneau denied what Roubaud calls "the mystical belief that freedom can arise from the chance erasure of constraints" (Roubaud, 57). In "Fruitful Ambiguity," Caillois goes further, though, to demystify this very "belief" as a deliberate "wish to perplex" on the part of Surrealism.

There is a world protected from the threat of resorption by virtue of its irreducible obscurity. It is the world of the confused aspirations of the soul, of its desires and disappointments. Neither words nor images can accurately grasp these inner realities without form or stability, which defy any description or picture. They require circumlocution. To better know them and to make others yearn for them, one must resort to an intermediary language, using a mode of knowledge best defined—even more so than what Saint Paul described to the Corinthians—as the sight of an enigma reflected in a mirror.[1]

Here both poetry and fantastic art alike bring into play that fruitful ambiguity I am close to viewing as their true vocation. For that matter, the process they propose is merely an indirect way of taming what, by nature, escapes language and representation. But there is no other way. As a crowning misfortune, this is a realm in which all pretenses are easy, tempting, and even quite pleasurable. They give rise to the same enchantment as that produced in its early days by the magic lantern's colored plates. I would not dream of denying their charm. Grave and authentic mystery nonetheless remains something that is not frivolously created by any one person; it is a mystery that must be suffered insofar as it cannot be dispelled. Some highly strung sensitivities are besieged by it, and it does not fail to disturb everyone else on occasion. Some artists seek to set traps for the invisible; like poets, they would like to force it to betray a few of its secrets. They hope it will leave a trace in their works, a shimmer of its silence. In my opinion, it is no coincidence that these artists and poets hence express themselves by means of what we call, in both cases, *images*.

In the realm of both discourse and painting, only *images* (that is, an approximate, fictional, metaphorical mode of expression) can somehow satisfy an ambition that is so awkward to sustain. This particular kind of image is located in the very heart of the fantastic, midway between what I have elsewhere termed "infinite" images and "impeded" images. . . . Infinite images strive for incoherence as a matter of course and reject all meaning out of hand. Impeded images translate specific texts into symbols that the proper dictionary then enables us to reconvert, term by term, back into the equivalent discourse; these closed images are simply mysterious by accident, because their key has either been lost or become a matter of indifference. At the outset, they were not mysterious at all. Nor is there any greater mystery in infinite images, which are excessively open, exclusively composed for the sake of surprise and quick to lose

---

1. 1 Corinthians 13:12: *Per speculum in aenigmate* [through a glass, darkly].

their effect. How could we be usefully surprised—and would we remain so—if we knew that the shock the author sought to make us feel was actually *the only thing* he wanted to achieve? Granted, he may obtain what he wanted, but I'm convinced that his short-lived venture leaves little room for mystery.

Luckily, this venture is never entirely pure. For the painter cannot help but introduce some marker, unwittingly at times, that betrays a significant private predilection. Because his wish to perplex far outweighs this involuntary confession, any information thus supplied inevitably gets lost and distorted. However, if it does reoccur, and if it seems coordinated with other markers, then against this background of organized nonsense there do occasionally begin to stand out the less arbitrary elements of some hidden coherence. These scattered signals restore to "infinite" images the possibility of harboring some distant message. Thereby, they become similar to the metaphorical images I have discussed elsewhere and that I could just as well have termed conjectural and allusive. In the end, I chose to term them *analogous* or *analogical* (I would say *anagogical* were I sure that they did grant access to some higher reality). This is because their value (if they have any) or at least their efficacy rests on a network of concordances and exclusions, multiple interferences, correspondences between one level and another—which in this empire of allegory replaces the raw light of analytical knowledge.

The irreducible dimension noted in poetry is of a similar kind and avails itself of a similar prerogative. Sometimes the system of relationships can be discerned not merely in terms of procedure or intent but even in matters of content. For example, the sonnets of *Les Chimères* have been interpreted with the help of alchemical keys. I do not deny that the specific relations thus uncovered between these poems and the forgotten symbology might be real or conceivably plausible. Nerval might well have drawn from this source. But these correlations strike me as relatively insignificant. The crucial similarity lies in the fact that Nerval had recourse to an emblematic world with multiple equivalences, which was both composite and coherent. It was populated by gods, kings, and heroes who met the challenges of destiny or circumstance with solemn, metaphorical deeds; the latter's literal meaning only serves to refer us to absent, perhaps inexpressible realities.

I do not think that Nerval (and he himself suggests this) assigned a fixed meaning to these sonnets. This would amount to saying that he contented himself with disguising a transparent discourse. But it is even more unlikely that he composed the sonnets at random, merely trying to keep them from the disgrace of being intelligible. I suspect, instead, that he was not entirely clear about what he sought to convey; that he resorted to a labyrinth of allegories, convincing himself that readers would find whatever it was they sought—as long as they were sufficiently enticed by the subterranean coherence of a network of disconcerting images. It remains that this coherence might well delude us and not give onto anything. Yet even then, by virtue of the fact that it is a coherence and translates or announces some kind of order, it will not have been pointless for us to lose our way seeking to uncover the latter. The intellectual effervescence of a mind pursuing a secret being kept hidden from it does tend to develop agility and sensitivity—which will never cease to provide their strengths and joys. What greater good may we expect from art if not this very kind of enrichment?

Certain prose works fulfill the same purpose. The Märchen genre, typical of German Romantic literature, readily interweaves symbols that are culled (when the occasion arises, as in Goethe's *Green Snake*) from some initiatory tradition or, at least, that are usually interpreted as such. Raymond Roussel's novel *Locus Solus* offers the example of a riddle without a key. A meticulous mystery branches out and crystallizes from one thing to another, while what is inexplicable starts taking on some kind of unity itself—which saves the work's many systematically bizarre elements from utter arbitrariness.

Olivier de Magny has forcefully and successfully shown that most of the fascination such works are uniquely able to exert specifically stems from the internal coherence they make us suspect. *"Locus Solus,"* he recently writes,

> stands before the reader's interrogation as a hieroglyphic monument closed in upon itself; each section and detail refers us to another detail in the convolutions and inner labyrinths of its legendary masonry. And yet, the strange brilliance radiating from this monument reveals that it is transparent and allows us to deduce the presence of meanings concealed within the sparkling enigma. Sparkling and above all, coherent; an enigma that is indefinitely prismatic. Each and every one of the amazing conceits that Roussel sets before the reader—from the flying maiden composing, tooth by tooth, her mosaic of *The Roughneck Soldier Dozing in a Dark Crypt*; to the gigantic diamond in which there floats a dancer with musical hair; or the huge glass case where corpses, still intact, perform the crucial scene of their human lives. Each, then, of these *mechanical extravaganzas* weaves outrageous correspondences. Each is the correlation of causes and effects that seem light years apart; each is a network of the effects produced by the most disparate things upon one another; each articulates a system of complicities, reactions, and repercussions that are established and linked from zenith to nadir in the realm of matter. In short, each "machine" is the objective analysis of an impossible and yet blatant analogy. Quite meticulous in their delirious complexity, these de-

scriptions are generally followed by a demonstration of how the object operates, as well as an explanation of its origin, its raison d'être, and its allusions to various layers of the historical or legendary past. They take us into the prospects of some fantastic cohesion. Even though we sense that it is intelligible, its meaning withdraws at our approach. It abandons us, so that we are like travelers stranded at the center of a labyrinth of conjectures, prisoners in the heart of a problematic world.

I insisted on quoting this analysis in full, for I think it could equally well apply to certain sets of images. With only a few minor excisions (the specific references to Roussel's work) it could seem instead to describe Piranesi's *Prisons*, or the empty towns painted by Chirico around 1925, or some other world that is both closed off and enigmatic, filled with curious beings and objects, a world whose latent geometry obeys laws that are unknown and yet dimly perceptible. The mystery always arises just as much from the order we divine as from the apparent lunacy it arranges. This is precisely because the mystery suggests that the madness is only apparent, and that the disconcerting chessboard (pieces and squares) is used for some game whose rules it should be possible to reconstruct. . . .

This kind of painting that deliberately devotes itself to the fantastic is necessarily discursive or, as one says, literary, in the sense that it clearly undertakes to recount something. And it is often reproached for this, although this means one is insufficiently aware that the taste for conveying messages by pictorial means can avail itself of formal painterly features—just as symbolic literary narratives can deploy stylistic ones. Bellini is just as great a painter in his allegories, and Raimondi is no less expressive in his etched engravings with a hidden meaning. Likewise, it is in *Les Chimères* that Nerval is most admirable as a poet, and Kafka's prose is most transparent in the labyrinths of *The Castle*.

Introduction to "Surrealism as a World of Signs"

As Hollier has explained, referring to Bataille's famous essay "Le Sens moral de la sociologie" (1946), the College of Sociology derived its "moral sense" from the collective nature of the Surrealist movement. This Surrealist "moral summons," in Bataille's words, is one that he sought to safeguard after the war from what Hollier calls any "aestheticizing deviationism."[1] For Caillois, on the other hand, writing in 1968, the Surrealist legacy seems to have rested largely on the filiation with Baudelaire, in whose wake "one [began] to speak of a work's authenticity." By this, Caillois meant "professional ethics": "Baudelaire's glory, just like that of André Breton later on, stems just as much from his moral *parti pris* as it does from his art. Here again, he was an innovator. Poetry does not entail putting the results of knowledge into verse—in and of itself poetry is both a method and knowledge. Nor is it meant to illustrate morals. Poetry should let us perceive the results of its author's faultless conduct—as a poet—here gathered and assimilated, made into style and authority."[2] So Baudelaire (and Breton) now feature in Caillois's constellation as exemplary models of poetic authenticity—hardly as mythical precedents for Luciferian revolt.[3]

Yet if poetry for Breton, after Baudelaire, is hence "a method and knowledge," the two part company in the actual performance of this task. "Surrealism as a World of Signs" criticizes the movement for having betrayed its stated purpose and more or less accuses it of bad faith. Caillois first offers a genealogy of "vacant metaphor," an object that has been naturally, accidentally, or intentionally deprived of meaning. He then provides a list of the incoherent or deceptive attitudes of Breton (and the Surrealists) toward the image, which destroy any true revelation, as he sees it. Marc Eigeldinger suggest, "In Surrealism, images are basic and original; they invent poetic ideas by the play of sparks and *flashes* which they produce."[4] However, Caillois posits an a priori collective framework, "*an objective common ground of the imagination*" as the criterion for the accuracy or *justesse* of poetic correspondences: "The resonance of

"Le Surréalisme comme univers de signes," in *Obliques: précédé de Images, images . . .* (Paris: Gallimard, 1987), 238–247.

the analogies one sets forth is not totally subjective, because if it were, then they could not be confirmed, and it would be impossible to convey the beauty of any image."[5] Like "Surrealism as a World of Signs," his *Approches de la poésie* thus inveighs against Surrealism's "systematic refusal of coherence and emotion, in sum, of all transparency or evidence, even perceptible," and he adds that "this ostracism rejected everything, including naïve sensation." For Caillois, the "chief characteristic" of the Surrealist imagination is hence to be "literally 'un-imaginable.'"[6] Let us distinguish these "un-imaginable" images from fantastic science fiction, which, according to him, transgresses the boundary of what can be imagined, thereby rendering the unimaginable available to the imagination (see introduction).

SURREALISM AS A WORLD OF SIGNS

In my opinion, it is no exaggeration to characterize Surrealism relative to other literary movements by means of its privileged, almost exclusive connivance with painting. In the areas of both verbal and figurative expression, Surrealism grants absolute supremacy to the image. In the literary domain, this movement hardly acknowledges anything else but poetry—and dream transcriptions. It tolerates the essay, has little interest in theater, and scorns the novel. In the domain of painting, it likewise rejects landscape and still life. It ventures into abstract art only as long as there are some incipient shapes, a kind of trampoline for reverie. That these forms should suggest a parallel world is better yet. At times, Surrealist painters do depict human figures, but these are always engaged in baffling activities, in mysterious circumstances and settings: they seem to be illustrating an episode from some enigmatic adventure that no one will ever know anything about. In both cases, the image and the image alone is what counts, or the image comes first; whether poetic or visual, this image seeks to surprise, to question. In short, this image is a sign without any certain, perceptible, or unambiguous meaning—it is an image that simply seeks to alert us.

Surrealism is not interested in architecture and is frankly hostile to music. Insufficiently noted, in this respect, is that it already differs from preceding styles whose manner often covered the full spectrum of the arts. There exists a Classical style in music, architecture, and oratory: the disposition of the Versailles gardens, the façade of the Louvre. The compositions of Couperin or Lully correspond to the paintings of Poussin, the tragedies of Racine, the sermons of Bossuet, and even to the series of "moments" in *La Princesse de Clèves*. These works are all harmonics of one sensibility, of one single will to achieve an apparent serenity, which is imposed on the disorder of desires and passions, while it presupposes them as well.

This also holds true for the creations of the Baroque; Romanticism also dominated most of the arts, except perhaps architecture. It is with Symbolism that the field began to narrow. Symbolism was always closely tied to music; that Debussy collaborated with Mallarmé or Maeterlinck is proof enough, in and of itself. But their alliance may seem more personal than essential: the common ground is no longer quite so clear. On the other hand, as if there were arising a new layout of complicit fervors, the new school developed a taste for occult correspondences, barely decipherable seals, for magical, cabalistic, and esoteric systems; these required and justified a constant, universal decoding of the "signature of things," to cite the ancient alchemists' phrase.

As soon as it emerged from Dadaist nihilism, Surrealism claimed and radicalized traditional combinatorial logic, which had been restricted to accepted symbols until that point. This tendency became increasingly pronounced. Henceforth everything was a potential sign—for the *voyant*, it actually was a sign. Above all, it *gave sign* to the elect. To capture the fleeting message, somnambulism was deemed better than wakefulness: once it has cast away the constraints and prejudices of reason, morality, and aesthetics, the mind accedes to the authentic world and can listen to the dictation of the unconscious. In addition to the outside world (already woven through with signs for mutual recognition) there also exists the secret language of private depths, which the controls of daytime work to stifle and disguise. Therefore, the images issuing from sleep, automatic writing, and pure chance (which is adept at breaking every kind of continuity, and thus coherence) spring up like rockets—hallucinatory and illuminating. A secondary world arises from forbidden shades. By its very nature, this world (which constitutes surreality strictly speaking) surfaces only through partial or ambiguous forms of expression serving as signals. The addressee (or at least, the person who thinks he is the addressee, who feels concerned by the wink of fate) welcomes these as condensed simulacra, as vehicles of messages that, when correctly interpreted, can moreover provide a kind of mysterious investiture, nearly a messianic unction.

Here we must note an extraordinary turnabout. In the past, *sign* was the name given to something that carried, transmitted, and spread information devoid of value until after it was explained. Henceforth, however, a bold reversal meant that any sign, coincidence, or open metaphor; any object whose use was still unknown or that had been diverted from its real purpose; any unintelligible utterance contravening the laws of perception or the demands of logic—henceforth, all this bizarre disparity acquired its own proper fascination, precisely on that account. Every disturbing element was granted a blank check drawn on the general surrounding mystery—that is, so long as the strangeness had not been explained away. And people did not have any desire to find the solution, for this might have broken the spell. They wished that there would be no solution and quickly managed to ensure that there could be none.

In other words, the privileged element was not a sign because it conveyed a message. It was elevated to the status of sign because it still seemed to demand one, despite having been naturally or accidentally deprived (or deliberately wrung dry) of any conceivable signification; and it was hence well-suited to supplying a vehicle for endless reverie.

Given this curious bias, Surrealism inevitably went on to exalt the superior dignity of the dazzling, solitary image at the expense of all other resources available to the writer or artist. The movement chiefly devoted itself to non-narrative literature. In painting, it attended only to the capacity for representation, while neglecting the strictly pictorial studies of form and color relationships. It thus totally rejected music, which is incompatible with representation and demands continuity. This bias also informed the movement's revealing taste for replacing words with objects (as interchangeable signs); for sewing a penknife or slipper into a poem to replace the term denoting them. Conversely, it explained the recourse to written as well as figurative expression in the same painting. I would certainly ascribe to the same tendency the exceptional importance of titles in Surrealist painting. The titles, always literary, were often stretched out the length of an entire sentence, including subject, verb, and complements; they were not mere titles but the verbal equivalents of painted composition—elaborately written, preferably lyrical, and reflecting the school's particular rhetoric. In fact, they often recalled the textual fragments reproduced in quotation marks under the corresponding plates of book illustrations. But here there was no book (except for Max Ernst's collage compilations), so that both captions and images remained suspended in a state of insolent solitude.

In this way, Surrealism presented itself as an evocative sorcery predicated on the use of the image; not of symbol or allegory, which refer to a specific object or defined entity, but of vacant metaphor. It does not symbolize anything; however, it magnetically attracts all available sensitivities, troubled like lost souls. At the same time, vacant metaphor betrays the artist's fantasies, whether displayed or disguised, and uses them as decoys. In certain cases, the recurrent images eventually come to constitute an additional language, a repertoire of expected references—just as there had previously been the Harlequin, the guitar, or the newspaper headline for the Cubists.

—Thus, in Max Ernst's work, with particular emphasis, there tended to recur discs or solar rings in a deserted sky, along with jagged rocks, fearful or ferocious birds, and triangular faces.

—In Chirico, artists' or dressmakers' dummies, prancing horses with flowing manes, arcades, statues with disproportionately long shadows, stations, clock towers, paltry local railways, and red brick chimneys drifting above dead towns.

—In Magritte, painted landscapes that prolong or complete, duplicate or replace the real landscape; an easel, set up in open fields, supports a canvas dotted with clouds merging with those in the actual sky; the locations of the light source slyly invert the natural zones of shadow and light; every commonplace expression is either taken literally or (rather monotonously) turned inside out like a glove; the cage is inside the bird instead of the bird being inside the cage; a girl becomes an antimermaid with the bust and head of a fish (admittedly, Antiquity never quite decided whether the Minotaur was a bull with a man's head or a man with a bull's head).

—In Dali (whose use of obsessional motifs could provide the basis of a chronology) we find, in turn, William Tell already close to death; fried eggs without a frying pan; soft watches; Millet's *Angélus*; the lobster-telephone; the *chou-fleur* [flowering cabbage] or rhinoceros; some unexpected item or other that develops, at an accelerated pace, an inventiveness that soon becomes more insouciant than stupefied.

—Last, in Tanguy, a population of giant amoebas, pouches quivering from a common frost despite their watertight membranes; wheezy ganglions, suckers and feelers, all crawling, exploring, and sucking; a tentative growth of mushrooms and elastic, tenacious warts that are unbalanced and bloated, the crust of a planet disinfected by its acid colors (what Breton called "the Neptunian light of clairvoyance"). An unfinished fauna crawls and swarms about, a kind of immunized vermin. It is neither terrestrial nor human. It does not have any familiar or intelligible form. It is merely disorienting. It functions by threatening us with distant biologies that are irremediably foreign, sealed off, lazy, and corrosive.

I have no idea how the future will look back on this kind of stubborn indulgence of personal simulacra. Perhaps it will merely see, as I am tempted to, a type of infantilism laboriously refined by maturity. For now, though, I am struck by Surrealism's nearly unanimous quest for signs that were both private and yet rapidly conventionalized, as if it had been a matter of uniting their fated conditions of individual isolation through an irresistible urge for display. A need to convince or almost to convert people, as much as any thoughts of glory.

Given the nature of things, painting is a privileged art, in that it can make the represented object serve as a sign. Unlike words, painting does more than indicate or evoke its object but forces us to see it, adorning it with a mysterious halo. One could almost say that it has the power to give the object the guise of an apparition and hence persuade us that it is really a sign. The writer knows that he lacks any resource that is so direct, efficacious, and seemingly unimpeachable.

It is not by chance that Surrealism turned to the spells of photography to make confession more convincing. Struck and *alerted* by some revealing fact (or one that he finds to be so at the time), an author can then furnish the visible proof of his prior emotional agitation. With this precise and incontestable document he tries to make the reader at least understand how he himself was overwhelmed, if not experience the same astonishment or confusion.

In *Nadja* and *L'Amour fou*, page after page, Breton thus inserted photographs of the Hôtel des Grands Hommes, of the Tour Saint-Jacques, of some sybilline shop sign or disconcerting object that had "alerted" him. The only example I will evoke here is the fragmentary metal mask designed to protect even its wearer's eyes with oblique strips through which he could see. I doubt that Breton was pleased when I brought him the complete object: a fencing mask worn by German students during the Romantic era. Indeed, conjecture is endless and varied, whereas reality is exclusive and intolerant. Whence, in a neighboring domain, the fragrance of sadness that always lingers "after plucking a dream, in the heart that has just done so," according to Mallarmé. The path from premonitions to the notion of predestination shaping their entire lives is traced in advance. Breton recognized his own initials, A and B, in the number 1713, which he distorted as

using the suitable graphic style to decompose each letter into two numbers. To strengthen this sense of identification, he even wrote the fateful number on his apartment door. He wondered about events that had occurred in the year 1713, events that necessarily concerned him. Without offering much in the way of explanation, he obtained from the Star, the seventeenth card of the Tarot, the title *Arcane 17* for his long meditation on the ultimate goals of mankind. Here Breton not only reappropriated for Surrealism the different traditions of the universal symbolic system—the Kabbalah, Pythagoras, Sweden-borg, Claude de Saint-Martin and Fabre d'Oliver, Saint-Yves d'Alveydre and Eliphas Lévi—but he also derived a questionable and dangerous conclusion from the doctrine (p. 153): "With all due respect to certain people who can only enjoy what is fixed and clear, in art this relation has always been maintained and is not about to cease." Here again, André Breton showed that he mistook the function of clarity and that there was hence an unavowed, characteristic distrust on his part of the real value of obscurity, which he had accepted all too soon and thoughtlessly. I persisted in fighting him on this point whenever I could. I did not deny that obscurity had value but I located it elsewhere, convinced that it would help to exalt future clarity rather than be dispelled by it.

To return to Breton's warning, I can hardly doubt that I am included among those being rebuked, and it is certainly no fortuitous conjunction that the dedication to my copy of *Arcane 17* invites me to "continue the duel in Tierra del Fuego." Nor is it a coincidence that in the work's concluding "Ajours," the author refers to a parable of Fabre d'Oliver that recalls, if remotely, our quarrel over the jumping beans. Breton observes that the fable's final sentences, in which a crushed acorn inaugurates a new fate, tend to lead one's thoughts down "a melancholy slope."

For Breton, signs do not end with the visible universe. He projects them into the world of wonders, where the Woman-Child blossoms without growing old and the Great Transparent Ones pass by, both as mediators of a hidden reality and as kindly ectoplasms, whose silent intercession guides visionaries who are attuned to the fascination of marvels. The entire universe is marked out with signs. The point is to know how to identify them or, rather, to learn how to *charge* them, in the electrical and also magical senses of the term. There is nothing that cannot act as a sign, if only the conditions are right and if only the subject, suddenly alerted, recognizes the wonder, selects it, and almost commandeers it with a kind of "Open sesame"—which is both an implicit encouragement from fate and a key to the stubborn enigma.

Whether one admits it or not, all of existence—its settings and events—is then regarded as something that is docile and can be interpreted. If not a phantasmagoria, the world is at least a cryptogram: a web of ineluctably ratified connivances. During an imaginary discussion with President de Brosses, at a "succulent" dinner in New York to which Montesquieu's illustrious correspondent supposedly invited him in 1942, Breton expressed himself as follows: "Well, at a time when I had broken with everything that garnered but empty tokens of reverence or respect, I dare say I witnessed the embryonic formation—oh! ever so hazardous—of a new signification. Why should we not look to the poets and artists of today for what we have always found—with the distance of hindsight—in their precursors? Could their evolution not reflect in coded but decodable language what *should*, what *will* be?"

I shall disregard the sleight of hand (however significant and frequent for this writer) that turns on the phrase *with the distance*. "Distance" presents itself as precisely what is required here to transform private fantasy into accepted mythology. I will confine myself to the notion of the "coded but decodable language," which, in this instance, is supposed to reflect, if not bring about, a more or less imminent future. We have seen that unconsciously and even explicitly, Breton never stopped wishing that this language should remain undecoded—although he asserted its decipherability. In his view, the poet faces a world (or magical mumbo-jumbo) that was first conceived by Paracelsus, if not by the *Hieroglyphica* of Horapollo and the Gnostics, and to which Hugo agreed to subscribe. All the Great Transparent Ones and every esoteric tradition have helped enrich it, that is, to leave further confused and inextricable an arsenal of traps for reverie that was limitless to begin with: a repertoire of symbols from which everyone can draw as he likes, according to every passing whim.

I have often suspected that Breton was aware of the dangers inherent in a subjectivity that was so welcoming and, strictly speaking, impossible to constrain. This would explain certain awkward conceptions, perhaps the most significant example being *objective chance*—an expression whose redundancy has always amazed me. For after all, it is not possible rigorously to conceive of a chance event unless it is objective, that is, unless it is the remarkable and unpredictable (in any case unforeseen, albeit strictly mechanical) interference of two independent causal series. In principle, the Surrealist position was unconditionally scientific, but its aesthetics—not to say, its metaphysics—presupposed a world of coincidence and revelation. Under the circumstances, it was necessarily and paradoxically bound to call "objective," in order to justify and valorize them, certain signs that were likely fortuitous but annexed by the blind workings of greed—to whose vain expectations they held out the promise of fallow pastures.

Poetic creation admirably tolerates such specular games. It is occasionally intoxicated by a certain facility, without perceiving its danger. Premonitions and yearnings, harmonics and recurrences, metaphors and images—all constitute poetry's natural and legitimate prerogative. Moreover, this is the only one that cannot be taken away. Yet, having attained the extremes of liberty, poetry should presently invent rules for its own usage—strict ones, at last—to decipher the palimpsest of the world. In its patience lies its strength; in its rigor, its glory. The point is to reveal outside our own mind (always quick to be mistaken) the reiterated legislation of the totality we are part of, that encloses and comprehends us, and that we try, in turn, to understand in the specular manner of a tiny concave lens that is our lot.

If the pursuit of surreality consists in this meticulous undertaking (like an asymptote, I'm afraid: a curve drawing near without ever actually reaching), then I have always been surrealist; what is more, I was surrealist before even becoming one. The fact would still remain, though, that in my philosopher's quest I did not rely on the parallel tradition, on the Emerald Tables and Hermes Trismegistus, but on the lucidity of Plato and the lesson received from Mendeleyev's table.

Diagonal Science

Introduction to "The Great Bridgemaker"

Caillois's 1950 eulogy for Mauss remained unpublished at the time.[1] It presented him as the sole response to the query "Everybody today feels the need
for a new humanism. But whom can we call upon to construct it?"[2] Among
other options, of course, there was Sartre, with *Existentialism Is a Humanism*
(1946), and Heidegger's response, the famous "Letter on Humanism" (1947):
"In defining the humanity of man humanism not only does not ask about the
relation of Being to the essence of man; because of its metaphysical origin humanism even impedes the question by neither recognizing nor understanding
it."[3] Without even acknowledging such choices, Caillois points to Mauss, who
illuminated "certain basic yearnings of human beings, which are obscure, persistent, inextinguishable and which seem to recur in different guises at different levels of civilization."[4] That is, Mauss offered not the "essence" of man but,
perhaps better, what we might call his emotional "generalization": the hidden
identities of his deepest motives. For Caillois to endorse the Maussian oeuvre
as a "slogan" rather than a mere "heritage" gave it polemical status against "totalitarian" Marxism and Freudianism (see introduction): "Mauss hated in the
same way both depth and hypotheses: remote and absolute causes, such as sex
or economics, which all too readily allow one to explain everything indiscriminately; and lightweight conjectures that are always easy to put forth and almost impossible to check. . . . He sought to establish uncontestable and clear
truths that were perfectly interrelated."[5] Indeed, Caillois's view of Mauss was
already a stand against the *sciences humaines* and his "frère-ennemi" (enemy-
twin), Lévi-Strauss, who was claiming to appropriate the Maussian legacy
in that very same year.[6] His well-known "Introduction à l'oeuvre de Marcel
Mauss" (1950) was "a very personal interpretation," according to Georges Gurvitch.[7] Lévi-Strauss cast Mauss as Moses, poised on the threshold of the structuralist sciences humaines, destined to incorporate "the most recent developments of the social sciences, which let us hope that the latter will be gradually
put into mathematical form."[8]

In the 1930s, Caillois had been an attentive student of the rationalist, neo-
Kantian anthropologist, who believed, together with his uncle, Durkheim,

"Le Grand Pontonnier," in *Cases d'un échiquier* (Paris: Gallimard, 1970), 17–27.

that Lévy-Bruhl was wrong: that primitive man did not possess a "primitive mentality" but rather a rational and logical mind, whose categories reflected those of his social structure.[9] Yet because Caillois's early writings often privileged biology and coherence rather than society and rationalism, Mauss had mixed feelings about his work. As noted earlier, he admired "The Praying Mantis" but criticized Caillois's correlation of the "philosophy of biology" with that "of society"; more seriously, he assailed the "complete irrationalism" of such essays as "Paris, a Modern Myth," attributing both to Caillois and to his unspecified milieu the general "influence of Heidegger, a Bergsonian who is lingering behind the times in Hitlerism, who is legitimizing Hitlerism, who is infatuated with irrationalism." He concluded, "In short, I do not think that you are a philosopher, not even by training. Believe me, keep to your sphere as a mythologist."[10] Mauss may have lacked the nuanced grasp of avant-garde writing to discern that, at least when compared to Bataille, "Paris, a Modern Myth" hardly professed "complete irrationalism." And the remark with respect to Heidegger is misleading because by 1936 Caillois had adopted an explicitly anti-Heideggerian stance in "L'Alternative (Naturphilosophie ou Wissenschaftlehre)"—which his postwar claim to the New Humanism of Mauss would affirm once again.

But when he wrote "The Great Bridgemaker," Caillois had moved to the new, poetic "diagonal science" (see introduction). And his essay does nothing if not underscore Mauss's creative license, his haphazard pedagogical style, based on free association and "endless digressions." Elsewhere, Caillois describes this "truly extraordinary man, whose utter lack of talent was almost embarrassing. . . . But he had genius. Every sentence stimulated somebody's thoughts."[11] (That is, perhaps, Mauss could make it easy for Bataille to misunderstand potlatch and the "total social fact"!) In short, playing with the image of the bridge as the basis of religion, but also as a secular symbol of interdisciplinary studies, Caillois suggests that the great bridgemaker could also inspire the poetic analogies and conjectures of a complementary imagination.

THE GREAT BRIDGEMAKER

I can still hear Marcel Mauss making the surprising revelation to me in the courtyard of the Sorbonne in 1937. Twice a week, he would speak to a few students about myths regarding the conquest of heaven and about corresponding rituals, whose chief implements were the kite and the greasy pole. This was actually a series of endless digressions, where Mauss's personal experience blended with his scholarly erudition in a way that was always unexpected and fruitful. After class, I would often walk him to the bus stop.

On that particular day, I announced to him that I had chosen "the religious vocabulary of the Romans" as the topic of the thesis I was planning to write (but never did). He congratulated me on my choice, while warning of the pitfalls that awaited me:

> To begin with, the word *religio* itself. The etymology of *relegere* is not in doubt. But people become dangerously excited about what it hides or reveals. Even though *relegere* never signified "to bind," it's nonetheless taken for granted that this meaning is the very essence of religion. But what does it bind? Everyone invents bonds reflecting their particular inclination: heaven and earth; nature and the supernatural; men and gods; or simply men among themselves, united within and through a common faith. In short, religion could bind almost anything. I'll skip the speculations as to the ancient meaning of *religio*: "scruple." That's all worthless. The truth is in Festus (Festus is the name I recall, but Mauss may have quoted some other lexicographer), who has this to say on the topic of *religio*: "*Religiones tramenta erant.*" "Religions" were "straw knots." Nobody, it seems, has ever noticed this little phrase. But which straw knots? Well, of course! The ones used to stabilize the beams of bridges. The proof is that in Rome, the chief of religion, the supreme priest, was called "the builder of bridges": *pontifex*. But nowadays, when people refer to the Pope as the Sovereign Pontif, are they aware that they're calling him the Great Bridgemaker!

I was dazzled by this discovery. But I was still unclear as to why a modest carpentry construction should have deserved such an extraordinary destiny. I was just asking him this when the bus arrived. He bid me a hurried goodbye and, from the platform, tossed back by way of reply, "The *ordo rerum*." I had been taking his courses for more than three years and knew what he meant by the "order of things." He meant the arrangement of the elements of the world (and also of institutions), as conceived and established by the gods. The nature of religion consisted in protecting this arrangement against every kind of assault: eclipses, twins, albinos, marvels, sweating statues, bestiality, and the variable (and interminable) list of taboos and blasphemies. The equilibrium was precarious; the mechanism delicate. Violating an interdiction brought about catastrophes—such as floods or epidemics, calamities and famines—unless a priest was there to suggest in time how to repair the damage: in other words, how to expiate the anomaly, sin, error, crime, or misfortune (here the same thing) so as to restore the regularity that had been upset.

Returning to the question of ancient Rome, the administration of the sacred was both familial and juridical. It generally devolved upon the college of pontifs, represented by a single dignitary, the *pontifex maximus*, named for life, who embodied the entire corps. His responsibilities were wide-ranging. He appointed flamines and Vestal Virgins. He supervised the phrasing of prayers, the correctness of rituals. He presided over games and the worship of the dead. He guaranteed the protection of temples, altars, and consecrated places, and he consulted the sibylline books. He set up the calendar of festivals and interpreted prodigious events, which he would then list in the annual catalogue. Control over the religious domain (clergy, ceremonies, buildings, and liturgical objects) was almost exclusively in his hands. How could such an important personage derive his name from the occupation—which seems so extremely profane—of an engineer or handyman? This has seemed such a shocking paradox that the etymology of *pontifex*, however obvious, has been contested (without success, for that matter). Is the enigma really so insoluble?

At that early stage when incipient forms of observation were combined with religious emotion, mankind took pleasure in discerning the effect in the world of such primary substances as air, water, earth, and fire. Each obeyed its own laws and occupied the place assigned to it. Piety meant respecting the implicit, general legislation and keeping it from being impaired by some accident. From this perspective, a waterway was clearly not something intended to be crossed; at least, not with dry feet. *In* the water, one could swim about like a fish; *on* the water, one could float about like wood. But to build a bridge was a sacrilegious subterfuge that, as such, jeopardized the world's order and could only bring down some terrible punishment upon its perpetrator, his family, and the nation. There would be a price to pay. Traces of this belief persist even into the Christian Middle Ages: according to some legends, the first soul to cross over a new bridge should be promised to Satan. Still, prevention is better than a cure, not to mention the fact that the building of bridges is extremely useful, —indeed, almost indispensable.

When it was thus decided to disrupt the world's arrangement to connect the two banks of a river, just imagine the anxiety of the specialists responsible for managing the sacred. What ruses could they use, what penance could they promise to prevent the wrath of the gods from ravaging the city?

If an arm of the sea happened to be involved, they were even more worried. When Xerxes marched his army from Asia to Europe, crossing on vessels moored side by side over the Hellespont, no one doubted his impending defeat. In the terms of Aeschylus's vivid image, he had dared place a yoke upon the neck of the sea. Such an offense could not remain unpunished. What the

Athenian triremes destroyed at Salamis was merely a fleet already doomed by the barbarian king's outrageous act.

Even striding across a small trickle of water without the proper propitiation was deemed culpable. Nothing less than the knowledge of the most prestigious exorcists could remove the danger from the impious audacity of securing passage across a river or waterway in a manner that annulled and defied their liquid state, whether it was accomplished by means of suspended lianas, projected onto the other shore with arrows or javelins; or by making use of swollen goatskins, which propped up some makeshift platform; by fitting rafts together; or, later on, by means of squared timbers or heaps of stones—stable and massive pieces of work, which were all the more sinful. In any event, a bridge, by virtue of its very essence, undermines some secret and inextricable economy, in which everything is interlinked and complementary. When disturbed in some spot, this suffers a progressive upheaval that could well destroy it altogether, or at least cause a degree of damage disproportionate to the initial blow.

Perhaps things have changed less than we think. Of course, many bridges have been built, from the three spans of the sturdy Pont du Gard to the aerial, spidery bridges of the San Francisco Bay. There come to mind the bridges of Venice, Florence, Prague, Paris, and London, all laden with history; the Avignon bridge that collapsed because some reckless fellow went dancing on it with his sister, who was wearing a white dress and golden belt. Or there was the bridge of San Luis Rey, which suddenly broke and plunged seven people who happened to be crossing it into the river Rimac; their fates were unrelated but parallel, according to an American novelist. One even recalls the nine anonymous bridges of Königsberg, which, it is said, caused Euler to discover the principles of topology. In every time and place, the history of mankind is linked to that of the bridges it has built. Instead of fear, there has evolved a kind of competitive daring. And yet, the fear of building other bridges in other domains, invisible bridges rising above the tenacious sediment of received opinion, remains just as reverential as ever—it is profound, powerful, paralyzing, and difficult to supplant.

It is not without melancholy, but then again not without a certain pride in our species, that I consider how one of the first sacrileges it conceived, undertook, and then legitimized was the building of bridges. And it is not unimportant that this sacrilege occurred just when mankind was first beginning to act on nature. Finally, and without irony, I note that our century's highest moral and religious authority bears the title of Sovereign Bridgemaker, without anyone remembering the obscure magic that explains its mystery.

*　*　*

The next week after class, I tried to pursue my conversation with Marcel Mauss, which had started out so well. Actually, I sensed ahead of time that it would be hopeless. And so it was. He didn't let me get a word in edgewise. Instead, he enumerated the merits of the book (fundamental, in his opinion) that Granet was working on at the time. Its title was supposed to be *Le Roi boit* [The king drinks]. This wasn't really a non sequitur. Festivals are bridges as well, though of a different kind.

Introduction to "A New Plea for Diagonal Science"

As noted in the introduction, diagonal science increasingly moved toward poetry and perceptible analogies. In *Méduse et Cie* (1960), Caillois clarified his methodological approach: "It is fine with me that each of these parallels, when viewed alone, should resemble one of those rigorous deliria that are typical of rational delirium. But in return, you must let the convergence of the different things I have presented cast some doubt on the accuracy of such a quick and absolute verdict. This convergence invites us to consider revising the judgment; it advises us to generalize our investigation and undertake a general comparison of the human and insect worlds. I will never tire of saying this: both belong to the same world." To this extent, he had not lost sight of science, allowing that when viewed outside of a vaster system, without a critical or total mass of evidence, any individual patterns might well seem "personal reverie or chance similarity"; the projected task was hence to "multiply similar examples . . . of the same type, meaning the same thing, which are in complicity with and reinforce one other."[1] However, by 1970, the revised version, "A New Plea for Diagonal Science," contrasted science, with its "truly economical criteria," and the diagonal sciences, whose imaginative leaps would have to be followed up by the most rigorous kinds of control and verification. This being the case, Caillois had no need to apologize for his "bold," subjective, and multidisciplinary approach.

A NEW PLEA FOR DIAGONAL SCIENCE

Progress in the sciences has been achieved at the cost of their increased specialization. A scientist is one who knows everything, or almost everything, about an ever more restricted domain—which is now almost infinitesimal compared to the full scope of knowledge. As for what remains outside his field, each scientist relies on other scholars; whether these fields are distant or nearby,

"Nouveau plaidoyer pour les sciences diagonales," in *Cases d'un échiquier* (Paris: Gallimard, 1970), 53–59.

he knows that they are just as narrow as his own. By definition, they are closed off to him, but he knows and relies on the fact that others like him are leading the same fight on other fronts. Inspired by the same ideal, they are applying comparable methods and submitting their intuitions to similar kinds of controls. Infinitely ramified, today's scientific knowledge is very fragmented. It forms an immense puzzle, and everybody is acquainted with a single piece that has been oddly and often arbitrarily (if not maliciously) carved out. However, almost no one can perceive or suspect its general physiognomy, the coherent picture that would give unity and meaning to the whole.

Things could not be otherwise. It remains that research itself suffers when each scientist, burrowing away in his own special tunnel as if he were some efficient and myopic mole, operates like a complete maverick, like a miner who is digging ever deeper, almost utterly unaware of the discoveries made by fellow workers in neighboring galleries, and even more so of the results in distant quarries. What we need are relay stations at every level: anastomosis and coordination points, not only for assembling the spoils but above all for comparing different processes. When it comes to rigorous investigation, genius almost always involves borrowing a proven method or fruitful hypothesis and using it in a field where no one had previously imagined that it could be applied.

Nature is one. Its laws are everywhere the same, or at least, they are in accord and coherent and correspond to each other in the different kingdoms, longitudes, and latitudes. Each science explores a specific segment, that is, examines a set of phenomena, data, individuals, or reactions displaying similar or parallel properties. But without being arbitrary, the limits that determine these sets often are still deceptive. In any case, they were determined by means of a criterion that, even if it were the best one, necessarily excluded all the rest. Before classifying vertebrates as mammals, birds, batrachians, reptiles, or fish, they were grouped according to the number of feet they had. Horses were put into the same category as frogs and turtles. A more thoroughgoing analysis subsequently led people to select other, less evident but more important discriminants. The evolution of science partly lies in the progress of its own classifications: in the determination of basic and truly economical criteria, which gradually take the place of superficial characteristics that "seem obvious," as one says, and are thus all the more deceptive. These mislead, divide, and delude researchers, instead of guiding them toward the profound, secret, and fruitful relationship. Nonetheless, it should be said that having four feet is an interesting feature as well, with certain specific and ineluctable consequences, which is almost eliminated as an object of study, though, by the new, improved taxonomy. Residual characteristics that have been legitimately disqualified surely give rise to remarkable relationships that are indubitably worth detecting and establishing. Even though they have been excluded, they are by no means insignificant. From another perspective, they might suddenly turn out to be decisive; rather than sterile impasses and labyrinths, they might prove to be major arteries and lines of force. The universe is radiant. It supports any secant, median, chord, or bisectrix. The problem is that specialization encourages scientists to penetrate ever more deeply in the same direction, making it harder for them to discover, observe, or imagine revolutionary perspectives.

Mythography studies the fabulous beliefs connected with certain rituals; psychopathology studies obsessions and deliria; and entomology, the behavior of insects. I thought that I could compare the habits of the praying mantis (or of other animal species in which the female devours the male before or after mating) with the fear of the toothed vagina (a fear often found in certain types of neuropaths) and with the myths of goddesses or femmes fatales whose embrace proves deadly. This is certainly a bold approach, but does that mean it should be rejected out of hand? Aesthetics studies the harmony of lines and colors. Could it not conceivably compare paintings with butterfly wings, for example? Of course, one must keep in mind that a painting is an external work, produced by an individual's free will and skill, whereas the design of a butterfly's coloring is programmed into the organism; it is that species' immutable fate. These distinctions are fundamental. They must be made clear from the very outset. But once we have defined and measured such undeniable differences, it may be useful to seek to uncover the common denominator for all harmonies of line and color. Such an expansion of our mental field of vision should, in all likelihood, lead to a general theory of beauty in nature and in art.

Similarly, the phenomena of mimicry shows how certain animals assimilate into the background and become almost invisible, while others imitate, and are mistaken for, species that are sometimes very distant. Still others terrify their enemies or paralyze their prey by suddenly unveiling their *ocelli*—impressive fake eyes—or by sporting useless and monstrous appendages; on occasion, by parading veritable masks, like the *fulgora* or lantern fly. Here it is impossible not to think, first, of those legends concerning hats or cloaks that make their wearer invisible, and of camouflage techniques; second, of the impulses expressed in mankind by the phenomena of fashion and disguise, carnivals and theater; and finally, of the sacred, institutional terror aroused by the masked and disguised officiants in primitive ceremonies.

"Anthropomorphism!" people will say, but it is exactly the opposite. It should be realized that the point is not to explain certain puzzling facts observed in nature in terms of man. On the contrary, it is to explain man (governed by the laws of this same nature, to which he belongs in almost every respect) in terms of the more general behavioral forms found widespread in nature throughout most species. This attitude prompts one to greatly vary the principles of biological explanation and to assert that nature (which is no miser) pursues pleasure, luxury, exuberance, and vertigo just as much as survival. Hence it seems justified to break the framework predicated on the struggle for survival and natural selection. These mainsprings are too strictly and exclusively utilitarian and, in this sense (which contradicts received opinion), they are very closely anthropomorphic; they stem from an ephemeral, local, and dated image mankind once had of itself under very specific conditions. The time has come to invoke "motives" that are just as pressing on a universal scale, such as profusion, play, *ivresse*, and even aesthetics, or at least the need for ornament and decoration.

Productive exchanges between the human sciences and the natural sciences can be established and developed. The dialogue should be even broader and include the physical sciences. Crystal, for example, has properties akin to those of living matter. For one thing, it can scar over a break through heightened regenerative activity, in much the same way that a lobster regenerates its claw or a Saurian its tail; for another, it can gradually eliminate foreign bodies accidentally trapped in its well-ordered, homogeneous substance. Last, it seems that the lattices determining the immutable regularity of crystals are identical to those revealed on a cross-section of striated muscle fiber by electron microscope, or to those determining the disposition of leaves on a stalk or of grains on an ear of corn. Here we have auspicious and promising connivances among mineralogy, botany, anatomy, and the sciences of the future that would organize their disparate contributions.

It was not a Hellenist, nor even a philologist, but a specialist in cryptography who managed to decipher the Minoan alphabet: running out of texts to decipher, he happened to have some spare time. If my memory serves, not military strategists but botanists discovered how to most effectively deploy destroyers and thus protect Allied convoys at the height of the Battle of the Atlantic in 1942. The botanists were inspired by the helicoidal leaf pattern on stalks noted above. There are many other examples, even from times past. When Newton discovered that the moon does not fall down to earth whereas an apple inevitably does so owing to the very same force, he connected two facts from realms that were then utterly distinct. Today, nothing remains of this connection, scandalous at the time, except for the anecdote of the dreamer enlightened by falling fruit. But even this trivial relic shows just how original this step was.

*   *   *

Generally speaking, one may already declare that it would not be pointless—quite the contrary—to undertake a thorough study of symmetry, right-handed and left-handed, in everything from man to tartaric acid crystals. And it would be interesting to explore spiral developments (both in shells and nebulae), focusing on the fact that the spiral is the only module in which the demand for symmetry is subject to the constraint of growth. At the same time, we should also look for dissymmetry wherever it occurs and view it as a factor of life, independence, and ultimately freedom—in short, as a force of negative entropy. Probably another useful field of research would be to compare the organizational stages in inanimate, animate, psychological, and social realms, as well as the modalities involved in shifting from one to the other. These are so many fields for the sciences, both permanent and novel, that I have in the past suggested calling "diagonal."

These sciences bridge the older disciplines and force them to engage in dialogue. They seek to make out the single legislation uniting scattered and seemingly unrelated phenomena. Slicing obliquely through our common world, they decipher latent complicities and reveal neglected correlations. They wish for and seek to further a form of knowledge that would first involve the workings of a bold imagination and be followed, then, by strict controls, all the more necessary insofar as such audacity tries to establish ever riskier transversal paths. Such a network of shortcuts seems ever more indispensable today among the many, isolated ouposts spread out along the periphery, without internal lines of communication—which is the site of fruitful research.

Introduction to "The Natural Fantastic"

The prospective poetics of Caillois's late writing recall Baudelaire's theory of the imagination. "When Baudelaire thinks about the functions of the 'queen of faculties,' he defines its specific domain as that of the *possible*," notes Eigeldinger.[1] *L'Ecriture des pierres* (1970) thus describes the "limited museum of the fantastic in nature," with its "rare examples of impossible similarities" that "repeat and do not imitate," and which are, in fact, new poetic possibilities pointing the way to a more expansive coherence.[2]

"The Natural Fantastic" here initiates a new stage in Caillois's thinking about stones. In *L'Ecriture des pierres*, the striking surprise or revelation had involved dissymmetry, or what Caillois called "pattern" perceived against the norm of symmetrical markings. "A calm design is miraculous," he wrote, likening it to Chinese calligraphy.[3] However, "The Natural Fantastic" would refute this analogy, noting that such pictures in stones were all too frequent—no mysterious miracle or fantastic transgression here! And Caillois develops a crucial distinction between animate and inanimate nature. Unlike the other natural kingdoms, informed by the boundary of death, the mineral kingdom has "no apparent order to destroy." It is the emergence of order—of symmetry—that constitutes the miracle or scandalous transgression, like the fantastic appearance of a ghost under normal or animate circumstances.[4] With such markers of the mineral realm, what Caillois seeks to discern, in any event, is the path he described in 1966 as leading from a "universe in which nothing is intelligent, yet" toward the "feats of conscience [*conscience*] and doubt."[5]

These late formal speculations forgo the "hypermoral" enthusiasm of Bataille's thoughts about humanity, a process of "awakening" to the ways in which "what is possible in man" always "goes beyond the bounds of reason."[6] But in what he calls his "materialist mysticism," Caillois grasps for the cosmos. In so doing, he both dehumanizes man's creation within the natural order, in the Taoist tradition, and humanizes nature by recasting it in his own terms, in the Western tradition.[7] *Pierres* (1966) thus describes his meditation: "My thought tries to seize [stones] at the ardent moment of their birth. I then experience a very special kind of excitement. I feel myself becoming a bit like

"Le Fantastique naturel," in *Cases d'un échiquier* (Paris: Gallimard, 1970), 61–73.

stones. At the same time, I liken them to myself by means of the unsuspected properties I sometimes attribute to them in the course of my speculations, which are alternatively precise and lax, and which combine the web of dreams with the chain of knowledge."[8]

THE NATURAL FANTASTIC

As opposed to fairy tales or to the Marvellous, which involves a world of enchantment, of constant metamorphoses and miracles where everything is always possible, I think the Fantastic presumes a well-ordered universe ruled by the immutable laws of physics, astronomy, and chemistry. This world is one in which like causes produce like effects, and which consequently excludes the slightest chance of miracles. The fantastic appears as the disruption of a natural order that is deemed impossible to disturb. This natural order, not to say nature itself in the strong sense of the word, can be defined only as a form of regularity so fundamental that it is beyond the reach of any manipulation. By definition, it is so strong that human skill can modify it only by obeying it.

It follows from this point of view that the fantastic can never be "natural," for it is presented, on the contrary, as the inadmissible breach wrought in nature by some mysterious power that is specifically viewed as *supernatural*. It has to be *imaginary*, that is, a deliberate invention of the mind, which recognizes it as such. Therefore, the fantastic cannot *exist*, properly speaking: it cannot be part of nature, of the attested universe.

Yet common parlance allows that a landscape may seem fantastic, as frequently occurs where some erosion has carved out simulacra of towers, palaces, or gigantic animals. Likewise, a tree or a flower may be termed fantastic (or the details of a flower, such as the passion flower, in which a certain naïve piety has long discerned the nails, hammer, and lance of Christ's Crucifixion) and an anthropomorphic root such as the mandrake. And, so too, an insect (or one of its features, such as the skull pattern on the corselet of the *Acherontia atropos*), a fish, a bird, or a Saurian may all be termed fantastic, even though they are products of nature, if their appearance is so surprising, baffling, or disquieting that it does not seem they could really be what they are.

Under these conditions, it is surely useful to try to define how animate or inanimate nature can give the impression of escaping its own norms, and even of mocking them outright. Rarity and strangeness here play a crucial role. For example, simply considering the world of vertebrates, alongside the animals that are the stuff of legend (sphinxes, chimeras, centaurs, mermaids, griffons, etc.), there exist animals, such as the unicorn, that natural science catalogued and described for a long time. Conversely, certain animals catalogued only quite recently actually do exist. Their morphology is so bizarre that an observer would readily judge them more thoroughly unreal and inadmissible than the legendary hybrids.

Of course, to name them "fantastic" is a misuse of language, but a significant one. In any event, being subject myself—perhaps unwittingly—to the diffuse pressure exerted by language, I was induced to launch the idea (surprising, to say the least, especially to me) of the *natural fantastic*.[1] I first used the term in connection with an insect from northeast Brasil, the lantern fly, and a North American mammal, the star-nosed mole or *Condylura*. These two animals' appearances made me resort to a category whose specious nature I could easily perceive. Quite obviously, these creatures were not fantastic because they were a part of nature. Just as obviously, they seemed fantastic, and even gave quite an exceptional sense of the fantastic: the tree-dwelling homopteron, on account of its frontal protuberance, which is almost as big as its body and deceptively suggests a crocodile's muzzle; and the subterranean vertebrate, on account of its snout, which sports a crown of twenty-two short tentacles of live pink flesh, all mobile, sensitive, and retractable, flaccid or tensed at will, and very vaguely like an intricate starfish or some horrible corolla.

In both cases, the observer can hardly believe his own eyes and thinks himself in the presence of nightmarish creatures that contradict reality more than they emerge from it. Upon consideration, the surprise effect is not caused by the same mechanism in the two cases. With the lantern fly, the disconcerting element results from the presence of a hollow and weird mask. This is the spitting image of the snout of some animal from which its flying bearer differs in all other respects and with which it could never in any way be confused, even in terms of size. The resemblance is stunning and seems inexplicable, insofar as it is indeed exact, striking, and, at the same time, useless. The undulating halo of the Condylura is terrifying, on the contrary, because it does not recall any known form and because it draws on dissimilar elements to compose a repugnant and novel entity.

---

1. In *Méduse et Cie* (1958), *Au coeur du fantastique* (1965), and *Images, images* (1966). Feeling my way, I gradually developed the idea of the "natural fantastic," for which I am now seeking to provide a better foundation. This idea, I think, was already implicit in my very early study, *La Mante religieuse* (1935), attempting to establish the existence of bizarre-privileged items in the universe, which served as objective guarantors for lyrical emotion and the poetic image at the same time. This essay presents an expanded version of this theory.

One could give numerous examples of such phenomena and show that in each case, there is a certain mythology or specific fascination attached to the bizarre animal, whether this is a spider, octopus, bat, praying mantis, or seahorse.

The seahorse may perhaps warrant a separate analysis, because this fish does not really look much like an actual horse. The way it is sculpted, so to speak, its lack of feet and almost of body (not to mention its vertical displacements and diagonal bounds), these all more readily recall a man-made horse: *the knight in the game of chess.*

We may note an identical convergence of natural and man-made effects in a spider from Florida, the *Cyclocosmia truncata*, which has been photographed by Andreas Feininger — but this is carried to paroxystic heights, exceeding even the ambiguities of the lantern fly and the Condylura mole.[2] The upper side of its abdomen is flattened into a kind of shield, shaped like a perfect circle. This forms a roof above the insect. When the spider digs itself into the ground, the shield closes like a tightly fitting trapdoor over the hole where it is buried; all that one can see is the amazing circle, marked by a rim of short prickly spines, grouped in tufts. In slightly raised but flattened relief, radiating lines are affixed around this circumference, like a sunburst or hair standing up on end. A mythical face is engraved in the center, the thick, impassive mask of the savage Mexican divinities: we see two enormous, empty orbs, without pupils or irises. Vertical lines extend down from the forehead, and with their full length mark the separation of the two nostrils, as if to emphasize the face's symmetry: its mouth is sinuous and well chiseled, although deformed by cruelty. For an informed observer, this is definitely the effigy of an implacable star that demands a human sacrifice.

Perhaps most surprising is the accomplished artistry whereby the rays prolong the features of the solar mask on the medallion without any break in the overall design. The composition is just as skillful, the chiseling just as clear as those of the Aztec calendar or of the related Tiahuanaco portico. But here, the terrible black sun is nothing but an assemblage of superficial and meaningless excrescences on a spider's integument.

The shell of the marine turtle *Caretta caretta gigas* provides an example that is equally disconcerting. On the dark brown, almost black shield appears a single heraldic mold, which takes up most of the functional surface. It suggests a two-headed eagle with compact, simplified wings and four large flight feathers. Joined together and virtually the same size, these *remiges* are almost

2. Andreas Feininger, *The Anatomy of Nature* (London, 1956), 136–137.

perpendicular to the bird's body, though slightly inclined in the direction of its flight (and the direction in which the turtle is swimming). The bright orange pattern looks more woven or plaited than painted: a tapestry or basket-weaving design. The color was not spread out to traced limits set beforehand. It permeates a rough, broken substance, just as the color in stained glass windows penetrates the glass paste, or like the colors in enamel or mosaics. Each element thus has its own uniform tint. Whence the abrupt, angular aspect of the effigy.

Yet this is simply an illusion. The picture does not fully coincide with the outline of the tortoise-shell polygons composing the swimmer's shield. It spreads out like a jagged stain, even though it gives the impression of spanning the whole plate. Moreover, like the Cyclocosmia mentioned above, it irresistibly brings to mind another simulacrum—of a style, rather than of any particular motif. It recalls the tribal and clan emblems, the pictograms decorating Indian tents in the American West. The legendary animal gods often form pairs, in which one roams the water and the other the skies. Their respective empires complement the world of man's dominion. His alliance with and worship of these gods grants him access to kingdoms where he nonetheless remains an intruder and that are difficult for him to explore.

Of course, the eagle is not the only bird that glides, and the salmon appears as the lord of the waters more often than the turtle. In Alaska, we find an alliance between the frog and the crow. This is not what matters, but rather the stylization of the worshipped bird. It corresponds perfectly to the natural image displayed by the Caretta caretta. That it should appear on a turtle's shell (a highly mythical animal, with a prominent role in many cosmogonies) simply constitutes a kind of extra coincidence in this case. The eagle's features on the turtle are characteristic in other ways as well. It is peaceful, fluffy, and massive, with a head that is replicated owing to the demands of symmetry, but that is somewhat self-effacing, lacking in aggressivity. Rather soft despite its clear outlines, this bird is dramatically opposed to the rapacious predator of Western heraldry, with its crooked beak, open claws, and erect feathers—a cruel bird, always watchful and quick even when at rest. The eagle is equally remote from the forceful classical form of the Egyptian sparrow hawk and from the baroque aspect of the Garouda bird, Vishnu's mount. It is strikingly apparent that it belongs to the pictographic writing of North America, which is precisely the place where the turtle almost entirely disappears from the legends—especially, by necessity, the species of turtle that haunts the Indian Ocean and the South Pacific, far from the shoreless plains of the prairies. Here, then, we have a convergence and nothing but a convergence, which would be futile to mention if it did not add to the number of such cases. But like the others, it draws its strength from its very implausibility and from the vast gap (an immeasurable one, as it yawns from zoology to the graphic arts) dividing the disparate facts it compares. In a different domain, this is the mainspring of poetic imagery. I shall return to this point.

In the animal kingdom, I suppose, the natural fantastic finds its most pronounced expression in the Cyclocosmia and the Caretta. In any event, these extreme cases show that any natural entity (whether animal, plant, stone, or landscape) belongs to the realm of the fantastic whenever its appearance seizes and effectively mobilizes our imagination in ways that are always the same. In some cases, this appearance sets the being in question apart from the neighboring species it should most resemble. Like the lantern fly, it is rather mysteriously relegated to the remoter branches of taxonomy. It suddenly appears where it should not, and thus produces an inexplicable confusion in the natural order. In other cases, on the contrary (as with the Condylura), its appearance does not recall any other and seems to have issued from some unknown universe, subject to an unfamiliar and thus threatening form of organization. Finally, the sense of disarray is sometimes aroused by nature's anticipatory replication of a human object—a chess piece, pictogram, or liturgical mask—that was fabricated quite on its own, requiring plans, calculations, and choices, unrelated to its phantom model, which suddenly emerged in nature by contrary means.

At first glance, the mineral world appears to abound in wonders of these different kinds. Moreover, they seem more significant here than elsewhere. Blind and insensate stone, lacking consciousness and initiative, deprived of the fluidity of life, makes the least exchange or hybridization seem inconceivable. However, the frequency of such wonders, and their ease, are so excessive as to be made thereby inoperative. It is all too clear that in this kingdom there is no obvious order to demolish. As for dreaming up ghost stones endowed with life, consciousness, and will, stones that eat, fly through the skies, reproduce, attack or embrace human beings—mythology is full of such events. Similarly, literature has not refrained from imagining ghostly animals and evil plants. But this is precisely the point: they are deliberate fictions created in play, not some fantastic dimension inscribed in the universe itself.

No doubt agate patterns (of birds or fish, monsters or calligraphies) constantly suggest vague similarities. The same holds true for the flames and moss of jaspers, for the ruined cities in the stones of crumbling houses, and for the landscapes within marble. Sometimes the parallel festoons of onyx seem to outline fortified enclosures with polygonal bastions. But none of these analogies, however startling they may seem, really constitutes a mystery. Rather, they are miracles, semiwondrous encounters for which chance alone is responsible. If not the indulgence of perception that is ever eager to identify and connect any shape it finds surprising with another more familiar one. There is nothing here to make one shudder.

On the other hand, what is truly unusual among stones is to find a design that is neither roughly geometric nor somehow figurative. Each image they offer involves a more or less regular network of lines and vague figures, or the more or less legible evocation of a creature or object in the world. There are no inventions here, one might say, no appearances that strike us as original, enigmatic, and inconceivable, as if from some other world, that are also sufficiently developed and coherent to impose the representation of some creature or scene similar to what the fantastic imagination can produce when it delights in troubling or fascinating the mind.

Basically, although the mineral kingdom abounds in disconcerting similarities, almost nothing really recalls such prodigious aberrations as the Condylura (the mole with the star-shaped nose), the Cyclocosmia (the spider with the sun-shaped shield), or the Caretta caretta (the marine turtle with the heraldic eagle). The only exceptions that come to mind are certain *septaria* I have described elsewhere, which mimic a Chinese character with an equal degree of insolence.[3] But this case is almost unique. As a general rule, it seems that stone, which can easily produce miniature models of the gods, stars, and architecture, cannot trigger that very special kind of alarm produced by an inadmissible offense against the universal legislation. Because here, as in other kingdoms, there would have to be some shrewd fissuring of the laws in effect, or some clearly flouted necessity. But then, what order exists in the mineral kingdom, aside from the overly complicated geometry of crystals? Besides, a fracture in a crystal is never more than a simple accident that destroys but does not negate anything. Far from contravening any laws, phenomena such as twinned crystals obey them meticulously. No one but a mineralogist would shudder if something truly impossible, such as a seven-sided quartz needle, were to be observed. On the contrary, though, with the advent of life, we can clearly make out the line that no "ghost" could cross without arousing anguish and fear. The specter, or resuscitated ghost, would then be a prime example of what we find unacceptable. But when there is only inertia, what novelty is capable of outraging a chaos that by definition suffers every injury without a wound—except precisely order itself, the birth of a tentative norm, inagurating in the tumult the wondrous calm of regularity, conquered at last?

In the kingdom of undifferentiated matter, we find a certain symmetry taking shape. In the heart of the din that it negates and organizes, the ruling effigy

3. See "Un Caractère chinois," in *Cases d'un échiquier*, 110.

is emerging, the extravagant emblematic seal (either polyhedron or sphere, polygon or circle, exact angle or perfect curve), which draws to itself a portion of the floating mass. The admirable innovation acts as a ghost, providing a ghost's astonishing presence. In an environment without axis, pole, or center arises unexpectedly the principle of balanced distribution. A mineral imposing the idea of such a contrast supplies, at last, that which alone in this impassive realm can correspond to an apparition, in the strong sense of the term. Perhaps it is not only due to the white veil visible through the transparency of its needles, and which announces their definitive contours, that one variety of quartz is called "spectral." It is also because the clear image of the captive needle (a pure silhouette, immaterial in the bosom of nature) manifestly proclaims the scandalous, still tremulous intrusion of geometry. In this most protected retreat, the ghostly design attests to the sudden presence of something highly disturbing, which is, paradoxically, order. Later on, to be sure, the fantastic will assume the contrary guise of a breach in the order that it established in the first place. For now, in the universe of the indistinct, it can fulfill its mission of rupture only by introducing into this confused substance the absolute horror entailed by the emergence of a strict and unpredictable legislation.

Let me return to my meditation on the topic of inadmissible similarities: the lantern fly, seahorse, spider, mole, and turtle. I would be the first to declare them the results of coincidence. But there are too many: they must necessarily comply in turn with some kind of law. For the actual number of forms and forces, compensations and competitions governing all things is relatively small, and so they reoccur, even down to their rarest repercussions. From the very outset, every design and structure, however complex, could have met with potential interference. Some of these surfaced at several sites in the inextricable labyrinth of the kingdoms, which is therefore bestrewn with a secondary maze of echoes and reflections.

These mysterious relays (inevitable, upon reflection) leave the mind perplexed. At times, it is enchanted by false connivances that are deceptive; at others, it panics when recognizing signs seen before at the most distant crossroads, as if the world's cartography were replicated there. It suspects that these are traps set for its own naïveté. Admittedly, they do not indicate true correlations. They simply affect us. They disturb. Their lesson is that because the universe has only a limited number of structures, privileged models must necessarily reoccur.

At this point, I would like to specify exactly what is implicated and excluded by my recklessness. I would at once consider the present conjecture to be null and void if it were demonstrated to me that the silhouette of the knight in chess had been historically inspired by the seahorse; that the artists who sculpted the figures of Tiahuanaco took the Cyclocosmia's dorsal shield as their model; or that the Indians who drew the eagle pictogram had ever seen the Caretta caretta's shell. In other words, I think that convergence is more plausible than influence. Similarly, I've had occasion to note a coincidence between the regular polyhedrons in Plato and the structures of radiolarians. My audacity goes so far that rather than accept the influence hypothesis, I prefer to assert that Plato or some other geometer appears as a distant avatar of the radiolarian. Moreover, if I skip several stages—unwisely, it is true—and take account of the parameters to be modified (notably, the passage from an external to an internal skeleton, from automatism to image, and from the organic to the speculative), this assertion strikes me as seductive and almost irrefutable.

The mystery resides in this reversal—the fact of which simply cannot be denied. I am willing to concede that the hypothesis seems insane. However, due reflection ultimately does find that it is the most economical one. After all, it merely draws the conclusions ensuing from a postulate that can hardly be avoided in rigorous research: that of the unity of the world. This postulate leads, in turn, to a further wager: that the world is finite. For if it is infinite, not with regard to dimension or scale, but if some unpredictable and novel event can be observed, such as an entity with no place in Mendeleyev's periodic table or in any more general scheme, then the lot of mankind is simply confusion, absurdity, and impotence. The precondition of useful thought is that the world is finite. And, in a finite, teeming world, things are repeated and respond to each other. There are discernable cycles and symmetries, homologies and recurrences. Everything fits into one or several series. There is nothing that does not have its own counterpart or double, the cypher that recalls to our mind a certain premonition of it, or nostalgia for it.

At such times, nature gives the impression of ruffling its immutable order. Within its framework, it sets up perplexing shortcuts and short-circuits, all sorts of unexpected echoes that seem the product of hallucination. The calm, slow ramification of kingdoms and subkingdoms, of classes, orders, and families, of genuses, species, and their minor varieties is thrown into disarray. The fantastic deploys its show of splendors and signals even into the realm of the inanimate.

The fantastic stems from the resurgence of seals that, through the workings of totally external mechanisms, provide the images (distant or nearby, they are always wondrous) of other phenomena scattered among the inventory of things. This insistence or dedication is not an illusion. It betrays the supremacy of rare elements amid the multitude of common appearances. It designates them clearly among the general commotion that tends to conceal the profound unity of nature. For its part, the imagination has always let itself be spellbound by these ambiguous encounters. It likes to superpose things and is even enraptured by making things coincide that are only superposable on an infinitesimal point—and even then it is often only through reckless conjecture, almost prejudice. The signs avariciously conceded by the natural fantastic do more than stimulate the demon of analogy. They show it the way. They precede it and nourish its mania for interpretation. They fulfill it by revealing, or at least by allowing it to presume the existence of an underlying imaginary that is part of the real. This is a springboard and guarantee for that other imaginary, woven by the mind, which is perhaps only an uncertain echo of the first or its lyrical mirage—half-proffered, half-solicited, misleading, but not fully a lie.

Letters left adrift, terms without a lexicon, these boundary markers, whose aberrant arrangement does not correspond to any register or cadastral survey on the order of man, nonetheless figure among the indications that move him most, and the most obscurely. In the end, more or less alone, they guarantee the wagers and resources for the images of tenacious poetry. The network of surprising markers constitutes a secret and inexhaustible warranty, a sort of intellectual gold supporting all fiduciary transactions of the intellect and imagination.

In exchange for this repository (insofar as he accepts its reality) man is dispossessed of the ancient preeminence he briefly claimed as his own—an instant that is immemorial for him but very swift for geological time. Henceforth, man knows that he is neither alone nor a monarch. In the infinite game of Snakes and Ladders without a well, jail, or fruitful stops, man is not a player— nor even the dice—but an almost passive counter that is moved from square to square in its turn, together with other reiterated emblems. Sometimes he is stopped by an image that disturbs him, an image reminding him of another or else holding out the promise of different ones. The return of the simulacrum lets him glimpse the tattered shreds of a concealed order he can barely reach, and never with certainty. Dazzled or enlightened, he tries to understand and, at times, to expand the rules of a game he never asked to take part in, and that he is not allowed to renounce.

Roger Caillois Timeline

1913   Born in Reims on March 3.

1914–19   Childhood in Maisons-Alfort (Seine).

1920–29   High school in Reims.

1927–28   Befriends Roger Gilbert-Lecomte and René Daumal of Le Grand Jeu; discovers Lautréamont, Rimbaud, and Saint-John Perse.

1929–32   Studies philosophy at the Lycée Louis-le-Grand, preparing for the entrance exams to the Ecole Normale Supérieure.

1932–34   Meets André Breton; joins the Surrealist movement; writes *La Nécessité d'esprit*.

1933   Enters the Ecole Normale Supérieure. Attends the classes of Marcel Mauss and Georges Dumézil at the Ecole Pratique des Hautes Etudes.

1933–35   Studies at the Ecole Normale Supérieure.

1934   Meets Gaston Bachelard at a philosophy conference in Prague; breaks with Surrealism.

1935   Publishes *Procès intellectuel de l'art*. Meets Jean Paulhan and becomes a regular contributor to the *Nouvelle revue française*.

1936   Academic degrees: the Agrégation de grammaire competition; diploma from the Ecole Pratique des Hautes Etudes (studies in religion). Also founds the journal *Inquisitions* with Aragon, Tzara, Monnerot.

1936–38   Teaches at the Ecole Normale and the Lycée de Beauvais; publishes *Le Mythe et l'homme* and articles from *Les Démons de midi*.

1938   Founds the College of Sociology with Georges Bataille and Michel Leiris.

1939   Publishes *L'Homme et le sacré*. Meets Victoria Ocampo.

1939–40   Resides in Buenos Aires, Argentina; founds the Institut Français de Buenos Aires; founds the journal *Les Lettres françaises*. Publishes *Patago-*

nie, *La Róca de Sísifo*, *La Communion des forts*, *Les Impostures de la poésie*, *Ensayo sobre el espíritu de las sectas*, *Le Rocher de Sisyphe*.

1941   Marries Yvette Billod.

1945   Returns to Paris; replaces Raymond Aron at the helm of *La France libre*.

1946   Publishes *Fisiología de Leviatán*, *Sur l'enjeu d'une guerre*, *Circonstancielles*, *Vocabulaire esthéthique*, and an introduction to the complete works of Lautréamont. Translates and edits *Poèmes* by Gabriela Mistral.

1947   Joins the editorial committee of *Confluences*; codirects *La Licorne*; joins the editorial committee of Gallimard. Lectures at the Ecole Pratique des Hautes Etudes; teaches at the Lycée Michelet.

1948   Joins the Office of Ideas at UNESCO. Publishes *Babel* and a critical edition of Montesquieu's *Histoire véritable*. Founds the Latin American Croix-du-sud series at Gallimard. Divorces Yvette Billod.

1949   Runs UNESCO's program of translating representative works. Publishes *Espace américain*, *Description du marxisme*, *Quatre essais de sociologie contemporaine*, and a revised, amplified version of *L'Homme et le sacré*. Produces an annotated edition of Montesquieu's complete works for the Bibliothèque de la Pléiade at Gallimard.

1952   Founds the journal *Diogène*.

1953   Translates *Labyrinthes* by Borges. Writes a preface for Saint-Exupéry's complete works.

1954   Publishes *Poétique de Saint-John Perse*.

1956   Publishes *L'Incertitude qui vient des rêves*.

1957   Marries Alena Vichrova.

1958   Publishes *Art poétique*, *Les Jeux et les hommes*; coedits *Trésor de la poésie universelle*; edits *Manuscrit trouvé à Saragosse* by Potocki.

1959   Preface to *Masques*, a catalogue for the Musée Guimet.

1960   Publishes *Méduse et Cie*.

1961   Publishes *Ponce-Pilate*. Presents and translates *Hauteurs de Macchu-Pichu* by Neruda; introduction to *Les Littératures contemporaines à travers le monde*.

1962   Publishes *Esthétique généralisée*; coedits *Puissances du rêve*.

1963   Publishes *Bellone ou la pente de la guerre*, *Le Mimétisme animal*, *Instincts et sociétés*; translates *L'Auteur et autres textes* by Borges.

1965   Publishes *Au coeur du fantastique*. Runs the department of "diffusion culturelle" at UNESCO.

1966   Publishes *Pierres, Images, images . . .*

1967   Publishes *Obliques*; coedits *Le Rêve et les sociétés humaines*.

1968   Visiting writer at the University of Texas in Austin; seminars on the poetics of Saint-John Perse and the French avant-garde between the wars.

1970   Zaharoff lecture at Oxford on dissymmetry; publishes *Cases d'un échiquier*, *L'Ecriture des pierres*.

1971   Elected to the Académie Française; leaves UNESCO, while remaining a consultant for their program on translating representative works.

1972   Inducted into the *Académie Française*. Publishes *Discours de réception à l'Académie française et réponse de René Huyghe*.

1973   Publishes *La Dissymétrie*, *La Pieuvre*, and preface with André Masson to the Malraux exhibit at the Maeght Foundation.

1974   Publishes *Approches de l'imaginaire*.

1975   Publishes *Obliques, précédé de Images, images, Pierres réfléchies, Randonnées, Malversations*.

1976   Publishes *Cohérences aventureuses* (*Esthétique généralisée*, *Au coeur du fantastique*, *La Dissymétrie*).

1977   Publishes *Petit Guide du XVe arrondissement à l'usage des fantômes*.

1978   Publishes *Le Fleuve Alphée*; *Trois Leçons des ténèbres*; *Rencontres*; *Le Champ des signes: récurrences dérobées: aperçu sur l'unité et la continuité du monde physique, intellectuel et imaginaire ou premiers éléments d'une poétique généralisée*; *Approches de la poésie*. Caillois dies on December 21.

This chronology is based on the one published in *Roger Caillois: "Cahiers pour un temps"* (Paris: Centre Georges Pompidou and Pandora, 1981). For a detailed biography, see Odile Felgine, *Roger Caillois*.

Notes

Introduction

1. Maurice Blanchot, *Michel Foucault tel que je l'imagine* (Paris: Fata Morgana, 1986), 10.

2. See Denis Hollier, ed., *The College of Sociology 1937–39*, 2d ed., trans. Betsy Wing (Minneapolis: University of Minnesota Press, 1988); and Denis Hollier, ed., *Le Collège de Sociologie 1937–1939*, 3rd ed. (Paris: Gallimard, 1995); see also Denis Hollier, *Absent without Leave* (Cambridge, MA: Harvard University Press, 1997). These volumes contain crucial information regarding Caillois and this intellectual milieu, which I do not seek to reproduce here.

3. Roger Caillois, *Pierres réfléchies* (Paris: Gallimard, 1975), 11.

4. Monographs devoted to Caillois include Alain Bosquet, *Roger Caillois* (Paris: Seghers, 1971); Dominique Autié, *Approches de Caillois* (Toulouse: Privat, 1981); Odile Felgine, *Roger Caillois* (Paris: Stock, 1994); and Stéphane Massonet, *Les Labyrinthes de l'imaginaire dans l'oeuvre de Roger Caillois* (Paris: L'Harmattan, 1998). Collections of essays include special issues of the *Nouvelle revue française*, "Hommage à Roger Caillois" (Sept. 1979), *SUD*, "Roger Caillois ou la traversée des savoirs" (1981); and *Europe*, "Roger Caillois," 859–860 (Nov.–Dec. 2000); see also *Roger Caillois: "Cahiers pour un temps"* (Paris: Centre Georges Pompidou and Pandora, 1981); Jean-Clarence Lambert, ed., *Les Cahiers de Chronos: Roger Caillois* (Paris: Editions de la Différence, 1991); Laurent Jenny, ed., *Roger Caillois, la pensée aventurée* (Paris: Belin, 1992).

5. Roger Caillois, *La Nécessité d'esprit* (Paris: Gallimard, 1981); *The Necessity of Mind*, trans. Michael Syrotinski, afterword by Denis Hollier (Venice, CA: Lapis Press, 1990); Roger Caillois, *L'Homme et le sacré* (Paris: Ed. Leroux, 1939); 2d ed. (Paris: Gallimard, 1963); *Man and the Sacred*, trans. Meyer Barash (Glencoe, IL: Free Press, 1960); Roger Caillois, *Les Jeux et les hommes* (Paris: Gallimard, 1958); *Man, Play and Games*, trans. Meyer Barash (New York: Free Press, 1961); Roger Caillois and G. E. von Grunebaum, eds., *Le Rêve et les sociétés humaines* (Paris: Gallimard, 1967); *The Dream and Human Societies* (Berkeley: University of California Press, 1966); Roger Caillois, *The Writing of Stones*, trans. Barbara Bray, introduction by Marguerite Yourcenar (Charlottesville: University of Virginia Press, 1985); Roger Caillois, *Puissances du roman* (Marseille: Sagittaire, 1942); rpt. in *Approches de l'imaginaire* (Paris: Gallimard, 1970). The central section, originally published as Roger Caillois, *Le Roman policier* (Buenos Aires: Ed. Lettres Françaises, 1941), has been translated by Roberto Yahni and A. W. Sadler as *The Mystery Novel* (Bronxville, NY: Laughing Buddha Press, 1984). Roger Caillois, *Ponce Pi-*

late (Paris: Gallimard, 1960); *Pontius Pilate*, trans. Charles Lam Markmann (New York: Macmillan, 1963).

6. There is helpful material, though, in Roger Caillois, interview with Jean-Jose Marchand, videotape, dir. Michel Latouche, Archives du XXème siècle Société Française de Production, Paris, 1971. All further references are to Archives interview. See also Jeannine Worms, *Entretiens avec Roger Caillois* [interview taped in 1970], (Paris: Editions de la Différence, 1991).

7. Roger Caillois, *Cases d'un échiquier* (Paris: Gallimard, 1970), 10.

8. Roger Caillois, *Le Fleuve Alphée* (Paris: Gallimard, 1978), 215.

9. Caillois, *Approches de la poésie* (Paris: Gallimard, 1978), 245.

10. Caillois, *Fleuve*, 201.

11. Caillois, *Fleuve*, 15, 10.

12. Caillois, *Fleuve*, 29.

13. Caillois, *Man and the Sacred*, 138 (trans. modified).

14. The most resounding and influential attack on Caillois in this respect, and still widely quoted to this day, is Meyer Schapiro, "French Reaction in Exile," *Kenyon Review* 7 (winter 1945): 29–42, a review of Caillois's essays in *La Communion des forts* (Mexico City: Quetzal, 1943).

15. Roger Caillois, "Lettre du rédacteur en chef sur le role de *Diogène* et les conditions d'un humanisme rénové," *Diogène* 4 (1953): 141. In 1954–1955, Caillois launched a notorious attack on "Surrealist ethnography" and "inverse ethnocentrism" in *Race et histoire*. See Roger Caillois, "Illusions à rebours I," *Nouvelle nouvelle revue française* 25 (Dec. 1954): 1010–24; and "Illusions à rebours II," *Nouvelle nouvelle revue française* 25 (Jan. 1955): 58–70. Among the first to level a frontal assault on the "inverse ethnocentrism" of Lévi-Strauss's early work, Caillois explained to Lévi-Strauss that his hostility to the West presupposed the very fruits of its existence: "archaeology, ethnography and museums" ("Illusion à rebours II," 70), and that despite denying cultural evolutionism and value judgments, he was nonetheless quick to praise primitive cultures over his own. According to David Pace, Lévi-Strauss's reply, "Diogéne couché" in *Les Temps modernes*, dealt effectively with the "substantive" issues of this attack "from the right," explaining, for example, that the comparative evaluation of cultures was entirely possible, albeit in terms of individual traits rather than the whole. *Claude Lévi-Strauss, Bearer of Ashes* (1983; Boston: ARK, 1986), 94–95.

16. Felgine, *Caillois*, 365; she adds that "Caillois was apparently more drawn to Africans who had been extensively trained by the French educational system, such as Léopold Sedar Senghor, and Tchicaya U' Tamsi, a talented autodidact, felt slighted" (365).

17. A reasonable refutation is Alexandre Pajon, "L'Intrépidité politique de Roger Caillois avant-guerre," in Lambert, *Les Cahiers de Chronos: Roger Caillois*, 373–387.

18. Hollier, *Absent*, 33.

19. Georges Bataille, letter to Roger Caillois, 7 Oct. 1935, in *Georges Bataille: Lettres à Roger Caillois 4 août 1935–4 février 1959*, ed. Jean-Pierre Le Bouler (Paris: Folle Avoine, 1988), 49. See also Jean-Pierre Le Bouler, "Bataille et Caillois: Divergences et complicités," *Magazine littéraire* 243 (June 1987): 47–49.

20. I have surmised that he published a travestied version of the text as "L'Ordre et l'empire" in *Europe* (1936); see C. Frank, "Contre-Attaque de Caillois? A propos de 'L'Ordre et l'empire,'" *Europe* 859–860 (Nov.–Dec. 2000): 72–82.

21. Georges Bataille, letter to Roger Caillois, 13 Nov. 1939, in *Georges Bataille: Lettres à Roger Caillois*, 121.

22. Bataille, letter to Roger Caillois, 13 Nov. 1939, 121.

23. Aldous Huxley, letter to Roger Caillois, 3 Oct. 1939, C.H. 20, Special Collections, Bibliothèque Municipale, Vichy, France.

24. Susan Rubin Suleiman, *Subversive Intent* (Cambridge, MA: Harvard University Press, 1990), 74.

25. David Coward, "The Apostles of Anguish," *Times Literary Supplement* 4–10 (Aug. 1989): 858. For a refreshingly temperate view, see Peter Tracey Connor, *Georges Bataille and the Mysticism of Sin* (Baltimore, Md.: Johns Hopkins University Press, 2000).

26. Jean-Michel Heimonet sadly remarks, "Applying rigorous sociological principles to Poetry or filtering or tempering the Revolution by means of a program involves one and the same gesture. . . . It is aesthetically and politically identical to a real exorcism, in which the desired magic dissolves away." *Politiques de l'écriture Bataille/Derrida* (Paris: Jean-Michel Place, 1990), 68.

27. Felgine's biography paints Caillois as a man who finally succumbs to the life-long lure of vertigo and irrationalism. Laurent Jenny cites a contradiction "that is clearly legible in certain insoluble tensions informing his oeuvre. For example, this rigid style, which imbues his sentence with the strained manner that psychoanalysis would call a *reaction-formation*. Or else this paradoxical repugnance for the subjects he favors most." "La Fêlure et la parenthèse," in Lambert, *Les Cahiers de Chronos: Roger Caillois*, 351. Jenny's excellent commentaries lack an attentiveness to diachronic shifts that make Caillois's thought less intransigent, compulsive, and confused than Jenny often implies.

28. Caillois, Archives interview.

29. On Paulhan and Dumézil, in this respect, see Roger Caillois, *Rencontres* (Paris: Presses Universitaires de France, 1978).

30. I henceforth use the term "sacred" in the sociological—rather than theological or metaphysical—sense that characterized its usage at the College of Sociology.

31. Alan Sokal and Jean Bricquemont, *Impostures intellectuelles* (Paris: Odile Jacob, 1997).

32. Bataille wrote to Caillois after a clash regarding Contre-Attaque, "I also hope that this unfortunate event will let us see the extent to which essential matters still derive from the god *polemos*." Letter to Caillois, 9 Oct. 1935, in *Georges Bataille: Lettres à Roger Caillois*, 51.

33. Roger Caillois, "The Winter Wind," in Hollier, *The College of Sociology*, 32–43. In *Absent without Leave*, Hollier writes, "No matter how mimesis is interpreted, death is a mask for life, a mask behind which life protects its difference by pretending to renounce that difference"(43), and "An aristocrat is not an exhibitionist. He is not about to reveal

his difference to the first person who comes along. The trace fades: all his distinction lies in his reserve"(45). See Peter F. DeDomenico's "Revenge of the Novel: Roger Caillois's Literary Criticism in the Wake of the 1930s," *Romanic Review* 89.3 (May 1998): 381–409, for a decontextualized and overly suspicious reading of Caillois, which argues that critics who resist viewing him as somehow allied to fascism or Nazism "make the mistake of trusting the content of a writer for whom meaning is no more important than rhetorical effect" (406).

34. Jean Paulhan, *Les Fleurs de Tarbes ou La Terreur dans les lettres* (1941; Paris: Gallimard, 1990), 168.

35. See Shadia Drury, *Leo Strauss and the American Right* (New York: St. Martin's Press, 1997).

36. René Etiemble, "Deux masques de Roger Caillois," *Nouvelle revue française* 142 (Sept. 1979): 142.

37. James Clifford, *The Predicament of Culture* (Cambridge, MA: Harvard University Press, 1988).

38. See, in particular, Georges Bataille, "La Guerre et la philosophie du sacré," rev. of *L'Homme et le sacré*, by Roger Caillois, *O. C.* 12 (Feb. 1951): 52.

39. Roger Caillois, *Le Champ des signes: récurrences dérobées* (Paris: Edition Hermann, 1978), 78.

40. Roger Caillois, "En toute sévérité," *Volontés* 12 (Dec. 1938): 48–50; Roger Caillois, *Babel: Précédé de vocabulaire esthétique* (1946; Paris: Gallimard 1978), 370.

41. [Caillois], "Debates sobres temas sociologicos: Comentario a 'Los irresponsables,' de Archibald Macleish," *Sur* 83 (Aug. 1941): 104. Although his journal *Diogenes* integrated these two roles, there was perhaps a greater division between his publications and his UNESCO career after the war than if Caillois had been teaching at the Ecole des Hautes Etudes.

42. Caillois, *Pierres réfléchies*, 122; this may recall the final image of collective treasure in "Patagonia," although that is a social—rather than natural—accumulation.

43. Wahl, qtd. in C. Frank, "Contre-Attaque," 80; Breton, qtd. by Caillois in the Archives interview, reading the letter on camera; Edmond Jabès, letter to Roger Caillois, 7 Oct. 1974, C. J. 6, Special Collections, Bibliothèque Municipale, Vichy, France.

44. See Marcel Granet, *La Civilisation chinoise* (1929; Paris: Albin Michel, 1968), and *La Pensée chinoise* (1934; Paris: Albin Michel, 1999).

45. Personal interview with André Chastel, Cambridge, MA., May 1988.

46. See Odile Felgine and Claude Perez, eds., "Correspondance Jean Paulhan–Roger Caillois 1934–1967," in *Cahiers Jean Paulhan*, vol. 6 (Paris: Gallimard, 1991); on August 18, 1938, Paulhan wrote to Caillois of plans to establish an advisory committee for the *Nouvelle revue française* composed of Sartre, Caillois, and Armand Petitjean (89).

47. See Marc Thivolet, *Le Grand Jeu* (Paris: L'Herne, 1968), for a reproduction of the group's publications.

48. Gérard de Cortanze, "L'Irréductible Hostilité de Bataille au surréalisme," *Magazine littéraire* 243 (June 1987): 35.

49. Despite Caillois's efforts, the work remained unpublished at the time.

50. Caillois, qtd. in Jean-François Sirinelli, *Génération intellectuelle: Khâgneux et Normaliens dans l'entre-deux-guerres* (Paris: Fayard, 1988), 524.

51. Along with other new recruits (René Char, Pierre Yoyotte, Salvador Dali, and Jules Monnerot), Caillois witnessed the years of *Le Surréalisme au Service de la révolution*, loosely framed by Breton's *Second manifeste* and the Surrealists' formal expulsion from the Communist Party in 1933. He then saw the transition to the apolitical, luxurious art journal *Minotaure* (1933–1939), which the Surrealists eventually came to control.

52. Caillois, Archives interview.

53. The phrase was "qui réduirait les dimensions de la *petite psychologie romanesque.*" Chastel recalls that Caillois ironically sent him the manuscript of *The Necessity of Mind*; Chastel opposed its publication at the time but now finds it "better than" Lévi-Strauss, and relates it to his own study of Cassirer in his preface to *Fables, formes, figures* (Paris: Flammarion, 1965), Personal interview.

54. Marcel Mauss, "Rapports réels et pratiques de la psychologie et de la sociologie" (1924), in *Sociologie et anthropologie* (Paris: Presses Universitaires de France, 1989), 296. Here, he discusses "phenomena of *totality* in which the group takes part but also, thereby, all the various people, all the individuals in their moral, social, mental and especially bodily or material integrity" (303).

55. Marcel Mauss, letter to Roger Caillois, 22 June 1938, in *Roger Caillois*: "*Cahiers pour un temps,*" 54.

56. See Henri Béhar, "Roger Caillois 'Boussole mentale' du surréalisme," in Jenny, *Roger Caillois, la pensée aventurée*, 15.

57. Roger Caillois, *Approches de la poésie*, 10. For other commentary on Caillois's use of analogy, see Annamaria Lasserra, *Materia et imaginario, il nesso analogico nell'opera di Roger Caillois* (Rome: Bulzoni, 1990); see also her "L'Art du pontonnier," *Europe* 859–860 (Nov.–Dec. 2000): 183–195.

58. Georges Bataille, "Le Sens moral de la sociologie," *Critique* 1 (1946); rpt. in *Critique* 591–592 (Aug.–Sept. 1996): 585.

59. Caillois, *Nécessité*, 24. Roger Shattuck comments that Caillois was "the writer and critic best equipped to reassess the role of dreams, games, psychic experiments, and the occult in Surrealism." *The Innocent Eye* (New York: Washington Square Press, 1986), 55.

60. Marc Eigeldinger, "La Poétique hugolienne de l'image et de l'imagination," in *Du romantisme au surnaturalisme: Hommage à Claude Pichois* (Neuchâtel: A la Baconnière, 1988), 90.

61. Pierre Reverdy, qtd. by Breton in André Breton, *Manifestoes of Surrealism*, trans. Richard Seaver and Helen Lane (1969; Ann Arbor: University of Michigan Press, 1972), 20 (trans. modified).

62. Pierre Reverdy, *Nord-Sud, Self-Defence, et autres écrits sur l'art et la poésie* (Paris: Flammarion, 1975), 75.

63. André Breton, *Point du jour* (1934; Paris: Gallimard 1970), 57; Louis Aragon, *Traité de style* (1928), qtd. and trans. in Margaret Cohen, *Profane Illumination* (Berkeley: University of California Press, 1993), 194.

64. Roger Caillois, *Approches de l'imaginaire* (Paris: Gallimard, 1974), 45.

65. Caillois, *Approches de l'imaginaire*, 51.

66. Louis de Broglie, preface to *Essais*, by Emile Meyerson (Paris: Vrin, 1936), viii.

67. Georges Bataille, "The Solar Anus," in *Visions of Excess: Selected Writings, 1927–1939*, ed. and trans. Allan Stœkl (Minneapolis: University of Minesota Press, 1985), 5.

68. Georges Bataille, "The Sacred," in *Visions of Excess*, 242.

69. See Lucien Lévy-Bruhl, *The Primitive Mentality*, trans. Lilian A. Clare (New York: Macmillan, 1923); see also Emile Durkheim and Marcel Mauss, "De quelques formes primitives de la classification" (1903), in Marcel Mauss, *Essais de sociologie* (Paris: Minuit, 1969). Roger Caillois, rev. of *L'Expérience mystique et les symboles chez les primitifs*, by Lucien Lévy-Bruhl, *Nouvelle revue française* (Aug. 1938): 322, 323.

70. Dominique Parodi, "Le Sentiment de ressemblance," *Revue philosophique* 109 (1930): 210. Parodi here seems to deny Bergson's fundamental opposition between "spiritual energy" (l'énergie spirituelle) and "science"; so too did Caillois, as André Chastel confirmed to me (personal interview).

I have consistently translated *spirituel* by the English term "spiritual," even though "spirituel" in French does not necessarily have the religious connotations of the English "spiritual," as it derives from *esprit*, which can mean "spirit" or "mind." This intellectual sense, as opposed to the religious sense, is its general meaning throughout the book. Of course, such an ambiguity inherent in Caillois's use of the term *pouvoir spirituel* (spiritual power) reflects that of the College of Sociology itself, with its secular sociological "sacred."

71. Walter D. Wetzels, "Aspects of Natural Science in German Romanticism," *Studies in Romanticism* 10 (winter 1971): 45.

72. Contrary to what Hollier suggests in *Absent without Leave*, Caillois does not begin with a "plea for distinction" (41) but the reverse.

73. Parodi writes: "These strange 'correspondences' [he] discovers . . . are simply the juxtaposition of psychological states that are utterly different but that, on some level, blend together and are the same within the continuous flow of a certain impression, that is to say, of one single subjective attitude" ("Sentiment," 207). In 1936, having moved from *l'instinct d'abandon* to "militant orthodoxy," Caillois would praise Baudelaire's efforts to coordinate "intellectual research and vital reaction": "[He] seeks to gather into one single order of efforts everything that can be of interest to the human being and his most varied tendencies." Rev. of *L'Esthétique de Baudelaire*, by André Ferran, *Nouvelle revue française* (Nov. 1936): 902.

74. See Felgine, *Caillois*, 87.

75. Georges Bataille, "The Notion of Expenditure," in *Visions of Excess*, 116–129.

76. See Georges Bataille, "Le Problème de l'état," *Critique sociale* 9 (Sept. 1933); "La Structure psychologique du fascisme," *Critique sociale* 10, 11 (Nov. 1933, Mar. 1934); and a review of *La Condition humaine*, *Critique sociale* 10 (Mar. 1934); they are all reproduced in Georges Bataille, *Oeuvres complètes*, 12 vols., ed. Michel Foucault (Paris: Gallimard, 1970–1988). The Popular Front was Léon Blum's ill-fated left coalition.

77. "'Contre-Attaque' Union de lutte des intellectuels révolutionnaires," in *Histoire*

du surréalisme: Suivie de documents surréalistes, by Maurice Nadeau (Paris: Seuil, 1964), 437. This was a manifesto signed by Adolphe Acker, Pierre Aimery, Georges Ambrosino, Georges Bataille, Bernard, Roger Blin, Jacques-André Boiffard, André Breton, Jacques Brunius, Claude Cahun, Louis Chavance, Jacques Chavy, René Chenon, Jean Dautry, Jean Delmas, Henri Dubief, Jean Duval, Paul Eluard, Jacques Fischbein, Lucien Foulon, Reya Garbarg, Arthur Harfaux, Maurice Heine, Maurice Henry, Georges Hugnet, Janine Jane, Marcel Jean, Pierre Klossowski, Loris, Dora Maar, Léo Malet, Suzanne Malherbe, Georges Mouton, Henry Pastoureau, Benjamin Péret, Germaine Pontabrie, Robert Pontabrie, Yves Tanguy, Robert Valançay. Henri Dubief, who participated in the group, later explained that although Bataille had no doubt as to the "perversity" of fascism, "he was observing that in the course of politics and history, it was superior to a worker's movement that had gone awry and to a corrupt liberal democracy. It was hence less a matter of defending oneself, while retreating, against fascism, than of overcoming it by mobilizing the popular masses freed from the supervision of ossified workers organizations." "Témoignage sur Contre-Attaque," *Textures* 6 (Jan. 1970): 57; see also Robert Stuart Short, "Contre-Attaque," in *Entretiens sur le surréalisme*, ed. Ferdinand Alquié (Paris: Mouton, 1968); Jean Piel, *La Rencontre et la différence* (Paris: Fayard, 1982); and Marina Galletti, *Georges Bataille: L'Apprenti sorcier* (Paris: Editions de la Différence, 1999).

78. Roger Caillois, letter to Gurnaud, n.d., c. 8, Special Collections, Bibliothèque Municipale, Vichy.

79. Roger Caillois, "L'Ordre et l'empire," in *Le Mythe et l'homme* (Paris: Gallimard, 1938), 134, 133; see also C. Frank, "Contre-Attaque de Caillois?"

80. Roger Caillois, rev. of *Propos de Georges Sorel*, ed. Jean Variot, *Nouvelle revue française* (Apr. 1936): 602.

81. Georges Sorel, *Reflections on Violence* (1908), trans. T. E. Hulme, introduction by Edward A. Shils (New York: Free Press, 1974); on Breton's "collective myth," see André Breton, *Position politique du surréalisme* (1935; Paris: J-J. Pauvert, 1971), 11.

82. See Jules Monnerot, "A partir de quelques traits particuliers à la mentalité civilisée," *Le Surréalisme au service de la révolution* 5–6 (1933): 35–37; and his "Remarques sur le rapport de la poésie comme genre et comme fonction," *Inquisitions* 1 (June 1936): 14–20. On Jules Monnerot, see Jean-Michel Heimonet, *Jules Monnerot, ou la démission critique, 1932–1990* (Paris: Editions Kime, 1993).

83. Jean Wahl, rev. of *Inquisitions* and *Acéphale*, *Nouvelle revue française* 275 (Aug. 1936): 403.

84. *Inquisitions* 1 (June 1936), rpt. in Henri Béhar, ed., *Inquisitions: Fac-simile de la revue augmenté de documents inédits* (Paris: Editions du CNRS, 1990); all further references are to this edition.

85. See Schapiro, "French Reaction in Exile."

86. Wahl, rev. of *Inquisitions* and *Acéphale*, 403.

87. Caillois, *Approches de l'imaginaire*, 33; he specifies that his use of the terms "rational" and "irrational" derives from Meyerson. According to de Broglie, Meyerson proposed to "let some irrational elements slip into our theoretical constructions; this

more or less surreptitious insertion will prevent the set of our successive identifications from simply constituting a huge tautology" (preface, xi). This surreptitious mode is absent from Caillois's "militant" theory.

88. Société Française de Philosophie, *Vocabulaire technique et critique de la philosophie* (1902–1923), 9th ed. (Paris: PUF, 1962), 381.

89. Caillois repeats, forty years later, in terms close to Bachelard's *Le Nouvel esprit scientifique* and *La philosophie du non*, that he does not favor reason, which he equates with common sense, received opinion, and prejudice: "What I believe in is coherence. I believe that the data out of which we construct a system should all be congruent to each other. That is what I consider the work proper to intelligence" (Archives interview).

90. On the contagious nature of the sacred in Durkheim, as well as in Hubert and Mauss, see Philippe Borgeaud, "Le Couple sacré/profane: Genèse et fortune d'un concept 'opératoire' en histoire des religions," *Revue de l'histoire des religions* 211 (1994): 402–405.

91. Jean Paulhan, letter to Marcel Jouhandeau, 29 June 1936, no. 313, in, *Jean Paulhan: Choix de lettres 1917–1936*, ed. Dominique Aury and Jean-Claude Zylberstein (Paris: Gallimard, 1986), 385.

92. Roger Caillois, "Touches pour un portrait sincère," *Nouvelle revue française* 197 (May 1969): 737; rpt. in Caillois, *Rencontres*, 49–54.

93. Paulhan, *Les Fleurs de Tarbes*, 253.

94. Rpt. in Caillois, *Approches de l'imaginaire*, 25–34. See Isabelle Thomas-Fogiel, *Fichte: Nouvelle présentation de la doctrine de la science 1797–1798* (Paris: Vrin, 1999), for a study of this epistemological dimension.

95. Caillois, *Approches de l'imaginaire*, 32, 33; Reichenbach, qtd. in Caillois, *Approches de l'imaginaire*, 33.

96. Caillois, *Approches de l'imaginaire*, 32, 33; Reichenbach, qtd. in Caillois, *Approches de l'imaginaire*, 33; Caillois also cites Niels Bohr, Ph. Frank, and Carnap and Reichenbach's journal *Erkenntniss*.

97. Rudolf Carnap, "The Elimination of Metaphysics through Logical Analysis of Language," in *Logical Positivism*, ed. A. J. Ayer (New York: Free Press, 1959).

98. Caillois, *Fleuve*, 219.

99. Caillois, "L'Alternative," 30.

100. Roger Caillois, "L'Aridité," *Mesures* (Apr. 1938): 9.

101. Roger Caillois, "Places et limites de la poésie jusqu'à, selon et depuis Baudelaire," *Preuves* (Dec. 1968): 19; rpt. in Caillois, *Cases*.

102. Roger Caillois, "La Hiérarchie des êtres," "Le Fascisme contre l'esprit" (Fascism against the mind), special issue of *Les Volontaires* 9 (Apr. 1939): 317–326; rpt. in Caillois, *Communion*, 133.

103. Roger Caillois, rev. of *Nouvelles conversations de Goethe avec Eckermann; L'Exercice du pouvoir; Du Mariage*, by Léon Blum; *En lisant M. Léon Blum* by Marcel Thiébaut, *Nouvelle revue française* (Oct. 1937): 674, 675.

104. See Jean-Louis Loubet del Bayle, *Les Non-conformistes des années 30, une tentative de renouvellement de la pensée française* (Paris: Editions du Seuil, 1969). Caillois never re-

published certain essays he wrote during these years, such as "The Birth of Lucifer," "Aggressiveness as a Value," and "Dionysian Virtues."

105. Caillois, Archives interview.

106. Emile Durkheim, *The Elementary Forms of Religious Life*, trans. Joseph Ward Swain (New York: Free Press, 1965), 466.

107. Piel, *Rencontre*, 164.

108. See, for example, Raymond Charmet, rev. of *La Sociologie allemande contemporaine*, by Raymond Aron, rpt. in Béhar, *Inquisitions*, 52–54. Philippe Borgeaud succinctly explains: "The sacred, according to Rudolph Otto, is an agent of repulsion and seduction at the same time; it reveals a reality that is discordant but infinitely richer and deeper than the propositions of reason. It inevitably appealed to those people from the school of Durkheim and Mauss, who thereby understood that a magical world of fearsome and foundational powers challenged the bourgeois world of daily banality. For Durkheim himself, the sacred appeared as the product of collective effervescence—but to guarantee a peaceful and legitimately bourgeois form of civil practice. And yet, it became the time of 'sacred transgression' (to cite Roger Caillois's expression), parallel to that of mystical spirituality. A sacred that is no longer the product but the cause, origin, and even the motor of effervescence. . . . The being of the sacred comes to oppose the bourgeois state of non-being" (*Couple sacré/profane*, 413).

109. Georges Bataille, Roger Caillois, and Michel Leiris, "Declaration of the College of Sociology on the International Crisis," in Hollier, *The College of Sociology*, 45.

110. Caillois, "Winter," 35, 36.

111. Hollier, *Le Collège de sociologie*, 218.

112. Caillois, "Winter," 33. See Heimonet, *Politiques*, 98.

113. Hollier, *The College of Sociology*, 73.

114. Prevost, qtd. in Hollier, *Le Collège de sociologie*, 449; see Hollier's complex and interesting commentary of this discussion on the relation between democracy and the sacred.

115. Georges Bataille, "Nietzsche et les fascistes: Une réparation," *O.C.* 1 (1970): 465.

116. Aron, qtd. in Jacques Le Rider, *Nietzsche en France: De la fin du XIXe siècle au temps présent* (Paris: Presses Universitaires de France, 1999), 157; Le Rider is himself quoting from Vincent Descombes, *La Philosophie par gros temps* (Paris: Editions de Minuit, 1989), 82. Noting that one could hardly "suspect [Aron] of unreasoned Nietzscheism," Le Rider evokes the recent debate in which Descombes, hostile to the "irrationalism" of the College of Sociology, nonetheless said that Habermas lacked "historical sensibility" in condemning the demise of "ethical rationalism" in Bataille and others at the time (82).

117. Roger Caillois, "Naturaleza del hitlerismo," *Sur* (Oct. 1939): 106; emphasis added. See Hermann Rauschning, *The Revolution of Nihilism*, E. W. Dickens (1938; New York: Alliance, Longmans, Green, 1939); according to Stanley G. Payne, Rauschning "maintained that cultural and political deterioration had produced a condition of cultural and moral nihilism." *A History of Fascism 1914–1945* (Madison: University of Wisconsin Press, 1995), 452. See Hans Mayer, "The Rituals of Political Associations in Ger-

many of the Romantic Period" (1939) in Hollier, *The College of Sociology*, 267; and Roger Caillois, "Conséquences du nihilisme," in *Circonstancielles* (Paris: Gallimard, 1946).

118. Caillois, "Hiérarchie," 135, 125. Etiemble wrote to Caillois in August 1940: "Since you have so clearly written that there do not exist only two types of government, the fascist and the anarcho-democratic, why don't you try to define the general principles of the 3rd type, as you see it?" Letter to Roger Caillois, 28 Aug. 1940, c.e. 9, Bibliothèque Municipale, Vichy. Caillois's distrust of democracy also echoes Sorel's warning to the proletariat not to become "an inert mass destined to fall, as democracy, under the direction of politicians who live on the subordination of their electors" (*Reflections*, 271); see also Hollier, *Le Collège de sociologie*, 219–220.

119. Caillois, "Hiérarchie," 129–135.

120. Caillois, "Winter," 38.

121. Caillois, "Winter," 37 (trans. modified).

122. Qtd. in Michel Winock, *Le Siècle des intellectuels* (Paris: Seuil, 1999), 65.

123. Winock, *Siècle*, 65.

124. Nicole Racine makes an important point: "The tragic nature of the period [the 1930s] is amply illustrated by the fact that the great moral lesson bequeathed by the Dreyfus Affair—the defense of the individual against the reason of State—was clouded over by the political stakes of the day." "Références dreyfusiennes dans la gauche française," in *La Postérité de l'affaire Dreyfus*, ed. Michel Leymarie (Orléans: Presses Universitaires du Septentrion, 1998), 120. Replacing state with community could perhaps allow for an apt commentary on Caillois's views at the time.

125. In 1941, Caillois said that Lenin had been less inspired by Marx than by "Clausewitz, Netchaiev or certain Russian nihilists who formulated the principles of action of the 'active minorities.' To these names must be added that of Sorel." [Anon.], "Debates sobre temas sociológicos: Nuevas perspectivas en torno a 'Los irresponsables,' de Archibald Macleish," *Sur* (Sept. 1941): 87; see also Hollier, *The College of Sociology* 347–350; Hollier, *Le Collège de sociologie*, 847–851.

126. Sorel, *Reflections*, 271.

127. See Vilfredo Pareto and Arthur Livingston, *The Mind and Society: A Treatise on General Sociology* (1916), ed. and trans. Andrew Bongiorno(1935; New York: Harcourt Brace and Co., 1963).

128. Roger Caillois, letter to Jean Paulhan, 16 Dec. 1939, in Felgine and Perez, "Correspondance Jean Paulhan–Roger Caillois," 129; Roger Caillois, letter to Jean Paulhan, 5 Nov 1937, in Felgine and Perez, "Correspondance Jean Paulhan–Roger Caillois," 60.

129. In *Puissances du roman*, he explains that he is taking the word "whirlwind" from Moeller van den Brück (*Approches de l'imaginaire*, 230).

130. See Hollier, *Le Collège de Sociologie*, 849. "La Hiérarchie des êtres" thus cited communism as a potential new "order" for the future (326); this footnote was integrated into the body of the text when republished in *La Communion des forts*.

131. Caillois, introduction, to Hollier, *The College of Sociology*, 11.

132. Caillois, "Hiérarchie," 135.

133. See Bataille's two talks, "Attraction and Repulsion I: Tropisms, Sexuality and Tears"; "Attraction and Repulsion II: Social Structure," in Hollier, *The College of Sociology*, 103–124; see also Robert Hertz, *Death and The Right Hand* (Glencoe, Ill.: Free Press, 1960).

134. Caillois, Archives interview.

135. Caillois, *Man and the Sacred*, 13–37.

136. Caillois, *Man and the Sacred*, 37 (trans. modified).

137. Caillois, *Man and the Sacred*, 37.

138. Caillois, Archives interview.

139. I am adopting the English translation of these terms in *Man and the Sacred*.

140. Caillois, *Man and the Sacred*, 15.

141. Caillois, *Man and the Sacred*, 132. These sections are virtually identical. Caillois writes in both editions, "The dichotomy of sacred and profane no longer seems bound to the concept of the order of the universe, to the rhythm of its aging and regeneration, and to the opposition between neutral and/or inert objects, energies that animate or destroy them, that inherently attract or repel" (135).

142. Roger Caillois, *L'Homme et le sacré* (Leroux: Presses Universitaires de France, 1939), 139.

143. Caillois, *Man and the Sacred*, 136.

144. Two years earlier, Caillois and Paulhan had compared "The Winter Wind" to *Les Fleurs de Tarbes*; see Felgine and Perez, "Correspondance Jean Paulhan–Roger Caillois."

145. Laurent Jenny, preface, to "Correspondance Jean Paulhan–Roger Caillois," by Felgine and Perez, 18. An excellent, brief introduction to Paulhan is Silvio Yeschua, "Jean Paulhan et la 'rhétorique' du secret," in *Le Texte, le secret et l'exégèse*, intro. by Jean Starobinski (Paris: Champion, 1992), 29–50.

146. Caillois, *Man and the Sacred*, 132 (emphasis in 1st ed.; trans. modified).

147. Caillois, *Man and the Sacred*, 133, 175, 135 (emphasis in 1st ed.; trans. modified).

148. Caillois, *L'Homme et le sacré* (1st ed.), 135; the reference to the Nazis was excised from the postwar version and replaced by a clear reference to communism, or "party militants" (*Man and the Sacred*, 134).

149. Bataille, "'La Guerre,'" 52; Bataille, letter to Roger Caillois, 20 July 1939, in *Georges Bataille: Lettres à Roger Caillois* 113; see 115.

150. Louis Pinto writes that Bataille's apparent "*parti pris* of general and extreme subversion . . . ended up worrying his allies of the time [in particular Caillois, Kojève, Wahl]." *Les Neveux de Zarathoustra: La Réception de Nietzsche en France* (Paris: Seuil, 1995), 111.

151. Caillois, *Approches de l'imaginaire*, 59.

152. Caillois, "Hiérarchie," 128.

153. Georges Bataille, letter to Roger Caillois, 20 July 1939, in *Georges Bataille*, 110.

154. For the most informative survey, see Michel Surya, *Georges Bataille: La mort à l'oeuvre*, 2d ed. (Paris: Gallimard, 1992); see also Galletti, *Georges Bataille*.

155. Henri Dussat, letter to Jacques Chavy, 12 Jan. 1936, personal archives of Jacques Chavy.

156. Among the most important activities of Acéphale were the night-long, ritualized meditations in the Marly forest. Each member would stand next to one tree; altogether, these formed a circle around Bataille, who was standing next to an oak tree that had once been struck by lightning. This has been recounted in Surya, *Georges Bataille*; Galletti, *Georges Bataille*; and Patrick Waldberg, "Acéphalogramme," *Magazine littéraire* 321 (Apr. 1995): 158–159. This formation recalls Mauss's examples of potlatch: "One who has given a potlatch is compared to a tree or a mountain: 'I am the only great tree, I the chief. You here are right under me, . . . You surround me like a fence, . . . I am the first to give you property, . . . 'Raise the unattainable potlatch-pole, for this is the only thick tree, the only thick root.'" Marcel Mauss, *The Gift: Forms and Functions of Exchange in Archaic Societies* (1907), trans. Ian Cunnison (New York: Norton, 1967), 108.

157. René Chenon, personal archives; the original text reads: "Reproche de B.[a-taille] à Heid[egger]. Ce dernier atteint trop *rapidement* le néant." See also Galletti, *Georges Bataille*.

158. Jules Monnerot, letter to Roger Caillois, Nov. 1935, in Caillois, *Roger Caillois: "Cahiers pour un temps,"* 196.

159. Georges Ambrosino, letter to Imre Kelemen, personal archives of Jacques Chavy.

160. "Constitution du 'journal intérieur,'" in Galletti, *Georges Bataille*, 341. Galletti suggests they were responding to "For a Militant Orthodoxy." Dubief's remarks, in particular, suggest that Caillois was already more specifically concerned with the attitudes of an elective aristocracy and its relation to power. See Galletti, "Un Inédit de la société secrète Acéphal: Georges Ambrosino, *La constitution de l'être est éminemment para-doxale*," *Europe* 859–860 (Nov.–Dec. 2000): 85.

161. Georges Ambrosino qtd. in Galletti, "Inédit," 88.

162. Henri Dubief, "Critique d'une position de Roger Caillois," Lia Andler personal archives (3 pp.): 1, 2. In the epigraph to "For a Militant Orthodoxy" and in "The Winter Wind," Caillois refers to Baudelaire "imagining the formation of a new aristocracy, based on a mysterious grace that would involve neither work nor wealth" ("Winter," 38). See also "Paris, a Modern Myth."

163. Georges Bataille to Isabelle Waldberg" [*L'Etoile Alcool: Texte de méditation*], in Galletti, *Georges Bataille*, 537. See Georges Bataille, "Joy in the Face of Death," in Hollier, *The College of Sociology*, 322–327.

164. Personal interview with a former member of Acéphale, 1992, who requested anonymity; what he said, in the original French: "La chose fondamentale, c'est *que* il devait y avoir une victime, tuée, par un des membres du groupe, volontaire. *Mais*, ça n'a pas fonctionné pour une raison simple, c'est *que* on n'a pas trouvé de volontaire pour exécuter. . . . Dans le *groupe* on s'engageait à être la victime *possible* et l'assassin *possible* mais *sans* qu'il y ait d'autres précisions." The term *adeption* was explained in a personal interview with Jacques Chavy, a former member of Acéphale, Jan. 1998, Paris.

165. Caillois, Archives interview 4. On the tensions between Caillois and Bataille, see Bataille, *Georges Bataille*.

166. Qtd. in Hector Bianciotti, "Le Dernier Encyclopédiste: Roger Caillois," *Le Nouvel Observateur* 521 (4 Nov. 1974): 73.

167. Caillois, *Approches de l'imaginaire*, 59.

168. Marina Galletti, "Secret et sacré chez Leiris et Bataille," in *Bataille–Leiris: L'intenable assentiment au monde*, ed. Francis Marmande (Paris: Belin, 1999), 133.

169. Roger Caillois, rev. of *Nietzsche, suivi de textes choisis*, by Henri Lefebvre, *Sur* (Nov. 1939): 78 ("it would be abhorrent that the doctrine of the man who said, 'Reject consolations,' should become a consolation, and of the worst kind").

170. Georges Bataille, "Ce que j'ai à dire. . . ." in Galletti, *Georges Bataille*, 332, 333.

171. Roger Caillois, "Résurrection de Corneille," *Nouvelle revue française* (Oct. 1938): 662.

172. Caillois, *Approches de l'imaginaire*, 59.

173. Personal interview with former member of Acéphale. What he said, in the original French: "Effectivement le bourreau devait . . . être protégé vis-à-vis de la loi, et [il] y avait eu des discussions effectivement entre nous pour trouver . . . *que* c'était quelque chose qui n'était pas bien, que d'essayer de protéger celui qui allait procéder au meurtre."

174. Caillois, "L' Aridité," 10.

175. In this respect, I disagree with Hollier (*Le Collège de sociologie*, 541), who says that Caillois is challenging Bataille by differentiating anthropological carnival from political revolution. It seems to me that Caillois, while confirming this distinction, is nonetheless intent to chart an enduring structure in the collective imagination.

176. Hollier, *Absent*, 13.

177. Roger Caillois, *Ponce Pilate* (1960; Paris: Gallimard, 1978), 142–145.

178. Roger Caillois, "Notes pour un itinéraire de Roger Caillois," in *Roger Caillois: "Cahiers pour un temps,"* 168.

179. Caillois, *Communion*, 13. Meyer Schapiro's review of this work in "French Reaction in Exile" is not inaccurate in its condemnation of Caillois's ideal of a "spiritual power," although this is to some extent a Trotskyist attack, declaring that "the victory or defeat of socialism in France will be felt everywhere" (40), or decrying Caillois's "shallow and ignorant critique of Marxism, confused for the most part with Stalinism" (36). Schapiro is wrong, though, about Caillois's debt to Renan (see "Duties and Privileges of French Writers Abroad") and in warning that Caillois's "call for the creation of a secret, militant group, hating the masses" is preparing a "practical and sinister role" for intellectual "doctrinaire[s] of order" in postwar France (42). Schapiro also errs when he says that Caillois, like Auguste Comte, "lays great weight on the cohesion of society through sacraments, and I am told that he has attempted, together with certain surrealists, to create modern rites and rituals" (31). Schapiro is presumably confusing Caillois with Bataille and rumors about Contre-Attaque and/or Acéphale. Indeed, his essay could well be read, in large part, as an unwitting discussion of the College of Sociology (with which he was clearly unfamiliar). For one thing, Schapiro condemns the ahistorical as well as formal, aesthetic, and cultural emphasis of Caillois's essays, which reflect "the growing incapacity or unwillingness of sociolo-

gists to deal with class conflict" (34). And he proffers criticism—justified, albeit doctrinaire—of Caillois's lack of sociological rigor. What would he have said about Bataille's
writings!

180. Roger Caillois, "The Art of St.-John Perse," trans. Haakon M. Chevalier, *Sewanee Review* 53.2 (spring 1945): 202.

181. Felgine, *Caillois*, 205.

182. Caillois, qtd. in Felgine, *Caillois*, 203.

183. See Felgine, *Caillois*, 207.

184. Roger Caillois, letter to Victoria Ocampo, 17 Aug. 1939, in *Correspondance Roger
Caillois–Victoria Ocampo*, ed. Odile Felgine (Paris: Stock, 1997), 77. In 1935, Caillois,
unlike Bataille, had already hinted at the self-destructive nature of fascist leadership
(C. Frank, "Contre-Attaque").

185. Caillois, Archives interview. See also Felgine, *Caillois*, 207.

186. For details on Caillois's relation to Ocampo, see, in particular, Felgine, *Correspondance Roger Caillois–Victoria Ocampo*.

187. See John King, *Sur: A Study of the Argentine Literary Journal and Its Role in the
Development of a Culture, 1931–1970* (Cambridge, England: Cambridge University Press,
1986).

188. See Marina Galletti, "Roger Caillois en Argentine," in Jenny, *Roger Caillois, la
pensée aventurée*, 139–174.

189. King, *Sur*, 61, 64.

190. King, *Sur*, 95.

191. Roger Caillois, "Testimonio francés," *Sur* (Oct. 1939): 51.

192. Roger Caillois, letter to Jean Paulhan, 11 Nov. 1939, in Felgine and Perez, "Correspondance Jean Paulhan–Roger Caillois," 125.

193. Roger Caillois, "Défense de la république," in *Circonstancielles*, 20.

194. See Claude Nicolet, *L'Idée républicaine en France: Essai d'histoire critique (1789–
1924)* (Paris: Gallimard, 1982).

195. Caillois, *Circonstancielles*, 24.

196. Louis Tillier, rev. of *Lettres françaises*, *France libre* 18 (Apr. 1942): 506.

197. Caillois, *Circonstancielles*, 12.

198. Caillois, "Testimonio," 51.

199. Caillois, *Circonstancielles*, 129.

200. *Sur* published a list of detective writers censored by the fascists in Rome,
surmising, "Perhaps fascism considers that a certain inquisitive desire awakened by
detective novels is unhealthy." "El detective en desgracia—'Roma'" *Sur* 59 (Aug.
1939): 81.

201. Jorge Luis Borges, rev. of *Le Roman policier*, *Sur* 91 (Apr. 1942): 57; trans. Emir
Rodriguez Monegal and Alastair Reid and rpt. in *Borges: A Reader* (New York: Dutton,
1981), 148. Borges criticized Caillois's sociohistorical, and what he considered determinist, claims about the genre arising with the French secret police because he himself
defined it as an Anglo-Saxon creation (originating with Poe).

202. Paulhan, *Fleurs*, 168.

203. René Etiemble, rev. of *Le Roman policier*, by Roger Caillois, *Lettres françaises* 10 (1 Oct 1943): 68.

204. Caillois, *Approches de l'imaginaire*, 167, 230.

205. Caillois, *Approches de l'imaginaire*, 230 (emphasis added); 152.

206. Caillois, *Communion*, 13. Sounding closer here to "Sociology of the Intellectual" than to "The Winter Wind," he defines such virtue as the capacity for renunciation, or detachment from social goods.

207. Jean Wahl, letter to Roger Caillois, Mount Holyoke College, 6 Mar. 1944, c.w. 3, Special Collections, Bibliothèque Municipale, Vichy.

208. Roger Caillois, *Ensayo sobre el espíritu de las sectas* (Mexico City: El Colegio de Mexico, "Jornadas," 1945); rpt. in Roger Caillois, *Instincts et sociétés* (Paris: Gonthier, 1964), 114, 72; this section was first published in New York as "Esprit des sectes," *Renaissance* 2–3 (1944–1945).

209. *Le Monde*'s future editor, Hubert Beuve-Méry, ran Uriage in 1941 until it was suppressed by Laval in January 1943 after the unification of France.

210. Bernard Comte, "Uriage [Ecole des cadres d']," in Jacques Julliard and Michel Winock, *Dictionnaire des intellectuels français* (Paris: Seuil, 1996), 1136.

211. [Caillois], "Pronunciou Sua Anunciada Conferencia o Famoso Escritor Francês Roger Caillois," *Diario* 16 Sept. 1943, Special Collections, Bibliothèque Municipale, Vichy.

212. Claire Paulhan, "Desjardins (Paul)," in Julliard and Winock, *Dictionnaire des intellectuels français*, 358–359.

213. [Caillois], "Prononciou." For Caillois's less idealized comments about Pontigny in 1937, see Felgine, *Caillois*, 144–145. Given his inquiry about spiritual power to Jean Wahl, note that the previous year "L'Actualité littéraire" of *Lettres française* records: "Mount Holyoke *(Massachusetts)*. Gustave Cohen is organizing meetings of the sort Paul Desjardins ran at Pontigny. Jean Wahl reads poems, there, that he wrote in France, during his stay in a concentration camp [Drancy]." *Lettres francaises* (Feb. 1943): 82. See also Jeffrey Mehlman, *Emigré New York: French Intellectuals in Wartime Manhattan, 1940–1944* (Baltimore, Md.: Johns Hopkins University Press, 2000), 101.

214. Roger Caillois, letter to Victoria Ocampo, 26 Oct. 1945, in Felgine, *Correspondance Roger Caillois–Victoria Ocampo* 243.

215. Caillois replaced Raymond Aron at the helm of *La France libre*, joined the journal *Confluences*, and codirected the short-lived journal *La Licorne*, while also publishing in *Fontaine, Arche, Constellation, Terre des hommes, Cahiers de la Pléiade, Table ronde*, and *Liberté de l'esprit*, among others.

216. He also translated such writers as Gabriela Mistral, Antonio Porchia, Josep Carner, and Pablo Neruda.

217. See Felgine, *Caillois*, 296.

218. Personal interview with Chastel.

219. Here, he encountered Alena Vichrova, a Czeckoslovakian refugee, who became his new wife in 1957; the marriage to Yvette Billod had dissolved soon after their return to France.

220. Alexandre Pajon, "In Search of a Journal; Caillois and *Diogenes*," *Diogenes* 160 (Oct.–Dec. 1992): 114.

221. Roger Caillois, *Babel: Orgueil, confusion et ruine de la littérature* (Paris: Gallimard, 1948), 148, 375.

222. Roger Judrin (Aimé Patri), rev. of *Babel*, by Roger Caillois, *Paru* 47 (Oct. 1948): 54. He calls Caillois's book the third "great trial of contemporary literature"—the others being Julien Benda's *La France byzantine* (with "metaphysical views about the primacy of reason over sensitivity" and Sartre's *Qu'est-ce que la littérature?* (or "revolutionary *engagement*") (54).

223. Caillois, Archives interview.

224. Michel Beaujour, *Terreur et rhétorique: Breton, Bataille, Leiris, Paulhan, Barthes & Cie* (Paris: Jean-Michel Place, 1999), 21.

225. Roger Caillois, letter to Jean Paulhan, 13 Aug 1947, in Felgine and Perez, "Correspondance Jean Paulhan–Roger Caillois," 172.

226. Maurice Blanchot, *La Part du feu* (Paris: Gallimard, 1949), 316, 328.

227. Caillois, *Babel*, 160.

228. Roger Caillois, "Sur l'indépendance du poète," *Bouteille à la mer* 66 (1950): 12.

229. See the essays in Roger Caillois, *Chroniques de Babel* (Paris: Denoël/Gonthier, 1981).

230. Caillois, *Chroniques*, 77

231. Jean Paulhan, *De la Paille et du grain*, vol. 5 of *Jean Paulhan: Oeuvres complètes* (Paris: Cercle du Livre Précieux, 1970); an initial version was published in the *Cahiers de la Pléiade* (1947–1948). The "Actualité littéraire" of *Lettres françaises* already voiced similar views in January 1945: "The National Council of Writers votes to ratify a motion that would draw 'the Government's attention to the danger incurred by letting the complicity on the part of a certain number of writers during the Occupation go unpunished.' During the discussion, a voice is heard, rising to defend 'the writer's right to error': it is the voice of Jean Paulhan, whose attitude was precisely, as we know, courageous and exemplary. Coquettishness? No, the concern not to resemble those whom we have fought" (54).

232. In Caillois, *Circonstancielles*.

233. Caillois, qtd. in Felgine, *Caillois*, 293.

234. Georges Bataille, "Problèmes du surréalisme," *O.C.* 7 (1976): 456.

235. Bataille, "La Guerre," 48.

236. Denis Hollier, "La Fin de sommations," *Critique* (Aug.–Sept. 1996): 593.

237. Georges Bataille, letter to Georges Ambrosino, Vézelay, 2 Nov. 1946, Esther Ambrosino, private archives. The original French reads: "quiconque ne fait pas essentiellement de son temps et de ses [forces et] ressources un usage dilapidateur [est en train de] se réduit lui-même [à la] en servitude. . . . [l]organisation ne devrait avoir aucune consistance saisissable: le *collège* devrait même être davantage qu'un *collège* une *absence de collège*."

238. Georges Bataille, "La Religion surréaliste (24 février 1948)," *O.C.* 7 (1970): 393.

239. Caillois, *Rencontres*, 26.

240. Caillois, "Lettre du rédacteur en chef," 142.

241. Roger Caillois, *Quatre essais de sociologie contemporaine* (Paris: Olivier Perrin, 1951), 7.

242. Caillois, *Man and the Sacred*, 173, 179.

243. Caillois, *Man and the Sacred*, 171, 158, 207 (trans. modified), 162, 162 (trans. modified). See Johan Huizinga, *Homo ludens: A Study of the Play Element in Culture* (1944; New York: J. and J. Harper Editions, 1970).

244. Caillois, Archives interview; see also Pajon, "In Search."

245. See Caillois, *Man, Play and Games*; in particular, the category of controlled vertigo, *ilinx*.

246. Roger Caillois, "De la Féerie à la science-fiction," in *Obliques* (Paris: Stock, 1975), 18; originally published as preface, to *Anthologie du fantastique* (Paris: Club Français du Livre, 1958).

247. Roger Caillois, introduction, to *Contes Étranges*, by Prosper Mérimée (Paris: Vialetay, 1972), xi. See Tzvetan Todorov, *The Fantastic: A Structural Approach to a Literary Genre* (Ithaca, NY: Cornell University Press, 1973).

248. Caillois, "Féerie," 18, 34.

249. Caillois, *Approches de l'imaginaire*, 105.

250. Roger Caillois, "Actualité des Kenningar," *Nouvelle nouvelle revue française* 30 (June 1955); rpt. as "L'Enigme et l'image," in *Approches de la poésie*, 175–191.

251. Roger Caillois, *Approches de la poésie*, 180, 179, 186, 102. Caillois described "l'un dans l'autre" as "a kind of experimental generalization, or systematization of Reverdy's famous thesis about the image"—calling for the maximum distance between the two terms of the comparison (177). See André Breton, *L'Un dans l'autre* (Paris: Eric Losfeld, 1970).

252. Roger Caillois, "Problèmes du rêve," *Bulletin de la société française de philosophie* (July–Sept. 1957): 112.

253. Roger Caillois, *L'Incertitude qui vient des rêves* (Paris: Gallimard, 1956), 87.

254. Jenny, preface to "Correspondance Jean Paulhan–Roger Caillois," by Felgine and Perez, 21.

255. Montesquieu, qtd. in Caillois, *Rencontres*, 105; we also find this quote in Caillois's introduction to *Quatre essais de sociologie contemporaine*. Moreover, at UNESCO he could not sign "any kind of manifesto or participate in any kind of political activity" (Caillois, Archives interview).

256. Felgine, *Caillois*, 363; she is paraphrasing Roger Caillois, "La Révolution cachée" (The hidden revolution), *Le Monde* 13 June 1968.

257. Alain Peyrefitte, letter to Roger Caillois, Jan. 1975, C.P. 8, Bibliothèque Municipale, Vichy.

258. Popper, qtd. in Lévi-Strauss, Claude (and Roger Caillois), "Discours prononcés dans la séance publique tenue par l'Académie Française pour la réception de M. Claude Lévi-Strauss le . . . 27 juin 1974, Institut de France, Académie Française" (Paris: Institut de France, 1972), 35.

259. In 1936 he already viewed "generalization" as a rigorous counterpart to what he deemed the "supple" Hegelian dialectics deployed by his entourage.

260. Caillois, "Illusions à rebours II," 66, 68, 67. He refers, for example, to the Surrealists' common "transference" to the Dalai Lama in rejection of the Pope. Clearly, this did not involve the ironic juxtapositions charted by Clifford's "ethnographic surrealism": "For every local custom or truth there was always an exotic alternative, a possible juxtaposition or incongruity" (*Predicament*, 120).

Caillois's assertions prompted Lévi-Strauss's angry response that he only frequented Breton and the Surrealists in New York during the war, and thus well after the start of his ethnographic career in 1936.

261. Pace, *Claude Lévi-Strauss*, 95.

262. Qtd. in Christine Ockrent, "Qu'avez-vous fait de vos vingt-ans," interview with Claude Lévi-Strauss, Paris, Antenne 2, 21 May 1990.

263. Caillois, "Illusions à rebours II," 68. I think Caillois is referring to Lévy-Bruhl's category of "primitive mentality" rather than to actual people and their cognitive framework; throughout the 1930s, he frequently questioned the validity of this very category (see, for example, "The Function of Myth"). Denis Saurat was a writer who suggested that the Mayan Indians had achieved greater breakthroughs than those of Western mathematicians.

264. Roger Caillois, "After Six Years of a Doubtful Combat," trans. Muriel McKeon, *Diogenes* 26 (Apr.–June 1959): 3–5 Here he wrote: "It is clear that it cannot be a question of returning to the superficial and qualitative analogies from which the sciences have had to free themselves in order to institute a system of methodical, controlled, and perfectible knowledge. From this point of view the ambitions of the philosophers of the Middle Ages and of the scholars of the Renaissance constitute a lure which is the more formidable because it corresponds to a permanent need of the spirit, particularly binding today, and seems, therefore, to offer a quick solution that is fascinating to minds seduced in advance. The tables of concordances, in which a Paracelsus distributes the qualities of the phenomena, are no longer admissible, nor is even the analogical, essentially visual science of which Leonardo dreamed when he drew a head of hair like a river, a mountain like drapery. . . . Leonardo sought out the archetypes of the phenomena, as did Goethe at a later date. He was wrong to seek them with the senses, and particularly with sight, the sense most easily victimized by appearances. That was the work of the painter and the poet, not of the scientist, since for the latter the real task consists, on the contrary, to determine the hidden correspondences—invisible and unimaginable to the profane. They will very rarely be those which seem evident, logical, and probable. These hidden relations articulate, rather, phenomena which seem at first to have nothing in common" (5).

265. Gaston Bachelard, *Le Nouvel Esprit scientifique* (1934; Paris: Presses Universitaires de France, 1984).

266. Jenny, preface to *Roger Caillois, la pensée aventurée*, 7.

267. Caillois, *Approches de la poésie*, 10.

268. Caillois, quoting himself in *Approches de la poésie*, 224.

269. Caillois, "Places et limites de la poésie jusqu'à, selon et depuis Baudelaire," 18–19.

270. Caillois, *Fleuve*, 163. See Breton's famous Hegelian dictum in the *Second Manifesto*: "Everything tends to make us believe that there exists a certain point of the mind at which life and death, the real and the imagined, past and future, the communicable and the incommunicable, high and low, cease to be perceived as contradictions" (*Manifestoes*, 123).

271. Roger Caillois, "Thèmes fondamentaux chez Jorge Luis Borges," *Cahiers de l'Herne* 2 (1964): 218; rpt. in Caillois, *Rencontres*. Other "perfect encyclopedists"—"Jules Verne, Arnold Toynbee, Saint-John Perse (a deliberately disparate list)"—are likewise "eccentric authors, because they do not take any particular, local or temporal center of references as absolute. They are and wish to be the beneficiaries of the world's totality, the heirs of a universal humanism, from which they freely choose what they need" ("Thèmes," 229).

272. Roger Caillois, "'Le Dernier Encyclopédiste': Roger Caillois," interview with Hector Bianciotti, *Nouvel Observateur* (4 Nov. 1974): 72.

273. Roger Caillois, "Les Traces," *Preuves* (July 1961): 24.

274. Caillois, *Récurrences*, 67.

275. Caillois, *Approches de la poésie*, 14.

276. Paul Ricoeur, "The Power of Speech: Science and Poetry," trans. Robert F. Scuka, *Philosophy Today* (spring 1985): 69. He claims that the language of science, which is "exact, coherent and verifiable," lets us "fashion a model of reality transparent to our logic, homogeneous with our reason and, in this sense, with ourselves"; whereas poetry "creates or induces a new manner of finding oneself, of feeling oneself living in the world" (69). He concludes that "poetry preserves science by impeding the production of this fanaticism of the manipulable" (69).

277. Paul de Man, "Poetic Nothingness: On a Hermetic Sonnet by Mallarmé," trans. Richard Howard, in *Paul de Man: Critical Writings 1953–1978*, ed. and introduction by Lindsay Waters (Minneapolis: University of Minnesota Press, 1989), 28.

278. For example, for all that he criticized Breton's astrology, Caillois lists "ancient Chinese" theories of microcosms, the models or *signatures* of Paracelsus, together with Pascal's idea of the two infinites as conceptual guidelines for his lapidary meditations in *Pierres réfléchies* (9).

279. Roger Caillois, "La Dissymétrie" (1973), rpt. in *Cohérences aventureuses* (Paris: Gallimard, 1976); Caillois, *Approches de la poésie*, 252; here, he writes that metaphor "presupposes both a hidden identity and an apparent disparity that makes the comparison of the metaphor's two terms unexpected, if not scandalous. At the same time, the metaphor reveals the concealed connivance of this comparison, whereby the metaphor is justified and celebrated, ultimately becoming one of the many and interconnected signs of the world's coherence" (*Approches*, 252).

280. Referring to the hermetic, ironic, and aesthetic formalism of the avant-garde in the wake of Mallarmé, José Ortega y Gasset had championed the "style" of "dehumanized" art, by which he meant, in 1925, "aesthetic sentiments" at the expense of "hu-

man pathos": "the art of which we speak is inhuman not only because it contains no things human, but also because it is an explicit act of dehumanization," *The Dehumanization of Art and Other Essays on Art, Culture, and Literature*, trans. Helene Weyl (1948; Princeton, NJ: Princeton University Press, 1968), 22. Caillois entirely disagreed with Ortega's theory of the novel *(Ideas sobre la novela)* during the war, but in 1960 he and Camus planned to coedit Ortega y Gasset's *Oeuvres choisies* (Selected works) in an eight-volume translation project (never carried out) for Gallimard. See Roger Caillois, letter to Victoria Ocampo, 31 July [1960], in Felgine, *Correspondance Roger Caillois–Victoria Ocampo*, 360.

281. Caillois, *Fleuve*, 207, 216.

282. Jean Starobinski, "Saturne au ciel de pierres," *Nouvelle nouvelle revue française* 320 (1979): 178; rpt. in *Europe* 859–860 (Nov.–Dec. 2000).

283. Caillois, *Approches de la poésie*, 83.

1. Introduction to "Testimony (Paul Eluard)"

This piece was reprinted in *Les Cahiers de Chronos: Roger Caillois*, ed. Jean-Clarence Lambert (Paris: Editions de la Différence, 1991).

1. See Helena Lewis, *The Politics of Surrealism* (New York: Paragon House, 1988).

2. Caillois, Archives interview.

2. Introduction to "The Praying Mantis"

This essay was revised and reprinted in *La Mante religieuse* (Paris: Aux amis du livre, 1937); in *Le Mythe et l'homme* (Paris: Gallimard, 1938). See *The Necessity of Mind* for the first, unpublished version.

1. Esther Ambrosino, who attended this lecture, recalled that Caillois talked about the praying mantis, perhaps among other things (personal interview, May 1992, Paris). See "Animal Societies," *Roger Caillois* (18 Dec, 1937), in Hollier, *The College of Sociology*, 94–97.

2. Roger Caillois, "Un Roman cornélien," *Nouvelle revue française* (Mar. 1938): 481.

3. Caillois notes in *The Necessity of Mind* that in 1924 Breton was planning to found a publishing house whose insignia (hence on every book) was the sketch of a praying mantis he had commissioned from Max Ernst (*Nécessité*, 170).

4. André Breton, "Introduction aux *Contes bizarres* d'Achim d'Arnim," in *Oeuvres complètes*, ed. Marguerite Bonnet (Paris: Gallimard, 1992), 359.

5. On this use of the term "lyrical," see Laurent Jenny: "'Lyricism' no longer refers either to a subjective outpouring nor to any specific literary form. As early as 1929, Dali redefined it as 'one of man's most violent [aspirations]' which can be approached only by 'instinct' and 'the most irrational faculties of the mind.' This renewed acceptation of the word *lyricism* is made still more precise by Roger Caillois, who, since 1933, had been working on an essay on 'mental necessity.'" "From Breton to Dali: The Adventures of Automatism," *October* (winter 1989): 109.

6. Caillois, Archives interview.

7. Caillois, *Nécessité*, 27.

8. Nadeau, *Histoire du surréalisme*, 153.

9. Elisabeth Roudinesco, *Histoire de la psychanalyse en France 1925–1985* (Paris: Seuil, 1986), 2: 126; Nadeau, *Histoire*, 148.

10. Caillois, *Nécessité*, 24.

11. Pierre Janet, *Les Névroses* (Paris: Flammarion, 1909), 367, 288.

12. Caillois's essay "The Natural Fantastic" (1970) offers a broad sense of the seminal role played by his early writings on the praying mantis without recalling his conceptual framework of 1932–1934.

13. Caillois, *Nécessité*, 153.

14. André Gide, *Corydon* (Paris: Gallimard, 1924), 52–78; see his lengthy footnote 76–77.

3. Introduction to "Letter to André Breton" and "Literature in Crisis"

First published in *Procès intellectuel de l'art* (Marseille: Cahiers du Sud, 1935).

1. Gaëtan Picon, "Les Essais de Roger Caillois," *Fontaine* 54 (summer 1946): 268.

2. Caillois, *Approches de l'imaginaire*, 51.

3. Bachelard, *Le Nouvel Esprit scientifique*, 11, 10, 17.

4. I am drawing from W. H. Auden's poem *Rimbaud*: "His senses systematically deranged." *W. H. Auden: A Selection by the Author* (London: Penguin, 1958), 63. For Bachelard's comments about Caillois's contribution to exploring the imaginative dimension of biological evolution, see his *Lautréamont* (Paris: José Corti, 1939), 144.

5. Caillois, *Approches de l'imaginaire*, 39; emphasis added. He illustrates such a "vital" perspective with the familiar paradigm of modern physics, that of infinitely flat beings placed on a huge sphere: "They can only *imagine* it as finite, which it is indeed for three-dimensional creatures; but for them, everything *vital* occurs as if it were infinite" (40).

6. In "Literature in Crisis" Caillois contrasts "pure science" and a "science of art's imaginative content"; without elaborating, he implies elsewhere in *Art on Trial by Intellect* that "pure science" studies the mathematical, formal structures of man and his milieu, and that it involves "the principle of economy" (*Approches de l'imaginaire*, 44). Without naming any poet or theory, *The Necessity of Mind* refers to "the exceptionally unintelligent notion of *pure poetry*" (Caillois, *Nécessité*, 18).

7. Caillois, *Approches de l'imaginaire*, 46–47. Such complexity makes art useless as strategic, political propaganda, argues Caillois, specifically questioning, in this regard, Sorel's *Reflections on Violence* (*Approches de l'imaginaire*, 47); a few years later, his views had apparently changed (see "Paris, a Modern Myth," in this volume).

8. Given that Ortega y Gasset was widely discussed in France in the 1920s, it is not inconceivable that Caillois had this social approach to art in mind.

9. Ortega y Gasset, "Dehumanization," 52.

10. Caillois, *Approches de l'imaginaire*, 50.

4. Introduction to "Mimicry and Legendary Psychasthenia"

This essay was revised and reprinted in *Le Mythe et l'homme* (Paris: Gallimard, 1938). For a different translation, see "Mimicry and Legendary Psychasthenia," trans. John Shipley, *October* 31 (winter 1984): 17–32.

1. Caillois, *Approches de l'imaginaire*, 45.

2. It was thus a forerunner to the "profane environment of conservation and economy," which *Man and the Sacred* would later oppose to "the fundamental ambiguity of the sacred" (Caillois, *Man and the Sacred*, 136).

3. This example challenges Hollier's earlier cited claim that "no matter how mimesis is interpreted, death is a mask for life, a mask behind which life protects its difference by pretending to renounce that difference" (*Absent*, 43).

4. Bataille, "Notion" 311, 310. For psychoanalysis, "[the gift] symbolizes excretion which itself is linked to death in conformity with the fundamental connection between eroticism and sadism" (122).

5. Rosalind Krauss, *The Optical Unconscious* (Cambridge, MA: MIT Press, 1994), 179, 155, 183.

6. Bachelard, *Nouvel*, 182.

7. Gaston Bachelard, *L'Expérience de l'espace dans la physique contemporaine* (Paris: Presses Universitaires de France, 1937), 5–6.

8. When Bachelard contributed "Le Surrationalisme" to *Inquisitions*, he offered a more radical view of scientific subjectivity: "If one does not put one's reason at risk in the course of an experiment, then this experiment is not worth experiencing" (Béhar, *Inquisitions*, 5).

9. Jacques Lacan, "The Mirror Stage as Formative of the Function of the I," in *Ecrits: A Selection*, trans. Alan Sheridan (New York: Norton, 1977), 3.

10. Jacques Lacan, rev. of *Le Temps vécu*, by E. Minkowski, *Recherches philosophiques* 5 (1935–1936): 431.

5. Introduction to "Review of L'Homme, cet inconnu, by Dr. Alexis Carrel"

1. Denis Pelletier, "Carrel (Alexis)," in Juilliard and Winock, *Dictionnaire des intellectuels français*, 221.

2. Jean Paulhan, letter to Roger Caillois, 15 Jan. 1936, in Fergine and Perez, "Correspondance Jean Paulhan–Roger Caillois," 34.

6. Introduction to "The Function of Myth"

This essay was first published as "Le Mythe et l'homme," *Recherches philosophiques* 5 (1935–1936).

1. Sorel, *Reflections*, 128.

2. Raymond Aron praised Caillois's "philosophical intent" to "show the complementary nature of sociological, psychological, and psychoanalytic explanations that too

many specialists like to pit against each other," Rev. of *L'Expérience mystique et les symboles chez les primitifs*, by Lucien Lévy-Bruhl; *La Conscience morale et l'expérience morale* and *La Loi morale: les lois naturelles et les lois sociales*, by Gaston Richard; *Le Mythe et l'homme*, by Roger Caillois; *Psychologie des masses*, by André Joussain; *Morphologie sociale*, by Maurice Halbwachs; *Le Problème des classes*, by Jean Lhomme; *La Notion de progrès devant la science actuelle*, by Centre International de Synthèse; *La Civilisation*, by Félix Sartiaux; *Essai d'une histoire comparée des peuples d'Europe*, by Charles Seignobos, *Zeitschrift für Soziologie* 7 (1938): 414.

3. Caillois, *Rencontres*, 205; the essay originally appeared in *Le Monde*, 4 Jan. 1969. Dumézil recalled for Didier Eribon how he began with the concept of "cycle" and then moved to "system"; his subsequent shift to "structure" led him to be later viewed, erroneously so, in his opinion, as a "precursor, if not as the first theoretician of structuralism." *Entretiens avec Didier Eribon* (Paris: Gallimard, 1987), 118.

4. René Etiemble, "Einstein, Dumézil," in *Hygiène des lettres* (Paris: Gallimard, 1958), 243; his final phrase evokes Breton's famous appropriation of Lautréamont's image.

5. Roger Caillois, rev. of *Mythologie universelle*, by Alexandre Haggerty Krappe, *Cahiers du Sud* (Apr. 1935): 331; he adds that this project is "chimerical, in the current state of documentation" (331).

6. On the general shift from Bergson to Nietzsche as the dominant form of philosophical anti-intellectualism at this time, see Pinto, who explains that "heroic pathos seemed more attuned to the intellectual demands of a somber period than were those cautiously optimistic lessons of wisdom proposed by . . . [Bergson's] *Les Deux sources de la morale et de la religion* [The two sources of morality and religion] (1932)" (*Neveux*, 86).

7. Marcel Mauss, *The Gift*; Mauss, "Essai sur le don," in *Sociologie et anthropologie* (Paris: Presses Universitaires de France, 1989), 273 (not in English version). In his "Place de la sociologie appliquée ou politique" (1927), the committed socialist wrote: "We will have achieved our primary goal when a positive political policy—distinct from but inspired by a thoroughgoing and concrete sociology—will be able to put it into practice." *Essais de sociologie* (Paris: Minuit, 1969), 79.

8. Roger Caillois, rev. of *Le Tabou de l'inceste*, by Lord Raglan, *Cahiers du Sud* (Nov. 1935): 778; emphasis added.

9. See Georges Bataille, "Chronique nietzschéenne," *O.C.* 1 (1970): 489.

10. Georges Bataille, "The Sorcerer's Apprentice," in Hollier, *The College of Sociology*, 22.

11. Georges Bataille, *Literature and Evil*, trans. Alastair Hamilton (1973; New York: Marion Boyars, 1985), 25.

7. Introduction to "The Noon Complex"

The articles constituting Caillois's study as a whole include "Les Spectres de midi dans la démonologie slave: les faits," *Revue des études slaves* 16 (1936): 18–37; "Les Spectres de midi dans la démonologie slave: interprétation des faits," *Revue des études slaves* 17 (1937):

81–92; "Les Démons de midi," *Revue de l'histoire des religions* 115 (March–June 1937): 142–173; 116 (July–August 1937): 54–83; 116 (September–December 1937): 143–186. Reprinted in toto as *Les Démons de midi* (Montpellier: Fata Morgana, 1991).

1. Roger Caillois, *Les Démons de midi* (Montpellier: Fata Morgana, 1991), 11.
2. He visited the Ukraine and Czechoslovakia in 1934 with the ethnographer P. Bogatyrev, a member of the Prague Linguistic Circle.
3. See Caillois, *Démons*, 10.
4. Caillois, *Démons*, 10.
5. Philippe Borgeaud, "Spectres et démons de midi," *Europe* 859–60 (Nov.–Dec. 2000): 114–25.
6. Georges Bataille, *La Part maudite* (1949; Paris: Minuit, 1967), 66.
7. "Préface," *Minotaure* 9 (15 Oct. 1936).
8. Roger Caillois, "Théorie de la fête," *Nouvelle revue française* (Jan. 1940); qtd. in Hollier, *The College of Sociology*, 302. See also Marcel Mauss, *Seasonal Variations of the Eskimo* (Boston: Routledge and Kegan Paul, 1979).

8. Introduction to "For a Militant Orthodoxy"

This essay was reprinted as "Conclusion: Pour une fonction unitaire de l'esprit," in *Le Mythe et l'homme* (Paris: Gallimard, 1938); in *Inquisitions: Fac-similé de la revue augmenté de documents inédits*, ed. Henri Béhar (Paris: Editions du CNRS, 1990).

1. Caillois, *Mythe*, 41.
2. Caillois, rev. of *L'Esthétique de Baudelaire*, by André Ferran, 901.
3. Tristan Tzara, "Compte-rendu," in Béhar, *Inquisitions*, 65. *Inquisitions* fell apart by the second issue over disagreements regarding the Spanish Civil War; although Caillois signed an anti-Franco manifesto in *Europe* (Aug. 15, 1936), he opposed Aragon's wish to politically commit *Inquisitions* in this respect.
4. Caillois, Archives interview.
5. In 1941, for example, Caillois remarked: "I think . . . that with figures like Auguste Comte, who created . . . determinist doctrines, there were nonetheless many activist elements, although that is not what was ultimately operative." "Debates sobre temas sociológicos: Nuevas perspectivas en torno a 'Los irresponsables,' de Archibald Macleish," 90.
6. Caillois, Archives interview; Caillois, *L'Homme et le sacré*, 2 ed., 1985, 8.
7. Caillois, Archives interview: 4.
8. Granet, *Civilisation*, 23. This last sentence appears in the *Man and the Sacred* postwar version as: "The ideal is that he should not do anything, that he should reign and not govern" (93; trans. modified).

9. Introduction to "Interview with Gilles Lapouge, June 1970"

The interview was first published in *La Quinzaine littéraire* 97 (June 1970).

1. Caillois, *Approches de l'imaginaire*, 59. "Mimicry and Legendary Psychasthenia"

had evoked "an *incantation frozen at its height* and that has caught the sorcerer in his own trap"; Raymond Aron's review of *Le Mythe et l'homme* had queried this point in particular. However, by 1937, Caillois's Fichtean, Vienna School scientist aimed for self-conscious mastery and lucidity (see introduction).

2. Pierre Andler, letter to Jacques Chavy, 18 June 1947, Jacques Chavy, personal archives.

10. Introduction to "First Lecture"

1. Hollier, *Le Collège de sociologie*, 32.
2. Bataille, qtd. in Hollier, *Le Collège de sociologie*, 32.
3. See also Hollier, *Le Collège de sociologie*, 54–55.
4. Cuvillier, *Introduction* 95.
5. Caillois, *Man and the Sacred*, 137.
6. Bataille, qtd. in Hollier, *Le Collège de sociologie*, 32.
7. Wilhelm Reich, *The Mass Psychology of Fascism* (1934), trans. Theodore Peter Wolfe (New York: Orgone Institute Press, 1946). Payne write, "Reich viewed fascism as the product of sexual repression in bourgeois society when combined with compensatory and aggressive impulses. He thus interpreted fascism as the 'natural' consequence of bourgeois society, which was grounded in sexual repression, but thought it capable of involving other social classes as well" (*History*, 452).
8. Caillois, *Man and the Sacred*, 136. See Caillois, *L'Homme et le sacré*, 1st ed. (1938), 138.
9. Personal conversation with Jacques Chavy, Paris, Jan. 2001.

11. Introduction to "Dionysian Virtues"

This essay was reprinted in *Acéphale: religion, sociologie, philosophie, 1936–1939*, by Georges Bataille (1939; Paris: Jean-Michel Place, 1995).

1. Manfred Frank, *Le Dieu à venir*, trans. from the German by Florence Vatan and Veronika von Schenck (Paris: Actes Sud, 1989), 15, 30, 46 (paraphrasing Bloch).
2. See *Acéphale* 2 (21 Jan, 1937), rpt. in Georges Bataille, *Acéphale: Religion, sociologie, philosophie, 1936–1939* (1939; Paris: Jean-Michel Place, 1995); Bataille, "Nietzsche et les fascistes: Une réparation," 463; Le Rider, *Nietzsche*, 167.
3. Roger Caillois, rev. of *Poisons sacrés, ivresses divines*, by Ph. de Felice, *Cahiers du Sud* (Apr. 1937): 305, 306.
4. Roger Caillois, rev. of *Les Paradis artificiels*, by Louis Lewin, *Cahiers du Sud* (Jan. 1937): 57–59. See also his review of *Les Échecs artistiques*, by André Chéron; *L'Opposition et les cases conjuguées sont réconciliées*, by Marcel Duchamp and V. Halberstadt, *Nouvelle revue française* (Sept. 1937): 511–514; and "L'Aridité," 7–12.
5. Caillois, rev. of *Les Paradis artificiels*, 59. He cites a now forgotten work, *Le Peyotl*, by a certain Roubier.

6. Caillois, *Approches de l'imaginaire*, 58. Caillois cites the influence on him, at the time, of *The Plumed Serpent* "because it contained a whole theory of the sacred, and of the living sacred, the active sacred." This influence was also perhaps partly due, he says, to the "lyricism of the hymns in the work" (Archives interview).

7. This was stated to me unequivocally (personal interview with a former member of Acéphale).

8. Personal interview with a former member of Acéphale. In the original French: "C'était quelque chose de finalement *non-violent*, absolument. . . . Si on peut parler d'excès c'est dans la mesure où chacun de *nous* pouvait donc se diriger vers le . . . en cherchant, en cherchant . . . finalement, disons *l'extase—que* je n'ai pas trouvée, et que certainement *peu* de participants à Acéphale ont trouvée, mais enfin, c'était dans cette direction-là que nous allions."

12. Introduction to "Aggressiveness as a Value"

1. Sorel, *Reflections*, 270.

2. Georges Bataille, [*Programme*], 4 Apr. 1936, in Galletti, *Georges Bataille*, 281.

3. Galletti, *Georges Bataille*, 239.

4. Bataille, "Ce que j'ai à dire . . . ," 331.

5. Descombes, *La Philosophie par gros temps*, qtd. in Le Rider, *Nietzsche*, 163.

6. Galletti, *Georges Bataille*, 247.

7. Caillois, "Winter," 39 (trans. modified).

8. Caillois, "L'Aridité," 10.

9. Hollier, *Le Collège de sociologie*, 66.

10. Alexandre Kojève, *Introduction to the Reading of Hegel: Lectures on the Phenomenology of the Spirit* (1947), comp. Raymond Queneau, ed. Allan Bloom, trans. James H. Nichols Jr. (1969; Ithaca, NY: Cornell University Press, 1980), 19.

11. Caillois, "L'Aridité," 12.

12. Le Rider, *Nietzsche*, 154; Walter Benjamin [J. E. Mabinn, pseud.], rev. of "L'Aridité," by Roger Caillois; *Un Régulier dans le siècle*, by Julien Benda; *Les Grands Cimetières sous la lune*, by Georges Bernanos; *Le Dialogue catholico-communiste est-il possible?* by G. Fessard, *Zeitschrift für Sozialforschung* 7 (1938): 404.

13. See Roger Caillois, *L'Aile froide* (1938; Montpellier: Fata Morgana, 1992).

14. Hollier, *Absent*, 33. Caillois had remarked as an extreme deductive argument that if Luciferian "researchers" were to commit a rape, it would be neither by instinct nor for pleasure, "but to make the victim experience pleasure despite herself, and because they themselves are seduced by this strange cruelty of imposing pleasure itself" (rev. of *Les Échecs*, 513). I earlier attributed this to Baudelaire's "sinister view" of sexual love (see "The Praying Mantis"); see also "Metamorphoses of Hell."

15. Caillois, "Un Roman cornélien," 479–481. Caillois's edition of *Le Cid* (Paris: Hachette, 1939) foreshadows Octave Nadal's later theory of Corneillean "amour d'estime," or love based on mutual aristocratic respect, in *Le Sentiment de l'amour dans l'oeuvre de Pierre Corneille* (1948; Paris: Gallimard, 1991).

16. Caillois, "L'Aridité," 12.

17. Kojève, *Introduction*, 20.

13. Introduction to "The Birth of Lucifer"

For a different translation, see "The Birth of Lucifer," trans. Robert Sage, *Verve* (New York) 1 (December 1937).

1. Caillois, *Mythe*, 11.

2. Caillois's "First Lecture: Sacred Sociology and the Relationships among 'Society,' 'Organism,' and 'Being'" and his "Paris, a Modern Myth" refer to Frazer's *The Magic Art and the Evolution of Kings* and *The Magical Origin of Kings*.

3. Caillois, *Mythe*, 11, 9.

4. Caillois, *Man and the Sacred*, 38 (trans. modified); both editions are identical.

5. Caillois, Archives interview.

6. Caillois, "Winter," 36. On this shift, see Heimonet's discussion in "Des 'mythes humiliés' aux 'mythes triomphants,'" in Jenny, *Roger Caillois, la pensée aventurée*, 104.

7. Roger Caillois, rev. of *Essai sur le titanisme dans la poésie romantique occidentale entre 1815 et 1850*, by Vačlav Černy, *Nouvelle revue française* (November 1937): 847–49.

8. Caillois, "Résurrection de Corneille," 659, 665.

9. Caillois, "Winter," 39.

10. Roger Caillois, rev. of *Service inutile*, by H. de Motherlant, in Béhar, *Inquisitions*, 56.

11. Roger Caillois, rev. of *L'Équinoxe de Septembre*, by H. de Motherlant, *Nouvelle revue française* (Jan. 1939): 151.

12. Bataille, "La Conjuration sacrée," *O.C.* 1 (1970): 443.

13. See Caillois, "L'Aridité"; see also his *L'Aile froide*.

14. Georges Bataille, "Van Gogh Prométhée," *O.C.* 1 (1970): 500.

15. Caillois, Archives interview.

16. See D. H. Lawrence, *The Plumed Serpent* (1926; New York: Vintage International, 1992). For a recent discussion of the novel, see Marianna Torgovnick, *Gone Primitive: Savage Intellects, Modern Lives* (Chicago and London: University of Chicago Press, 1990), 159–76. Georges Ambrosino's wife recalls reading and enjoying *The Plumed Serpent* with her husband and sister in the 1930s (after *Lady Chatterley's Lover*) (Personal conversation with Esther Ambrosino, Paris, July 2002). Several sketches and paintings by Jacques Chavy might also conceivably be interpreted as illustrations of this work. Both Chavy and Ambrosino were members of Acéphale.

14. Introduction to "Paris, a Modern Myth"

This essay was first published in the *Nouvelle revue française* (May 1937).

1. See Caillois, rev. of *L'Esthétique de Baudelaire*, by André Ferran, 901; see also his review (part 1) of *La Comédie humaine*, by Balzac, ed. Marcel Bouteron, *Nouvelle revue française* (March 1937): 452–455; part 2 (January 1938): 136–38.

2. Caillois, "Winter," 342.

3. Victoria Ocampo, "Roger Caillois," *Sur* 59 (Aug. 1939): 50; these last references to "soul" and "psychoanalysis" better characterize Ocampo's intellectual orientation than that of Caillois.

4. On this topic, see, in particular, Denis Hollier's commentary to René Guastalla's talk on "Naissance de la littérature," in *Le Collège de sociologie*, 460–472. For a recent discussion, see Philippe Sellier, "Qu'est-ce qu'un mythe littéraire?" *Littérature*, no. 55 (1984).

5. Caillois wrote, "*The Human Comedy* is . . . the illustration of a system of taste rather than of ideas, and . . . tries to be as commanding as possible; it considers passion—which includes both thoughts and feelings—as the foundation of social existence but also, at the same time, as its supreme mode of dissolution" (rev. of *La Comédie humaine*, 454).

6. Hollier writes, "In the spring of 1937, Caillois spoke before the Convention of Aesthetics and the Science of Art that was held in Paris. . . . Myth, which is of interest to me, he told his colleagues, does not fall within your province. I am removing it from your sphere. It is of the greatest importance to preclude an aesthetic approach to myth" (*The College of Sociology*, xxv). Hollier is referring to Roger Caillois, "Le Mythe et l'art: Nature de leur opposition," in *Congrès international d'esthétique et de science de l'art* (Paris: F. Alcan, 1937). Movies, which Caillois addressed after the war, are notably absent from his "mass culture," perhaps given the lack of a critical mass and data for sociological research.

7. Caillois, rev. (part 2) of *La Comédie humaine*, 137.

8. Caillois, rev. (part 2) of *La Comédie humaine*, 137.

9. See Benjamin, rev. of "L'Aridité." See also my discussion of "The Myth of Secret Treasures in Childhood," in this volume.

10. Gérard Raulet, *Walter Benjamin* (Paris: Ellipses, 2000), 154, 54.

15. Introduction to "Sociology of the Intellectual"

This essay was first published in *Nouvelle revue française* (Aug. 1939): 291–301. Rpt. in *La Communion des forts* (Mexico City: Quetzal, 1943). Rpt. in *La Communion des Forts*, 2nd ed. (texte edit) (Marseille: Sagittaire, 1944).

1. Caillois, *Man and Sacred*, 134 (trans. modified).

2. See Julien Benda, *The Treason of the Intellectuals* (1928; New York: Norton, 1969).

3. This talk took place at the Union pour la vérité, which, like other important intellectual forums, such as the Abbey of Pontigny, had been created and was still being run by Paul Desjardins, whom Caillois later held up as the model creator of a new, secular, "monastic order" (see introduction). See also Hollier, *Le Collège de sociologie*, 870–871.

4. Winock, *Siècle*, 240.

5. Allan Stoekl, *Agonies of the Intellectual* (Lincoln: University of Nebraska Press, 1992), 10.

6. Roger Caillois, letter to Jean Paulhan, 27 Mar. 1938, in Felgine and Perez, "Correspondance Jean Paulhan–Roger Caillois," 73.

7. Roger Caillois, "Hommage à Georges Bidault," in *Cironstancielles*, 116. This influential figure for Caillois's early life was a Catholic reformer, a fervent enemy of the Action Française; he became a leader of the Parti Démocrate Populaire in the late 1930s, served heroically in the Resistance, and was minister of Foreign Affairs under De Gaulle. Later exiled, he was subsequently amnestied for his involvement with the OAS and the defense of French Algeria.

8. Georges Dumézil, *Flamen-Brahman* (Paris: Librairie Orientaliste Paul Geuthner, 1935), 39, 44.

9. Caillois, Archives interview.

16. Introduction to "Preamble to the Spirit of Sects"

This essay was first published as "Actualité des sectes," *Lettres françaises* 14 (Oct. 1944): 40–46. Rpt. in *Ensayo sobre el Espíritu de las Sectas* (Mexico City: El Colegio de Mexico, collection Jordanas), 1945. Rpt. in *Fisiología de Leviatán* (Buenos Aires: Editorial Sudamericana, 1946). Rpt. in *Instincts et société; essais de sociologie contemporaine* (Paris: Gonthier, 1964).

1. Patrick Waldberg, "'Vers un nouveau mythe? Prémonitions et défiances': Patrick Waldberg à Isabelle Waldberg (Extraits d'une lettre écrite à bord d'un cargo en convoi sur l'Atlantique)," *V.V.V.* (4 Feb. 1944): 41–42; see also Patrick Waldberg, *Un Amour Acéphale: Correspondance, 1940–1949* (Paris: Editions de la Différence, 1992).

2. Caillois's lengthy monograph, *Ensayo sobre el Espíritu de las Sectas* (Essay on the spirit of sects) was first published in separate sections: "Actualité des sectes" (Topicality of sects), *Lettres françaises* 14 (Oct. 1944); "Recours à la secte" (Recourse to the sect), *France libre* 8, no. 46 (1944); "La Secte au pouvoir" (The sect in power), *France libre* 8, no. 43 (1944); "L'Esprit des sectes" (The spirit of sects), *Renaissance II+III* (1944–1945).

3. Roger Caillois, *Instincts et société: Essais de sociologie contemporaine*, 8.

4. See Caillois, Archives interview.

5. Roger Caillois, *Le Rocher de Sisyphe* (Paris: Gallimard, 1946), 146, 147. According to Felgine, "he wrote toward the end of his life that it was 'an ambiguous act of contrition, which was much more inspired by regret than by remorse'" (*Caillois*, 238).

6. "Etres du crepuscule" was published as "Seres del anochecer" in *Sur* (Dec. 1940). Jean-Pierre Le Bouler suggests that "Etres du crépuscule," or an initial draft, might be the text Caillois sent to Bataille to be read at the final session of the College of Sociology (Bataille, *Georges Bataille: Lettres à Roger Caillois*, 116); indeed, Bataille's letter of July 20, 1939 indicates his refusal to read this text publicly, describing it to Caillois as "your 'examination of conscience' regarding cheap cerebral agitation" (111).

7. Roger Caillois, "Seres del anochecer," *Sur* (Dec. 1940): 96, 97–99. See Caillois, "Marginalia," in Hollier, *The College of Sociology*, 377.

8. This phrase was cut from "Etres du crépuscule" in *Le Rocher de Sisyphe*.

9. Caillois, "Seres," 97–99.

10. Caillois, "Seres," 99.

11. Caillois, *Rocher*, 175, 164. See Roger Caillois, *La Roca de Sísifo* (Buenos Aires: Sudamericana, 1942).

12. Georges Auclair, "Roger Caillois: Le Collège de sociologie," "Hommage à Roger Caillois," special issue of *Nouvelle revue française* (Sept. 1979): 93.

17. Introduction to "Discussions of Sociological Topics"

1. "Debates sobre temas sociológicos," *Sur* (June 1941): 85; responding to an inquiry sent out in the name of the journal by Eduardo Mallea, José Bianco, and Caillois, various Argentinian intellectuals had indicated which topics "in the sociological, political and literary spheres, according to them, were of the most pressing interest in national and global terms"(85). The following discussions at *Sur* were "Commentario a 'Los irresponsables, de Archibald Macleish,'" *Sur* (Aug. 1941); "Nuevas perspectivas en torno a Archibald Macleish," *Sur* (Sept. 1941); "Tienen las Americas una historia común?" *Sur* (Nov. 1941); "El problema Gandhi," *Sur* (Nov. 1942); and "Moral y literatura," *Sur* (Apr. 1945).

2. See Galletti, "Roger Caillois en Argentine," 150. Mendoza's only other notable contribution in this forum was the list of topics she proposed for the questionnaire of June 1941, uniquely addressing the construction of "a *collective consciousness* in the course of contemporary events" in Argentina and America, as well as in Mexico and Peru ("Debates sobre temas sociológicos," 87).

3. Roger Caillois, "Défense de la république," 23.

18. Introduction to "The Nature and Structure of Totalitarian Regimes"

The studies of Hitler were taken up in expanded form in *Quatre essais de sociologic contemporaine* (Paris: Gonthier, 1964).

1. *La Nación* (20 Aug. 1940) (Spanish-language version), Caillois Archives, Bibliothèque Municipale, Vichy.

2. Elie Halévy, *L'Ere des tyrannies: Études sur le socialisme et la guerre* (1938; Paris: Gallimard, 1990).

3. Rev. of *France libre* 25 (16 Nov. 1942), *Lettres françaises* 9 (July 1943): 60. On *L'Ere des tyrannies*, see François Furet, *Le Passé d'une illusion: essai sur l'idée communiste au xxe siècle* (Paris: R. Laffort, 1995), 347; and Hollier, *Le Collège de sociologie*, 847–851.

4. Published in *Bulletin de la Société Française de Philosophie* 2 (April–May 1946): 41–92; rpt. in Raymond Aron, *Machiavel et les tyrannies modernes* (Paris: Fallois, 1993), 165–183.

5. Furet, *Le Passé d'une illusion*, 513.

6. Francisco Ayala, "El Curso de Roger Caillois," *Sur* (Nov. 1941): 86–88.

7. "Las Conferencias de Roger Caillois," *Crisol* (22 Sept. 1940), Caillois Archives, Bibliothèque Municipale, Vichy.

19. Introduction to "Duties and Privileges of French Writers Abroad"

Reprinted in *Circonstancielles* (Paris: Gallimard, 1946).

1. Sartre, *Situations* 2 (Paris: Gallimard, 1948), qtd. in Anna Boschetti, *The Intellectual Enterprise: Sartre and Les Temps Modernes*, trans. Richard C. McCleary (Evanston, IL: Northwestern University Press, 1988), 110.

2. Boschetti, *The Intellectual Enterprise*, 110.

3. See Hollier's discussion of Bataille and Blanchot: "Impossibility is literature's essential attribute, its condition of possibility" (*Absent*, 8).

4. Tillier, rev. of *Les Lettres françaises*, 156.

5. Rev. of *Fonction universelle de la France*, by Henri Focillon, *Lettres françaises* 2 (Oct. 1941): 51.

6. Rev. of "Au service de l'ennemi" (*France libre* 25 [16 Nov. 1942]) *Lettres francaises* 9 (July 1943): 61.

7. "Review of *Lettres françaises*," *Times Literary Supplement* (31 Oct. 1942), Caillois Archives, Bibliothèque Municipale, Vichy. Given what Caillois says about Jünger in "The Nature and Structure of Totalitarian Regimes," the publication of his writing was instructive rather than "exemplary." As for Ernest Renan's "Lettre à David Strauss" (1871), *Lettres françaises* 2 (Oct. 1941): 25–36, this does not entirely support Jeffrey Mehlman's insinuations about Renan and Caillois in *Emigré New York: French Intellectuals in Wartime Manhattan, 1940–1944*, 35–36, 73. Renan's letter attacks Germany's "ethnographic and archaeological politics," which have replaced "liberal politics": "Our politics are those of the right of nations; yours, the politics of race. Aside from the fact that it is scientifically unsound to divide humanity into races, since few countries contain a truly pure race, this can only lead, furthermore, to wars of extermination, to 'zoological' wars. . . . It would put an end to that fruitful mixture called humanity, made up of numerous and equally necessary elements" (Renan, 31). Renan's skepticism about "pure democracy" and communism (34)—explicitly shared by Caillois, as we have seen—then leads him to propose that the Germans should "create for man an association outside of the State, above and beyond the family, that would elevate, support, correct, assist him, and make him happy—what the Church once was and is no longer. Either reform the Church or find some substitute for it"(35).

20. Introduction to "Patagonia"

First published as *Patagonie* (Buenos Aires: Editions de l'Aigle, 1942). Rpt. as "Patagonia," in *La Roca de Sísifo* (Buenos Aires: Sudamericana, 1942). Rpt. in *Le Rocher de Sisyphe* (1946). Rpt. in *Confluences* 5. 8 (1945). Rpt. in *Espace Américain* (1949; Montpellier: Fata Morgana, 1983).

1. Georges Bataille, "Attraction and Repulsion I," 106.

2. Picon, "Les Essais de Roger Caillois," 277.

3. Caillois, *Rocher*, 150. He wrote in the 1946 preface: "At that time, I did not know that the Sisyphus fable had been simultaneously serving to express the absurd, which some people see as the characteristic of the human condition" (145).

4. Paulhan, qtd. in Hollier, *The College of Sociology*, 305.

5. Germaine de Staël-Holstein, *Germany* (1813), trans. and ed. O. W. Wright (Boston: Houghton, Mifflin, 1887), 367.

6. Caillois, "Notes pour un itinéraire," 168.

7. See also Felgine, *Caillois*, 288–290.

8. Roger Caillois, *Espace américain* (1949; Montpellier: Fata Morgana, 1983), 12.

9. "I am indeed aware," responds the Minister of Culture to some prior letter, "that the artistic documentation, as one says, of pre-Columbian America is a joke. . . . Like you, I believe that from the French point of view, there would be something extremely important and intelligent to undertake, and with a very minimal capital outlay," André Malraux, letter to Roger Caillois, 15 Dec. 1947, C.M. 45, Special Collections, Bibliothèque Municipale, Vichy. This joint project was never pursued.

10. "Debates sobre temas sociológicos? Tienen las Americas una historia común?'" *Sur* 86 (Nov. 1941): 86, 87.

11. "Above all, I liked this mastery of a language that finds its end in itself without ceding to self-indulgence. Beneath your modern vision, there is a live discipline that knows how to return to the French tradition in other ways than by a game of pure culture," wrote Alexis Léger in a letter to Caillois, 2 July 1942, qtd. in Felgine, *Caillois*, 236.

12. The available evidence suggests that Caillois sent "Patagonia" to Alexis Léger in May 1942, after having received a copy of *Exile*. Perse's poem had just appeared in the journal *Poetry*; it would be republished in *Lettres francaises* 5 (1 July 1942) and as a separate "booklet" by *Lettres françaises* in August 1943 (see Felgine, *Caillois*, 236, 247). On Léger's stay in New York, see Mehlman, *Emigré*, 164–180.

13. Caillois, "Art of St.-John Perse," 204.

14. Rev. of *France libre* 27 (15 Jan, 1943), *Lettres françaises* 9 (July 1943): 65.

15. André Chastel, "Loyautés de l'intelligence," in Caillois, *Roger Caillois: "Cahiers pour un temps,"* 40.

16. Caillois, "Paul Valéry: Le 'Je' et le jeu" (16 July 1946), in Caillois, *Chroniques de Babel*, 106, 104; on his appreciation for as well as divergences from this poet, see also his "Eloge de Paul Valéry," *Cahiers du Sud* 276–278 (1946): 299–306.

17. Caillois, *Pierres réfléchies*, 34.

21. Introduction to "The Myth of Secret Treasures in Childhood"

Reprinted in *La Communion des forts: Etudes de sociologie contemporaine* (Mexico City: Quetzal, 1943). Rpt. in *La Communion des forts: études de sociologie contemporaine*, 2d ed. (texte edit) (Marseille: Sagittaire, 1944).

1. Roger Caillois, letter to Victoria Ocampo, 16? Apr. 1941, in Felgine, *Correspondance Roger Caillois–Victoria Ocampo*, 121.

2. Roger Caillois, letter to Victoria Ocampo, 18 Apr. 1941, in Felgine, *Correspondance Roger Caillois–Victoria Ocampo*, 124.

3. Victoria Ocampo, letter to Roger Caillois, 1941, in Felgine, *Correspondance Roger Caillois–Victoria Ocampo*, 138, 139.

4. Caillois, *Man and the Sacred*, 133.

5. Caillois, "L'Aridité," 9.

6. Benjamin, rev. of "L'Aridité," 404. Bataille didn't like the miser either, but for different reasons, sharply noting in his postwar review of *Man and the Sacred*, which decried Caillois's insufficient emphasis on sacrifice, "Caillois comes to believe that gold is sacred for the miser (and this is actually not his most profane example)" ("La Guerre," 52).

7. Bataille, *Literature*, x.

8. In early 1941, Breton and Caillois exchanged letters leading to the publication of Breton's "Dialogue créole" in *Les Lettres françaises* (Jan. 1942) and Caillois's contributions to *V.V.V.* In October 1941, Breton wrote again, lamenting the attack against Surrealism in Caillois's "Pour une esthétique sévère," *Lettres françaises* 1 (July 1941). Caillois read the following letter from Breton out loud in the Archives interview: "Then I considered what had distanced us from each other, at the close of a conversation at my place, in Paris, where I believe that both you and I had nonetheless sought to be genuine, to the point of exaggerating out point of view: it is all the more regrettable that this should have led to a break. After all, it was better than the silence that ensued; and what was there for you to find so blameworthy, I remained what I had always been, most likely with my reasons and faults, at least *myself* and you were also yourself, that is, someone in whose authenticity I have never ceased to believe and with whom I have several things in common. I believe, let me repeat, that we were worth more than that mutual neglect and hostility we endeavored to maintain, from that point on, and fortunately, I hope, to little effect."

9. Michel Leiris, "The Sacred in Everyday Life," in Hollier, *The College of Sociology*, 24.

10. Caillois, *Man and the Sacred*, 37.

11. Caillois, "Pour une esthétique sévère," 39.

12. See Mehlman, *Emigré*, 145–164.

13. Antoine de Saint-Exupéry, *The Little Prince* (1943), trans. Richard Howard (1971; San Diego: Harcourt, 2000), 68.

22. Introduction to "The Situation of Poetry"

This essay was first published as "Introduction," *Lettres Françaises* 7–8 (February 1943): 1–6. Rpt. in *Impostures de la poésie* (Buenos Aires: Ed. Lettres françaises, 1944; Paris: Gallimard, 1945, 1962).

1. Roger Caillois, Response to "Enquête sur la poésie indispensable," *Cahiers G.L.M.* (Oct. 1938): 56.

2. Roger Caillois, *Les Impostures de la poésie* (1944), in *Approches de la poésie*, 42. The essay's title echoed Tristan Tzara's "Essai sur la situation de la poésie" published in *SASDLR* 4 (1931), and cited in *The Necessity of Mind*.

3. See, in particular, Caillois, *Impostures*.

4. Roger Caillois, "Aventures de la poésie moderne," in *Approches de la poésie* 64, 63.

5. Roger Caillois, "Un Visionnaire," *Liberté de l'esprit* (Feb. 1952): 43.

6. See, in particular, Paulhan's talk to the College of Sociology, "D'un langage sacré," in Hollier, *Le Collège de sociologie*, 694–728.

7. Caillois clearly viewed Léger as a crucial arbiter in literary matters. "In the nearly three years that I have been here [Buenos Aires] now," he wrote to the French poet, "I have had no point of reference for judging . . . what I write" (qtd. in Felgine, *Caillois*, 236).

8. Caillois, "The Art of St.-John Perse," 202.

9. Caillois's major work on Perse was *Poétique de Saint-John Perse* (Paris: Gallimard, 1954).

10. See Roger Caillois, "Reconnaissance à Saint-John Perse," in *Approches de la poésie*, 217–228.

23. Introduction to "Pythian Heritage"

This essay was first published in *Lettres Françaises* 10 (1 October 1943). Rpt. in *Impostures de la poésie* (Buenos Aires: Ed. Lettres Françaises, 1944; Paris: Gallimard, 1945, 1962). For an alternative English translation, see "Pythian Heritage (On the Nature of Poetic Inspiration)," [no translator listed] *Books Abroad* 17 (spring 1943): 207–11.

1. Caillois, *Approches de la poésie*, 47.

2. Rev. of *V.V.V.* 2–3 (Mar. 1943), *Lettres françaises* 10 (1 Oct. 1943): 57. Although the ideas expressed here coincide with those of Caillois, the vitriolic style might point to the pen of his important collaborator, René Etiemble.

3. Paul Valéry, qtd. in Jean Hytier, *La Poétique de Valéry* (Paris: Armand Colin, 1953), 136; Hytier is quoting from Valéry's *La Création artistique* in *Bulletin de la Société Française de Philosophie* (1928): 14–17.

4. Rev. of "Combat de l'homme," by Jean Mahan (*France libre* 22 [15 Aug. 1942]), *Lettres françaises* 7–8 (Feb. 1943): 86.

24. Introduction to "Loyola to the Rescue of Marx"

1. Caillois, *Approches de l'imaginaire*, 98.

2. Caillois, "L'Ordre," 125; see also C. Frank, "Contre-Attaque de Caillois?"

3. Caillois, *Les Jeux et les hommes*, 24. Before the war, Loyola had given Caillois a definition of self-mastery as freedom—which could then become despotism.

4. Winock, *Siècle*, 606.

25. Introduction to "Paroxysms of Society"

Previous versions of this essay include "Le Sacré de transgression: Théorie de la fête," in *L'Homme et le sacré* (Paris: Ed. Leroux, 1939); "Théorie de la fête," *Nouvelle revue française* (January 1940): 49–56; "El Culto de la guerra," in *Fisiología de Leviatán* (Buenos Aires: Editorial Sudamericana, 1946), 77–106; "Guerre et sacré," in *L'Homme et le sacré* (Paris: Gallimard, 1950); "Paroxysme de la société" in *Quatre essais de sociologie contemporaine* (Paris: Oliver Perrin, 1951), 140–153.

1. Hollier, *Le Collège de sociologie*, 642. These terms conclude both editions of the main text; see Caillois, *Man and the Sacred*, 138.

2. Caillois, Archives interview.

3. Borgeaud, *Couple sacré/profane*, 414; his only other reference, though, is to Dumézil.

4. See Hollier's discussion of carnival and revolution in *Le Collège de sociologie;* see also the references to war in Galleti, *Bataille*. Shortly before his death, the anthropologist Louis Dumont wrote to me about meeting Bataille "on the eve of the war. I got angry at Bataille, who was exulting at the prospect that Hitler, the butcher, would soon be unleashing torrents of blood."

5. Caillois, *Man and the Sacred*, 165 (trans. modified).

6. See also Roger Caillois, "Del culto de la guerra," in *Fisiología de Leviatán*, trans. Julián Calvo and C. A. Jordana (Buenos Aires: Editorial Sudamericana, 1946), 77–106.

7. Caillois, *Quatre*, 7.

8. Caillois, *Man and the Sacred*, 176, 179, (trans. modified).

9. Bataille, "La Guerre," 57.

10. Georges Bataille, letter to Roger Caillois, Oct. 1945, *Georges Bataille: Lettres à Roger Caillois*, 133; see also 134.

11. Bataille, *La Part maudite*, 62–63.

12. In Bataille, *Visions of Excess*, 122.

13. Mauss, *Gift*, 108, 40 (emphasis added). I here concur with Jean-Michel Heimonet, *Le Mal à l'oeuvre; Georges Bataille et l'écriture du sacrifice* (Marseille: Parentheses, 1986), 31.

14. Caillois, *Man and the Sacred*, 121.

15. Roger Caillois, *Bellone ou la pente de la guerre* (1963; Paris: Editions Nizet, 1973), 9, 8.

26. Introduction to "Metamorphoses of Hell"

This piece was first published in *Diogène* 85 (1974). For a different translation, see "Metamorphoses of Hell," trans. Mary Burnet, *Diogenes* 85 (1974).

1. See Felgine, *Caillois*, 161; see also Felgine and Perez, "Correspondance Jean Paulhan–Roger Caillois," 60–61.

2. Roger Caillois, "La Mort dans le cinéma américain," in *Quatre*, 17–23.

3. Bataille, *Literature*, 24.

4. Bataille thanked Caillois in *L'Erotisme* (1957) for having provided the first theoretical elaboration of "transgression" with *Man and the Sacred*; on the difference between Bataille's attitudes and the theory of sexual liberation, see Surya, *Georges Bataille*, 548.

5. See my introduction to "Aggressiveness as a Value," in this volume.

6. Bataille, "Guerre," 50; such a response to death differs from that of animals, religious people, or rational scientists.

7. Maurice Blanchot, "Réflexions sur l'enfer," in *L'Entretien infini* (Paris: Gallimard, 1969), 70. Heidegger's *Letter on Humanism* had claimed that Sartre never reached authentic Being; Blanchot argues that Camus's *Le Myth de Sisyphe* does not reach authentic death.

8. Philippe Ariès, "La Mort inversée: Le changement des attitudes devant la mort dans les sociétés occidentales," *Archives européennes de sociologie* 8 (1967): 187, 194. He says that prior to Edgar Morin's *L'Homme et la mort devant l'histoire* (1951), there was no "real history or sociology of death" above and beyond iconographic studies of death, Huizinga's *The Waning of the Middle Ages*, and Caillois's article (169).

9. Georges Bataille, "Du Rapport entre le divin et le mal," (1996) rev. of *Le Dualisme dans l'histoire de la philosophie et des religions*, by Simone Pètrement, O.C. 11 (1988): 206.

10. Georges Bataille, "Réflexions sur le bourreau et la victime," (1947) rev. of *Jours de notre mort*, by David Rousset, O.C. 11 (1988): 266. Perhaps the experience of Acéphale should have revealed that he and his friends were simply *incapable* of being executioners.

11. See the sense of "hypermoral" in Bataille, *Literature*, 9.

27. Introduction to "The Image"

This piece was first published in *Vocabulaire esthétique* (Paris: Fortaine, 1946).

1. Caillois, *Babel*, 7, 19.

2. Caillois, *Approches de la poésie*, 238.

3. Caillois, "Image," in *Vocabulaire esthétique* (Paris: Fontaine, 1946), 65–66.

4. Jean Paulhan, *Clef de la poésie* (1944; Paris: Gallimard, 1984), 81–89.

5. Caillois, "Actualité des Kenningar," 187.

6. Caillois, *Approches de la poésie*, 168.

7. Jean Paulhan, "Le Langage sacré," in Hollier, *Le Collège de sociologie*, 694–728.

28. Introduction to "Fruitful Ambiguity"

This essay was first published in *Au Coeur du fantastique* (Paris: Gallimard, 1965).

1. André Breton and Jean Schuster, "Art poétique," *Bief, jonction surréaliste* 7 (1 June 1959). See André Breton and Paul Eluard, "Notes sur la poésie," in Breton, *Oeuvres complètes*, 1:1014–19.

2. Roger Caillois, *Art poétique, ou confession négative* (1958), in *Approches de la poésie*, 74.

3. Breton and Schuster, "Art poétique."

4. Roger Caillois, *Au coeur du fantastique* (1965), in *Cohérences aventureuses* (Paris: Gallimard, 1976), 105.

5. Caillois, *Cohérences*, 11.

6. Caillois, *Cohérences*, 105.

7. Raymond Queneau, *Le Voyage en Grèce* (Paris: Gallimard, 1973), 94.

8. Jacques Roubaud, "Raymond Queneau et l'amalgame des mathématiques et de la littérature," in *Atlas de Littérature Potentielle*, by OULIPO (1981; Paris: Gallimard, 1988), 56.

29. Introduction to "Surrealism as a World of Signs"

1. Hollier, "La Fin des sommations," 597.

2. Caillois, "Places," 20, 19.

3. The essay was republished as "Intervention surréaliste" in *Cases d'un échiquier*. Caillois published an important eulogy for Breton, "Divergences et complicités," in the *Nouvelle revue française* (April 1967).

4. Eigeldinger, "Poétique," 89.

5. Caillois, "Places," 19.

6. Caillois, *Approches de la poésie*, 10.

30. Introduction to "The Great Bridgemaker"

1. See Caillois, *Rencontres*, 295.

2. Caillois, *Rencontres*, 27.

3. Martin Heidegger, *Basic Writings: Revised and Expanded Edition*, ed. David Farrell Krell (1977; New York: HarperCollins, 1993), 226.

4. Caillois, *Rencontres*, 26.

5. Caillois, *Rencontres*, 27.

6. See Michel Panoff's polemical work, *Les Frères ennemis: Roger Caillois et Claude Lévi-Strauss* (Paris: Payot, 1993).

7. Georges Gurvitch, "Avertissement," in Mauss, *Sociologie et anthropologie*, viii. According to David Pace, Lévi-Strauss admitted that, "as a latecomer to ethnology, he had barely known Mauss" and had never attended his courses (*Lévi-Strauss*, 150).

8. Claude Lévi-Strauss, "Introduction à l'oeuvre de Marcel Mauss," in Mauss, *Sociologie et anthropologie*, xxxvi.

9. See Durkheim and Mauss, "De quelques formes primitives de la classification."

10. Marcel Mauss, letter to Roger Caillois, 22 June 1938, in *Roger Caillois: "Cahiers pour un temps,"* 205.

11. Caillois, Archives interview.

31. Introduction to "A New Plea for Diagonal Science"

Previous versions include "After Six Years of a Doubtful Combat," trans. Muriel McKeon, *Diogenes* 26 (April-June 1959): 3-8; "Sciences diagonales," *Nouvelle nouvelle revue française* (April 1959); "Préface," *Méduse et Cie* (Paris: Gallimard, 1960).

1. Roger Caillois, *Méduse et Cie* (Paris: Gallimard, 1960), 31, 30.

32. Introduction to "The Natural Fantastic"

1. Baudelaire (Salon de 1859), qtd. in Eigeldinger, "Poétique," 81.

2. Caillois, *L'Ecriture des pierres*, in *Pierres, suivi d'autres textes* (Paris: Gallimard, 1970), 108.

3. Caillois, *Pierres, suivi d'autres textes*, 147.

4. Later, *Pierres réfléchies* (1975) would come back on that claim, because Caillois encounters a stone evoking two things at the same time: a bird and a Mayan priestess. This oscillation so captures his imagination that he reinstates stone designs within the "fantastic in nature," with the following caveat: "I am interested only in those stone designs that—like those of clouds, tree bark, or cracks in the wall—tempt the whims of reverie due to some ambiguity that is inherent in their nature" (102).

5. Caillois, *Pierres, suivi d'autres textes*, 101.

6. Bataille, "Réflexions sur le bourreau et la victime," 266.

7. In an early distinction that informs all his writings on stones, Caillois contrasts the Western artist, "who takes a legible resemblance in the stone as his point of departure and strives to accentuate this to make it into a painting," and the Chinese painter, who "uses his art to deceive the viewer and persuade him that his painting is a natural, unadulterated piece of marble, which he merely titled—that is, interpreted and signed." "Les Traces," *Preuves* (July 1961): 24. In *Pierres*, he then suggests that abstract expressionism ("*l'art informel*") converges with Taoism and talks of the apocryphal (and aptly named) Chinese painter, Mi-Fou, who gave up, overwhelmed by nature's perfection (see Caillois, *Pierres*, in *Pierres, suivi d'autres textes*, 85–108).

8. Caillois, *Pierres, suivi d'autres textes*, 91.

Bibliography

Ariès, Philippe. "La Mort inversée: Le changement des attitudes devant la mort dans les sociétés occidentales." *Archives européennes de sociologie* 8 (1967).

Aron, Raymond. *Machiavel et les tyrannies modernes*. Paris: Fallois, 1993.

———. Rev of *L'Expérience mystique et les symboles chez les primitifs*, by Lucien Lévy-Bruhl; *La Conscience morale et l'expérience morale* and *La Loi morale: les lois naturelles et les lois sociales*, by Gaston Richard; *Le Mythe et l'homme*, by Roger Caillois; *Psychologie des masses*, by André Joussain; *Morphologie sociale*, by Maurice Halbwaches; *Le Problème des classes*, by Jean Lhomme; *La notion de progrès devant la science actuelle*, by Centre International de Synthèse; *La Civilisation*, by Félix Sartiaux, *Essai d'une histoire comparée des peuples d'Europe*, by Charles Seignobos. *Zeitschrift für Soziologie* 7 (1938).

Auclair, Georges. "Roger Caillois: le collège de sociologie." "Hommage à Roger Caillois." Special issue of *Nouvelle revue française* (Sept. 1979).

Auden, W. H. *W. H. Auden: A Selection by the Author*. London: Penguin, 1958.

Aury, Dominique, and Jean-Claude Zylberstein, eds. *Jean Paulhan: Choix de lettres 1917– 1936*. Paris: Gallimard, 1986.

Autié, Dominique. *Approches de Caillois*. Toulouse: Privat, 1981.

Ayala, Francisco. "El Curso de Roger Caillois." *Sur* (Nov. 1941).

Bachelard, Gaston. *L'Expérience de l'espace dans la physique contemporaine*. Paris: Presses Universitaires de France, 1937.

———. *Lautréamont*. Paris: José Corti, 1939.

———. *Le Nouvel Esprit scientifique*. 1934. Paris: Presses Universitaires de France, 1984.

———. *La Philosophie du non, essai d'une philosophie du nouvel espirit scientifique*. Paris: Presses Universitaires de France, 1940.

Balzac, Honoré de. *Le Père Goriot*. Paris: Gallimard, 1971.

Bataille, Georges. *Acéphale: religion, sociologie, philosophie, 1936-1939*. 1939. Paris: Jean-Michel Place, 1995.

——— "Attraction and Repulsion I: Tropisms, Sexuality and Tears." In *The College of Sociology 1937–39*, ed. Denis Hollier, trans. Betsy Wing. 2d ed. Minneapolis: University of Minnesota Press, 1988.

———. "Attraction and Repulsion II: Social Structure." In *The College of Sociology 1937– 39*, ed. Denis Hollier, trans. Betsy Wing. 2d ed. Minneapolis: University of Minnesota Press, 1988.

———. "Ce que j'ai à dire . . ." In *Georges Bataille: L'Apprenti sorcier*, ed. Marina Galletti. Paris: Editions de la Différence, 1999.

———. "Chronique nietzschéenne." *O.C.* 1 (1970).

———. "La Conjuration sacrée." *O.C.* 1 (1970).

———. *Georges Bataille: Lettres à Roger Caillois 4 août 1935 – 4 février 1959.* Ed. Jean-Pierre Le Bouler. Paris: Folle Avoine, 1988.

———. "La Guerre et la philosophie du sacré." Rev. of *L'Homme et le sacré*, by Roger Caillois. *O.C.* 12 (Feb. 1951).

———. "Joy in the Face of Death." In *The College of Sociology 1937–39*, ed. Denis Hollier, trans. Betsy Wing. 2d ed. Minneapolis: University of Minnesota Press, 1988.

———. *Literature and Evil.* Trans. Alastair Hamilton. 1973. New York: Marion Boyars, 1985.

———. "Nietzsche et les fascistes: Une réparation." *O.C.* 1 (1970).

———. "The Notion of Expenditure." In *Visions of Excess: Selected Writings, 1927–1939*, ed. and trans. Allan Stoekl. Minneapolis: University of Minnesota Press, 1985.

———. *Oeuvres complètes.* 12 vols. Ed. Michel Foucault. Paris: Gallimard, 1970.

———. *La Part maudite.* 1949. Paris: Minuit, 1967.

———. "Le Problème de l'état." *Critique sociale* 9 (Sept. 1933).

———. "Problèmes du surréalisme." *O.C.* 7 (1976).

———. "Du Rapport entre le divin et le mal." Rev. of *Le Dualisme dans l'histoire de la philosophie et les religions*, by Simone Pètrement. *O.C.* 11 (1946).

———. "Réflexions Sur le bourreau et la victime." Rev. of *Jours de notre mort*, by David Rousset. *O.C.* 11 (1947).

———. "La Religion surréaliste (24 février 1948)." *O.C.* 7 (1976).

———. Rev. of *La Condition humaine*, by André Malraux. *Critique sociale* 10 (Mar. 1934).

———. "The Sacred." In *Visions of Excess: Selected Writings, 1927–1939*, ed. and trans. Allan Stoekl. Minneapolis: University of Minnesota Press, 1985.

———. "Le Sens moral de la sociologie." *Critique* 1 (1946). Rpt. in *Critique* 591–592 (Aug.–Sept. 1996).

———. "The Solar Anus." In *Visions of Excess: Selected Writings, 1927–1939*, ed. and trans. Allan Stoekl. Minneapolis: University of Minnesota Press, 1985.

———. "La Structure psychologique du fascisme." *Critique sociale* 10–11 (Nov. 1933, Mar. 1934).

———. "Van Gogh Prométhée." *O.C.* 1 (1970).

———. *Visions of Excess: Selected Writings, 1927–1939*, ed. and trans. Allan Stoekl. Minneapolis: University of Minnesota Press, 1985.

Bataille, Georges, Roger Caillois, and Michel Leiris. "Declaration of the College of Sociology on the International Crisis." In *The College of Sociology 1937–39*, ed. Denis Hollier, trans. Betsy Wing. 2d ed. Minneapolis: University of Minnesota Press, 1988.

Bayle, Jean-Louis Loubet del. *Les Non-conformistes des années 30, une tentative de renouvellement de la pensée française.* Paris: Editions de Seuil, 1969.

Beaujour, Michel. *Terreur et rhétorique: Breton, Bataille, Leiris, Paulhan, Barthes & Cie.* Paris: Jean-Michel Place, 1999.

Béhar, Henri. "Roger Caillois 'Boussole mentale' du surréalisme." In *Roger Caillois, la pensée aventurée*, ed. Laurent Jenny. Paris: Belin, 1992.

———, ed. *Inquisitions: Fac-similé de la revue augmenté de documents inédits.* Paris: Editions du CNRS, 1990.

Benda, Julien. *The Treason of the Intellectuals.* 1928. New York: Norton, 1969.

Benjamin, Walter [J. E. Mabinn, pseud.]. Rev. of "L'Aridité," by Roger Caillois; *Un Régulier dans le siècle*, by Julien Benda; *Les Grands Cimetières sous la lune*, by Georges Bernanos; *Le Dialogue catholico-communiste est-il possible?* by G. Fessard. *Zeitschrift für Sozialforschung* 7 (1938).

Bianciotti, Hector. "Le Dernier Encyclopédiste: Roger Caillois." *Le Nouvel Observateur* 521 (4 Nov. 1974): 73.

Blanchot, Maurice. *L'Entretien infini.* Paris: Gallimard, 1969.

———. *Michel Foucault tel que je l'imagine.* Paris: Fata Morgana, 1986.

———. *La Part du feu.* Paris: Gallimard, 1949.

Borges, Jorge Luis. Rev. of *Le Roman policier*, by Roger Caillois. *Sur* 91 (Apr. 1942). Trans. Emir Rodriguez Monegal and Alastair Reid and rpt. in *Borges: A Reader*. New York: Dutton, 1981.

Boschetti, Anna. *The Intellectual Enterprise: Sartre and* Les Temps Modernes. Trans. Richard C. McCleary. Evanston, IL: Northwestern University Press, 1988.

Bosquet, Alain. *Roger Caillois.* Paris: Seghers, 1971.

Borgeaud, Philippe. "Le Couple sacré/profane: Genèse et fortune d'un concept 'opératoire' en histoire des religions." *Revue de l'histoire des religions* 211 (1994): 402–405.

———. "Spectres et démons de midi." *Europe* 859–60 (Nov.–Dec. 2000): 114–25.

Breton, André. *Manifestoes of Surrealism.* Trans. Richard Seaver and Helen Lane. 1969. Ann Arbor: University of Michigan Press, 1972.

———. *Oeuvres complètes.* 3 vols. Ed. Marguerite Bonnet. Paris: Gallimard, 1988.

———. *Point du jour.* 1934. Paris: Gallimard, 1970.

———. *Position politique du surréalisme.* 1935. Paris: J.-J. Pauvert, 1971.

———. *L'Un dans l'autre.* Paris: Eric Losfeld, 1970.

Breton, André, and Jean Schuster. "Art poétique." *Bief, jonction surréaliste* 7 (1 June 1959).

Broglie, Louis de. Preface to *Essais*, by Emile Meyerson. Paris: Vrin, 1936.

Caillois, Roger. "Actualité des Kenningar." *Nouvelle nouvelle revue française* 30 (June 1955). Rpt. as "L'Enigme et l'image." In *Approches de la poésie.* Paris: Gallimard, 1978.

———. "After Six Years of a Doubtful Combat." Trans. Muriel Mckeon. *Diogenes* 26 (Apr.–June 1959).

———. "L'Agressivité comme valeur." *L'Ordre nouveau* (June 1937): 56–58.

———. *L'Aile froide.* 1938. Montpellier: Fata Morgana, 1992.

———. *Approches de la poésie.* Paris: Gallimard, 1978.

———. *Approches de l'imaginaire.* Paris: Gallimard, 1974.

———. "L'Aridité." *Mesures* (Apr. 1938).

———. "The Art of St.-John Perse." Trans. Haakon M. Chevalier. *Sewanee Review* 53.2 (spring 1945).

———. *Babel: Orgueil, confusion et ruine de la littérature.* Paris: Gallimard, 1948.

———. *Babel: Précédé de vocabulaire esthétique.* 1946. Paris: Gallimard, 1978.

———. *Bellone ou la pente de la guerre.* 1963. Paris: Editions Nizet, 1973.

———. *Cases d'un échiquier.* Paris: Gallimard, 1970.

———. *Chroniques de Babel.* Paris: Denoël/Gonthier, 1981.

———. *Le Cid.* Paris: Hachette, 1939.

———. *Circonstancielles.* Paris: Gallimard, 1946.

———. *Cohérences aventureuses.* Paris: Gallimard, 1976.

———. *La Communion des forts.* Mexico City: Quetzal, 1943.

———. "Le Complexe de midi."*Minotaure* 9 (October 1936): 9–10.

———. "Conséquences du nihilisme." In *Circonstancielles.* Paris: Gallimard, 1946.

———. "Crise de la littérature." In *Approches de l'imaginaire.* Paris: Gallimard, 1974: 52–54.

———. "Debates sobres temas sociológicos: Comentario a 'Los irresponsables,' de Archibald Macleish." *Sur* 83 (August 1941).

———. "Debates sobre temas sociológicos: Nuevas perspectivas en torno a 'Los irresponsables,' de Archibald Macleish." *Sur* (September 1941).

———. "Défense de la république." In *Circonstancielles.* Paris: Gallimard, 1946.

———. "De la Féerie à la science-fiction." In *Obliques.* Paris: Stock, 1975. Originally published as preface to *Anthologie du fantastique* (Paris: Club Français du Livre, 1958).

———. *Les Démons de midi.* Montpellier: Fata Morgana, 1991.

———. "'Le Dernier Encyclopédiste': Roger Caillois." Interview with Hector Bianciotti. *Nouvel Observateur* (November 4, 1974).

———. "Devoirs et privilèges des écrivains français à l'étranger." *Lettres francaises* 2 (October 1941): 1–4.

———. "La Dissymétrie." 1973. In *Cohérences aventureuses.* Paris: Gallimard, 1976.

———. "Divergences et complicités." *Nouvelle nouvelle revue française* (April 1967).

———. "Eloge de Paul Valéry." *Cahiers du Sud* 276–278 (1946).

———. *Ensayo sobre el espíritu de las sectas.* Mexico City: El Colegio de Mexico, "Jornadas," 1945. Rpt. in *Instincts et sociétés.* Paris: Gonthier, 1964.

———. "Entretien avec Gilles Lapouge." In *Roger Caillois: "Cahiers de Chronos,"* ed. Jean-Clarence Lambert. Paris: Ed. de la Différence, 1991: 134–137.

———. "En toute sévérité." *Volontés* 12 (Dec. 1938).

———. *Espace Américain.* 1949. Montpellier: Fata Morgana, 1983.

———. "Le Fantastique naturel." In *Cases d'un échiquier.* Paris: Gallimard, 1970: 61–73.

———. "Fertilité de l'ambigu." In *Cohérences aventureuses: esthétique généralisée; au coeur du fantastique; la dissymétrie.* Paris: Gallimard, 1976: 184–90.

———. *Fisiología de Leviatán.* Trans. Julián Calvo and C. A. Jordana. Buenos Aires: Editorial Sudamericana, 1946.

———. *Le Fleuve Alphée.* Paris: Gallimard, 1978.

———. "Fonction du mythe." In *Le Mythe et l'homme.* Paris: Gallimard, 1938: 13–32.

———. "Le Grand Pontonnier." In *Cases d'un échiquier.* Paris: Gallimard, 1970: 17–27.

———. "L'Héritage de la Pythie." *Approches de la poésie.* Paris: Gallimard, 1978: 34–42.

———. "La Hiérachie des êtres." "Le Fascisme contre l'esprit" (Fascism against the mind). Special issue of *Les Volontaires* 9 (Apr. 1939). Rpt. in *La Communion des forts*. Mexico City: Quetzal, 1943.

———. *L'Homme et le sacré*. Paris: Ed. Leroux, 1939.

———. *L'Homme et le sacré*. 2d ed. Paris: Gallimard, 1950.

———. "Illusions à rebours I." *Nouvelle nouvelle revue française* 24 (Dec. 1954).

———. "Illusions à rebours II." *Nouvelle nouvelle revue française* 25 (Jan. 1955).

———. "L'Image." In *Babel, précédé de Vocabulaire esthétique*. Paris: Gallimard, 1978: 66–69.

———. *L'Incertitude qui vient des rêves*. Paris: Gallimard, 1956.

———. *Instincts et société: Essais de sociologie contemporaine*. Paris: Gonthier, 1964.

———. Interview with Jean-José Marchand. Videotape. Dir. Michel Latouche. Archives du XXème siècle, Société Française de Production, Paris. 1971.

———. Introduction to *Contes étranges*, by Prosper Mérimée. Paris: Vialetay, 1972.

———. *Les Jeux et les hommes*. Paris: Gallimard, 1958.

———. "Lettre à André Breton." In *Approches de l'imaginaire*. Paris: Gallimard, 1974: 35–38, 52–54.

———. "Lettre du rédacteur en chef sur le role de *Diogène* et les conditions d'un humanisme rénové." *Diogène* 4 (1953).

———. "Loyola au secours de Marx." *Liberté de l'esprit* 6 (summer 1949): 123–24.

———. *Man and the Sacred*. Trans. Meyer Barash. Glencoe, IL: Free Press, 1960.

———. *Man, Play and Games*. Trans. Meyer Barash. New York: Free Press, 1961.

———. "La Mante religieuse." *Minotaure* 5 (1934): 23–26.

———. *Méduse et Cie*. Paris: Gallimard, 1960.

———. "Métamorphoses de l'enfer." In *Obliques*. Paris: Stock, 1975: 213–47.

———. "Mimétisme et psychasthénie légendaire." *Minotaure* 7 (1935): 5–10.

———. *The Mystery Novel*. Trans. Roberto Yahni and A. W. Sadler. Bronxville, NY: Laughing Buddha Press, 1984.

———. "Le Mythe et l'art: nature de leur opposition." In *Congrès international d'esthétique et de science de l'art*. Paris: F. Alcan, 1937.

———. *Le Mythe et l'homme*. Paris: Gallimard, 1938.

———. "The Myth of Secret Treasures in Childhood," trans. Lawrence Krader. *V.V.V.* 1 (June 1942): 4–8.

———. "La Naissance de Lucifer." *Verve* (Paris) 1 (December 1937): 32.

———. "Naturaleza del hitlerismo." *Sur* (Oct. 1939).

———. *La Nécessité d'esprit*. Paris: Gallimard, 1981.

———. *The Necessity of Mind*. Trans. Michael Syrotinski. Afterword by Denis Hollier. Venice, CA: Lapis Press, 1990.

———. "Notes pour un itinéraire de Roger Caillois." In *Roger Caillois: "Cahiers pour un temps."* Paris: Centre Georges Pompidou and Pandora, 1981.

———. "Nouveau Plaidoyer pour les sciences diagonales." In *Cases d'un échiquier*. Paris: Gallimard, 1970: 53–59.

———. "L'Ordre et l'empire." In *Le Mythe et l'homme*. Paris: Gallimard, 1938.

————. "Paris, mythe moderne." In *Le Mythe et l'homme* (1938): 150–171.

————. "Paroxysmes de la société." In *Bellone ou la pente de la guerre*. Bruxelles: Renaissance du livre, 1963; Paris: Nizet, 1973: 209–23.

————. "Patagonie." *Renaissance* 1.3 (July–September 1943): 419–428.

————. *Pierres, suivi d'autres textes*. Paris: Gallimard, 1970.

————. *Pierres réfléchies*. Paris: Gallimard, 1975.

————. "Places et limites de la poésie jusqu'à, selon et depuis Baudelaire." *Preuves* (Dec. 1968). Rpt. in *Cases*. Paris: Gallimard, 1970.

————. *Poétique de Saint-John Perse*. Paris: Gallimard, 1954.

————. *Ponce Pilate*. 1960. Paris: Gallimard, 1978.

————. "Pour une esthétique sévère." *Lettres françaises* 1 (1 July 1941).

————. "Pour une orthodoxie militante: les tachs immédiates de la pensée moderne." *Inquisitions* 1 (June 1936): 6–14.

————. "Préambule pour l'esprit des sectes." In *Approches de l'imaginaire*. Paris: Gallimard, 1974: 89–94.

————. "Problèmes du rêve." *Bulletin de la société française de philosophie* (July–Sept. 1957).

————. "Pronunciou Sue Anunciada Conferencia o Famoso Escritor Francês Roger Caillois." *Diario*, 16 Sept. 1943.

————. *Puissances du roman*. Marseille: Sagittaire, 1942. Rpt. in *Approches de l'imaginaire*. Paris: Gallimard, 1970.

————. *Quatre essais de sociologie contemporaine*. Paris: Olivier Perrin, 1951.

————. *Le champ des signes: récurrences dérobées*. Paris: Edition Hermann, 1978.

————. *Rencontres*. Paris: Presses Universitaires de France, 1978.

————. Response to "Enquête sur la poésie indispensable." *Cahiers G.L.M.* (Oct. 1938).

————. "Résurrection de Corneille." *Nouvelle revue française* (Oct. 1938).

————. Rev. of *La Comédie humaine*, by Balzac, ed. Marcel Bouteron. *Nouvelle revue française* (Mar. 1937).

————. Rev. of *L'Equinoxe de septembre*, by H. de Montherlant. *Nouvelle revue française* (Jan. 1939).

————. Rev. of *Les Echecs artistiques*, by André Chéron; *L'Opposition et les cases conjuguées sont réconciliées*, by Marcel Duchamp and V. Halberstadt. *Nouvelle revue française* (Sept. 1937).

————. Rev. of *L'Homme, cet inconnu*, by Dr. Alexis Carrel. *Nouvelle revue française* (March 1936): 438–39.

————. Rev. of *Les Paradis artificiels*, by Louis Lewin. *Cahiers du Sud* (Jan 1937).

————. Rev. of *Essai sur le titanisme dans la poésie romantique occidentale entre 1815 et 1850*, by Václav Černy. *Nouvelle revue française* (November 1937): 847–849.

————. Rev. of *L'Esthétique de Baudelaire*, by André Ferran. *Nouvelle revue française* (Nov. 1936).

————. Rev. of *Le Tabou de l'inceste*, by Lord Raglan. *Cahiers du Sud* (Nov. 1935).

————. Rev. of *L'Expérience mystique et les symbols chez les primitifs*, by Lucien Lévy-Bruhl. *Nouvelle revue française* (Aug. 1938).

———. Rev. of *Mythologie universelle*, by Alexandre Haggerty Krappe. *Cahiers du Sud* (Apr. 1935).

———. Rev. of *Nietzsche, suivi de textes choisis*, by Henri Lefebvre. *Sur* (Nov. 1939).

———. Rev. of *Nouvelle Conversation de Goethe avec Eckermann; L'Exercice du pouvoir; Du Mariage*, by Léon Blum; *En lisant M. Léon Blum*, by Marcel Thiébaut. *Nouvelle revue française* (Oct. 1937).

———. Rev. of *Poisons sacrés, ivresses divines*, by Ph. de Felice. *Cahiers du Sud* (Apr. 1937).

———. Rev. of *Propos de Georges Sorel*, ed. Jean Variot. *Nouvelle revue française* (Apr. 1936).

———. Rev. of *Service inutile*, by H. de Montherlant. Rpt. in *Inquisitions*, ed. Henri Béhar. Paris: Editions du CNRS, 1990.

———. "La Révolution cachée." *Le Monde* 13 June 1968.

———. *La Roca de Sísifo*. Buenos Aires: Sudamericana, 1942.

———. *Le Rocher de Sisyphe*. Paris: Gallimard, 1946.

———. "Un Roman cornélien." *Nouvelle revue française* (Mar. 1938).

———. *Le Roman policier*. Buenos Aires: Ed. Lettres Françaises, 1941.

———. "Seres del anochecer." *Sur* (Dec. 1940).

———. "Situation de la poésie." In *Approches de la poésie*. Paris: Gallimard, 1978: 23–27.

———. "Sociologie du clerc." *Approches de l'imaginaire*. Paris: Gallimard, 1974: 61–69.

———. "Sociology of the Executioner." In *The College of Sociology 1937–39*, ed. Denis Hollier, trans. Betsy Wing. 2d ed. Minneapolis: University of Minnesota Press, 1988.

———. "Sur l'indépendance du poète." *Bouteille à la mer* 66 (1950).

———. "Le Surréalisme comme univers de signes." In *Obliques*. Paris: Stock, 1975: 238–47.

———. "Témoignage." *Europe* 525 (1973): 79–84.

———. "Testimonio francés." *Sur* (Oct. 1939).

———. "Thémes fondamentaux chez Jorge Luis Borges." *Cahiers de l'Herne* 2 (1964). Rpt. in *Rencontres*. Paris: Presses Universitaires de France, 1978.

———. "Touches pour un portrait sincère." *Nouvelle revue française* 197 (May 1969). Rpt. in *Rencontres*. Paris: Presses Universitaires de France, 1978.

———. "Les Traces." *Preuves* (July 1961).

———. "Les Vertus dionysiaques." *Acéphale* 3-4 (July 1937): 24–26.

———. "Un Visionnaire." *Liberté de l'esprit* (February 1952).

———. "The Winter Wind." In *The College of Sociology 1937–39*, ed. Denis Hollier, trans. Betsy Wing. 2d ed. Minneapolis: University of Minnesota Press, 1988.

———. *The Writing of Stones*. Trans. Barbara Bray. Introduction by Marguerite Yourcenar. Charlottesville: University of Virginia Press, 1985.

Caillois, Roger, and G. E. von Grunebaum, eds. *The Dream and Human Societies*. Berkeley: University of California Press, 1966.

———, eds. *Le Rêve et les sociétés humaines*. Paris: Gallimard, 1967.

Carnap, Rudolf. "The Elimination of Metaphysics through Logical Analysis of Language." In *Logical Positivism*, ed. A. J. Ayer. New York: Free Press, 1959.

Charmet, Raymond. Rev. of *La Sociologie allemande contemporaine*, by Raymond Aron. Rpt. in *Inquisitions*, ed. Henri Béhar. Paris: Editions du CNRS, 1990.

Chastel, André. *Fables, formes, figures*. Paris: Flammarion, 1965.

Clifford, James. *The Predicament of Culture*. Cambridge, MA: Harvard University Press, 1988.

Cohen, Margaret. *Profane Illumination*. Berkeley: University of California Press, 1993.

Comte, Bernard. "Uriage [Ecole des cadres d']." In *Dictionnaire des intellectuels français*, by Jacques Julliard and Michel Winock. Paris: Seuil, 1996.

Cortanze, Gérard de. "L'Irréductible Hostilité de Bataille au surréalisme." *Magazine littéraire* 243 (June 1987).

Coward, David. "The Apostles of Anguish." *Times Literary Supplement* (4–10 Aug. 1989).

Cuvillier, Armand. *Introduction à la sociologie*. 1936. 6th ed. Paris: Armand Colin, 1960.

"Debates sobre temas sociológicos." *Sur* (June 1941).

"Debates sobre temas sociológicos? Tienen las Americas una historia común?" *Sur* 86 (Nov. 1941).

De Domenico, Peter F. "Revenge of the Novel: Roger Caillois's Literary Criticism in the Wake of the 1930s." *Romanic Review* 89.3 (May 1998): 381–409.

de Man, Paul, "Poetic Nothingness: On a Hermetic Sonnet by Mallarme." Trans. Richard Howard. In *Paul de Man: Critical Writings 1953–1978*. Ed. and introduction by Lindsay Waters. Minneapolis: University of Minnesota Press, 1989.

Descombes, Vincent. *La Philosophie par gros temps*. Paris: Editions de Minuit, 1989.

de Staël-Holstein, Germaine. *Germany*. 1813. Trans. and ed. O. W. Wright. Boston: Houghton, Mifflin, 1887

"El detective en desgracia—'Roma.'" *Sur* 59 (Aug. 1939).

Drury, Shadia. *Leo Strauss and the American Right*. New York: St. Martin's Press, 1997.

Dubief, Henri. "Témoignage sur Contre-Attaque." *Textures* 6 (Jan. 1970).

Dumézil, Georges. *Entretiens avec Didier Eribon*. Paris: Gallimard, 1987.

———. *Flamen-Brahman*. Paris: Librarie Orientaliste Paul Geuthner, 1935.

Durkheim, Emile. *The Elementary Forms of Religious Life*. Trans. Joseph Ward Swain. New York: Free Press, 1965.

Durkheim, Emile, and Marcel Mauss. "De quelques formes primitives de la classification." 1903. In *Essais de sociologie*, by Marcel Mauss. Paris: Minuit, 1969.

Eigeldinger, Marc. "La Poétique hugolienne de l'image et de l'imagination." In *Du romantisme au surnaturalisme: Hommage à Claude Pichois*. Neuchâtel: A la Baconnière, 1988.

Etiemble, René. "Deux masques de Roger Caillois." *Nouvelle revue française* 142 (Sept. 1979).

———. *Hygiène des lettres*. Paris: Gallimard, 1958.

———. Rev. of *Le Roman policier*, by Roger Caillois. *Lettres françaises* 10 (1 Oct. 1943).

Felgine, Odile. *Roger Caillois*. Paris: Stock, 1994.

———, ed. *Correspondance Roger Caillois–Victoria Ocampo*. Paris: Stock, 1997.

Felgine, Odile, and Claude Perez, eds. "Correspondance Jean Paulhan–Roger Caillois 1934–1967." In *Cahiers Jean Paulhan*, vol. 6. Paris: Gallimard, 1991.

Frank, Claudine. "Contre-Attaque de Caillois? A propos de 'L'Ordre et l'empire.'" *Europe* 859–860 (Nov.–Dec. 2000): 72–82.

Frank, Manfred. *Le Dieu à venir*. Trans. from the German by Florence Vatan and Veronika von Schenck. Paris: Actes Sud, 1989.

Furet, François. *Le Passé d'une illusion: essai sur l'idée communiste au XXe siècle*. Paris: R. Laffont: Calmann-Lévy, 1995.

Galletti, Marina. *Georges Bataille: L'Apprenti sorcier*. Paris: Editions de la Différence, 1999.

———. "Un Inédit de la Société secrète Acéphale: Georges Ambrosino *La Constitution de l' être est éminemment paradoxale*." *Europe* 859–860 (Nov.–Dec. 2000).

———. "Roger Caillois en Argentine." In *Roger Caillois, la pensée aventurée*, ed. Laurent Jenny. Paris: Belin, 1992.

———. "Secret et sacré chez Leiris et Bataille." In *Bataille–Leiris: L'intenable assentiment au monde*, ed. Francis Marmande. Paris: Belin, 1999.

Gide, André. *Corydon*. Paris: Gallimard, 1924.

Granet, Marcel. *La Civilisation chinoise*. 1929. Paris: Albin Michel, 1968.

———. *La Pensée chinoise*, 1934. Paris: Albin Michel, 1999.

Grenier, Jean. "L'Ordre nouveau." *Nouvelle revue française* 263 (Aug. 1935).

Halévy, Elie. *L'Ere des tyrannies: Etudes sur le socialisme et la guerre*. 1938. Paris: Gallimard, 1990.

Heidegger, Martin. *Basic Writings: Revised and Expanded Edition*. Ed. David Farrell Krell. 1977. New York: Harper Collins, 1993.

Heimonet, Jean-Michel. *Jules Monnerot, ou la démission critique, 1932–1990*. Paris: Editions Kime, 1993.

———. *Le Mal à l'oeuvre: Georges Bataille et l'écriture du sacrifice*. Marseille: Parentheses, 1986.

———. *Politiques de l'écriture Bataille/Derrida*. Paris: Jean-Michel Place, 1990.

Hertz, Robert. *Death; and The Right Hand*. Glencoe, IL: Free Press, 1960.

Hollier, Denis. *Absent without Leave*. Cambridge, MA: Harvard University Press, 1997.

——— "La Fin de sommations." *Critique* (August–September 1996).

———, ed. *Le Collège de sociologie 1937–1939*. 3d ed. Paris: Gallimard, 1995.

———, ed. *The College of Sociology 1937–39*. 2d ed. Trans. Betsy Wing. Minneapolis: University of Minnesota Press, 1988.

Huizinga, Johan. *Homo ludens: A Study of the Play Element in Culture*. 1944. New York: J. and J. Harper Editions, 1970.

Hytier, Jean. *La Poétique de Valéry*. Paris: Armand Colin, 1953.

Janet, Pierre. *Les Névroses*. Paris: Flammarion, 1909.

Jenny, Laurent. "La Fêlure et la parenthèse." In *Les Cahiers de Chronos: Roger Caillois*, ed. Jean-Clarence Lambert. Paris: Editions de la Différence, 1991.

―――. "From Breton to Dali: The Adventures of Automatism." *October* (winter 1989): 109.

―――, ed. *Roger Caillois, la pensée aventurée.* Paris: Belin, 1992.

Judrin, Roger (Aimé Patri, pseud.). Rev. of *Babel*, by Roger Caillois. *Paru* 47 (October 1948).

King, John. *Sur: A Study of the Argentine Literary Journal and Its Role in the Development of a Culture, 1931–1970.* Cambridge, England: Cambridge University Press, 1986.

Kojève, Alexandre. *Introduction to the Reading of Hegel: Lectures on the Phenomenology of the Spirit.* 1947. Comp. Raymond Queneau, ed. Allan Bloom, trans. James H. Nichols Jr. 1969. Ithaca, NY: Cornell University Press, 1980.

Krauss, Rosalind. *The Optical Unconscious.* Cambridge, MA: MIT Press, 1994.

Lacan, Jacques. "The Mirror Stage as Formative of the Function of the I." In *Ecrits: A Selection.* Trans. Alan Sheridan. New York: Norton, 1977.

―――. Rev. of *Le Temps vécu*, by E. Minkowski. *Recherches philosophiques* 5 (1935–1936).

Lambert, Jean-Clarence, ed. *Les Cahiers de Chronos: Roger Caillois.* Paris: Editions de la Différence, 1991.

Lasserra, Annamaria. "L'Art du pontonnier." *Europe* 859–860 (November–December 2000): 183–195.

―――. *Materia et imaginario, il nesso analogico nell'opera di Roger Caillois.* Rome: Bulzoni, 1990.

Lawrence, D. H. *The Plumed Serpent.* 1926. New York: Vintage International, 1992.

Le Bouler, Jean-Pierre. "Bataille et Caillois: Divergences et complicités." *Magazine littéraire* 243 (June 1987): 47–49.

Le Rider, Jacques. *Nietzsche en France: de la fin du XIXe siècle au temps présent.* Paris: Presses Universitaires de France, 1999.

Lévi-Strauss, Claude (and Roger Caillois). "Discours prononcés dans la séance publique tenue par l'Académie Française pour la réception de M. Claude Lévi-Strauss le . . . 27 juin 1974, Institut de France, Académie Française." Paris: Institut de France, 1972.

Lévy-Bruhl, Lucien. *The Primitive Mentality.* Trans. Lilian A. Clare. New York: Macmillan, 1923.

Lewis, Helena. *The Politics of Surrealism.* New York: Paragon House, 1988.

Massonet, Stéphane. *Les Labyrinthes de l'imaginaire dans l'oeuvre de Roger Caillois.* Paris: L'Harmattan, 1998.

Mauss, Marcel. *Essais de sociologie.* Paris: Minuit, 1969.

―――. "Essai sur le don." In *Sociologie et anthropologie.* Paris: Presses Universitaires de France, 1989.

―――. *A General Theory of Magic.* Trans. Robert Brain. 1972. New York: Routledge, 2001.

―――. *The Gift: Forms and Functions of Exchange in Archaic Societies.* Trans. Ian Cunnison. 1907. New York: Norton, 1967.

―――. "Rapports réels et pratiques de la psychologie et de la sociologie." 1924. In *Sociologie et anthropologie.* Paris: Presses Universitaires de France, 1989.

――――. *Seasonal Variations of the Eskimo.* Boston: Routledge and Kegan Paul, 1979.

Mayer Hans. "The Rituals of Political Associations in Germany of the Romantic Period." 1939. In *The College of Sociology 1937–39*, ed. Denis Hollier, trans. Betsy Wing. 2d ed. Minneapolis: University of Minnesota Press, 1988.

Mehlman, Jeffrey. *Emigré New York: French Intellectuals in Wartime Manhatten, 1940–1944.* Baltimore, Md.: Johns Hopkins University Press, 2000.

Meyerson, Emile. *Essais.* Paris: Vrin, 1936.

Monnerot, Jules. "A partir de quelques traits particuliers á la mentalité civilisée." *Le Surréalisme au service de la révolution* 5–6 (1933).

――――. "Remarques sur le rapport de la poésie comme genre et comme fonction." *Inquisitions* 1 (June 1936).

Montherlant, Henry de. *L'Equinoxe de septembre suivi de Le Solstice de juin et de Mémoire* [texte inédit]. Paris: Gallimard, 1975.

Nadal, Octave. *Le Sentiment de l'amour dans l'oeuvre de Pierre Corneille.* 1948. Paris: Gallimard, 1991.

Nadeau, Maurice. *Histoire du surréalisme: suivie de documents surréalistes.* Paris: Seuil, 1964.

Nerval, Gérard de. *Oeuvres complètes.* 2 vols. Ed. and intro. Albert Béguin and Jean Richer. Paris: Gallimard, 1960.

Nicolet, Claude. *L'Idée républicaine en France: Essai d'histoire critique (1789–1924).* Paris: Gallimard, 1982.

Ocampo, Victoria. "Roger Caillois." *Sur* 59 (Aug. 1939).

Ortega y Gasset, José. *The Dehumanization of Art and Other Essays on Art, Culture, and Literature.* Trans. Helene Weyl. 1948. Princeton, NJ: Princeton University Press, 1968.

Pace, David. *Claude Lévi-Strauss, Bearer of Ashes.* 1983. Boston: ARK, 1986.

Pajon, Alexandre. "In Search of a Journal: Caillois and *Diogenes.*" *Diogenes* 160 (Oct.–Dec. 1992).

――――. "L'Intrépidité politique de Roger Caillois avant-guerre." In *Les Cahiers de Chronos: Roger Caillois*, ed. Jean-Clarence Lambert. Paris: Editions de le Différence, 1991.

Panoff, Michel. *Les Fréres ennemis: Roger Caillois et Claude Lévi-Strauss.* Paris: Payot, 1993.

Pareto, Vilfredo and Arthur Livingston. *The Mind and Society: A Treatise on General Sociology.* 1916. Ed. and trans. Andrew Bongiorno. 1935. New York: Harcourt Brace and Co., 1963.

Parodi, Dominique. "Le Sentiment de ressemblance." *Revue philosophique* 109 (1930).

Paulhan, Jean. *Clef de la poésie.* Paris: Gallimard, 1984.

――――. *Les Fleurs de Tarbes ou La Terreur dans les lettres.* 1941. Paris: Gallimard, 1990.

――――. *Jean Paulhan: Oeuvres complètes.* 5 vols. Paris: Cercle du Livre Précieux, 1970.

――――. *De la paille et du grain.* Vol. 5 of *Jean Paulhan: Oeuvres complètes.* Paris: Cercle du Livre Précieux, 1970.

Payne, Stanley G. *A History of Fascism 1914–1945.* Madison: University of Wisconsin Press, 1995.

Picon, Gaëtan. "Les Essais de Roger Caillois." *Fontaine* 54 (summer 1946).

Piel, Jean. *La Rencontre et la différence*. Paris: Fayard, 1982.

Pinto, Louis. *Les Neveux de Zarathoustra: La réception de Nietzsche en France*. Paris: Seuil, 1995.

"Préface." *Minotaure* 9 (15 October 1936).

Queneau, Raymond. *Le Voyage en Grèce*. Paris: Gallimard, 1973.

Racine, Nicole. "Références dreyfusiennes dans la gauche française." In *La Postérité de l'Affaire Dreyfus*, ed. Michel Leymarie. Orléans: Presses Universitaires du Septentrion, 1998.

Raulet, Gérard. *Walter Benjamin*. Paris: Ellipses, 2000.

Rauschning, Hermann. *The Revolution of Nihilism*. 1938. New York: Alliance, Longmans, Green, 1939.

Reich, Wilhelm. *The Mass Psychology of Fascism*. 1934. Trans. Theodore Peter Wolfe. New York: Orgone Institute Press, 1946.

Renan, Ernest. "Lettre à David Strauss." 1871. *Lettres françaises* 2 (October 1941).

Rev. of "Au service de l'ennemi" (*France libre* 25 [16 Nov. 1942]) *Lettres françaises* 9 (July 1943).

Rev. of "Combat de l'homme," by Jean Mahan (*France libre* 22 [15 August 1942]). *Lettres françaises* 7–8 (Feb. 1943).

Rev. of *Fonction universelle de la France*, by Henri Focillon. *Lettres françaises* 2 (Oct. 1941).

Rev. of *V.V.V.* 2–3 (Mar. 1943). *Lettres françaises* 10 (1 October 1943).

Reverdy, Pierre. *Nord-Sud, Self-Defence, et autres écrits sur l'art et la poésie*. Paris: Flammarion, 1975.

Ricoeur, Paul. "The Power of Speech: Science and Poetry." Trans. Robert F. Scuka. *Philosophy Today* (spring 1985): 69.

Roger Caillois: "Cahiers pour un temps." Paris: Centre George Pompidou and Pandora Editions, 1981.

Roubaud, Jacques. "Raymond Queneau et l'amalgame des mathématiques et de la littérature," in *Atlas de Littérature Potentielle* by OULIPO. 1981. Paris: Gallimard, 1988.

Roudinesco, Elisabeth. *Histoire de la psychanalyse en France 1925–1985*. 2 vols. Paris: Seuil, 1986.

Saint-Exupéry, Antoine de. *The Little Prince*. 1943. Trans. Richard Howard. 1971. San Diego: Harcourt, 2000.

Schapiro, Meyer. "French Reaction in Exile." *Kenyon Review* 7 (winter 1945): 29–42.

Sellier, Philippe. "Qu'est-ce qu'un mythe littéraire?" *Littérature*, no. 55 (1984).

Shattuck, Roger. *The Innocent Eye*. New York: Washington Square Press, 1986.

Short, Robert Stuart. "Contre-Attaque." In *Entretiens sur le surréalisme*, ed. Ferdinand Alquié. Paris: Mouton, 1968.

Sirinelli, Jean-François. *Génération intellectuelle: Khâgneux et Normaliens dans l'entre-deux-guerres*. Paris: Fayard, 1988.

Société Française de Philosophie. *Vocabulaire technique et critique de la philosophie*. 1902–1923. 9th ed. Paris: PUF, 1962.

Sokal, Alan, and Jean Bricquemont. *Impostures intellectuelles*. Paris: Odile Jacob, 1997.

Sorel, Georges. *Reflections on Violence*. 1908. Trans. T. E. Hulme. Introduction by Edward A Shils. New York: Free Press, 1974.

Starobinski, Jean. "Saturne au ciel de pierres." *Nouvelle nouvelle revue française* 320 (1979). Rpt. in *Europe* 859–860 (November–December 2000).

Stoeckl, Allan *Agonies of the Intellectual*. Lincoln: University of Nebraska Press, 1992.

Suleiman, Susan Rubin. *Subversive Intent*. Cambridge, MA: Harvard University Press, 1990.

Surya, Michel. *Georges Bataille: La mort à l'oeuvre*. 2d ed. Paris: Gallimard, 1992.

Thivolet, Marc. *Le Grand Jeu*. Paris: L'Herne, 1968.

Thirion, André. *Révolutionnaires sans révolution*. Trans. Joachim Neugroschel. 1972. New York: Macmillan, 1975.

Thomas Fogiel, Isabelle. *Fichte: Nouvelle présentation de la doctrine de la science 1797–1798*. Paris: Vrin, 1999.

Tillier, Louis. Rev. of *Lettres françaises*. *France libre* 18 (April 1942).

Todorov, Tzvetan. *The Fantastic: A Structural Approach to a Literary Genre*. Ithaca, NY: Cornell University Press, 1973.

Toussenel, Alphonse. *L'Espirit des bêtes: zoologie passionelle: mammifères de France*, 2d ed. Paris: Librairie Phalanstérienne, 1855.

Tzara, Tristan. "Compte-rendu." Rpt. in *Inquisitions*, ed. Henri Béhar. Paris: Editions du CNRS, 1990.

———. "Essai sur la situation de la poésie." *SASDLR* 4 (1931).

Wahl, Jean. Rev. of *Inquisitions* and *Acéphale*. *Nouvelle revue française* 275 (August 1936).

Waldberg, Patrick. "Acéphalogramme." *Magazine littéraire* 321 (April 1995): 158–159.

———. *Un Amour Acéphale: Correspondence, 1940–1949*. Paris: Editions de la Différence, 1992.

———. "'Vers un nouveau mythe? Prémonitions et défiances': Patrick Waldberg à Isabelle Waldberg (Extraits d'une lettre écrite à bord d'un cargo en convoi sur l'Atlantique)." *V.V.V.* (4 February, 1944).

Wetzels, Walter D. "Aspects of Natural Science in German Romanticism." *Studies in Romanticism* 10 (winter 1971).

Winock, Michel. *Le Siècle des intellectuels*. Paris: Seuil, 1999.

Worms, Jeannine. *Entretiens avec Roger Caillois*. Pairs: Editions de la Différence, 1991.

Ycschua, Silvio. "Jean Paulhan et la 'rhétorique' du secret." *Le Texte, le secret et l'exégèse*, ed. Jean Starobinski. Paris: Champion, 1992.

Index

Bergery, Gaston, 61
Bergson, Henri, 16, 19, 68, 89, 115n, 117, 236, 338, 368 n.70, 385 n.6
Beuve-Méry, Hubert, 377 n.209
Bianco, Jose, 213, 215, 392 n.1
Bianquis, Geneviève, 153
Bidault, Georges, 191, 391 n.7
Billod, Yvette, 34, 360, 377 n.219
Binet, Léon, 77, 78
Bioy Casares, Adolfo, 298
Blanchot, Maurice, 41–43, 299, 398 n.7
Blin, Georges, 40
Bloch, Ernst, 155
Blum, Léon, 20, 125, 175, 368 n.76
Bodin, Jean, 75n
Bogatyrev, P., 386 n.2
Bolyai, János, 135n
Borgeaud, Philippe, 124, 285, 371 n.108
Borges, Jorge Luis, 2, 6, 37, 40, 50, 263, 298, 316, 360–361, 376 n.201
Boschetti, Anna, 235
Bossuet, Jacques Bénigne, 281, 328
Bourget, Paul, 124
Bouvier, E. L., 79n, 99n
Brasillach, Robert, 167
Brauner, Victor, 86
Brehm, A. E., 70
Breton, André, 4, 8, 9, 10, 11, 12, 14, 47, 59, 60, 61, 62, 63, 64, 65, 66, 69, 76, 82, 84, 89, 145, 174, 253, 268, 269, 316, 320, 326, 330, 331, 332, 359, 367 n.51, 380 nn.260, 270, 381 n.278, 382 n.3, 385 n.4, 395 n.8, 399 n.3
Bricquemont, Jean, 6
Broglie, Louis de, 12, 369 n.87
Brontë, Emily, 299
Bruno, Giordano, 302
Bychowski, Gustav, 76
Byron, G. G., Lord, 170

Caesar, Julius, 184
Campanella, Tommaso, 310

Camus, Albert, 40, 382 n.280, 394 n.3, 398 n.7
Carner, Josep, 377 n.216
Carrel, Alexis, 107–108
Cartesian subject, 89
Cassirer, Ernst, 115n, 367 n.53
Cassian, John, 128
Catholicism, 23, 35, 40, 160, 215, 391 n.7
Černy, Václav, 153n, 154, 167
Char, René, 65, 367 n.51
Chardonne, Jacques, 235
Chastel, André, 9, 10, 41, 243, 367 n.53, 368 n.70
Chateaubriand, F.-R. de, 184
Chateaubriant, Alphonse de, 210
Chavy, Jacques, 147–149, 389 n.16
Chesterton, G. K., 181, 236
China, 4, 9, 41, 132, 197, 287, 348, 381 n.278, 400 n.7. See also Taoism
Christianity, 19, 34, 40, 161, 194, 197, 222, 254, 287, 294, 298, 305, 340
Christ, 19, 32, 40, 75, 349
Christoffel, E. B., 100
Clausewitz, Karl von, 229, 372 n.125
Clifford, James, 7, 380 n.260
Cohen, Gustave, 377 n.212
College of Sociology, 1, 3–5, 8, 11, 15, 17, 20–22, 24, 26–28, 30, 32–35, 38–39, 66, 112, 125, 130–131, 141–145, 147–148, 160, 173, 175, 203, 205–206, 210, 240, 254, 284–286, 317, 326, 359, 368 n.70, 371 n.116, 375 n.179, 391 n.6
Combelle, Lucien, 39
Communism, 10, 14–16, 24, 28, 36, 42–43, 59–60, 63, 142–143, 160, 207–208, 218, 223, 225, 279–283, 300, 372 n.130, 373 n.148, 376 n.51, 393 n.7
Comte, Auguste, 191, 375 n.179, 386 n.5
Comte, Bernard, 40
Contre-Attaque, 4, 8, 14–15, 22, 28–29, 59, 110, 112, 149, 365 n.32, 369 n.77, 375 n.179

Fascism, 4, 14–15, 21–23, 35, 64, 121, 148, 154–155, 160, 173, 205, 218, 366 n.33, 368 n.76, 369 n.77, 371 n.117, 376 nn.184, 200, 387 n.7. *See also* Franco, Francisco; Hitler, Adolph; Mussolini, Benito; Nazism

Faulkner, William, 38

Faust, 111, 148, 153

Febvre, Lucien, 41

Feininger, Andreas, 351

Felgine, Odile, 4, 365 n.27, 391 n.5

Fichte, J. G., 18, 135, 387 n.1

Ficino, Masilio, 302

Finsler, Paul, 100

Flaubert, Gustave, 75n, 101, 241

Focillon, Henri, 38, 235

Foucault, Michel, 1, 5, 320

Franco, Francisco, 35, 218, 386 n.3

Frank, Manfred, 155

Frank, Waldo, 35

Frazer, J. G., 19, 72, 73n, 97, 152–153, 166, 186n, 285, 389 n.2

Freud, Sigmund, 9, 11, 42, 59, 66, 68, 73, 89, 111, 119n, 337

Fréville, Jean, 63–65

Furet, François, 218

Galletti, Marina, 30, 374 n.160

Gandhi, Mahatma, 215–216

Giacometti, Alberto, 65

Gide, André, 68–69, 263, 298

Gilbert-Lecomte, Roger, 9, 48, 60, 359

Goethe, J. W., 122n, 192, 195, 324, 380 n.264

Gorer, Geoffrey, 300

Goya, Francisco, 305

Grand Jeu, Le, 9, 12, 68, 91, 156, 359

Granet, Marcel, 9, 132, 152, 342

Grenier, Jean, 160

Guastalla, René, 390 n.4

Gunther, Hans F., 222

Gurvitch, Georges, 337

Habermas, Jürgen, 371 n.116

Halbwachs, Maurice, 152

Halévy, Elie, 217

Hecate, 74, 126

Hegel, G. W. F., and Hegelianism, 17, 42, 52, 131, 135n, 141, 161–162, 240, 378 n.259, 380 n.270

Heidegger, Martin, 18, 28, 337–338, 398 n.7

Heimonet, Jean-Michel, 21, 365 n.26, 397 n.13

Heine, Maurice, 5, 86

Hemingway, Ernest, 38

Henry, Maurice, 65

Henry, Victor, 115n

Hercules, 118

Hermes Trismegistus, 333

Hertz, Robert, 25, 152

Hitler, Adolf, 4–5, 15, 20, 22, 24, 28, 34, 35, 42, 44, 64, 107, 119n, 173, 205, 209, 218, 222n, 227n, 229, 231n, 269, 298, 338, 397 n.4. *See also* Fascism; Nazism

Hoffmansthal, Hugo von, 2, 122n

Hollier, Denis, 4, 6, 20–21, 24, 32, 147, 161–162, 206, 241, 284, 285, 326, 365 n.33, 375 n.175, 384 n.3, 390 nn.4, 6, 397 n.4

Horapollo, 333

Hubert, Henri, 97, 98n, 152, 154, 370 n.90

Hugnet, Georges, 86

Hugo, Victor, 11, 178, 183, 185, 186n, 189n, 263, 266, 333

Huizinga, Johan, 44–45, 398 n.8

Huxley, Aldous, 5, 310

Huyghe, René, 360

Inquisitions, 16, 125, 130–131; *Inquisitions*, 16–17, 65, 130–131, 142, 359, 384 n.8, 386 n.3

Ishtar, 301

Jabès, Edmond, 8

Janet, Pierre, 12, 59, 67–68, 100, 128n

Maurras, Charles, 23, 186n, 191, 236; Action Française, 391 n.7

Mauss, Marcel, 9–10, 13–14, 20, 24, 26, 41, 43–44, 49, 97, 98n, 110–112, 125, 132, 144, 152, 153–154, 156, 166, 286–287, 337–338, 342, 359, 367 n.54, 370 n.90, 371 n.108, 374 n.156, 385 n.7, 399 n.7

Mecklin, John Moffatt, 119n. *See also* Ku Klux Klan

Mehlmann, Jeffrey, 393 n.7

Mendeleyev, Dmitry, 51, 263, 334, 356

Mendoza, Angelica, 213–214, 392 n.2

Messac, Régis, 178–179

Meyerson, Emile, 12, 17, 89, 369 n.87

Mi-Fou, 400 n.7

Millet, Jean François, 76

Milne-Edwards, Henri, 151

Minkowski, Eugène, 90, 100–101

Minos, 73

Minotaur, 330

Mistral, Gabriela, 360, 377 n.216

Mitre, Emilio, 215

Moeller van der Brück, Arthur, 24, 372 n.129

Monnerot, Jules, 16, 21, 29, 43, 62, 65, 142, 367 n.51

Monte Cristo, Count of, 260

Montesquieu,C.-L. de Secondat, Baron de, 43, 47, 162, 171, 236, 332, 360

Montherlant, Henry de, 38, 167, 210, 212

More, Sir Thomas, 310

Morin, Edgar, 398 n.8

Moses, 337

Mouffet, Thomas, 70

Mounier, Emmanuel, 35, 237, 239

Müller, Max, 114

Musset, Alfred de, 78n

Mussolini, Benito, 15, 218, 230

Nadal, Octave, 388 n.15

Nadeau, Maurice, 67

Napoleon I, 111, 143, 148, 170

Nazism, 15, 22, 24, 27, 36, 42, 64, 107, 205, 207, 218, 223–225, 284, 298, 300, 366 n.33, 373 n.148. *See also* Hitler, Adolph; Totalitarianism

Neruda, Pablo, 360, 377 n.216

Nerval, Gérard de, 85, 113, 266, 321, 323, 325

Netchaiev, Serguei, 372 n.125

Newton, Sir Isaac, 135n, 346

Nietzsche, Friedrich, 7, 19, 21, 23–24, 28, 31, 38, 111–112, 117, 124, 136, 152, 155, 157, 160, 161, 205, 235, 371 n.116, 375 n.169, 385 n.6. *See also* Le Rider, Jacques; Pinto, Louis

Noulet, Emilie, 235

Novalis, 122n

Nozières, Violette, 86

Ocampo, Victoria, 1, 34, 35, 40, 173, 215, 242, 244, 252, 359, 390 n.3. See also *Sur*

Oedipus, 111, 118, 122, 185

Old Man of the Mountain (Rashid ad-Din as-Sinan), 187, 208, 257

Omphale, 118

Origen, 302

Orpheus, 301

Ortega y Gasset, José, 52, 83, 381–382 n.280, 383 n.8

Orwell, George, 310

Osiris, 73

Otto, Rudolf, 20, 25, 371 n.108

OULIPO (Ouvroir de littérature potentielle), 321

Ovid, 176

Pace, David, 48, 399 n.7

Pajon, Alexandre, 364 n.17

Pan, 126

Pandora, 118

Paracelsus, Theophrastus, 333, 380 n.264, 381 n.278

Pareto, Vilfredo, 24

Parodi, Dominique, 13, 14, 368 nn.70, 73

Pascal, Blaise, 381 n.278
Paul, Saint, 322
Paulhan, Jean, 1, 5–6, 9, 16–18, 24, 26–27, 36–38, 41–42, 46–47, 107, 191, 241, 263, 279, 316–317, 359, 366 n.41, 378 n.231
Payne, Stanley, 371 n.117, 387 n.7
Péguy, Charles, 40
Pelorson, Georges, 39
Péret, Benjamin, 64
Péri, Gabriel, 63
Personalism, 35, 40
Pétain, Henri-Philippe, 34
Petitjean, Armand, 366 n.41
Peyrefitte, Alain, 47
Philostratus, Flavius, 75
Picon, Gaëtan, 40, 80, 240
Piel, Jean, 20
Piéron, Henri, 117n
Pindar, 179
Pinto, Louis, 373 n.150, 383 n.6
Piranesi, G. B., 325
Pittard, Eugène, 147, 151
Plato, 115n, 128, 161, 310, 334, 356
Plisnier, Charles, 38
Plutarch, 120, 121n
Poe, E. A., 376 n.201
Polycrates, 118, 121
Ponson du Terrail, P. A., 178
Pontigny, l'Abbaye de, 40, 377 n.212, 390 n.3
Pontius Pilate, 32
Popper, Karl, 48, 52
Porchia, Antonio, 377 n.216
Potocki, Jean, 360
Poussin, Nicolas, 327
Prévost, Pierre, 21
Prometheus, 31, 167
Pythagoras, 103, 332

Queneau, Raymond, 321
Quetzalcoatl, 168. *See also* Lawrence, D. H.

Rabaud, Etienne, 77, 94
Racine, Jean, 178, 266, 327
Racine, Nicole, 372 n.124
Raglan, F. R. S., Lord, 112
Raimondi, Marcantonio, 325
Rais, Gilles de, 305
Rank, Otto, 73n
Rastignac, Eugène de, 185
Raulet, Gérard, 175
Rauschning, Hermann, 22, 217, 371 n.117
Reich, Wilhelm, 148, 154, 387 n.7
Renan, Ernest, 236, 375 n.179, 393 n.7
Restif de la Bretonne, N.-E., 189n
Reverdy, Pierre, 11, 315–316, 379 n.251
Ricoeur, Paul, 52, 381 n.276
Riemann, G. F. B., 17, 100, 135
Rimbaud, Arthur, 9, 11, 60, 67, 83, 87–88, 133n, 134, 136, 176, 185, 189n, 268, 318, 359, 383 n.4
Rolland, Eugène, 73
Rollin, Jean, 161
Romains, Jules, 208, 212
Roubaud, Jacques, 321
Roudinesco, Elisabeth, 67
Rousseau, Jean-Jacques, 3, 220
Roussel, Raymond, 320–321, 324–325
Rousset, David, 300
Rouveyre, André, 162
Russell, Bertrand, 18

Sade, D. A. F., Marquis de, 63, 66, 86, 305
Saint-Exupéry, Antoine de, 37, 254, 360
Saint-John Perse (Alexis Léger), 34, 50, 236, 242, 263, 267, 359–361, 381 n.271, 394 nn.11, 12, 396 n.7
Saint-Just, L.-A. de, 20, 30, 59, 62, 186n
Saint-Simon, C. H. de Rouvroy, Comte de, 161
Samson, 73, 128, 212
Sarmiento, Domingo Faustino, 215
Sartre, Jean-Paul, 2, 37, 40, 42, 190–191, 235, 337, 366 n.41, 378 n.222, 398 n.7. See also *Temps modernes, Les*

Satan, 31, 37, 166–172, 298, 340. *See also*
    Devil; Lucifer
Saurat, Denis, 49, 380 n.263
Schaeffle, Albert, 151
Schapiro, Meyer, 16, 375 n.179
Schelling, F. W. J., 13, 18, 124
Schiller, J. C. F., 141
Schlegel, A. W., 115, 121n
Schuster, Jean, 320
Sebillot, Paul, 70–71
Senancour, E. P. de, 184
Senghor, L. S., 364 n.16
Serge, Victor, 236
Servius, M. H. G., 125
Shattuck, Roger, 367 n.59
Simiand, François, 147, 151, 154
Simmel, Georg, 151
Sirens, 126
Sirinelli, Jean-François, 9
Sisyphus, 33
Smith, Adam, 147
Soca, Susana, 65
Sokal, Alan, 5
Solomon, King, 128
Solzhenitsyn, Aleksandr Isaevich,
    300
Sorel, Georges, 15–16, 19, 23, 110, 131,
    148, 154, 160, 387 n.118, 372 nn.118, 125,
    383 n.7
Souvarine, Boris, 14, 28
Spencer, Herbert, 151
Spengler, Oswald, 240
Stalin (J.V. Djusgashvili), 22, 143, 227n,
    375 n.179
Starobinski, Jean, 53
Stirner, Max (J. C. Schmidt), 167
Stoekl, Allan, 190
Strauss, David, 236
Strauss, Leo, 7
Structuralism, 6, 18, 47, 49, 337, 385 n.3.
    See also Bogatyrev, P.; Lévi-Strauss,
    Claude
Stucken, Eduard, 114

Sue, Eugène, 178–179, 183
Suleiman, Susan, 5
Supervielle, Jules, 62
Sur, 1, 34–35, 37, 173, 213, 376 n.200
Surrealism, 1, 4–6, 9–12, 16–17, 20, 33,
    37, 42, 46, 48–52, 59–67, 82–87, 89,
    110–111, 132, 142, 144–145, 156, 173–
    175, 236, 253, 262, 268–269, 315–316,
    320–321, 326–334, 359, 364 n.15,
    367 nn.51, 59, 379 n.260, 395 n.8.
    See also Aragon, Louis; Breton, André;
    Dali, Salvador; Eluard, Paul; Tzara,
    Tristan
Surya, Michel, 374 n.156, 398 n.4
Swedenborg, Emanuel, 332

Tanguy, Yves, 64–65, 330
Taoism, 18, 348, 400 n.7. *See also* China
Tarde, Gabriel, 24
Temps modernes, Les, 40, 110, 364 n.15
Theocritus, 80n
Thirion, André, 61
Tillier, Louis, 36, 235
Tocqueville, Alexis de, 287
Todorov, Tzvetan, 46
Tönnies, Ferdinand, 151
Totalitarianism, 36, 46–48, 122, 160,
    213–214, 217–232, 280, 287, 337
Toussenel, Alphonse, 66
Toynbee, Arnold, 263, 381 n.271
Trotskyist, 375 n.179
Tylor, Edward, 97
Tzara, Tristan, 16, 65, 130–131, 142,
    396 n.2

UNESCO, 1, 4, 41, 366 n.41, 379 n.255
Uriage (Ecole national des cadres de la
    jeunesse), 40
Ureña, Pedro Henriquez, 213–215
U'Tamsi, Tchicaya, 4, 364 n.16

Vailland, Roger, 60
Vaillant-Couturier, Paul, 4, 63–64

Valéry, Paul, 87, 236, 243, 265, 269, 320, 394 n.16
Van Gogh, Vincent, 167–168
Vautrin, 185–186
Verne, Jules, 263, 381 n.271
Véry, Pierre, 180, 181n
Vichrova, Alena, 360, 377 n.219
Vienna School, 18, 387 n.1; Frank, Ph., 135n. *See also* Logical positivism
Vierkandt, Alfred, 152
Vignon, Paul, 92, 103n
Vigny, Alfred de, 170, 189n
Villiers de l'Isle Adam, 260
Virgil, 121n, 125
Voltaire, F. M. A., 37, 190
von Salomon, Ernst, 24, 38, 206, 209
von Wiese, Leopold , 152

Wahl, Jean, 5, 8, 16, 39, 373 n.150, 377 n.212
Waldberg, Patrick, 205, 374 n.156
Weber, Max, 151
Weissmann, A., 129n
Westermarck, Edward A., 152
Wetzels, Walter D., 13
Wheeler, W. Morton, 117n, 152
William the Taciturn, 171
Winock, Michel, 23, 154n, 190, 280

Xerxes, King, 340

Yoyotte, Pierre, 64 – 65, 367 n.51

Zola, Emile, 190

French sociologist ROGER CAILLOIS (1913–1978) was founder, with Bataille and Leiris, of the College of Sociology of the French Institute of Buenos Aires, and founder of the journal *Diogène*. He wrote and edited more than two dozen books. CLAUDINE FRANK is Assistant Professor of French at Barnard College. CAMILLE NAISH is a translator of several books and the author of *Death Comes to the Maiden: Sex and Execution, 1431–1933*, and *A Genetic Approach to Structures in the Work of Jean Genet*.

Library of Congress Cataloging-in-Publication Data

Caillois, Roger.

The edge of surrealism : a Roger Caillois reader / Roger Caillois ; edited by Claudine Frank.

p. cm.

Includes bibliographical references and index.

ISBN 0-8223-3056-3 (cloth : alk. paper)

ISBN 0-8223-3068-7 (pbk : alk. paper)

1. Sociology—Philosophy. 2. Religion and sociology. 3. Tales—Themes, motives. 4. Rites and ceremonies. I. Frank, Claudine. II. Title.

HM590.C35 2003

301′.01—dc21   2002015808